THE FIRST UNITARIAN SOCIETY OF ALBANY
A UNITARIAN-UNIVERSALIST CONGREGATION

The Social World of the First Christians

The Social World
of the First Christians

Essays in Honor of Wayne A. Meeks

Edited by
L. Michael White
and
O. Larry Yarbrough

FORTRESS PRESS

THE SOCIAL WORLD OF THE FIRST CHRISTIANS
Essays in Honor of Wayne A. Meeks

Library of Congress Cataloging-in-Publication Data

The social world of the first Christians ; essays in honor of Wayne A.
   Meeks / L. Michael White & O. Larry Yarbrough, editors.
     p. cm.
   Includes bibliographical references and index.
   ISBN 0-8006-2585-4 (alk. paper)
   1. Sociology, Biblical—History—Early church, ca. 30–600.
2. Bible. N.T.—Social scientific criticism.   3. Bible. N.T.—
Criticism, interpretation, etc.   I. Meeks, Wayne A.   II. White, L.
Michael.   III. Yarbrough, O. Larry.
BS2545.S55S63   1995
225.6'7—dc20   95-2033
                                CIP

Manufactured in the U.S.A.   AF 1-2585

99   98   97   96   95   1   2   3   4   5   6   7   8   9   10

IN HONOREM

WAYNE A. MEEKS,

SCHOLASTICI, PAEDAGOGI, AMICI,

SEMPER QUAERENTI,

PRO VITA LONGA ET FELICITATE

SEMPITERNA SUPPLICEMUS

Contents

PART ONE
PAUL AND HIS COMMUNITIES

PART TWO
EARLY CHRISTIANS IN THEIR SOCIAL WORLD

PART THREE
THE RELIGIOUS AND SOCIAL ENVIRONMENT
OF EARLY CHRISTIANITY

PART FOUR
THE SHAPING OF EARLY CHRISTIAN CULTURE

Contributors

David L. Balch
Professor of New Testament
Brite Divinity School
Texas Christian University
Fort Worth, Texas

Jouette M. Bassler
Professor of New Testament
Perkins School of Theology
Southern Methodist University
Dallas, Texas

Elizabeth A. Clark
John Carlisle Kilgo Professor of
  Religion
Department of Religion
Duke University
Durham, North Carolina

Nils Alstrup Dahl
Buckingham Professor of New
  Testament, Emeritus
Yale Divinity School
Oslo, Norway

John T. Fitzgerald
Associate Professor of New Testament
Department of Religious Studies
The University of Miami
Coral Gables, Florida

Susan R. Garrett
Lillian Claus Associate Professor of
  New Testament
Yale Divinity School
New Haven, Connecticut

Rowan A. Greer
Professor of Anglican Studies
Yale Divinity School
New Haven, Connecticut

Ronald F. Hock
Professor of Religion
University of Southern California
Los Angeles, California

Luke Timothy Johnson
Professor of New Testament
Candler School of Theology
Emory University
Atlanta, Georgia

Marinus de Jonge
Professor of New Testament and
  Ancient Christian Literature, Emeritus
Faculty of Theology
University of Leiden
Leiden, The Netherlands

Leander E. Keck
Winkley Professor of Biblical Theology
Yale Divinity School
New Haven, Connecticut

Helmut Koester
John H. Morrison Professor of New
  Testament Studies and Winn
  Professor of Ecclesiastical History
Harvard Divinity School
Cambridge, Massachusetts

Bentley Layton
Professor of Ancient Christianity
Department of Religious Studies
Yale University
New Haven, Connecticut

Abraham J. Malherbe
Buckingham Professor of New
  Testament
Yale Divinity School
New Haven, Connecticut

J. Louis Martyn
Edward Robinson Professor of Biblical
  Theology, Emeritus
Union Theological Seminary
New York, New York

Paul W. Meyer
Helen H. P. Manson Professor of New
  Testament Literature and Exegesis,
  Emeritus
Princeton Theological Seminary
Princeton, New Jersey

Jerome H. Neyrey, S.J.
Professor of New Testament
Department of Theology
University of Notre Dame
Notre Dame, Indiana

J. Paul Sampley
Professor of New Testament
School of Theology
Boston University
Boston, Massachusetts

Alan F. Segal
Professor of Judaic Studies
Department of Religion
Barnard College
Columbia University
New York, New York

Stanley K. Stowers
Professor of Religious Studies
Brown University
Providence, Rhode Island

L. Michael White
Professor of Religion in New
  Testament and Christian Origins
Department of Religion
Oberlin College
Oberlin, Ohio

O. Larry Yarbrough
Associate Professor of Religion
Department of Religion
Middlebury College
Middlebury, Vermont

Preface

THIS COLLECTION of essays is presented to Wayne A. Meeks on the occasion of his sixty-third birthday. Written by former students, colleagues, and friends, these studies explore four facets of the first Christians and their social world, areas of research to which Professor Meeks has himself made significant and lasting contributions.

The nine essays in Part One deal with Paul and his communities. The first five of these treat patterns of argument in Paul's letters as they relate to the social and interpretive context of his communities. Nils Dahl, Wayne Meeks's teacher at Yale, discusses the case of Euodia and Syntyche in Phil 4:2–3 and suggests that their dispute provided the occasion for much of the letter and the particular tone of Paul's parenesis. J. Louis Martyn reconsiders the background of the phrase "the elements of the cosmos" in the argument of Galatians by suggesting that Paul understood the Law as one of the creaturely elements. Paul Sampley analyzes the rhetorical pattern of indirect or schematized speech in order to understand both the argument of Romans 14–15 and the social situation to which it might have been addressed. In her study of the troublesome term σκεῦος (vessel) in 1 Thess 4:4, Jouette Bassler argues that the inherently flexible nature of metaphorical language relied on a common ground of understanding between Paul and his hearers and that, therefore, the most likely point of reference is Paul's own teaching regarding the practice of "spiritual" marriage.

The remaining four articles treat Paul's modes of community organization and exhortation. Ronald F. Hock examines another problematic case of terms in the Philemon letter and argues that the more literal rendering of πρεσβύτης as "old man" (rather than "ambassador," as typically assumed in most English versions) is both lexicographically and contextually preferable. Susan Garrett discusses Paul's ability to blend cultural models derived from his complex moral world in order to locate his own sense of suffering on behalf of the gospel and especially in the enigmatic reference to his "thorn in the flesh" (2 Cor 12:7). Marinus de Jonge demonstrates that traditional assumptions regarding the use of the pseudepigraphic literature as "backgrounds" to Paul are misguided, and that it would be better to see Paul and other early Christian literature as traducers of this common pattern of Hellenistic-Jewish parenesis. Abraham Malherbe shows how Paul uses familial terminology in his parenetic language in order to inculcate a notion of the church or community as the new and eternal family of God. Larry Yarbrough concludes this section by treating the social and metaphorical function of language regarding parents and children in Paul's communities, in his relations to them, and in the theology of his letters.

The six essays in Part Two concentrate on other early Christian communities or writings in their social contexts. The first two deal with the Matthean Gospel. Leander Keck argues that the notion of the spirit offers an important link between theological and social contexts in the Gospel by seeing its role in the internal tensions of the Matthean community. John Fitzgerald takes up the notion of perjury and oaths from the Sermon on the Mount and, through a detailed study of the patterns of usage from the social environment, suggests that the breaking of oaths to God, not just false swearing, is the key to understanding the Matthean context. Next, Luke Johnson discusses the social context of James and argues for a situation, both historically and intellectually, proximate to the supposed Palestinian environment of the Q document, a situation consistent with the namesake. Jerome Neyrey uses ritual analysis to argue that the footwashing episode from the Johannine last supper is really an interweaving of two rites symbolic for the community, the first a ceremony for communal solidarity and the other a transformative ritual for the status of Peter. The section then concludes with two studies on Luke-Acts. David Balch discusses the concepts of rich and poor (and related oppositions) to show that they come in fact from standard motifs among Greek and Roman historians and, thereby, to suggest both a literary and social framework for understanding Luke-Acts as political historiography. Finally, Michael White takes Acts 16 as a test case for applying archaeological data and sociohistorical analysis to fictionalized narrative and argues that the conventions of the author's social environment are integral with the fictive "real world" of the text, but that both are removed from the situation of Paul.

Part Three of the volume contains four studies dealing with the broader religious and social environment. Helmut Koester offers a careful analysis of the architectural plan of the so-called Red Hall at Pergamon, an imperially supported sanctuary for the Egyptian cults which marks a significant religious counterpoint to the spread of Christian groups in western Asia Minor. In a report of his dialogue with a sociologist, Alan Segal raises issues regarding the definition of magic that have implications not only for the study of religion but also for the intellectual climate of the early Christian world. Stan Stowers offers an anthropological approach to the Greek religious environment by discussing the social and conceptual underpinnings of sacrificial practice with an eye toward its permeation into all areas of life and toward the implications of refusals to sacrifice. Finally, Bentley Layton offers a series of reflections on the study of Gnosticism in the early Christian world and proposes directions and cautions for future study of its diverse forms with both intellectual and social dimensions.

The final section of the work focuses on the impact of Paul and Pauline traditions in shaping later Christian life and thought, especially as mediated through Augustine. First, Elizabeth Clark discusses early Christian use of the Abraham stories, showing how Augustine's interpretation of them in his anti-Manichaean polemics established the ascetic ideal of later Western culture while at the same time legitimating the suppression of opposing views. Paul Meyer argues that one of Augustine's early anti-Pelagian treatises, *On the Spirit and the Letter,* was largely based on his reading of Romans and is thus a kind of commentary on the letter refracted through the context of Augustine's polemic. Finally, Rowan Greer deals with one of the most central of Pauline formulations for the shaping of medieval Western Christendom—Rom 5:12; he discusses the different interpretation of the verse in the early patristic period before showing how Augustine's shift of emphasis (and translation) marks a turning point for later Western considerations of the doctrine of sin.

All translations of biblical passages, unless otherwise noted, are from the *New Revised Standard Version.* Translations of Latin and Greek texts follow that of the Loeb Classical Library, abbreviated LCL (Cambridge: Harvard University Press; London: William Heinemann), unless otherwise indicated. Titles for Greco-Roman and early Christian texts follow the *Oxford Classical Dictionary* wherever possible.

L. Michael White   O. Larry Yarbrough
Oberlin College   Middlebury College

Abbreviations

AB	Anchor Bible
AGJU	Arbeiten zur Geschichte des antiken Judentums und des Urchristentums
AJP	*American Journal of Philology*
AJS	*American Journal of Sociology*
AnBib	Analecta Biblica
AncSoc	*Ancient Society*
ANET	*Ancient Near East in Texts Relating to the Old Testament* (ed. J. B. Pritchard; Princeton: Princeton University Press, 1969)
ANF	Ante-Nicene Fathers
ANRW	*Aufstieg und Niedergang der römischen Welt* (ed. W. Haase and H. Temporini; Berlin: de Gruyter)
BA	*Biblical Archaeologist*
BAGD	W. Bauer, W. F. Arndt, F. W. Gingrich, and F. W. Danker, *Greek-English Lexicon of the New Testament* (2nd ed. Chicago: University of Chicago Press, 1979)
BCH	*Bulletin Correspondence Hellenistique*
BETL	Bibliotheca ephemeridum theologicarum lovaniensium
BFCT	Beiträge zur Förderung christlicher Theologie
Bib	*Biblica*
BJRL	*Bulletin of the John Rylands Library*
CBQ	*Catholic Biblical Quarterly*
CCL	Corpus christianorum latinorum
CIG	*Corpus inscriptionum graecarum*
CIJ	*Corpus inscriptionum judaicarum*
CIL	*Corpus inscriptionum latinarum*
CMG	*Corpus Medicorum Graecorum*
ConBNT	Coniectanea biblica, New Testament
CR	*Classical Review*

CSEL	Corpus scriptorum ecclesiasticorum latinorum
DGE	*Dialectorum Graecarum exempla epigraphica potiora*, ed. E. Schwyzer
DRev	*Downside Review*
Ebib	Etudes bibliques
EKKNT	Evangelisch-katholischer Kommentar zum Neuen Testament
EPRO	Etudes préliminaires aux religions orientales dans l'empire Romain
EvT	*Evangelische Theologie*
ExpT	*Expository Times*
FRLANT	Forschungen zur Religion und Literatur des Alten und Neuen Testaments
GCS	Griechische christliche Schriftsteller
GRBS	*Greek, Roman, and Byzantine Studies*
HNT	Handbuch zum Neuen Testament
HR	*History of Religions*
HSM	Harvard Semitic Monographs
HTKNT	Herders theologischer Kommentar zum Neuen Testament
HTR	*Harvard Theological Review*
HTS	Harvard Theological Studies
HUT	Hermeneutische Untersuchungen zur Theologie
ICC	International Critical Commentary
IE	*Inscriptiones Ephesos*
IG	*Inscriptiones Graecae*
IGRR	*Inscriptiones Graecae ad res Romanas pertinentes*
ILS	*Inscriptiones Latinae Selectae*
JAAR	*Journal of the American Academy of Religion*
JAC	*Jahrbuch für Antike und Christentum*
JBL	*Journal of Biblical Literature*
JHS	*Journal of Hellenic Studies*
JSHRZ	Jüdische Schriften aus hellenistisch-römischer Zeit
JSNT	*Journal for the Study of the New Testament*
JSNTSup	Journal for the Study of the New Testament, Supplement
KD	*Kerygma und Dogma*
LCC	Library of Christian Classics
LCL	Loeb Classical Library
LSA	*Lois sacrées de l'Asie Mineure*
LSCG	*Lois sacrées des Cités grecques*
LSG	*Lois sacrées des Cités grecques, supplément*
LSJ	H. G. Liddell, R. Scott, and H. S. Jones, *Greek-English Lexicon* (Oxford: Oxford University Press, 1966)
LXX	Septuagint
MNTC	Moffatt New Testament Commentary
NCB	New Century Bible
NCBC	New Century Bible Commentary
NedTTs	*Nederlands theologisch tijdschrift*
NICNT	New International Commentary on the New Testament
NovT	*Novum Testamentum*
NovTSup	Novum Testamentum, Supplement

NPNF	Nicene and Post-Nicene Fathers
NTAbh	Neutestamentliche Abhandlungen
NTD	Das neue Testament Deutsch
NTS	*New Testament Studies*
OGIS	*Orientis Graeci Inscriptiones Selectae. Supplementum Sylloges Inscriptionum Graecarum*
PG	J. Migne, *Patrologia graeca*
PL	J. Migne, *Patrologia latina*
PVTG	Pseudepigrapha Veteris Testamenti graece
RAC	*Reallexikon für Antike und Christentum*
RB	*Revue biblique*
RE	*Realencyklopädie für protestantische Theologie und Kirche*
REG	*Revue des Études Grecques*
RevScRel	*Revue des sciences religieuses*
RhM	*Rheinisches Museum für Philologie*
RHR	*Revue de l'histoire des religions*
RNT	Regensburger Neues Testament
RSR	*Recherches de science religieuse*
SBLDS	Society of Biblical Literature Dissertation Series
SBLMS	Society of Biblical Literature Monograph Series
SBLSBS	Society of Biblical Literature Sources for Biblical Study
SBT	Studies in Biblical Theology
SC	Sources chrétienne
SEG	*Supplementum Epigraphicum Graecum*
SJT	*Scottish Journal of Theology*
SNTSMS	Society for New Testament Studies Monograph Series
SR	*Studies in Religion/Sciences religieuses*
SVTP	Studia in Veteris Testamenti pseudepigrapha
TAPA	*Transactions of the American Philological Association*
TDNT	*Theological Dictionary of the New Testament*
TF	Theologische Forschung
TSC	*The Second Century*
TLZ	*Theologische Literaturzeitung*
TZ	*Theologische Zeitschrift*
VC	*Vigiliae Christianae*
WBC	Word Biblical Commentaries
WMANT	Wissenschaftliche Monographien zum Alten und Neuen Testament
WUNT	Wissenschaftliche Untersuchungen zum Neuen Testament
ZAW	*Zeitschrift für die alttestamentliche Wissenschaft*
ZKG	*Zeitschrift für Kirchengeschichte*
ZNW	*Zeitschrift für die neutestamentliche Wissenschaft*
ZPE	*Zeitschrift für Papyrologie und Epigraphik*
ZTK	*Zeitschrift für Theologie und Kirche*

An Appreciation

THIS COLLECTION of essays reflects the high esteem in which Wayne Meeks is held by students and colleagues alike. We celebrate a distinguished career in which he has played many roles—as scholar, editor, teacher, advisor, colleague, and friend—all with patience, attentiveness, and consummate skill. In all these roles, moreover, he has been the proverbial Proteus, whose very image he himself conjured up for understanding Paul. Questioning conventional wisdom and approaches through his scholarship, while forcing students and colleagues alike to question their own assumptions, he has made a lasting impact.

Wayne Atherton Meeks was born on January 8, 1932, in Aliceville, Alabama. He is married to the former Martha Evelina Fowler, and they have three daughters, Suzanne, Edith, and Ellen. After graduating from the University of Alabama (1953) Phi Beta Kappa, with a B.S. degree in physics, he earned the B.D. degree from Austin Presbyterian Seminary (1956) and then spent a year at Tübingen as a Fulbright Scholar. After serving as Presbyterian University Pastor to colleges in Memphis, he entered the graduate program at Yale in 1961. He earned the M.A. degree in 1964 and the Ph.D. in 1965. After returning to Yale in 1969, he was promoted to full professor in 1973 and named to the Woolsey Professorship in Biblical Studies in 1984.

Wayne Meeks, for all his own modesty, has made pioneering contributions to scholarship on the Fourth Gospel, Paul, and early Christianity itself. He has led the way in probing new modes of historical analysis and insight, most notably in his studies of the social world of Paul and of his probing of the inner workings of the often unspoken, but nonetheless real, dimensions of moral world formation.

The publication of *The Prophet-King: Moses Traditions and the Johannine Christology*, a revision of his Yale dissertation under the direction of Nils

Dahl and Paul Meyer, quickly established Wayne Meeks as an important scholar of the New Testament. Its sensitive exegesis of the text, erudite survey of the traditions, balanced critique of existing scholarship, and carefully wrought conclusions made *The Prophet-King* a model dissertation—and more. Indeed, nearly thirty years after its appearance, it is still regarded as a seminal study; few contemporary treatments of the Fourth Gospel have failed to draw on its insights.

During the decade of the seventies, Meeks produced a number of characteristically insightful articles. Three of these are especially important, however, for they broke new ground in the study of the social world of early Christianity, which was just then reemerging as an area of interest among American scholars. In "The Man from Heaven in Johannine Sectarianism," he began to explore through his finely tuned awareness of nuances in Johannine language the connection between theological expression and social context, especially in the way christological formulations reflect sectarian self-consciousness. In "The Image of the Androgyne: Some Uses of a Symbol in Earliest Christianity" and "'Since then you would have to go out of the world': Group Boundaries in Pauline Christianity," Meeks demonstrated what could be gained from reading ancient texts using theories and models developed by modern anthropologists and sociologists. From his reading of Clifford Geertz, Mary Douglas, Victor Turner, and others, Meeks refashioned many of the questions we bring to the study of Paul and the early Christians, inviting the reader to look from a different angle and thus gain a new perspective. Here again, his approach was exemplary, for he never allowed himself to be enslaved by theories. Always the exegete, he did not import theories and models to the ancient text, but instead allowed modern theories to illuminate the text. His anthology *The Writings of St. Paul*, also from this period, reflects his interest in the changing traditions, perceptions, and influences of Paul in later Christian history and scholarship, an interest that also informs his treatment of the historical questions.

The First Urban Christians: The Social World of the Apostle Paul brought together many of the insights Meeks had won in these early studies, showing how Paul and his churches were shaped by the world around them and in turn created a world of their own. First published in 1983, the book is already a classic study of Pauline Christianity. Winner of the American Academy of Religion Award for Excellence (1986) and the *Biblical Archaeology Review* Award for Best Book in New Testament (1984), it has been translated into Spanish, Japanese, Italian, Portuguese, and German.

More recently, Professor Meeks has begun to explore how the social worlds of early Christianity affected issues of morality and ethics. This was the theme of his 1986 Presidential Lecture for the Society of Biblical Literature, entitled "Understanding Early Christian Ethics," and of other recent articles, "The Polyphonic Ethics of the Apostle Paul" and "The Circle of Reference in Pauline Morality." These essays, along with *The Moral World of the*

First Christians, probe a new direction in the study of early Christian ethics by moving beyond treatment of individual issues or questions to the experiential contexts and the forces that shaped early Christian practices and responses. Professor Meeks refers to this approach as "cultural linguistics," by which he means that culturally defined mores are a learned grammar of beliefs, behaviors, and expectations. Culminating this effort is his most recent work, *The Origins of Christian Morality: The First Two Centuries,* which appeared as this collection of essays goes to press. Based on his Speakers Lectures at Oxford University, this book will doubtless influence the field for decades to come.

Professor Meeks has also contributed significantly to scholarship through his numerous editorial activities. He has served on the editorial boards of *New Testament Studies,* the *Journal of Biblical Literature, Biblical Interpretation,* and the Society of Biblical Literature Monograph Series; as editor of the Society of Biblical Literature Sources for Biblical Study Series, as associate editor of the *Harper Bible Commentary,* and as general editor of the Library of Early Christianity for Westminster Press. His most recent, and potentially most far-reaching editorial contribution, however, is his work as general editor for the *HarperCollins Study Bible.* Through this work countless scholars, students, and general readers will benefit from his learning and insight. He will no doubt seek to minimize his own role in this effort, pointing rightly enough to the contributions of many members of the Society of Biblical Literature; however, his own contribution in shaping and guiding the project is evidence of the high regard in which he is held by his colleagues.

In addition to his repute as a scholar, Wayne Meeks has been a well-respected teacher, first at Dartmouth, then at Indiana University, and, since 1969, at Yale. His essay "Imagining the Early Christians: Some Problems in an Introductory Course in the New Testament," his preface to *The First Urban Christians,* and his two National Endowment for the Humanities Seminars for college and secondary teachers are reflective of his commitment to teaching. Indeed, his doctoral students have learned not only from his graduate seminars but also from observing the methods and approaches with which he introduced undergraduates to the study of the New Testament and early Christianity and how seriously he takes his students.

For all these contributions to scholarship and teaching, Wayne Meeks has received numerous awards, including the National Endowment for the Humanities Fellowship (1974), John Simon Guggenheim Memorial Fellowship (1979–80), an honorary doctorate from the University of Uppsala (1990), and election to the British Academy as a Corresponding Fellow (1992).

Professor Meeks, with this collection of essays, we as colleagues, friends, and former students, seek to honor you for a long and distinguished career. We wish for you and Martha a long, happy, and productive life.

BIBLIOGRAPHY

The Writings
of Wayne A. Meeks

BOOKS

1993

The Origins of Christian Morality: The First Two Centuries. New Haven and London: Yale University Press, 1993.

General editor, *HarperCollins Study Bible (Society of Biblical Literature)*, 1989–93.

1990

(joint editor with David L. Balch and Everett Ferguson) *Greeks, Romans, and Christians: Essays in Honor of Abraham J. Malherbe.* Minneapolis: Fortress Press, 1990.

1987

General Editor, *Library of Early Christianity.* Philadelphia: Westminster, 1982–87.

1986

The Moral World of the First Christians. Library of Early Christianity. Philadelphia: Westminster Press, 1986.

1983

The First Urban Christians: The Social World of the Apostle Paul. New Haven and London: Yale University Press, 1983. Spanish edition, Salamanca: Sigueme, 1989. Japanese edition, Tokyo: Jordan Press, 1989. Italian edition, Bologna: Mulino, 1992. Portuguese edition, São Paulo: Edições Paulinas, 1992. German edition, Munich: Chr. Kaiser, forthcoming.

1979

Zur Soziologie des Urchristentums. Theologische Bücherei, Historische Theologie 63. Munich: Kaiser, 1979.

1978

(joint author, editor, and translator with Robert L. Wilken) *Jews and Christians in Antioch in the First Four Centuries of the Common Era.* Sources for Biblical Study 13. Missoula, Mont.: Scholars Press, 1978.

1977

(joint editor with Jacob Jervell) *God's Christ and His People: Essays Presented to Nils Alstrup Dahl.* Oslo: Universitetsforlaget, 1977.

1973

(joint editor and translator with Fred O. Francis) *Conflict at Colossae: A Problem in the Interpretation of Early Christianity Illustrated by Selected Modern Studies.* Sources for Biblical Study 4. Missoula, Mont.: Scholars Press, 1973; 2nd ed. 1975.

1972

The Writings of St. Paul. A Norton Critical Edition. New York: Norton, 1972.

1967

The Prophet-King: Moses Traditions and the Johannine Christology. NovTSup 14. Leiden: Brill, 1967.

1964

Go From Your Father's House: A College Student's Introduction to the Christian Faith. Richmond: John Knox, 1964.

ARTICLES

1992

"Il cristianesimo [to A.D. 235]." In *Storia di Roma* II.3, 283–319. Turin: Einaudi, 1992.
"The Social World of the New Testament." *The Oxford Study Bible,* 79*–89*. New York: Oxford University Press, 1992.

1991

"The Man from Heaven in Paul's Letter to the Philippians." In *The Future of Early Christianity: Essays in Honor of Helmut Koester,* edited by Birger A. Pearson et al., 329–36. Minneapolis: Fortress, 1991.

"On Trusting an Unpredictable God: A Hermeneutical Meditation on Romans 9–11." In *Faith and History: Essays in Honor of Paul W. Meyer*, edited by John T. Carroll, Charles H. Cosgrove, and E. Elizabeth Johnson, 105–24. Atlanta: Scholars Press, 1991. An abridged Swedish translation in *Svensk Exegetisk Årsbok* 56 (1991) 101–17.

1990

"Equal to God." In *The Conversation Continues: Studies in Paul and John in Honor of J. Louis Martyn*, edited by Robert T. Fortna and Beverly R. Gaventa, 309–22. Nashville: Abingdon, 1990.

"The Circle of Reference in Pauline Morality." In Balch, Ferguson, and Meeks [see above] 1990. Pp. 305–17.

1988

"The Polyphonic Ethics of the Apostle Paul." *Annual of the Society of Christian Ethics* 1988: 17–29.

1987

"Judgment and the Brother: Romans 14:1–15:13." In *Tradition and Interpretation in the New Testament: Essays in Honor of E. Earle Ellis*, edited by Gerald F. Hawthorne, 290–300. Grand Rapids, Mich.: Eerdmans; Tübingen: Mohr-Siebeck, 1987.

"Studying the Bible as Memory and Imagination." In *The Bible and the Liberal Arts*, edited by Raymond B. Williams. Papers from a Conference October 16–17, 1986. Crawfordsville, Ind.: Wabash College, [1987].

1986

"St. Paul of the Cities." In *Civitas: Religious Interpretations of the City*, edited by Peter S. Hawkins, 15–23. Atlanta: Scholars Press, 1986.

"A Hermeneutics of Social Embodiment." In *Christians among Jews and Gentiles: Essays in Honor of Krister Stendahl on His Sixty-fifth Birthday*, edited by George W. E. Nickelsburg and George W. MacRae, 176–86. Philadelphia: Fortress, 1986.

"Understanding Early Christian Ethics." *JBL* 105: 3–11.

1985

"Die Rolle des paulinischen Christentums bei der Entstehung einer rationalen ethischen Religion." In *Max Webers Sicht des antiken Christentums: Interpretation und Kritik*, edited by Wolfgang Schuchter, 363–85. Frankfurt a.M.: Suhrkamp, 1985.

"Breaking Away: Three New Testament Pictures of Christianity's Separation from the Jewish Communities." In *"To See Ourselves as Others See Us": Christians, Jews, "Others" in Late Antiquity*, edited by Jacob Neusner and Ernest S. Frerichs, 93–115. Chico, Calif.: Scholars Press, 1985.

1983

"Social Functions of Apocalyptic Language in Pauline Christianity." In *Apocalypticism in the Mediterranean World and the Near East*, edited by David Hellholm, 687–705. Proceedings of the International Colloquium on Apocalypticism, Uppsala, August 12–17, 1979. Tübingen: Mohr-Siebeck, 1983.

1982

"'And Rose Up to Play': Midrash and Paraenesis in 1 Corinthians 10:1–22." *JSNT* 16: 64–78.
"The Social Context of Pauline Theology." *Interpretation* 3: 266–77.

1978

"'Since then you would have to go out of the world': Group Boundaries in Pauline Christianity." In *Critical History and Biblical Faith: New Testament Perspectives*, edited by Thomas J. Ryan, 4–29. Villanova, Penn.: College Theology Society, 1978.
"Hypomnemata from an Untamed Skeptic: A Response to George Kennedy." In *The Relationships Among the Gospels: An Interdisciplinary Dialogue*, edited by William O. Walker, Jr., 157–73. Trinity University Monograph Series in Religion 5. San Antonio: Trinity, 1978.

1977

"The Unity of Humankind in Colossians and Ephesians." In Meeks and Jervell, eds., *God's Christ and His People* (see above). Pp. 209–21.

1976

"The Divine Agent and His Counterfeit in Philo and the Fourth Gospel." In *Aspects of Religious Propaganda in Judaism and Early Christianity*, edited by Elisabeth Schüssler Fiorenza, 43–67. Notre Dame: University of Notre Dame Press, 1976.
"Jews and Christians in Antioch." In *Society of Biblical Literature 1976 Seminar Papers*, edited by George W. MacRae, 33–65. Missoula, Mont.: Scholars Press, 1976.
"Moses, in the NT." In *The Interpreter's Dictionary of the Bible*. Supplementary Volume, 605–7. New York and Nashville: Abingdon, 1976

1975

"'Am I a Jew?'—Johannine Christianity and Judaism." In *Christianity, Judaism, and Other Greco-Roman Cults: Studies for Morton Smith at Sixty*, edited by Jacob Neusner, vol. 1, pp. 163–86. Studies in Judaism in Late Antiquity 12. Leiden: Brill, 1975.

"Imagining the Early Christians: Some Problems in an Introductory Course in the New Testament." *Perspectives in Religious Studies* 2/1: 3–12.

1974
"The Image of the Androgyne: Some Uses of a Symbol in Earliest Christianity." *HR* 13: 165–208.

1972
"The Man from Heaven in Johannine Sectarianism." *JBL* 91: 44–72.
"The Christian Proteus." In *The Writings of St. Paul* [see above]. Pp. 435–44.

1971
"True Spirituality: A Study of Opposition to Paul in Corinth." *Enquiry* 3 (March-May): 21–50.

1970
"Paul as Heretic: A Study of Opposition to the Apostle in Galatia." *Enquiry* 3 (Sept.-Nov.): 21–48.

1968
"Moses as God and King." In *Religions in Antiquity: Essays in Memory of Erwin Ramsdell Goodenough*, edited by Jacob Neusner, 354–71. Studies in the History of Religions 14. Leiden: Brill, 1968.

1966
"Galilee and Judea in the Fourth Gospel." *JBL* 85: 159–69.

REVIEWS

In the *Journal of Biblical Literature, Journal of Roman Studies, Gnomon, Interpretation, Religious Studies Review, Journal of the American Academy of Religion, Heythrop Journal, Association for Jewish Studies Newsletter, Union Seminary Quarterly Review,* and *Theology Today.*

Part One

Paul and His Communities

CHAPTER 1

Euodia and Syntyche
and Paul's Letter to the Philippians

Nils A. Dahl

IN THE DAYS of Paul, two women, Euodia and Syntyche, lived in Philippi, a Roman colony in the province of Macedonia. Their names happen to be known to us because they did not agree. To Paul, the conflict must have been a serious matter; he addresses each of them and exhorts them to be of the same mind, pursuing a common purpose. He even asks a third person to come to their assistance and adds a reference to Clement and other fellow workers (Phil 4:2–3). Both the identity of the persons and the nature of the conflict were, no doubt, familiar to the first recipients of the letter.

Later readers, however, including modern scholars, can at best satisfy their curiosity on this matter by means of more or less plausible inferences and guesses. As far as possible, conjectures should take account of what we know about the city of Philippi and, more generally, about the status and role of women in Greco-Roman cities in the first century.[1] At the same time, the paragraph about Euodia and Syntyche must be carefully interpreted in the context of Philippians and other Pauline letters. I shall not discuss all the proposals that have been made nor present relevant new data. What I would like to do is to turn the question around: How far may close attention to the paragraph about Euodia and Syntyche contribute to a better understanding of the problems of the literary unity, composition, and scope of the Epistle to the Philippians.

NAMES AND PERSONS

Clement, who has a Latin name (*Clemens*), is likely to have been a descendant (or perhaps a freedman/client) of the Roman veterans who were settled at Philippi when Antonius founded and Octavian reorganized the

---

1. See especially Lilian Portefaix, *Sisters Rejoice: Paul's Letter to the Philippians and Luke-Acts as Seen by First-Century Philippian Women* (ConBNT 21; Stockholm: Almqvist & Wiksell, 1988).

city as a Roman colony (42 and ca. 30 B.C.E.). As Euodia and Syntyche are Greek names, the two women would have belonged rather to the local Macedonian population or, perhaps more likely, have been Greek immigrants from Asia Minor, like Lydia from Thyatira, the dealer in purple cloth who according to Acts 16:14–15 became the first convert and Paul's hostess in Philippi. As she may have been called the "Lydian," it is conceivable that she might be identical with either Euodia or Syntyche, but that is a conjecture without any proof. The many and diverse attempts to identify the "true yokefellow" (γνήσιε σύζυγε) remain pure guesswork; I tend to think that he, or possibly she, must have been closely associated with Paul as a "true partner" (TEV).

What is beyond reasonable doubt is that Euodia and Syntyche were prominent members of the Christian community at Philippi and, to use the words of Wayne Meeks, "were women who had sufficient independence to have been recognized in their own rights as activists in the Pauline mission."[2] The *ius italicum* granted to a Roman colony may have favored their independence, but their civil status remains, unfortunately, unknown to us.

The majority of female names in the Pauline epistles are to be found in the last chapter of Romans, which begins with a commendation of Phoebe, the deacon of the church at Cenchreae and a patron to many and to Paul himself (Rom 16:1–2). The chapter makes best sense if she was also the carrier of Paul's letter to Rome. According to the attractive suggestion of Robert Jewett, her task was to prepare for Paul's arrival and to gain support for his intended mission to Spain. If so, the following list of greetings names influential persons who were representatives of various Christian groups in the big city.[3]

The list begins with the well-known couple Prisca and Aquila; similarly, both Andronicus and Junia (*sic*) and Philologus and Julia are likely to have been married couples (16:3–5, 7, 15). Paul also extends greetings to Rufus and his mother, who had acted like a mother to Paul himself, and to Nereus and his sister (16:13, 15b). Four names of women are not associated with any male; in all these greetings Paul adds a commendatory phrase like "who has/have toiled in the Lord" (16:6, 12). Whereas Maria and the beloved Persis are greeted separately, Tryphaena and Tryphosa are mentioned together, as sisters or members of the same household.

Both in Rome and in the cities of the Pauline mission, the activity of Christian women was to a variable degree interconnected with their customary role in household management. Some of them may in fact have been in charge of their own houses and affairs, for example, Phoebe, the

2. W. A. Meeks, *The First Urban Christians: The Social World of the Apostle Paul* (New Haven: Yale University Press, 1983) 57.

3. R. Jewett, "Paul, Phoebe, and the Spanish Mission," in *The Social World of Early Christianity* (Festschrift H. C. Kee; ed. J. Neusner et al.; Philadelphia: Fortress, 1990) 142–61.

mother of Rufus, Chloë, and Lydia (Rom 16:1f., 13; 1 Cor 1:11; Acts 16:14–16). A large house could also provide room for the assembly of an ecclesial community, as in the houses of Prisca and Aquila in Ephesus and Rome, Philemon in Colossae, and Nympha in Laodicea (1 Cor 16:19; Rom 16:5; Phlm 1–3; Col 4:15 MSS B 1739 al.).[4]

Women are hardly likely to have proclaimed the gospel on streetcorners and in marketplaces, but other forms of communication have from an early time on contributed more to the spread of Christianity. For women like Lydia and Priscilla, trade and workshop offered ample opportunities to make contacts and bear testimony to the faith (see Acts 16:14; 18:3). So did the synagogues; Acts reports that Prisca/Priscilla gave Apollos more adequate instruction about "the way (of God)" after she had heard him speak boldly in the synagogue (Acts 18:26).

Christian women as well as men were also active outside their own houses in ways that drew public attention and caused trials and persecution. Paul's fellow workers Prisca and Aquila risked their own necks for his sake, and Andronicus and Junia had been his fellow prisoners (Rom 16:4, 7). The preceding survey illustrates a variety of activities in which women like Euodia and Syntyche may have been engaged, in and outside their own households. What is without analogy in their cases is that commendatory remarks are not connected with a greeting but with an appeal that implies an indirect reproach.

ADMONITION AND COMMENDATION

The admonition of Euodia and Syntyche is introduced with παρακαλῶ, a word that in similar contexts is a polite yet urgent form of request and is translated with words such as "entreat," "exhort," or "appeal to" (in KJV mostly "beseech"). In the letter to Philemon, Paul uses the same verb to call for a free, voluntary obedience, rather than to command (ἐπιτάσσειν). Only when his relationship with the addressees is in trouble, Paul may write "I beg" (δέομαι, Gal 4:12; 2 Cor 10:2). Addressing the anonymous person who is to assist the two women, he uses the more colorless form "I ask you" (ἐρωτῶ σέ, Phil 4:3). It is quite unusual for Paul to exhort three individuals by name and in each case explicitly state that he is doing so. By contrast, the general exhortations in Philippians begins with an imperative (2:1), while parenetic sections in his other letters are regularly introduced with a metaphrase, mostly with παρακαλῶ. All such observations indicate that the disagreement between Euodia and Syntyche has been a matter of concern

---

4. On the "household assemblies," see Meeks, *First Urban Christians*, 75–77, and also L. M. White, *Building God's House in the Roman World: Architectural Adaptation among Pagans, Jews, and Christians* (Baltimore and London: Johns Hopkins University Press, 1990).

for the well-being of the whole Christian community at Philippi, not merely a personal quarrel between the two women.

Using a fairly common expression, Paul urges them to be of the same mind (τὸ αὐτὸ φρονεῖν, as in Phil 2:2 and 2 Cor 12:11; cf. Rom 12:16; 15:5). This implies not only that they should agree and live in harmony with each other but also that they ought to have the same concern in mind. That is especially clear in Philippians, where the verb (φρονεῖν) occurs more often than in any other Pauline letter (ten times, over against eight in Romans and five elsewhere).

The urgent appeal is followed by a relative clause which states that Euodia and Syntyche have been Paul's companions in an athletic contest (συν-ήθλησάν μοι) and—according to the most natural syntax—that they have done this together with Clement and other fellow workers of Paul. The metaphor can suggest a fight with adversaries like wrestling or boxing, as it does in Phil 1:27–30, but the image can also be drawn from a race (see Phil 2:16; 3:14). In any case, the main point is that Christians are like athletes, who have to make their utmost effort, train hard, and exercise rigid self-discipline, even if it causes pain and agony, in order to be victorious and gain the prize (cf. 1 Cor 9:24–28). The athletic metaphors yield a perspective on Christian life and activity, agony and suffering, and even prayer and intercession (see also Rom 15:30; Col 1:29–2:1; 4:12; 1 Thess 2:2).

The explicit statement that Clement, and other fellow workers too, have also been Paul's partners in the athletic contest allows for the inference that Euodia and Syntyche were likewise among Paul's "fellow workers" (συν-εργοί). This does not mean that they had, like Timothy and probably Titus, accompanied Paul on extended missionary journeys. Paul can use the term "fellow worker" (συνεργός) about persons like Prisca and Aquila, Philemon and others who did not. Like Clement and others, Euodia and Syntyche were residents of Philippi at the time of Paul's writing. They may have continued and extended his work and also faced trials after he had left, but nothing indicated that they, like Epaphroditus, also acted as delegates to and from the apostle. The terms used do, however, indicate that they had collaborated with Paul personally and that must have been at a time when Paul was in Philippi. If he wrote from Ephesus, rather than from Rome or Caesarea, the cooperation must go back to Paul's first visit. If so, Euodia, Syntyche, and Clement are representatives of the Philippian Christians for whose "partnership (κοινωνία) in the gospel from the first day" onward Paul gives thanks (Phil 1:3–6).

In some respect, what Paul writes about Euodia and Syntyche is similar to the commendations added to several names in the greeting list in Romans (esp. 16:3–4, 7) and to commendations of Timothy, Epaphroditus, and other persons who are to be welcomed and highly esteemed (Phil 2:20–22, 25, 29–30; cf. Rom 16:1–2; 1 Cor 16:13–18; Col 1:7; 4:12). By contrast, the merits of Euodia and Syntyche were so well known that Paul did not need to repeat them. In spite of a commendatory form, Paul's remarks serve much more to point out the scandalous nature of the conflict between the two distinguished women who have been Paul's companions in his struggle, like the other fellow workers, whose names are in the book of life. This is an expression of Paul's confidence in God, who will bring to completion the good work that he has begun (cf. Phil 1:5–6; 3:15). Yet the relative clause is appended in a way that leaves room for the possibility that the names of Euodia and Syntyche might be blotted out from the book of life unless they heed correction and get back on the right track (cf. Rev 3:5; Ps 69:28/29).

My analysis does not yield precise answers to questions about the activity and experiences of the two women, but it does allow for one conclusion: The conflict between Euodia and Syntyche was not merely a personal quarrel but was related to their work and trials for the sake of the gospel. They are more likely to have worked independently, as did Maria and Persis, than to have been closely associated with one another like Tryphaena and Tryphosa. Consideration of the immediate context and the broader setting in Philippians makes me think of the disagreement as a conflict between two rivals.

LITERARY CONTEXT

The paragraph about Euodia and Syntyche is self-contained without any explicit link to what precedes or follows. It has its natural place toward the end of the letter, and the somewhat loose combination of various injunctions and other items in a concluding section is not without analogy in other Pauline letters (see esp. 1 Cor 16:1–23; 1 Thess 5:12–28). Proponents of the theory that the canonical shape of Philippians is due to a secondary combination of parts of two or three letters disagree widely among themselves about what parts of Phil 4:1–9 belong to which letter. The simplest solution is to connect all the short paragraphs in 4:1–9 with the preceding section (3:2–21). Yet several observations favor the view that at least the appeals in 4:1, 2–3 belongs to the same letter as 1:1–2:30 (or 3:1). I am therefore going to discuss the place and function of Phil 4:2–3 in the context of the letter that we know from the manuscripts.[5]

5. Arguments in favor of the integrity of Philippians are based on a variety of specific observations; see, for example, T. E. Pollard, "The Integrity of Philippians," *NTS* 13 (1966–67) 57–66; R. Jewett, "The Epistolary Thanksgiving and the Integrity of Philippians," *NovT* 12 (1970) 40–53; M. D. Hooker, "Philippians 2:6–11," in *Jesus und Paulus* (Festschrift W. G. Kümmel; ed. E. E. Ellis and E. Grässer; Göttingen: Vandenhoeck & Ruprecht, 1975) 151–64; H. Gamble, *The Textual History of the Letter to the Romans* (Studies and Documents 42; Grand Rapids: Eerdmans, 1977) Appendix II (pp. 145–46).

The paragraph is fairly clearly related to the immediately preceding verses. The assertion that Paul's beloved brothers (and sisters) are his joy and wreath of victory introduces a general injunction to stand firm in the Lord (4:1). Thus it serves as a transition from the preceding section (3:2–21) to the special appeal to Euodia and Syntyche, especially by anticipating the metaphor of an athletic context in 4:3. The book of life (4:3), is a list of the citizens of the commonwealth (πολίτευμα) in heaven (3:20). As the Roman colonists in Philippi have the rights of citizenship even though they do not live in Rome, so the members of the church at Philippi are citizens of heaven who still live on earth, expecting Christ to come from heaven and transform their mode of existence.

The interconnection between the special appeal of 4:2–3 and the general exhortations in 4:4–7 and 8–9 is less obvious, but it is at least conceivable that Paul continued to keep the most burning issue in mind. Constant rejoicing in the Lord, prayer, and thanksgiving should overcome the anxious concern for one's own advantage that is a cause of strife. The injunction to let the mutual forbearance among Christians be known to all people would be especially appropriate if outsiders paid unfavorable attention to the conflict between some outstanding members of the community. If so, this would also provide a background for the concluding exhortation to take generally accepted moral standards into consideration (4:8). Not only the accumulation but also the choice of terms for whatever is true, noble, just, and worthy of praise departs so much from Paul's normal language that he probably had some special reason to stress human decency as well as Christian love.

The exhortation to a common decency that does not cause offense is followed by a reference to Paul's own example (4:9). The entire, albeit otherwise diverse, segment Phil 3:17–4:9 is thus enclosed by appeals to imitate Paul. Even in the appended thanksgiving for the gift of the Philippians, Paul presents himself as a model (4:10–18). The thanksgiving is very cordial but does at the same time stress that he was not really in need of the gift. He is self-sufficient (αὐτάρκης), content with what he has, whether abundance or want, able to do and to endure everything in him who gives him strength. Already the opening thanksgiving anticipates Paul's gratitude for the gifts by which the Christians at Philippi have displayed their partnership (κοινωνία, 1:5; συγκοινωνήσαντες, 4:14) with Paul, both in past and in more recent times.

Such arguments for the literary integrity do not, however, answer the question of what, if any, importance the inserted paragraph about Euodia and Syntyche has for the composition of the letter as a whole. The paragraph restates an injunction that earlier in the letter has a general form, to be of the same mind (or have the same concern, τὸ αὐτὸ φρονῆτε, 2:2; τὸ αὐτὸ φρονεῖν, 4:2). Most commentators have tended to regard the appeal to the two women as a special application of the general exhortation. Only a few have suggested "that when Paul wrote the more general exhortation, he already had this quarrel [between Euodia and Syntyche] in mind."[6] The arguments that favor this suggestion have, to my knowledge, never been laid out in detail.

Paul may have found that the conflict between Euodia and Syntyche violated generally accepted standards of decent behavior as well as Christian love. That would explain why he exhorts all Christians to consider whatever is true, honorable, just, and so on, in a way that is without analogy in his other letters. The Philippians, who know this from the example set by Paul, should put it into practice (4:8–9). This restates a preceding injunction (3:17) to follow Paul's example so that the specific appeals of 4:2–9 are tied by *imitatio Pauli* to the general exhortations of 3:17–4:1.

The specific appeals are followed by the thanksgiving for the gift Paul has received, a thanksgiving that was already anticipated in the opening of the letter (1:3–7). It may also be related to how Euodia and Syntyche had proved to be Paul's fellow athletes in several ways—even as benefactors who had contributed to the gifts by which the Christians at Philippi displayed their fellowship or partnership (κοινωνία, 1:5; see also 1:7; 4:14) with Paul both in the past and more recently. The form of the thanksgiving is somewhat curious. It is very cordial but does at the same time stress that he was not in need of the gift (see especially 4:11–13, 17–18a). He is "self-sufficient" (αὐ-τάρκης), content with what he has, in both abundance and want. Able to do and to endure everything in him who gives him strength, he is indeed a model, perhaps especially for people like Euodia and Syntyche.

My tentative reading between the lines is not based on exact arguments that allow for any precise verification—or refutation. It does, however, gain some probability from the observation that was my point of departure, namely, that there is a remarkable correspondence between the initial, general exhortations in Phil 1:27–2:5 and the special appeal to Euodia and Syntyche in the context of 3:20–4:3. These can be seen especially in Paul's use of citizenship language, athletic imagery, and the weight given to the key thematic phrase "Be of the same mind."

As the phrase "be of the same mind" was in common use, it is not very significant that it occurs twice in a letter such as Romans (12:16; 15:5). What is remarkable is the extraordinary weight that is given to the appeal, not only in Phil 4:2–3 but also in 2:1–2. Here the appeal is introduced by four parallel clauses, "So if there is any encouragement in Christ," and so on. Thereby Paul conjures the addressees to heed his appeal: "Make my joy complete by being of the same mind!" The form of the exhortation is friendly, as is the whole letter, in which expressions of joy, cordial sentiments and con-

6. G. B. Caird, *Paul's Letters from Prison* (New Clarendon Bible; New York: Oxford University Press, 1976) 149–50.

fidence abound. The letter does not contain explicit reproaches or complaints. It does contain stern warnings against some alien teachers (3:2, 18–19), but there is no evidence that there existed opposing factions within the congregation. The only conflict about which we get any information is the disagreement of Euodia and Syntyche; it may have been the main reason why Paul's joy was less than complete.

Having admonished the addressees to be of one mind, Paul spells out what this implies: to share the same love and, being inwardly united (σύμ-ψυχοι), to have one concern and goal in mind (τὸ ἓν φρονοῦντες, 2:2). He further proceeds to adduce attitudes that will either hinder or promote unity among Christians: selfishness (ἐρίθεια) and empty conceit (κενοδοξία) in contrast to the humble attitude (ταπεινοφροσύνη) in which one regards others higher than oneself. One should look out not only for one's own interests but for what is good for the others (2:3–4). All of this pertains to personal relations, not to conflicting doctrines or ritual praxis. The difference between this section of Philippians and Rom 14:1–15:6 and parts of 1 Corinthians increases the probability that Paul formulated the exhortations with Euodia and Syntyche in mind.

The main hortatory section of Philippians begins with the thematic admonition to behave in a manner that is worthy of the gospel of Christ (1:27). The word for behave is here not the usual "walk" (περιπατεῖν) but a verb (πολιτεύεσθαι) that carries connotations of the duties of a citizen and thus corresponds to the notion that Christians have their commonwealth (πολίτευμα) in heaven (3:20). In the latter part of 1:27, Paul spells out implications of a conduct worthy of the gospel in a way that prepares for his insistence in 2:2 and 4:2 on unity among Christians and exhibits striking similarities to formulations in 3:20–4:2. The believers in Philippi are encouraged to stand firm (στήκετε) in one spirit (1:27) or in the Lord (4:1). They are, moreover, to continue to struggle as fellow athletes (συναθλοῦντες) for the faith of the gospel (1:27), as Euodia and Syntyche have done in the past (συνήθλησάν μοι, 4:3; the verb occurs nowhere else in the New Testament). Thus, not only the urging appeals in 2:1–5 but also the initial exhortations in 1:27–28 are especially applicable to the two women.

After the exhortations in Phil 1:17–28, Paul adds some remarks about the enmity and the sufferings that the Philippians have experienced and still experience (1:28–30). He concludes that they thus have part in the same athletic contest (ἀγών) as Paul himself, whose struggle they once observed and later heard about (1:30). In the last exhortation of the letter (4:9), Paul uses a strikingly similar phraseology in the appeal to act according to the paradigm set by Paul's teaching and behavior. My suggestion that even the general exhortations in Philippians have been formulated in a way that relates to the conflict between Euodia and Syntyche would be further confirmed if the same holds true for the presentation of models and warning examples.

MODELS AND WARNING EXAMPLES

The prime model is Jesus Christ, whose self-abasement and exaltation are
recounted in Phil 2:6-11. Since the time of E. Lohmeyer (1927-28) it has
been widely assumed that Paul is here quoting a hymn.[7] Whether Paul is
quoting a single hymn or adapting a conventional hymnic style, form, and
phraseology to the context of the letter is uncertain. In the context of the
main hortatory part of the letter (1:12-2:18), the function of the inserted
"hymn" is to undergird the preceding and following exhortations by means
of a hymnic commemoration of Christ.

The first part of the hymn (2:6-8) clearly corresponds to the preceding,
urgent admonitions in 2:1-5. The admonitions contrast selfishness
(ἐριθεία) and vanity (κενοδοξία) with a humble disposition (ταπεινοφροσύνη) to count others higher than oneself and not look for one's own interests but for those of others (2:3-4). Christ is the model for this attitude:
being "in the form of God" (ἐν μορφῇ θεοῦ) he did not count equality with
God a prize (ἁρπαγμός) to grasp or keep for himself, but he emptied himself,
taking on the form of a slave (μορφὴν δούλου) and, as a human being, he
humbled (ἐταπείνωσεν) himself, obedient until his death on the cross
(2:6-8).

I tend to read the controversial verse 2:5 as two steps in the gradual transition from exhortations to hymnic predications. In the imperatival main
clause, v. 5a, the demonstrative pronoun τοῦτο is placed before the predi-
cate and probably refers to what precedes: "This you should think (=be concerned about) among yourselves" (τοῦτο φρονεῖτε ἐν ὑμῖν). The appended
relative clause contains only the words "that/which also in Christ Jesus" (ὃ
καὶ ἐν Χριστῷ Ἰησοῦ). The simplest understanding of the syntax is to
explain this as one among several examples of an adjectival relative clause
without the copula "is" (ἐστιν, not ἦν, "was"; see, e.g., 1 Cor 5:1; Phil 4:3
[end]). In any case, the sequence of thought presupposes that Christ is the
model to emulate just because he is the redeemer (2:6-8) and the Lord
(2:9-11).[8] As always in Paul's letters, the reference to the cross signifies the

7. E. Lohmeyer, *Kyrios Jesus: Eine Untersuchung zu Phil. 2,5-11* (Heidelberg: C. Winter, 1928).
For further bibliography on the hymn, see also L. M. White, "Morality between Two Worlds: A
Paradigm of Friendship in Philippians," in *Greeks, Romans, and Christians: Essays in Honor of
Abraham J. Malherbe* (ed. D. L. Balch; Minneapolis: Fortress, 1990) 207-9 and nn.

8. A paraphrase such as "Have the same mind that Jesus Christ had" does not adequately
render the best attested Greek text. The analogy with Paul's use of "in me" in Phil 1:30 and 4:9,
however, makes me willing to consider the proposal of Wayne Meeks, who renders Phil 2:5
thus: "Base your practical reasoning on what you see in Christ Jesus" (*The Origins of Christian
Morality: The First Two Centuries* [New Haven: Yale University Press, 1993] 206; see also Meeks,
"The Man from Heaven in Paul's Letter to the Philippians," in *The Future of Early Christianity:
Essays in Honor of Helmut Koester* [ed. B. A. Pearson; Minneapolis: Fortress, 1991] 329-36;
White, "Morality between Two Worlds," 209-10). The general meaning would have been suffi-
ciently clear to the first readers, who hardly reflected on the syntax.

death of Jesus as a saving event, and even God's enthronement of Jesus as
Lord contributes to the content of the formula "in Christ Jesus" (cf., e.g.,
Rom 3:24–26; 1 Cor 1:30).

The first part of the hymn (Phil 2:6–8) states the reasons why the
addressees ought to relate to one another in the way that Paul has recommended. A similar rhetorical pattern occurs several times in the Pauline letters and elsewhere. Christians are exhorted that their mutual relations to
each other should conform to what Christ has done for them. Christians
should please their neighbors, for Christ did not please himself (Rom
15:2–3; see also 15:7). "He loved us and gave himself up for us" (Eph 5:2; see
also 4:28; Col 3:13; 1 Pet 2:20–25; etc.). The connection between the second
part of the hymn and the resumed exhortations in Phil 3:12–18 is more like
another rhetorical pattern, which does not represent Christ as a model. It
does rather refer to the purpose (or consequences) of his coming death
and/or resurrection, in order to draw a moral lesson, that is, "Christ died
and came to life again in order to rule as lord of the dead and the living"
(Rom 14:9; see also 1 Thess 4:14; 5:9–10; 2 Cor 13:4; etc.).[9]

This pattern can be applied not only to warnings (see Rom 14:4–12) but
also to statements of comfort and encouragement (see 1 Thess 4:13–15;
5:9–11). In Philippians 2 there is a striking shift of mood from the conjuring
injunctions in 2:1–5 to a confident outlook toward a blameless, even lumi-
nous, existence of the children of God in the midst of a perverse generation
(2:14–18). God, who has exalted Christ in order that he should be universally acclaimed as Lord, is also at work among those who work for their
own salvation with fear and trembling (2:12–13). The same confident outlook reappears in 3:12–16 and even more clearly in the expectation that the
Lord Jesus Christ will come from heaven and transform our humble body to
become like (σύμμορφον) his body of glory (3:20–21).

Like Christ, Paul is himself a model to emulate, not in the least because he
has renounced the privileges he once enjoyed. He was a circumcised
Israelite of pure descent, blameless according to the righteousness of the
Law. But whatever gain he had he counted as loss for the sake of Christ
(3:4–11). This account of the great change in Paul's life is remarkably similar
to, and yet different from, the version of the same event in Galatians
(1:11–2:21). There Paul stresses that God through a revelation of his Son

9. Already long ago (1954) I distinguished between the two patterns of christological references in moral instruction; see Nils Dahl, "Form-critical observations in Early Christian
Preaching," in English in *Jesus in the Memory of the Early Church* (Minneapolis: Augsburg, 1976)
30–36. A more detailed study would have demonstrated that both patterns can have a general
scope, but in some cases also have a very specific address. See especially 2 Cor 8:7–11; cf., e.g.,
Eph 5:2, 25; Rom 14:5–12; 15:1–8. The insertion of the "hymn" in the hortatory context in Phil
2:1–18 has analogies in 1 Pet 1:16–22; 2:18–25; and 3:16–19(–22). Even though domestic slaves
are the addressees in 1 Pet 2:18, the recollection of Christ's work and its purpose in 2:21–25
has a general scope.

commissioned him to preach the gospel to the Gentiles, as he did in Galatia. Paul argues in detail that in his relation to Peter, the authorities in Jerusalem, and the Christians in Judea, he has without any compromise stood for the same gospel that he preached to the Gentiles (1:16–2:21). Moreover, he adds complicated arguments from scripture to prove that the Gentiles have a full share of God's promise to Abraham (3:1–29; 4:21–5:1). He asks them to become as he is; this means that they should practice the same freedom from the Law as he himself does (4:12). In Philippians we find no corresponding argumentation. Paul is a model because he has abandoned his former pride and boasting in order to pursue the goal that is set before him in Christ. The Philippians are to imitate Paul's selfless renunciation of all his own advantages and privileges (3:10–17).

Paul is, moreover, a model because he meets general human standards of decency (4:8–9). He is content with what he has, whether plenty or little, abundance or want (4:11–13), and his attitude to death or continued life is equally relaxed (1:18b–26). In a similar way Timothy is a model because he does not (like so many others) look after his own interests, and Epaphroditus is to be highly regarded because he came close to death in his service to Paul (2:20–21, 27–30).

Even Philippians contains some references to opponents of Paul: "evil workers" (3:2–3) and "enemies of the cross of Christ" (3:18–19). The letter does not, however, contain any real discussion or refutation of the arguments of these opponents. They are simply characterized by stereotyped invectives, and scholars have argued whether they represent one or two groups. The opponents are known from the reports and have, apparently, had much in common with the opponents of Paul in 2 Corinthians (see 11:22–30; 13:4).[10] There seems to be an increasing agreement that Paul uses them as examples to warn against selfish pride and boasting of circumcision and other this-worldly advantages (Phil 3:3, 19).[11]

CONCLUSIONS

My remarks concerning models and warning examples suggest that it is likely that 3:3–17 and 20–21, and probably also 4:1–3, were from the begin-

10. On similar features in Philippians 3 and 2 Corinthians, see H. Koester, "The Purpose of the Polemic of a Pauline Fragment (Philippians iii)," *NTS* 8 (1961–62) 317–32. There is, however, no evidence that Paul and his ministry were attacked in Philippi as they were in Corinth. In Philippians, the picture of the heretics, who are proud and boast over their own privileges and achieved glory, remains abstract, shaped by the contrast to Paul's attitude (see 3:7–14). Paul suspects that not all of the addressees share his conviction; he fears that he has not reached the goal but is hoping for the future resurrection of the dead (3:15–16; 3:11–14; cf. 3:20–4:1). The Philippians, possibly including Euodia and Syntyche, may, however, have tended toward a perfectionism of which the "enemies of the cross of Christ" were the extreme example, without accepting the heretical doctrines.

11. See especially W. S. Kurtz, S.J., "Kenotic Imitation of Paul and Christ in Philippians 2 and 3," in *Discipleship in the New Testament* (ed. F. F. Segovia; Philadelphia: Fortress, 1985) 103–26.

ning part of the same letter as the hymn in 2:6–11. The remark in 3:1 (that it is not irksome to Paul to write the same things) causes in any case a problem that is not solved by the theory that a fragment of another letter is inserted at this point. One might guess that the Philippians have expected that Paul would castigate their lack of unity and that he thus responds by stressing his mood of joy in writing.

It has long been customary to regard the letter to the Philippians as a spontaneous expression of joy and friendship. More recent studies have shown that what we find is rather a rhetoric of friendship. Paul stresses mutual joy, confidence, and friendship as strongly as he possibly can, in order to stimulate these attitudes among the recipients.[12] Robert T. Fortna has called Philippians "Paul's most egocentric letter."[13] In fact, one can find elements of egocentricity in most of Paul's letters, and what Paul writes about himself in Philippians is closely related to the unselfish attitude that he wishes to stimulate among the recipients.

My attempt has, I think, proved that is makes sense to read the letter with the assumption that the disagreement between Euodia and Syntyche is the chief problem Paul faces and the main reason why his joy over the Philippians is less than complete. This should not be stressed to the exclusion of other possibilities. A closer examination of the "pattern of conformity" and the "teleological pattern" would prove that similar formulations can have a general as well as a specific aim. What seems certain is that the two women were outstanding and influential members of the church of Philippi. The conflict between them was obviously more than a personal quarrel, but there is no direct evidence that it was due to differences of teaching or attitude to Paul. Euodia and Syntyche were most likely rivals who wanted to get as much recognition and honor for their work in the gospel as possible. Questions about who had suffered the most for her faith or who had contributed the most to the gift to Paul may perhaps have been part of their conflict.[14]

In the beginning of his letter Paul gives brief reports of the situation where he is himself imprisoned (Rome or Ephesus). This inspired other preachers to speak the word of God with boldness, out of genuine love for Paul. Others, however, reacted with envy, hoping that their activity would profit from Paul's enforced public silence (Phil 1:12–18). Paul stresses that in any case he rejoices that Christ is proclaimed, whether in pretense or in truth. I dare to think that even in this respect Paul presents himself as a

---

12. See L. T. Johnson, *The Writings of the New Testament* (Philadelphia: Fortress, 1986) 338–49; White, "Morality between Two Worlds," 201–15.

13. R. T. Fortna, "Philippians: Paul's Most Egocentric Letter," in *The Conversation Continues: Studies in Paul and John in Honor of J. Louis Martyn* (ed. R. T. Fortna and B. R. Gaventa; Nashville: Abingdon, 1990) 220–34.

14. See also the suggestion of White, "Morality between Two Worlds," 214 and n. 59.

model. Moreover, Euodia and Syntyche should learn to disregard motivation and honors and rejoice whenever Christ is proclaimed.[15]

15. I owe great thanks to L. Michael White for his patience and assistance in bringing this manuscript into shape for publication, and to my daughter Eva, without whose help I would, owing to temporary illness, never have been able to complete it at all. Most of all, I want to thank Wayne for many years of cooperation, mutual influence, and friendship.

CHAPTER 2

Christ, the Elements of the Cosmos, and the Law in Galatians

J. Louis Martyn

THE DATA IN THE LETTER

IN GAL 4:3 AND 4:9 Paul mentions τὰ στοιχεῖα τοῦ κόσμου, "the elements of the cosmos."[1] In both cases he speaks of two contrasting periods, distinguished from each other by a radical change in the relationship human beings have to these elements. The earlier of these periods is that prior to the advent of the Christ; the second is the one since that event.

We begin with the reference in Gal 4:3-5. Drawing on the picture of the boy who is held under the authority of guardians and overseers during his minority, even though he is the heir of his father's household, Paul formulates his application:

> Something very like this is true of us. When we were children, we were held in a state of slavery under the power of the elements of the cosmos. But when the fullness of time arrived, God sent his Son, born of a woman, born under the power of the Law, in order that he might redeem those held under the Law; in order, that is, that we might receive adoption as sons.[2]

One sees immediately four striking motifs: (a) The elements of the cosmos had the power to enslave, and they exercised that power. (b) God has terminated that enslavement by sending his Son. (c) In their enslaving activity the elements had some kind of connection or relationship with the Law. At the minimum, the elements and the Law were functionally parallel entities: both enslaved, and God's sending of Christ has effected liberation from both. (d) The elements enslaved "us," and the Law enslaved "them." Do these

---

1. The references to cosmic elements in Colossians, Hebrews, and 2 Peter (cf. *Herm. Vis.* 3.13.3) will be mentioned only in passing; it is important to read Galatians in its own right before making comparisons.

2. Translations of NT passages herein are those of the author, except in a few cases, mostly citations of parallel wording in Greek, where the NRSV rendering has been supplied.

pronouns indicate a reference to Gentiles and Jews respectively? Or is Paul of the opinion that prior to Christ's advent the human race was essentially a monolith, enslavement under the elements of the cosmos and under the Law being characteristic of all human beings? The answer is given in Gal 3:13–4:6, for in this passage Paul's careful alternation of pronouns and verb subjects (sometimes first person plural; sometimes second person plural) is surely a psychologically effective means of insisting on the undifferentiated monolith of humanity before Christ.[3]

A few sentences after this first reference to the elements of the cosmos, Paul speaks of them a second time (Gal 4:8–11). Now, instead of referring to "us" and "them," he narrows the focus, addressing the Galatians as "you," thus depicting two contrasting epochs in their life:

> It is true that formerly, not knowing God, you were enslaved to things that in nature are not gods; but now, knowing God—or rather being known by God— how can you possibly turn back to the weak and impotent elements, wishing once again to be their slaves? You observe special days and months and sea-sons and years. I am anxious about you, worrying that the labor I have spent on you might prove to have no effect!

Three of the motifs mentioned above are repeated here, connecting this ref-erence to the earlier one: (a) enslavement to the elements; (b) the termina-tion of that enslavement by something God has done (he has known the Galatians); (c) the close connection drawn between enslavement to the ele-ments and the keeping of the Law through the observance of ritual times. Moreover, the third motif is clarified: Gentiles who have been known by God and who now *turn* to the Law by following its prescription of holy times are not thereby confirming the end of their veneration of the ele-ments. On the contrary, they are *returning* to that veneration.[4] The elements and the Law are therefore more than functionally parallel entities, both hav-ing the power to enslave. If veneration of the Law is one form in which human beings venerate the cosmic elements, it is highly probable that in some fashion or other the Law *is* one of those elements. Thus, the universal "we" who were held under the power of the elements (4:3) are the same per-sons as "those" who were held under the power of the Law (4:5).[5]

3. The exegetical debate pertinent to this matter up to 1983 is well presented in Richard B. Hays, *The Faith of Jesus Christ* (Chico, Calif.: Scholars Press, 1983). See also Charles B. Cousar, *A Theology of the Cross* (Minneapolis: Fortress, 1990) 115–17; R. N. Longenecker, *Galatians* (Dal-las: Word, 1990) 164; N. T. Wright, *The Climax of the Covenant* (Edinburgh: Clark, 1991).

4. That the holy times mentioned by Paul have to do with the Galatians' incipient accep-tance of the Law is clear from the context. See also D. Lührmann, "Tage, Monate, Jahreszeiten, Jahre (Gal 4,10)," in *Werden und Wirken des Alten Testaments* (ed. R. Albertz et al.; Göttingen: Vandenhoeck & Ruprecht, 1980) 428–45.

5. See, e.g., B. Reicke, "The Law and This World According to Paul: Some Thoughts Concern-ing Gal 4:1–11," *JBL* 70 (1951) 259–60. Other interpreters have argued that the "we" of 4:3 are Gentiles, whereas the "those" of 4:5 are Jews, supporting their reading in part by referring to

There are also three new accents: (d) By addressing the Galatians directly, Paul now specifies their former enslavement as their worship of the elements. (e) He denies that the elements are deities, implying that in the Galatians' original religious life they worshiped the elements as gods. (f) He insists that the elements are, on the contrary, weak and impotent.

These two references to the elements pose one of the more interesting and also one of the more important issues of Galatians, especially if one asks how they may be related to Paul's christology and to his view of the Law.[6] Why should Paul speak to the Galatians about the elements of the cosmos, and how does he intend the audience to construe his reference? What, precisely, are these elements, how did they enslave, and how is it that their universally enslaving power has been broken by the advent of Christ? Was it not sufficient in Paul's mind to characterize the period prior to Christ as one of imprisonment under *the Law* (3:23, 25)? Why speak also of imprisonment under the elements, somehow identifying the Law as one of them?

These are exceedingly thorny questions, as one can see from the extraordinary number of studies given to them and from the striking absence of a consensus.[7] As to the identity of the elements, we may begin with the four major possibilities listed by W. Bauer in his lexicon:[8]

---

1 Cor 9:20–21. It is indeed clear that in this latter passage Paul differentiates Gentiles from Jews, identifying the former as persons "not under the Law" (οἱ ἄνομοι) and the latter as persons "under the Law" (οἱ ὑπὸ νόμον). But those very expressions show that in 1 Cor 9:20–21 Paul is following the tradition according to which all persons are identified by their relation to the Law, it being a cosmic entity by virtue of having been a pre-cosmic one. According to tradition, God created the Law before the cosmos, used it then as the instrument with which he made the heavens and the earth, and subsequently offered it to all peoples of the earth (Prov 8:22–31; *Gen. Rab.* 1.1; *Sifre Deut* §343, etc.). Thus, in the terms of 1 Cor 9:20–21 Jews (and the circumcision party in the Jerusalem church) are indeed *those of the Law*. But in the same terms Gentiles also derive their identity from the Law by being *those of the not-Law*. Different from both, Paul declares himself to be "in the Law of Christ" (ἔννομος Χριστοῦ), an affirmation that sounds the note struck in Gal 6:2. That is to say, to be in the Law of Christ is to be altogether beyond the distinction between the Law and the not-Law.

6. The author of Colossians considers the relationships among the elements, the Law, and Christ to pose issues requiring explicit discussion. Regarding corresponding issues in Galatians, see the conclusion below.

7. The basic bibliography is given in the commentaries; see H. D. Betz, *Galatians* (Hermeneia; Philadelphia: Fortress, 1979); U. Borse, *Der Brief an die Galater* (RNT; Regensburg: Pustet, 1984); and Longenecker, *Galatians*. See especially J. Blinzler, "Lexicalisches zu dem Terminus τὰ στοιχεῖα τοῦ κόσμου bei Paulus," in *Studiorum Paulinorum Congressus Internationalis Catholicus 1961* (AnBib 18; Rome: Pontifical Biblical Institute, 1963) 2:429–43; John G. Hawkins, "The Opponents of Paul in Galatia" (Ph.D. dissertation, Yale University, 1971) 181–250. Several studies of Eduard Schweizer are especially helpful for the role of the elements in the Colossian heresy, but one must take care not to allow the study of the elements in Colossians to set the agenda for the investigation of their role in Galatians; see most recently Schweizer, "Slaves of the Elements and Worshipers of Angels: Gal 4:3, 9 and Col 2:8, 18, 20," *JBL* 107 (1988) 455–68; see also the constructive critique of Richard E. DeMaris, *Colossian Controversy* (Sheffield: JSOT Press, 1994).

8. For additional possibilities, see Blinzler and Hawkins in the preceding note.

1. "Elements (of learning), fundamental principles." As this is almost certainly the meaning of στοιχεῖα in Heb 5:12, numerous exegetes, noting the motif of immaturity in Gal 4:1-2, have proposed it for the references in Galatians as well: human beings were formerly given to the elementary forms of religion, Jewish and Gentile; these have now been surpassed by the new revelation in Christ.[9] But such a reading is precluded by the context, and notably by the clause "we were held in a state of slavery under the power of the elements of the cosmos," scarcely a reference to an immature stage of religious development that has been merely transcended by the maturing advent of Christ. In a word, there is here no thought of progress *from* elementary forms of religion *to* mature ones.[10]

2. "Elemental substances, the basic elements from which everything in the natural world is made and of which it is composed," presumably the traditional four: earth, water, air, fire. The lexicographical labors of J. Blinzler have shown this to be the most common meaning of the term στοιχεῖα, and the only meaning attested for the expression στοιχεῖα τοῦ κόσμου. One should accept it for any text of Paul's time, unless there is good reason not to do so.[11]

3. "Elementary spirits which the syncretistic religious tendencies of later antiquity associated with the physical elements." This is the meaning favored by Bauer, H. D. Betz, and others, but the sources for it are mostly later than Paul.[12]

4. "Heavenly bodies." A number of interpreters link this meaning with the preceding one; Betz, for example, speaks of "demonic entities of cosmic proportions and astral powers which are hostile towards man."[13] It is a reading that honors Paul's insistence that the elements held humanity in a state of slavery, clearly viewing them as inimical powers of some sort. Again, however, the thought that the astral elements are demonic and hostile to human beings is difficult to show by drawing on early sources.[14]

---

9. See, e.g., E. D. Burton, *The Epistle to the Galatians* (ICC; Edinburgh, Clark, 1921) 518; recently Longenecker finds Paul to be "building on the view of τὰ στοιχεῖα as being 'first principles' or 'elemental teachings.'" Gal 4:3 is thus a reference to "the Mosaic law ... [as the] 'basic principles' given by God in preparation for the coming of Christ," while Gal 4:9 is a reference to the "veneration of nature and cultic rituals that made up the Gentiles' 'basic principles' of religion" (*Galatians*, 165–66).

10. Hawkins, "Opponents of Paul," 183–85, 210–12.

11. Blinzler, "Lexicalisches," 439–41. Examples include Philo, *Quis rerum divinarum heres sit* 134 (cf. note 40 below); Wis 7:17; 19:18; 4 Macc 12:13; and, among Christian texts, 2 Pet 3:10, 12, where the author refers to the dissolution of the world's elements in a final cosmic conflagration, a Stoic motif.

12. See Derek R. Moore-Crispin, "Galatians 4:1-9: The Use and Abuse of Parallels," *Evangelical Quarterly* 60 (1989) 211.

13. Betz, *Galatians*, 205.

14. See Longenecker, *Galatians*, 165. Astutely leaving aside the motif of demonic hostility, Hawkins opts at the end of his investigation for "the heavenly bodies which determine the

We can already draw an initial and tentative conclusion: lexicographical observations strongly favor the second meaning listed by Bauer, the four traditional cosmic elements, earth, water, air, fire. As we have already noted, one must have a strong reason to read τὰ στοιχεῖα τοῦ κόσμου in some other way.[15]

Interpretive disarray remains widespread, however, and, in any case, lexicography cannot settle an issue of such exegetical complexity. Looking about, therefore, for a new way of approaching the subject, one may ask whether the history of the Galatians' linguistic experience may not offer a key. Paul employs the expression "the elements of the cosmos" without explanation; he may very well be using the expression in his own way, but he seems able to assume that it already has some meaning in the Galatians' vocabulary. What can we say, first of all, then, about the Galatians' experience with the expression prior to their hearing Paul's use of it in his letter?

THE GALATIANS PROBABLY KNEW THE EXPRESSION "THE ELEMENTS OF THE WORLD" BEFORE ENCOUNTERING EITHER PAUL OR THE TEACHERS[16]

H. D. Betz is correct to say that we can know relatively little about the religion of the Galatians before they were seized by the Pauline gospel.[17] Taking them to have been located in the tribal centers of Ancyra, Tavium, and Pessinus, nestled in the rustic Anatolian highlands, one can assume that some of them, at least, may have been adherents of an old Celtic religion.[18]

---

sequence of calendrical observances" ("Opponents of Paul," 249). As we will see, that may very well be the major meaning the term had for the Teachers who invaded Paul's Galatian churches; it is not central to Paul's view. For evidence, albeit later, of this type of syncretism in the region of western Asia Minor (including Galatia), see A. R. R. Sheppard, "Pagan Cults of Angels in Roman Asia Minor," *Talanta* 12–13 (1980–81) 77–101 (esp. 94–96).

15. The lexicographical conclusions reached by Blinzler have been supported by further research: D. Rusam, "Neue Belege zu dem *stoicheia tou kosmou* (Gal 4,3.9; Kol 2,8.20)," *ZNW* 83 (1992) 119–25. It is worth mentioning that over a period of some years Eduard Schweizer has written several pieces to show that both in Colossians and in Galatians the reference is to the traditional four elements. That is surely the reading with which to begin one's work, but as we will see below, the study of Galatians cannot come to rest there.

16. On the use of the expression "the Teachers" to refer to the persons whose incursion into Paul's Galatian churches caused the writing of the letter, see J. Louis Martyn, "A Law-Observant Mission to Gentiles: The Background of Galatians," *SJT* 38 (1985) 307–24.

17. Betz, *Galatians*, 3 n. 11.

18. For reasons that cannot be developed here I think it likely that the churches were in ethnic Galatia. See W. A. Meeks, *The First Urban Christians: The Social World of the Apostle Paul* (New Haven: Yale University Press, 1983) 42–43. See further David Magie, *Roman Rule in Asia Minor to the End of the Third Century after Christ* (2 vols.; repr. New York: Arno, 1975); R. Chevallier, *Roman Roads* (Berkeley: University of California Press, 1976); A. H. M. Jones, *The Cities of the Eastern Roman Provinces* (rev. ed. by M. Avi-Yonah et al.; Oxford: Clarendon, 1971); R. K.

One would certainly bear in mind, however, that Pessinus was the site of a major sanctuary dedicated to Cybele, the Great Mother of Life and the lover of Attis.[19] We can be confident that the Galatians had been enthusiastic adherents of one or several cults characterized by severe devotion to deities very probably represented—at least in some cases—by statues placed in their temples.

Equally important is the fact that Paul can formulate an argument in the letter that presupposes for its effectiveness a certain amount of intellectual sophistication. As noted above, the Galatians evangelized by Paul did not live in large, thoroughly hellenized cities, but a number of them were clearly persons of some education.[20] The letter shows that Paul can assume their acquaintance with certain rhetorical conventions and with some expressions and terms that had acquired a degree of technical denotation, such as the verb συστοιχεῖν ("to correspond to," Gal 4:25). Thus, whatever the form of their native religion(s), they were probably in command of some of the common philosophical theories about the structure of the cosmos. Specifically, they had almost certainly heard of and pondered some form of the ubiquitous speculation about the elements that constitute the world's foundation. If, as noted above, one of Paul's Galatian churches was in Pessinus, it may be of some importance that Apuleius mentions the temple of Cybele there as the place in which the Phrygians reverence Isis under the name of "the Pessinuntine Mother of the Gods." For in the same passage Apuleius identifies Isis as *elementorum omnium domina* ("mistress of all the elements," *Metamorphoses* XI, 5; cf. XI, 25).

Taking these observations into account, one notes in particular the second of Paul's references to the elements. There he says—apparently without fear of being effectively controverted—that in their past life the Galatians worshiped the elements as though they were gods. To be sure, the Galatians will almost certainly have referred to their gods—at least the major ones—by proper names. A newcomer to their cities will not have found them worshiping earth, air, fire, and water.[21] Yet, looking back on that earlier period,

---

Sherk, "Roman Galatia: The Governors from 25 B.C. to A.D. 114," *ANRW* 2.7.2 (1980) 954–1052; S. Mitchell, "Population and the Land in Roman Galatia," *ANRW* 2.7.2 (1980) 1053–81.

19. See A. D. Nock, *Essays on Religion and the Ancient World* (Cambridge, Mass.: Harvard University Press, 1972) 2:893; M. J. Vermaseren, *Cybele and Attis: The Myth and the Cult* (London: Thames & Hudson, 1977) 13–31; Helmut Koester, *History, Culture, and Religion in the Hellenistic Age* (Philadelphia: Fortress, 1980) 191.

20. G. Schöllgen is correct to accent the autochthonal character of the residents of these relatively small and only partially hellenized cities, "Was wissen wir über die Sozialstruktur der paulinischen Gemeinden?" *NTS* 34 (1988) 71–82; cf. the works listed in n. 18 above. The point, however, can be overdone, Ancyra was no village, and contact with major urban centers in western Asia Minor is well documented.

21. In this sense P. Vielhauer is right to follow G. Delling in saying: "Von einem Stoicheia-kult in Galatien fehlt jede Spur," in *Geschichte der urchristlichen Literatur* (Berlin: de Gruyter,

they may have concluded (especially under the tutelage of the Teachers; see below) that in their cults they were somehow reverencing the elements, at least as subordinate deities. That would represent nothing more than the insight of Philo, for example, who, continuing a tradition evident in Homer and Empedocles, speaks of persons who revere the elements as gods: they

> call fire Hephaestus . . . , air Hera . . . , water Poseidon . . . , and earth Demeter (*De vita contemplativa* 3).[22]

In Paul's time it is the common *Jewish* view that when Gentiles worship idols, they are in fact worshiping the elements. Thus, the Galatians may have held, for example, to some form of the common belief that changes in the elements, including the movements of the stars, cause the turning of the seasons, thus affecting the growing of the food necessary for the sustenance of life.[23] If they were adherents of the cult of the Great Mother, they may have engaged in orgiastic rites designed to assure the fertility of the earth.[24] However this may be, the Galatians are almost certain to have known the expression "the elements of the cosmos" long before they laid eyes on either Paul or the Teachers—very probably as earth, air, fire, water, with the possible addition of the stars—and Paul is able to assume some retrospective comprehension on their part when he links these elements with gods they worshiped before his arrival.

THE TEACHERS MAY HAVE COMMENTED ON "THE ELEMENTS"

None of the letter's explicit references to the Teachers and to their message indicates that they spoke to the Galatians about the elements of the

---

1975) 117; cf. idem, "Gesetzesdienst und Stoicheiadienst im Galaterbrief," in *Rechtfertigung: Festschrift für Ernst Käsemann zum 70. Geburtstag* (ed. J. Friedrich et al.; Tübingen: Mohr, 1976) 543–55.

22. Homer, *Iliad* 20.67 (from G. Delling, στοιχεῖον, *TDNT* 7:675); Empedocles, Fr 6; Diels and Kranz, *Die Fragmente der Vorsokratiker*, 1:311; K. Freeman, *Ancilla to the Presocratic Philosophers* (Cambridge, Mass.: Harvard University Press, 1948) 52; the Greek text of the fragment of Empedocles is given also in G. S. Kirk and J. E. Raven, *The Presocratic Philosophers* (Cambridge: Cambridge University Press, 1971) 323. Here and below (nn. 28, 39, 40) I cite Philo from LCL, sometimes making minor changes in the translation.

23. E. Schweizer ("Slaves of the Elements," 457–58) cites and translates a very interesting text from Alexander Polyhistor (Diels, 1:449); for the most part I follow Schweizer's translation: "among the sensible bodies are the four elements, fire, water, earth, air, which throughout undergo changes and are altered. And from them there came into being the animate, intellectual world. . . . Light and darkness, warm and cold, dry and wet have equal shares in the world (ἰσόμοιρα . . . ἐν τῷ κόσμῳ); [but there are variations in their strength]. By a predominance of warm, summer comes, by a predominance of cold, winter. . . ." On this text see now DeMaris, *Colossian Controversy*, 88–97.

24. On the different forms of the Magna Mater/Cybele cult and their development, see Giulia Sfameni Gasparro, *Soteriological and Mystical Aspects in the Cults of Cybele and Attis* (EPRO 103; Leiden: Brill, 1985) passim.

world. One cannot limit oneself to those explicit references, however, when one is attempting to reconstruct the major motifs of the Teachers' theology. Passages in which Paul makes no direct reference to the Teachers suggest strongly, for example, that they tied their instruction about the Law to affirmations they made about Abraham.[25] Might they have spoken about the elements, even though Paul does not mention their having done so? Two factors suggest that they did:

1. We know that comments about the elements played a role not only in some Jewish portraits of Gentiles but also in corresponding forms of Jewish apologetic directed to Gentiles. One thinks, for example, of Wisdom 13, a text strangely overlooked in most of the attempts to understand Paul's references to the cosmic elements:

> For all men who were ignorant of God were foolish by nature; and they ... did not recognize the craftsman, while paying heed to his works; but they supposed that either fire or wind or swift air, or the circle of the stars, or turbulent water, or the luminaries of heaven were the gods that rule the world. If through delight in the beauty of these things, men assumed them to be gods, let them know how much better than these is their Lord, for the author of beauty created them. And if men were amazed at their power and working, let them perceive from them how much more powerful is he who formed them. For from the greatness and beauty of created things comes a corresponding perception of their Creator. (Wis 13:1–5)[26]

Reading this text, one is again reminded of Paul's charge that in their native religious life the Galatians worshiped the elements, holding them to be gods (Gal 4:8). One also notes three further motifs: (a) The author of Wisdom lists not only fire, wind, air, and water, but also the stars, perhaps reflecting the widespread linking of the activity of the elements with the turning of the seasons and thus with the demarcation of sacred times.[27]

25. On the role of Abraham in the Teachers' theology, see C. K. Barrett, "The Allegory of Abraham, Sarah, and Hagar in the Argument of Galatians," in *Rechtfertigung: Festschrift für Ernst Käsemann zum 70. Geburtstag* (ed. J. Friedrich et al.; Tübingen: Mohr, 1976) 1–16; J. Louis Martyn, "A Law-Observant Mission to Gentiles"; B. H. Brinsmead, *Galatians–Dialogical Response to Opponents* (Chico, Calif.: Scholars Press, 1982); G. Walter Hansen, *Abraham in Galatians* (Sheffield: JSOT Press, 1989).

26. Trans. F. V. Filson. See also Wis 7:17; 19:18; 4 Macc 12:13; *1 Enoch* 80:7. Disdain of those who revere the elements as quasi deities is not an exclusively Jewish motif. G. Delling mentions as an example Menander's mocking of those who divinize the elements (*TDNT* 7:677).

27. The finding that there is no pre-Pauline text in which the elements are said to include the stars can be literally maintained even in the face of Wisdom 13, for the term στοιχεῖα does not occur there. It seems clear, however, that in this text the author expands his other references to the elements (7:17; 19:18) to include the stars and, more broadly speaking, the luminaries of heaven. That the heavenly bodies created on the fourth day mark the holy times is said, for example in *Jub.* 2:8–10 (cf. *1 Enoch* 82:9). One notes also that Philo speaks of the four physical elements as the material out of which God created both κόσμος and οὐρανός, four also being the number of the seasons determined by the stars (*De opificio mundi* 52). See also Ben Sira, who relates the distinguishing of holy times to the elemental polarity set in the

(b) He is concerned to bring the Gentiles to the true knowledge of God (note the imperative verbs—"let them know" and "let them perceive"). And (c) he is convinced that the elements do indeed provide the route to God: Gentiles can ascend the ladder of perception *from* contemplation of the world's elements *to* the knowledge of God. There is ample evidence that this proselytizing reference to the world's elements was characteristic of numerous diaspora Jews of Paul's time. And the following observation leads one to think that the same may be true of the Christian-Jewish missionaries who made their way into Paul's Galatian churches:

2. Some Jewish apologists formulated this teleological (and sometimes proselytizing) argument by referring to Abraham's understanding of the elements. Two examples will suffice: (a) Philo, recalling that Abraham was reared in the religion of the Chaldeans, speaks of the patriarch's ladderlike journey to the perception of the true God, doing so in a way quite similar to that portrayed in Wisdom 13:

> The Chaldeans were especially active in the elaboration of astrology and ascribed everything to the movements of the stars. . . . Thus they glorified visible existence, leaving out of consideration the intelligible and invisible. . . . . They concluded [indeed] that the world itself was God, thus profanely likening the created to the Creator. In this creed Abraham had been reared, and for a long time remained a Chaldean. Then opening the soul's eye as though after profound sleep, and beginning to see the pure beam instead of the deep darkness, he followed the ray and discerned what he had not beheld before, a charioteer and pilot presiding over the world and directing in safety his own work. (*De Abrahamo* 69–70)[28]

(b) Josephus speaks in a similar way of Abraham's teleological journey from polytheism to monotheism:

> He (Abraham) began to have more lofty conceptions of virtue than the rest of mankind, and determined to reform and change the ideas universally current concerning God. He was thus the first boldly to declare that God, the creator of the universe, is one, and that, if any other being contributed aught to man's welfare, each did so by His command and not by virtue of its own inherent power. This he inferred from the changes to which earth and sea are subject, from the course of sun and moon, and from all the celestial phenomena; for, he argued, were these bodies endowed with power, they would have provided for their own regularity, but since they lacked this last, it was manifest that even those services in which they cooperate for our greater benefit they render not in virtue of their own authority, but through the might of their commanding

---

cosmos by God (Sir 33:7–9, 14–15). On the great spring festival of Attis, March 15–27, see Vermaseren, *Cybele and Attis* (n. 19 above) 113–23, and Koester, *History, Culture, and Religion of the Hellenistic Age*, 192–94.

28. Trans. Colson, LCL. Cf. E. R. Goodenough, *By Light Light* (New Haven: Yale University Press, 1935) 137 n. 87.

sovereign, to whom alone it is right to render our homage and thanksgiving. (*Jewish Antiquities* 1.155–56; trans. Thackeray, LCL)

Bearing in mind the weighty role played by Abraham in the Teachers' Gentile mission, we may make several suggestions with some degree of plausibility:[29]

The Teachers are almost certain to have shared the Jewish view of Gentiles as people who ignorantly worship the visible parts of creation, and they may have spoken in this connection of the Gentile tendency to confuse the elements with God (cf. again Wisdom 13 and Gal 4:8). It is not difficult to imagine their saying to the Galatians themselves:

> The presence of idols in the temples of your former religion shows that you Gentiles ignorantly reverenced the elements as though they were gods. More tragic still, Paul did nothing really to terminate your ill-informed relation to the elements. It is true that, like other peoples, you were apparently aware of the role of the astral elements in signaling the seasons you celebrated as holy. You did not know, however, the true calendar established by God, and Paul did not convey it to you. In truth the stars are nothing other than servants of the God of Israel who made them and who gave them a role in relation to his holy Law. As servants of this God, the elements shift the seasons in order to fix the correct times for the true feasts, those ordained by him.

The Teachers would not have spoken in this vein, however, simply in order to charge their Gentile hearers with ignorance. If they referred to the elements, they would probably have spoken of them in an evangelistic way: "You are to ascend from the foolish and idolatrous worship of the elements themselves to the knowledge of the true God, celebrating the holy times ordained by him in his Law, and doing so at the junctures fixed by the activity of his servants, the astral elements."

Would they have offered the Gentiles a paradigm of this crucial ascent? We have already referred to grounds for thinking that the Teachers made extensive use of traditions that present Abraham as the first Gentile to come to the true knowledge of God, being thus the paradigmatic proselyte. What can now be added is the possibility that, in presenting this picture of Abraham, they would not have overlooked the traditions in which (a) the patriarch is said to have made the journey to the knowledge of God by an astrological contemplation of the elements, (b) being the first to observe the holy feasts at the correct times (e.g., *Jubilees* 16).

Thus, it may have been as part of the Galatians' new understanding of the season-causing elements that they took up the calendrical observances laid out by the Teachers. That is one reading of the connection Paul draws between two of his charges: the Galatians, he says, are (re-)turning to the worship of the elements (4:9), and they are taking up from the Teachers the

---

29. Regarding the role of Abraham in the Teachers' theology, see n. 25 above.

observance of holy times (4:10). Thus one might hazard an imaginary encapsulation of one paragraph in the Teachers' message:

> In making the ascent from the pagan contemplation of the elements to the true knowledge of God, you follow in the steps of Abraham, for he did the same. You become, indeed, Abraham's true, Law-observant descendants, knowing for the first time why the constantly changing elements cause the turning of the seasons. As servants of God, they do that to enable us to observe at the correct time the holy feasts ordained by God (Gal 4:10).[30]

THE GALATIANS LISTEN TO PAUL'S LETTER

Now, imagining ourselves seated in one of the Galatian congregations as Paul's messenger reads his letter aloud, we may begin with the initial part of the second reference to the elements: "you [Galatians] were enslaved to things that in nature are not gods." If the suggestions offered above are cogent, it follows that in two regards Paul and the Teachers are in agreement: (a) The Galatians were—from the Jewish point of view—typical Gentiles, in that, directly or indirectly, they viewed the elements as divinities; (b) this worship was altogether foolish.

When, however, we take into account the whole of Paul's second reference to the elements, and when we combine it with the first, we see that between the Teachers and Paul there is a radical parting of the ways. Paul does not for a moment entertain a form of ladder theology, encouraging Gentiles to acquire true knowledge of God by lifting their gaze from the elements to their maker. More dramatically still, he refuses to speak of the elements from the Jewish point of view, finding in element worship a characteristic of Gentiles. On the contrary, he says that prior to Christ's advent all human beings venerated the elements and were in fact enslaved by them.[31] As we have noted early in this essay, Paul considers the elements of the cosmos somehow to include the falsely deified idols of Gentile religion and the Law. Indeed, the formerly Jewish members of the church (in Jerusalem, in Antioch, etc.)—no less than the formerly Gentile ones (in Galatia)—were once enslaved to those elements. Further, it follows that, if

30. The Galatians' attraction to the ladder theology basic to the journey from contemplation of the elements to knowledge of God may be reflected in Gal 4:9. One notes that, in order to make his own point, Paul has to reverse himself in mid-sentence: "But now, having come to know God, or rather, since 'coming to know God' is an expression fundamental to the ladder theology of the Teachers, let me put it a different way: now that you have been known by God, . . ." That the Teachers spoke explicitly of the elements is asserted also by Lührmann, "Tage, Monate, Jahreszeiten, Jahre," 431 n. 15.

31. As we have noted in n. 5 above, this point has been seen by many interpreters, although most admit that it is difficult to explain. It is one of the major aspects of the στοιχεῖα puzzle; see below.

formerly Gentile members *turn* to the Law, they in fact *return* to the worship of the falsely deified elements (4:9-10). One hardly needs to say that vis-à-vis the theology of the Teachers these statements of Paul constitute strong and explicitly polemical medicine.

It is clear, to be sure, that Paul cannot intend to refer to Jewish Christians (and by implication to Jews) as persons who in the past literally worshiped idols, images they held incorrectly to be gods. (Note again the change to "you [Galatians]" in 4:8-9; cf. Rom 2:22.) Nor can he mean that Gentile Christians, in their former life, literally observed and were enslaved by the Law (cf. Rom 2:14-16, 26-27).[32] That he speaks of universal enslavement is, however, unmistakable; and this point will have been in itself enough to incite outrage on the part of the Teachers and their followers in the Galatian churches. Joining one of the Galatian congregations again, we can imagine hearing the Teachers' retort:

> Paul is suggesting that prior to the advent of God's Messiah the world was a monolith of enslavement to the elements; he is saying that Jews no less than Gentiles were held in bondage to them, indeed that the holy and just and good Law of God *is* one of these enslaving elements! Such talk is outrageous. *We* have never considered the elements to be Gods; we know that the Law of God is not one of them; and being Abraham's seed, we ourselves have never been enslaved to anyone (cf. John 8:33).

A Major Puzzle

We can also imagine that Paul anticipated such outrage. Not at all easy to understand is his expectation that his inclusion of the Law among the enslaving elements of the cosmos would prove even momentarily worthy of consideration when his letter was read aloud to the Galatians. This expectation is, in fact, one of the persistent puzzles of the letter.[33] Can it be made less puzzling?

An answer may lie in our noting again that Paul does not speak merely of the elements, but specifically in Gal 4:3 of the elements *of the cosmos*. It is, to be sure, a traditional way of referring to the elements of nature.[34] This expression may provide, however, a clue to the character of Paul's startling

---

32. Correctly recognizing this point, Blinzler unfortunately flees from Galatians to Romans, concluding that by the elements of the cosmos Paul meant flesh, sin, and death ("Lexikalisches," 442-43).

33. P. Vielhauer is more right than wrong to say that Paul includes the Law among the enslaving elements "[um] Heidentum und Judentum auf den gleichen begrifflichen Nenner [zu] bringen" ("Gesetzesdienst," 553). One is left, however, with the puzzle mentioned in the text.

34. Aristotle, for example, can use as an equivalent the expression στοιχεῖα τῆς φύσεως ("elements of nature," *Metaphysics* 986b), and Philo follows suit (*De vita Mosis* 2.251). Cf. Blinzler, "Lexikalisches," 440-41.

universalism, provided we allow it to pose a simple question: *Of what cosmos*, specifically, were these enslaving elements the fundamental parts?

The Cosmos of Which Paul Speaks

We note first that Paul employs the word "cosmos" at only one other point in the letter:

> ... the cross of our Lord Jesus Christ, by which the cosmos was crucified to me and I to the cosmos. For neither is circumcision anything nor is uncircumcision anything; what is something is the new creation. (6:14–15)[35]

I have commented elsewhere on these sentences, noting Paul's affirmation that the cosmos from which Christ's cross has separated him consisted of pairs of opposites.[36] What is gone with the crucifixion of the cosmos is not simply circumcision, but rather both circumcision and uncircumcision, and thus the distinction of Jew from Gentile. Or, to take the matter to its root, what has suffered eclipse is not simply the Law, but rather the cosmos that had at its *fundamentum* both the Law and the not-Law.[37]

Equally important for our present concern is the background of this affirmation: In form it is a traditional way of referring to the totality of the cosmos, evident, for example, in Ben Sira: "all the works of the Most High are in pairs, one the opposite of the other" (33:15). In this tradition the word "cosmos" or its equivalent is intimately linked with pairs of opposites. It is obvious that in Gal 6:14–15 Paul shapes this tradition to his own theological concern, speaking of a *religious* pair of opposites so fundamental to life as to be called "cosmos." Given the identity of this pair, it is not difficult to see that its erasure brought about loss of cosmos for Paul, the Pharisee; but one sees also that Paul considers the erased cosmos to have been the cosmos of all human beings (Gal 3:26–28).

Do we have here, then, an approach to the puzzle that we found to be posed by Gal 4:3, 8–9: What cosmos was it whose elements enslaved human beings and whose hegemony has been terminated in Christ? Was it a cosmos composed of elements that were themselves pairs of opposites? Is

35. Comparison with Col 2:20 is revealing: "If you died with Christ, parting from (ἀπό) the elements of the world, why do you submit to rules as though you were living in (ἐν) the world." As DeMaris observes, this text connects the στοιχεῖα τοῦ κόσμου with *cosmos*: "both terms seem to denote a sphere of existence ... that one can part *from* or live *in*" (*Colossian Controversy*, 53).

36. J. L. Martyn, "Apocalyptic Antinomies in Paul's Letter to the Galatians," *NTS* 31 (1985) 410–24. Burton, in considering the expression "elements of the cosmos," felt strangely compelled to look outside the letter to ascertain the meaning of the prepositional phrase "of the cosmos," thus concluding that it refers "most naturally ... to the world of humanity" (*Galatians*, 518).

37. In speaking of the crucifixion of the cosmos "to me," Paul doubtless intends his pronoun to refer to all members of God's church. For those incorporated into Christ, the cosmos of the Law/the not-Law has suffered death in the cross.

there precedent for linking pairs of opposites not only to the word "cosmos" (so Gal 6:14–15) but also to the term "elements" (Gal 4:3, 8–9) and thus to "the elements of the cosmos?" These prove to be significant questions because they point to an area in which we do in fact have information.

The Elements of That Cosmos

Among the widely varied speculations about the elements of the cosmos we find a significant number in which the traditional four elements are compared with one another; and, being compared, the elements are then arranged in pairs of opposites (in Greek often called τἀναντία). This is, in fact, an ancient way of speaking not only of the cosmos but also explicitly of its elements, not least when one wishes to refer to the elements' effects on (and in) human beings.[38] In Paul's own time, Philo drew on Pythagorean tradition in order to develop the pattern at some length. Dealing with God's act of creation, he speaks of the division of the elements of the cosmos into equal parts, referring to the elements themselves as pairs of opposites:

> First he [God] made two sections, heavy and light, thus distinguishing the element of dense from that of rare particles. Then again he divided each of these two, the rare into air and fire, the dense into water and land, and these four He laid down as first foundations, to be the sensible elements of the sensible world (στοιχεῖα αἰσθητὰ αἰσθητοῦ κόσμου).[39] Again He made a second division of heavy and light on different principles. He divided the light into cold and hot, giving to the cold the name of air and to the naturally hot the name of fire. The heavy He divided into wet and dry, and He called the dry "land" and the wet "water." . . . observe how God in "dividing in the middle," actually did divide equally. . . . First, as to equality of number, he made the light parts equal in number to the heavy parts, earth and water which are heavy being two, and

38. The notion of opposition among the elements (sometimes στοιχεῖα sometimes ἀρχαί) can be seen as early as Anaximander, Heraclitus, and Empedocles, the last being credited with the view that the changes among the four material elements are caused by numbers five and six, love and strife (see Kirk and Raven, *Presocratic Philosophers*, 327–30; Diels frgs. 424–26). A particularly clear exposition is given by Aristotle; see, e.g., *Metaphysics* 986b, where, having cited the Pythagorean tradition of the opposites, he continues his account by the summarizing remark: τἀναντία ἀρχαὶ τῶν ὄντων, an affirmation in which, as is often the case, τὰ στοιχεῖα are represented by one of the synonyms (e.g., μέρη, "parts"). Aristotle is a clear witness, therefore, for the continuation of the ancient tradition in which the elements are the opposites (τὰ στοιχεῖα = τἀναντία); cf. also 1005a, πάντα γὰρ ἢ ἐναντία ἢ ἐξ ἐναντίων.

39. Philo seems consistently to have thought of the four traditional elements as earth, air, water, and fire—sensible elements, that is, of the sensible cosmos. As far as one can see from the works we have, he did not think of a second set of elements for the noetic cosmos, suggesting, let us say, that the four sensible elements symbolize four noetic ones. On the contrary, speaking of the tabernacle, for example, Philo says that it is a house perceived by the mind (ὁ μὲν δὴ νοητὸς οἶκος οὗτος); but when he adds that the tabernacle (or its adornment, its curtains) is also perceived by sense (αἰσθητὸς δ' ὁ κόσμος ἐστιν), he says that that is so because the curtains are woven from four materials that are symbols *of the four (sensible) elements*, earth, air, water, and fire (*De congressu eruditionis gratia* 117).

fire and air which are naturally light being two also. . . . In the same way we
have one and one in darkness and light, in day and night, in winter and summer, in spring and autumn. . . . (*Quis rerum divinarum heres sit* 134–35, 146)[40]

Philo arranges these columns of element-opposites in various ways, each
involving the traditional four elements:

the rare		*the dense*		
air	versus	earth		
fire	versus	water		

the light			*the heavy*		
cold	versus	hot	wet	versus	dry
air	versus	fire	water	versus	earth[41]

Thus from Philo—and from other authors as well—we see the tradition in
which the elements *are* the pairs of opposites (τὰ στοιχεῖα = τἀναντία) that
constitute the foundation of the cosmos, including the seasonal cycles. A
number of thinkers close to Paul's time, including both Ben Sira and the
author of Wisdom, would have readily agreed with the traditional statement: The elements of the cosmos *are* pairs of opposites.[42]

When, now, we bring together two points in Galatians at which Paul
speaks of the old cosmos—6:14–15 and 3:28—we can see that, in his own
way, he has in mind precisely this tradition. In writing Gal 6:14–15, Paul
expects the Galatians to understand his testimony: the cross of Christ separated him from a *cosmos* that consisted of a pair of opposites: *circumcision*
and *uncircumcision*. That statement leads us back to 3:28, where the same
pair—Jew and Greek (Gentile)—introduces the baptismal tradition focused
on pairs of opposites that have disappeared: for those who are incorporated
into Christ, there is no Jew and Gentile. Moreover, the baptismal formula is
broader than the affirmation of 6:14–15, including the social pair of slave
and free, and the creational pair of male and female.[43] Thus, a Christian bap-

40. Trans. Colson, LCL. Cf. also 207: "Having taught us the lesson of equal division, the
Scripture leads us on to the knowledge of opposites (τὴν τῶν ἐναντίων ἐπιστήμην), by telling us
that 'He placed the sections facing opposite each other' (Gen xv.10). For in truth we may take
it that everything in the world is by nature opposite to something else." (Cf. the citations from
Aristotle in n. 38 above.)

41. Another traditional scheme depicted these oppositions as an integrated order of the
natural elements, using a wheel with *air, water, earth,* and *fire* at the four compass points and
with *wet, cold, dry,* and *hot* located in between each adjacent pair. Thus, *hot* is between *air* and
fire and stands opposite *cold,* which is between *earth* and *water.* There are here three matters
that are intimately interrelated and that are pertinent to our interpretation of Gal 4:3, 8–9: (1)
the elements, (2) the pairs of opposites, (3) the seasons, and thus times of special celebration.

42. See, e.g., Sir 33:15; Wis 19:18–21.

43. Both of these additional pairs figure in the tradition ascribed variously to Thales,
Socrates, Plato, and the later Rabbi Judah; more important is the fact that male and female

tizand acquainted with a traditional list of oppositional pairs—in whatever form—would easily have heard in the baptizer's words a list of the oppositional *elements* that have now found their terminus in Christ, and thus a declaration of the end of the cosmos constituted by those elements.

Moreover, the formula of Gal 3:28—with its announcement of liberation from enslaving pairs of element-opposites—constitutes a key part of the context in which, in 4:3–5, Paul explicitly speaks of liberation from the enslaving elements of the cosmos. It is, then, a reasonable hypothesis that, when he speaks in 4:3 and 9 of the elements of that cosmos, Paul himself has in mind not earth, air, fire, and water, but rather the elemental pairs of opposites listed in 3:28, and emphatically the first pair, Jew and Gentile, and thus the Law and the not-Law.

To be sure, I have suggested above that, prior to hearing Paul's letter, the Galatians will have connected the expression τὰ στοιχεῖα τοῦ κόσμου with the traditional earth/air and fire/water, the stars being added. Can Paul expect them suddenly to sense a reference to the elements of *religious* polarity? That is the sort of question that arises at a number of junctures in this extraordinarily dense letter, each of which reflects Paul's assumption that the Galatian congregations will listen to the whole of the letter several times and with extreme care. Paul assumes not only great perspicacity but also considerable patience. In regard to what he calls the elements of the old cosmos, he seems to think that the baptismal reference to the termination of pairs of opposites (3:28), coupled with his climactic reference to the death of the cosmos made up of the first of those pairs (6:14–15) will alert the Galatians to his intention in 4:3, 9. From those other passages, then, one finds a reasonable reading of Paul's line of thought in 4:3, 9:

(a) Having accented the baptismal confession of 3:28, with its reference to the dissolution in Christ of certain pairs of opposites—Jew/Gentile, slave/free, male/female, (b) Paul takes for granted the widespread tradition in which pairs of opposites are themselves identified as "the elements of the cosmos," in order that (c) in 4:3 he might use that expression itself to refer to the pairs of opposites that are passé, noting indeed that these oppositional elements had in fact enslaved all human beings prior to Christ.[44] (d) And just as he has said that the opposition of Law to not-Law affected the whole of humanity, thus being a true element of the cosmos (4:3), so he can finally say that for the not-Law Galatians to turn to the Law—employing careful observation of what they identify as the cosmic elements in

---

stand in the Pythagorean list of the elemental pairs of opposites: Aristotle, *Metaphysics* 986a, where the fifth pair in the Pythagorean list is ἄρρεν [καὶ] θῆλυ. On the connection with the seasons, see also the passage from Alexander Polyhistor quoted in n. 23 above.

44. By juxtaposing Gal 3:28 and 4:3 Paul instructs the Galatians as to the identity of the oppositional elements; cf. Philo's concern that people be led to knowledge of the opposites: τὴν τῶν ἐναντίων ἐπιστήμην (n. 40 above; cf. Wis 7:17).

order to distinguish holy times from profane ones—is for them to return to
the old cosmos of Law/not-Law (4:9–10).

Heard in this way, Gal 6:14–15; 3:28; and 4:3, 8–9 constitute a typical
instance of Paul's transformation of language.[45] In a word, the equation of
the world's elements with archaic pairs of opposites is an ancient tradition
which Paul now employs in his interpretation of the *religious* impact of
Christ's advent. Following the baptismal formula, to say it again, he applies
that tradition not to the sensible elements but rather to the elements of
religious distinction.[46] These are the cosmic elements that have found their
termination in Christ. Specifically, the cosmos that was crucified on the
cross is the cosmos that was founded on the distinction between Jew and
Gentile, between sacred and profane, between the Law and the not-Law.[47]

THE LAW AS ONE OF THE COSMIC ELEMENTS
AND THE LAW AS THE LAW OF CHRIST

The essence of the conclusion is before us, and to some degree it seems
to unpuzzle the puzzle of Paul's references to the elements of the cosmos in
Galatians. That conclusion is of such a nature, however, as to suggest that it
is the proverbial tip of the iceberg; from it numerous weighty questions follow, and some of them lead into areas into which many interpreters of Paul

45. Cf. Paul's eschatological interpretation of Stoic maxims in Gal 6:2–10.

46. As noted above, when Paul connects the Galatians' veneration of the elements with
their observance of holy times (4:9–10), he may seem momentarily to follow the Teachers in
assuming the elements to include the stars. In fact he adheres here also to the view that the
elements are the religious pairs of opposites. For to say that the elements play a role in distinguishing holy times from profane ones is simply to specify yet another way in which they are
related to the religious pairs of opposites that belong to the cosmos terminated by Christ's
advent.

47. I am instructed by Paul W. Meyer's use of the expression "binary categorizations of religious human beings" in his perceptive study "The Worm at the Core of the Apple: Exegetical
Reflections on Romans 7," in *The Conversation Continues: Studies in Paul and John in Honor of J.
Louis Martyn* (ed. R. T. Fortna and B. R. Gaventa; Nashville: Abingdon, 1990) 62–84 (e.g., p. 69).
Especially on the basis of Gal 3:28 one might suggest that in Galatians Paul intends to speak of
nothing more than the nomistic separation of human beings into insiders and outsiders, thus
referring to a curse *produced* by the Law rather than to the Law itself. It seems to me correct to
say that that binary religious categorization of human beings is the fundamental identity of
the curse pronounced by the Law (on the anthropological use of the terms "circumcision" and
"uncircumcision," see Joel Marcus, "The Circumcision and the Uncircumcision in Rome," *NTS*
35 [1989] 67–81). But in Galatians there is also the issue of the relationship between anthropological categorization and cosmic antinomies, both those of the old cosmos and those of the
dawning new creation. For Paul, as for the Teachers, the Law is a cosmic power to be reckoned
with in its own being. Thus he discusses not only its effects, but also its genesis (3:19–20).
Moreover, in the cosmic terms of 6:14–15, the Law (circumcision) produces anthropological
effects *in its opposition to* the not-Law (uncircumcision), and it is in that paired existence that
the Law itself proves to be an element of the old *cosmos*. See further n. 49 below.

should perhaps prefer not to go. In Paul's mind how old is the old cosmos with its pairs of opposites? Were one to look simply at the third pair in the baptismal formula, one could think this cosmos as old as the distinction of male and female (Gen 1:27). That is a matter to which Wayne Meeks has devoted a characteristically learned and penetrating essay, speaking of the erasure of sexual distinction as "a potent symbol of social criticism or even of total rejection of the existing order ... [a symbol for] 'metaphysical rebellion,' an act of 'cosmic audacity,' attacking the conventional picture of what was real and what was properly human."[48] As he doubtless recognized, however, and as I have emphasized above, in writing to the Galatians, Paul focuses his concern on the first pair, Jew and Gentile. In interpreting this letter, then, the major issue connected with the age of the old cosmos—with its cursing Law!—is whether Paul thought the nomistic distinction of Jew from Gentile to have been an enslaving power from its inception.[49] And if so,

48. Wayne A. Meeks, "The Image of the Androgyne: Some Uses of a Symbol in Earliest Christianity," *HR* 13 (1973–74) 165–208 (207). As the Corinthian correspondence shows, the baptismal symbol was subject to a nondialectical reading of "no male and female," and that reading caused Paul great concern in his dealings with the church in Corinth. In that reading Paul recognized, as Meeks says, "an implicit rejection of the *created* order and not only of its existing demonic distortion" (p. 208). As I will suggest below, a similar issue is raised when, focusing one's attention on the Jew/Gentile pair, one compares Galatians with Romans. Did Paul himself pen in Galatians a nondialectical reading of "neither Jew nor Greek," failing adequately to distinguish between (a) a covenantal-nomistic act by which God himself created a special people, Israel, and (b) the enslaving, demonic powers of the present evil age that have distorted that elective act of God? And was he compelled, in writing Romans, to correct his own earlier nondialectical reading? See Wayne A. Meeks, "On Trusting an Unpredictable God: A Hermeneutical Meditation on Romans 9–11," in *Faith and History: Essays in Honor of Paul W. Meyer* (ed. John T. Carroll et al.; Atlanta: Scholars Press, 1990) 105–24.

49. The age of the Law's curse is an intriguing question. In current research an interesting thesis has been advanced by James D. G. Dunn: The Law's curse is to be seen quantitatively. It consists of "the ill effects of the *too narrow* understanding of covenant and law" characteristic of the post-Maccabean period ("Works of the Law and the Curse of the Law [Galatians 3:10–14]," *NTS* 31 [1985] 537 [emphasis added]; cf. idem, "The Theology of Galatians," in *Pauline Theology, Volume I* [ed. Jouette M. Bassler; Minneapolis: Fortress, 1991] 125–46). But was the curse of the Law considered by Paul to be of recent vintage, having arisen with the zealotic intensification of the Maccabean heritage? Clearly the line of interpretation pursued in the present essay suggests no such thing. One might hazard the guess that, faced with the question, and reasoning consistently from the event of the cross, Paul would have said (when he was writing to the Galatians) that the Law had its paired existence from its genesis at Sinai, and that its curse—the binary distinction of Jew from Gentile—was consequently no younger than the Mosaic Law itself.

But also no older. Here one is reminded of yet another important difference between Paul's theology and that of the Teachers. If it is important to see that for Paul the curse of the Law is as old as the Law itself, then it is equally important to note that unlike the Teachers Paul is sure that the Law does not go back to Abraham. What does originate there is God's promise, and that promise to Abraham—a pre-proclamation of the gospel—is explicitly directed against the polarization of Jew and Gentile, as Gal 3:8 shows. The Law and its curse prove, then, to constitute an angelic parenthesis lodged between and differentiated from two punctiliar acts

what conclusion did he draw—as he wrote Galatians—about ancient Israel, the people set apart from all others (Deut 10:15; Amos 3:2; *Jub.* 16:17; cf. Gal 3:16; 6:16)? Did he think that act of corporate, elective separation to have been a mistake from the beginning—involving enslavement both for Israel and for the Gentile nations—and thus an event of which God could scarcely have been the direct and immediate author (cf. Gal 3:19–20)?[50] Finally, did he see matters differently when he wrote to the Roman churches?[51]

These are complex issues demanding treatment elsewhere; in the present conclusion we can briefly address no more than one question, and even that one only in outline: In Galatians precisely what picture of the Law emerges from Paul's identification of the Law/not-Law as one of the cosmic element-pairs terminated in the cross of Christ? When the issue is posed in that way, one sees that in this letter Paul's references to the Law (there are thirty-two of them in six chapters) fall into two fundamental groups closely related to his certainty regarding there being two periods in the history of the elements of the old cosmos. In its elemental existence—paired with the

---

of God himself: (a) the uttering of the promise to Abraham and to Abraham's singular seed, and (b) the sending of that seed, Christ. Neither of these divine acts involves the religious separation of one people from others, the separation that creates the *homo religiosus*. Both are indeed antithetical to that separation, God's act in Christ being the climactic erasure of all marks of the religious separation introduced by the parenthetical Law in its paired existence. Noting, then, that in writing Galatians Paul is concerned to speak of the end of religion's (viz., the Law's) distinction of sacred from profane, Jew from Gentile, one is compelled to speak of much more than some intensified sociological factors of the post-Maccabean era. One may be led, in fact, in the direction of Robert G. Hamerton-Kelly's negative reference to the Law's "embeddedness in the realm of the sacred" ("Sacred Violence and Sinful Desire," in *The Conversation Continues: Studies in Paul and John in Honor of J. Louis Martyn* [ed. R. T. Fortna and B. R. Gaventa; Nashville: Abingdon, 1990] 49; cf. idem, *Sacred Violence: Paul's Hermeneutic of the Cross* (Minneapolis: Fortress, 1992).

50. With these questions we are on the threshold of Marcion's concerns (see also the preceding note), not least those having to do with the genesis of the Law. P. Vielhauer is right to hint that with the expression τὰ ἀσθενῆ καὶ πτωχὰ στοιχεῖα ("weak and impotent elements," 4:9) Paul may intend to deny that the elements are of divine origin ("Gesetzesdienst," 554). In the terms of the present essay the question then becomes: If Ben Sira was confident that "all the works *of the Most High* are in pairs," can one attribute the same confidence to Paul, naming as one of the pairs of divine origin the Law/the not-Law? Some dimensions of the issues are addressed in J. Louis Martyn, "Paul and His Jewish-Christian Interpreters," *USQR* 42 (1988) 1–15; idem, "Covenant, Christ, and Church in Galatians," in *The Future of Christology: Essays in Honor of Leander E. Keck* (ed. A. J. Malherbe and W. A. Meeks; Minneapolis: Fortress, 1993) 137–51; idem, "On Hearing the Gospel Both in the Silence of the Tradition and in Its Eloquence," in *From Jesus to John: New Testament Christologies in Current Perspective: Festschrift M. de Jonge* (ed. M. De Boer; Leiden: Brill, 1993) 129–47.

51. From Galatians 3–4 one may indeed turn to the dialectic of Romans 9. After including the giving of the Law among the signs of God's grace to Israel (Rom 9:4), a motif absent from Galatians, Paul traces God's elective grace in the generations of the patriarchs; but he does not go beyond Jacob and Esau, thus failing explicitly to include Sinai in the history of God's elective grace (Rom 9:7–13). It is, finally, because of the patriarchs, not because of the Law, that Israel is the beloved of God (Rom 11:28).

not-Law—the Law had a past. Loosed from that paired existence, it also has a present. In light of this temporal distinction, one sees that the two groups of references to the Law answer, for the most part, two questions: What did the Law do and not do? And what has now been done to the Law?[52]

What Did the Law Do, and What Did It Not Do, in Its Paired Existence with the Not-Law?

The first group of references to the Law is introduced by the expression ἔργα νόμου, "observance of the Law" (2:16); and for the most part this group is linguistically marked by that expression and by its companion ὑπὸ νόμον εἶναι, "to be under the power of the Law" (the group consists of all twenty-four instances prior to 4:21b, plus 5:3, 4, 18, 23; 6:13). As the expression ἔργα νόμου indicates, the consistent reference here is to the Law in its paired existence, the Law observed by some and not observed by others, the Law that, in the company of its opposite, distinguished the sacred from the profane (2:17–18; 4:10), dividing humanity into two camps, Jews and Gentiles (2:15).

In its paired existence, the Law was both impotent and potent. (a) To a considerable extent Paul ties the first of these motifs to the expression ἔργα νόμου. The Law that is observed and not observed was impotent to make things right (2:16; 3:2, 5, 10–12), being unable to counter the fleshly impulse (a task for which only the Spirit of Christ is competent [5:16]). It was added by angels to the scene marked by God's own covenantal act of issuing the promise to Abraham. And if God's own covenantal promise did not create a corporate people of God in the generations following Abraham (3:16), there is not the slightest hint that the Law filled this lacuna. On the contrary, it merely functioned to provoke transgressions (3:19). To be sure, God could and did use it—in its paired existence—to close every route to rectification except the one he employed in sending his Son (note the purpose clauses of Gal 3:22, 24). As to making people alive, however, the Law was impotent; nor is there any hint that God intended to use it for the providing of life (3:21; cf. Rom 7:10).

(b) Impotent to set things right, the Law was in other regards quite powerful, as one sees from Paul's expression "to be under the power of the Law." In speaking of the Law's power, Paul uses various tenses, but when he refers with emphasis to things done by it—one of his major concerns in connection with it—he uses for the most part (or implies) the past tense, indicating, as we have already noted, that the nomistic pair of opposites is a matter belonging to what is called, in the perspective of apocalyptic dualism, "the old age." It was precisely in its paired existence with the not-Law that the

---

52. Exegetical details underlying what follows here will be given in a future work.

Law separated observers from nonobservers, placed all of humanity under the power of its curse (3:10), spoke the false promise of Lev 18:5 (Gal 3:12), and climaxed the inimical demonstrations of its power by pronouncing a curse on Christ himself, as he hung on the cross (3:13).[53] It confined everyone, functioning as a universal prison warden (3:23, 24), thus making slaves of all human beings (4:3, 5). Moreover, to say it again for emphasis, the Law did all of these things in its paired existence with the not-Law, in its inimical power as one of the paired elements of the old cosmos.

WHAT HAS NOW BEEN DONE TO THE LAW BY CHRIST?

Paul's answer to this question is also complex, for he refers both to Christ's defeat of the Law as it existed in its paired arrangement and to his loosing of the Law from that arrangement, with the result that, as the Law of Christ, it now raises its voice to testify to the truth of the gospel. (a) Precisely where the Law's curse fell on him with its full power, Christ silenced that cursing voice, liberating human beings from the enslaving power of the Law/not-Law (note especially ἐξαγοράζω ["redeem"] in 3:13; 4:5; and ἐλευθερόω ["set free"] in 5:1). It is crucial to see that this liberating deed of Christ is something he did to the Law as one of the old world's elements. What met its death in the cross of Christ was the curse pronounced by the Law in its paired existence, as Paul emphasizes both in 3:28 and in 6:14–15.

(b) Finally, given the consistently malignant portrait of the Law in Gal 2:16–4:21a, one may be surprised to see Paul's conviction that the Law has survived the crucifixion of the old cosmos, thus having a life beyond the cross. That is the conclusion one has to draw in considering three instances in which the apostle speaks apocalyptically and positively of the Law in its second period, in the period since the crucifixion of Christ. *Post Christum* the Law bears witness to the birth of children by the power of the promised Spirit of Christ (4:21b). The Law is fulfilled in Christ's church, as that community is corporately obedient to the levitical commandment to love the neighbor (5:14). Finally, in its role as the love commandment, it is even identified as the Law of Christ (6:2). How are these three references to be understood?

A clue of considerable import is given by the fact that the first reference comes at the point at which Paul speaks twice in one sentence of the Law.

Tell me, you who desire to be under the authority of the Law (ὑπὸ νόμον . . . εἶναι) and thus, although you seem not to know it, under the power of the

---

53. In Gal 3:11–12 Paul employs the rhetorical form of the textual contradiction in order to distinguish the true promise of Hab 2:4 from the false one of Lev 18:5, as I will argue elsewhere, drawing on the labors of J. S. Vos, but reaching a conclusion quite different from his ("Die hermeneutische Antinomie bei Paulus [Gal 3.11–12; Röm 10.5–10]," *NTS* 38 [1992] 254–70). On the basis of Gal 3:21b and Rom 8:3 Richard Hays concluded a number of years ago that Paul considered Lev 18:5 to be "unconditionally false" (*Faith of Jesus Christ*, 221).

Law's cursing voice: Do you really hear what the Law says when it bears its evangelistic witness? (paraphrase of Gal 4:21)

In Gal 4:21a Paul repeats his earlier portrait of the Law as one of the enslaving elements of the old cosmos. But for the first time in this letter he also refers, in 4:21b, to the Law to which the Galatians are to listen carefully. This Law is neither the Law that is to be observed (ἔργα νόμου), thus implying its opposite, nor the Law that imprisons (ὑπὸ νόμον εἶναι). On the contrary, Paul introduces here a new kind of reference to the Law, linguistically indicating that new reference by means of a univocal echo of the *shema*— " . . . do you *hear* what the Law says?"[54] Demanding to be heard, this Law is the voice of Torah as scripture (5:14; cf. 4:22, 27, 30), the Law of Christ (6:2), the Law that, freed of its paired existence, contains the promise (4:23, 28)!

In these instances, then (4:21b; 5:14; and 6:2), Paul speaks of the Law that no longer belongs to the elements of the old cosmos.[55] Referring to this Law one would even be correct to supply the eschatological expression "but now." For to take into account both Galatians and Romans is to see that the contrasting—and even dualistic—references to the Law in Gal 4:21 are spelled out in greater detail in Rom 3:21.

Tell me, you who desire to be under the authority of the Law (ὑπὸ νόμον . . . εἶναι) and thus, although you seem not to know it, under the power of the Law's cursing voice: Do you really hear what the Law says when it bears its evangelistic witness? (paraphrase of Gal 4:21)

The Law has shown all to be under the power of Sin (ὑφ᾽ ἁμαρτίαν εἶναι), thus silencing every mouth. . . . But now, apart from the Law, God's rectifying power has been revealed; yet that rectifying power is also witnessed to by the Law and the prophets. (paraphrase of Rom 3:9 and 21)

The temporal distinction—"but now"—suggests again that a major key to Paul's references to the Law in Galatians lies in the relationship between the Law and the elemental opposites of the old cosmos.[56] What did Christ do to the Law when he took it in hand, making it the νόμος τοῦ Χριστοῦ,

---

54. Similar observations of scriptural echoes are noted and analyzed at length in Richard B. Hays, *Echoes of Scripture in the Letters of Paul* (New Haven: Yale University Press, 1989) passim.

55. I have earlier tried to speak of the duality evident in Gal 4:21 by crediting Paul with the view that with the advent of Christ an antinomy opened up *internal to the Law*; the result being that the Law has both a cursing voice and the voice of an evangelical witness. Since the voice of the cosmic element I have here called the Law/the not-Law can still bewitch and enslave (Gal 3:1), I will not wholly abandon that earlier formulation. It must be clear, however, that for those who have been incorporated into him, Christ has silenced that enslaving voice, showing in his death the Law's true, evangelical voice.

56. One is reminded of the seminal article by N. A. Dahl, "Form-critical Observations on Early Christian Preaching," in *Jesus in the Memory of the Early Church* (Minneapolis: Augsburg, 1976) 30–44. In each of the four formulaic patterns identified by Dahl the Christ-event is a kind of pivot point, seen especially in the temporal force of his "soteriological contrast pattern."

"the Law of Christ"? He defeated it in its paired existence (its power to curse); but he also loosed it from its opposite, binding it, so to speak, to his cross as the enactment of love (6:14; 2:20; cf. Col 2:14). To recapitulate, it is this loosed Law—lacking the two linguistic markers characteristic of the references to the Law in its paired existence—of which Paul speaks in 4:21b; 5:14; and 6:2. It is, then, the Law loosed from its opposite that has survived the death of the old cosmos.

To be sure, one may pause briefly to ask whether Paul is really speaking of the Mosaic Law in all three of these positive references. Is it not better to see in 6:2 a reference to a different Law or to a principle? By no means! All thirty-two instances of the term νόμος in Galatians refer to the Law of Moses.[57] Paul simply sees, to say it again, that, surviving the crucifixion of the old cosmos, the Law is no longer caught in the paired existence it had in the "evil age"; it is thus free to bear its evangelistic witness as scripture, and as scripture it is to be listened to.[58] Having been delivered by Christ from the company of its opposite, the not-Law (6:14–15), it now neither pronounces the curse of Deut 27:26 nor speaks the false promise of Lev 18:5. Instead, it tells the true story of Sarah and Hagar, thus preaching the gospel, just as, seen now in retrospect, it did in speaking God's promise to Abraham in the past (3:8).

This is the scripture-Law that is to be fulfilled—rather than observed—by the community of faith (5:14), being the Law of a quite specific love: the love Christ enacted by dying in our behalf; the love of neighbor spoken of in Lev

57. This assertion is debatable, as one notes especially in the literature on Gal 6:2 (e.g., n. 60 below). See now Michael Winger, *By What Law? The Meaning of Nomos in the Letters of Paul* (Atlanta: Scholars Press, 1992) 43–44, 74–75, 195. The details of my own reading will be given elsewhere; meanwhile see John M. G. Barclay, *Obeying the Truth: A Study of Paul's Ethics in Galatians* (Edinburgh: Clark, 1988) 125–35. That even the ἕτερος νόμος ("another law") of Rom 7:23 is the Mosaic Law is convincingly argued by Paul W. Meyer, "The Worm at the Core of the Apple," 79.

58. In some instances nomenclature is a matter of importance. Speaking of the two Gentile missions, that of the Teachers and that of Paul and his fellow workers, I have earlier employed the expressions "Law-observant gospel" and "Law-free gospel." In a private communication Paul W. Meyer has kindly offered the caveat that the latter expression—a time-honored one—is open to serious misunderstanding. As usual, his comment is instructive. In assessing Paul's view of the Law, we are dealing with a matter that cannot be adequately grasped in a simple slogan, such as "Law-free gospel." The argument formulated above should suffice to show that one does not have to go to Romans to see the Law playing a constructive and crucially important role in Paul's theology. Yet, in Gal 5:1, for example, it is from the tyranny of the Law's cursing and enslaving voice that Christ is said to have *set us free*. Respecting this matter, Luther was far more right than wrong. Meyer's warning reminds one, however, that abbreviations can seriously mislead. One might even add that, knowing that very well, Paul often filled out his abbreviations with discourses of considerable complexity (e.g., the two exegetical passages in Galatians: 3:6–4:7 and 4:21–5:1!). With the understanding, then, that all encapsulations demand qualifying exposition, one might offer a suggestion: As regards the Law's cursing voice, Paul's gospel is Law-free; as regards its witnessing voice, Paul's gospel is Law–fulfilling.

19:18; the love that is the first mark of the fruit borne by the Spirit (5:22); the love that can be defined as faith active in the community in which each bears the other's burdens (6:2; 5:6).[59] Freed of its element-opposite, this is explicitly and emphatically the *whole* Law, the Law of Christ.[60]

When one ponders the surprising turn Paul takes in Gal 4:21b; 5:14; and 6:2—a turn showing that the author of Galatians does not formulate an antinomian theology—one is reminded of the care with which, in writing Romans, he speaks of the Law as God's Law.[61] Was it Paul's discovery of the Law's identity *in the hands of the crucified Christ* that enabled him ultimately to insist on its identity as the holy and just and good Law *of God*, radically distinguishing it from the Law in the hands of Sin (Rom 7:12, 22, 23)?[62] However the historical unfolding of Paul's theology is to be imagined, would one perhaps say that Galatians and Romans converge at one point of great importance: To a considerable extent the Law was inimical by being in the wrong company, that of its opposite, the not-Law (Galatians), and that of Sin (Romans).[63] When it fell into the right company, freed both from its paired existence and from Sin, it lifted its evangelical voice as the Law of Christ, testifying to the freedom that is known in the truth of the gospel, and thus in the commandment to love the neighbor as Christ loved us.

---

59. By speaking in 5:14 of "the whole Law," Paul takes pains to preclude the thought that with the advent of Christ the Law was simply quantitatively reduced (cf. 5:3). We may say, perhaps, that, for Paul, the *whole* Law *emerged* by being loosed from its paired existence with the not-Law, having thereafter nothing to do with the distinction of sacred from profane.

60. As I have hinted in n. 55 above, the connection between Gal 5:14 and 6:2 seems to me essentially to settle the question of the reference of νόμος in the latter verse; Paul means the Law of Moses as it has fallen into the hands of Christ (linguistically analogous to νόμος τῆς ἁμαρτίας, "the Law as it had fallen into the hands of Sin," Rom 7:23 etc.). That is not the way in which Gal 6:2 is read by Richard B. Hays ("Christology and Ethics in Galatians: The Law of Christ," *CBQ* 49 [1987] 268–90), but the christological dimensions of his study seem to me nevertheless quite illuminating.

61. Paul can scarcely have thought that he would be preaching the good news *in the Galatian situation* by speaking explicitly of "the Law of God." That observation reminds one that the issue of antinomianism in Paul's theology must be assessed by reading each letter in its own context before one attempts the synthetic task. There is, however, one obvious constant: Paul always considers the Law impotent to handle the fleshly Impulse (so Gal 3:21; 5:16; Rom 8:3). If one were to say that that view was in itself sufficient to warrant the charge of antinomianism, then one would use the term to characterize the theology of Galatians, and that of Romans as well. One would still have to account, however, for the impact of Gal 4:21b; 5:14; and 6:2. And it is on the basis of these passages that I have refused to speak of Galatians as an antinomian document.

62. See again Meyer, "The Worm at the Core of the Apple."

63. I have refrained from saying "the Law *became* inimical only by falling into the wrong company." Did Paul think—when he wrote Galatians—that the holy and just and good Law came into being at Sinai (Gal 3:19; cf. Rom 5:20), only subsequently falling into bad company, and later still falling into the hands of Christ? See nn. 48–49 above.

CHAPTER 3

The Weak and the Strong:
Paul's Careful and Crafty Rhetorical Strategy
in Romans 14:1–15:13

J. Paul Sampley

SCHOLARS HAVE MISREAD Paul's references to the strong and the weak in Rom 14:1–15:13 and have misconstrued the force and purpose of his accompanying argument. Typically, interpreters, taking the strong and the weak to refer to two specific Roman groups, have raced to identify potential parties.[1] Further, as they considered Paul's mention of vegetarians (14:2, 21), scholars have scoured about for *religionsgeschichtliche* counterparts;[2] finding vegetarians who are also teetotalers (14:21) has proved a daunting challenge![3] It is perhaps an ironic tribute to Paul's rhetorical strategy that modern scholars have been divided in their claims that the strong or the weak are Jewish or Gentile believers[4]—ironic because such an identification was never Paul's rhetorical purpose.

As a way of honoring Wayne Meeks, I will first assess the identification of the weak and the strong in 14:1–15:13[5] and then move to the Greco-Roman rhetorical tradition for assistance in understanding Paul's purpose

1. Some, however, have considered 14:1–15:13 to be largely theoretical and general, with little or no connection to any real circumstances in Rome. See R. J. Karris, "Romans 14:1–15:13 and the Occasion of Romans," in *The Romans Debate* (rev. ed., ed. K. P. Donfried; Peabody, Mass.: Hendrickson, 1991), 75–76, 80–81.

2. R. J. Karris uses the term "bankrupt" to describe "the history of religions approach" on this issue ("Occasion," pp. 69–70).

3. F. Watson makes a most extensive effort to maintain that Jewish abstention from meat and wine was a credible possibility ("The Two Roman Congregations: Romans 14:1–15:13," in *The Romans Debate*, 204).

4. For the history of scholarship on such identifications, see Karris, "Occasion," 68 n. 25.

5. It is appropriate that, with other concerns, Wayne Meeks has treated the passage on which this essay is focused. See his "Judgment and the Brother: Romans 14:1–15:3," in *Tradition and Interpretation in the New Testament: Essays in Honor of E. Earle Ellis* (ed. Gerald F. Hawthorne; Grand Rapids: Eerdmans, 1987) 290–300.

in this section of his letter. I will close with some observations on how this section, newly interpreted, fits into the entirety of the letter to the Romans.

IDENTIFICATION OF THE WEAK AND THE STRONG IN ROMANS 14:1-15:13

The weak are explicitly named only three times: τὸν ἀσθενοῦντα (14:1) ὁ ἀσθενῶν (14:2), and τῶν ἀδυνάτων (15:1), the former two echoing Paul's description of Abraham in 4:19-20.[6] What is Paul's profile of the weak person? First, he is weak τῇ πίστει, weak in faith or with respect to faith (14:1). Second, he is a vegetarian (14:2). Without further characterization of the weak person, Paul rules out anyone's meddling—either in the form of disdain or condemnation—in the relationship of a house servant (οἰκέτης) with his master (κύριος). Having established that preferences regarding meat and vegetables are extraneous to one's relationship to one's Lord, Paul turns to another disparity: "one prefers one day over another; another prefers all days alike" (14:5).[7] Scholars have leapt to identify weak and strong here, but Paul has not. For Paul, keeping or not keeping days and eating and abstaining (14:6) are *adiaphora* (indifferent matters),[8] just as are life and death (14:7-9), because regardless of how different people's preferences and practices are, "we are the Lord's" (14:8).[9] Because believers belong to the Lord, days do not matter one way or the other. What does matter is doing or not doing with respect to the Lord. Giving thanks to God matters (14:6). Even if a modern interpreter insisted on carrying Paul's mention of weak and strong in 14:1-2 into the topic of honoring days, it is not a priori clear who might better be identified as the weak person: the one who reckons all days the same or the one who honors special days.

What does Paul tell us about the strong (οἱ δυνατοί, 15:1)? They believe they can eat anything (φαγεῖν πάντα, 14:2) and they are the ones who "ought to bear the weaknesses of the unstrong" (τὰ ἀσθενήματα τῶν ἀδυνάτων, 15:1; cf. Gal 6:1-2). These references exhaust the identifiable characteristics of

---

6. Abraham is paradigmatic for Paul as the one who did not weaken in faith (μὴ ἀσθενήσας τῇ πίστει, 4:19) but whose faith grew stronger through giving glory to God (4:20). Note the striking connections of Abraham with the one who is weak in faith in Rom 14:1 and the thrice repeated mention of glorifying God in 15:6, 7, 9.

Paul's use of similar terminology in 1 Corinthians is of no help in understanding Romans because the situations and purposes of the rhetoric are so different.

7. NT translations are the author's unless otherwise noted.

8. On *adiaphora* in Paul's letters, see my *Walking Between the Times: Paul's Moral Reasoning* (Minneapolis: Fortress, 1991) 77-83.

9. 14:9 is an echo of the lordship claim of 14:4 and is followed by a noninterference formula in 14:10-12, forming a *chiasmus*: A (nonintervention, expressed in terms of disdain or condemnation [14:3-4a-b]), B (relation to Lord [14:4c]), B´ (relation to Lord [14:8-9]), A´ (condemnation and disdain [even the order of these is reversed] are questioned [14:10-11]).

the weak and strong in Romans[10] and surely give us scant basis to assign them to either extreme of what was more likely a continuum among the house-churches of Rome.

While Rom 14:1–15:13 gives us little about the identity of the "weak" and the "strong," these verses are laced with exhortations and definitional declarations that are designed to be equally applicable to all the Roman believers: "Let each one be fully persuaded in his own mind" (14:5); "Not one of us lives to himself; not one of us dies to himself" (14:7); "Whether we live or die, we belong to the Lord" (14:8); "Consequently each of us shall make an accounting concerning himself" (14:12); "Consequently, therefore, let us pursue the things that make for peace and edification of one another" (14:19); "Let each of us please the neighbor unto the good, for edification" (15:2); "May God . . . grant you the same mind among yourselves" (15:5); and "Therefore, welcome one another just as Christ has welcomed you" (15:7). These claims rehearse the common ground and calling that all believers share, and they give a powerful context in which to consider anew individual differences with regard to practice on this issue or that.

It is instructive to consider more closely the rather vague formulation about evaluating days (14:5–6). We may suppose that one point of contention among Roman believers was in fact the sabbath, although Paul never says so; indeed, he does not even mention the sabbath. Consider Paul's rhetorical strategy. In the most deft fashion, Paul moved any confrontation regarding the sabbath onto neutral ground: assuredly most Jews must have reckoned the sabbath fundamental, but contemporary Gentiles were notorious for honoring special days. Given Paul's casting of the issue, honoring days is not simply a Jewish problem. Paul's rhetorical strategy moves the discussion away from the hot issue of sabbath-keeping, where steely positions are likely already forged on all sides, to the widespread problem of honoring special days. Paul's oblique approach puts no Roman group in the spotlight. In fact, Paul employed the same oblique rhetorical strategy earlier in the text, when he artfully moved any discussion of keeping *kashrut*–or not doing so—onto neutral and mutually accessible grounds of vegetarianism-by-choice versus the omnivorous life.

Paul's approach cloaks the actually divisive practices of the ethnically different Roman believers under the garb of putative practices with which no group has an entrenched position. This rhetorical maneuver of oblique approach is designed to enable the Roman believers to consider afresh, and without already established prejudices, the relative insignificance of diverse practices and moral decisions when seen in the light of their common standing in the Lord. When Paul finally brings to the surface—even then for

10. The reference in Rom 5:6 is to the pre-reconciled common condition of helplessness or weakness due to sin's power.

only one sentence—what indeed must have been a contentious issue, viz., what is κοινός (common, base, unclean [14:14]), he has assiduously prepared a context within which it can be considered afresh and on different grounds by all the parties among the Roman believers. On the basis of scant data, scholars have been all too ready to identify weak and strong as accurate denominators for the contending groups—and that without serious consideration of Paul's rhetorical strategy in this section of the letter to the Romans. Let us now consider what we can learn about Paul's oblique approach by looking at the rhetorical handbooks and other contemporary reflections about the art of persuasion.

THE RHETORICAL TRADITIONS:
FRANK SPEECH VERSUS OBLIQUE SPEECH

A comparison with 2 Corinthians 1–7 will help us understand Paul's situation and strategy in Romans. Paul wrote a "painful letter" to the Corinthians (2 Cor 2:4). In it he called them to task, openly and directly. His letter grieved them (2 Cor 7:8) and produced repentance (7:9–11) which Titus has reported to Paul's great joy (7:7, 13b–16). We learn from 2 Corinthians 1–7 that Paul describes himself as relating to the Corinthians "by the open statement of the truth" (7:4 RSV). In his *apologia*, Paul identifies with the Psalmist: "I believed, therefore I spoke" (7:13; Ps 116:10). He links his "truthful speech" (ἐν λόγῳ ἀληθείας) with the power of God (6:7). Using the term παρρησία, which in rhetorical traditions describes frank or direct speech, Paul says "I am perfectly frank with you" (7:4 NEB) and "we make use of much frank speech" (3:12). They know he used frank speech (παρρησία) with them.

As others roughly contemporary recognize, frank speech is not to be used in all circumstances. Plutarch has general counsel about the time to use frank speech:

> In what circumstances, then, should a friend be severe, and when should he be emphatic in using frank speech (χρῆσθαι τῆς παρρησίας)?[11] It is when occasions demand of him that he check the headlong course of pleasure or of anger or of arrogance, or that he abate avarice or curb inconsiderate heedlessness. (*Moralia* 69E)[12]

---

11. The expression in Plutarch (χρῆσθαι τῆς παρρησίας) even employs the same verb as Paul in 2 Cor 3:12 (πολλῇ παρρησίᾳ χρώμεθα). Frankness as a mode of parenesis or exhortation was also common among the philosophic moralists of the day. See A. J. Malherbe, *Moral Exhortation: A Graeco-Roman Sourcebook* (Philadelphia: Westminster, 1986) 48–55; idem, *Paul and the Thessalonians* (Minneapolis: Augsburg-Fortress, 1987) 29, 42, 84–89.

12. This and all subsequent translations of Plutarch are from *Plutarch's Moralia*, trans. by F. C. Babbitt (LCL). Another confirmation that Paul and his readers know he uses frank speech with them is also found in Plutarch: "so it may well be that every man's frank speaking [παρρησία] needs to be backed by character [ἤθους], but this is especially true in the case of those who admonish others and try to bring them to their sober senses. . ." (*Moralia* 71E). The

Plutarch knows that when frank speech is applied "to errors that are being committed" pain results (*Moralia* 59D); the Corinthians and Paul know that also (2 Cor 1:23–2:4). Paul's long relationship with the Corinthians—even though he and they have had better and worse moments—gives him a basis for dealing with them in frank speech, and judging from 2 Corinthians 1–7 it has proved somewhat effective.[13] Frank speech may be appropriate for one situation, however, but not for another.

For Paul, Rome is not Corinth. Paul is an outsider to the Roman churches without any basis for the friendship necessary for frank speech;[14] he was not the one whose preaching founded them; he is known directly by relatively few people (Romans 16). Nevertheless, as "apostle to the Gentiles" (1:1–6; 11:13) Paul feels a special responsibility that differences between Jewish and Gentile believers must not split the body of Christ[15] and accordingly declares how and why he writes the Roman believers. Why does he write? He says he has written them "on some points" (ἀπὸ μέρους) to help them "remember something again" (ἐπαναμιμνῄσκων), something he suggests they must already know (15:15). How does he write? "Rather boldly" (τολμηροτέρως, 15:15), he says. Any intervention in Roman church affairs is rather bold of Paul. Nevertheless he is compelled to intervene, hoping to help them "live in such harmony with one another, in accord with Christ Jesus, that together you may with one voice glorify the God and Father of our Lord Jesus Christ" (15:5–6 RSV).

In a rhetorical handbook entitled *On Style*, Demetrius of Phalerum (ca. fourth century B.C.E.) envisages that three options are open to someone in a circumstance like Paul's: "Flattery no doubt is shameful, while adverse criticism (ἐπιτιμᾶν) is dangerous. It is best to pursue the middle course, that of the covert hint (figured speech; ἐσχηματισμένον)" (294).[16] Paul does not

---

need to certify one's ethos as a warrant for frank speech is abundantly evident in 2 Corinthians 1–7, passim.

13. 2 Corinthians 10–13, which I take to be subsequent to 2 Corinthians 1–7 (V. P. Furnish, *II Corinthians* [AB 32A; Garden City, NY: Doubleday, 1984] 37–41) shows that Paul thought frank speech had been effective with the Corinthians, because he employs it once again.

14. Of the extant assuredly Pauline letters, this is the only one where he is the sole author; many in Rome may have heard (unflattering?) things about him.

15. For the details of Paul's zeal regarding inclusion of the Gentiles into one body of Christ which is "neither Jew nor Greek," see my paper, "A Response to Robert Jewett's 'Ecumenical Theology for the Sake of Mission: Romans 1:1–17 + 15:14–16:24'" (delivered in the Paul Seminar at the SBL Annual Meeting in San Francisco, 1992, and to be included in *Pauline Theology*, vol. 3) 5–6.

16. This and all subsequent translations of Demetrius are from *Demetrius, On Style*, trans. W. R. Roberts (LCL). Quintilian notes that "*schema* may be employed under three conditions: first, if it is unsafe to speak openly; secondly, if it is unseemly to speak openly; and thirdly, when it is employed solely with a view to the elegance of what we say..." (9.2.66). This and all subsequent translations from Quintilian are from *The Institutio Oratoria of Quintilian*, trans. H. E. Butler (LCL).

employ flattery as his basic approach in Romans. In an *inclusio* that frames the letter, Paul affirms his high regard for the Romans (1:8–12; 15:14), but this is hardly flattery in the sense that Plutarch has detailed.[17] Likewise Paul avoids direct or adverse criticism in Romans. Paul has no choice but to "pursue the middle course." "Blunt speech [παρρησία] gives way to oblique speech [figured speech; ἐσχηματισμένος λόγος or σχῆμα][18] in situations where the speaker is (or feels) threatened or unsure of his audience."[19]

Figured speech maintains good taste and keeps the speaker safe from reprisal (Demetrius, *On Style* 287), yet it allows the speaker to counsel others regarding their foibles and wrongdoings. "Since great lords and ladies dislike to hear their own faults mentioned, we shall therefore, when counseling them to refrain from faults, not speak in direct terms (οὐκ ἐξ εὐθείας ἐροῦμεν) . . ." (*On Style* 292). Figured speech, "speech by indirection,"[20] is "criticism from which the speaker or writer himself stands back. He is safe because the critical links in thought must be established by his reader or listener: the text is incomplete until the audience completes the meaning."[21]

With direct speech (παρρησία) the speaker or writer applies the critique directly; in figured speech the readers or hearers must apply *to themselves* what has been said. Direct speech is argumentative and confrontational while figured speech is allusive and evocative; direct speech needs proofs, while figured speech invites the hearer to establish its veracity by self-application.[22]

Ahl delineates the advantages of figured speech. It is a "strategy of convenience" when one is unsure of one's audience, and it is at the same time a "strategy of power" due to "the greater persuasiveness of oblique suggestion."[23] Figured speech delivers reproach without scoring a direct hit; it allows, even encourages, the readers to apply its point to themselves. Rhetoricians knew that by figured speech "the judge [or any hearer] will be led . . . to believe in that which he thinks he has found out for himself" (Quintilian 9.2.71).

17. Plutarch, "How to Tell a Flatterer From a Friend," *Moralia* 48E–74.

18. Frederick Ahl suggests that figured speech "was the normal mode of discourse throughout much of Greek and Roman antiquity" ("The Art of Safe Criticism in Greece and Rome," *American Journal of Philology* 105 [1984] 204).

19. Ibid. 184.

20. Ibid. 187. For a brief history of the technical use of the term *schema*, see ibid., 187–89.

21. Ibid., 187. Special attention must be paid to Ahl's argument that figured speech is not plain speech merely gussied up (p. 191) but is "expressing the complexity of reality by complexity of language" (p. 192): "in figured speech the speaker wishes us to understand something beyond, or something different from, what the superficial meaning of his words suggests" (p. 192).

22. Quintilian distinguishes speaking *palam* (directly) from speaking *operte* (in a concealed fashion). "For at times such hidden shafts [as figured speech] will stick, and the fact that they are not noticed will prevent their being drawn out, whereas if the same point were stated openly [*palam*], it would be denied by our opponents and would have to be proved" (9.2.75).

23. Ahl, "Art of Safe Criticism," 184.

Figured speech was the ideal, indeed the only, avenue open to Paul as he wrote to the Romans. Uncertain how much authority any contending faction at Rome might accord him, he had to proceed cautiously. Yet proceed he must because his calling as apostle to the Gentiles convinced him that he had some special responsibility for seeing that Gentile believers—whether they have come to faith because of his preaching or not—and Jewish believers not suffer a schism.[24] The body of Christ could not be sundered. Rather than proceed directly to the assuredly sensitive issues of *kashrut* and sabbath, where positions were no doubt hardened and where Paul's apostolic leverage might be stymied, he creatively moved the discussion to matters that in principle were equally open both to Jews and to Gentiles. Paul can hope that all of his readers and hearers in Rome, like Quintilian's judge, apply to their own differences what they find out for themselves: what they eat or do not eat, what days they honor or do not honor are, like life and death, *adiaphora* (indifferent matters) in the Lord. As modern readers of Paul, we must realize that teetotaling vegetarians are not a reality among Roman believers, that the Romans are not torn in disputes between vegetarians and omnivores, and that the question of days is purposefully put in a vague and oblique fashion. Apart from the κοινόν ("unclean," NRSV) of 14:14, none of the issues as they are listed in Romans 14 can be read on a one-for-one basis as directly reflective of the contentions among the Roman believers. Paul has written in a way designed to maximize the chance that the Romans will be able to apply his thoughts to their own conflicts. The truly divisive points of contention among the Roman believers are not overtly listed in Rom 14:1–23; they are only latently or indirectly represented there. Likewise, there are not two Roman groups called "strong" and "weak." Paul has introduced that terminology so that his rhetorical purposes may serve his evangelical convictions that divisiveness in the body of Christ is not acceptable.

PAUL'S ADMONITIONS TO THE "STRONG" CONSIDERED ONCE AGAIN

The "strong" are addressed regarding how they are to relate to those other people, viz., the "weak" (14:1; 15:1). Of course, Paul includes himself among those who are strong. Because the strong are identified by contrast with those who are "weak with respect to faith" (τῇ πίστει, 14:1), we can assume that the "strong" are "strong with respect to faith." Thus, it is notable that the strong "believes" or "has faith (πιστεύει) that he may eat anything" (14:2).

---

24. His apostleship to the Gentiles also included Spain (Rom 15:24, 28). Direct speech might result in such Roman antagonism toward Paul that any future Roman support of his Spanish mission might also be placed in jeopardy.

There should be no surprise that Paul speaks of stronger and weaker faith.[25] The Romans know from several points in the letter that Paul understands that faith, though a gift (cf. 1 Cor 12:9), is variable in strength: (a) Abraham, their collective father in the faith, "grew strong with respect to faith" (Rom 4:20); (b) Paul has encouraged each of the Romans not to overestimate himself or herself but to think "as God has measured a measure of faith to each" (12:3); (c) Paul has noted that certain gifts (χαρίσματα) must be employed "in proportion to faith" (κατὰ τὴν ἀναλογίαν τῆς πίστεως); and (d) faith is individuated, as shown in the construction "the faith which you (sing.) yourself have" (14:22).

At the first mention of "the one weak with respect to faith" Paul enjoins the readers to "welcome" such a person (14:1); to do less is not to recognize that God has already welcomed that person (14:3; cf. 15:7). Demetrius's discussion of figured speech reckons with just such a possibility as Paul seizes on in Rom 14:1.

> At times we . . . shall remind an irascible person that yesterday he was praised for the indulgence he showed to So-and-So's errors, and that he is a pattern to the citizens among whom he moves. Every man gladly takes himself as a model and is eager to add praise to praise, or rather to win one uniform record of praise. (*On Style* 295)

Rhetorically, Paul has thrown wide the gate with his formulation of 14:1, encouraging *each* of the Roman auditors to think of himself or herself as "strong with respect to faith" and to adopt a posture of acceptance and encouragement toward all other believers. In so doing, Paul employs a strategy that he has used widely in his ministry: he paints the best picture and invites his audience to imagine themselves into the living of it. Like Demetrius, Paul assumes that his readers will be "eager . . . to win one uniform record of praise" (cf. 1:11–13; 15:14).

Much has (rightly) been made in studies of the letter to the Romans regarding the connection of 12:1–2 to all that follows, but 14:1–15:13 cannot be understood apart from its connections to 12:3. Two factors in 12:3 prepare the way for 14:1–15:13. The first is the already noted individuated "measure of faith," which provides the conceptual framework within which one could recognize stronger and weaker faith. The second is a caution against *over*-evaluation. Paul urges "every one who is among you not to think too highly of oneself beyond what it is necessary to think" (12:3; cf. Phil 2:3–4). Significantly, *there is no warning against low self-evaluation;* neither here nor anywhere else in the letter (cf. 11:25; 12:16).[26] Paul's estimate of the contentions at Rome must lead him to suppose that unreasonably high self-

25. For a fuller explication of Paul's view of the life of faith as one of growth from weaker to stronger faith, see my *Walking Between the Times*, 46–51.

26. 1 Cor 12:14–19 shows that Paul is quite capable of addressing low self-evaluation among his believers when he thinks it is a problem.

evaluation is the problem: all sides think they are right! The Roman Jewish believers can rightly look to their heritage as God's chosen people; the Roman Gentile believers can see favor and power being connected to their ascendancy, which was realized in the leadership vacuum created by the Claudian edict. Accordingly, when Paul broaches the Roman divisiveness with his figured speech in 14:1–15:13, he urges the strong to welcome the one who is weak in faith—and in so doing assumes that all parties may well identify themselves as strong in faith. Each of the Roman believers is free to regard himself or herself as strong in faith; and each must understand that Paul believes the Romans should welcome those who are weaker in faith, or those whom they consider weaker in faith. Each believer has the obligation to welcome and nurture others, just as "Christ did not please himself" (15:1–3; cf. Phil 2:6–8). The theme is reprised in 15:7: "Therefore, welcome one another just as Christ welcomed you, unto the glory of God."

So there is not one strong group in the Roman churches; likewise there is not a group that would identify itself as weak. The rhetorical notations of "weak" and "strong" have no objective referents in the Roman congregations. Likewise, we must also dismiss the putative identification of eating and drinking patterns as reliable markers of the Roman disputes. Paul's rhetorical purposes are to build bridges across Roman divisiveness, and he uses oblique, figured speech as a means of achieving those goals.

While figured speech avoids a direct hit and therefore does not give an interpreter a one-for-one picture of what was actually going on in the Roman churches,[27] it must, if it is to be effective, give the readers and hearers at once enough distance from reified positions to allow for fresh reflection and at the same time enough similitude to their situations as to invite self-application. Effective indirect discourse must operate within the window framed on the one side by the author's necessity not to score a direct hit[28] and on the other by a need to be close enough to the really divisive issues to encourage the hearers' self-application.

Knowing how indirect or schematic speech functions, we can at least deduce what Paul supposes to be the general shape of the Roman contentions.[29] First, Paul assumes that the contending groups are locked in an ethnically grounded struggle—and that that is sufficient cause for him to intervene. Second, his choices of dietary preferences and the honoring of days suggest that *kashrut* and sabbath are probably at the heart of the contention, though he does not feature them (cf. 14:14, 20). His introduction of

27. The implication of this finding for our efforts to reconstruct early Roman believers' practices and beliefs should be sobering because Romans is, after all, one of the best sources we have for such an undertaking.

28. Direct rebuke would require proofs, could easily be rejected as meddling, and might even exacerbate already present antagonisms.

29. Paul may not be privy to all the complexities of the divisiveness among the Roman churches.

wine drinking (14:21) late in the section dominated by questions of *eating* serves to move the discussion more to the middle of the rhetorical window. It is as if Paul, sensitive to the drift of his comments more toward the issue of eating and its proximity to the hot issues at Rome, generalizes his immediacy by mentioning the drinking of wine.[30] In his correspondence with Corinthian believers on the question of eating of meat offered to idols, Paul has already shown a ready disposition to link drinking to eating practices; in Romans he makes the same connection and thereby ensures that his speech stays indirect and schematic. Third, his recitation of indifferent matters (14:6–9) challenges the Roman auditors to make a careful discernment between what makes a difference and what does not. Being fully convinced and without waverings, giving thanks to God, knowing that "we are the Lord's," being one in Christ in such a way that gives glory to God—or as the formulation of 14:17 puts it, "righteousness and peace and joy in the Holy Spirit"—*these are important matters;* these are not optional for believers. What one eats or drinks and what days are kept or not are not the central issues.[31]

Quintilian warns against making one's figures obvious to the audience (9.2.72); judging by the scholarly blindness to Paul's use of them in Rom 14:1–15:13, Paul did not violate Quintilian's caution. Scholars have missed Paul's use of figured speech, but Paul's readers would most surely have known how to read it.[32]

THE REST OF ROMANS IN LIGHT OF THE OBLIQUE SPEECH OF 14:1–15:13

Because Paul's standing with most of the Roman believers is not assured, and is indeed perhaps even suspect,[33] his most direct treatment of their intramural differences comes as late as chapter 14—and, as we have seen, even that is not direct. If in Romans when Paul is most direct he is oblique, then our consideration of the rest of the letter must be undertaken with a radically readjusted hermeneutical scale from the ones we would apply to other Pauline letters. Paul did not wait until 14:1 to make contact with the readers' struggles. All of Romans, from beginning to end, is an apostolic intervention, pastoral in style, in an intramural, ethnically grounded struggle over leadership and position in the Roman house-churches.[34] The entire

30. To be sure, this move is made easier because of his already having cited what I suppose to be the traditional formulation of 14:17, which links food and drink.

31. For the interplay of conviction and faith, doubt and waverings, see my study of Paul's moral reasoning in *Walking Between the Times*, 57–62.

32. Ahl, "Art of Safe Criticism," 179, 192, 204.

33. See my detailing of the hermeneutic of suspicion potentially present among both the Jewish and Gentile Roman believers, in "A Response to Robert Jewett," 2.

34. Here I suppose that Paul writes the Roman churches at a time when the Claudian edict has expired and when the Jewish believers (among whom are, e.g., Prisca and Aquila) who did

letter is directed toward helping all of Paul's readers and hearers to recognize and affirm their unity in the powerful gospel of God. Rom 1:18–8:39 is not, as has too often been assumed, the doctrinal base from which Paul will subsequently build ethical implications. In chapters 1 through 8, indeed in 1 through 11, Paul's interest is not doctrine *per se* but the establishment of the broadest possible ground upon which all of the Roman believers, no matter what their ethnic background, can see that they stand in common.[35] Let us now briefly look at the major sections of Romans as a sustained, cohesive, comprehensive address of the Roman factions, as a quest for unity.

Romans 1:18-4:25 elaborates the thesis of 1:16–17. The section has a negative and a positive thrust. The negative argument is designed to remind the Roman believers, *both Jews and Gentiles*, that their pre-faith story was the same: each of them was subject to the power and rule of sin. The positive argument reminds Paul's readers, whether Gentile or Jew, that they are utterly dependent on God's grace; they all became right with God and therefore children of Abraham when they believed God as Abraham did. Far from Paul's enunciation of doctrines of sin, grace, and faith for the sake of doctrinal clarity, 1:18–4:25 is Paul's establishment and rehearsal—a genuine remembering afresh (cf. Rom 15:15)—of the common ground that he knows is shared equally by all of his Gentile and Jewish audience in Rome.[36] Paul's positive treatments of Abraham (Romans 4) and of the strange Gentiles (2:14–16), which do not mention sin, make clear that Paul's contention about all being under the power of sin is a porous argument whose primary purpose is not to answer all questions about sin but to depict the common ground that Paul knows is shared equally by all of his Gentile and Jewish readers and hearers in Rome. The same motivation lies behind Paul's amplification of the common paternity of Abraham.

Romans 5-8 unfold for Paul's audience the scope of God's design, of which they are now a part. The section opens with the newly established peace with God (5:1), closes with the awesome apocalyptic picture of God's cosmic redemptive purposes (8:18–25, 28–30) wherein the lost glory of 3:23 is restored beyond compare, and, in the bracketed chapters, details some of the factors bearing on how believers are to comport themselves between their new-found peace and the parousia. This vast story is rehearsed—again

leave Rome ca. 49 C.E. have returned to find that Gentile believers have flourished and even achieved ascendancy.

35. As Paul constructs his comprehensive argument relevant to Roman believers' disputes, he also contributes to his own ethos, thus making more likely his effectiveness but also increasing the chances that some Romans may want to assist Paul in his Spanish mission. Rhetoric can function simultaneously on several different levels and to different purposes.

36. Generally Paul's assertions are so inclusive as to make sure that he is not misunderstood to be saying that the Roman believers' story is different from his or that of others who have come to faith: for example, "both Jews and Greeks, all are under sin" (3:9); "for all have sinned and come short of God's glory" (3:23).

the "recalling to mind" of Rom 15:15—as the shared narrative of their present lives and ultimate destiny as God's children. All the Roman believers are called to see their own stories as a part of God's unfolding drama. Consider how the disputing factions might have heard Paul's questions: "Who shall bring charges against God's elected ones? It is God who justifies; who is the one who condemns?" (8:33–34; cf. the echo in 14:4). If no cosmic powers can disrupt one's standing in God's cosmic redemptive purposes, surely no believer may dare to oppose or even despise God's other elected ones. When God justifies (cf. 5:9 as the established common story of all the Roman hearers), who dares condemn? How can some Roman believers condemn or scorn other believers there?

Chapters 9-11 address some of the implications and assumptions underlying what Paul has said in the preceding chapters. The issues coalesce around the faithfulness and freedom of God: faithfulness because God's promises, gifts, and call are not subject to revocation (11:29; cf. 3:3–4); freedom because God's mercy and call may gain expression in ways that surprise people and that move creatively around and through human obduracy. This section continues Paul's effort to help the Romans understand how God's faithfulness and freedom have impacted them. Jewish believers have a fundamental primacy because of God's faithfulness; they are part of the root stock onto which these "wild branches" have been grafted (11:18; cf. 15:27). Likewise, Gentile believers, the product of God's freedom, though they have been grafted into God's tree, are there only because of faith; φόβος (respect), not ὑψηλός (proud feeling), is the more fitting response (11:20).

In *12:1-15:13* Paul calls upon the Roman believers, as children of God, to live their lives individually and collectively in such a way as to reflect their gratitude to God and their loving acceptance of one another. It is little wonder, given contention among the worshipers of the different house-churches in Rome, that the section moves toward a climax in which Paul three times mentions "welcoming" (14:1, 3; 15:7). God has welcomed (14:3); Christ has welcomed (15:7); now it is incumbent upon all the Roman believers to welcome one another as they have been welcomed (15:7). Then God will surely be glorified (15:7). Indeed, the final exhortation of this section of the letter is the one calling upon all the believers in Rome to "welcome one another, therefore, as Christ has welcomed you, for the glory of God" (15:7 RSV). Προσλαμβάνω (welcome) is the perfect admonitory term to sum up Paul's purposes *throughout* Romans, meaning as it may "receive or accept in one's society, in(to) one's home or circle of acquaintances."[37] Paul exhorts the Roman believers to reach across the barriers that their separate house-

---

37. BAGD, 717. For the role of hospitality in the house-church context, see also Wayne Meeks, *The First Urban Christians: The Social World of the Apostle Paul* (New Haven and London: Yale University Press, 1983) 75–77, 109; idem, *The Moral World of the First Christians* (Philadelphia: Westminster, 1986) 108–14, 121.

churches have come to represent. Paul's call is grounded in the most basic cause or premise: "just as Christ has welcomed you" (15:7).

We interpreters of Paul have been accustomed, and rightly so, to read Paul as a master of direct speech, as a person who engages issues, opponents, and even his own churches with head-on straightforwardness. Surely the Corinthians and the Galatians must have understood him that way—as indeed must have Paul's rivals who insinuated themselves into those Pauline churches. Many of our interpretive models—quite properly generated off of Galatians and the Corinthian letters for the interpretation of *those* letters—simply do not fit Paul's letter to the Romans, force them as we may. Paul proves more flexible than we. He knows he is in a distinctive situation with the Romans, for all the reasons already detailed. Accordingly, he draws upon the conventions of persuasion available in his time and known to him and to his audience. Flattery will not do; censure is out. Figured speech, oblique address, suggestion, encouragement of the readers to make application to themselves—these are the only avenues open to Paul, and he takes them with great care and skill as he seeks to live up to his calling as apostle to the Gentiles. It is for these reasons that we can no longer read Rom 14:1–15:1— and indeed all of Romans!—as we used to.

CHAPTER 4

Σκεῦος: A Modest Proposal for Illuminating Paul's Use of Metaphor in 1 Thessalonians 4:4

Jouette M. Bassler

IT IS FAIR TO SAY, I think, that scholars have reached a virtual impasse over 1 Thess 4:4. The lines are clearly drawn between two different interpretations of this verse, but neither has been able to prevail because neither is able definitively to resolve the ambiguities that plague the text. Because of these pervasive ambiguities, the following "Modest Proposal"[1] cannot claim to be any more definitive than its predecessors. Some developments in the interpretation of the Pauline letters do, however, render it a possible, if not a plausible, alternative. Perhaps, like Swift's essay, it will cause us to reconsider the prevailing situation even if it is not itself considered to be a palatable alternative. A fresh approach to an old topic seems a fitting tribute to Wayne Meeks, who has throughout his career forced us to rethink familiar New Testament texts by subjecting them to new modes of inquiry.

THE PROBLEM WITH METAPHORS

εἰδέναι ἕκαστον ὑμῶν τὸ ἑαυτοῦ σκεῦος
κτᾶσθαι ἐν ἁγιασμῷ καὶ τιμῇ (1 Thess 4:4)

The primary difficulty with this verse is the word σκεῦος. Literally a "vessel" or "instrument," the term is used metaphorically here, but Paul nowhere in the letter defines its meaning. This, of course, was no problem for the Thessalonians, for Paul is here repeating instructions he had previously given to that church (4:2), and in that earlier, oral discussion Paul must have used and defined the now-problematic term. So Paul and the Thessalonians knew what σκεῦος referred to. We, however, do not.

---

1. With apologies to Jonathan Swift.

Two proposals have been made as to its meaning, and each has its ardent defenders.[2] The contours of this debate are well known and need only a brief rehearsal here.[3] On the one hand, there are those who, following a number of patristic writers and influenced by 2 Cor 4:7, interpret the metaphor in terms of the body.[4] Since, however, the usual meaning of the verb κτᾶσθαι ("to acquire") is excluded by this interpretation of σκεῦος, it becomes necessary to appeal to some rare instances in which the present tense of the verb seems to take on the meaning of the perfect ("to keep, guard, or control").[5] Thus construed, the message of the verse, "that each of you knows how to control his (or her) own body in holiness and honor," seems to anticipate the argument of 1 Cor 6:12–20, which is often cited as a parallel. This interpretation has met with wide acceptance,[6] but the rather strained reading of κτᾶσθαι that it requires limits its appeal.[7]

Another line of interpretation, influenced by 1 Pet 3:7 and rabbinic parallels, interprets the σκεῦος as the wife. The usual meaning of κτᾶσθαι is possible here,[8] and the resultant translation ("that each of you knows how to acquire his own wife in holiness and honor") seems to echo the argument of 1 Cor 7:1–7, which is often cited as a parallel.[9] This interpretation too has

2. A third proposal, that σκεῦος is a euphemism for the penis, has few followers; see J. Whitton, "A Neglected Meaning for Σκεῦος in 1 Thessalonians 4.4," *NTS* 28 (1982) 142–43. The 1970 edition of the NAB reflects this interpretation ("each of you guarding his member in sanctity and honor"), but the 1986 edition follows the σκεῦος-as-wife interpretation.

3. For a fuller discussion of these proposals, see Raymond F. Collins, "'This is the Will of God: Your Sanctification.' (1 Thess 4:3)," in *Studies on the First Letter to the Thessalonians* (BETL 66; Leuven: Leuven University Press, 1984) 299–325; and O. Larry Yarbrough, *Not Like the Gentiles: Marriage Rules in the Letters of Paul* (SBLDS 80; Atlanta: Scholars Press, 1985) esp. 65–87.

4. This is the preferred reading, for example, of the NEB, REB, NRSV (cf. RSV mg), NJB, NIV. Unless otherwise indicated, translations in this article are the author's own.

5. Paul uses the verb only here. All other New Testament occurrences of the verb (six in all) are in the present, aorist, or future tense and have the ingressive meaning "get" or "acquire." MM (p. 362) cites one text that allegedly lends support to the meaning "gradually obtain complete mastery of the body" for 1 Thess 4:4. The support, however, is very weak: the cited text has the compound verb ἀνακτᾶσθαι (not κτᾶσθαι) with its usual present tense meaning "reconcile."

6. See Collins, "Will of God," 312; Yarbrough, *Not Like the Gentiles*, 68 n. 8.

7. There are other problems as well. Collins notes that with this reading the reflexive pronoun (ἑαυτοῦ) is problematic, "since it is difficult to understand in what sense Paul would be petitioning each of the Thessalonian Christians 'to acquire *his own* body'" ("Will of God," 315).

8. This is the preferred reading of the RSV. Oddly, Collins, who acknowledges the usual ingressive sense of κτᾶσθαι and prefers the interpretation of σκεῦος as wife, ultimately renders the verse in such a way that this meaning of κτᾶσθαι is completely obscured: "each one of you know how *to live with* his wife in holiness and honor" ("Will of God," 314, emphasis mine). Note that the sense of the reflexive pronoun has also been obscured.

9. See especially Raymond F. Collins, "The Unity of Paul's Paraenesis in 1 Thess. 4.3–8: 1 Cor. 7.1–7, A Significant Parallel," in *Studies on the First Letter to the Thessalonians* (BETL 64; Leuven: Leuven University Press, 1984) 326–35.

met with wide acceptance, but there are some serious difficulties here as well. The word σκεῦος is not attested in Greek literature with this meaning,[10] and the limited application of the exhortation (to unmarried men) seems incompatible with the more general precepts that surround it.[11] Scholars favoring this interpretation note that, though evidence is lacking in the Greek literature, rabbinic literature clearly documents the use of the corresponding Hebrew word כְּלִי ("vessel") as a metaphor for a woman or wife. These parallels, however, introduce an unsettling element into the passage. It is not so much that the texts usually cited are late,[12] but that they are implicitly or explicitly pornographic. The text that Collins quotes is typical:

> Some say that Medes are more beautiful, while others say that Persians are more beautiful. Then Assuerus said: The כְּלִי which I use is neither a Mede nor a Persian. Do you want to see her? Yes, they answered, provided that she's naked.[13]

Yarbrough argues that σκεῦος κτᾶσθαι in 1 Thess 4:4 is "Paul's rendering" of the Hebrew phrase found in passages like this one.[14] Paul's argument in 1 Thess 4:3–8, however, centers on the concepts of holiness and honor. It is difficult to concede that, with all the other terms available to him, Paul would use in this context one that originates in—and conveys—a view of women as containers for semen.

Neither interpretation, then, gives a completely satisfying resolution to the problem presented by Paul's metaphorical use of the word σκεῦος in this verse. Nor is it likely that further perusal of the Greco-Roman and rabbinic literature will resolve the impasse. A metaphor involves a flexible use of the language, and while certain metaphorical uses of a word may become common, they do not exhaustively define the possibilities.[15] Thus in 1 Thess 4:4, σκεῦος does not necessarily mean what it meant in the Greco-Roman or

10. In 1 Pet 3:7 the wife is described using the *analogy* (not the metaphor) of "the weaker vessel" (ὡς ἀσθενεστέρῳ σκεύει).

11. Recognizing this problem, Helmut Koester argues that Paul chose the neuter term σκεῦος to emphasize the mutuality of sexual control ("1 Thessalonians—Experiment in Christian Writing," in *Continuity and Discontinuity in Church History: Essays presented to George Hunston Williams* [ed. F. F. Church and T. George; Studies in the History of Christian Thought 19; Leiden: Brill, 1979] 33–44, esp. 43 n. 23). His translation of the difficult verse, however, skims over a number of other exegetical difficulties: "treat your marriage partner [σκεῦος] with respect, not in blind passion."

12. They *are* late, but they have rather clear antecedents in some OT texts that convey the idea of a woman as a container, but without using the specific word כְּלִי (see, e.g., Prov 5:15–18; Sir 26:12).

13. *B. Meg.* 12b; see also *m. Ketub.* 3:4–5; *b. B. Meṣ.* 84b.

14. Yarbrough, *Not Like the Gentiles*, 70.

15. Thus I find Collins's approach too restrictive when he says, "The term [σκεῦος] is rarely used by Paul, but when it is used it is always used in the figurative sense. The question then becomes: which of the metaphorical senses ["body," "wife," or "male sexual organ"] is appropriate to the interpretation of v. 4?" ("Will of God," 311).

rabbinic literature. It means what Paul and the Thessalonian church agreed that it meant in their earlier discussions of the matter, and this could have been a completely idiosyncratic usage! Before rejecting this exegetically alarming possibility out of hand, let us see where it leads us.

Paul uses σκεῦος metaphorically in only two other places in the uncontested letters, but even this small sample reveals considerable creativity with its application. In Rom 9:22–23, for example, the σκεύη ὀργῆς ("vessels of wrath") and the σκεύη ἐλέους ("vessels of mercy") refer to unbelieving Israel and believing Jews and Gentiles respectively;[16] and in 2 Cor 4:7, which is often cited in support of the interpretation of 1 Thess 4:4 in terms of the body, the words ἐν ὀστρακίνοις σκεύεσιν ("in earthen or clay vessels") refer not to the mortal body *per se* but to the frailty of those chosen to proclaim the gospel, that is, to Paul and his associates.[17] In both of these passages, the metaphor is qualified by an adjective or a genitive noun, and the qualifier together with the surrounding argument clearly indicates the intended referent. The word is not qualified in 1 Thess 4:4, but that does not mean that Paul is following some *standard* usage there. He may be following a metaphorical use of the word every bit as creative as that in Romans or 2 Corinthians, but one so well known to the Thessalonians that he felt no need to clarify it. If this is the case, we will not find the answer in the contemporary literature. The answer lies in those earlier instructions to the Thessalonians, but since these are lost to us, we must approach the problem in a different way. We will, of course, look for clues in the argument of 1 Thess 4:1–8, but first we need to look more closely at the parallels between the Thessalonian and Corinthian texts.

THE PROBLEM WITH PARALLELS

I start with the assumption that κτᾶσθαι has its usual present tense meaning here: "to get or acquire." That is, I assume more flexibility with the metaphorical σκεῦος than with the verb. Only if the usual meaning of this fairly common verb yields no intelligible results should an obscure usage be assumed. This eliminates for the moment any interpretation of 1 Thess 4:4

---

16. This application of the metaphor reverses Israel's expectations: according to Wisdom 15–16, it is Israel who is the object of God's mercy while pagan idolators face God's implacable wrath.

17. See Victor P. Furnish, *II Corinthians* (AB 32A; Garden City, N.Y.: Doubleday, 1984) 278–80; see also John T. Fitzgerald, *Cracks in an Earthen Vessel: An Examination of the Catalogues of Hardships in the Corinthian Correspondence* (SBLDS 99; Atlanta: Scholars Press, 1988) 167–74. Outside the Pauline corpus, the flexibility of the metaphor remains well attested: see Acts 9:15 (the "chosen vessel" is Paul), 2 Tim 2:21 (the "vessels for honor" are the tested and purified church leaders, the "vessels for dishonor" are the false teachers), 1 Pet 3:7 (the "weaker vessel" is the wife).

in terms of body, for, as Collins notes, "to acquire one's own body" makes no sense at all.[18]

Those who interpret σκεῦος in this verse as a reference to a wife have seen here, as we have noted, a close parallel to the argument of 1 Cor 7:1–7. Yarbrough, for example, claims that the rule for marriage that Paul gives in 1 Cor 7:2a is "exactly the same, except in more direct speech," as that found in 1 Thess 4:4.[19] He demonstrates the point by juxtaposing the two verses 1 Thess 4:4 (εἰδέναι ἕκαστον ὑμῶν τὸ ἑαυτοῦ σκεῦος κτᾶσθαι, "that each one know how to acquire his own vessel") and 1 Cor 7:2 (ἕκαστος τὴν ἑαυτοῦ γυναῖκα ἐχέτω, "let each one have his own wife"). Yet, as Michael McGehee has observed, the verbal parallelism consists only of two pronouns.[20] Moreover, the parallelism rests on an interpretation of 1 Cor 7:2 that has recently come under some criticism.

It has usually been assumed that 1 Cor 7:2 refers to entering into marriage, that "let each man have his own wife" means, quite simply, let him get married. With this reading, the verse is construed as providing significant support for interpreting σκεῦος as wife in 1 Thess 4:4. Yet several scholars have challenged this interpretation of 1 Cor 7:2, arguing that neither the terminology nor the context really supports it.[21] Instead, Paul seems to be dealing in this verse with a significantly different issue: the question of sexual relations within established marriages. Paul is thus to be understood as saying in this verse: "Let each man have (sexual relations with) his own wife and let each woman have (sexual relations with) her own husband." If this is the case, then the verse no longer provides support for interpreting σκεῦος as wife; indeed, Paul's advice in the whole of 1 Corinthians 7 actually seems to *undermine* that interpretation.

The argument in 1 Corinthians 7 is very complex because Paul deals with so many subgroups within the community (those married to believers, those married to unbelievers, the unmarried, the widowed, some "virgins") and treats men and women separately within each group. Yet it is clear that "in view of the impending crisis" (v. 26) Paul always holds out celibacy as the preferred option for the unmarried (7:8, 25–28, 32–35, 38, 40). To be sure, he also insists that marriage is a valid option for those who cannot control their passions—that is, those who do not have his gift of celibacy (v. 7)—but

18. Collins, "Will of God," 313.

19. Yarbrough, *Not Like the Gentiles*, 69; so, too, William Klassen, "Foundations for Pauline Sexual Ethics as Seen in I Thess. 4:1–8," in *SBL 1978 Seminar Papers* (ed. P. J. Achtemeier; Missoula, Mont.: Scholars Press, 1978) 167.

20. Michael McGehee, "A Rejoinder to Two Recent Studies Dealing with 1 Thess 4:4," *CBQ* 51 (1989) 83.

21. See, e.g., Gordon D. Fee, *The First Epistle to the Corinthians* (NICNT; Grand Rapids: Eerdmans, 1987) 278–79; so, too, John C. Hurd, Jr., *The Origin of 1 Corinthians* (Macon, Ga.: Mercer University Press, 1983) 162. Hans Conzelmann seems to leave both options open; see *1 Corinthians* (Hermeneia; Philadelphia: Fortress, 1975) 116.

marriage is thus rather clearly understood as an outlet for these passions (7:9, 36–37; see also v. 5). Paul's ranking here of celibacy and marriage is, of course, shaped by his strong conviction that "the present form of this world is passing away" (7:31). His apocalyptic convictions, however, are at least as strong in 1 Thessalonians (see 4:13–5:11), yet there, if σκεῦος means wife, he gives quite different advice. He makes no mention of the option of celibacy and, far from viewing marriage as a (valid) outlet for sexual desire, he insists that the Thessalonian men obtain their wives in holiness and honor and quite apart from lustful passion (v. 5). Thus, when 1 Cor 7:2 is understood to refer to sexual relations within marriage instead of to marriage itself, all support for the interpretation of 1 Thess 4:4 in terms of acquiring a wife vanishes. Some verses at the *end* of this chapter, however, may provide the background for a somewhat different interpretation of σκεῦος.

It has often been noted that in 1 Corinthians 7, where Paul clearly responds to questions of marriage and sexual ethics, he takes great pains to address both men and women in parallel clauses. In 1 Thess 4:4, however, if the σκεῦος refers to the wife, only the man is addressed, a state of affairs that more than one scholar has deemed "unusual" or "unlikely."[22] This argument assumes, of course, that Paul's balanced treatment of women and men in 1 Corinthians 7 is normative for him and not evoked by special circumstances in that community.[23] Moreover, and more seriously, it overlooks the fact that even in 1 Corinthians 7 there is one portion of the chapter where Paul addresses only the male member of a male–female pair: his advice to the man pondering whether to marry "his virgin" (7:36–38).

These verses are exceedingly difficult. The older view—that the "virgins" were the marriageable daughters of fathers who were here assured by Paul that it was "no sin" to give them in marriage—finds few advocates today. There is still a lively debate, however, among proponents of two other interpretations. Some argue that the situation Paul addresses involves engaged couples who had "frozen" their relationship when they became convinced about the apocalyptic urgency of the times but were now reconsidering the merits of proceeding with the marriage. Others understand Paul's advice to be directed toward couples who had deliberately entered into "spiritual marriages" but were now experiencing some difficulties with the temptations created by this intimate but chaste relationship.[24] The two situations are

22. See McGehee, "Rejoinder," 84; Dieter Lührmann, "The Beginnings of the Church at Thessalonica," in *Greeks, Romans, and Christians: Essays in Honor of Abraham J. Malherbe* (ed. D. L. Balch et al.; Minneapolis: Fortress, 1990) 245–46.

23. See, e.g., Fee's comments on the reason for the balanced treatment of women and men in 1 Corinthians 7 (*1 Corinthians*, 270). Antoinette C. Wire agrees that Paul's balanced treatment has a specific rhetorical goal here, but she defines that goal differently; see *The Corinthian Women Prophets: A Reconstruction through Paul's Rhetoric* (Minneapolis: Fortress, 1990) 72–97.

24. See the discussions by Hurd, *Origin*, 169–80; Fee, *1 Corinthians*, 325–27; J. K. Elliott,

similar in several respects: both involve an ongoing celibate relationship and both involve a vow or binding agreement of some sort, whether to live (together) in this celibate relationship or to prolong indefinitely their engaged status. At issue is whether the couple initially entered into a "normal" engagement and then decided to prolong it or deliberately entered into an "abnormal," ascetic relationship.[25]

Here, as in 1 Thessalonians 4, Paul does not clearly define the nature of the relationship he is discussing because it was well known to his readers. Several things, however, emerge from his comments. First, the "virgins" are treated separately from Paul's earlier discussion of married couples and divorced, unmarried, and widowed people, and thus, as Hurd notes, they probably constituted a special group within the church.[26] Second, to refer to a man's fiancée as "his own virgin" (7:36) is rather unusual[27] and suggests at the very least that virginity, not betrothal, was the significant aspect of the relationship. Finally, only in his remarks concerning "virgins" does Paul insist—not once but twice—that marriage (to one's "virgin") is not a *sin* (7:28, 36), which suggests rather strongly that some in the congregation thought the opposite. Whatever the nature of the relationship between the man and "his virgin," converting it to a normal marriage was viewed as a very serious error by at least a vocal few.

Certainty is elusive here, but these factors lend some support to the hypothesis that the situation Paul was addressing in these verses involved some sort of spiritual marriage.[28] We will never know the exact nature of

---

"Paul's Teaching on Marriage in 1 Corinthians: Some Problems Considered," *NTS* 19 (1972–73) 219–25; Wire, *Corinthian Women Prophets*, 224–25.

25. Hurd claims that the "key difference" between these two hypotheses is "whether or not the couple were actually living together" (*Origin*, 176). This seems to me to be less significant for defining the nature of the relationship than the couple's intention when they entered it.

26. The περὶ δέ ("now concerning") of 7:25 suggests that in this verse Paul begins to address a new, but related, topic. Hurd argues that 7:25–38 concerns a single problem, that generated by spiritual marriages (*Origin*, 169–82). Interestingly, though Elliott argues for a different understanding of the situation that Paul addresses, he too regards the argument of vv. 25–38 as a unity ("Paul's Teaching on Marriage," 220–23).

27. *Pace* Elliott, who claims that "in the rest of the New Testament παρθένος is commonly used of a betrothed girl" ("Paul's Teaching on Marriage," 221). The evidence he cites, however, includes the story of the birth of Jesus (Luke 1:27; Matt 1:18, 23); the highly symbolic parable of the ten virgins (Matt 25:1–13); and the equally symbolic statement in 2 Cor 11:2. None of these texts provides evidence for what was common parlance in the Pauline churches, which is the relevant question here. Various phrases are found in the writings of this period: ἁρμοστής ("betrothed husband"; cf. ἡρμοσάμην in 2 Cor 11:2); ἡ ἐμνηστευμένη αὐτῷ [γυνή] ("his betrothed wife"; Luke 2:5); μνηστήρ (fem. μνήστρια; "wooer, suitor").

28. The terminology "spiritual marriage" is probably misleading. Fee is quite right to point out that γαμίζειν ("to marry"—even if the causative force is absent) is a strange way to refer to consummating a *marriage* that had taken place much earlier (1 *Corinthians*, 352). Paul's argument will be better served if we refer instead to virgin partners, though that terminology may suggest too much mutuality. Paul's argument in 7:36–38 reveals that the man had the decisive voice in terminating the arrangement.

the relationship as it existed in Corinth, though the phenomenon seems to have become rather widespread in the church, even though officially censured, from the second century on.[29] Such a relationship would have had a number of practical advantages, especially for those convinced that the end of the age was fast approaching. Hurd, for example, mentions the advantages of marriage "without the care and burden of children," and Clark notes that in the period before convents were known or widespread the relationship solved the problem of domestic arrangements for women committed to celibacy.[30] The relationship may have had positive symbolic overtones as well. In a later letter to the Corinthians, Paul speaks of his desire "to present [the church] as a chaste virgin to Christ" (2 Cor 11:2), and it is possible that the virgins mentioned in this earlier letter symbolized in some way this relationship. This certainly seems to have been the case in the post-Pauline churches addressed by the Pastoral Epistles (1 Tim 5:11–12),[31] and such a view of the relationship would help explain why breaking it was opposed so vigorously by the Corinthians.

One thing that is certain is that Paul did not disapprove of these spiritual marriages; he disapproved only of those who would impose their inflexible view of them on others. Did Paul *instigate* them? Hurd thinks so:

> Indeed we strongly suspect that Paul was instrumental in inaugurating these relationships. We have argued that the vow undertaken by these couples was a result of their Christian enthusiasm. This peculiar institution, therefore, was created during Paul's original stay in Corinth. It is doubtful whether anything so significant for the life of the congregation could have been inaugurated without his full consent and approval. Moreover, since Paul was at that time the undisputed leader of the Corinthian Church, it is natural to suppose that he himself was responsible for creating this new Christian institution.[32]

If Paul introduced the concept of "spiritual marriages" to the Corinthians, would he not have introduced it in other churches as well? This intriguing possibility encourages me to make the following proposal.

---

29. See, e.g., Elizabeth A. Clark, "John Chrysostom and the Subintroductae," *Church History* 46 (1977) 171–85; reprinted in *Ascetic Piety and Women's Faith: Essays on Late Ancient Christianity* (Studies in Women and Religion 20; Lewiston, N.Y.: Mellen, 1986) 265–90.

30. Hurd, *Origin*, 179; Clark, "Subintroductae," 278–79. See also *Ps-Diogenes* 47 (in A. J. Malherbe, *The Cynic Epistles: A Study Edition* [SBLSBS 12; Missoula, Mont.: Scholars Press, 1977]).

31. See also J. M. Bassler, "The Widows' Tale: A Fresh Look at 1 Tim 5:3–16," *JBL* 103 (1984) 23–41.

32. Hurd, *Origin*, 276. McGehee finds such a proposal "incredible" ("Rejoinder," 88); see also Wolfgang Schrage (*Der erste Brief an die Korinther* [EKK 7/1; Neukirchen-Vluyn: Neukirchener Verlag, 1991] 49), who calls the idea "höchst fraglich." I am not as willing as these scholars are to reject the idea out of hand.

THE MODEST PROPOSAL

I propose that 1 Cor 7:36–38, not 1 Cor 7:1–7, is the closest parallel to 1 Thess 4:4 and that, as a result of his earlier teaching on the topic, Paul and the Thessalonians understood the word σκεῦος in 1 Thess 4:4 as a metaphorical reference to virgin partners, "vessels," perhaps, "of holiness." His advice, then, to the members of this church was that to achieve the goal of pleasing God each of them should know the benefits of acquiring a virgin partner. What, beyond sheer speculation, constitutes the evidence for this reading of the text?

There is at least as much verbal and structural parallelism between the relevant clauses of 1 Thess 4:4 and 1 Cor 7:37 as that claimed for 1 Cor 7:2, and much greater congruence in their arguments: τὸ ἑαυτοῦ σκεῦος κτᾶσθαι, "acquire his own vessel" (1 Thess 4:4); τηρεῖν τὴν ἑαυτοῦ παρθένον, "keep his own virgin" (1 Cor 7:37). We saw above that 1 Cor 7:2 and 1 Thess 4:4 create the *impression* of correspondence, but the two verses actually contain quite different sorts of statements. One refers to acquiring a "vessel," the other to having sexual relations with one's wife. Quite apart from the different terms (σκεῦος, "vessel," and γυναικός, "wife"), the correspondence in content was more apparent than real. Here, however, though the terms are still different (σκεῦος and παρθένος, "virgin"), the statements *are* analogous. If σκεῦος and παρθένος refer to the same relationship, one text refers to inaugurating (1 Thess 4:4), the other to maintaining (1 Cor 7:37), this relationship.

In both passages, the one concerning virgins and the one concerning vessels, the same motifs are present. In 1 Thess 4:1, the general rubric for the instructions that follow is "how . . . to live and to please God" (ἀρέσκειν θεῷ). Paul speaks elsewhere of the need to please God. Earlier in the letter to the Thessalonians, Paul has insisted that his apostolic labors are devoted to the single goal of pleasing God (2:4). It may not be irrelevant to note that Paul, unlike Peter and other apostles (1 Cor 9:5), was not married, for in 1 Cor 7:32, Paul argues that only "the unmarried man" (ὁ ἄγαμος) is able to focus on "the affairs of the Lord, how to please the Lord" (πῶς ἀρέσῃ τῷ κυρίῳ). He does not use precisely the same phrase when speaking of "the unmarried woman and virgin" (ἡ γυνὴ ἡ ἄγαμος καὶ ἡ παρθένος),[33] but the concern she has to be "holy in body and spirit" (v. 34) is equivalent to the unmarried man's concern "to please the Lord." Clearly Paul believes that

---

33. It is not clear whether καί has a copulative or epexegetical function here—that is, whether Paul is speaking of one or two categories of women; see Margaret Y. MacDonald, "Women Holy in Body and Spirit: The Social Setting of 1 Corinthians 7," *NTS* 36 (1990) 171. The verb that follows (μεριμνᾷ) is singular.

pleasing God is facilitated by a celibate life-style, and since acquiring a "vessel" is urged as part of a program to please God, celibacy may be involved here as well.

Though holiness characterizes the Christian as such (1 Cor 1:2; 6:11; 1 Thess 5:23), the particular phrase used in 1 Cor 7:34 to define the life-style of the unmarried women and virgins, "holy in both body and spirit" (ἁγία καὶ τῷ σώματι καὶ τῷ πνεύματι),[34] indicates that holiness is also intimately connected in Paul's mind with celibacy. Being "holy in body" (i.e., celibate) is what sets *these* women apart from their married sisters, who were, like all Christians, holy in spirit. This link between holiness and celibacy is supported by 1 Cor 7:5–6, where Paul links sexual abstinence within a marriage with special periods of prayer, and is confirmed by 2 Cor 11:2, where Paul expresses his desire to present the church "as a *holy virgin* (παρθένον ἁγνὴν) to Christ."[35] In 1 Thess 4:3–8 Paul presents his instructions concerning the σκεῦος, as well as the admonitions to abstain from fornication and not to wrong a brother in some matter,[36] under the category of "your sanctification" (ὁ ἁγιασμὸς ὑμῶν). He repeats the reference to sanctification or holiness in vv. 4 and 7 and concludes the section with the reminder that God has given the *Holy* Spirit to them (v. 8). Holiness, then, is the leitmotif of this portion of the letter, and insofar as Paul sees holiness enhanced by chastity, the interpretation of σκεῦος as virgin partner is encouraged.

One must also consider the remarkable attention Paul gives to motivation in this passage. He opens (4:1) with the unusual and emphatic double exhortation: "We ask and urge you in the Lord Jesus" (ἐρωτῶμεν ὑμᾶς καὶ παρακαλοῦμεν ἐν κυρίῳ Ἰησοῦ). The passage then concludes with a striking series of motivational clauses:

> . . . because the Lord is an avenger in all these things, just as we have already told you beforehand and solemnly warned you. For God did not call us to impurity but in holiness. Therefore whoever rejects this rejects not human authority but God, who also gives his Holy Spirit to you. (4:6–8)

Paul provides here five separate grounds for obedience: God's avenging justice, Paul's earlier instructions, God's call to holiness, the divine authority behind the instructions, and the transforming gift of the Holy Spirit. This remarkable emphasis on motivation has not gone undetected, but Malherbe, for example, explains it as Paul's way of highlighting the distinctive-

---

34. See MacDonald's article ("Women Holy in Body and Spirit") for a discussion of this life-style.

35. Collins cites 1 Cor 7:12–16 to demonstrate that sanctification is realized in marriage ("Will of God," 316), but Paul refers there to the possible sanctification (i.e., salvation) of the currently unbelieving spouse. This is substantially different from the special "holiness in both body and spirit" that Paul affirms for the celibate Christian.

36. See below, pp. 64–65.

ness of the Christian moral life.[37] The exhortations, Malherbe argues, reflect traditional moral instructions. It was only in the motivational clauses that the distinctive aspect of the Christian moral life—its theological grounding—could be made clear and thus these clauses are emphasized.

Certainly Paul is concerned in this letter with distinguishing the new Christians from their pagan neighbors and from their own pagan past (see, e.g., 1:9–10; 4:5; 4:13; 5:4–10). It seems at least possible, however, that it is not just through the motivational rhetoric that Paul hopes to contribute to their sense of distinctiveness but also through the behavior that he seeks so diligently to motivate. That is, Paul could be stressing motivation in these exhortations not simply because of the nature of the motivation but because of the nature of the exhortation. If Paul was promoting virgin partnerships rather than consummated marriages, that could require a lot of motivation.

It is important to note, however, that Paul does not seem to be insisting on a celibate life-style for everyone. Few have commented on the peculiar formulation of the second clause of the exhortation, the one concerning the σκεῦος, but it is, I think, significant. In 1 Thess 4:3–6, Paul defines the "will of God" for the Thessalonians through three specific precepts, each presented as an infinitive clause. The first is straightforward: ἀπέχεσθαι ὑμᾶς ἀπὸ τῆς πορνείας ("that you abstain from fornication"). The last precept uses two articular infinitives, but again God's will seems to be directly presented: τὸ μὴ ὑπερβαίνειν καὶ πλεονεκτεῖν ἐν τῷ πράγματι τὸν ἀδελφὸν αὐτοῦ ("not to overstep and defraud his brother in the matter"). The middle precept, however, is not presented as a direct instruction but is mediated by the additional infinitive εἰδέναι: εἰδέναι ἕκαστον ὑμῶν τὸ ἑαυτοῦ σκεῦος κτᾶσθαι ἐν ἁγιασμῷ καὶ τιμῇ.

This construction (using some form of εἰδέναι plus an infinitive) is very unusual for Paul: he uses it elsewhere only in Phil 4:12, but there he uses it twice and surrounds it with other verbs that clarify its meaning.

> οἶδα καὶ ταπεινοῦσθαι ("I know what it is to have little")
> οἶδα καὶ περισσεύειν ("and I know what it is to have plenty")
> ἐν παντὶ καὶ ἐν πᾶσιν μεμύημαι ("in any and all circumstances I have learned the secret")
> καὶ χορτάζεσθαι καὶ πεινᾶν καὶ περισσεύειν καὶ ὑστερεῖσθαι ("of being well-fed and going hungry, of having plenty and of being in need" [NRSV])

The three finite verbs in parallel clauses—οἶδα . . . οἶδα . . . μεμύημαι—develop the same idea: to "know" is to learn the secret of. This idea is also communicated by the verb ἔμαθον ("I have learned"), which introduces the statement, and by ἰσχύω ("I am strong enough"), which concludes it. Paul is

---

37. Abraham J. Malherbe, "Exhortation in 1 Thessalonians," in *Paul and the Popular Philosophers* (Minneapolis: Fortress, 1989) 60–61; see also Yarbrough, *Not Like the Gentiles*, 76–87.

thus saying to the Philippians that during his imprisonment he has learned the lesson of self-sufficiency, has been instructed in the secret of adjusting to circumstances, has discovered he is strong enough (with God's help) to endure all things. This suggests that when Paul says in 1 Thess 4:4 εἰδέναι . . . κτᾶσθαι, he is not insisting that each Thessalonian immediately acquire a "vessel," but that each know about, know the secret of, know the advantages of, be able if the opportunity arises—to acquire a vessel in holiness and honor. There is room here for the more carefully nuanced understanding of the different obligations of those already married or widowed or divorced that we find in 1 Corinthians 7.[38]

The last of the three precepts in 1 Thess 4:3-6 raises an auxiliary set of questions. It too is phrased enigmatically: τὸ μὴ ὑπερβαίνειν καὶ πλεονεκτεῖν ἐν τῷ πράγματι τὸν ἀδελφὸν αὐτοῦ ("not to overstep and defraud his brother in the matter"). Some claim that Paul is addressing a new issue here: the subject of fraud in the marketplace. Others argue for the unity of the section: the πρᾶγμα ("matter" or "business") that Paul mentions here is that mentioned in the preceding verses.[39] There is much in favor of the argument for the unity of the section: the common concern for sexual matters in the first and second precepts encourages one to expect a reference to them in the third as well; the overarching theme of holiness seems more appropriate to sexual issues than commercial ones; and there are no clear indicators to the reader or hearer that a new topic is being introduced in v. 6.[40] Indeed, the way πρᾶγμα is mentioned in the argument suggests that the antecedent is obvious from the immediate context. It is customary among those who see continuity in Paul's argument here to find in this word a reference to the general subject of sexual relations raised in v. 3. Thus Yarbrough translates the precept, "Let no man transgress against his brother by defrauding him in the matter of sexual relations,"[41] and understands it to be a reference to adultery. But Paul has a word for adultery (μοιχεύω, μοιχός) and he does not use it here. Instead, the wording ἐν τῷ πράγματι suggests a more specific reference to the matter just mentioned in the second precept,

38. An interesting suggestion made by L. M. White in an oral communication preserves the flexibility of Paul's position even more clearly. If σκεῦος in 1 Thess 4:4 refers to the marriage relationship itself, as it does in Plutarch's "Advice to Bride and Groom" (*Moralia* 138e), then Paul could be understood as exhorting each Thessalonian Christian to secure his or her own marriage relationship—whether virginal or "normal"—in holiness and honor.

39. See the summary of the debate by Collins, "Will of God," 317–19, and by Yarbrough, *Not Like the Gentiles*, 73–76.

40. Gottlieb Lünemann argued that the articular infinitive in v. 6 "imperatively requires us to consider τὸ . . . αὐτοῦ as parallel to ὁ ἁγιασμὸς ὑμῶν, ver. 3, and, accordingly, as a second object *different* from the first" (emphasis his) (*Critical and Exegetical Hand-Book to the Epistles to the Thessalonians* [MeyerK; New York: Funk & Wagnalls, 1885] 518). This seems to overinterpret the significance of the article, which most scholars take to be resumptive (after the interruption in v. 5 to the list of precepts).

41. Yarbrough, *Not Like the Gentiles*, 76.

the matter of acquiring a "vessel." What would be the connection between these two precepts?

There are some conceivable opportunities for fraud if the second precept speaks of acquiring a wife: one could woo someone betrothed to another, though this would be a relatively rare event. The opportunities for overstepping boundaries (ὑπερβαίνειν) and taking advantage of another's credulity (πλεονεκτεῖν) are far greater, however, if the situation is one of celibate partnerships. A father, brother, or male relative would be gravely defrauded if his female relative were committed to a celibate relationship that became compromised by πάθος ἐπιθυμίας ("passion of lust," 4:5). And if Paul uses the masculine τὸν ἀδελφόν in v. 6 to refer to either the (Christian) brother *or* sister,[42] as he does elsewhere frequently in the plural (1 Thess 1:4; 2:1; etc.) and occasionally in the singular (1 Cor 8:11, 13), then he could be speaking here of taking advantage of the virgin partner her or himself. I propose, then, as a possible translation of these enigmatic verses the following:

> This is the will of God, your sanctification: That you abstain from sexual immorality; that each of you know about acquiring a vessel/virgin partner in holiness and honor, not in lustful passion like the Gentiles who do not know God; and that [each of you know] not to overstep [the limits of the relationship] and defraud his brother (or sister) in this matter.

CONCLUSION

1 Thess 4:4 presents us with a puzzle. Various solutions have been proposed, but none has proved to be entirely satisfactory. The modest proposal offered here is highly speculative and purely exploratory. Let me review its salient features.

It assumes the inherent flexibility of metaphorical language: Paul was not restricted here to what σκεῦος "usually" meant. It assumes some continuity in Paul's thoughts on marriage in the Thessalonian and Corinthian correspondence.[43] It assumes that the issue Paul addresses in 1 Cor 7:36–38 was that of spiritual marriages and that John Hurd is probably correct in his hunch that Paul himself introduced the practice during his visit to Corinth.[44] From there it is an easy step to argue that if Paul introduced the practice in Corinth it is likely that he also did so in other communities. This provides the necessary background for proposing that 1 Thess 4:4 refers to precisely this aspect of Paul's ethical instructions.

---

42. Note the NRSV translation of this verse: "that no one wrong or exploit a brother or sister in this matter."

43. It is useful to recall here that Paul was probably in Corinth when he wrote the letter to the Thessalonians.

44. I am not willing to concede *all* aspects of Hurd's argument, especially the hypothesis of a reversal in Paul's position as a result of the Apostolic Decree.

The proposal thus rests on a delicate pattern of assumptions. Even worse, it bases the interpretation of one problematical text (1 Thess 4:4) on another, equally problematical one (1 Cor 7:36–38). This is a risky business, but it does allow us to view this much-disputed text, if only for a moment, from a new perspective. And the proposal itself does have some advantages over previous proposals, for it does not generate the logical and grammatical problems that plague the more familiar readings. One does not need to strain the meaning of κτᾶσθαι ("to acquire") or struggle with accommodating this advice to that Paul tenders in 1 Corinthians 7. If this proposal is correct, however, it will require us to rethink some of our assumptions about early Christianity. It may be that while Paul borrowed the language and the style of the Hellenistic moralists, novel elements could lie hidden behind familiar—or metaphorical—language. If correct, the proposal also renders more comprehensible the persistent association of Paul with an ascetic message. The widows of the Pastoral Epistles and the tradents of the apocryphal Acts may have linked Paul's message with celibacy because Paul himself had emphatically done so. Whether they appreciated the implications and flexibility of Paul's position is, of course, a different matter.

CHAPTER 5

A Support for His Old Age:
Paul's Plea on Behalf of Onesimus

Ronald F. Hock

"WHAT WAS IT LIKE to become and be an ordinary Christian in the first century?" Wayne Meeks asks this question at the beginning of his *First Urban Christians* [1] and answers it in two steps. First, he provides informative but general accounts of urban life in the early Roman Empire and in the specific cities in the Pauline missionary orbit. Then he turns to Acts and Paul's letters for the clues they give of the social level of Pauline Christians, but especially for the evidence they contain about the Pauline churches themselves. Here we see Meeks at his masterful best—making deft use of the methods and categories of the social sciences for organizing his analysis and teasing out every bit of social information he can from the letters that pertains to the formation of these churches—their means of governance, their several rituals, and the social force of their beliefs. Even when formally stated, Meeks's answer to the question he posed at the outset is impressive indeed—for its breadth, its sophistication, and its many insights.

But the question itself, while in some respects very revolutionary, is in others quite traditional, in that the focus is still internal, viewing the Pauline Christians from within, first on their "becoming" Christian and then on their being "Christian." The result is that the "social" world of Paul's churches that Meeks describes turns out to be an ecclesiology in a social key—and a sectarian ecclesiology at that. For the internal focus may be taken to emphasize the separation of Christians from the world, their subsequent resocialization, their sense of solidarity and unity, and their distinctive beliefs and ethos. Meanwhile, the larger outside world is not merely different but becomes hostile and in need of a radical change in

---

1. W. A. Meeks, *The First Urban Christians: The Social World of the Apostle Paul* (New Haven: Yale University Press, 1983) 2.

ethos and symbols—in need of that very new world that the Pauline churches themselves were constructing.

What is missing in this sectarian view that emerges from an almost exclusive use of the evidence in Paul's letters, however, is the control and balance that would be provided by an equally detailed and nuanced analysis of the urban world of the Greek East from which the Pauline churches drew their members and in which they continued to exist. To be sure, Meeks is doubtful that such an analysis is even possible. Ancient writers, he says, ignored what we most want to know about the texture of life in these cities, and modern archaeologists have too often preferred famous monuments and mosaics to the residential quarters where Pauline house-churches stood. Accordingly, Meeks concludes: "We thus have no comprehensive, detailed picture of life in a first-century provincial town into which we could fit our few early-Christian puzzle pieces."[2]

There is, however, a group of documents that, if properly analyzed, could fill in much of that picture. The Greek romances provide us with a detailed, comprehensive, and coherent account of life in precisely the provincial cities of Paul's missionary territory: Tarsus, Antioch, Ephesus, Miletus, Priene, Mitylene, Rhodes, Paphos, Alexandria—to name just a few.[3] One romance, Chariton's *Callirhoe*, is especially important, for it is the most contemporary document we have for Paul's world in the Greek East of the first century. This romance was written in Aphrodisias in Asia Minor and probably in the mid-first century; three other romances—Xenophon's *Ephesian Tale*, Achilles Tatius's *Cleitophon and Leucippe*, and Longus's *Daphnis and Chloe*—belong to the early, middle, and late second century and, even if they are somewhat later, they nevertheless document much the same urban life as the letters of Paul and the narrative of Chariton.[4] In these romances we find firsthand accounts of a myriad of specific, daily activities that went on in aristocratic households, marketplaces, theaters, gymnasia, temples, gardens, inns, harbors, workshops, brothels, prisons, and cemeteries. By

---

2. Ibid., 28.

3. The focus of the following analysis is on literary sources. For a parallel attempt using documentary sources, emphasizing the city of Ephesus, see G. H. R. Horsley, "The Inscriptions of Ephesos and the New Testament," *NovT* 34 (1992) 105–68.

4. For the dates see my "The Greek Novel," in *Greco-Roman Literature and the New Testament* (ed. D. Aune; SBLSBS 21; Atlanta: Scholars Press, 1988) 127–49, esp. 128–29. Translations of these romances as well as later and fragmentary ones are now readily available in *Collected Ancient Greek Novels* (ed. B. P. Reardon; Berkeley: University of California Press, 1989) 17–124 (Chariton), 128–69 (Xenophon), 175–284 (Achilles Tatius), and 288–348 (Longus). All translations in this article, however, are my own. For texts of these romances, see W. Blake, ed., *Aphrodisiensis de Chaerea et Callirhoe Amatoriarum Narrationum Libri Octo* (Oxford: Clarendon, 1938); A. D. Papanikolaou, ed., *Xenophon Ephesius Ephesiacorum Libri V* (Leipzig: Teubner, 1973); E. Villborg, ed., *Leucippe and Cleitophon* (Stockholm: Almqvist & Wiksell, 1955); M. D. Reeve, ed., *Longus Daphnis et Chloe* (Leipzig: Teubner, 1982). The best one-volume discussion of the romances is T. Hägg, *The Novel in Antiquity* (Oxford: Blackwell, 1983).

observing these activities we can begin to identify the conventions of thought and behavior that governed the daily lives of individuals from leading aristocrats down to marginalized fishermen, runaways, and brigands. Here can be found the larger social world within which to set Pauline Christianity—a Christianity, I submit, that will have surprisingly more in common with this larger society than is usually supposed.

It is clearly beyond the scope of this essay to provide a picture of life in the cities of Paul from the Greek romances, but a modest beginning can be made by looking again at Paul's most modest letter, the letter to Philemon, and in fact at only one puzzle piece in it—the word πρεσβύτης in v. 9. For it was by reading the romances that I was able to find the rightful place for this disputed piece of the puzzle.

In his recent monograph on Philemon, Norman Petersen observes that "with one exception, the pertinent language [in Philemon] is readily translatable."[5] That exception is, of course, πρεσβύτης in v. 9, which scholars translate either as "old man" or as "ambassador." The aims of this paper are to argue on behalf of the translation "old man" and, by so doing, to point out the various implicit social conventions from the larger Greco-Roman world that Paul was trading on when using this word and that make this translation the obvious one in the context of the argument of the letter.

PAUL, "AN AMBASSADOR": THE INTERPRETIVE TRADITION

Petersen is not the first to acknowledge this lexical problem. Indeed, the debate over whether to render πρεσβύτης as "old man" or as "ambassador" is more than a century old. The key figure in the debate is widely regarded to be J. B. Lightfoot, whose arguments for the translation "ambassador" at the end of the last century have dominated the discussion ever since. But before presenting Lightfoot's arguments, a brief review of his own exegetical tradition is required.

As becomes apparent from Lightfoot's exegetical contemporaries, for example, C. J. Ellicott and H. A. W. Meyer, Paul's apparent reference to his age in Philemon 9 had long become problematic—going back, they say, to John Calvin.[6] That problem, as Lightfoot phrased it, is why Paul should "make his age a ground of appeal to Philemon who, if Archippus [cf. v. 2]

---

5. N. Petersen, *Rediscovering Paul: Philemon and Sociology of Paul's Narrative World* (Philadelphia: Fortress, 1985) 22.

6. See C. J. Ellicott, *Critical and Grammatical Commentary on St. Paul's Epistles to the Philippians, Colossians, and Philemon* (Andover, Mass.: Draper, 1872) 223; and H. A. W. Meyer, *Critical and Exegetical Handbook to the Epistles to the Philippians and Colossians, and to Philemon* (trans. W. P. Dickson; New York: Funk & Wagnalls, 1885) 405.

70   The Social World of the First Christians

was his son, cannot have been much younger than himself."[7] Calvin's solution was to claim that πρεσβύτης denoted *non aetatum, sed officium.*[8] R. Bentley and others actually changed Paul's words to fit Calvin's meaning by proposing an ever so slight emendation—adding one letter to the problematic word πρεσβύτης ("old man") in order to form the seemingly intended word πρεσβευτής ("ambassador").[9]

With this exegetical tradition in mind we can now present Lightfoot's proposal, the genius of which was to make even so slight an emendation unnecessary. Πρεσβύτης itself, Lightfoot claimed, could on occasion be used with the meaning "ambassador," as is apparent from several passages in 1 Maccabees, 2 Chronicles, and other writings, where the manuscripts have both πρεσβύτης and πρεσβευτής, though the meaning is clearly "ambassador."[10] That Paul too was using πρεσβύτης in the sense of "ambassador" is further supported, Lightfoot added, by the language of Eph 6:20, where the clause "on behalf of [the mystery of the gospel] I am an ambassador in chains (πρεσβεύω ἐν ἁλύσει)," parallels closely the phraseology of Phlm 9: "Paul, an ambassador, and now also a prisoner, of Christ Jesus."[11] Lightfoot had, in short, resolved a long-perceived problem—the inappropriateness of a reference to age in Phlm 9—by making not even so slight an emendation necessary but with a deft lexical argument supported by the parallel thought in Ephesians.

Lightfoot's proposal has found many adherents ever since.[12] and his arguments still dominate the discussion, although they have been modified and

7. J. B. Lightfoot, *Saint Paul's Epistles to the Colossians and Philemon* (8th ed.; London: Macmillan, 1886) 337.

8. Calvin's quote is taken from Ellicott, *Philemon*, 223.

9. For discussion of the emendation, see Lightfoot, *Philemon*, 336. This emendation still appears in the *apparatus criticus* of the most recent edition of Nestle-Aland, *Novum Testamentum Graece* (26th ed.; Stuttgart: Deutsche Bibelgesellschaft, 1979) 561.

10. Lightfoot, *Philemon*, 336–37, citing, e.g., 2 Chr 32:31; 1 Macc 14:21; 15:17; 2 Macc 11:34 from the LXX as well as some early Christian writings, e.g., Ignatius, *Smyrn.* 11.

11. Lightfoot, *Philemon*, 337.

12. A sampling of commentators who favor "ambassador": E. Haupt, *Die Gefangenschaftsbriefe* (MeyerK 8–9; 8th ed.; Göttingen: Vandenhoeck & Ruprecht, 1902) 188–89; C. F. D. Moule, *The Epistles of Paul the Apostle to the Colossians and to Philemon* (Cambridge: Cambridge University Press, 1957) 144; E. Lohmeyer, *Die Briefe an die Philipper, an die Kolosser und an Philemon* (MeyerK; 13th ed.; rev. by W. Schmauch; Göttingen: Vandenhoeck & Ruprecht, 1964) 185; R. P. Martin, *Colossians and Philemon* (NCB; Greenwood, S.C.: Attic, 1973) 144, 163; J. Ernst, *Die Briefe an die Philipper, an Philemon, und die Epheser* (RNT 7; Regensburg: Pustet, 1974) 133–34; A. Suhl, *Der Brief an Philemon* (Zürcher Bibelkommentare; Zurich: Theologischer Verlag, 1981) 31; and P. T. O'Brien, *Colossians, Philemon* (WBC 44; Waco, Tex.: Word, 1982) 289–90. Among recent specialized studies, where the issue is discussed, the following favor "ambassador": U. Wickert, "Der Philemonbrief—Privatbrief oder apostolisches Schreiben?" *ZNW* 52 (1961) 231–38, esp. 233–35; C. J. Bjerkelund, *ΠΑΡΑΚΑΛΩ: Form, Funktion und Sinn der ΠΑΡΑΚΑΛΩ-Sätze in den paulinischen Briefen* (Oslo: Universitetsforlaget, 1967) 119; R. Gayer, *Die Stellung des Sklaven in den paulinischen Gemeinden und bei Paulus* (Bern: Lang, 1976) 251 n. 572; F. F. Church, "Rhetorical Structure and Design in Paul's Letter to Philemon," *HTR* 71 (1978) 17–33, esp. 25 n. 41;

expanded. The lexical argument in particular is repeated, though usually in a stronger form than Lightfoot's. C. F. D. Moule and many others ever since have claimed that the meanings "old man" and "ambassador" are equally possible or virtually interchangeable renderings of πρεσβύτης.[13] Consequently, only context can decide, but instead of Lightfoot's simple query about why Paul should appeal to his age in this context, scholars have made several positive contextual arguments for "ambassador" in Phlm 9. For example, E. Lohmeyer understands δέσμιος Χριστοῦ Ἰησοῦ ("a prisoner for Christ Jesus") in v. 9 as a title, so that πρεσβύτης, its syntactical partner, must also be a title, a condition that is met only if πρεσβύτης means "ambassador."[14] Similarly, U. Wickert understands the two circumstantial participles in vv. 8 and 9 (ἔχων and ὤν) to be compositionally parallel and logically concessive, so that Paul waives both his authority to command (v. 8) and his being a πρεσβύτης (v. 9), a circumstance that makes sense only if πρεσβύτης means "ambassador"—a conclusion further buttressed by Wickert's general assessment of the letter as an *apostolisches Schreiben.*[15]

Recently, Petersen has provided the most elaborate contextual argument yet for "ambassador." He argues that in vv. 8–16 there is "a series of semantic contrasts between two terms, the second of which is contrasted with the first."[16] He points to ten such contrasts—for example, "bold enough to command" with "I prefer for love's sake to appeal" (vv. 8–9a), "my son" with "whom I fathered" (v. 10), "formerly useless" with "now useful" (v. 11), "whom I sent to you" with "whom I wanted to keep with me" (vv. 12–13), "not by necessity" with "by free will" (v. 14). Within this series of semantic contrasts is πρεσβύτης and "a prisoner of Christ Jesus" (v. 9b). What is more, Petersen points out that the grammatical construction of this last pair is the same as that for "formerly useless" and "now useful" (v. 11), in that both are connected by νυνὶ δέ ("but now"). Consequently, since "formerly useless" and "now useful" are clearly contrastive, πρεσβύτης must mean "ambassador" since "old man" and "prisoner" are "not a contrast at all."[17]

W.-H. Ollrog, *Paulus und seine Mitarbeiter: Untersuchungen zu Theorie und Praxis der paulinischen Mission* (WMANT 50; Neukirchen: Neukirchener Verlag, 1979) 102 n. 39; Petersen, *Rediscovering Paul,* 125–28; and J. D. M. Derrett, "The Function of the Epistle to Philemon," *ZNW* 79 (1988) 63–91, esp. 86–87. Meeks also favors "ambassador" (*First Urban Christians,* 233 n. 62).

13. Moule, *Philemon,* 144. See also Lohmeyer, *Philemon,* 185 n. 2; Ernst, *Philemon,* 133; Martin, *Philemon,* 163; Gayer, *Stellung,* 251 n. 572; O'Brien, *Philemon,* 290; and Petersen, *Rediscovering Paul,* 125.

14. Lohmeyer, *Philemon,* 185.

15. Wickert, "Philemonbrief," 233 n. 8 and 235. Wickert's emphasis on Philemon not as a *Privatbrief* (where, he argues, "old man" would make more sense) but as an *apostolisches Schreiben* (where "ambassador" makes better sense) has been especially persuasive among scholars; see, e.g., Bjerkelund, *ΠΑΡΑΚΑΛΩ,* 210 n. 3; Gayer, *Stellung,* 251 n. 572; Church, "Rhetorical Function," 25 n. 41; and Ollrog, *Mitarbeiter,* 102 n. 39.

16. Petersen, *Rediscovering Paul,* 126.

17. Ibid., 127.

Lightfoot's appeal to Pauline usage—in particular to Eph 6:20—has also received wide support, although recently scholars have added 2 Cor 5:20, where Paul does use the verb πρεσβεύειν ("to be an ambassador") in the expression "we are ambassadors for Christ."[18] In addition, Petersen looks father afield—to Romans, Galatians, and Philippians—and argues that since Paul elsewhere calls himself an apostle and a slave or prisoner (Rom 1:1; Gal 1:1, 10; Phil 1:1, 12–18; 2:22), then his reference to himself in Phlm 9 as πρεσβύτης is likely a functional equivalent, in that πρεσβύτης, which is paired with prisoner, must be the equivalent of "apostle"—hence "ambassador."[19]

For all these reasons, then, many scholars have concluded that in Phlm 9, to use Petersen's words, "'old man' is simply not a viable translation of πρεσβύτης."[20] Many scholars, but not all—for the translation "old man"[21] has continued to have its defenders. Their defense, however, has often conceded too much, or attempted too little, to be persuasive.

On the lexical side, for example, defenders of the translation "old man" have conceded too much. They often grant the interchangeability of "old man" and "ambassador" as the rendering of πρεσβύτης.[22] And when it comes to a contextual case for "old man," there is, on the one hand, all too often nothing but some vague reason for this preference—for example, that "old man" is more appropriate in a private letter, which can appeal to compassion[23]—and, on the other hand, there is all too seldom any attempt to counter the supporting arguments on behalf of "ambassador"—for example, Wickert's oft-cited appeals to the grammar of vv. 8–9 and to the character of the letter as an *apostolisches Schreiben*.[24] Equally seldom is there any argument against the relevance of the ambassador language elsewhere in Paul's

---

18. See, e.g., Suhl, *Philemon*, 31; O'Brien, *Philemon*, 290; Petersen, *Rediscovering Paul*, 126; and Derrett, "Functions," 86.

19. Petersen, *Rediscovering Paul*, 127–28.

20. Ibid., 128.

21. A sampling of commentators who favor "old man": M. R. Vincent, *A Critical and Exegetical Commentary on the Epistles to the Philippians and to Philemon* (ICC; New York: Scribner, 1911) 184; E. F. Scott, *The Epistles of Paul to the Colossians, to Philemon and to the Ephesians* (MNTC; London: Hodder & Stoughton, 1930) 107; M. Dibelius, *An die Kolosser, Epheser, an Philemon*, rev. and ed. H. Greeven (HNT 12; 3rd ed.; Tübingen: Mohr, 1953) 104–5; G. Friedrich, *Die kleineren Briefe des Apostels Paulus, Der Brief an Philemon* (NTD 8; 10th ed.; Göttingen: Vandenhoeck & Ruprecht, 1965) 193; E. Lohse, *Colossians and Philemon* (Hermeneia; Philadelphia: Fortress, 1971) 199; P. Stuhlmacher, *Der Brief an Philemon* (EKK; Neukirchen-Vluyn: Neukirchener Verlag, 1975) 37–38; and J. Gnilka, *Der Philemonbrief* (HTKNT 10; Freiburg: Herder, 1982) 43. Among specialized studies, where the issue is discussed, see also G. Bornkamm, "πρεσβύτης," *TDNT* 6 (1968) 683, W. Schenk, "Der Brief des Paulus an Philemon in der neueren Forschung (1945–1987)," *ANRW* 2.25.4 (1987) 3439–95, esp. 3463.

22. See, e.g., Vincent, *Philemon*, 184; Dibelius-Greeven, *Philemon*, 104; Lohse, *Philemon*, 199; Stuhlmacher, *Philemon*, 37; and Schenk, "Philemon," 3463 n. 61.

23. See, e.g., Vincent, *Philemon*, 184; Scott, *Philemon*, 107; and Stuhlmacher, *Philemon*, 37.

24. See n. 14 above.

letters.[25] Too much of the argument for "ambassador," therefore, remains unchallenged.

In other words, it is clear that the case for "old man" as the correct rendering of πρεσβύτης in Phlm 9 has not yet been made, and to that task I now turn.

FROM LEXICAL ARGUMENTS TO SOCIAL CONTEXTS

In making the case for "old man" as the correct translation of πρεσβύτης in Phlm 9, it will be necessary first to assess anew the arguments made on behalf of the rendering "ambassador." With that assessment completed it will then be possible to argue more strongly than before on behalf of "old man."

The principal argument for "ambassador" has always been the lexical one: confusion in the manuscripts between πρεσβύτης and πρεσβευτής for the word "ambassador" means that πρεσβύτης can, on occasion, mean "ambassador" (so Lightfoot) or can, on virtually any occasion, mean "ambassador" (so Moule and many others). Lightfoot himself provided most of the evidence of such confusion, largely from the LXX, and other examples from Polyaenus and Plutarch can also be cited.[26] Still, it needs to be emphasized how rarely the confusion arises. In the case of Plutarch, who uses πρεσβύτης or πρεσβευτής some 150 times, the manuscripts are confused only once—less than 1 percent of the time![27] In addition, standard lexica, such as LSJ, do not recognize "ambassador" as a meaning of πρεσβύτης, and in H. J. Mason's study of Greek and Roman political terms, the discussion of πρεσβευτής as an equivalent for the Latin *legatus* does not even hint at the possibility of πρεσβύτης as a variant spelling.[28] Hence, in Greek sources of the period there appears to be no such ambiguity in the meaning of πρεσβύτης. In other words, far from having "old man" and "ambassador" as interchangeable meanings that can be decided only from the context, πρεσβύτης should virtually always be read as meaning "old man"—and certainly in Phlm 9, where, after all, there is not even any confusion in the manuscripts.

---

25. An exception is Dibelius-Greeven, *Philemon*, 104: he rejects the appeals to Eph 6:20 and 2 Cor 5:20, in that the former is Deutero-Pauline and the latter stands the argument of Philemon on its head.

26. BAGD 700 (s.v. πρεσβύτης) cites Polyaenus 8.9.1. See also Plutarch, *Crassus* 27.5.

27. I wish to thank my friend and colleague Professor Edward N. O'Neil for letting me use his complete index to Plutarch. Each instance of πρεσβύτης and πρεσβευτής was checked against the apparatus in the appropriate Teubner volume of Plutarch. For a broader lexical study, emphasizing how rarely υ was written for ευ, see J. N. Birdsall, "Πρεσβύτης in Philemon 9: A Study in Conjectural Emendation," *NTS* 39 (1993) 625–30.

28. See H. J. Mason, *Greek Terms for Roman Institutions: A Lexicon and Analysis* (Toronto: Hakkert, 1974) 153–55.

Once the lexical argument falls, the supporting arguments from the immediate context and from Pauline usage elsewhere also appear less compelling. For example, Lohmeyer's argument, that δέσμιος Χριστοῦ Ἰησοῦ is a title and so must its syntactical partner πρεσβύτης be, fails to convince, since both terms, as we will see, do not refer to Paul's apostolic status but describe rather his condition—or, better, his plight—at the time of writing the letter. Wickert's claim, that the circumstantial participles ἔχων (v. 8) and ὤν (v. 9) are both concessive, forming a tautological parallelism, is not the only way of construing these participles, since the second one can just as easily be seen as causal. Wickert's further claim about Philemon being an *apostolisches Schreiben* and not a *Privatbrief,* while correct in the main, does not mean that Paul could only speak as an apostle (i.e., as an "ambassador") in v. 9 and not, as we will see, more personally (i.e., as an "old man").

Also, Petersen's broader analysis of vv. 8–16 in which he finds a series of ten semantic contrasts, making only "ambassador," and not "old man," a contrast with "prisoner" in v. 9, is weakened by the fact that at least three of the pairs are not contrasts—for example, "especially to me" and "so much more to you" (v. 16) is clearly an ascensive pair. Petersen's further claim that the pair "formerly useless" and "now useful" (v. 11), which is contrastive, uses the same grammatical construction (νυνὶ δέ) as the pair πρεσβύτης and "a prisoner of Christ Jesus" (v. 9), which must now also be contrastive, fails to note that the first pair also contains πότε ("once"), so that the construction is not the same after all. Consequently, when Petersen concludes that "the relationship 'old man' and 'prisoner' . . . is not a contrast at all,"[29] he is right; they are ascensive, which is perfectly acceptable in the context of vv. 8–16.

With the lexical and contextual arguments less compelling than often supposed, the appeal to Pauline usage is even less relevant. Eph 6:20 is Deutero-Pauline, and 2 Cor 5:20 and the other passages do not address the same situation as Philemon. In short, the case for "ambassador" as the meaning of πρεσβύτης in Phlm 9, which has been built up over the last century, is subject to criticism at every level and particularly on the lexical level. If this assessment is correct, then it is time to re-read Philemon and see more clearly why Paul spoke of himself as an "old man" in v. 9.

PAUL'S APPEAL TO "OLD AGE": THE SOCIAL CONVENTIONS

The thesis to be argued here is that Paul referred to himself as a πρεσβύτης because it would help him in some way in the plea he was making to Philemon on behalf of the latter's slave, Onesimus. In other words, this thesis requires that the investigation of πρεσβύτης and its context be rhetorical, focuses on the letter's foreground, its moment of delivery to Philemon in the presence of both Onesimus and the church that met in Philemon's household. How did Paul's reference to his age function rhetorically in

---

29. Petersen, *Rediscovering Paul,* 127.

Paul's appeal to Philemon? I emphasize the foreground—the rhetorical situation of the letter and the rhetoric of its argument—because scholars have tended to focus more on the background of the letter, on how Onesimus first met Paul in prison,[30] or on where Paul was imprisoned.[31] In addition, this thesis requires that the approach be that of the social historian, of one who is familiar with the texture of life in the cities of the Greek East, familiar with the daily lives of people and the conventions of thought and behavior that governed them. I emphasize social history because scholars look only to theological and history-of-religions categories when reading the letter, and I emphasize the daily lives of people in general because scholars have read the letter almost exclusively in terms of the institution of slavery and even then in terms that are often too general or abstract to illuminate the *specific* slave conventions that Paul is using. To be sure, introductory questions, theological meanings, and slavery as an institution are all important to an understanding of Philemon, but they do not exhaust that understanding and, indeed, they have so far not allowed us to appreciate the meaning and function of πρεσβύτης in v. 9. We need, therefore, to be able to recognize—with the help of the Greek romances and other contemporary sources—the specific *rhetorical* and *social* conventions that can explain Paul's use of his age in his plea for Onesimus.

When Paul concludes his argument in Phlm 21 with a note of confidence that Philemon will do even more than what Paul has asked for, it may not be clear what it was that Paul wanted Philemon to *do*—most likely the manumission of Onesimus and his return to Paul (vv. 13–16)—but it is clear that the argument is, in rhetorical terms, deliberative. Indeed, F. Forrester

---

30. This issue has attracted the most attention recently. The scholarly tradition has long assumed that Onesimus was a runaway who somehow reached Paul in prison. Recently, however, S. Winter ("Paul's Letter to Philemon," *NTS* 33 [1987] 1–15) has argued that Onesimus was not a runaway at all but a slave who was sent to Paul in prison, and P. Lampe ("Keine 'Sklavenflucht' des Onesimus," *ZNW* 76 [1985] 135–37) has also argued that Onesimus was not a runaway but rather a slave who had wronged his master and then sought out Paul deliberately in order that, as Philemon's friend, Paul could intercede on his behalf and help restore him to his master's good graces. This latter scenario is quite plausible and indeed has received the support of B. M. Rapske ("The Prisoner Paul in the Eyes of Onesimus," *NTS* 37 [1991] 187–203) and S. S. Bartchy ("Not a Runaway after all: The Case of Onesimus, Philemon, and Paul," a paper read at the Pauline Epistles Section of the Annual Meeting of the Society of Biblical Literature, Kansas City, Mo., November, 1991; see also his article "Philemon, Paul's Letter to," in the *Anchor Bible Dictionary*, 5:305–10. I wish to thank Professor Bartchy for making copies of these two articles available to me. For a reassertion of the traditional view, see J. G. Nordling, "Onesimus Fugitivus: A Defense of the Runaway Slave Hypothesis in Philemon," *JSNT* 41 (1991) 97–119,

31. The traditional site of Rome as Paul's place of imprisonment is being challenged by scholars who favor Caesarea or Ephesus, with Ephesus the clear favorite today. See, among recent proponents, Lohse, *Philemon*, 165–67; Martin, *Philemon*, 147–49; Stuhlmacher, *Philemon*, 21; Suhl, *Philemon*, 20; Gnilka, *Philemonbrief*, 4–5; and Schenk, "Philemon," 3480–81. For a defense of Rome, see O'Brien, *Philemon*, xlix–liv. The place of Paul's imprisonment has a bearing on the dating of the letter—the mid-50s if he was in Ephesus, the early 60s if in Rome.

Church has identified the letter to Philemon as an example of deliberative rhetoric—a speech in which the speaker persuades someone *to do* something or dissuades someone *from doing* something. Church also divides the letter according to the three parts of a deliberative speech—exordium (vv. 4–7), proof (vv. 8–16), and peroration (vv. 17–22)—and he analyzes each part of the letter to see how it fulfills the functions of a deliberative speech.[32] For example, in the second part, or proof, and especially in v. 9, where the word πρεσβύτης appears, he identifies two rhetorical figures: ἀντίφρασις, or the abandonment of a strong argument, in vv. 8–9 and *conduplicatio*, or repetition of words, in vv. 9–10.[33]

Yet, despite its many virtues, Church's analysis remains too formal. The specific rhetorical situation of the letter is not discussed, and the social roles and values that lie behind the letter's rhetorical moves are not identified. In addition, Church follows Wickert's grammatical analysis of vv. 8–9, which means that he accepts "ambassador" as the meaning of πρεσβύτης.[34] This decision casts Paul in a narrowly apostolic or ecclesiastic role and thus effectively keeps Church from sensing any social roles that Paul may have assumed in this portion of the argument. Thus, while Church has made an excellent beginning in the rhetorical analysis of Philemon, there is still much to do. The first step is to clarify the rhetorical situation in which the argument as a whole and Paul's use of πρεσβύτης in particular are to be viewed. Then the rhetorical function of Paul's reference to his age must be investigated.

To set the stage for identifying the rhetorical situation, we need to see the letter, as Petersen has emphasized, as part of a larger and ongoing "story," whose characters are the writer, the recipients, and any others named in the letter.[35] In the case of the letter to Philemon the story, so far as it can be reconstructed and so far as it concerns us, began with Paul's conversion of Philemon (v. 19), which was followed at some point by his slave Onesimus's departure from his household—for whatever reason (v. 15)—and his arrival some time later where Paul was imprisoned—wherever that was (vv. 1, 9, 13). During this imprisonment Paul also converted Onesimus (v. 10) and at some point decided to send him back but with hopes that he would return and continue his service to Paul (vv. 11–13). To realize those hopes Paul wrote a letter on behalf of Onesimus, who then carried it back to his master. When the latter opened the letter and read it, we come to the rhetorical situation of the letter, or the specific setting within which Paul's plea was made.[36]

32. See Church, "Rhetorical Function," 17–33.
33. Ibid., 25–26.
34. Ibid., 25 and n. 41.
35. See Petersen, *Rediscovering Paul*, 65–78.
36. I wish to thank Professor James D. Hester of the University of Redlands for his discussing with me the notion of the rhetorical situation.

What was that rhetorical situation? A clue comes immediately in the opening address. The letter is addressed not only to Philemon but also to Apphia, Archippus, and the ἐκκλησία in Philemon's house (vv. 1–2). The word ἐκκλησία is universally translated as "church." For one who reads the letter in the light of social conventions in the cities of the Greek East, however, a less ecclesiological rendering comes to mind, namely, "assembly." Indeed, when the word is so rendered, I am reminded of the various ἐκκλησίαι, or assemblies, that play an important role in the Syracuse of Chariton's romance. The leading citizen of Syracuse is the general Hermocrates; each time an issue arises that affects him or his household or his city an assembly is called and the issue is resolved in this public forum, whether in the theater or in the marketplace. For example, when Chaereas and Callirhoe, the principal characters in the romance, fall in love, but seemingly cannot marry because of the rivalry between their respective households (Chariton 1.1.3, 9), the people of Syracuse call an ἐκκλησία, in which the only business is to persuade Callirhoe's father, Hermocrates, to consent to the marriage. He listened to the people's plea on behalf of Chaereas and agreed—out of his love for Syracuse (φιλόπατρις)—to the marriage (1.1.11–12). Later in the romance other issues arise, other assemblies are called, and actions are taken after such public deliberation (see esp. 3.4.4–17; 8.7.1–8.14).

This social convention of putting household matters up for public decision making may lie behind Paul's decision to include the ἐκκλησία, or assembly, that met in Philemon's house in his epistolary plea on behalf of Onesimus. The letter might have been addressed solely to Philemon and the matter decided by Philemon alone. But Paul's broader address puts the matter before the Christian ἐκκλησία, or assembly. This assembly, like that in Syracuse, thus becomes a participant in the deliberations, or at least a witness to them. To be sure, the scale differs: Hermocrates is the leading citizen of the city, Philemon only of his own household, so that the size of the ἐκκλησία differs. But otherwise the rhetorical situations are similar. Both Hermocrates and Philemon are asked to do something, and both must decide on their actions in a public forum. In addition, just as Hermocrates was motivated by his love for Syracuse (as demonstrated earlier by his spectacular defeat of the Athenian navy; see Chariton 1.1.1 etc.), so Paul reminds Philemon and the ἐκκλησία of Philemon's past acts of love toward the saints (v. 5), as demonstrated in his "refreshing of the saints" (v. 7), and makes such love (v. 9) the basis of his plea on behalf of Onesimus. Paul has, like the people of Syracuse, made his request a test of Philemon's public reputation and honor. Thus, even though Paul's plea is directed explicitly at Philemon, as shown by the second person singular in vv. 4–22, Paul's argument nevertheless is calculated to be heard by the ἐκκλησία as a whole.

It is not possible here to analyze the argument as a whole; indeed, Church has shown how ably Paul crafted the argument throughout the letter. Our concern is focused on the word πρεσβύτης in v. 9, which, as we have seen, occurs early in the proof (vv. 8–16). Church correctly emphasizes the importance of *ethos* and *pathos* in constructing a persuasive argument, but because of his dependence on Wickert for his rendering of πρεσβύτης as "ambassador," his analysis falters precisely at the point of our concern.

The rhetorical function of πρεσβύτης becomes clearer if we try to answer these social historical questions: What images are prompted by a reference to old age? What does the combination of old age and imprisonment (v. 9) suggest? How does this combination help to characterize Paul? How is old age related to the characterization of Onesimus as Paul's child (v. 10)? How does the familial language affect the relation of Onesimus and Philemon as slave and master? Is such language often used in deliberations with a master regarding his slave?

Images of old age are numerous. Most frequent, perhaps, is the image of a garrulous old man or woman.[37] Another image is that of old age as a difficult burden, involving the loss of bodily strength, hearing, sight, beauty, and pleasure, as one maxim bluntly puts it.[38] Or old age is a time all too often characterized by ἀπορία, or the lack of a means of support, as expressed in a chreia attributed to Diogenes: On being asked whose life is truly miserable, he said, "An old man with no means of support" (Diogenes Laertius 6.51).

Of these images the last may be that intended by Paul. For ἀπορία is suggested by the following reference to his imprisonment—an old man and also a prisoner for Christ Jesus (v. 9). Prisoners had to depend on others for basic care, both physical and emotional, as is poignantly shown by Demetrius for his imprisoned friend Antiphilus.[39] But this suggestion is confirmed by Paul's further reference to Onesimus as his child (τέκνον) (v. 10)—itself a widely attested convention.[40] In any case, with this reference we are able to identify the precise social convention intended by Paul in his use of πρεσβύτης. The image of Paul as an old man whose means of support in prison would have been difficult, to say the least, along with a reference to the child he has begotten in prison, reminds us of the social convention of children's responsibility to support their parents in old age.

This convention is widely attested, as in this maxim: "Blessed is the one

37. A sampling from various sources: Aristotle, *Rhet.* 2.13.12; Plutarch, *Quaest. conviv.* 631B; Dio, *Or.* 7.1; and Philostratus, *VS* 541.

38. Ps.-Menander, *Mon.* 39–40 (p. 35 Jaekel). Cf. also *Mon.* 830 (p. 81 Jaekel) and Teles, *Frag.* V (p. 56 O'Neil).

39. For Demetrius and Antiphilus, see Lucian, *Toxaris* 28–33. Cf. also Xenophon of Ephesus 2.7, and Achilles Tatius 6.14.1.

40. It was conventional for old people—free or slave—to regard a younger slave as a child (τέκνον), a convention found frequently in the romance by Xenophon of Ephesus (1.14.4; 2.10.4; 3.12.2, 4; 5.1.2, 4).

who is fortunate to have children."[41] But Longus's romance, *Daphnis and Chloe*, will illustrate it concretely. The shepherd Dryas, Chloe's father, talks briefly with Daphnis and says of his parents, the retired goatherder Lamon and his wife Myrtale, that they have been blessed because they have in Daphnis a γηροτρόφος, that is, one who can support them in their old age. Later, when there is talk of the marriage of Daphnis and Chloe, Lamon also recognizes the value of this marriage and hence of gaining a daughter-in-law, since, he says, he is getting old (ἡμιγέρων) and so needs another hand for his work. Finally, even the wealthy landowner Dionysophanes thinks of his sons as χειραγωγοί, or "supports" in his old age (see Longus 3.9.1; 31.2; 4.24.2).

In other words, whether one is a lowly goatherd or a wealthy landowner, old age is a time of vulnerability, of becoming dependent on others—particularly on one's children, if so blessed. By trading on this convention,[42] Paul begins his argument to Philemon by evoking considerable *pathos* for himself—as an old man and prisoner in need of support—and at the same time by establishing Onesimus's *ethos*—as his child who is now responsible for his support. In other words, within the quasi-public rhetorical situation in which Philemon has been cast by Paul as a man of generosity and kindness, we now see that Paul has presented himself and Onesimus as an aged parent and child, with the latter responsible for the support of the former.

By trading on this convention, however, Paul not only presents Onesimus as essential to himself, as the child with the duty to support him, but Paul also uses this familial imagery in his role as mediator on behalf of Onesimus before his master. The role of Paul as πρεσβύτης is less operative in this familial imagery, but since his age prompted the father–son support convention we will investigate this familial imagery further.[43] Once again, the Greek romances make us aware of specific and subtle conventions that operated between slaves and masters. And the particular convention on which Paul depends in his plea on behalf of Onesimus involves the use of familial language by the mediator in his plea with a master over a slave who has angered him. The function of this familial language is to recast the rela-

41. Ps.-Menander, *Mon.* 489 (p. 61 Jaekel). See also Xenophon, *Oec.* 7.12, 19; Plutarch, *Consol. ad Apollon.* 111E; Ps.-Diogenes, *Ep.* 47 (p. 178 Malherbe).

42. In 2 Cor 12:14-15 Paul trades on the reverse of this convention—the expenses parents incur when their children are young, as Larry Yarbrough shows elsewhere in this volume.

43. Scholarly treatment of Onesimus's being Paul's τέκνον has been limited to perfunctory references to other places in Paul's letters where Paul uses similar imagery—of Timothy (1 Cor 4:17) or Christians generally (1 Cor 4:14; Gal 4:19) (so, e.g., Vincent, *Philemon*, 184–85; Lohmeyer, *Philemon*, 186 n. 1; Lohse, *Philemon*, 199; Ernst, *Philemon*, 134; and Stuhlmacher, *Philemon*, 38–39). The only historical backgrounds suggested are rabbinic (so recently Stuhlmacher, *Philemon*, 38; O'Brien, *Philemon*, 290–91; and Gnilka, *Philemonbrief*, 44–45) and history of religions, in particular mystery religions (so Dibelius-Greeven, *Philemon*, 105, but otherwise usually rejected).

tionship of master and slave, where much harsher treatment was tolerated, into one involving family members, where forgiveness and indulgence were much more likely.[44]

Chariton's romance illustrates this slave convention nicely. To set the stage: The heroine Callirhoe has been kidnapped by brigands and later sold to the administrator of the leading household in Miletus, that belonging to Dionysius. Plangon, the wife of Phocas, the manager of Dionysius's seaside properties, is ordered to care for her and in fact treats her as her child (τέκνον; cf. Chariton 2.8.6; 11.6). Later, when Dionysius visits these properties and is inspecting the herds and crops, he has occasion to criticize Phocas (2.7.2). Plangon, on hearing of her master's anger toward her husband, runs to Callirhoe's room and seeks her help as a mediator. Callirhoe agrees and makes a plea on behalf of Phocas. She introduces her plea by expressing her gratitude for Plangon's many kindnesses and by saying that Plangon has loved her like a daughter (φιλεῖ γάρ με ὡς θυγατέρα). Having recast the slave Plangon into her mother, Callirhoe then makes her specific request: Do not be angry with her husband (2.7.5–7). The whole plea, therefore, is made without any hint that Plangon and Phocas are slaves; instead, familial language is used—mother and daughter, husband and wife. And Dionysius's anger was assuaged.

Similarly, Paul presents Onesimus as his child, and later as Philemon's brother (v. 16), and in so doing recasts the relationships among the principals. Paul's plea—that Philemon welcome Onesimus as he would Paul and that Philemon allow Onesimus to return to Paul in order that he may continue to serve him in his apostolic work—is thus no longer stated in terms of a slave before his master but as a father on behalf of his child. The greater persuasiveness of this recasting of the relationships is obvious and shows that Paul, like Callirhoe, is able to mitigate the harsh reality of master–slave relations by drawing on this particular convention of adopting familial terms when mediating on behalf of a slave with his angry master.

Paul still has other arguments—that Philemon's action could be done willingly (v. 14), that Onesimus's departure was necessary (v. 15), that Paul himself will pay for any losses (vv. 18–19), that Philemon himself is in debt to Paul (v. 19). But it is likely that already with the appeal to Onesimus's responsibility to support his aged father and to Onesimus's status as a family member (vv. 9–10) Philemon is well on the way to being persuaded.

CONCLUSIONS

The appropriateness of the word πρεσβύτης in Phlm 9 in the sense of "old man" should now be clear. It is not problematic, as exegetes since Calvin

---

44. See now R. Saller, "Corporal Punishment, Authority, and Obedience in the Roman Household," in *Marriage, Divorce, and Children in Ancient Rome* (ed. B. Rawson; Oxford: Oxford University Press, 1991) 144–65.

have claimed, and hence there is no need to resort to emendation, as Bentley did with his admittedly ingenious suggestion of πρεσβευτής, nor is there any need to fall back on the smallest of probabilities, that πρεσβύτης can itself, on occasion, mean "ambassador," as Lightfoot first claimed. Rather, the standard meaning "old man" makes perfectly good sense. When the letter to Philemon is read in the light of the conventions of thought and behavior that governed the lives of people in the cities of Paul's missionary orbit, then the meaning and functions of "old man" emerge quite unmistakably.

The letter itself was read in the rhetorical situation of a quasi-public ἐκκλησία, or assembly, in which Philemon's action regarding Paul's plea on behalf of Onesimus was witnessed by those Christians who met in his house (vv. 1–2) and who were to judge this action against the honor that Philemon had gained by his love toward the saints (v. 5). With Philemon thus characterized by his past benefactions, Paul then turns to himself and to Onesimus, identifying himself as an old man and prisoner (v. 9) and Onesimus as his child (v. 10). These characterizations, when seen in combination, cast Paul in the role of an old father who is in need of his child's support—an accepted convention of children toward their aged parents. Philemon can hardly deny Onesimus's return to Paul, given his familial responsibility—a responsibility that supersedes any slavish role he may have served in Philemon's household. In addition, Paul's use of his age and familial relationship with Onesimus that made Onesimus essential to him for his support has the further function of mitigating any anger that Philemon may have had toward his slave, since Paul's rhetoric also draws on the convention of using familial relations in master–slave deliberations.

It is not possible here to analyze the other features of Paul's argument in Philemon in relation to the larger urban world of the Greek East, but the effect of this investigation of one word, πρεσβύτης in Phlm 9, should be sufficient to indicate that the relations with that larger world will be numerous and close. Moreover, those relations should serve to cast doubt on the widespread scholarly tendency to separate Pauline Christianity too much from its Greco-Roman urban context and therefore to make that Christianity seem too sectarian. But if one puzzle piece, Paul's use of πρεσβύτης in Phlm 9, is any indication, becoming a Christian, to recall Wayne Meeks's question, did not involve too much of a change, and being a Christian, as a result, was in many respects a rather ordinary existence, of the same texture as the existence of most other people in the urban world of the Greek East.

CHAPTER 6

Paul's Thorn and
Cultural Models of Affliction

Susan R. Garrett

W AYNE A. MEEKS has observed that, for persons in the Pauline communities, the Messiah's crucifixion and resurrection provided a "new and controlling paradigm of God's mode of action."[1] Meeks writes that the paradox of the crucified Messiah was the key to various aspects of communal life, including Christians' experiences of suffering or hostility. When afflicted, Pauline Christians obtain comfort by remembering the action of God in the cross/resurrection. They "are called to rejoice in being permitted to imitate Christ (as in Rom. 5:1–11; 2 Cor. 1:3–7) and at the same time receive reassurance that it is in weakness that the power of God manifests itself."[2] Meeks argues, however, that the extant Pauline letters offer no general theodicy. Rather, when Paul discusses evil, he emphasizes factors affecting the life of the church. For example, when Paul remarks about death in 1 Thess 4:13–18; 1 Corinthians 15; and 2 Cor 5:1–10, he does not address the general human problem of mortality, but "the continuing solidarity of the Christian community transcending death, or present solidarity of those who must not pretend that death is no longer real, or the right understanding of apostolic power."[3] As Paul responds to the various social problems or predicaments resulting from Christians' experiences of affliction, the paradigm of the cross/resurrection proves to be a remarkably flexible tool.

2 Cor 12:7–10 supplies interesting material for reflection on the role of this central paradigm in Pauline theodicy (such as it is). Here Paul discusses a specific instance of personal affliction, which he refers to obliquely as a

1. Wayne A. Meeks, *The First Urban Christians: The Social World of the Apostle Paul* (New Haven: Yale University Press, 1983) 180. Several people gave me helpful suggestions for this article; I would especially like to thank Richard Hays, Dale Martin, and Allen Hilton.

2. Ibid., 181.

3. Ibid., 189.

"thorn in the flesh, an angel of Satan." The precise identity of this "thorn" has eluded interpreters for centuries, and this question is, finally, unresolvable. The strongest hypotheses involve some sort of human enemy or physical ailment.[4] Either way, the affliction bore directly on Paul's stature and authority before the Corinthians, and so had (as Meeks would suggest) social consequences within the Corinthian community. If the thorn was a human opponent known to the Corinthians, then the challenge to Paul's authority was direct and obvious. If the thorn was, rather, a physical affliction, then the Corinthians must have taken offense at Paul's inability to rid himself of the malady—in that case Paul was, as Jacob Jervell has argued, the "weak" or "sick" charismatic.[5] Whatever the identity of the thorn, the cross/ resurrection paradigm governs Paul's reading of the divine response, for Christ's resurrection had shown "power made perfect in weakness" (12:9) to be God's characteristic design for Christian life.

But the paradigm of the cross/resurrection cannot by itself account for all the interpretive moves that Paul makes in 2 Cor 12:7–10. In particular, this paradigm cannot explain Paul's labeling of the affliction as an "angel of Satan" and his emphatic statement of God's purpose in sending this "angel" or "messenger" ("to keep me from exalting myself," v. 7 [twice]). How is one to account for these interpretive moves? The question is methodologically difficult because, as Meeks has noted, the letters present "neither a systematic doctrine nor a comprehensive myth of evil's nature and origin"; hence, attempts to reconstruct a systematic view behind express statements (such as 12:7) remain "highly problematical."[6] On the other hand, one must surely say *something* about the conceptual background to Paul's assertion that an angel of Satan was sent to "torment" or "buffet" (κολαφίζειν) him, inasmuch as the statement raises an array of questions: How does Satan's service for God as described in this passage relate to his opposition as described in, for example, 2 Cor 2:11 and 4:4? Why was Paul afraid of "exalting himself"? How would the thorn/angel prevent him from doing so? etc. A way must be found to illuminate the conceptual background to v. 7 without resorting to a grand (and therefore suspect) reconstruction of "the Pauline worldview."

I will draw on recent work in cognitive anthropology (a subdiscipline

4. See the review of the various arguments in Ralph P. Martin, *2 Corinthians* (WBC 40; Waco, Tex.: Word, 1986) 413–16. Scriptural precedents for the metaphor of the thorn are discussed in Terence Y. Mullins, "Paul's Thorn in the Flesh," *JBL* 76 (1957) 299–303; also David M. Park, "Paul's ΣΚΟΛΟΨ ΤΗ ΣΑΡΚΙ: Thorn or Stake? (2 Cor XII 7)," *NovT* (1980) 179–83. More recently, Jerry W. McCant has argued that the thorn in the flesh "was the Corinthian Church's rejection of the legitimacy of Paul's apostolate" ("Paul's Thorn of Rejected Apostleship," *NTS* 34 [1988] 572).

5. Jacob Jervell, "Der schwache Charismatiker," in *Rechtfertigung: Festschrift für Ernst Käsemann zum 70. Geburtstag* (ed. Johannes Friedrich et al.; Tübingen: Mohr-Siebeck, 1976) esp. 191–94.

6. Meeks, *First Urban Christians*, 184.

concerned with how cultural knowledge is organized)[7] in an effort to provide such illumination of this conceptual background. Specifically, I propose to substitute the more formal anthropological concept of "cultural model" for the notion of "paradigm" as used above. I hope that my approach will shed light not only on Paul's reference to the angel of Satan, but also on how Paul's musings in 2 Cor 12:7–10 serve his larger rhetorical aims in chapters 10–13 and respond to the particular social situation in Corinth.

"Cultural models" are socially transmitted, taken-for-granted mental representations of different aspects of the world, "shared cognitive schemas through which human realities are constructed and interpreted."[8] Such models shape human experience by imposing culturally distinct patterns of order on the world. They supply interpretations of events and inferences about them, and provide a framework for remembering, reconstructing, and describing experiences. Because cultural models are shared by the members of a social group, a great deal of information related to them need not be made explicit in discourse among those members.[9] Indeed, many who use a given cultural model struggle when asked to articulate its overall organization, precisely because they take the model so fully for granted. Such persons are like a child who speaks in a syntactically correct fashion but cannot articulate a single rule of grammar. Or, as Dorothy Holland and Naomi Quinn remark, such persons "*use* the model but they cannot produce a reasonable *description* of the model. In this sense, the model is like a well-learned set of procedures that one knows how to carry out rather than a body of fact one can recount."[10] Studies of cultural models from various modern cultures indicate that alternative, even conflicting, paradigms often coexist, but without being integrated into a globally consistent whole. Members of a given culture easily and regularly switch from one model to another within a given domain of experience, combine components of different models, or invoke different models for different problems. "That there is no coherent cultural system of knowledge, only an array of differ-

7. On the early development of cognitive anthropology, see Susan R. Garrett, "Sociology of Early Christianity," in *The Anchor Bible Dictionary* (ed. David Noel Freedman et al.; 6 vols.; New York: Doubleday, 1992) 6:91–92, and the works cited therein.

8. Cited from the back cover of Roy D'Andrade and Claudia Strauss, eds., *Human Motives and Cultural Models* (Cambridge: Cambridge University Press, 1992). An earlier collection of essays that has especially influenced my thinking is that of Dorothy Holland and Naomi Quinn, eds., *Cultural Models in Language and Thought* (Cambridge: Cambridge University Press, 1987). Though the essays in this multidisciplinary collection pursue diverse questions, their authors are united in their insight "that culturally shared knowledge is organized into prototypical event sequences enacted in simplified worlds" (Quinn and Holland, "Culture and Cognition," in ibid., 24). The uniformity of the collection's essays in holding this presupposition enables me to make eclectic use of the various contributors' findings.

9. Roy D'Andrade, "A folk model of the mind," in Holland and Quinn, eds., *Cultural Models*, 113.

10. Ibid., 114.

ent culturally shared schematizations formulated for the performance of particular cognitive tasks, accounts for the co-existence of the conflicting cultural models encountered in many domains of experience."[11] For my purposes, these findings suggest that the early Christians could alternate among different cultural models of affliction, or combine elements from different models, without perceiving what may strike us as "logical contradictions" in thought.

Typically, cultural models are organized as "prototypical event sequences enacted in simplified worlds."[12] For example, Eve Sweetser has shown that in Western usage the English word "lie" presupposes a conceptualized social world in which a culturally standardized and normative pattern guides communication between individuals: speakers speak in order to transmit correct information. "In this simplified world, the telling of false information has certain consequences, such as harm to the recipient of the lie, and thus is clearly a reprehensible act."[13] This conceptual world is "simplified" because it does not always match the actual contexts in which real-life communication takes place: speech may have other goals besides the transmission of information, and speakers may speak falsely without malicious intent to deceive, or even without cognizance of their own misinformation.[14] As a second example, American society's cultural model of "sexual harassment" presupposes a prototypical event sequence, or mini-plot, in which a male worker propositions or makes lewd remarks to a (subordinate) female coworker, with overt or implied threats regarding her job security if she takes any kind of action. In real life the social context of sexually tinged interactions may be more complex: his remarks may be ambiguous; what begins as innocent flirtation may only evolve to more inappropriate interactions; she may not see anything wrong with his behavior at the time; the sexual roles may be reversed.

I will argue below that, in his excursus on the thorn in the flesh, Paul combined components not only from the cross/resurrection model of God's mode of action but also from two *cultural models of affliction*, which I have labeled the *Job model* and the παιδεία (or "discipline") *model* (described

---

11. Quinn and Holland, "Culture and Cognition," 10; see especially Allan Collins and Dedre Gentner, "How people construct mental models," in Holland and Quinn, eds., *Cultural Models*, 243–65. A modern example might be the combination of elements from both the Freudian and Jungian psychological models in popular discourse about the human mind.

12. Quinn and Holland, "Culture and Cognition," 22–24.

13. Dorothy Holland and Debra Skinner, "Prestige and intimacy: The cultural models behind Americans' talk about gender types," in Holland and Quinn, eds., *Cultural Models*, 88. The reference is to Eve E. Sweetser, "The definition of *lie*: an examination of the folk models underlying a semantic prototype," in Holland and Quinn, eds., *Cultural Models*, 43–66.

14. As part of her study, Sweetser examines English words for "false nonlies" or "palliated/justified lies," which mark deviations from the simplified world of the cultural model, as a way of elucidating the model itself (ibid., 52–59). Such words include, for example, *white lie, social lie, exaggeration, tall tale, (honest* or *careless) mistake.*

more fully below). Each of these models of affliction is widely attested in contemporaneous Jewish and/or pagan literature, and each corresponded to some aspect of the experience Paul wished to describe or the rhetorical goals he sought to achieve.

A "cultural-models approach" to the study of Pauline statements about suffering and hostility offers at least two methodological benefits.[15] First, as noted above, such an approach acknowledges the existence of both complementary and competing models within a given domain of experience. Thus the approach can take into account the similarity or overlap of some Jewish and Christian treatments of affliction as divine discipline or training (παιδεία), which exhibits the sufferer's own worthiness, to Hellenistic (especially Stoic) discussions of affliction. One can here speak of a dominant cultural model of the era, given nuanced adaptation in particular cultural streams and by particular writers. One way that some Jewish and Christian authors adapted this model was by mingling elements from it and from the alternative models of suffering and hostility that had grown out of their respective myths, texts, and collective memories. Such mingling occurred despite the various models' incommensurate premises about divine and human realities.[16] Second, a cultural-models approach is more consonant with the dynamic, multifunction character of cultural knowledge than is an approach employing the more familiar concept of "world-

15. I am presently writing a book on trials of faith in Pauline Christianity, in which I will elaborate on these and other first-century cultural models of affliction and/or temptation (the two overlap) and will show how they were used by Paul. I hope in the book to be able to reflect on the methodological implications of a cultural-models approach more fully than space permits me to do here, but at least a brief remark about my use of the term "model" is needed in the present essay. In arguing that Paul employed certain "cultural models," I am myself utilizing a model of how cognition works and how experience is shaped and interpreted. My assumption here is that the principles of cognition identified in studies of modern cultural models transfer across centuries and cultures. The problem of incommensurability is, however, less than in many recent modeling approaches to New Testament study, because I do not base my sketches of the relevant cultural models on findings from modern societies, but, rather, imaginatively construct the models' designs from ancient sources. (To complicate the issue, one could say that my sketches are themselves "models" of cultural models; see further Quinn and Holland, "Culture and Cognition," 32; on modeling approaches in New Testament studies, and on the problem of incommensurability, see Garrett, "Sociology," 90 [col. ii], 92–93).

16. In "The God of This World and the Affliction of Paul: 2 Cor 4:1–12" (in *Greeks, Romans, and Christians: Essays in Honor of Abraham J. Malherbe* [ed. David L. Balch et al.; Minneapolis: Fortress, 1990] 99–117), I tried to show how, in 2 Cor 4:1–12, Paul integrated elements from a Stoic view of the endurance of hardships with a (more typically Jewish) portrayal of himself as a suffering righteous one, scorned by the devil's allies. Although I did not explicitly employ a cultural-models approach in that article, its argument about how Paul used different cultural traditions to contrast himself and his opponents is consistent with the argument offered in the present essay (with regard to both my methodology and my delineation of the thrust of Paul's rhetoric in each passage). I hold that 2 Corinthians 1–9 and 10–13 were originally separate letters; see ibid., 102 n. 16.

view" (which may suggest a static and all-encompassing "thing," fully consistent in all its parts). By assuming that Paul drew on flexible, small-scale symbolic constructs, rather than on a "grand theory" of suffering and hostility, one is better able to make sense of the inconsistencies or variant emphases in the apostle's scattered remarks on this subject. Paul thinks and writes about affliction in a problem-oriented way, invoking various cultural models as demanded by the diverse social and cognitive tasks he must perform vis-à-vis his readers.

THE JOB MODEL OF AFFLICTION

Ancient readers viewed Job not as an existential hero who courageously held his ground against God but as a paragon of the virtue of *patient endurance* (ὑπομονή). By the Hellenistic period the story had been transformed from what it had been in its ancient Near Eastern cultural context in accommodation to the eschatological and dualistic concerns of apocalyptic. The translators of the LXX had already softened the near-blasphemous edges of Job's outcries to God, and the epistle of James and the *Testament of Job* both cite Job as the virtual embodiment of ὑπομονή (Jas 5:11; *T. Job* 1:5). As ever more blame for the world's ills was ascribed to the character of Satan, the paradigmatic value of Job's patient endurance of satanic affliction grew. Increasingly the plot of the prologue to Job provided a template or schema of the structure of relationships among God, satan, and humans in times of suffering, into which persons could insert their own experiences of suffering and so render them meaningful. According to this schema, Satan uses suffering to lead the righteous astray from single-minded commitment to God.[17] He does so by afflicting persons (physically or otherwise) and then offering them an "easy out." The choices that afflicted persons make here and now will have eschatological relevance: for the righteous to take Satan's "out" (e.g., by "cursing God," committing apostasy, or otherwise disobeying God's will) would supply evidence with which Satan could accuse them before God's judgment throne. Instead, those who are afflicted must withstand Satan's onslaught by placing their trust in God, as Job was thought to have done.

The *Testament of Job* can be viewed as an expansive elaboration of "the Job model."[18] In this text, Satan is given a motive for attacking the righteous

---

17. On the virtue of "single-mindedness" (ἁπλότης) in ancient Judaism and Christianity, see Susan R. Garrett, "'Lest the Light in You Be Darkness': Luke 11:33–36 and the Question of Commitment," *JBL* 110 (1991) 93–105, and the references contained therein. For other references to Satan as "tester," see Garrett, "God of This World," 105 n. 28.

18. I am in agreement with Berndt Schaller (*Das Testament Hiobs* [JSHRZ 3.3; Gütersloh: Mohn, 1979]) that the *Testament of Job* was most likely written by a Hellenistic Jewish author sometime between the beginning of the first century B.C.E. and mid-second century C.E. (on

man: Job has destroyed an idol's temple, wherein Satan was worshiped. Job knows from the outset that Satan is his combatant and that if Job exhibits endurance he will receive eternal life. Satan asks God for the authority to attack Job, but God gives Satan authority only over Job's body. Job must himself forfeit authority over his soul by cursing God (*T. Job* 16:7; 20:1–3; 26:3; cf. Job 1:11–12; 2:5–6). Because Job withstands Satan's attacks, at last the devil tearfully concedes that Job is the stronger. Thus, by his endurance Job actually *triumphs over* the Adversary. Some of the most interesting presuppositions of this melodramatic account can be traced to a particular way of reading canonical Job. These include the assumptions: (1) that human righteousness and service for God may prompt satanic attack; (2) that Satan views his affliction of humans as a contest in which honor and authority are at stake; and (3) that Satan stands in an ambiguous relationship to God, authorized by God but seeking to lead God's faithful astray.[19]

These presuppositions turn out to be constituent elements of the Job model of affliction as it appears also in other Jewish and Christian texts from this era. For example, in the *Jubilees* account of the testing of Abraham, "Prince Mastema" responds to a heavenly report about Abraham's uprightness by inviting God to order the patriarch to sacrifice Isaac. Mastema says, "Tell him to offer him [Isaac] (as) a burnt offering upon the altar. And you will see whether he will do this thing. And you will know whether he is faithful in everything in which you test him" (*Jub.* 17:16[20]; the echoes of the Job account are obvious). Thereafter the story proceeds as in Genesis. But, significantly, when Abraham passes the test by showing his willingness to sacrifice Isaac, *Jubilees* reports that "Prince Mastema was shamed" (18:12). The motif of "shame" implies that the Satan figure viewed Abraham's obedience as a personal defeat.

---

date and provenance, see further Garrett, "God of This World," 106 n. 35; for more general remarks on the worldview presupposed by this document, see Susan R. Garrett, "The 'Weaker Sex' in the *Testament of Job*," *JBL* 112 [1993] 55–70).

19. The notion of Satan's opposition to God probably derives from (non-Joban) traditions about an Archfiend who is the "Lord of this world" or the "Prince of darkness" and who seeks to undermine God's work. By the first century, such traditions (which ultimately derive from ancient Near Eastern myths and perhaps from Zoroastrian beliefs) had merged with those from Job and from elsewhere, resulting in an image of Satan that was multifaceted and not entirely self-consistent (one could argue that there were "competing cultural models" of Satan). For an account of the various narrative streams of tradition that influenced ancient Jewish and Christian views of Satan (which, however, does not take adequate account of possible Zoroastrian influence), see Neil Forsyth, *The Old Enemy: Satan and the Combat Myth* (Princeton: Princeton University Press, 1987). Karl Georg Kuhn errs in the opposite direction, overstressing Persian influence to the neglect of traditions from Job and from the rest of the Hebrew scriptures ("New Light on Temptation, Sin, and Flesh in the New Testament," in *The Scrolls and the New Testament* [ed. Krister Stendahl; New York: Harper & Brothers, 1957] 94–113).

20. Translation by O. S. Wintermute, in James H. Charlesworth, ed., *Old Testament Pseudepigrapha* (2 vols.; Garden City, N.Y.: Doubleday, 1983, 1985) 2.90 (hereafter *OTP*).

Christians of Paul's time and subsequent years sometimes recast their own experiences of suffering along the lines provided by the Job cultural model of affliction. They put themselves in Job's place, just as the author of *Jubilees* recast the story of Abraham, putting Abraham in Job's place. It is not necessary to assume that Christians who interpreted their affliction in this way intended to allude specifically to the story of Job. More likely they did not give conscious thought to the ultimate source of their language or imagery, so fully had the Job model (and the other cultural models discussed here) passed into their common cultural idiom. Cultural models are often transparent to those who use them.[21]

One example of a text in which Christians' suffering is interpreted using the "Job model" is 1 Pet 5:8–9. The passage runs as follows:

> Discipline yourselves, keep alert. Like a roaring lion your adversary [ὁ ἀντί-δικος ὑμῶν] the devil prowls around, looking for someone to devour. Resist him, steadfast in your faith, for you know that your brothers and sisters in all the world are undergoing the same kinds of suffering.[22]

Like the authors of *Testament of Job* and *Jubilees*, this author assumes that a righteous life may actually induce satanic affliction. In contemporaneous writings the word ἀντίδικος generally designates a legal adversary in a court of law.[23] This is precisely the role assigned to the *śāṭān* in the Job account, where he accuses Job before the divine court (cf. Zech 3:1). For first-century Christian readers, the reference to the devil as ὁ ἀντίδικος would have elicited images of Satan before the judgment throne of God, accusing the righteous of being unfaithful (cf. Rev 12:10). The reference to the devil as one who "prowls around, looking for someone to devour," also evokes the Job account. Twice in the prologue of Job, God asks the *śāṭān* "Where have you come from?" Each time the *śāṭān* answers, "From going to and fro on the earth, and from walking up and down on it" (Job 1:7; 2:2). By the first century, this impersonal *śāṭān* had become the Archfiend Satan, and the character's "going to and fro" upon the earth was being intepreted as a hunt for victims—persons whom Satan might justifiably accuse before God.[24]

Paul's familiarity with the Job model of affliction is evident in 1 Thess

21. Quinn and Holland, "Culture and Cognition," 14.

22. All biblical quotations follow the NRSV, occasionally with slight modifications.

23. Cf. Matt 5:25 (parallel Luke 12:58); Luke 18:3 (note the judicial context). The word is also used with this sense in contemporaneous literature (e.g., *POxy.* 37.I.8 [first century C.E.]; Josephus, *Antiquities* 8.30).

24. See Charles Bigg, *Epistles of St. Peter and St. Jude* (ICC; New York: Scribner, 1901) 102. Bigg points out that Ps 21:14 LXX has also contributed to the image of Satan in 1 Pet 5:8. For the argument that the *śāṭān* was an impersonal figure at the time of the composition of the prologue to Job, see Peggy L. Day, *An Adversary in Heaven: śāṭān in the Hebrew Bible* (HSM 43; Atlanta: Scholars Press, 1988).

3:1–5.[25] Here Paul describes his former anxiety about whether the young Thessalonian church would be able to withstand the suffering inflicted by their compatriots (2:14). He had wanted to visit them to see for himself how they were faring, but "Satan blocked our way" in this effort (2:18). Therefore Paul sent Timothy to exhort them not to be shaken by their afflictions. Paul continues,

> In fact, when we were with you, we told you beforehand that we were to suf-
> fer affliction; so it turned out, as you know. For this reason, when I could bear
> it no longer, I sent to find out about your faith; I was afraid that somehow the
> tempter had tempted you and that our labor had been in vain. (1 Thess 3:4–5)

Paul had feared that Satan—"the tempter"—had used the Thessalonians' affliction as a means to seduce them away from their fidelity to the Christian God. Specifically, Paul may have worried that some or all of his converts had reverted to their former belief in idols (cf. 1:9). In that case, Paul and his coworkers' efforts to save the Thessalonians from God's righteous wrath at the judgment would have been for nought. In his remarks to the Thessalonians, Paul has instantiated the details of their situation into the "structure of relationships among things and actors and actions" provided by the Job model, thereby producing a culturally legitimate interpretation of the causes and reasons for their suffering.[26]

In 2 Cor 12:7–10, Paul's reference to his thorn in the flesh as an "angel/ messenger of Satan" indicates that here, too, he is interpreting his experience using the categories of the Job model. As I noted above, the historical referent of the "thorn" can no longer be identified. For my purposes it is sufficient to note that Paul regarded Satan as in some way responsible for this personal tribulation. I say "in some way" responsible, because the agency behind the tribulation is made ambiguous by Paul's use of the passive verb "was given" (ἐδόθη). I have already suggested that such ambiguity typifies the Job model.[27] Here the passive construction and the reference to an angel of Satan imply that *God has granted Satan the authority to harass Paul.* The

---

25. See also Garrett, "God of This World," 111–15.

26. The quoted phrase is taken from Edwin Hutchins, "Myth and experience in the Trobriand Islands," in *Cultural Models*, 279. Hutchins writes, "If we ignore the specific identities of the things and actors and actions [in the myth under study] and concentrate instead on the organization of the relationships among them, we see a structure I call a *schema.* When particular instances are plugged into the slots in the schema, we say the schema is instantiated, and the result is a proposition that is an assertion about the world" (ibid.).

27. See Hans Josef Klauck, *2 Korintherbrief* (Würzburg: Echter-Verlag, 1986) 94. Note that twice in the prologue of canonical Job, God gives the devil the authority to test Job (1:12; 2:6). The detail is repeated (and elaborated) several times in *Testament of Job,* and also occurs (sometimes in the form of a divine passive) in other texts that tell of the devil's exercising of authority. See, e.g., *T. Job* 8:1–3; 16:2; 20:2–3; Luke 4:6; and 22:31, where Satan had presumably demanded of God that the disciples (the "you" is plural) be remanded to his authority. See also n. 28 below.

actual deed is then carried out by Satan's "messenger" or "angel."[28] Why would God allow Satan to afflict Paul? In order, Paul deduces, to keep him from "exalting himself"—from being puffed up or arrogant on account of his visionary experiences. God permits Satan's intervention because it will keep Paul humble, inasmuch as Paul cannot remove the affliction by himself. Like the patient Job, Paul must rely on divine grace for the strength to endure the trial.

Notice that, according to the logic of the Job model, Satan would not have shared God's positive purpose. The devil sometimes *serves* God's aims, but he does not *sympathize* with them (cf. 2 Cor 2:11). Satan has his own motives for attacking Paul: the apostle is the faithful servant of God, whose work undermines Satan's authority.[29] According to the Job model, Satan would have desired that Paul prove unable to endure the divine chastisements. Paul's endurance is, then, a shameful defeat for Satan.

In assuming that his affliction serves a positive purpose, the apostle draws on a second cultural model of affliction: that of affliction as divine "chastisement" or "discipline" (παιδεία), done to make the faithful fit for judgment.

THE Παιδεία MODEL OF AFFLICTION

Research has shown that within a given culture, alternative and even conflicting cultural models may govern a particular domain of experience. In Jewish culture of the late Second Temple era, an alternative to the "Job model" of affliction envisioned suffering as a pedagogical process. (In Greek contexts παιδεία could be understood as *education* or even *culture* in an

---

28. Paul's reference in 2 Cor 11:15 to his opponents as "ministers of Satan" is often cited as support for a theory of the "angel" as a human opponent. But the expression could also refer to a demon-underling of Satan that Paul supposes to be the immediate source of his affliction. Note that, according to the Greek fragment of *Jub.* 10:8–9, ὁ διάβολος asks that God permit him to retain a portion of the demons under his control for the testing of humans. Accordingly, a tenth were given over (ἐδόθη) to him, so that he might "test humans for the purpose of proving each one's inclination toward God" (ὥστε πειράζειν τοὺς ἀνθρώπους πρὸς δοκιμὴν τῆς ἑκάστου πρὸς θεὸν προαιρέσεως [cited from A. M. Denis, ed., *Fragmenta pseudepigraphorum quae supersunt graeca* [Leiden: Brill, 1970] 87). New Testament references to "angels of Satan" are found at Matt 25:41 and Rev 12:7, 9; cf. *T. Asher* 6:4; *Barn.* 18.1.

29. Compare the similar argument regarding 2 Cor 4:1–12 in Garrett, "God of This World," esp. 109–15. Some scholars (including, e.g., Erhardt Güttgemanns, *Der leidende Apostel und sein Herr: Studien zur paulinischen Christologie* [FRLANT 90; Göttingen: Vandenhoeck & Ruprecht, 1966] 164–65; and Hans Dieter Betz, "Eine Christus-Aretalogie bei Paulus [2 Kor 12, 7–10]," *ZTK* 66 [1969] 290–91 [cf. 303]) argue that in referring to attack by an angel of Satan, Paul must be citing the charge of his opponents (because presumably he would not initiate such a damaging assertion). But, according to the structure of the Job model, being the victim of satanic testing actually attests to one's *righteousness:* witness the cases of Job, Jesus, and Abraham (see n. 43 below).

idealized sense—and was often personified as such—but, as here, it could also be viewed as the learned *discipline* that makes one a cultured person.) According to the παιδεία model, God is a father who tests his beloved children with suffering so as to "chastise" or "discipline" them. The παιδεία model makes sense of suffering by identifying God as its agent and the sufferers' own correction, purification, or improvement as God's purpose. Thus, whereas the Job model views tests of affliction as salvation-threatening, and so to be avoided, the παιδεία model views such tests as serving the positive end of preparing persons for judgment, and so to be accepted (if not actually embraced).[30] Such a positive view of testing/discipline is conveyed, for example, by the following passage from the Wisdom of Solomon:

> But the souls of the righteous are in the hand of God, and no torment will ever touch them. . . . For though in the sight of others they were punished, their hope is full of immortality. Having been disciplined a little [ὀλίγα παιδευθέντες], they will receive great good, because God tested them [ἐπείρασεν αὐτούς] and found them worthy of himself; like gold in the furnace he tried them [ἐδοκίμασεν αὐτούς], and like a sacrificial burnt offering he accepted them. (Wis 3:1, 4-6)

The foregoing passage is interesting for two reasons: first, it conjoins the παιδεία metaphor with that of the refiner's fire;[31] and, second, it follows immediately after a description of the righteous man's test of affliction as the work of the devil's allies (Wis 2:21-24),[32] thus illustrating how ancient authors could shift from one cultural model of affliction to another in a very short space.

In the New Testament, no text illustrates the model of affliction as divine παιδεία better than Heb 12:3-11.[33] After quoting Prov 3:11-12 (itself a fundamental text for this cultural model), the author continues,

> Endure trials for the sake of discipline [εἰς παιδείαν ὑπομένετε]. God is treating you as children; for what child is there whom a parent does not discipline?

---

30. Mark 14:38 and parallels, and Matt 6:13 and parallel indicate that one way to avoid πειρασμός is through prayer. Contrast the relatively positive view of πειρασμός in Sir 2:1-6 (which employs the παιδεία model). On ancient views of divine παιδεία, see further Charles H. Talbert, *Learning Through Suffering: The Educational Value of Suffering in the New Testament and in Its Milieu* (Collegeville, Minn.: Michael Glazier, 1991) esp. 15-16; and Judith M. Gundry Volf, *Paul & Perseverance: Staying In and Falling Away* (Philadelphia: Westminster, 1990) 107-12. For other passages in which it is said that God (or the gods) test the righteous (or virtuous) through affliction, see John T. Fitzgerald, *Cracks in an Earthen Vessel: An Examination of the Catalogues of Hardships in the Corinthian Correspondence* (SBLDS 99; Atlanta: Scholars Press, 1988) 43-44; and Garrett, "God of This World," 100 n. 7.

31. In general on the important role of metaphor in many cultural models, see Quinn and Holland, "Culture and Cognition," 27-30.

32. On the best translation for these verses, see Garrett, "'Lest the Light in You Be Darkness,'" 102 n. 26.

33. See Talbert, *Learning Through Suffering*, 58-74.

If you do not have that discipline in which all children share, then you are illegitimate and not his children. (Heb 12:7–8)

We should be even more willing to accept discipline by God than we are to accept it from our human parents, the author explains, "for they disciplined us for a short time as seemed best to them, but he disciplines us for our good, in order that we may share his holiness" (v. 10).

The passages from Wisdom and from Hebrews share the widespread assumption that *successful endurance of tests of affliction makes one acceptable to God.* As Joseph says in the *Testament of Joseph*, God "may stand aside in order to test the disposition of the soul. In ten testings [πειρασμοί] he showed that I was approved [δόκιμος], and in all of them I persevered, because perseverance [ἡ μακροθυμία] is a powerful medicine, and endurance [ἡ ὑπομονή] provides many good things" (*T. Jos.* 2:6–7).[34] Paul expresses a similar view when he writes to the Romans that "suffering produces endurance [ἡ ὑπομονή], and endurances produces character" (ἡ δοκιμή, a state or quality of being approved [Rom 5:3–4]). The Lord's commendation in the present (2 Cor 10:18) anticipates approval at the judgment (cf. 1 Cor 4:5). I will argue below that this "proving" effect of tribulation or testing is relevant for the interpretation of 2 Cor 12:7–10, inasmuch as the passage addresses the Corinthians' desire for Paul to "prove" that Christ operates through him (2 Cor 13:3; cf. 3:1).[35]

In 1 Cor 11:27–32, Paul shows that he is familiar with the παιδεία model of affliction. Here Paul is trying to make sense of the recent sickness and death of some of the Corinthian Christians. He infers that the unfortunate events reflect God's present judgment of the Corinthians for unholy conduct, and he further informs them that their affliction ought to prompt them to examine or test themselves (δοκιμαζέτω δὲ ἄνθρωπος ἑαυτόν, v. 28). If they tested themselves, then they would conduct themselves in an approved way, and so God would not *need* to judge them (εἰ δὲ ἑαυτοὺς διεκρίνομεν, οὐκ ἂν ἐκρινόμεθα, v. 31; cf. Gal 6:1–5). But as it is, Paul explains, "when we are judged, we are being disciplined [παιδευόμεθα] by the Lord so that we may not be condemned along with the world" (v. 32). In making this last assertion, Paul reasons that the present affliction endured by the Corinthians is clearing away their impurities (like the refiner's fire), and so rendering them approved. They will therefore not have to be condemned along with the world.

When Paul experienced his thorn in the flesh, he apparently heeded his own advice to engage in self-examination or self-testing: only by such intro-

---

34. Trans. Howard Clark Kee, in *OTP* 1:819. Note the ambiguity with regard to the agent behind the testing.

35. See further Talbert, *Learning Through Suffering,* 14–15 and the passages cited therein; for attestations in pagan philosophical literature of the notion that afflictions prove character or worth, see Fitzgerald, *Cracks,* 42–43.

spection could he have deduced that God was using this affliction to teach him not to "exalt [ὑπεραίρεσθαι] himself." His successful endurance of the thorn (and other apostolic afflictions [12:10]) qualify Paul as one whom God has approved.

Why did Paul think it important that he not "exalt himself"? This is a question that neither the Job nor the παιδεία model of affliction is able to answer. It requires that we turn to yet a third cultural model, that of the cross/resurrection.

THE CROSS/RESURRECTION MODEL

The cross/resurrection model posits a connection between lowliness/ weakness and exaltation/strength. As Meeks has pointed out, it is not quite right to characterize this connection as paradoxical:

> That is, things ordinarily taken as signs of weakness are not simply redefined as powerful because they emulate the weakness of the crucified Jesus, although some of the statements by Paul may plausibly be taken that way. More often the pattern is dialectical or sequential: the Christ was first weak, then powerful; so, too, the Christians are weak and afflicted today, but will be vindicated and glorious.[36]

Meeks notes that "very early the declaration of Jesus' death and resurrection was mixed with a different symbolic pattern, that of descent from heaven followed by exaltation and enthronement there."[37] The two patterns reinforced one another, inasmuch as both envisioned the one who is or who becomes "lowly" as being "raised up" by God (see esp. Phil 2:8–9). Interestingly, the cross/resurrection model (in more abstract terms, a "low-to-high" pattern) appears to be the inverse of another cultural model of God's mode of action (a "high-to-low" pattern) current in Judaism of Paul's day. According to this other cultural model, exalting oneself or putting oneself on a par with God leads inevitably to a fall. The classic biblical exemplar of the high-to-low model is Isa 14:3–20, about the king of Babylon, who says "I will ascend to the tops of the clouds, I will make myself like the Most High" (v. 14), and so was cast down to Sheol. This and other biblical texts (including Daniel 4 and passages throughout Ezekiel 28–32) were used to explain Satan's fall: he had dared to make himself equal to God and so was cast down.[38] Significantly, Paul—or whoever wrote 2 Thessalonians—draws on

36. Meeks, *First Urban Christians*, 182.

37. Ibid., 183. Meeks notes (242 n. 49) that many New Testament scholars now believe that the descent/enthronement pattern is rooted in Jewish myths or metaphors about divine wisdom.

38. See the discussion of the relevant traditions from the Hebrew scriptures, the Pseudepigrapha, and the New Testament in Susan R. Garrett, "Exodus from Bondage: Luke 9:31 and

the high-to-low model in describing the "lawless one," who "opposes and exalts himself (ὁ ἀντικείμενος καὶ ὑπεραιρόμενος) above every so-called god or object of worship, so that he takes his seat in the temple of God, declaring himself to be God" (2 Thess 2:4; it is noteworthy that ὑπερ-αίρεσθαι ["to exalt oneself"] appears only here and in 2 Cor 12:7 in the New Testament). The lawless one will be annihilated by the Lord Jesus at his coming (2:8). Other authors of the period, both Jewish and Christian, utilized the high-to-low model in portrayals of such doomed figures as Antiochus Epiphanes, Julius Agrippa I (= the "Herod" of Acts 12), and Simon Magus.[39] The message was obvious: "exalting oneself" in this life can only lead to one's fall.

It is clear that Paul viewed the "thorn" of 2 Corinthians 12 in the light of his exalting revelatory experiences. Paul's ascent to the third heaven placed him in a precariously high position. He implies that the ascent endangered him by encouraging arrogance, which would in turn bring about his own fall. The apostle interprets the thorn in the flesh as God's/Christ's way of humbling or lowering him. The affliction ensures that Paul will not think more of himself than he ought to think (cf. 2 Cor 12:6; Rom 12:3); he cannot by his own power remove the thorn, or even persuade the Lord to remove it, but must depend on the Lord for the strength to endure. "My grace is sufficient for you, for my power is made perfect in weakness" (2 Cor 12:9). Paul does not here suggest that weakness has been arbitrarily renamed as strength. Nor does he even imply, in apocalyptic fashion, that his weakness will *one day* give way to strength. Rather, Paul's weakness requires him to endure the affliction (since he is powerless to remove it), and *by his very endurance* he exhibits strength. Paul here presupposes a model of "endurance" as active engagement with affliction (rather than passive subjugation to it).[40] Persons who practiced endurance were often likened to sparring athletes, who endure pain and so win the crown (cf. *T. Job* 4:10; 4 Macc 17:11–16). This point would not have been lost on the Corinthians, inasmuch as Paul has earlier portrayed himself to them as one who, like the Stoic σοφός ("wise man"), exhibits virtue and strength by enduring hardships.[41] The Pauline nuance is, of course, that in his case endurance attests

---

Acts 12:1–24," in *CBQ* 52 (1990) 666–67, 676–77. On whether the high-to-low pattern was applied to Satan already in the first century C.E., see ibid., 667 n. 42.

39. For discussion of the Acts 12 account of Herod's fall, see Garrett, "Exodus," 675–77. On Simon Magus, see Susan R. Garrett, *The Demise of the Devil: Magic and the Demonic in Luke's Writings* (Minneapolis: Fortress, 1989) 61–78. Note that in *T. Job* 41–43, Elious (= Elihu) utters "presumptuous words" (λόγοι θρασοί) against Job and so is denied salvation. Elious is explicitly described as "filled with Satan" (41:5). Elsewhere the author of the *Testament of Job* condemns pride (ὑπερηφανία, 15:8) and arrogance (ἀλαζονεία, 21:3).

40. F. Hauck writes that, in the Greek world, "there predominates in ὑπομένειν the concept of the courageous endurance which manfully defies evil. Unlike patience, it thus has an active component" (*TDNT* 4:581–82).

41. On endurance by athletes, see Seneca, *Ep.* 78.16; 80.3; Epictetus, *Dis.* 3.15.2–4; see also

not to his own strength but to the δύναμις ("power") of Christ, which the Lord graciously bestows on Paul (χάρις [v. 9; cf. 2 Cor 1:11: τὸ εἰς ἡμᾶς χάρισμα, "the blessing or gift granted us"]). Paul's endurance is therefore proof of Christ's χάρις ("grace") toward him, in the same way as are the "signs and wonders and mighty works" that he performed among the Corinthians (2 Cor 12:12).[42] In the remainder of the letter Paul will argue that Christ can and will manifest his power through Paul in yet another way: in Paul's "powerful" dealing with his errant children (13:4, 10).

Paul's excursus on the thorn demonstrates his participation in Christ's crucifixion; the recounting of Christ's word to him shows that he likewise shares in the resurrected Christ's power (cf. 2 Cor 4:7–15). By thus underscoring the magnitude of Christ's strength in him, Paul's remarks about his affliction further his aim of persuading the Corinthians to modify their attitude and behavior toward him and toward the "superapostles" who exalt themselves through boasting (2 Cor 11:12, 21). In other words, his remarks have certain social consequences in the Corinthian setting. To identify these consequences more precisely, it is necessary to see how the excursus on the thorn functions rhetorically within 2 Corinthians 10–13.

PAUL'S THORN IN THE CONTEXT OF 2 CORINTHIANS 10–13

Paul easily and freely drew elements from what I have described as three distinct cultural models, in part because each gave symbolic expression to particular aspects of his experience. The Job model reflected Paul's subjective sense of being tempted to stray from his trust in God. The παιδεία model expressed his conviction (confirmed, he says, by revelation) that God permitted him to suffer for his own good. The cross/resurrection model corresponded to his belief that God worked mightily in him, despite his afflicted condition. But, in addition, Paul drew on these cultural models

---

Victor C. Pfitzner, *Paul and the Agon Motif* (NovTSup 16; Leiden: Brill, 1967) 30–35; Fitzgerald, *Cracks*, 87–100. The most extensive and useful discussion of the Stoic and Pauline views of affliction (but without reference to 2 Cor 12:7–10 specifically) is Fitzgerald, *Cracks*, esp. 117–201. Fitzgerald argues that in 2 Corinthians 1–7, Paul repeatedly exhibits his own capacity and worth by referring to his God-enabled endurance of affliction. See also Garrett, "God of this World"; and Rudolf Bultmann, *Der zweite Brief an die Korinther* (Göttingen: Vandenhoeck & Ruprecht, 1976) 228–32.

42. Here I am basically in agreement with Jervell, "Der schwache Charismatiker," 197 n. 63 (against Güttgemanns, *Der leidende Apostel*, 168–70). But Jervell seems to equate ὑπομονή with the difficult situations in which charismatic deeds of power take place ("Der schwache Charismatiker," 197 n. 64). Rather, ὑπομονή is itself one manifestation of divine χάρις. Compare 4 Macc 17:11–16 and *T. Job* 27:2–5, both of which use athletic imagery to describe (in Stoic fashion) the "victory" or "conquering" by the one who endures severe trials. For an earlier overview of ways to interpret Christ's oracle to Paul, see Gerald G. O'Collins, "Power Made Perfect in Weakness: 2 Cor 12:9–10," *CBQ* 33 (1971) 528–37.

because their implicit assumptions furthered his rhetorical aims in chapters 10–13.

According to the Job model of affliction, Satan tends to single out *God's righteous servants* for attack. The devil seeks to lead the righteous astray, and so to obtain evidence with which he can accuse them before God. Thus, Satan had accosted Abraham, Job, and Jesus immediately after God had declared each one to be worthy.[43] By describing himself as the victim of diabolical affliction, Paul implies that he, too, is a worthy servant of God. He, too, is one who opposes Satan's work and so elicits Satan's animus. Paul's claim to be a victim of satanic assault is therefore an oblique but positive assertion about himself. It is consistent with his self-portrayal in 2 Cor 4:1–12, where Paul suggests that he is the afflicted righteous one, since he is being opposed by the "god of this world" and this "god's" human allies ("the perishing").[44] By making such an assertion in 2 Cor 12:7, Paul clearly intends to influence the way the Corinthians interact with him. They should recognize that he is not a weak person of no account, but a suffering righteous one through whom God manifests power—and they should behave in an appropriately obedient fashion.

According to the παιδεία model, God tests the righteous through affliction as a way of chastising or disciplining them in preparation for judgment. By recounting how he has endured the chastisement of the thorn (not to mention his other afflictions [12:10]), Paul shows the Corinthians that he has been tested by God and by himself and has passed the test (cf. 10:18). Paul's demonstration that he is "tried and true" anticipates his own reference a few verses later to the Corinthians' desire for "proof" (δοκιμή) that Christ speaks in him (13:3). That demonstration also gives Paul moral ground on which to stand as he turns the tables on the Corinthians, informing them that it is *they* who ought to worry about showing "proof":

> Examine yourselves [ἑαυτοὺς πειράζετε] to see whether you are living in the faith. Test yourselves [ἑαυτοὺς δοκιμάζετε]. Do you not realize that Jesus Christ is in you?—unless, indeed, you fail to meet the test [εἰ μήτι ἀδόκιμοί ἐστε]! I hope you will find out that we have not failed [to meet the test] [ὅτι γνώσεσθε ὅτι ἡμεῖς οὐκ ἐσμὲν ἀδόκιμοι]. (2 Cor 13:5–6; cf. Gal 6:1–5)

Paul's preceding description of his endurance of the thorn has already shown that he most certainly is not ἀδόκιμος ("unproven," or "having failed to meet the test"; cf. 1 Cor 9:27). The measures he has met are the standards not of the Corinthians but of God. By the Corinthians' canon Paul may appear to have failed the test, but by God's standards it is not Paul but the Corinthians who are at risk of failure.[45] Inasmuch as Paul has spent almost

---

43. Job 1:8–11; 2:3–5; Matt 3:17–4:1; Mark 1:11–13; Luke 3:22; 4:1–2; *Jub.* 17:15–16.
44. See Garrett, "The God of This World," 110–11.
45. To be sure, Paul may here be implying that he himself will be held accountable by God if

all of chapters 10–13 defending his own worthiness, his insistence here that the Corinthians bear the burden of proof is a moral and rhetorical *tour de force*. I have tried to show how Paul's reliance on the παιδεία model and its unstated assumptions enabled him to make that shift.

According to the cross/resurrection model, Christians imitate Christ in his suffering, confident that they will also share in the power of the resurrection. By portraying himself as someone who is lowly and weak, Paul shows that he participates in Christ's cross. Simultaneously, he places himself in antithesis to the superapostles, whom the Corinthians regard as exalted and strong. Repeatedly in chapters 10–13, Paul emphasizes his humility, weakness, or abasement and his opponents' self-commendation or arrogance.[46] The very name he gives them serves to advance the contrast: they are the *superlative* (ὑπερλίαν) apostles (11:5; 12:11), whereas Paul will not *exalt* (ὑπεραίρεσθαι) himself (12:7). They boast in their own accomplishments (11:21), but Paul will boast only of his weakness, for he does not want the Corinthians to think more of *him* than they ought to think (12:5–6). Paul's spatial metaphors and imagery woven through this section also underscore the contrast. Paul uses divine power "to *pull down* [καθαιρεῖν] arguments and *every proud obstacle raised up* [πᾶν ὕψωμα ἐπαιρόμενον] against the knowledge of God" (10:5).[47] Paul was *lowered* in a basket (11:33). When Paul *ascended* to heaven God immediately had him brought down (12:2–3, 7). The inverse cultural models sketched above govern the respective statuses and eventual destinies of the opposed parties as portrayed by Paul: Paul is the "low" one whom God will make "high," whereas the superapostles—who lord it over the Corinthians and put on airs (11:20)—must yet be laid low. "They have done Satan's work; to Satan's fate they will go."[48] Again, Paul's rhetoric has social consequences: the Corinthians are to realign their values to conform to the pattern of the cross, which requires them to turn away from the superapostles and become obedient to Paul.

---

the Corinthians fail to be obedient to the Gospel. Their continued faithfulness is reckoned to Paul's credit. Cf. 2 Cor 11:2–3; 1 Thess 2:19–20; also the discussions in Victor Paul Furnish, *II Corinthians* (AB 32A; New York: Doubleday, 1984) 578; A. T. Lincoln, "'Paul the Visionary': The Setting and Significance of the Rapture to Paradise in II Corinthians XII. 1–10," *NTS* 25 (1979) 210; and Volf, *Paul & Perseverance*, 218–19.

46. Paul's humility, weakness, or abasement: 10:1, 10, 13–18 (Paul does not overstep his limits in boasting or commend himself); 11:7, 21, 29–33; 12:7–10, 11, 21 (Paul will be humbled if they deprive him of his grounds for boasting); 13:4, 9. The superapostles' self-commendation or arrogance: 10:12, 13–18 (implies that they overstep their limits in boasting and commend themselves); 11:5, 12, 20; 12:11.

47. On the philosophical background of this language, see Abraham J. Malherbe, "Antisthenes and Odysseus, and Paul at War," in *Paul and the Popular Philosophers* (Minneapolis: Fortress, 1989) 91–119.

48. Martin, *2 Corinthians*, 353 (in reference to 2 Cor 11:15).

CONCLUSION

In Meeks's treatment of "patterns of belief and patterns of life" in the Pauline communities, he suggests that the paradigm of the crucified Messiah, raised by God to new life, proved to be "one of the most powerful symbols that has ever appeared in the history of religions."[49] Meeks calls the pattern a "master symbol,"[50] in recognition of its pervasive effect throughout many areas of early Christian life and thought. Anthropologists Dorothy Holland and Naomi Quinn have argued that it is just such "cultural models of wider applicability" that give a culture (or, in the case of the early Christians, a subculture) its distinctiveness or "thematicity."[51] Meeks has begun the important work of showing how this central paradigm functioned in various domains of experience in the Pauline communities. In this paper, I have tried to elaborate on Meeks's suggestion about the role of the cross/resurrection paradigm in the domain of affliction, by showing how Paul uses this cultural model and others in an interpretation of his personal tribulation or "thorn." What Paul is doing in 2 Cor 12:7–10 is not "theodicy" in any general or absolute sense: Paul does not here make a broadly applicable theological statement about God's goodness in the face of evil. Rather, as I have tried to show, he constructs an argument specific to the unique circumstances that have brought him to this point in his ongoing social and epistolary discourse with the obstreperous but beloved Corinthians.

Yet Paul's argument in this passage is not irrelevant to early Christian theodicy in a broader sense, for the *elements* of that argument—the cultural models sketched in Meeks's work and above—reappear often in ancient Christian writings about affliction. These models and others were the "structures of signification"[52] that guided the first Christians in their comprehension of and responses to the hardships that typified their communal existence. Meeks's work teaches us to search out both what was culturally shared and what was distinctive in such experiences and to ask how the early Christians' writings about them not only reflected but also affected the texture of everyday life.

49. Meeks, *First Urban Christians*, 180.
50. Ibid., 191.
51. Quinn and Holland, "Culture and Cognition," 34–35.
52. The phrase is taken from Clifford Geertz, *The Interpretation of Cultures* (New York: Basic Books, 1973) 9.

CHAPTER 7

Light on Paul from the *Testaments of the Twelve Patriarchs?*

M. de Jonge

THE *TESTAMENTS* AND THE NEW TESTAMENT

ONE OF THE FEATURES of the 26th edition of Nestle-Aland's *Novum Testamentum Graece* is the expansion of the number of references to the Pseudepigrapha of the Old Testament in the outer margin in comparison with the 25th. On p. 81* of the English introduction to N.-A.[25] we find a list of abbreviations of the books of the Bible (including the deuterocanonical/apocryphal books of the Old Testament), followed by the statement: "Besides these occur: Ps(almi) Sal(omonis), Ascensio Isaiae, Ass(umptio) Mosis, Apc (Apocalypsis) Eliae, 4 Esra, Henoch; Aratus (Act 17,28), Epimenides (Tit 1,12), Menander (1 K 15,33)." A similar list is given on pp. 67*–68* of N.-A.[26], but this time the books are divided between those of the Old Testament (with special mention of LXX titles) and of the New Testament with a special section "Apocrypha and Pseudepigrapha of the Old Testament" in between. As Pseudepigrapha are listed *Jubilees, Martyrdom of Isaiah, Psalms of Solomon, Enoch, Assumption of Moses, Apocalypse of Baruch, Testaments of the Twelve Patriarchs* (cited individually), *Life of Adam and Eve,* plus the *Apocalypse of Elijah* (according to Origen).

At the end of N.-A.[25] there is an "Index locorum" with Old Testament texts quoted in the New Testament or mentioned in the margin for other reasons. In N.-A.[26] we find Appendix III "Loci citati vel allegati," divided into two sections: (A) "Ex Vetero Testamento" and (B) "E Scriptoribus Graecis." The Old Testament section mentions first the books of the Hebrew Bible, next those found only in the LXX plus 4 Ezra, and finally, somewhat surprisingly, the so-called Pseudepigrapha of the Old Testament. For the editors of N.-A.[26] texts from the Old Testament Pseudepigrapha mentioned in the outer margin are clearly of a comparable nature and of the same exegetical value as texts found in the Hebrew and the Greek Bibles.[1]

Appendix III just mentioned gives sixteen passages from the *Testaments of the Twelve Patriarchs* as parallels to eighteen passages from the New Testament (pp. 774–75); the same list is now found in N.-A.[27], pp. 805–6. In twelve cases they appear in the margin of texts in the letters of Paul (ten of them in Romans); otherwise two are in Acts, one in Hebrews, and three in the Letter of James. This distribution makes a one-sided impression, and one wonders why particularly Paul's Letter to the Romans has received special attention.[2]

One of the best-known lists of parallels between the writings of the New Testament and the *Testaments of the Twelve Patriarchs* is found in R. H. Charles's translation and commentary on the *Testaments*.[3] He gives them in §26 under the heading "Influence of the Testaments on the New Testament," adding as §27 a survey entitled "Teaching of the Author on Forgiveness, the Two Great Commandments, Universalism, the Messiah, the Resurrection, the Antichrist, and its Influence on the N.T." (pp. xcii–xcix). The list in §26 gives parallels to twenty passages in Matthew, thirteen in Luke, five in Acts, three in John, thirty-eight in the Pauline[4] and Deutero-Pauline epistles (plus a long list of words common to the *Testaments* and the Pauline epistles, but not found in the rest of the New Testament), ten in the Catholic Epistles (four in James[5]), five in the Apocalypse.

For Charles, as for the editors of N.-A.[26], the *Testaments* are a Jewish writing comparable to the Apocrypha of the Old Testament, like other Pseudepigrapha. He realized, of course, that within the *Testaments* there are a number of clearly Christian passages, but those he regarded as Christian interpolations that could be identified easily. In his very influential edition of the text he identified those Christian interpolations by putting them between brackets.[6] Parallels found in these interpolations are not included

1. The Pseudepigrapha are not especially mentioned in the short section on Appendix III in Kurt Aland and Barbara Aland, *Der Text des Neuen Testaments* (Stuttgart: Deutsche Bibelgesellschaft 1982; 2nd ed. 1989).

2. Nine of the ten parallels to Romans can be found in Ernst Käsemann's notes on the texts in his *An die Römer* (HNT 8a; Tübingen: Mohr-Siebeck, 1973). The exception is *T. Benj.* 4:3f. at Rom 12:21; at Rom 1:4 Käsemann refers to *T. Levi* 18:11 instead of 18:7, mentioned in N.-A.[26]. Käsemann mentions, however, many more passages from the *Testaments* than are mentioned in Nestle-Aland.

3. R. H. Charles, *The Testaments of the Twelve Patriarchs translated from the editor's Greek text and edited with introduction notes and indices* (London: A. and C. Black, 1908) lxxviii–xcii.

4. The parallels on Rom 12:1; 12:21; and 15:23 agree with those found in the margin of N.-A.[26].

5. Here there is agreement between Charles and the margin of N.-A.[26] in the case of Jas 4:7.

6. R. H. Charles, *The Greek Versions of the Testaments of the Twelve Patriarchs* (Oxford: Clarendon, 1908), reprinted several times. Only in 1978 was it succeeded by M. de Jonge et al., *The Testaments of the Twelve Patriarchs: A Critical Edition of the Greek Text* (PVTG 1,2; Leiden: Brill, 1978).

in his list; consequently, those taken from the rest of the document are self-evidently regarded as having influenced the ideas of the New Testament authors. On Paul, Charles writes: "From the evidence presently to be adduced, it will be clear that St. Paul was thoroughly familiar with the Greek translation of the Testaments."[7] In two instances, 1 Thess 2:16/*T. Levi* 6:11 and Rom 1:32/*T. Asher* 6:2, he speaks of direct quotations from the *Testaments*.

Before 1884, when F. Schnapp returned to the thesis of J. E. Grabe, the editor of the *editio princeps* (1698), that the *Testaments* were originally Jewish but had been interpolated by a Christian (and won the day), many scholars treated this writing as a Christian document.[8] They, too, paid attention to the parallels with the New Testament writings, trying to establish which of those had influenced the authors of the *Testaments* in particular. There was a lot of discussion on the question whether the *Testaments* should be regarded as a product of Jewish Christianity (Ebionite or Nazarene) or as belonging to Pauline Christianity.[9] One of the authors belonging to the pre-Schnapp period, J. M. Vorstman, whose Leiden dissertation *Disquisitio de Testamentis XII Patriarcharum Origine et Pretio* of 1857[10] has played only a modest role in subsequent discussions (no doubt because of its limited circulation), devoted a considerable part of his book to the subject "De Testamentorum XII Patriarcharum pretio in interpretatione librorum N.F." (pp. 101–78), and to this we now turn.

Vorstman lists "loquendi formulas, quae, observatione dignissimae, et in N.T. et apud Testamentorum auctorem inveniuntur." He mentions twenty-four passages in Matthew, three in Mark, sixteen in Luke, nine in John, three in Acts, fifty-three in the Pauline epistles and the Deutero-Pauline writings, four in Hebrews, nineteen in the Catholic Epistles (four in James, seven in the Johannine epistles mentioned under a separate heading) and, finally, six in the Apocalypse (pp. 101–47). He adds a list of *hapax legomena* and very

---

7. Charles, *Greek Versions*, lxxxv. Charles not only assumes that the Greek was translated from the Hebrew but also that the two families of the Greek text which he distinguishes go back to two different versions of a Hebrew text—a highly speculative theory. On the question whether the *Testaments* were translated from Hebrew or Aramaic, see H. W. Hollander and M. de Jonge, *The Testaments of the Twelve Patriarchs: A Commentary* (SVTP 8; Leiden: Brill, 1985) 27–29 (hereafter cited as *Commentary*).

8. F. Schnapp, *Die Testamente der Zwölf Patriarchen* (Halle: Max Niemeyer, 1884).

9. See H. Dixon Slingerland, *The Testaments of the Twelve Patriarchs: A Critical History of Research* (SBLMS 21; Missoula, Mont.: Scholars Press, 1971), particularly chapter 2: "The Testaments of the Twelve Patriarchs from the Beginning of Research until 1884" (pp. 5–18).

10. Published by P. C. Hoog, Rotterdam. On Vorstman's place in contemporary research, see W. A. van Hengel, "De Testamenten der Twaalf Patriarchen op nieuw ter sprake gebracht," *Godgeleerde Bijdragen* 34 (1860) 881–970. In this article van Hengel (1779–1871), who was professor of New Testament at Leiden from 1827 to 1849, gives a detailed review of Vorstman's book, interspersed with many observations of his own, clearly the result of extended study of the *Testaments*.

rare words in the New Testament which are also found in the *Testaments* (pp. 147–68), and concludes with a list of grammatical observations on a number of expressions found in the New Testament writings as well as in the *Testaments* (pp. 168–78). Notwithstanding the wealth of parallels adduced, Vorstman does not think literary dependence of the *Testaments* on any of the writings of the New Testament can be proved, except in the case of 1 Thess 2:16/*T. Levi* 6:11, which he discusses at some length (p. 146, cf. pp. 22–26).

The limitation of references in the margin of N.-A.[26] remains difficult to explain, because the suggested parallels are of the same nature as those found in the lists given by Charles and Vorstman. Between Charles and Vorstman there is only a limited overlap; fourteen of Charles's thirty-eight Pauline and Deutero-Pauline passages, for instance, figure in Vorstman's list.[11] Apart from the basic disagreement on the question whether the *Testaments* were influenced by the writings of the New Testament or vice versa, there is clearly difference of opinion on the degree of agreement in terminology and ideas required to make it worthwhile to list the instance concerned in a list of parallels.

The aim of the present paper is to illustrate the most important issues raised by consideration of Paul and the *Testaments of the Twelve Patriarchs* by means of a discussion of the limited selection of parallels found in the margins of the epistles of Paul in N.-A.[26] I shall, however, also have to say something about Rom 1:32/*T. Asher* 6:2 (important to Charles); 1 Thess 2:16/*T. Levi* 6:11 (important to Charles and Vorstman); and about *T. Benj.* 11, a passage in the *Testaments* referring to the apostle Paul, who was a Benjaminite, as he tells us in Phil 3:5.

As is well known, the discussion on the provenance and the literary history of the *Testaments* has by no means led to universally accepted conclusions. Forty years ago I defended the thesis that the *Testaments* were a Christian composition using a great variety of Jewish material.[12] In later years I became more cautious. In 1985 I wrote: "We are not able to prove that the *Testaments* were composed in Christian circles in the second half of the second century; they may also be the outcome of a thorough and to a considerable degree consistent redaction of an earlier Jewish writing. But it is extremely difficult to find convincing proof for the existence of such a document, nor are we in a position to determine its contents."[13] Others have continued in the footsteps of Schnapp and Charles and distinguished

11. Among them the three passages mentioned in n. 7. The N.-A.[26] margin and Vorstman also agree in the case of Rom 1:4 and 5:4.

12. M. de Jonge, *The Testaments of the Twelve Patriarchs: A Study of their Text, Composition and Origin* (Assen: Van Gorcum, 1953; 2nd ed. 1975).

13. M. de Jonge, "The Testaments of the Twelve Patriarchs: Christian and Jewish. A hundred years after Friedrich Schnapp," *NedTTs* 39 (1985) 265–75—now in M. de Jonge, *Jewish Eschatology, Early Christian Christology and the Testaments of the Twelve Patriarchs: Collected Essays* (NovTSup 63; Leiden: Brill, 1991) 233–43. The quotation is from p. 273 (*Collected Essays*, 241).

between different Jewish stages in the history of the composition of the *Testaments*, as well as a more or less protracted stage of Christian interpolation/redaction—without, however, reaching any significant degree of agreement.[14] For obvious reasons the wider ramifications of this problem cannot be dealt with here, but in the discussion of the individual parallels various aspects of it will be touched upon.

THE CASE FOR PARALLELS

A. In a number of cases, found in parenetic passages, we find the use of similar notions and expressions.

1. In Rom 1:26 Paul uses the expression πάθη ἀτιμίας ("degrading passions" NRSV). A comparable (but not identical) use of πάθος with a genitive is found in *T. Jos.* 7:8: "For when someone has submitted to the passion of an evil desire (πάθει . . . ἐπιθυμίας πονηρᾶς)."[15] In fact, "being a slave of two passions (πάθη) contrary to the commandments of God" one "cannot obey God" (*T. Jud.* 18:6). Passions and sins are closely connected (cf. *T. Jos.* 3:10 with 7:8, and *T. Asher* 3:2 with *T. Jud.* 18:6).

2. In Rom 2:15 Paul speaks about the function of conscience. "They show that what the law requires is written on their hearts, to which their own conscience also bears witness (συμμαρτυρούσης αὐτῶν τῆς συνειδήσεως)." Here Nestle-Aland's margin refers to the only instance of συνείδησις in the *Testaments*, *T. Reub.* 4:3: "even until now my conscience presses me hard on account of my sin." In two other passages in the *Testaments* the expression "his own heart" is used (*T. Jud.* 20:5; *T. Gad* 5:3) with a comparable meaning.

3. In Rom 2:17–24 Paul reproaches the Jews, instructed in the law and relying on their relation to God, for not practicing what they teach; they are no longer a guide to the blind nor a light to those who are in darkness. Here at v. 22 Nestle-Aland's margin mentions *T. Levi* 14:4: "What will all the Gentiles do, if you are darkened through ungodliness and bring a curse upon our

14. See J. Becker, *Untersuchungen zur Entstehungsgeschichte der Testamente der Zwölf Patriarchen* (AGJU 8; Leiden: Brill, 1970); A. Hultgård, *L'eschatologie des Testaments des Douze Patriarches I-II* (Acta Univ. Uppsaliensis, Hist. Rel. 6–7; Uppsala: Almqvist & Wiksell, 1977–1982); and, recently, J. H. Ulrichsen, *Die Grundschrift der Testamente der Zwölf Patriarchen: Eine Untersuchung zu Umfang, Inhalt und Eigenart der ursprünglichen Schrift* (Acta Univ. Uppsaliensis, Hist. Rel. 10; Uppsala, 1991).

15. Here, and elsewhere, my edition mentioned in n. 6 has been used. The translations have been taken from H. W. Hollander and M. de Jonge, *The Testaments of the Twelve Patriarchs: A Commentary*. For comments on the oldest attainable text of the *Testaments*, see this commentary, the introduction to the edition, and a number of detailed articles in M. de Jonge, ed., *Studies on the Testaments of the Twelve Patriarchs: Text and Interpretation* (SVTP 3; Leiden: Brill, 1975), esp. pp. 45–179 (hereafter cited as *Studies*). In a considerable number of instances differences in interpretation go back to different decisions in textual matters.

race. . . ." Levi's reproach to his offspring resembles that of Paul, but it is expressed differently.[16]

4. In Rom 5:3–4 Paul tells his readers that "suffering produces endurance (ὑπομονή), and endurance produces character (δοκιμή) and character produces hope." Here we are referred to a number of other New Testament texts (among which Jas 1:2–4), as well as to *T. Jos.* 10:1. In this testament Joseph concludes the elaborate story about his temptations and sufferings because of Potiphar's wife in chapters 3–9 with a disquisition in 10:1–4 which begins with the words: "You see, therefore, my children, how great things patience (ὑπομονή) works and prayer with fasting."[17] In addition, the second story about Joseph's troubles in 11:2–16:6 is followed by a reference to his patience and endurance in 17:1: "You see, children, how great things I endured, that I should not put my brothers to shame." Both ὑπομονή and μακροθυμία are central virtues in this testament (see also 2:7: "In ten temptations he [God] showed that I was approved [δόκιμος] and in all of them I endured [ἐμακροθύμησα], for endurance [μακροθυμία] is a mighty remedy, and patience [ὑπομονή] gives many good things").[18]

5. In 1 Cor 6:18 we find the exhortation φεύγετε τὴν πορνείαν ("shun fornication") which is also found in *T. Reub.* 5:5.[19] Comparable expressions are "that you may flee hatred and cleave to the love of the Lord" in *T. Gad* 5:2 and "flee the malice of Beliar" in *T. Benj.* 7:1 (cf. also *T. Benj.* 8:1; *T. Ash.* 3:2). The opposite is ἐγγίζετε δὲ τῷ θεῷ ("draw near to God") in *T. Dan* 6:2;[20] this verse is therefore mentioned in Nestle-Aland's margin at Jas 4:8, "draw near to God, and he will draw near to you." This follows on v. 7, "submit yourselves to God. Resist the devil and he will flee from you," where *T. Napht.* 8:4 is referred to, which reads "and the devil will flee from you and the wild beasts will flee from you and the Lord will love you, and the angels will cleave to you." Wherever God's commandments are obeyed, Beliar and evil spirits will flee (*T. Iss.* 7:7; *T. Dan* 5:1; *T. Benj.* 5:2; cf. 3:3–5). In the end Beliar

16. In their present form and context *T. Levi* 10, 14–15 and 16 are clearly directed against Israel's priestly leaders who opposed Jesus Christ (see *Commentary*; idem, "Levi, the sons of Levi and the Law in Testament Levi X, XIV–XV and XVI," originally published in *Mélanges Cazelles* (1981) and now in my *Collected Essays*, 180–90. One may note that MSS chij in *T. Levi* 14:4 characterize the Gentiles as "living in blindness" (cf. Rom 2:19).

17. For the combination of ὑπομονή ("endurance, patience") and prayer, see also Rom 12:12: "rejoice in hope, be patient in suffering, persevere in prayer."

18. For further details, see the introduction to *T. Joseph* in *Commentary*, 362–65.

19. See now also B. S. Rosner, "A Possible Quotation of *Test. Reuben* 5:5 in 1 Corinthians 6:18A," *JTS* n.s. 43 (1992) 123–27. Rosner finds similarities (in thought) also between *T. Jos.* 10:1–3 and 1 Cor 6:19, and *T. Jos.* 8:5 and 1 Cor 6:20.

20. Compare the (vain) declaration of the Egyptian woman in *T. Jos.* 6:7: "I do not come near to idols but to the Lord alone" and the characterization of πορνεία in *T. Reub.* 4:6 as "separating it (the soul) from God and bringing it near to the idols," and *T. Sim.* 5:3, "separating from God and bringing near to Beliar." See also the note on *T. Reub.* 4:6 in *Commentary*, 100.

and all evil spirits will be destroyed completely (*T. Sim.* 6:6; *T. Levi* 3:3; 18:12; *T. Jud.* 25:3; *T. Zeb.* 9:8). Concerning God: Dan admonishes his sons to keep his commandments "that the Lord may dwell in you and the devil may flee from you (*T. Dan* 5:1; cf. *T. Jos.* 10:2–3; *T. Benj.* 6:4[21]). In fact, "you will be in peace having the God of peace, and no war will prevail over you" (*T. Dan* 5:2). Further, in the eschatological future God will be near those who obey him (*T. Dan* 5:13; *T. Iss.* 7:7; *T. Zeb.* 8:2; *T. Napht.* 8:3).

6. *T. Dan* 5:2, just quoted, is mentioned in the margin of Rom 15:33, "the God of peace will be with all of you." Interestingly the expression ὁ θεὸς τῆς εἰρήνης is found only in this passage in the *Testaments* and in several places in Paul, as a somewhat solemn expression used in blessings, assurances, and wishes (see Rom 16:20; 1 Cor 14:33; 2 Cor 13:11; Phil 4:9; 1 Thess 5:23; cf. also 2 Thess 3:16 ["the Lord of peace"] and Heb 13:20).[22] *T. Dan* 5:2 combines an exhortation with an assurance and thus is nearest to 2 Cor 13:11 and Phil 4:9.[23] In the *Testaments* we find also the expression "the angel of peace" (ὁ ἄγγελος τῆς εἰρήνης). His functions are to conduct Israel and to protect it against falling into the extremity of evils (*T. Dan* 6:5, cf. v. 2); to guide the soul of the good man (*T. Benj.* 6:1); and to comfort with life the man who dies quietly and in joy (*T. Ash.* 6:5–6). Here we may point to Rom 16:20: "The God of peace will shortly crush Satan under your feet."

7. Also, in the last instance to be mentioned in this section there is a particularly close connection between the New Testament text and a passage in the *Testaments*. In Rom 12:21 Paul exhorts his readers: "Do not be overcome with evil, but overcome evil with good (νίκα ἐν ἀγαθῷ τὸ κακόν)." With this corresponds *T. Benj.* 4:3, which says about the good man "by doing good he overcomes the evil (οὗτος ἀγαθοποιῶν νικᾷ τὸ κακόν), because he is shielded by the good"; comparable notions are found in *T. Benj.* 5:2, 4 and *T. Jos.* 18:2 (the good man is modeled on Joseph), but *T. Benj.* 4:3 gives the nearest parallel to the Pauline expression.[24] Hence, it figures prominently in the commentaries on Rom 12:21, which mention hardly any further parallels.[25]

How do we explain these similarities in thought and diction between Paul (and James) and the *Testaments?* With regard to the exhortations of the *Testaments*, it should be noticed that they contain little that is distinctively

21. See *Commentary*, 428, note on *T. Benj.* 6:4.

22. See G. Delling, "Die Bedeutung 'Gott des Friedens' und ähnliche Wendungen in den Paulusbriefen," in *Jesus und Paulus: Festschrift für W. G. Kümmel zum 70. Geburtstag* (ed. E. E. Ellis and E. Grässer; Göttingen: Vandenhoeck & Ruprecht, 1975) 76–84. There is no Old Testament equivalent, but see Num 6:26; Judg 6:24.

23. So Delling, "Bedeutung," 80; he also points to Amos 5:14 and 1 Kgs 11:38. Compare also *Herm. Sim.* 9.32,2: "The Lord dwells among men who love peace, for in truth peace is dear to him" (Dominus habitat in viris amantibus pacem, ei enimvero pax cara est).

24. See also *T. Gad* 6–7, an elaboration of Lev 19:17–18.

25. *Commentary* (p. 423 on *T. Benj.* 4:2) points to Hippolytus, *Haer.* 9.23 describing the Essenes: μηδένα δὲ μήτε ἀδικοῦντα μήτε ἐχθρὸν μισήσειν, προσεύχεσθαι δὲ ὑπὲρ αὐτῶν ("and show hatred neither to any wrongdoer nor enemy but offer prayers on their behalf").

Jewish or Christian. They obviously want to teach what is universally good and to warn against vices which all persons, Jews and non-Jews, Christians and non-Christians should abhor. They testify to the continuity in ethical thought between Hellenistic-Jewish and early Christian circles and, given the fact that they have come down to us in a heavily redacted form, we can never be sure of the actual provenance of the wording of individual sayings.[26] It is quite possible, and even probable, that the close agreements between Paul and the *Testaments* in the last two cases point to influence of early Christian ideas and diction on the *Testaments* in their present form— but even this cannot be maintained with absolute certainty.

B. We now proceed to a number of nonparenetic passages. In four cases in Paul (and one in Hebrews) Nestle-Aland[26] mentions parallels from the *Testament of Levi*. This testament is different from the other eleven, insofar as it contains much specific material. It has long been noticed that parallels to this material are found in Aramaic fragments found (first) in the Cairo Genizah and (later) at Qumran, as well as Greek additions to MS Athos, Koutloumous 39 (=e) of the *Testaments*.[27] The nature of the relationship between these fragments and the present *T. Levi* is a matter of dispute, but to me it is clear that *T. Levi* "represents an abbreviated and heavily redacted version of the Levi-material, preserved in the various fragments of *Ar. Levi*."[28] The references in Nestle-Aland are, unfortunately, to two passages to which no Aramaic or Greek parallels are extant, chapter 18, the announcement of a new priest, and chapters 2–3, the description of a heavenly journey of the

26. See my essays "Die Paränese in den Schriften des Neuen Testaments und in den Testamenten der Zwölf Patriarchen," in *Collected Essays*, 277–89 (originally in Festschrift Schnackenburg, 1989) and "Rachel's Virtuous Behavior in the Testament of Issachar," in *Collected Essays*, 301–13 (originally in Festschrift Malherbe, 1990). See also "The Pre-Mosaic Servants of God in the Testaments of the Twelve Patriarchs and in the Writings of Justin and Irenaeus," in *Collected Essays*, 263–76 (originally in *VC* 39 [1985] 157–70), and also H. W. Hollander, *Joseph as an Ethical Model in the Testaments of the Twelve Patriarchs* (SVTP 6; Leiden: Brill, 1981).

Rosner sees no reason to assume that *Testament of Reuben* is a later interpolation influenced by Paul ("Possible Quotation," 124): hence, there are, according to him, two possible explanations for the parallels concerned. Either "the Testaments of the Twelve Patriarchs witnesses to a traditional interpretation of Gen. 39 which also influenced Paul" or "Paul was in 1 Cor 6:18a directly dependent on *Test. Reuben* 5:5, a text to which he was drawn because of the Twelve Patriarchs' effective use of Joseph, a stock biblical character, in its warnings against πορνεία" (p. 127). Rosner favors the second option. Those who dismiss the simplistic theory of the *Testaments* as a Jewish document interpolated by Christians and stress the continuity in ethical thought between Hellenistic Judaism and Christianity will explain the similarities noted by Rosner as dependent on common traditional interpretation. Rosner himself interestingly refers to the fact that Gregory of Nyssa in a homily on 1 Cor 6:18 uses Gen 39:11–14 as its major illustration.

27. See my "The Testament of Levi and 'Aramaic Levi,'" in *Collected Essays*, 244–56 (originally published in *Mémorial Jean Carmignac* = *RevQ* 13 [1988]) and, earlier, "Notes on Testament of Levi II–VII," in *Studies*, 247–60 (originally in *Festschrift M. A. Beek*, 1974), as well as the essay mentioned in n. 15.

28. *Collected Essays*, 253.

patriarch. Consequently there is considerable difference of opinion among scholars concerning the amount of redaction, especially Christian redaction, in the present text of these chapters.

1. At Rom 1:4, "declared to be Son of God with power according to the spirit of holiness (κατὰ πνεῦμα ἁγιωσύνης) by resurrection of the dead," the reader is referred to *T. Levi* 18:7: "And the spirit of understanding and sanctification (ἁγιασμοῦ) will rest upon him (=the new priest) in the water." Other commentators have pointed to v. 11, where this new priest is said to "give to the saints to eat from the tree of life, and the spirit of holiness (πνεῦμα ἁγιωσύνης) will be upon them." *T. Levi* 18:6–7 and its counterpart *T. Jud.* 24:2 are clearly influenced by the story of Jesus' baptism in the Gospels. In both passages the savior figure not only receives the Spirit of God, but also gives it to those who put their trust in him (*T. Jud.* 24:2: "and he will pour out the spirit of grace upon you").

In fact, whatever text may lie behind *T. Levi* 18, in its present form it has undergone heavy Christian redaction, just as *T. Judah* 24. One should note that, although Levi, as priest, occupies a central position in Israel, his priesthood is limited (5:2); he "will proclaim concerning him who will redeem Israel" (2:10) and he has to instruct his sons concerning Jesus Christ (4:5). It is against Jesus that Levi's sons will sin (see 4:4–6 and the sin-exile-return passages in chapters 10, 14–15 and 16).[29] Also *T. Levi* 18 follows on a sin-exile-return passage in 17:8–10: 17:11 mentions new priestly sins and 18:1 new divine punishment. Next 18:2 announces: "Then the Lord will raise a new priest to whom all the words of God will be revealed." Nowhere is it stated that he will be a levitical priest, whereas the parallel passage in *T. Judah* 24 declares that the one who will receive "the blessing of the spirit of the Holy Father" will arise from Judah's seed.

As commentaries on Romans do not fail to notice, the expression πνεῦμα ἁγιωσύνης occurs only in Rom 1:4 and *T. Levi* 18:11. In view of the heavy Christian redaction in this chapter, it is probable that the diction of *T. Levi* 18:11 was influenced by that of Rom 1:4, and not the other way around.[30]

2. Paul's mention in 2 Cor 12:2 of his being caught up to the third heaven has been compared by many exegetes to the description of the heavens seen by Levi on his heavenly journey in *T. Levi* 2–3; hence *T. Levi* 2 figures in Nestle-Aland's margin at this verse. The corresponding Aramaic fragment speaks about a vision of heaven(s) but breaks off before giving any details. The majority of Greek manuscripts give a complicated picture of seven

29. See *Commentary*, Introduction 7.2.1 (pp. 53–56) for a full survey and a characteristic of these passages.

30. Another part of the description of the blessings granted by the new priest, "during his priesthood all sin will fail" (*T. Levi* 18:9), is referred to in the margin of Heb 9:26: "he has appeared once and for all at the end of the age to remove sin by the sacrifice of himself." It should be noted that *T. Levi* 18 does not connect the new priesthood with any sort of sacrifice or with the self-sacrifice of the new priest.

(three plus four) heavens, both in 2:7–9 and, in far more detail, in chapter 3. This text is difficult and probably the result of a complicated process of redaction, but it is internally consistent. Manuscripts *(n)chij* reduce the number of heavens to three in 2:7–9, as well as in 3:1–4; (another?) three heavens are described in 3:5–8, but the connection between these and the ones previously mentioned is not clear in this group of manuscripts. Elsewhere I have argued in favor of the theory that the *(n)chij* text is secondary compared to that found in the other manuscripts.[31] Moreover, if the *stemma codicum*, painstakingly constructed during the preparation of the Leiden edition of 1978 and consistently applied during the reconstruction of the oldest attainable text, is taken seriously, no reading found in *nchij* alone can be regarded as representing the oldest text.

Other scholars, from R. H. Charles (who held *chi* in high esteem) to J. H. Ulrichsen,[32] favor the *chij* reading in 2:7–9 and regard it as nearer to the original text behind the complicated picture in *T. Levi* 2–3 than the text found in the other manuscripts. In my opinion, however, the reference to *T. Levi* 2 in commentaries on 2 Corinthians[33] and in Nestle-Aland's margin, is to a late, secondary version of this passage.

3. The second heaven described in *T. Levi* 3:2 is said to contain "fire, snow and ice ready for the day of the ordinance of the Lord in the righteous judgment of God (εἰς ἡμέραν προστάγματος κυρίου ἐν τῇ δικαιοκρισίᾳ τοῦ θεοῦ)." This text is mentioned in the margin of Rom 2:5, "you are storing up wrath for yourself on the day of wrath, when God's righteous judgment will be revealed (ἐν ἡμέρᾳ ὀργῆς καὶ ἀποκαλύψεως δικαιοκρισίας τοῦ θεοῦ)." Clearly, the use of the word δικαιοκρισία in both texts in connection with the last judgment,[34] is regarded as being of some significance, but this parallel does not enable us to draw any conclusions about the relationship between Paul and the *Testaments*.

4. In Rom 12:1 Paul exhorts his brothers "to present your bodies as a living sacrifice (θυσίαν), holy and acceptable to God, which is your spiritual worship (τὴν λογικὴν λατρείαν ὑμῶν)." To this corresponds the description of the angels of the presence of the Lord in *T. Levi* 3:(5–)6 who "offer to the Lord a pleasant odour, a reasonable and bloodless offering (λογικὴν καὶ ἀναιμάκτον προσφοράν)." Here the dependence is clearly on the part of *T. Levi*, for the combination of terms found there is quite common in early Christian texts.[35]

---

31. See *Studies*, 248–51.

32. Ulrichsen, *Grundschrift*, 190–92.

33. So still V. P. Furnish, *II Corinthians* (AB 32A; Garden City, N.Y.: Doubleday, 1984) 525.

34. It is also used in *T. Levi* 15:2, and compare 2 Thess 1:5: ἔνδειγμα τῆς δικαίας κρίσεως τοῦ θεοῦ ("evidence of the righteous judgment of God"). On the use of δικαιοκρίτης ("righteous judge") for God, see *Commentary*, 137 on *T. Levi* 3:2 (add there *Sib. Or.* 3:704).

35. See *Commentary*, 138, note on *T. Levi* 3:6.

5. The last Pauline passage with a parallel in the *Testaments* mentioned in Nestle-Aland[26] is Rom 11:25–26, a crucial text in Paul's argument concerning God's relation to Israel and the Gentiles.[36] Paul writes: "I want you to understand this mystery: a hardening has come upon part of Israel, until the full number of the Gentiles has come in. And so all Israel will be saved (καὶ οὕτως πᾶς Ἰσραὴλ σωθήσεται)." Here Nestle-Aland's margin mentions "Test Seb fin" without specifying the exact verse. E. Käsemann refers to *T. Zeb.* 9:6–9 and U. Wilckens to *T. Zeb.* 9:8, where he probably follows the longer text found in MSS *bkgldm*.[37]

T. Zeb. 9:5–7 forms one of the many sin-exile-return passages in the *Testaments*. On the return part of it in v. 7 follows a long, complicated and clearly Christian passage in v. 8, in which the clause "and he will convert all the nations to zeal for him (εἰς παραζήλωσιν αὐτοῦ) is of particular interest in view of Rom 11:25–26. One should note that it is followed by the prophecy of new sins and new punishment in v. 9, "And again through the wickedness of your words you will provoke him, and you will be cast away until the time of consummation (ἕως καιροῦ συντελείας)." At the time of consummation, as the next chapter tells us, the patriarch will rise in the midst of his sons, "as many as have kept the law of the Lord and the commandments of Zebulun their father" (*T. Zeb.* 10:2).

T. Zeb. 9:6–9 can be properly understood only if read alongside other passages in the *Testaments* where the sin-exile-return pattern is repeated, particularly *T. Asher* 7 and *T. Levi* 17:8–18:14 (mentioned above).[38] The present text of *T. Zebulun* 9 and 10 clearly represents a Christian view of the history of

36. In passing we have also briefly discussed the non–Pauline passages Heb 9:26; Jas 1:3; 4:7–8. The only other instance to be noted is the reference to *T. Jos.* 8:5 in the margin of Acts 16:23–25. Acts tells us how Paul and Silas in the prison of Philippi "were praying and singing hymns to God and the prisoners were listening to them." In *T. Jos.* 8:5 it is Joseph who sings hymns to the Lord in the prison of Pharaoh, and the Egyptian woman who listens to him. The agreements are general rather than particular. Vorstman remarks that ἐπακροᾶσθαι ("to listen or hearken to") used in Acts 16:25 is a *hapax legomenon* in the New Testament (*Disquisitio*, 115). So it is in the *Testaments*, but this fact is hardly sufficient to prove interdependence between the two texts mentioned.

37. Käsemann, *An die Römer*, 299–300, partly following a complicated and rather far-fetched theory by C. Müller about a tradition about a "Völkersturm" against Jerusalem/Israel, radically reinterpreted by Paul (see Müller, *Gottes Gerechtigkeit und Gottes Volk: Eine Untersuchung zu Römer 9-11* [FRLANT 86; Göttingen: Vandenhoeck & Ruprecht, 1964] 38–43). U. Wilckens, *Der Brief an die Römer* II (EKK VI/2; Zurich, Einsiedeln, and Cologne: Benziger; Neukirchen-Vluyn: Neukirchener Verlag, 1980) 255, esp. n. 1145. He refers to the tradition of the "Völkerwallfahrt" to Sion.

On the much-debated question of the originality of the longer or the shorter text in *T. Zebulun* 5–9, see my "Textual Criticism and the Analysis of the Composition of the Testament of Zebulun," in *Studies*, 144–60, esp. 149–52. In this essay I argue in favor of the longer text found in MSS *bkgldm*.

38. On this see also my "The Future of Israel in the Testaments of the Twelve Patriarchs," in *Collected Essays*, 164–79 (earlier published in *JSJ* 17 [1986] 196–211).

Israel, ultimately dependent on views like that expressed by Paul in Romans 9–11. In fact, as I have tried to show elsewhere, in the *Testaments* "there is great concern for Israel's final salvation, and the definite promise that Israel will share in God's salvation if it obeys God's commandments and/or believes in Jesus Christ."[39] In *T. Benj.* 10:11, at the very end of the exhortations in the *Testaments*, the patriarch, after having remarked that Israel will be convicted through the chosen ones of the Gentiles (v. 10), concludes:

> But you, if you walk in holiness before the face of the Lord,
> you will again dwell safely with me
> and all Israel will be gathered together unto the Lord
> (καὶ συναχθήσεται πᾶς Ἰσραὴλ πρὸς κύριον).

OTHER CASES: QUESTIONS OF INFLUENCE

We now turn to the three passages in the *Testaments* listed above that are not mentioned by Nestle-Aland (*T. Asher* 6:2; *T. Levi* 6:11; *T. Benj.* 11) but were considered of some importance in earlier treatments of the relationship between Paul and the *Testaments*.

1. Charles's theory that in Rom 1:32 Paul quoted from *T. Ash.* 6:2 rests on an incorrect text-critical decision and a highly questionable conjecture. In *T. Ash.* 6:1–2 the patriarch's children are exhorted to keep the commandments of the Lord "with a single face (μονοπροσώπως), because people with a double face (οἱ διπρόσωποι[40]) receive a double punishment." Hence the exhortation: "Hate the spirits of deceit which strive against men." The reason for this double punishment is not given, but a parallel in *Herm. Sim.* 9.18.2 helps us, which says: "but those who have knowledge of God . . . and act wickedly, will be punished doubly (δισσῶς κολασθήσονται)." Some scribes felt they had to clarify the issue by emending the text; after "double punishment" they added "for they both do the evil thing and have pleasure in them that do it" (see now MSS *dmeafchj*), a phrase reminiscent of that of Paul in Rom 1:32. In the present context it does not make any sense; also not if one reads the following clause as "following the example of the spirits of deceit" (with *eafchj*[41]). Even Charles is not happy with the longer version of the text as it stands. In his comments on this verse, both in his edition and in his commentary, he states that this is not a matter of double punishment but of double guilt. He therefore assumes a misreading of the Hebrew

---

39. De Jonge, "The Future of Israel," 178.

40. Μονοπρόσωπος corresponds with ἁπλοῦς ("single-minded, simple"), a prominent feature of good people in the *Testaments*; διπρόσωπος has two meanings, one negative (here, and in *T. Ash.* 3:1–2; 4:1) and one neutral, "having two aspects" (so in 2:2, 3, 5, 7, 8; 4:3, 4). See the introduction to *T. Asher* in *Commentary*, 338–41.

41. MSS *chj* continue with "and striving against humankind."

underlying the text[42] resulting in a wrong Greek translation. This high-handed dealing with the text results in the English translation, "For they that are double-faced are guilty of a twofold sin; for they both do the evil thing and they have pleasure in them that do it."

2. A very intriguing case is presented by the parallel between 1 Thess 2:16 and *T. Levi* 6:11, which, though not listed by Nestle-Aland, has received much, sometimes even detailed, attention in commentaries on 1 Thessalonians.[43] Paul, writing about the opposition of the Jews against the prophets, Jesus, and those sent out by him (including Paul preaching to the Gentiles) concludes: "Thus they have constantly been filling up the measure of their sins, but God's wrath has overtaken them forever" (1 Thess 2:16; NRSV marg.). The meaning of the last clause ἔφθασεν δὲ ἐπ᾽ αὐτοὺς ἡ ὀργὴ εἰς τέλος has been the subject of much discussion, but there is no doubt that it forms an integral part of the text. Paul follows here a pattern of thought used by him and other early Christians to explain Jesus' death as that of the final prophet sent by God to Israel and killed by the people—a horrible event calling for the eschatological judgment in the near future (compare also Mark 12:1–9 and Luke 11:49–51 par. Matt 23:34–36[Q]).[44]

In *T. Levi* 5–6 the last verse, 6:11, sums up why Levi and his brother Simeon had to kill the inhabitants of Shechem: "the wrath of God had come upon them, definitely (ἔφθασε δὲ ἡ ὀργὴ κυρίου ἐπ᾽ αὐτοὺς εἰς τέλος)."[45] This points back to 6:8, where Levi explains that he had to go against his father's wishes because he saw that "God's sentence upon Shechem was for evil." The inhabitants of that city had wanted to treat Sarah as they treated Dinah, and they had persecuted Abraham and maltreated other strangers (6:8–10). In fact, the whole episode in the *Testaments* starts with an express command to Levi to execute vengeance on Shechem because of Dinah (5:3), given by the angel who accompanied Levi on his heavenly journey. And, anticipating the story that follows, Levi tells his readers: "I destroyed (συνετέλεσα) the sons of Hamor at that time, as is written in the heavenly tables" (5:4). The angel identifies himself in v. 6 as "the angel who intercedes for the race of Israel that God will not smite them utterly, for every evil spirit attacks it." In

---

42. We should remember that he assumes that each of the two families of the Greek text which he distinguishes goes back to a Hebrew original (see n. 7).

43. See especially E. von Dobschütz, *Die Thessalonicher-Briefe* (MeyerK; 7th ed.; Göttingen: Vandenhoeck & Ruprecht, 1909; repr. with add. 1974) 115; and B. Rigaux, *Saint Paul: Les épîtres aux Thessaloniciens* (Ebib; Paris: Gabalda; Gembloux: Duculot, 1956) 455–56. A recent contribution to the discussion is found in T. Baarda, "The Shechem Episode in the Testament of Levi: A Comparison with Other Traditions," in *Sacred History and Sacred Texts in Early Judaism. A Symposium in Honour of A. S. van der Woude* (ed. J. N. Bremmer and F. Garcia Martínez; Kampen: Kok Pharos, 1992) 11–73, esp. 59–73.

44. On this see, for instance, my *Jesus: The Servant-Messiah* (New Haven: Yale University Press, 1991) 34–37.

45. In *T. Reub.* 4:4 the expression ἡ ὀργὴ κυρίου ("the wrath of God") is used for God's punishment of Reuben for his sin with Bilhah.

T. Dan 6:5 we read that "the angel of peace himself will strengthen Israel that it may not fall into the extremity of evils (εἰς τέλος κακῶν)." God may punish the children of Israel, but he will not allow them to be destroyed forever, like the inhabitants of Shechem, for whose sins there is no pardon (see also chapter 7). On this point this story in the *Testaments* is quite clear, and in keeping with what is found elsewhere.[46] Paul and other Christians, however, were so appalled by what their fellow Israelites had done to Jesus Christ (and were doing to those who preached the Gospel) that they interpreted this as the culmination of Israel's sins against God, bound to bring about a final and definitive judgment—on Israel.

How is the close relationship in thought and diction between 1 Thess 2:16 and *T. Levi* 6:11 to be explained? Direct dependence one way or the other is difficult to prove. Dependence on a common source would be possible, but already Vorstman, raising this possibility, added "quamvis fontem non possim indicare,"[47] and no one after him has been successful in finding one.[48] Do we, then, have to assume use of a current Jewish expression in similar contexts (but with a different application) by both Paul and the *Testaments?* This is possible, but the measure of agreement in terminology remains striking.[49] On the basis of what is found elsewhere I am inclined to think that the present wording of *T. Levi* 6:11 did indeed undergo influence from 1 Thess 2:1–16.[50]

3. The last passage to be discussed under this heading, *T. Benjamin* 11, follows immediately on *T. Benj.* 10:11 already mentioned above. When all the sons of Benjamin will dwell safely with their father, and all Israel will be gathered unto the Lord, says Benjamin,

> I shall no longer be called a ravening wolf on account of your ravages,
> but a worker of the Lord, distributing food
> to those who work that which is good;
> and there will arise from my seed in later times a beloved of the Lord,

---

46. See also Amos 9:8 LXX; 2 Chr 12:12; Ps 103 (102):9; Dan 3:34 LXX and Theod.; Jdt 7:30; Wis 16:5, 6.

47. Vorstman, *Disquisitio*, 23.

48. In his commentary on the text of this verse Charles follows H. Rönsch (in his *Das Buch der Jubiläen oder die kleine Genesis* [Leipzig: Fues's Verlag, 1874] 390–91 and, in more detail, in *ZWT* 18 [1875] 278–83) in assuming that *T. Levi* 6:11 and 1 Thess 2:16 go back to an (otherwise unattested) reading "and the wrath of God came upon them" in Gen 35:5.

49. Much attention has been given to variant readings in both texts, but I think that it is very difficult to prove that these are interrelated. We should note that the omission of *T. Levi* 6:11 in one branch of the Armenian version is due to the fact that the verse is defective in the rest of the Armenian witnesses; see M. E. Stone, *The Testament of Levi* (Jerusalem: St. James Press, 1969) 77.

50. Aramaic Levi fragments referring to the Shechem episode are extant, but unfortunately so defective that nothing can be said about an equivalent of the verse under discussion.

hearing his voice upon earth
and doing the pleasure of his will. (11:1–2a)

The first two lines allude to Gen 49:27 LXX; the first part refers to the sins of the Benjaminites (and of Israel as a whole); the second part to the preaching of the gospel among the Gentiles—clearly by the Benjaminite Paul,[51] who in the following lines is called "a beloved of the Lord" (cf. Deut 33:12), arising "from my seed in later times." This makes perfect sense in its present context.

There are significant textual variants. Manuscript *c* brings this passage in line with the other Levi-Judah passages at the end of a number of testaments[52] by reading in v. 2 "there will arise from the seed of Judah and Levi," and breaking off in the middle of this verse, continuing with a conventional report about the patriarch's death and burial. Manuscript *c* is clearly secondary here.[53] Next there is a very short text in the Armenian version (which omits many passages, particularly toward the end of the individual testaments, and even more so in the last testament, that of Benjamin). Scholars have argued in favor of progressive "christianization" of the short text represented by the Armenian. Why should the Armenian translator have omitted a reference to Paul? Perhaps because he wanted to shorten whatever text he had in front of him, or because this text had become mutilated by accident. In any case the Armenian passage is so short and so unexplicit, that it is difficult to see how the text in the Greek manuscripts could have arisen out of an original like the text now found in Armenian.[54]

The text of the Greek manuscripts (with the exception of *c*) continues in 11:2b–5 with a further description of Paul's activities. It cannot be discussed in detail, but three features call for some comment. First we find another allusion to Gen 49:27 LXX, when Paul is said to be "ravening from them (=Israel) like a wolf, and giving to the gathering of the Gentiles." The two parts of the verse from Genesis are no longer opposed to one another, but both refer here to actions of Paul.[55] Second, there is a clear reference to the Christian Holy Scriptures in general, and the book of Acts in particular, in

51. As (different) marginal notes in MSS *k, l,* and *d* explicate.

52. For a survey see *Commentary,* 56–61.

53. At the crucial point, the change of "from my seed" to "from the seed of Judah and Levi," *c* is not followed by the New Greek version, the only witness belonging to its group left at this stage.

54. For different points of view, see Becker, *Untersuchungen,* 49–51; A. Hultgård, *L'eschatologie,* 2:40, 235–36, 271–72; Ulrichsen, *Grundschrift,* 143; and my essay "The Greek Testaments of the Twelve Patriarchs and the Armenian Version," in *Studies,* 120–35, esp. p. 135 n. 56 (partly different from the treatment in my dissertation *A Study of Their Text, Composition and Origin,* 34).

55. On the early Christian interpretation of Gen 49:27 in its various forms—none of them entirely agreeing with the two found in the *Testaments* (see *Commentary,* 443, note on 11:2).

v. 4, where it is said that Paul "will be inscribed in the holy books, both his work and his word." The chapter ends with a reference to a word of Jacob concerning Paul, "He will supply the needs of your tribe"—using Pauline terminology (1 Cor 16:17; 2 Cor 9:12; 11:9; Phil 2:30; Col 1:24).

In view of the complexity of the chapter and the unevennesses in it, we may not exclude that the present text is the result of a process of redaction—which we can no longer unravel—during which new features were added. Already at the oldest stage, however, Paul, the Benjaminite, must have been mentioned as preacher to the Gentiles.

CONCLUSIONS

Looking back we may sum up:

1. The selection of passages from the *Testaments* in the margin of Nestle-Aland's 26th edition is very limited, and unevenly distributed. Yet inclusion in our investigation of the cases listed by Vorstman or Charles would not change our results and our conclusions.

2. Many parallels simply illustrate the continuity in content and diction between Hellenistic-Jewish and early Christian parenesis.

3. In cases where the *Testaments* reflect Christian ideas and terminology we cannot use them to illustrate the background of Paul or, indeed, other writers of books preserved in the New Testament. We will have to take seriously that the present *Testaments* are a Christian writing, transmitted in order to serve Christian needs.[56]

4. It should be borne in mind that also the great majority of the other so-called Pseudepigrapha of the Old Testament have come down to us exclusively through Christian channels; we shall have to take this fact into account when using parallels from these writings in interpreting the New Testament.

56. See my article "The Transmission of the Twelve Patriarchs by Christians," *VC* 47 (1993) 1–28.

CHAPTER 8

God's New Family in Thessalonica

Abraham J. Malherbe

FIRST THESSALONIANS has not impressed commentators for what it contributes to our understanding of Paul's view of the church. Such Pauline
images of the church as temple, field, and body are not used in the letter,
nor is the church's relationship with Christ of special interest.[1] If it is the
elaboration of such images or christological reflection that makes for a significant ecclesiology, then Paul indeed has not given much thought to the
nature of the church in this letter. I think the matter is otherwise and wish
to follow the lead of Wayne Meeks in examining the view of the church that
underlies Paul's exhortations in the letter.

We are all deeply in debt to Meeks for the light he has shed on the social
dimension of early Christianity, particularly of its Pauline wing, and I have
personally been enriched by a colleagueship that is now in its third decade.
Of special concern here is the interest he and his students have shown in
the household as the locus of Pauline churches, in matters of the family, and
in kinship language.[2] Exactly how these elements were related in Paul's
mind is still to be discovered, but already Meeks and his students have made
it possible for us to see more clearly how Paul's theology was inextricably
related to social reality, both his own and that of his churches. This, I wish to

1. The most extensive treatment of the ecclesiology of 1 Thessalonians of which I am aware
is R. F. Collins, "The Church of the Thessalonians," in idem, *Studies on the First Letter to the Thessalonians* (BETL 66; Leuven: University Press/Peeters, 1984) 285–98.

2. On the household, see W. A. Meeks, *The First Urban Christians: The Social World of the Apos-
tle Paul* (New Haven: Yale University Press, 1983) 75–77; idem, *The Moral World of the First
Christians* (Library of Early Christianity 6; Philadelphia: Westminster, 1986) 110–13; L. M.
White, *Building God's House in the Roman World: Architectural Adaptation among Pagans, Jews, and
Christians* (Baltimore: Johns Hopkins University Press, 1990). On the family, see O. L.
Yarbrough, *Not Like the Gentiles: Marriage Rules in the Letters of Paul* (SBLDS 80; Atlanta: Schol-
ars Press, 1985). On kinship language, see Meeks, *First Urban Christians*, 48–51.

argue, is the case in Paul's first letter to his converts in Thessalonica, whom Meeks calls "this new 'family of God.'"[3]

Paul appears in this letter in the first instance to be engaged in pastoral care rather than doing theology. He clearly has in view a group of recent converts from paganism who need direction on various aspects of the Christian life. In providing that direction, Paul stresses his relationship with them and on the basis of that relationship addresses their problems. Yet, in doing so, he emphasizes corporate dimensions of the faith which betray a particular view of the church. In what follows, I wish to show that a coherent view of the church, as the family of God, underlies his practical thinking in this pastoral letter.

THE FAMILY CREATED BY GOD

Throughout the letter, Paul stresses God's initiative and continuing activity. Paul knows that the Thessalonians, loved by God, were elected from the way in which they accepted the gospel (1:4–5). While Paul initially describes that gospel as "our gospel" (1:5), when he deals at greater length with his ministry, he is careful to specify that it is God's gospel (2:2, 4, 8, 9) with which he has been entrusted (2:4). He had been empowered by God to proclaim the gospel (2:2), and when he did so the gospel came to his hearers with dynamic force, the Holy Spirit and full conviction (1:5). Those who received the gospel received it not as human discourse but as what it truly is, God's word, which continues to be at work in them (2:13). Paul is thus at great pains to describe the founding of the Thessalonian church as a creation by God through the preaching of God's word.

The interest in God's creative work was also represented, but in a different way, in the initial message that Paul had preached in Thessalonica. Referring to that message in 1:9–10, Paul describes the God to whom the Thessalonians had converted from idols as θεὸς ζῶν καὶ ἀληθινός ("living and true God").[4] The description of God as θεὸς ζῶν ("living God") appears frequently in sources that reflect Hellenistic-Jewish propaganda to Gentiles, where it refers to God as the creator of the universe. It does so, for example, in Bel and the Dragon 5Θ, οὐ σέβομαι εἴδωλα χειροποίητα, ἀλλὰ τὸν ζῶντα θεὸν τὸν κτίσαντα τὸν οὐρανὸν καὶ τὴν γῆν ("I do not worship handmade idols, but the living God who created heaven and earth").[5] This

---

3. Meeks, *Moral World*, 129.

4. What follows is elaborated in a Yale Ph.D. dissertation by Mark Goodwin, "Conversion to the Living God in Diaspora Judaism and Paul's Letters" (1992). See also C. Bussmann, *Themen der paulinischen Missionspredigt auf dem Hintergrund des spätjüdisch-hellenistischen Missionsliteratur* (Bern: Herbert Lang, 1979). That 1 Thess 1:9–10 reflects Christian preaching to pagans, heavily informed by Jewish precedents, is now generally accepted. See T. Holtz, *Der erste Brief an die Thessalonicher* (EKK 13; Zurich: Benziger, 1986) 53–62.

5. See also Sir 18:1; *1 Enoch* 5; *Sib. Or.* 3:763; *Joseph and Aseneth* 8:5–6.

usage is also seen in Acts 14:15, where Paul and Barnabas urge the Lycaoni-ans ἐπιστρέφειν ἐπὶ θεὸν ζῶντα ὃς ἐποίησεν τὸν οὐρανὸν καὶ τὴν γῆν καὶ τὴν θάλασσαν καὶ πάντα τὰ ἐν αὐτοῖς ("to turn to the living God, who made heaven and earth and sea and everything in them").

The matter calls for further study, but it may already be observed that Paul in 2 Cor 3:3 uses this description of God when referring to the conver-sion of the Corinthians πνεύματι θεοῦ ζῶντος ("with the Spirit of the living God"). Also noteworthy is the complex of ideas in 2 Cor 6:16–18, where a contrast is drawn between Christians, who are ναὸς θεοῦ . . . ζῶντος ("a temple of the living God"), and idols. To confirm this contrast, Paul quotes a pastiche of Old Testament passages to describe God's offer to create a new people from among the unclean, from whom they should separate, and con-cludes with an allusion to Hos 2:1 LXX: καὶ ἔσομαι ὑμῖν εἰς πατέρα, καὶ ὑμεῖς ἔσεσθέ μοι εἰς υἱοὺς καὶ θυγατέρας, λέγει κύριος παντοκράτωρ ("And I will be a father to you, and you shall be my sons and daughters, says the Lord Almighty"). The same combination of ideas appears in Rom 9:24–25, Paul's claim that God had called vessels of mercy from among Gentiles as well as Jews, in support of which he combines and modifies Hos 2:1 and 2:25: "Those who are not my people I will call 'my people,' and her who was not beloved I will call 'my beloved.' And in the very place where it was said to them, 'You are not my people,' they will be called sons of the living God (υἱοὶ θεοῦ ζῶντος)."[6] To speak of the conversion of Gentiles, Paul here uses language used formerly of the return of apostatized Israel to God. It is important for Paul that God called the Gentiles because he loved them. Accordingly, he changes Hos 2:25 LXX, ἐλεήσω τὴν οὐκ ἠλεημένην καὶ ἐρῶ τῷ οὐ λαῷ μου λαός μου εἶ σύ ("I will show mercy to her who received no mercy and will say to those who were not my people, 'You are my people'"), to have it speak of God's love rather than God's mercy.[7]

These passages show that Paul thought of the God of creation as calling Gentiles into a new relationship with himself in which he would be their father and they his beloved children. This, according to 1 Thessalonians 1 and 2, God had accomplished through Paul's preaching of the gospel. The new relationships effected by the gospel are central to Paul's understanding of the church in Thessalonica, but before exploring that subject, a little more needs to be said about the notion of God as father. God is, of course, the father of Jesus Christ (1:10). It was also natural that, since a father was

6. For Paul's use and modification of Hosea, see Goodwin, "Conversion to the Living God," 12–15. Hosea also appears in *Jub.* 1:25, "And I shall be a father to them, and they will be sons to me. And they will all be called 'sons of the living God.' And every angel and spirit will know and acknowledge that they are my sons and I am their father in uprightness and righteous-ness. And I shall love them."

7. E. Pax has pointed out that proselytes to Judaism were described by the rabbis as being "loved by God" ("Beobachtungen zur Konvertitensprache im ersten Thessalonicherbrief," *Studii Biblici Franciscani Analecta* 21[1971] 234–35).

viewed as progenitor, God as creator would be referred to as father. This is already so in Plato; and Philo, under Platonic, and especially Stoic, influence, uses πατήρ ("father") as his favorite term to describe God as creator.[8] It is evidently such thinking that is behind 1 Cor 8:6, a tradition in which God the father was described as creator and Jesus Christ the agent of creation: ἀλλ᾽ ἡμῖν εἷς θεὸς ὁ πατήρ, ἐξ οὗ τὰ πάντα καὶ ἡμεῖς εἰς αὐτόν, καὶ εἷς κύριος Ἰησοῦς Χριστός, δι᾽ οὗ τὰ πάντα καὶ ἡμεῖς δι᾽ αὐτοῦ ("yet for us there is one God, the Father, from whom are all things and for whom we exist, and one Lord Jesus Christ, through whom are all things and through whom we exist"). The term πατήρ ("father") applied to God thus carries for Paul a creative connotation: God the Father is creator of both the universe and the new relationship(s) into which he calls those he loves.[9]

This is the way, I suggest, we should understand 1:1, the only place in the letter where Paul refers to the Thessalonians as a church: τῇ ἐκκλησίᾳ Θεσσαλονικέων ἐν θεῷ πατρὶ καὶ κυρίῳ᾽ Ἰησοῦ Χριστῷ (to the church of the Thessalonians in God the Father and the Lord Jesus Christ"). The church, or better, the assembly in Thessalonica, is described in a manner unusual for Paul. In the first place, the *nomen gentilicum* ("Thessalonians") rather than its geographical location is used to describe the church.[10] Attention is thus drawn to members of the church rather than the church's location. In the second place, and more importantly, the assembly's relationship to God is described with a dative ἐν θεῷ πατρί ("in God the Father"). The practical reason for relating the church to God and Christ in this way may be to make clear to the recent converts that their assembly is different from others by virtue of its relationship to God. I propose, however, that an additional nuance is present: the dative here is instrumental, as it is in 2:12 (ἐπαρρησιασάμεθα ἐν τῷ θεῷ ἡμῶν, "we were emboldened by our God"), and Paul modifies ἐκκλησία ("church") in this way to remind his readers that their assembly exists due to God the Father's action. Paul nowhere else speaks of being "in God,"[11] but in the Stoically influenced Acts 17:28 he is made to speak about the creator as a god who is the ground of human existence: ἐν αὐτῷ . . . ζῶμεν καὶ κινούμεθα καὶ ἐσμέν ("in him we live and move and exist"). Acts 17 uses traditions from Hellenistic-Jewish propaganda, as Paul did in Thessalonica (1:9–10) and in Romans 1 and 2.[12] It is possible that Paul

---

8. E.g., Plato, *Timaeus* 28C, 37C; Philo, *Cher.* 44; *Migr. Abr.* 28.193, 194; *Op. Mundi* 45, 46; *Spec. Leg.* 1.41; 2.225. Cf. *Mart. Pol.* 19.2, πατὴρ παντοκράτωρ ("Almighty Father"). On God as father in Stoicism, see G. Schrenk, "πατήρ," *TDNT* 5:955–56; and see further H. Hommel, *Schöpfer und Erhalter: Studien zum Problem Christentum und Antike* (Berlin: Lettner, 1956) 122ff.

9. Note also the collocation of θεὸς ζῶν, πατήρ and παντοκράτωρ in 2 Cor 6:16–18.

10. Contrast, for example, "to all those in Rome" (Rom 1:7); "to the church of God in Corinth" (1 Cor 1:2); "to the churches of Galatia" (Gal 1:2).

11. But see Rom 2:17; 5:11.

12. For Romans 1 and 2, see E. Weber, *Die Beziehung von Röm. 1–3 zur Missionspraxis des Paulus* (BFCT 9,4; Gütersloh: Bertelsmann, 1905); H. Daxer, *Römer 1,18–2,10 im Verhältnis zur*

derived this description of God as Father who creates and sustains the church from such traditions, which were indebted to Stoicism. Paul's use of prepositional formulations, here ἐν θεῷ πατρί ("in God the Father"), may also show the Stoic influence that is also evident in 1 Cor 8:6 (cf. Rom 11:36).[13] In that case, he would be combining scriptural, Jewish, and philosophical traditions to present a view of the creator of the cosmos as father to the new community. A. D. Nock notes that, although on the pagan side such views as that of the creator as father originated with the philosophers, in time they came to be held by the masses, so that Christian preaching of God as Father would have been easily acceped by them.[14]

THE MEMBERS OF GOD'S FAMILY

1 Thessalonians does not provide information on how people responded to the preaching of this message, as, for example, Gal 3:26–4:6 does. There, using an early tradition according to which the convert at baptism responds with the cry, "Abba! Father!" Paul employs the metaphor of adoption to describe the convert's introduction as God's new child into a new family who had responded in like fashion. According to Wayne Meeks, this "is a vivid way of portraying what a modern sociologist might call the resocialization of conversion. The natural kinship structure into which the person has been born and which previously defined his place and connections with the society are here supplanted by a new set of relationships."[15] We may safely assume that the Thessalonians were similarly initiated, for Paul calls God "our Father" (1:3; 3:11, 13) in a manner suggesting that his readers understood its significance.

Paul, whose preaching of the gospel was the means by which God called them, stresses the relationship between himself and the Thessalonians when he reminds them of their conversion (1:4–6). This stress is evident not only in the heavy preponderance of personal pronouns in these verses, as indeed elsewhere in the letter, but also in his reminder, unusual for him, that they had become imitators of him and the Lord when they received the

spätjüdischen Lehrauffassung (Naumburg: Pätz, 1914); G. Bornkamm, *Early Christian Experience* (New York: Harper & Row, 1969) 47–70.

13. E.g., Marcus Aurelius, *Med.* 4.23, ἐκ σοῦ, ἐν σοί, εἰς σε. But the formulation was used by other philosophers as well. See A.-J. Festugière, "Le 'compendium Timaei' de Galien," *REG* 65 (1952) 106ff.; R. M. Grant, "Causation and 'The Ancient World View,'" *JBL* 83 (1964) 34–40. Contra L. Cerfaux, *Christ in the Theology of St. Paul* (New York: Herder & Herder, 1959) 450. On 1 Cor 8:6, see H. Conzelmann, *1 Corinthians* (Hermeneia; Philadelphia: Fortress, 1975) 144–45.

14. A. D. Nock, *Conversion* (Oxford: Oxford University Press, 1933) 229–31.

15. Meeks, *First Urban Christians*, 87–88; see also idem, "The Image of the Androgyne: Some Uses of a Symbol of Early Christianity," *HR* 13 (1974) 165–208. On what follows, see Malherbe, *Paul and the Thessalonians*, 48–52.

Word.[16] The notion of imitation was widespread in Paul's day, and his use of it was informed by but not totally identical to that of the moral philosophers, who stressed the importance of having someone after whom to model oneself. People who imitated a leader, especially a teacher, held him in their memory so as to have a constant guide, especially when they were separated from him. Paul was anxious, after leaving Thessalonica, whether, having once looked to him as their example, the Thessalonians no longer did so. Timothy's report that they still remembered him (3:6), brought him great relief.[17] Such moral philosophical language continues in 2:1–12, when he recounts his ministry with them.[18]

Paul also uses familial terms to describe his relationship with the Thessalonians. As they had been loved by God (1:4), so they had become Paul's ἀγαπητοί ("beloved"; RSV "very dear"), in proof of which he did manual labor in order not to burden them (2:8–9). The letter teems with the language of family, but the picture that emerges is neither consistent nor hierarchical. This is clearest in 2:7, the only place where Paul mentions apostleship and its harsh prerogatives, only to forgo them in favor of treating his converts gently, like a wet nurse who nurses her own children. The imagery is derived from the moral philosophers.[19] But, then, a few verses later (2:11–12), he is like a father to them as he pays individual attention to them and adapts his pastoral care to their dispositions or emotional states. This, too, Paul derives from the psychagogy of the moral philosophers.[20] A few verses later, however, he is an orphan (ἀπορφανισθέντες; RSV "bereft") because he is separated from them (2:17), and this time he uses a Jewish tra-

---

16. Paul usually calls his readers to imitation: 1 Cor 4:16; 11:1; Phil 3:17; cf. 1:30; 4:9. For the parenetic use of imitation, see A. J. Malherbe, "Hellenistic Moralists and the New Testament," *ANRW* 2.26.1, 282; idem, *Moral Exhortation: A Greco-Roman Sourcebook* (Library of Early Christianity 4; Philadelphia: Westminster, 1986) 125, 135–37. For caution that imitation is not confined to parenesis, see M. M. Mitchell, *Paul and the Rhetoric of Reconciliation: An Exegetical Investigation of the Language and Composition of 1 Corinthians* (HUT 28; Tübingen: Mohr-Siebeck, 1991) 49–50. For Paul's distinctiveness in claiming that his converts had imitated him, see Malherbe, *Paul and the Popular Philosophers* (Minneapolis: Fortress, 1989) 56–58. For more extensive treatment, see B. Fiore, *The Function of Personal Example in the Socratic and Pastoral Epistles* (AnBib 105; Rome: Biblical Institute, 1986).

17. On remembering the model, see Ps.-Isocrates, *To Demonicus* 9–11; Lucian, *Nigrinus* 6–7; Malherbe, "Hellenistic Moralists," 282–83. On 1 Thess 3:7, see A. J. Malherbe, "'Pastoral Care' in the Thessalonian Church," *NTS* 36 (1990) 385–86.

18. See A. J. Malherbe, "Gentle as a Nurse," in *Paul and the Popular Philosophers*, 35–48.

19. See ibid. The role of the wet nurse is receiving considerable attention these days. See K. R. Bradley, "Wet-nursing at Rome: A Study in Social Relations," in *The Family in Ancient Rome: New Perspectives* (ed. B. Rawson; Ithaca, N.Y.: Cornell University Press, 1986) 201–29; idem, *Discovering the Roman Family: Studies in Roman Social History* (New York: Oxford University Press, 1991) chapter 2.

20. Malherbe, "Hellenistic Moralists," 283. Although 2:11–12 shares parenetic elements with 1 Cor 4:14–21, one notes the differences between the passages: for example, in the latter Paul *is* their spiritual father, *therefore* has the right to expect that they imitate him and to threaten punishment.

dition which he deftly twists: Proselytes were described as orphans because of the social ostracism and feeling of desolation that their conversion caused.[21] Paul identifies with his new converts by describing himself as an orphan. It is thus clear that Paul's kinship language, derived from pagan and Jewish traditions, does not describe a hierarchically structured community, but is part and parcel of the pathos of the letter, intended to strengthen the bond between Paul and his readers.

Paul, in addition, is the Thessalonians' sibling. Paul addresses them as ἀδελφοί ("brothers") thirteen times and describes various Christians as brothers three times. This is the highest incidence of the term in all of Paul's letters. Pagans as well as Jews described members of various conventicles and associations as brothers, and we do not know what Paul's source was for his usage.[22] In any case, what is more important is the way in which he uses the term.

Paul thinks of "brothers" as constituting the church's gatherings (5:25–27), but the directions on different aspects of life outside the assembly which he gives in the latter part of the letter also have in view relationships among the brothers. In giving advice on sexual morality, for example, he warns against transgressing and wronging one's brother, evidently by committing adultery with his wife (4:6). Paul prays that, as he loves them, so they would love one another (3:12), and when he exhorts them to social responsibility (4:9–12), he does so with the conviction that they have been divinely instructed about φιλαδελφία ("love of the brothers"), and already love all the brothers throughout Macedonia (4:9–10). The problem that 4:13–18 addresses is the grief caused by a surmise that Christians who had died would be separated from those who would be alive at the Parousia (4:15). In response, Paul emphasizes the eventual restoration of relationships with each other and the Lord, and ends with the injunction that they comfort one another with his words (4:17–18). So, membership in the family of brothers demands particular conduct.[23]

The most detailed and explicit instructions on how the Thessalonians are to relate to one another are given in 5:11–22.[24] As Paul had cared for each one of them individually (2:11–12), so are they to do, εἰς τὸν ἕνα, "one on one" (5:11), and Paul then proceeds to specify how the Thessalonian broth-

---

21. See, e.g., *Joseph and Aseneth* 12:11; 13:11; Malherbe, *Paul and the Thessalonians*, 43–45. But also see Plato, *Phaedo* 116A: "we felt that he was a father to us and that bereft of him we should pass the rest of our lives as orphans," of Socrates' disciples' anticipation of his death.

22. Meeks thinks Judaism was the more likely source (*First Urban Christians*, 87). For the most extensive discussion, see K. Schäfer, *Gemeinde als "Bruderschaft": Ein Beitrag zum Kirchenverständnis des Paulus* (Europäische Hochschulschriften 23.333; Frankfurt, Bern, and New York: Lang, 1989).

23. See also 1 Cor 5:11; 6:5–8; cf. Philemon 15–16.

24. Discussed in greater detail in Malherbe, "'Pastoral Care' in the Thessalonian Church."

ers are to treat one another as members of the congregation, at one time offering exhortation, at another receiving it. Love again enters the discussion, but, characteristically for Paul, here mutual concern expressed in reciprocal actions and attitudes is more important. He thus takes up various responsibilities: the brothers are to respect and love those who care for them pastorally (vv. 12–13); the brothers who engage in such care must, as Paul had done, adapt their treatment to the conditions of those they seek to benefit (v. 14); and they are all to exercise great prudence toward prophets in the Christian community: they must not devalue prophecy but must test it for the good that it contains and they must accept (vv. 19–22).

A FAMILY FOREVER

Eschatology suffuses 1 Thessalonians, and the eschatological language and images that Paul uses reinforce the point that this is not an ordinary group of people who happen to be called a family. God the Father's election of the Thessalonians became manifest in their reception of Paul's gospel (1:3–5), and Paul prays that together they will stand in holiness before their divine Father at the coming of the Lord Jesus and the heavenly host (3:12–13; cf. 2:19).[25] The community will then be reconstituted, so that even death will be seen to present no permanent danger to the fellowship (4:14–17).

God's call was not confined to the past event of their conversion. Paul twice describes God as ὁ καλῶν ("he who calls"), the one who continues his call in the present but does so with a view to the eschatological future. He who calls Paul's readers is faithful, and they can be confident that he will sanctify them and keep them secure at the coming of the Lord Jesus (5:23–24). Paul's pastoral care for them, as a father paying individual attention to his children, is aimed at fostering conduct worthy of God who calls them into his kingdom and glory (2:11–12). It is by virtue of being an eschatological community, children of the day and of the light (5:4–5), that they are likewise to continue their own edification and nurture (5:11). It is this eschatological dimension that makes the psychagogical description that follows different. Unlike pagans, who also engaged in admonition and comfort, and helped their fellows, the Thessalonian brothers were to do so because ("therefore") they believed in God's eschatological purpose for them.

God's call to holiness has not only a future referent (e.g., 5:23–24; cf. 3:13). Wayne Meeks has reminded us of the parenetic elements in apocalyptic and

---

25. On the church as the eschatological community, see R. Bultmann, *Theology of the New Testament* (2 vols.; New York: Scribner, 1951) 1:308–9.

suggested that the connection between the two in Thessalonians is more subtle.[26] It is also explicit when Paul speaks of God's call. God called them to a particular quality of life now, not to live in uncleanness, but ἐν ἁγιασμῷ ("in holiness," 4:7). What this call to holiness means, practically, is specified in 4:3–8, the warning to abstain from sexual immorality, to "take a vessel" (wife?) in holiness and honor and thus not to wrong one's brother. As children of the day (5:6), the ἀδελφοί ("brothers," 5:1, 4) further clothe themselves with faith, hope, and love (5:8–9). All this sets them apart from the society in which they live. Their behavior is to be different from that of the Gentiles who do not know God (4:5), and the Thessalonians should not live like the children of night and of darkness (5:6–7).

The references to their call and their life as a community of the last days thus distinguish them from others and reinforce their own sense of uniqueness, as Meeks has also emphasized.[27] This negative view is indeed evident elsewhere in the letter, where the eschatological element is also present: non-Christian Gentiles are idolators and will evidently experience the coming Wrath (1:9–10); they have no hope and therefore grieve in the face of death (4:13), and they oppose the gospel, thus already incurring, somehow, eschatological Wrath (2:14, 16).

Paul's view of the Thessalonians as an eschatological family does not, however, result in a consistently negative attitude toward non-Christians. One might expect that the more emphasis that is laid on the church as a unique family, the greater would be not only the contrast with, but the antipathy toward, non-Christians—yet the exact opposite is true. The readers are to love not only one another but all people (3:12). It is precisely in 4:9–12, which affirms that φιλαδελφία ("brotherly love") is divinely taught, and which compliments the Thessalonians for loving Christians throughout the province of Macedonia, that Paul, in terms derived from contemporary moral discourse, urges the Thessalonians to act εὐσχημόνως πρὸς τοὺς ἔξω ("becomingly to outsiders"). So, as the family instructed in proper behavior by God, the church is most clearly unique when it is viewed from an eschatological perspective. This love of the brethren does not, however, result in a disregard of society; on the contrary, it is the family members, who are taught by God to love each other and already do so throughout Macedonia, who engage in manual labor and so win the approval of outsiders.[28]

26. W. A. Meeks, "Social Functions of Apocalyptic Language in Pauline Christianity," in *Apocalypticism in the Mediterranean World and the Near East* (ed. D. Hellholm; Tübingen: Mohr-Siebeck, 1983) 689–95.

27. Meeks, "Social Functions," 694.

28. Paul makes a similar connection between love and manual labor in 2:8–9. It is striking that in 4:9–12 the only properly theological reason given for the love of the brethren is that

CONCLUSION

This survey reveals how Paul describes the Thessalonian church in familial terms even though he does not explicitly call the church the family of God. His reason for describing the church in this way may simply be that the traditions he used to describe their conversion spoke of the relationship between God and the elect in kinship language, and that Paul consistently applied it to the intracommunal relations of this young church, whose memory of their conversion was still fresh. The intensity with which he uses the language and images, however, and the wide range of pagan and Jewish traditions from which they are derived, suggest a more immediate reason for Paul's heavy emphasis on the various relationships he describes, and for the particular, familial way in which he describes those relationships.

It may very well be that it was the experience of new converts, who underwent a painful reorientation of social relationships, sometimes including marriage relations (cf. 4:2-8), that made Paul's approach particularly appropriate to the situation to which he wrote.[29] The Synoptic tradition reflects the domestic problems caused by the new missionary religion (e.g., Luke 12:51-53), but holds out promise for new relationships to substitute for the old ones in this age and the one to come (e.g., Mark 10:29-30).[30] Paul, too, appears to be aware of the problem, and he addresses it in this finely crafted pastoral letter by using language of kinship to describe the new fellowship. In literary terms, he achieves his pastoral purpose by writing a familial, parenetic letter to God's new family in Thessalonica, which quite possibly was still meeting in the house of Jason.[31]

---

they are taught by God to do so. For the philosophical traditions Paul employs in this section, see Malherbe, *Paul and the Thessalonians*, 12-20.

29. I have attempted to describe the feeling of alienation experienced by converts in general, and the Thessalonians in particular, in *Paul and the Thessalonians*, 36-52.

30. For Christianity viewed as a domestic troublemaker, see the material collected by A. Harnack, *Mission and Expansion of Christianity in the First Three Centuries* (New York: Putnam, 1909) 1:393-98; cf. E. R. Dodds, *Pagan and Christian in an Age of Anxiety* (Cambridge: Cambridge University Press, 1965) 115-16.

31. On the notion of familial letters, which were not identified as a separate type by ancient epistolary theorists, see S. K. Stowers, *Letter-Writing in Greco-Roman Antiquity* (Library of Early Christianity 5; Philadelphia: Westminster, 1986) 42-43, 71-76. It is possible that letters of friendship could assume a familial cast or be parenetic (which did receive a special classification), depending on the purpose the author had in mind. On 1 Thessalonians as a parenetic letter, see Malherbe, "Hellenistic Moralists," 278-93; on the pastoral function of the parenetic style, see Malherbe, *Paul and the Thessalonians*, 68-78. On the household of Jason, see Malherbe, *Paul and the Thessalonians*, 12-20.

CHAPTER 9

Parents and Children
in the Letters of Paul

O. Larry Yarbrough

FOR SOMEONE who argued so forcefully in favor of celibate life, the apostle Paul made a remarkable number of references to parents and children. Very few of these references address real parents and children or deal with concrete situations related to them. Most of the references are in fact metaphorical, serving to define the relationship between God and believers on the one hand and between Paul and his coworkers and churches on the other.

In this essay we will look at Paul's use of parent/child imagery, first surveying the occasions on which he treats concrete situations and then examining his use of parent/child imagery in the context of other arguments. Finally, we will consider the relationship between the concrete and the metaphorical, seeking to determine the extent to which the metaphorical references may be used to establish a Pauline ethic with regard to the family.[1] In a number of instances, we will make use of recent works on parents and children by historians of antiquity. These contribute significantly to our understanding of the social world in which early Christianity emerged and consequently aid us in setting Paul's references to parents and children in context.[2]

---

1. Because of the limits set for this volume, I focus on the question of Paul's ethical use of parent/child imagery, reserving for the conclusion a brief note on his theological use. I offer this essay as a tribute to Wayne Meeks, who has taught us so much about the moral world of Paul and the early Christians. See especially *First Urban Christians* (1983), *The Moral World of the First Christians* (1986), and *The Origins of Christian Morality: The First Two Centuries* (1993). Among his essays, see "The Circle of Reference in Pauline Morality" (1990), "The Polyphonic Ethics of the Apostle Paul" (1988), "A Hermeneutics of Social Embodiment" (1986) and "Understanding Early Christian Ethics" (1986). The bibliography of Professor Meeks's works in this volume provides details of publication.

2. The last decade has witnessed a veritable revolution in the study of the family in the ancient world. Among the works especially important for scholars of early Christianity are the two collections of essays edited by Beryl Rawson, *The Family in Ancient Rome: New Perspec-*

REFERENCES TO PARENTS AND CHILDREN

In all of his letters, Paul explicitly identifies only two parents and their children—Rufus and his mother (Rom 16:13) and the man living with his "father's wife" (1 Cor 5:1–5). The various "households" mentioned in the letters, however, would certainly have included parents and children.[3] Scholars have frequently speculated, for example, that Apphia was the wife of Philemon and that Archippus was their son (Phlm 2).[4] C. E. B. Cranfield has hazarded the guess that Philologus and Julia were the parents of Nereus and his (unnamed) sister (Rom 16:15),[5] though it is equally possible that Nereus's

---

tives (Ithaca, N.Y.: Cornell University Press, 1986); idem, *Marriage, Divorce, and Children in Ancient Rome* (Oxford: Clarendon, 1991); Suzanne Dixon, *The Roman Mother* (Norman, Ok., and London: Oklahoma University Press, 1988); idem, *The Roman Family* (Baltimore and London: Johns Hopkins University Press, 1992); Keith R. Bradley, *Discovering the Roman Family: Studies in Roman Social History* (New York and Oxford: Oxford University Press, 1991); John Boswell, *The Kindness of Strangers* (New York: Pantheon, 1988); Mark Golden, *Children and Childhood in Classical Athens* (Baltimore and London: Johns Hopkins University Press, 1990); and Thomas Wiedemann, *Adults and Children in the Roman Empire* (New Haven and London: Yale University Press, 1989). In addition to these book-length studies, there are numerous essays relevant to the topic by the same authors and others working in the field. Among the latter I would especially recommend the works of Richard Saller, B. D. Shaw, Susan Treggiari, Mireille Corbier, and Emiel Eyben. Both of the works edited by Rawson contain extensive bibliographies, including the works of these scholars. On a number of important points, these works provide important corrections to earlier treatments of the topic, including Philippe Aries's *Centuries of Childhood: A Social History of Family Life* (New York: Vintage, 1962). The widely publicized first volume of *A History of Private Life: From Pagan Rome to Byzantium* edited by Paul Veyne (Cambridge and London: Belknap, 1987) provides a readable and sometimes provocative introduction to many of the issues of family life in antiquity, but its usefulness is hampered by the lack of notation to works cited.

3. Among these are the households of Aristobulus and Narcissus (Rom 16:10 and 11), of Stephanas (1 Cor 16:15), and of Philemon (Phlm 1–2). The term for "children" Paul uses most frequently is τέκνα. It refers to a relationship and denotes nothing regarding age. (On this and other terms for "child," "children," etc., see Boswell, *Kindness of Strangers*, 22–39; Wiedemann, *Adults and Children*, 32–34.) Paul knew, and used, terms for young "children." Note his use of νήπιος, especially in 1 Cor 3:1 and 13:11; Gal 4:3; and 1 Thess 2:7.

4. See, e.g., Eduard Lohse, *Colossians and Philemon: A Commentary on the Epistles to the Colossians and to Philemon* (Hermeneia; Philadelphia: Fortress, 1971) 190; and J. B. Lightfoot, *Saint Paul's Epistles to the Colossians and to Philemon* (London and New York: Macmillan, 1892) 308–9. Norman Petersen points to Paul's use of the definite pronoun rather than the possessive pronoun in Phlm 2, claiming that "Paul is focusing on the social positions of brother and sister, not on personal relationships with him, even though that relationship is implied in v. 16" (*Rediscovering Paul: Philemon and the Sociology of Paul's Narrative Word* [Philadelphia: Fortress, 1985] 172 n. 5). This usage, he goes on to say, indicates "an egalitarian identification applicable to all members of the church, whereas the use of the possessive pronoun has . . . a hierarchical connotation because it links those of whom it is used to *Paul's* position." This, however, does not preclude the identification of Apphia as Philemon's wife or Archippus as their son. Nor do Florence Morgan Gillman's arguments in *ABD* 1:317–18. (Note that Gillman incorrectly identifies the italicized word in her quotation of Petersen.)

5. C. E. B Cranfield, *The Epistle to the Romans II* (ICC; Edinburgh: Clark, 1979) 795.

"sister" was in fact his wife and that Olympus was their son.[6] Whatever the case with regard to these two households, we must note Paul's silence on this score and use such speculations cautiously.[7]

In at least one instance, however, the absence of any reference to children raises some interesting questions. This is the case of Prisca and Aquila, with whom Paul had considerable contact both in Corinth and Ephesus and whom he greeted in his letter to Rome (Rom 16:3–5; Acts 18; 1 Cor 16:19). Because Jewish men were obligated to "be fruitful and multiply," it seems probable that Prisca and Aquila had children.[8] Still, Paul never mentions any, nor does the author of Acts, who reports that Paul met Aquila in Corinth "lately come from Italy with his wife Priscilla, because Claudius had commanded all the Jews to leave Rome" (18:2). Were the children grown and already established in their own households, choosing not to follow their parents as they moved from place to place in pursuit of their trade?[9] Were they still minors when Prisca and Aquila set out for Rome, and could they have been left in Pontus with other family members?[10] Were they estranged from their parents, because they did not accept Jesus as the Messiah? Or is it simply a case of children being neither seen nor heard? As tantalizing as they are, there is no way to answer any of these questions. To pose them, however, is not a matter of idle curiosity, for by doing so we begin to imagine more fully the lives of people who inhabited Paul's world, which may help us better understand both what Paul had to say and how it might have been received.[11]

If Paul rarely identifies parents and children in his greetings, it is equally

---

6. For Paul's use of "sister" as "wife," see 1 Cor 9:5.

7. That Paul says so little about the relationships of the people he greeted should not surprise us, for, after all, the recipients of the letters knew who they were and how they were related. If we are in the dark about them, it is but another example of our ignorance of the concrete situations behind Paul's letters.

8. There are few examples of failure to fulfill the obligation. See O. Larry Yarbrough, *Not Like the Gentiles: Marriage Rules in the Letters of Paul* (SBLDS 80; Atlanta: Scholars Press, 1985) 20–22.

9. The typical age for first marriages was early to mid teens for women and late teens to early twenties for men. At the time of marriage most couples would have established their own households separate from either set of parents. Prisca and Aquila could have had an empty nest by the time they were in their late twenties and mid-thirties.

10. The papyri include letters husbands wrote home to their wives while on business ventures. It would be interesting to learn if any exist from husbands *and* wives (or wives alone) addressed to a parent or some other person charged with minding their children.

11. Even if Prisca and Aquila did not have children, one wonders how Paul's relationship with them might have affected him. For example, did the time he spent in their household contribute to what he had to say about marriage in 1 Corinthians 7? (Prisca and Aquila presumably rented accommodations in Corinth and Ephesus. But were the accommodations detached from their work space or a couple of rooms above a shop?) And what might Prisca and Aquila have thought about Paul's opinions and advice regarding marriage? Though married, they were certainly actively engaged in mission with, and on behalf of, Paul!

rare for him to address specific issues involving them. Indeed, the brief reference to the children of "mixed marriages" in 1 Cor 7:12–16 is the only instance in all the letters in which Paul addresses a specific issue regarding familial relationships.[12] Even here, however, the argument focuses primarily on relations between the spouses. The believing partner, Paul says, should not instigate divorce with an unbelieving spouse so long as the latter desires to preserve the marriage, "since the unbelieving husband is consecrated through his wife, and the unbelieving wife is consecrated through her husband" (v. 14a).[13] He then applies a similar argument with regard to the children of the marriage: They are "holy" (ἅγια) so long as the couple remains together, but "unclean" (ἀκάθαρτά) if the marriage is dissolved (v. 14b). Although it is difficult to determine precisely what he means by this cryptic statement, it is clear Paul is of the opinion that "Christian" parents are obligated to consider the effect divorce will have on their children.[14] In essence, he argues that the marriage should be preserved "for the sake of the children." It is equally clear, however, that this argument is secondary. In any case, concern for the children is not determinative. For Paul goes on to say, "if the unbelieving partner desires to separate, let it be so; in

---

12. Apart from the highly unusual situation in 1 Cor 5:1–5 which presents too many thorny issues to be included here. In this essay I treat only those letters indisputably by Paul. Relations between parents and children are of course an issue in the household codes of Colossians and Ephesians. See Col 3:19–21 and Eph 6:1–4. They are also of concern to the author of the Pastoral Epistles; see esp. 1 Tim 3:4, 12; 5:4, 8; 2 Tim 1:5; Titus 1:6; 2:4.

13. In both instances the Greek for "consecrated" is ἡγίασται.

14. We must be careful, however, not to read too much into this. Paul expresses no concern here with the psychological effect divorce may have on children. All he mentions is their status with regard to "holiness." For discussion, with references to the literature, see Hans Conzelmann, *1 Corinthians: A Commentary on the First Epistle to the Corinthians* (Hermeneia; Philadelphia: Fortress, 1975) 121–23. In 1 Cor 7:14 Paul surely has in mind children who are still living with their parents, not children who are on their own. Indeed, one line of inquiry into the meaning of this passage that might be profitable is an examination of laws and practices regarding what we would call "custody." Normally, children in the Greco-Roman world belonged (quite literally) to their father and would remain in his household in the event of divorce. (The real "power" of the *patria potestas* was waning during Paul's day, however. See, for example, Rawson's essay "The Roman Family," in *The Family in Ancient Rome;* and Richard Saller's essay "Corporal Punishment, Authority, and Obedience in the Roman Household" in *Marriage, Divorce, and Children in Ancient Rome.*) If Paul was concerned with the status of children whose mother was a believer and whose father was not, as seems likely given the probability that the early Christian movement was especially attractive to women, might he have feared that the children would have been removed from the church's influence? On the question of the effect frequent divorce may have had on children in the Greco-Roman world, see Bradley, *Discovering the Roman Family*, chapters 6 and 7. He argues that the effects would have been less than might be imagined because of the provisions for child care. Children, that is, developed relationships with their nurses and paedagogues which remained strong throughout the comings and goings of their parents. This was true, moreover, at both the highest and lowest levels of society. The wealthy, that is, provided childcare not only for their own children but also for those of their slaves, since, otherwise, they lost the use of a good worker.

such a case the brother or sister is not bound" (v. 15a). Paul, it seems, is more concerned with peace between the spouses than with the status and disposition of the children.

The argument of 1 Cor 7:32–35 shows that children did not readily come to Paul's mind, even where one might expect them to. Here, "to promote good order and to secure . . . undivided devotion to the Lord" (πρὸς τὸ εὔσχημον καὶ εὐπάρεδρον τῷ κυρίῳ ἀπερισπάστως), Paul warns believers against marrying, since the married person "is anxious about worldly affairs" (μεριμνᾷ τὰ τοῦ κόσμου). But the only "worldly affair" Paul mentions is concern with "how to please" (πῶς ἀρέσαι) a spouse. He says nothing about the burdens imposed by having children. This silence is striking in light of the arguments against marriage in the moral tradition of the Greco-Roman world, which commonly listed children as one of the chief burdens of married life.[15] These two passages suggest that if children were of concern to Paul, they do not appear to have been of great concern—whether he is arguing against marrying or for preserving a marriage.

Still, we cannot dismiss 1 Cor 7:14b entirely, for it indicates that Paul was at least aware of the children within his churches, tells us something of the way he regarded them, and therefore gives us a concrete situation to which we may compare his metaphorical imagery. Before looking at the metaphorical imagery, however, there is one other passage we must examine briefly. Falling between the concrete and the metaphorical, it refers to the obligations children owe their parents.

In Rom 1:29–31 Paul gives a list of vices which characterize the Gentiles who did not acknowledge God and were thus given up "to a base mind and to improper conduct." Among them is being "disobedient to parents" (γονεῦσιν ἀπειθεῖς).[16] Because such lists were stock components in Greco-Roman literature, and because this list, like many of those found in the moral tradition, was so polemical, we should probably not make too much of the individual vices contained in it. Still, vice lists did vary from author to author, so that Paul's inclusion of disobedience to parents is at least worth noting. We will take up later what being disobedient to parents might have entailed. For the present we focus on a correlative question, whether Paul regarded the opposite of this vice, obedience to parents, as a virtue characteristic of those who do acknowledge God. That is, was it an element of Pauline parenesis? Unfortunately, evidence for answering the question is elusive. Obedience to parents does not appear in any of Paul's virtue lists, nor do any of his parenetic summaries include an admonition to obey one's parents.[17] The only possible evidence for determining whether obedience

---

15. See Yarbrough, *Not Like the Gentiles*, 33–41.

16. "Disobedience to parents" also appears in the vice list of 2 Tim 3:2.

17. To be sure, he may have the commandment to honor one's father and mother in mind when he refers to the other commandments that are fulfilled in loving one's neighbor (Rom 13:9), but this would be no more than an allusion.

to parents was of real concern to Paul derives from his discussions of what the churches owed him as their father. This, however, takes us into the realm of Paul's metaphorical use of parent/child imagery where we must tread with care, for though we may discover in these discussions explicit statements and general principles regarding parents and children, Paul uses them to make other arguments. Thus, we must ask yet another question: Would Paul necessarily have applied to real parents and their children the conventions he found useful in arguments concerning other issues? Would he, for example, have advised Prisca and Aquila to "lay up for their children"? Perhaps. But before deciding, we must look more closely at Paul's metaphorical use of parent/child imagery to determine what he had to say and why.

THE METAPHORICAL USE OF PARENT–CHILD IMAGERY

The saying to which we have just referred is, of course, from the maxim Paul cites in 2 Cor 12:14b: "Children ought not to lay up for their parents but parents for their children" (οὐ γὰρ ὀφείλει τὰ τέκνα τοῖς γονεῦσιν θησαυρίζειν ἀλλὰ οἱ γονεῖς τοῖς τέκνοις). Paul makes this claim as if its truth were obvious to anyone. No proof was necessary and none given. It implies, of course, that Paul is the father and the Corinthians his children, a claim Paul had made early in his correspondence with the church at Corinth.

Paul first used this imagery in his correspondence with the Corinthians in 1 Cor 4:14-21. At the end of the opening section, which seeks to reestablish his authority within the church,[18] Paul tells the Corinthians, "I do not write this to make you ashamed, but to admonish you as my beloved children (ὡς τέκνα μου ἀγαπητά). For though you have countless guides (παιδαγωγούς) in Christ, you do not have many fathers (οὐ πολλοὺς πατέρας). For I became your father (ἐγὼ ὑμᾶς ἐγέννησα) in Christ Jesus through the gospel."[19] This passage harks back to the argument of 3:4-17, where Paul contrasts himself to Apollos, using imagery of planter and skilled master builder for himself and of waterer and laborer for Apollos.[20] In both passages, Paul asserts that his is a role no one else can assume. What distinguishes them, in addition to the imagery, is that in chapter 3 Paul focuses on his rivals by referring to the final judgment all workers will undergo, while

18. See Nils A. Dahl, "Paul and the Church at Corinth according to 1 Corinthians 1:10–4:21," in *Christian History and Interpretation: Studies Presented to John Knox* (ed. William R. Farmer, C. F. D. Moule, and Richard R. Niebuhr; Cambridge: Cambridge University Press, 1967) 313–35.

19. See the similar thought, though without reference to Paul as "father," in 2 Cor 10:14b: "we were the first to come all the way to you with the gospel of Christ."

20. In 2 Cor 10:15–16 Paul refers to Corinth as a field belonging to himself and his coworkers.

in chapter 4 he focuses on his relationship with the Corinthians by referring to them as his beloved children. The paternal imagery, therefore, bespeaks the intimate feelings Paul has for the Corinthians.[21]

This intimacy is in fact the dominant motif in all of Paul's metaphorical applications of parent–child imagery. In his earliest letter, 1 Thessalonians, it appears as part of the parenetic reminder. "For you know," he tells the Thessalonians, "how like a father with his children (ὡς πατὴρ τέκνα ἑαυτοῦ) we exhorted each of you and encouraged you and charged you to lead a life worthy of God, who calls you into his own kingdom and glory" (2:11–12). This passage follows one in which Paul speaks of his manner as being "gentle, . . . like a nurse taking care of her children" (2:7),[22] an image that shows up again, to different effect, in the Corinthian correspondence.

In 1 Cor 3:1–2 Paul tells the Corinthians he had not been able to address them as adults but as "babes in Christ" (ὡς νηπίοις ἐν Χριστῷ), going on to say, "I fed you with milk, not solid food." This passage takes on new meaning in light of Keith R. Bradley's investigations of child care in the Roman world.[23] Bradley has shown, through painstaking analysis of numerous inscriptions, that it was not uncommon for men (usually freedmen) to play a signficant role in the tending of children, both in upper–class families and among those of servile origin. This role, moreover, was not limited to that of the familiar "custodian" (παιδαγωγός), but included the "nursing" of young children. Indeed, such men were referred to as *nutritor* or *nutricius*, masculine forms of the term *nutrix* (nurse).[24] Bradley concludes, further, that the tasks of the *nutritor* were essentially the same as those of the *nutrix*, namely, comforting children, telling them stories, rocking and singing them to sleep, and feeding them. Indeed, especially relevant to 1 Cor 3:2, one male nurse, C. Mussius Chrysonicus, was described as a *nutritor lactaneus*, which Bradley translates "an attendant who fed milk to his charges."[25] Needless to

21. Scholars of early Christianity who know only older works dealing with the *paterfamilias* may be inclined to make too much of Paul's emphasis on the intimate nature of parent–child relations, seeing it as distinctively Christian (or Jewish). Several recent studies of parents and children demonstrate that it was indeed an important feature of family life in the Greco-Roman world. See especially Suzanne Dixon, "The Sentimental Ideal of the Roman Family," Emiel Eyben, "Fathers and Sons," and Richard Saller, "Corporal Punishment, Authority, and Obedience in the Roman Household." All three essays are in Beryl Rawson's *Marriage, Divorce, and Children in Ancient Rome.*

22. On these two passages, see Abraham J. Malherbe "'Gentle as a Nurse': The Cynic Background to I Thess ii," *NovT* 12 (1970) 203–17. Malherbe argues that the imagery derives from the Hellenistic moral tradition.

23. See Keith R. Bradley, "Child Care at Rome: The Role of Men," in *Discovering the Roman Family,* 37–75.

24. The term *educator* was sometimes used along with *nutritor* or *nutricius* in the same inscription. Though all these terms could be used to describe a foster father, Bradley shows that in many instances the parents were living and on hand ("Child Care at Rome," 49).

25. Mussius Chrysonicus and his "companion" Aurelia Soteris worked for families of the equitorial class.

say, Mussius was not a wet-nurse, but he could well have fed a child the goat's milk sweetened with honey which Soranus, the Dr. Spock of his day, recommended for the first twenty days of a child's life and the breast milk mixed with cereal prescribed for the child of six months.[26] From Bradley's investigations we may conclude that even if Paul drew the image of a nurse from the moralists of his day, mundane experiences made the imagery real for him and his readers. Moreover, the fondness with which *nutritores* were remembered on funerary inscriptions indicates that, even if 1 Cor 3:1–2 is a rebuke, the underlying imagery should be taken as representative of the intimacy Paul feels toward the Corinthians.

We can see Paul's emphasis on the intimacy of the parent–child relationship in his other references to parents and children also. In 2 Cor 11:2 he presents himself as a(n) (overly?) solicitous father.[27] In Gal 4:19 he uses maternal imagery, which should be included here in light of the common convention that mothers loved their children more than fathers because of the great risk they endured in childbirth.[28] He describes Timothy on one occasion (1 Cor 4:17) as "my beloved child" (μου τέκνον ἀγαπητόν), saying on another (Phil 2:22) that Timothy worked with him "as a son with a father" (ὡς πατρὶ τέκνον). And when Paul returns Onesimus to Philemon, he does so regretfully, for Onesimus is his very own "child" (τὸν ἐμὸν τέκνον), "begotten" (ἐγέννησα) in chains (see Phlm 10, 12). Thus, Paul tells Philemon he is sending his "very heart" (τὰ ἐμὰ σπλάγχνα). Finally, in 2 Cor 6:11–13 Paul refers to his "open-hearted" conduct toward the Corinthians, concluding, "In return—I speak as to children—widen your hearts also." Though the interjection "I speak as to children" (ὡς τέκνοις λέγω) may appear to be condescending in tone, it is actually one of "endearment,"[29] not only in view of the passages just cited but because Paul's appeal for a "return" (ἀντιμισθίαν) surely derives from Jewish, Greek, and Roman moral traditions which held that children were obligated to pay parents back for the benefits they provided. Since the conventional wisdom in all three traditions held that no one could ever pay back these debts because they were so great, emphasis

26. For references and further discussion, see Aline Rouselle, *Porneia: On Desire and the Body in Antiquity* (Oxford: Blackwell, 1988) 54–58. There are problems with many of the conclusions Rouselle draws from the material she has collected, but her work is important for drawing attention to the medical texts of antiquity.

27. "I feel a divine jealousy for you, for I betrothed you to Christ to present you as a pure bride to her one husband."

28. "My children, with whom I am again in travail until Christ be formed in you" (τέκνα μου, οὓς πάλιν ὠδίνω μέχρις οὗ μορφωθῇ Χριστὸς ἐν ὑμῖν). The RSV translates the textual variant τεκνία. Τέκνα, however, is the better reading. For the claim that mothers loved children more than fathers, see, for example, Aristotle, *Nicomachean Ethics* 8.7.7: "This is why mothers love their children more than fathers, because parenthood (ἡ γέννησις) costs the mother more trouble" (trans. Rackham, LCL).

29. The term is used by Victor Paul Furnish in *II Corinthians* (AB 32A; Garden City, N.Y.: Doubleday, 1984) 361.

was placed on the greatest obligation, namely, to honor, respect, and love one's parents.[30] Thus in asking for a return of affection, Paul was only seeking what was due to him as the Corinthians' father.

Although Paul's metaphorical references to parents and children occur in many of his letters,[31] most of them in fact appear in his correspondence with the Corinthians. Indeed, the Corinthians could scarcely have missed the implication of 2 Cor 12:14b, since they had been told three separate times that Paul was their father and once that he was a nurse who had fed them milk. Here, yet again, he draws on this imagery, emphasizing now his parental duty to "lay up" for his children. But what does this mean?

The maxim itself apparently refers to parents' obligation to provide an inheritance for their children, Plutarch's *On the Love of Wealth* 526a and Philo's *Moses* 2.245 being the most frequently cited parallels. The former provides linguistic evidence for interpreting θησαυρίζειν as "lay up for an inheritance";[32] the latter supports Paul's claim that children should inherit from their parents and not parents from their children. Responding to Plutarch's criticism of the wealthy, an interlocutor says, "But they preserve and lay up (φυλάττουσι καὶ θεσαυρίζουσι) their goods for children and heirs." And commenting on the laws of inheritance found in Num 27:1–11, Philo writes that "in the natural order of things, sons are the heirs of their fathers and not fathers of their sons" (νομός φύσεως ἐστι κληρονομεῖσθαι γονεῖς ὑπὸ παίδων ἀλλὰ μὴ τούτους κληρονομεῖν).[33]

In addition to providing a parallel to "laying up," the passage from Plutarch is also important because it indicates that the view expressed in Paul's maxim was indeed quite common.[34] To be sure, fathers owned prop-

---

30. For references and discussion, see O. Larry Yarbrough, "Parents and Children in the Jewish Family of Antiquity," in *The Jewish Family in Antiquity* (ed. Shaye J. D. Cohen; Atlanta: Scholars Press, 1993) 49–55. The syntax of v. 13 is difficult. Blass-Debrunner-Funk (§154) suggest τὴν δὲ αὐτὴν ἀντιμισθίαν may be read τὸν αὐτὸν πλατυσμὸν ὡς ἀντιμισθίαν. Rudolf Bultmann adds ἀποδιδόντες to complete the thought (*The Second Letter to the Corinthians* [Minneapolis: Augsburg, 1985] 177). Though he does not note it, this is an apt rendering, since ἀποδιδόντες was commonly used when ancient writers referred to "repaying the debt" children owed their parents. He takes ὡς τέκνοις λέγω as simply another reference to Paul's love of the Corinthians. Jean Héring refers to "the proper reciprocity between parent and children," but does not appear to draw on ancient attitudes to establish this (*The Second Epistle of Saint Paul to the Corinthians* [London: Epworth, 1967] 49).

31. They are notably absent from Romans. This is not surprising, however, since Paul had not founded the church in Rome and thus would not have considered himself its "father."

32. The more common terms are καταλείπειν and ἀπολείπειν. In addition to the examples in Liddell and Scott, see Isocrates, *To Nicocles* 32 and Musonius Rufus, *Should Every Child That Is Born Be Raised?* 100.15 (references to Musonius Rufus are to the page and line number in Cora E. Lutz, *Musonius Rufus: The Roman Socrates* [New Haven: Yale University Press, 1947]). Paul can also use θησαυρίζειν in the metaphorical sense of storing up for the world to come (Rom 2:5) and in the literal sense of setting money aside (1 Cor 16:2).

33. Trans. Colson (LCL).

34. Plutarch would not have given the statement so much attention were it not reflective of

erty outright and could leave it to whomever they chose. Roman law and common sentiment, however, increasingly called for them to leave it to their children—both sons and daughters. Indeed, one legal opinion rendered shortly after Paul's time determined that the *paterfamilias* only held property in trust, thus limiting his power to bequeath it to someone outside the family.[35] Even when the *paterfamilias* did disinherit his children, moreover, they could contest the provisions of the will and reclaim the property by demonstrating that their exclusion was not warranted. One of the characters in Terence's play *The Self-Tormentor* illustrates how much some fathers agonized over this very question. He wants to leave his estate to his son but believes the latter's dissipated life has rendered him incapable of overseeing it. In the end, after much persuasion and to the father's great relief, the son "sees the light" so that the crisis is avoided.[36]

For the moralists and rhetoricians, this concern with leaving property to one's children was entirely misdirected. *On the Love of Wealth* 526a is noteworthy on this score also, for Plutarch's rejoinder to his interlocutor's claim that the wealthy store up for their children and heirs is exemplary of the criticisms moralists and rhetoricians frequently raised. "By the very means whereby they suppose that they are training their children," Plutarch says,

> misers ruin them instead and warp their characters all the more, implanting in them their own avarice and meanness, as though constructing in their heirs a fort to guard the inheritance. For their admonition and instruction comes to this: "Get profit and be sparing, and count yourself as worth exactly what you have." This is not to educate a son, but to compress him and sew him shut, like a money bag, that he may hold tight and keep safe what you have put in.

Isocrates' admonitions are more positive. He tells Demonicus, for example, that "it is fitting (πρέπει) that a son should inherit his father's friendships even as he inherits his estate."[37] And to Nicocles he declares, "Consider it more important to leave to your children a good name than great riches."[38] Musonius Rufus offers similar advice, claiming that parents who have only

---

common sentiment. As Wayne Meeks notes, Plutarch's interlocutor reflects the views of the wealthy (*First Urban Christians*, 67). His suggestion that Paul's maxim "does not sound like the ethos of people at the lowest end of the economic scale" is supported by Edward Champlin's assessment of the social status of the Romans who made wills (see *Final Judgments: Duty and Emothion in Roman Wills, 200 B.C.-A.D. 250* [Berkeley: University of California Press, 1991] chap. 3). See, however, J. A. Crook's review of Champlin's book in *Journal of Roman Studies* 82 (1992) 232–34. Crook argues that the question of the social status of testators warrants further study, noting a number of examples where their social status is lower than Champlin allows.

35. *Digest* 28.2.11. See Dixon, *Roman Family*, 41.

36. The plots of Terence's plays commonly turn on family relationships. They, and other Roman comedies, are an important source for reconstructing the social world of early Christianity and should be examined along with the moral traditions.

37. *To Demonicus* 2 (trans. Norlin, LCL).

38. *To Nicocles* 32 (trans. Norlin, LCL).

one or two children so that they may preserve their estates "rob them of brothers, never having learned how much better it is to have many brothers than to have many possessions." He concludes, "I believe that each one of us ought to try to leave (ἀπολείπειν) brothers rather than money to our children so as to leave (ἀπολείψοντα) greater assurances of blessings" (*Should Every Child* 100.2–3, 15–16).

This brief survey of common sentiment, legal opinions, and moral traditions illustrates something of the seriousness with which the Greco-Roman world took the issue of inheritance. In a recent work on Roman wills, Edward Champlin demonstrates that for many Romans making a will was in fact an all-consuming occupation, illustrated by Seneca's comment "How much time is spent, how long do we debate with ourselves to whom and how much we shall give!" The reason for taking such care was that a will revealed one's true nature. Consequently, as Champlin puts it, "wills [were], most obviously, expressions of emotion."[39]

This last observation is especially appropriate in considering Paul's reference to inheritance in the maxim of 2 Cor 12:14b, for the whole passage is charged with emotion. "Here for the third time I am ready to come to you. I will not be a burden, for I seek not what is yours but you," Paul writes, adding after the maxim, "I will most gladly spend and be spent for your souls. If I love you the more, am I to be loved the less?"

Such language echoes throughout 2 Corinthians 10–13. Paul first links his claim not to be a burden with a declaration of his love in 11:7–15. After reminding the Corinthians that he had not been a burden on his previous stays in the city and insisting that his boast of this would not be silenced, Paul declares, "And why? Because I do not love you? God knows I do!" Then, following a rehearsal of his hardships on behalf of the gospel (which are his credentials for true apostleship),[40] he returns to the theme of 11:7–11: "For in what were you less favored than the rest of the churches, except that I myself did not burden you?" He concludes with the pointedly ironic comment, "Forgive me this wrong!" (12:13). The issue at stake throughout this section appears in 11:7: the Corinthians were critical of Paul for refusing to accept financial assistance from them, a refusal that served only to exacerbate the already strained relationship between Paul and the Corinthians.

Though Paul asks whether by preaching the gospel to the Corinthians without cost he "abased" himself (2 Cor 11:7), Peter Marshall is probably right in arguing that it was in fact the Corinthians, or at least some of them, who felt "abased," seeing Paul's refusal of the gift as a spurning of their

39. Champlin, *Final Judgments*, 8; see especially chapter 1, "Motives." The translation of Seneca's *On Benefits* 4.11.4 is Champlin's modification of the LCL edition by Basore.
40. He also speaks of his heavenly vision, but even this is set over against Paul's "thorn in the flesh," so that the focus of 11:16–12:10 is on the apostle's weakness.

"friendship."[41] If this is correct Paul uses the maxim to defend himself by reminding the Corinthians of his duties as their father. In effect, he tells the Corinthians, "I am responsible for you, you are not responsible for me."

We may well ask, however, whether the argument had much chance of success, dependent as it is on the Corinthians' accepting status as dependent children. That this is in fact what Paul meant becomes clear in v. 15, where, by moving from "laying up" for children to "spending and being spent" on their behalf, Paul changes the metaphor. In v. 15, that is, he no longer speaks of providing an inheritance but of taking care of children. If he became their father by bringing the gospel to the Corinthians, he fulfilled the duties of a father by supporting himself and, more importantly, by enduring deprivation and hardship for their sakes. Their response, he states pleadingly, is to love him in return.

To this argument, however, other *topoi* treating relations between parents and children provided the Corinthians with a ready response. For whereas the topos *On Friendship* refers only to love, honor, and respect, others require children to repay their parents in more tangible ways. Among these, the most frequently mentioned is providing parents with food, clothing, and shelter. Two examples, one from the rabbis and the other from the Greco-Roman moralists, illustrate this. The first is from *b. Qiddušin* 31b

> Our Rabbis taught: What is "fear" and what is "honour"? "Fear" means that [the son] must neither stand in his [father's] place nor sit in his place, nor contradict his words, nor tip the scales against him. "Honour" means that he must give him food and drink, clothe and cover him, lead him in and out.

The second comes from Hierocles' comments entitled *What manner we ought to conduct ourselves towards our parents:*

> We should, therefore, procure for our parents liberal food ... a bed, sleep, unction, a bath, garments; and in short, all the necessaries which the body requires, that they may never at any time experience the want of any of these; in thus acting, imitating their care about our nurture, when we were infants.[42]

Whether any of the Corinthians thought of this counterargument we have no way of knowing; however, since the most frequently cited reason for having children was to provide for one's old age, it would be surprising had they not. For Paul to refrain from mentioning children's obligation to take care of their parents is, of course, no surprise at all. To speak of it would

---

41. Peter Marshall, *Enmity at Corinth: Social Conventions in Paul's Relationship with the Corinthians* (WUNT 2nd ser. 23; Tübingen: Mohr-Siebeck, 1987). Marshall draws heavily on book 8 of Aristotle's *Nichomachean Ethics,* which is concerned with friendship. The friendship between parents and children is a major theme of the latter half of book 8.

42. Trans. Thomas Taylor in his *Political Fragments* (Chiswick: Whittingham, 1822) 86. For further references and discussion, see Yarbrough, "Parents and Children in the Jewish Family of Antiquity."

have undermined his whole position. That Paul knew of this convention, and could indeed use it when occasion demanded, is suggested by his wish to keep Onesimus with him in prison "that he might serve me." The service he sought was that of a son, not a slave, for Onesimus was the child he had begotten in his chains (παρακαλῶ σε περὶ τοῦ ἐμοῦ τέκνου, ὃν ἐγέννησα ἐν τοῖς δεσμοῖς, v. 10). To be sure, Onesimus was to serve Paul on behalf of Philemon. But Paul regarded Philemon as a son too, as his claim that Philemon owed him his very self (σεαυτόν μοι προσοφείλεις, v. 19b) indicates.[43] The difference between the two situations determined why Paul could speak of children serving their parents in one letter but not in the other. Paul felt no threat to himself or his gospel in his relationship with Philemon, while it was one of his primary concerns in his relationship with the Corinthians. Thus, although Paul can admit to having been in need during his stay with the Corinthians (2 Cor 11:9), all that he requires of them—and all he will accept from them!—is to love him as their father.

In a number of situations, therefore, referring to commonly accepted sentiments regarding the relationship between parents and children served Paul well, even if on at least one occasion Paul's own argument could have been turned back on him. Again, however, we must bear in mind that we are speaking of Paul's *metaphorical* use of parent–child imagery. The question remains, therefore, whether Paul might have applied the conventions on which these metaphors were based to life as believers experienced it. To ask the question in its most pointed form: Could Paul have used common social conventions in addressing his relationship with the Corinthians if he did not hold them to be valid for the parents and children in his churches? To this issue we now turn.

THE MORAL FORCE OF PARENT-CHILD IMAGERY FOR PAUL

Neither form of the question just raised is easy to answer, given the complexity of Paul's thought. As we have seen, he is selective in his use of moral conventions and can unexpectedly change a metaphor when it suits his argument. Furthermore, because Paul rarely addresses parents and children directly and on no occasion gives general admonitions regarding them, we have little evidence to go on. What we do have is mostly negative: Paul regards disobedience to parents as a vice and treats the status of children as only a secondary issue in the question of divorce for couples of mixed marriages. All we can do, therefore, is test each case individually, seeking to determine whether the conventions Paul uses are in keeping with what he says elsewhere. We focus on the two aspects of Paul's metaphorical use of parent–child imagery that were so important in his relationship with the

43. On this topic, see the essay by Ronald Hock in this volume.

Corinthians: (1) parents should lay up for their children and (2) children should return their parents' affections.

Most likely, had occasion required him to speak of it, Paul would have encouraged children to love their parents. At first this seems so obvious as to be scarcely worth mentioning. In light of the way familial relations are treated in some of the traditions included in the Gospels, however, we cannot simply assume it.[44] Perhaps the strongest argument for maintaining that Paul would have encouraged children to return their parents' affection is that honoring one's parents is an essential element in the Greco-Roman and Jewish parenetic traditions of which he made so much use. To be sure, Paul did not take up every aspect of these traditions,[45] but there is no reason to question his use of this one. Indeed, it is in keeping with his admonition "to love one another" (1 Thess 4:9; Rom 13:9) and his castigation of the Gentiles for disobeying their parents (Rom 1:30). In all likelihood, and for the same reasons, Paul would even have extended the argument to encourage children to supply their parents' needs for food, clothing, and shelter. This not only would be in keeping with common parenetic traditions, but would fulfill his admonitions to "help the weak" (1 Thess 5:14) and "bear one another's burdens" (Gal 6:2). It is hard to believe, at any rate, that Paul would not have Rufus take care of his mother, were she in need.

The question is complicated somewhat if we consider what Paul might have said of cases in which parents were not believers. But his admonition to "do good to all" (Gal 6:10) coupled with his advising believers to remain with unbelieving spouses (1 Cor 7:14) suggest that he would have children love and support their parents even if they were unbelievers. Had the parents spoken against Paul's gospel, however, he would doubtless have responded as Musonius did to the father who forbade his son to study philosophy—there is finally a higher authority than one's parents.[46]

With regard to laying up for children, however, the matter is entirely different. For although providing an inheritance was widely held to be a duty parents owed their children, it seems unlikely Paul would ever have advised it. After all, in citing the maxim Paul is more concerned with "spending and being spent" than with "laying up" for the Corinthians. The primary reason for concluding that Paul would not advise parents to lay up for their children, however, is Paul's apocalyptic expectations. If he considered the end to be imminent, that is, could Paul ever have shown interest in inheritance, which by definition is a matter of the future? The parameters for Paul's discussion of what is to come are set by 1 Thess 4:13–5:11 and 1 Cor 7:25–31, and neither shows any concern with financial matters! This is not to say that Paul was never concerned with money. He in fact advises the Corinthi-

---

44. See, e.g., Mark 10:29; Matt 10:35//Luke 12:53; and Luke 14:26.

45. His treatment of divorce, for example, was unlike both Jewish and Greco-Roman views.

46. See *Must one obey one's parents under all circumstances* 104.37–106.6.

ans "to put something aside and store it up" (ἕκαστος ὑμῶν παρ᾽ ἑαυτῷ
τιθέτω θησαυρίζων). His object, however, is not an inheritance but the collection for the church in Jerusalem (1 Cor 16:2; see also Rom 15:25-29; Gal
2:10; 2 Corinthians 8-9). Similarly, he advises the Thessalonians to work
with their own hands, but this is so that they can be independent, not so
that they may store up wealth (1 Thess 5:11-12). Indeed, though the argument of 2 Corinthians 8-9 is exceedingly complex, portions of it suggest
that Paul had fundamental reservations about the storing up of wealth, at
least if it meant leaving other members of the church in need.[47]

We cannot be sure this is the way Paul would have argued had he
addressed the parents and children within his churches with regard to these
issues. Paul is rarely predictable. Had other issues impinged on individual
situations, he may well have deemed them more pressing and shaped his
argument accordingly. To explore the questions, however, is to discover the
dangers inherent in using Paul's metaphorical use of parent–child imagery
to construct a Pauline ethic of the family. This is especially true of the
maxim in 2 Cor 12:14b, for though it may tell us something of the social status of the Pauline churches, as Wayne Meeks so insightfully tells us, we cannot simply assume that Paul would have admonished his followers to put it
into practice. The maxim served Paul's argument with the Corinthians well,
but only as metaphor—a metaphor applied, moreover, in a very specific and
limited fashion.

If these conclusions regarding the use of Paul's parent–child imagery for
constructing a Pauline ethic are mostly negative, it is not to deny the importance of the metaphor for Paul and his churches. Indeed, in focusing on
Paul's use of parent–child imagery for defining his relationship with his coworkers and churches, we have neglected his theological use of it, which
finally may be even more central to his thought. For to Paul God is the
"Father" of the Lord Jesus and of all believers; adoption into the family of
God is a key metaphor for the new status believers have obtained; and "son-
ship," with its "glorious liberty," is to be contrasted to "slavery," with its
bondage to sin.

Much of Paul's imagery regarding parents and children he no doubt
derived from the Jewish traditions which shaped so much of his thought;
some of it he shared with the moralists, rhetoricians, and other religious
writers of his day. But it was also rooted in the day-to-day lives of the

47. See 2 Cor 8:13-15. This argument should not be pressed, however, since in his treatment
of the controversy over the Lord's Supper in 1 Cor 11:17-34 Paul declares that people should
satisfy their hunger at home, not that they should share their provisions. On the collection for
the Jerusalem church, see Dieter Georgi, *Die Geschichte der Kollekte des Paulus für Jerusalem* (TF
39; Hamburg-Bergstedt: Reich, 1965); Keith F. Nickle, *The Collection: A Study in Paul's Strategy*
(SBT 48; London: SCM, 1966); and Jouette M. Bassler, *God & Mammon: Asking for Money in the
New Testament* (Nashville: Abingdon, 1991) chapter 4. On 2 Corinthians 8-9, see the
Hermeneia commentary by H. D. Betz (Philadelphia: Fortress, 1985).

people to whom he proclaimed his gospel. In this essay we have tried to explore how Paul used this imagery and what the readers of his letters may have thought about it. Even if our answers are provisional and necessarily sketchy, they nonetheless allow us to imagine Paul and the lives of the early Christians for whom he wrote his letters with greater clarity. Wayne Meeks has taught us the benefits of asking such questions and has guided many of us in seeking answers to them. For this we honor him, even if we can never repay the debt.

Part Two

Early Christians
in Their Social World

CHAPTER 10

Matthew and the Spirit

Leander E. Keck

IF IT IS CLEAR anywhere in the New Testament that theological history, social history, and texts are intertwined, it is in the Gospels; for when they were created their contents were already more deeply embedded in early Christian communities than those of the epistles when they were dictated. While the epistles also used traditions and traditional motifs, the Gospels are far more the written results of the transmission and construal of traditions within the communities for which the texts were produced. Consequently, the community in which a given Gospel was created and first read would have recognized its traditions and customary themes, even if the new text ordered and construed them in unexpected ways. If we had a complete inventory of traditions and themes that circulated in a given early Christian community, we could infer more perceptively the actual import of what its evangelist included and excluded. As it is, we know neither his options nor his aims. Nonetheless, even the limited corpus of first-century Christian literature allows us to make some inferences about a given Gospel's possible functions in the community for which it was produced. These elemental observations prove to be especially suggestive for the Gospel according to Matthew.

No Gospel's context has been studied more intently in recent years than Matthew's, for the specificity of its contents makes it possible to infer a good deal about the readers and the problems they faced. Recent discussions have focused markedly on the community's tensions with formative Judaism. Indeed, the 1989 conference on the topic "The Social History of the Matthean Community in Roman Syria" put almost all of the emphasis on the community's external relationships, paying virtually no attention to its internal problems, despite the fact that in one participant's judgment

"Matthew's community is a sociological shambles."[1] Even if that judgment should prove to be somewhat overstated, it is evident that this Christian community, perhaps a network of house-churches, experienced serious internal problems as well. And it is with one of the latter that this essay is concerned—namely, the role of the Spirit. It is in just this regard that what Matthew does *not* say becomes significant. Silence is indeed ambiguous, though at times it provides an important clue—as in the well-known detective story, what merits attention is the dog that didn't bark.

GOSPEL ENDINGS AND CHURCH BEGINNINGS

Just as the beginnings of the Gospels provide important clues to the texts as a whole,[2] so their conclusions are important indicators of the evangelists' perspectives because a given ending is the nexus between a particular Jesus story and the story of the church, whether told or not. Noting briefly how two other Gospels end will bring into relief the distinctive feature of Matthew's ending with which this essay is concerned.

In Luke, the last thing the risen Jesus says to the disciples on Easter evening is, "And behold, I send the promise of my Father upon you; but stay in the city, until you are clothed with power from on high" (Luke 24:49). The problems of the brief narrative that follows in vv. 50–53, and its text variants, should not distract attention from the central point: the resurrected One pledges the gift of the Spirit-power to the disciples who had just been told "that repentance and forgiveness of sin should be preached in his [Christ's] name to all nations" (v. 48). The risen One authorizes the mission, and the Spirit is to empower it. What is said tersely at the end of Luke is elaborated in Acts 1:4–5, then summarized in v. 8, and subsequently supported by the narrative at key points, beginning with Pentecost (see 13:1–3; 16:6; 19:21). Also in John, Spirit and mission belong together. According to 20:21, Jesus having greeted the disciples, said, "As the Father has sent me, so I send you." To this the narrator adds, "When he had said this, he breathed on them and said to them, 'Receive the Holy Spirit. If you forgive the sins of any, they are forgiven; if you retain the sins of any, they are retained.'"[3]

1. The papers were edited by David L. Balch and published in 1991 by Fortress Press as *Social History of the Matthean Community: Cross-Disciplinary Approaches*; the quotation is from Robert H. Gundry, "A Responsive Evaluation of the Social History of the Matthean Community in Roman Syria," 60. See also Andrew J. Overman, *Matthew's Gospel and Formative Judaism: The Social World of the Matthean Community* (Minneapolis: Fortress, 1990); Bruce J. Malina and Jerome H. Neyrey, *Calling Jesus Names: The Social Value of Labels in Matthew* (Sonoma, Calif.: Polebridge, 1988); and Graham N. Stanton, *A Gospel for a New People: Studies in Matthew* (Edinburgh: Clark, 1992).

2. See the essays in *How Gospels Begin* (*Semeia* 52; Atlanta: Scholars Press, 1991).

3. The absence of any reference to the Spirit in the present ending of John in chapter 21 is understandable: Jesus commissions Peter to care for the church, not to oversee its mission.

Although Luke-Acts and John understand the Spirit quite differently, they agree that the Spirit is a hallmark of the Christian community. In Acts the Spirit's interventions are of a piece with other forms of divine guidance for the church (an angel in 8:26; the Lord himself in 9:10; 18:9); even the "Apostolic Decree" claims to have the approval of the Spirit, though the narrative leading up to it does not say so (15:28). For John, the Spirit manifests its presence neither in unusual events nor in turning points in the history of the community but in the steady unfolding of the meaning of Jesus as portrayed in this text. The Paraclete's major role is to bear witness to Jesus within the church itself. Even if Acts idealizes the generation whose experiences it reports, it is unlikely that its initial readers understood themselves as being informed of a Spirit-guided past that had wholly disappeared. In other words, for both of these roughly contemporary tradition-streams, it is self-evident that the Spirit is the mode in which the risen One is present, guiding and shaping the life of the church.

Even when the differences between the work of the Spirit in the Lukan and Johannine streams are taken into account, the significant point is that emphasizing the role of the Spirit is not simply the peculiar agenda of either evangelist but reflects a shared understanding of early church life; their agreement on the importance of the Spirit is therefore significant for the historian and for this essay's concern with the ending of Matthew.

MATTHEW 28:16–20

The importance of Matthew's concluding paragraph has been acknowledged ever since Otto Michel demonstrated its significance for understanding the whole Gospel.[4] Subsequently, however, interpreters have been so intrigued by what this paragraph says that they have neglected to explore the implications of one thing it does not say—Jesus neither promises nor imparts the Holy Spirit.[5] Instead, the Holy Spirit is confined to a liturgical formula to be used to mark one's entering the faith community, thereby replacing the link between Spirit and missionary with the link between Spirit and convert. Thus, the mission itself does not depend on the Spirit's empowering arrival as in Luke-Acts but can be undertaken immediately.

---

4. Otto Michel, "The Conclusion of Matthew's Gospel: A Contribution to the History of the Easter Message," in *The Interpretation of Matthew* (ed. Graham Stanton; Philadelphia: Fortress, 1983) 30–41; originally published in *EvT* 10 (1950) 16–26. The literature concerning this passage has become enormous.

5. The significance of the omission of the Spirit is not diminished by the fact that two themes important in Matthew are also omitted: forgiveness of sins (added to the cup saying in 26:28) and "the gospel of the kingdom"; none of the Gospel endings states everything that the evangelist's church said. It is the emphasis on the Spirit in Luke and John that makes the omission of it from Matthew significant.

Here the worldwide scope of the mission is the explicit reflex of the cosmic authority that God had conferred on Jesus through the resurrection/exaltation.

In view of Matthew's contemporaries, Luke-Acts and John, how is one to account for this marked silence about the Holy Spirit in connection with the church's life and mission? To attribute it to mere oversight would be patronizing, for that would imply that we know what the evangelist thought while excusing him for neglecting to say it. Nor will it do to attribute the silence to the fact that this evangelist, not knowing Luke and John but using Mark, which had no appearance story, simply had no precedent to guide him. True as this may be, that did not inhibit him from replacing Mark 16:1-8 altogether in order to end the Jesus story the way he thought it ought to end. Oddly, Hubbard argued that the evangelist used a "Proto-Commissioning" story which ended with "And I will send the Holy Spirit upon you" but which he rewrote as "And behold, I am with you. . . ."[6] Even though this hypothesis is neither necessary nor probable, in its own way it is sensitive to the problem and thereby invites closer scrutiny of the commissioning words themselves.

What Jesus says to the disciples falls into three parts: (a) self-presentation (v. 18a), the commission proper (vv. 19–20), (c) promise (v. 20b). The commission has but one imperative (μαθητεύσατε, "make disciples"), modified by two participial clauses: baptizing . . . teaching . . . . Just as the baptismal formula specifies the character of the baptism, so the content of the teaching too is specified: observing everything that Jesus had commanded. Given Matthew's marked interest in discipleship,[7] what Jesus had "commanded" surely embraces more than his *logia* in the imperative mood. The teachings of him who presented himself as the *kosmokrator* are obligatory, and his deeds (particularly his way of doing God's will) are mandatory precedents for the community being formed by the baptized. By requiring this obedience, we may surmise, Jesus himself will build his church (16:18).

According to Matthew, Jesus' last word is the promise that he himself will be present in the community-in-mission as long as this age lasts. The juxtaposition of the emphasis on obedience to Jesus and on the promise implies that he himself will be present as the disciples (including those who become disciples through them) live by what this Gospel records. Moreover, the theme of "presence" comes as no surprise, for it forms the climax of the angel's announcement to Joseph about Mary's child: "his name shall be called Emmanuel (which means God with us)" (1:23). Thus the story

6. Benjamin J. Hubbard, *The Matthean Redaction of a Primitive Apostolic Commissioning: An Exegesis of Matthew 28:16-20* (SBLDS 19; Missoula, Mont.: University of Montana Printing Department [Scholars Press], 1974) 120–21. His hypothesis is accepted by W. D. Davies and Dale C. Allison, Jr., *The Gospel According to Matthew* (ICC; Edinburgh: T. & T. Clark, 1988) 1:95.

7. Jack Dean Kingsbury, "The Verb *Akolouthein* ("To Follow") as an Index of Matthew's View of his Community," *JBL* 97 (1978) 56–73.

opens with the promise that through Jesus God will be present and concludes with the promise that Jesus, through this account of all he had commanded, will continue to mediate God's presence among the obedient. The inference is clear: if the risen Jesus himself will be present, there is no need for him to promise the Spirit. In other words, Hubbard rightly sensed that the presence of Jesus obviates the need of the Spirit's presence.

There is no reason to infer that the evangelist included the triadic baptismal formula because he wished to emphasize the reception of the Spirit in conjunction with baptism, as Paul assumes and Acts asserts (Acts 2:39) and reports (8:12-17; 9:17-18; 10:44-48). That the Matthean community understood baptism with this formula to summarize "the enthusiastic experience" itself, that it regarded baptism as "an insertion into the exaltation of Jesus," and that "it is the exaltation of the disciple, the disciple's sharing in the power given to Jesus"[8] are inferences wholly without foundation. Such construals attribute to the evangelist and his community the mind-set of Paul's Corinthians—precisely the opposite of what was probably the case for the evangelist. To see this, it is necessary to view the omission of the Spirit in the wider context of the First Gospel's attitude toward the work of the Spirit in the life of the church.

AMBIVALENCE TOWARD SPIRIT ACTIVITY

Here too, given the few references to the Spirit in Matthew, it is instructive to read the silences as well as the statements. Three considerations will bring into focus Matthew's ambivalence about the work of the Spirit: (1) the work of Jesus; (2) the attitude toward prophecy; and (3) the reluctance to celebrate present salvation.

1. Jesus is presented as Spirit-begotten (1:20) and as Spirit-endowed (3:16). Moreover, Matthew has Jesus explicitly claim that it is "by the Spirit of God" that he casts out demons (12:28; Q had "by the finger of God," retained in Luke 11:20). Blasphemy against the Holy Spirit is unforgivable because it is the ultimate repudiation of the divine (12:38). Further, among the several roles the Matthean Jesus plays is that of a charismatic prophet. When his erstwhile neighbors were puzzled by his audacity, he responded, "A prophet is not without honor—except in his own country and in his own house" (13:57). Oddly enough, however, when he commissioned the twelve disciples to undertake a mission that replicates his (preaching the kingdom's nearness, healing, raising the dead, cleansing lepers and expelling demons), he does not mention the Spirit (10:7-8). Nor has there been any previous hint that the Twelve had already received the Spirit. Matthew

---

8. So Jane Schaberg, *The Father, The Son and The Holy Spirit: The Triadic Phrase in Matthew 28:19b* (SBLDS 61; Chico, Calif.: Scholars Press, 1982) 332.

gives the impression that while Jesus' mission is empowerd by the Spirit, having the Spirit is not a prerequisite for the disciples' mission (though it is implied in the charge to exorcise). In short, Spirit-power appears to be restricted to Jesus, who shares his mission but not his power.

2. In Matthew, the prophet, whose endowment by the Spirit is presumed, is highly regarded. At the end of the mission discourse in chapter 10, Jesus promises those who receive an itinerant prophet "because he is a prophet" will have the same reward as the prophet. The same holds true of the one who plays host to the righteous man. Indeed, not even the simplest human gesture—a cup of water—toward a disciple will be overlooked by God. In this passage, the prophet appears to stand at the head of a three-tiered view of the community: prophet, righteous, disciple (10:41–42). The general esteem accorded prophets is reflected also in the final beatitude (5:11–12). Here one does not need to be a prophet or to receive one in order to have a prophet's reward, because what links the believer with the prophets of Israel is persecution.

At the same time, the First Evangelist is convinced that the phenomenon of (Spirit-empowered) prophecy requires of the community special discernment and caution because prophecy is not self-authenticating. The first reference to Christian prophets (7:15–23)[9] warns the church about travelers who, like Agabus (Acts 11:28; 21:10) and those known also to the author of the *Didache* (*Did.* 11), move from place to place (they "come to you"). Even the promise to those who receive prophets is subtly qualified, for in saying "he who receives a prophet because he is a prophet" itself implies the need to discern whether the itinerant is really a prophet. The text does not say, "because he claims to be a prophet" or even "because he does what prophets do." The need to detect who is and who is not a prophet is precisely the point of the warning in 7:15—some will arrive whose true nature is concealed beneath their prophetlike appearances; they are "wolves in sheepskins."[10] In terms of outward appearances, of observable authorizing signs, these rapacious ones look just like harmless sheep.

9. It is more likely that the evangelist has in view Christian prophets (so too É. Cothenet, "Les prophètes chretiens dans l'Évangile selon saint Matthieu," in *L'Évangile selon Matthieu: Rédaction et théologie* [ed. M. Didier; BETL 29; Gembloux: J. Duculot, 1972] 300) than that he thinks of Pharisees, as David Hill argues ("False Prophets and Charismatics: Structure and Interpretation in Matthew 7:15–23," *Bib* 57 [1976] 346). Hill's article begins with a useful survey of previous attempts to identify these persons. Because 7:15–23 brings together various logia with diverse histories, the passage (and its parallels in Luke and *Gospel of Thomas*) invites a careful tradition-historical analysis. Such an attempt was made by Michael Krämer, "Hütet euch vor den falschen Propheten: Eine Überlieferungsgeschichtliche Untersuchung zu Mt 7,15–23/Lk 6,43–46/Mt 12,33–7," *Bib* 57 (1976) 349–77. For a more recent, and quite different approach, see Hans Dieter Betz, "An Episode in the Last Judgment (Matt. 7:21–23)," in *Essays on the Sermon on the Mount* (Philadelphia: Fortress, 1985) chapter 7.

10. For the use of "wolves," which, in ancient polemic, are often associated with the demonic, see Otto Böcher, "Wölfe in Schafspelzen: Zum religionsgeschichtlichen Hintergrund von Matth. 7,15," *TZ* 24 (1968) 405–26, esp. 412ff.

The criteria for distinguishing the false from the true prophet, however, are scarcely adequate: "by their fruits you will know them" (7:16, repeated in v. 20 to form an *inclusio*). Not only is this agricultural metaphor (no grapes from thorns or figs from thistles) of little help in identifying wolves that look like sheep, but by the time the "fruits" would manifest themselves the damage would have been done. How useful is it to be told that when you see which ones attack (λύκοι ἅρπαγες) the others you will know who are sheep and who are wolves?[11]

The evangelist himself seems to have sensed the limited utility of this criterion, for he has Jesus go on to announce that only doers of God's will shall enter the kingdom and that he, Jesus, will say, "I never knew" those who somehow managed to prophesy, expel demons, and do many mighty deeds in Jesus' name while being "workers of lawlessness" (οἱ ἐργαζόμενοι τὴν ἀνομίαν, using the language of Ps 6:9). Apart from the unspecified ἀνομία, the rejected have been doing what Jesus commissions his emissaries to do in 10:8 (preach, heal, resurrect, cleanse lepers, and cast out demons)—plus prophesying in Jesus' name. In other words, the excluded have not been identifiable as rapacious wolves. The flow of thought in 7:15–23 implies that the criterion of "fruits" is of but relative, temporal value because who is truly sheep and who is actually sheeplike wolf cannot be known before the end.

At first glance, the fact that Jesus' final discourse twice mentions false prophets (24:11, 24) implies that here the evangelist returns to the theme that he had introduced into Jesus' inaugural sermon. At second glance, however, it is quite evident that the false prophets against whom Jesus warns in chapter 7 are to be distinguished from those predicted in chapter 24 because the latter are non-Christian figures. What is said here about false prophets, therefore, has no direct bearing on this Gospel's attitude toward Christian prophets who operate as Spirit-authorized figures.[12] It does, however, contribute indirectly to it—especially if one sees how it functions in the context of the final discourse, which probably comprises chapters 23–25.[13] Here the theme of the eschatological judgment, with which each of the preceding four discourses ends, becomes dominant.

In chapter 23 the seventh woe insists that the scribes, Pharisees, and hypocrites cannot distance themselves from their forebears who murdered the prophets (v. 29; similarly Q in Luke 20:47–48). After the transitional sayings

11. Hans Dieter Betz's assertion that "there can be no doubt that false prophets are Gentile Christian missionaries like Paul, who proclaim the gospel apart from the law" can be doubted. See his *Essays on the Sermon on the Mount*, 156 (also p. 21).

12. Cothenet, on the other hand, thinks that the evangelist applied the eschatological warning against zealot prophets in chapter 24 to Christian prophets in chapter 7 ("Les prophètes chrétiens," 302–3).

13. Interpreters continue to debate whether the fifth and final major discourse consists only of chapters 24–25 or includes chapter 23 as well.

in which Jesus taunts the hearers, "Fill up the measure of your fathers" so that escape is impossible (vv. 32–33), Matthew has Jesus speak in Wisdom's role,[14] saying that for this very reason (viz., to actualize vv. 32–33), *he* is sending "prophets and sages and scribes, some of whom you will flog in your synagogues and persecute from city to city" (v. 34)—a fate he had not only foretold for his emissaries but had linked with his own (10:17–25). Thus, the previous prophets, Jesus, and those sent by Jesus—for Matthew, the true prophets—share a single fate because the opposition is the same.

In chapter 24, however, the false prophets fare better: they will be believed by many. Not a word is said about their being rejected, even though what they say is false and leads many into error (24:5, 11, 24), whether by spurious claims to be "the Christ" (v. 5) or to know who (literally, where) he is (vv. 23, 26). Indeed, this whole series of warnings begins with the topic sentence, "Look out, so that you are not misled!" (24:4).[15] In other words, the sayings about the false prophets (and false Christs) in chapter 24 underscore the tragic history into which the evangelist placed the Jesus story: truth is rejected but error is accepted. The phenomenon of prophecy does not determine which is which, a point made already in chapter 7. A deeper skepticism about prophecy is hard to imagine.[16]

3. Also to be noted is the Matthean reluctance to celebrate the signs of present salvation, which in Paul, Luke-Acts, and John are signaled by the enabling presence of the Spirit. To be sure, Matthew is not accountable to them and so is not being measured by them. Nonetheless, can one overlook the fact that in this Gospel there is only one situation in which the disciples can count on the power of the Spirit—when they are to bear witness in court (10:20, a traditional saying slightly adapted from Mark 13:11; Luke 21:14 formulates a comparable point quite differently)? Assuring as this may be, it offers nothing for daily life in less extreme situations. One may, of course, note that the evangelist's predecessors did not mention the presence of the Spirit as a hallmark of Christian existence either. Yet the force of this observation is weakened considerably when one recalls that the creator of Matthew did not hesitate to introduce into the text a term he regarded as essential—righteousness.[17] This suggests that if the presence of

14. Matthew does not actually say that Jesus now speaks in Wisdom's role; nonetheless, this construal is generally accepted in view of the fact that in Q the saying was transmitted as Jesus' quotation of "the Wisdom of God" (Luke 11:49).

15. In Matt 24:5–25, the danger of being misled (πλανᾶν) appears three times: vv. 5 (taken from Mark 13:6), 11 (peculiarly Matthean), and 24 (taken from Mark 13:22). For the significance of πλανᾶν in early Christian material, see Herbert Braun, "Πλανάω," *TDNT* 6:228–53, esp. 242–53.

16. Eduard Schweizer, on the other hand, concluded that the evangelist "is not skeptical at all about a charismatic life in the Church" ("Observance of the Law and Charismatic Activity in Matthew," *NTS* 16 [1970] 226).

17. In Matthew, δικαιοσύνη appears in but seven passages (3:15; 5:6, 10, 20; 6:1, 33; 21:32), none derived from a known source. They express the evangelist's interest.

the Spirit had been important for him he would have found a way to say so, as did Luke in 11:13.

In a word, if for Paul, Luke-Acts, and John the presence of the Spirit is characteristic of Christian life, for Matthew it is reserved for a truly exceptional situation. Whereas both the Pauline ἀρραβών/ἀπαρχή and the Johannine presence that "dwells in you and will be in you" (14:7) assure the believer that one can live out of the future into the present, the Matthean view of the Spirit merely assures one that in future crises one will not fail. The Matthean Christian is earnest but not joyous, assured of forgiveness, if one forgives, but not of the enabling power of the Spirit to do daily what is required to enter the kingdom.

Matthew is consistent. For this refusal to celebrate the presentness of salvation, this restriction of the Spirit to crisis situations, is of a piece with the well-known Matthean distinction between the church and the kingdom of God, just as it is consonant with the pervasive concern with the coming judgment, when the sheep will be as surprised as the goats (25:31–46) because who is and who is not righteous will be manifest only then, as also the sayings about the threefold acts of righteousness make clear (6:1–18). One can enter the church (through baptism, using the triadic formula) and remain outside the kingdom, as even some who prophesy, exorcise, and work miracles in Jesus' name will discover when they hear the Judge dismiss them as workers of lawlessness (7:21–23).

Concluding Reflections

It is one thing to recognize the Matthean reticence about the Spirit in the life of the church and to see how that is consonant with other aspects of this Gospel (the exegetical task); it is another to account for it and to understand how it functioned in the evangelist's community (the historical/sociological task). One cannot avoid asking whether this reticence *reflects* the situation in the community or was designed to *correct* it. In the absence of clear evidence, one should be cautious in assuming the one or the other because either one entails reconstructing the history and dynamics of a Christian community that cannot be regarded as a conventical in a backwater but as part of what was becoming the mainstream. Here it must suffice, however, to identify some aspects of such an undertaking.

First, it is by no means clear whether the disparate and allusive data are to be construed as diverse ways of referring to one group within the Christian community or to several (or, for that matter, the extent to which one is justified in referring to *the* community, especially if one locates the evangelist in a cosmopolitan center such as Antioch).[18] For example, does the jux-

18. Wayne A. Meeks prudently observed that "there may have been many small household

taposition of the warning against false prophets (7:15–20) and the logia about the "Lord, Lord" sayers (vv. 21–23) point to one group or to two?[19] If the former, how are we to imagine prophecy, exorcism, and miracle working as part of the rapacious work of the false prophets who function in Jesus' name? Or do these passages refer to different problems in different clusters of house-churches, though traceable to reliance on the Spirit? Is it mere coincidence that this Gospel is simultaneously eclectic in the use of traditions, positively oriented to the institutionalization of the church, and reluctant to acknowledge the authority of the Spirit in daily life?

Second, the warning against itinerant charismatics ("who come to you," 7:15), whom the Matthean Jesus condemns as "false prophets," can also suggest that what the evangelist was coping with was more than diversity. As prophets, these figures would have asserted special authority because they were authorized by the Spirit. Nonetheless, from the evangelist's perspective, their impact on the community is destructive (rapacious wolves among [innocent] sheep). Unfortunately for us, he did not specify how that rapaciousness expressed itself. Nonetheless, are we amiss in seeing them as the rigorists who in the parable volunteered to pull the weeds from the field—that is, who disrupt the churches by forcing out those they deem not sufficiently faithful (13:28)? If that be the case, then the evangelist curbed such Spirit-authorized vigilante activity by having Jesus himself provide disciplinary procedures (18:15–20) and by framing them with the insistence that God wills the restoration of the wayward (vv. 10–14) and the parable of the fate of the unforgiving servant (vv. 23–25). At the same time, the evangelist made it clear that he was no less rigorous in his view of discipleship than the absolutists.

Third, in this context one cannot ignore the fact that many of the most demanding sayings of Jesus came into Matthew from that body of traditions called Q. Since the identity of the "Q-people" is not as clear as some bold reconstructions claim, one is not precluded from probing the possibility that they were, or at least included, the charismatic itinerant prophets. The more plausible such a hypothesis becomes, the more important are the consequences for the history and dynamics of the Christian community for which Matthew was created. To come right to the point: the customary view that the First Evangelist, in creating his Gospel by combining and editing Mark, Q, and M (the customary view), was engaged in far more than a literary and theological undertaking—he was at the same time engaged in a

---

groups in Antioch . . . and quite likely there was a certain diversity among them. Not all may have shared the history and perspectives that Matthew assumes" (*The Moral World of the First Christians* [Library of Early Christianity; Philadelphia: Westminster, 1986] 137). I suspect things were more turbulent than this.

19. Hill, for example, insists that two quite distinct groups are in view ("False Prophets," 340).

church-political process by which he dealt with groups who legitimated themselves by appealing to these respective Jesus traditions. Among them were those whose reliance on the Spirit threatened, in the evangelist's eyes, the stability of the church, which needed to consolidate itself for the future.

It is this possibility that makes the silence about the Spirit, especially in the Gospel's conclusion, so fascinating and so significant for our understanding of early Christianity as a whole.

CHAPTER 11

The Problem of Perjury in Greek Context: Prolegomena to an Exegesis of Matthew 5:33; 1 Timothy 1:10; and *Didache* 2.3

John T. Fitzgerald

THE PROBLEM OF PERJURY

PERJURY WAS NOT a new issue in the moral world of the first Christians.[1] It was mentioned already by Homer in the *Iliad*, a work that played an enormous role in the education and moral formation of individuals in the Greco-Roman world. As Wayne A. Meeks has astutely observed, "The heroes of the Iliad were patterns of life for the Greek; no educated person would ever be at a loss to cite a personal example of vice or virtue, drawn from Homer and the other classics."[2] This is certainly true in regard to the oath-takers of the *Iliad* and the *Odyssey*, for Homer provides examples of both those who commit perjury and those who speak truly and keep their oaths.

Perjury continued to be a pervasive phenomenon in the centuries following Homer, so that it evoked comment from all quarters, from poets and philosophers, moralists and satirists, tragedians and comedians, historians and rhetoricians, and lawmakers and litigants. In evaluating perjury, the ancient Greeks were not of one mind. Some regarded it as a most serious offense and vigorously denounced it; others viewed it as a minor indiscretion of no real consequence; and still others, such as Strepsiades in Aristophanes' *Clouds* (1226–41), did not hesitate to treat their oaths with utter contempt.[3]

---

1. For an introduction to the ethos and ethics of early Christianity, see especially Wayne A. Meeks, *The Moral World of the First Christians* (Library of Early Christianity 6; Philadelphia: Westminster, 1986).

2. Ibid., 62.

3. See K. J. Dover, *Aristophanes: Clouds* (Oxford: Clarendon, 1968) 240–41; idem, *Greek Popular Morality in the Time of Plato and Aristotle* (Berkeley and Los Angeles: University of California Press, 1974) 249.

Nor were all oaths judged the same. Some were to be taken with the greatest seriousness, whereas other oaths might be safely disregarded owing to the particular circumstances under which they were sworn. The latter included not only situations of danger and duress when a false oath served to save a person's life (Euripides, frg. 645) but especially those involving sexual passion. It was commonly believed that the gods were tolerant of perjury when sexual intercourse was involved; lovers were claimed to have "absolute authority" (πᾶσαν ἐξουσίαν) to break their vows, for "a lover's oath, they say, is no oath at all" (Plato, *Symp.* 183B).[4] In Aristophanes' *Lysistrata*, for instance, Kinesias desperately implores Myrrhine to break her vow of temporary chastity and promises to accept the responsibility (if any) for her offense (914–15).[5] False oaths could also be subsequent to intercourse. Philandering husbands, for example, could follow the example of Zeus, who, when confronted by an angry and jealous Hera, freely committed perjury by denying that he had sexual relations with Io (Apollodorus, *Bibl.* 2.1.3.1).[6]

Such circumstances, however numerous and potentially self-serving, were clearly regarded by the Greeks as exceptional.[7] On the whole, the Greeks viewed perjury as something that was self-evidently wrong and preferably to be avoided. This generally negative assessment of perjury allowed moralists to include it without discussion in various lists of vices.[8]

Given the widespread attention that the Greeks paid to perjury, one is not surprised to find it mentioned in both the New Testament and the Apostolic Fathers. Nor is one surprised to learn that the early Christian assessment of perjury is thoroughly negative. What is surprising to discover is that early Christian literature contains only three references to perjury. Furthermore, the standard Greek term for perjury (ἐπιορκία) does not

4. On the apparently conflated text of this Platonic passage, see K. J. Dover, *Plato: Symposium* (Cambridge: Cambridge University Press, 1980) 101; for the function of the passage in the work, see S. Rosen, *Plato's Symposium* (2nd ed.; New Haven and London: Yale University Press, 1987) 81–83.

5. Conversely, compare Aristophanes, *Eccl.* 1026, where the youth is willing to swear a false disclaimer oath in order to avoid having sexual relations with the old hag.

6. Apollodorus attributes the account of Zeus's perjury to Hesiod, who concluded from the story that "oaths concerning love do not draw down wrath from the gods." See Hesiod, frg. 124 and *Aegimius* 3: "And thereafter he ordained that an oath concerning the secret deeds of the Cyprian should be without penalty for men" (trans. Evelyn-White). For "adulterers' oaths," see Philonides 7 and Sophocles, frg. 694. See also Diogenes Laertius 1.36.

7. The divine's indulgence of perjury by lovers is treated as a unique dispensation in Plato, *Symp.* 183B.

8. See, for example, Ps.-Cebes, *Tabula* 9.4: "to commit all that is injurious, such as fraud, desecration, perjury, treason, pillage, and all that is like them." On this work, see J. T. Fitzgerald and L. M. White, *The Tabula of Cebes* (SBLTT 24; Greco-Roman Religion Series 7; Chico, Calif.: Scholars Press, 1983). For lists of vices in the ancient Mediterranean world, see J. T. Fitzgerald, "Virtue/Vice Lists," *The Anchor Bible Dictionary* (ed. D. N. Freedman; 6 vols.; New York: Doubleday, 1992) 6:857–59.

occur, but two of its cognates do. The verb ἐπιορκέω occurs in Matt 5:33 and *Did.* 2.3, and the adjective ἐπίορκος is used as a substantive in 1 Tim 1:10. Perjury is prohibited in the first two instances, and perjurers are included in a list of sinners in the third instance.

These data invite four initial observations. First, the references to perjury occur in three different literary genres—a Gospel, a letter, and a church order. This conforms to the Greek treatment of perjury in different kinds of genres and authors.

Second, all three references occur in contexts that are explicitly concerned with the moral life—the Sermon on the Mount, a list of sinners, and the Two Ways. In a similar way, perjury is a concern that is frequently mentioned in the Greek moralist traditions. On the other hand, there are many references to perjury in Greek documents that are not concerned with moral formation, such as the *Rhetorica* of Aristotle[9] and the speeches of the Attic orators. The latter are replete with references to the oath of the dicasts, who were both judges and jurors in the Athenian lawcourts.[10] This oath bound them to judge according to the laws and decrees of Athens, and, when there were no laws or decrees that applied to the case at hand, according to their best judgment.[11] Typically, both the plaintiff and the defendant would suggest to the dicasts that a decision against them would amount to a breach of the dicasts' oath. Such warnings against perjury were simply part of a litigant's rhetorical strategy and were issued solely in the interest of enhancing an individual's chances of success; they reflected no fundamental concern with the fidelity of the dicasts to their oath. Early Christian writings, by contrast, though often rhetorical, exhibit no interest in a rhetorical strategy that is designed to win a lawsuit. Indeed, the emphasis in several texts falls on nonretaliation and the forgoing of one's legal rights altogether (Matt 5:38–42; Luke 6:27–31; Rom 12:19–21; 1 Cor 4:12–13; 6:1–11; 9:1–27; 1 Thess 5:15; 1 Pet 2:23).[12]

9. See 1.15.12 (1375b.18); 1.15.28 (1377a.12); 1.15.29 (1377a.19); 1.15.32 (1377b.6); 3.3.1 (1405b.38); 3.15.8 (1416a.31).

10. See especially J. F. Cronin, *The Athenian Juror and His Oath* (Chicago: University of Chicago Libraries, 1936).

11. The fullest version of the oath appears in Demosthenes, *Or.* 24.149–51, but it is debated whether this passage contains the precise wording of the original oath. For discussion, see especially J. H. Lipsius, *Das attische Recht und Rechtsverfahren* (3 vols.; repr. Hildesheim: Olms, 1966) 1:150–53; and R. J. Bonner and G. Smith, *The Administration of Justice from Homer to Aristotle* (2 vols.; repr. New York: Greenwood Press, 1968) 2:152–56. Cronin (*Athenian Juror and His Oath*, 18) accepts the reconstruction of M. Fränkel, "Der attische Heliasteneid," *Hermes* 13 (1878) 464, and translates the pertinent section as follows: "I shall vote according to the laws and the decrees of the Athenian people and the Council of the Five Hundred, but concerning things about which there are no laws, I shall decide to the best of my judgment, neither with favor nor enmity." For Aristotle's discussion of how the speaker is to deal with this oath when the laws support his case and when they do not, see *Rhet.* 1.15.12.

12. Early Christian writers were not alone in this kind of emphasis. The Hellenistic moral-

Third, perjury is not the focal point in any of the early Christian texts. In Matt 5:33 the ancient prohibition serves as the foil for Jesus' own prohibition of oaths. In 1 Tim 1:10 perjurers are simply one item in a list of vicious persons, and in *Did.* 2.3 the prohibition of perjury belongs to a series of prohibitions in 2.2-3. This treatment coincides with the manner in which many Hellenistic moralists mention perjury. Both Dio Chrysostom and Maximus of Tyre, for instance, refer to perjury by name only four times, and Ps.-Cebes only once. Epictetus—though he advises his students to swear sparingly (*Ench.* 33.5)—does not even use any of the standard words for perjury. Nor do Teles and Marcus Aurelius. Lucian and Plutarch, on the other hand, refer to perjury twenty-four and fifteen times, respectively.[13] Yet even here, perjury is never the focal point of the work. The cursory treatment of perjury in early Christian literature, therefore, is not exceptional in the Greco-Roman moral world. It is only in the post-Constantinian period that Christian moralists such as John Chrysostom begin to make repeated references to perjury.[14]

Fourth, in all likelihood, even the references to perjury in early Christian literature do not derive from the earliest period. That is, the references to perjury are neither dominical nor apostolic but belong to the sub- or postapostolic period. Matthew, to be sure, prefaces Jesus' prohibition of oaths with an antithetical reference to the ancient prohibition of perjury, but it is unlikely that this antithesis derives from the historical Jesus. 1 Timothy purports to be written by Paul, but, as is generally recognized, is pseudepigraphic. In terms of content, it is closer to the church order tradition represented by the *Didache*. Dating the latter is difficult, because it appears to have evolved over the course of time. Its reference to perjury is absent from the Two Ways tradition preserved in Barnabas, so that it probably was added at a later stage in the document's history. In short, to the extent that usage of ἐπιορκία and its cognates provides a reliable index of early Christian concern with perjury, one may conclude that explicit attention to the problem by Greek-speaking Christians begins in the latter part

---

ists also extolled nonretaliation and the forgoing of one's legal rights as characteristics of the ideal philosopher; see J. T. Fitzgerald, *Cracks in an Earthen Vessel: An Examination of the Catalogues of Hardships in the Corinthian Correspondence* (SBLDS 99; Atlanta: Scholars Press, 1988) 103-7.

13. The number of references to perjury is based on the editions of the texts used by the Thesaurus Linguae Graecae. For Dio Chrysostom, see *Or.* 11.17; 55.15; 74.14, 16; for Maximus of Tyre, see *Or.* 29.2e; 34.9d; 35.5c; 36.2n; for Ps.-Cebes, see the *Tabula* 9.4. Lucian refers to perjury most often in *Timon*; see 2; 9; 23; 55. Of the references to perjury in Plutarch, see esp. *Mor.* 275C-D. The absence of the standard terms for perjury in Epictetus and other moralists does not necessarily imply a lack of concern for the problem. Epictetus, for example, refers to broken oaths in *Diss.* 1.14.15.

14. John Chrysostom uses the standard vocabulary for perjury at least 168 times. See, for example, his "Homilies on the Statues to the People of Antioch."

of the first century and continues in mostly cursory and occasional fashion into the second and third centuries.[15]

In order to appreciate the references to perjury in both polytheistic and Christian writings, we need to divest ourselves of some modern notions of perjury (such as the contemporary idea that it involves materiality and pre-supposes a legal or quasi-legal setting) and gain a better understanding of the practice of oath taking in antiquity. The latter, of course, forms the indispensable presupposition for the phenomenon of perjury. In the sections that follow, I shall first summarize briefly the ancient Greek practice of oath taking. After that, I shall turn to a discussion of three topics: the moralists' criticisms of oaths, Greco-Roman perspectives on perjury, and the meaning of the term "perjury."

THE OATH IN ANCIENT GREECE

Oath taking was one of the most pervasive practices of the ancient world. The use of oaths was not confined to individuals of high rank, to officials assuming the duties of public office, or to those engaged in specific occupations. On the contrary, oaths were taken by people of all social classes and were used for a wide variety of purposes. As a cross-cultural phenomenon, oaths played an important role not only in ancient Israel but in all societies of the ancient Mediterranean world, including those of the ancient Near East, Greece, and Rome.

In ancient Greece, for example, oaths were used in virtually all aspects of life.[16] The Greeks themselves recognized this. The Athenian orator Lycurgus, for example, once observed that "the oath is that which holds democracy together" (*Or.* 1.79). Although classical Athens differed in many ways from other Greek cities, it did not do so in regard to the power and importance of oaths.[17] Not all Greek cities swore the same oaths as the Athenians,

15. Early Greek apologists who mention perjury include Justin Martyr, *Dial.* 12.3; Tatian, *Oratorio ad Graecos* 10.2; and Clement of Alexandria, *Strom.* 7.8.50.4; 7.8.51.5; *Quis dives salvetur* 40.5.

16. On oaths in ancient Greece, see especially R. Hirzel, *Der Eid* (Leipzig: S. Hirzel, 1902); K. Latte, "Meineid," *Realencyklopädie für die klassische Altertumswissenschaft* 15.1 (1931) 346–57; and J. Plescia, *The Oath and Perjury in Ancient Greece* (Tallahassee: Florida State University Press, 1970). Other important works dealing with oaths in the ancient Mediterranean world include L. Wenger, "Der Eid in den griechischen Papyrusurkunden," *Zeitschrift der Savigny-Stiftung für Rechtsgeschichte*, Romantische Abteilung, 23 (1902) 158–274; and E. Seidl, *Der Eid im ptolemä-ischen Recht* (Munich: F. Straub, 1929), and *Der Eid in römisch-ägyptischen Provinzialrecht* (2 vols.; Münchener Beiträge zur Papyrusforschung und antiken Rechtsgeschichte 17 and 24; Munich: Beck, 1933–35).

17. For the use of oaths in Crete, see R. F. Willetts, *The Civilization of Ancient Crete* (Berkeley and Los Angeles: University of California Press, 1977) 157–58, 198, 205–9. Oaths appear already in the legal inscriptions from Dreros; see R. Meiggs and D. Lewis, *A Selection of Greek*

but all made an extensive use of oaths, and the oath enabled them to have dealings with one another and with other nations. This continued to be the case in the Hellenistic and Roman periods.

In discussing the use of oaths in Greek society, I shall draw extensively on evidence from Athens during the classical period. I do so for two reasons. First, the evidence is abundant and has been the focus of most studies of the Greek oath. Second, my purpose in this section is not to describe in detail the history and practice of any particular oath but to illustrate the scope and importance of oaths in the Greek world. In short, the following description is intended to be *illustrative*, not a description of either Athenian or universal Greek practice during the first century C.E.[18]

As Lycurgus's statement about the cohesive power of the oath indicates (*Or.* 1.79), citizenship and oath taking were particularly inseparable in ancient Athens. Children, for instance, could not be enrolled in the phratry unless their fathers and others swore to their legitimacy.[19] The ephebic oath in the temple of Agraulos was a necessary prerequisite for enrollment in the deme and the enjoyment of political rights; it was "a military, civic and religious contract"[20] that bound the citizen to the *polis* (city-state).[21] This pledge was later reinforced by an oath of loyalty to the *politeia* (constitution), so that all citizens swore their allegiance to the government in power and promised to obey its laws.[22] At one time, in fact, all Athenians were required

---

Historical Inscriptions (Oxford: Clarendon, 1969) No. 2 (pp. 2–3), and the interpretation of it recently advanced by M. Gagarin, *Early Greek Law* (Berkeley, Los Angeles, and London: University of California Press, 1986) 81–86.

18. My summary of ancient Greek oath taking is based primarily on Plescia, *Oath and Perjury*, whose organization of the material provides the outline for my own presentation. Plescia himself is primarily concerned with the period from Homer to Aristotle, though he occasionally refers to material from the Hellenistic and Roman periods.

19. See Andocides, *Or.* 1.127; Demosthenes, *Or.* 57.54; Isaeus, *Or.* 7.16; 8.19; and the discussions by G. Gilbert, *The Constitutional Antiquities of Sparta and Athens* (1895; repr. Chicago: Argonaut, 1968) 191–97; W. Wyse, *The Speeches of Isaeus* (Cambridge: Cambridge University Press, 1904) 559–60; Bonner and Smith, *Administration of Justice*, 2:160; and Plescia, *Oath and Perjury*, 15–16.

20. Plescia, *Oath and Perjury*, 17; for a similar assessment, see J. W. Taylor, "The Athenian Ephebic Oath," *Classical Journal* 13 (1917–18) 499. Dover terms it "the most comprehensive oath which an Athenian swore in his life" (*Greek Popular Morality*, 250).

21. See Taylor, "Athenian Ephebic Oath," 495–501; Bonner and Smith, *Administration of Justice*, 2:157–58; L. Robert, *Études épigraphiques et philologiques* (Paris: Champion, 1938) 296–307; M. N. Tod, *A Selection of Greek Historical Inscriptions* (2 vols.; Oxford: Clarendon, 1933–48) No. 204 (2:303–7); M. Ostwald, *Nomos and the Beginnings of the Athenian Democracy* (Oxford: Clarendon, 1969) 4, 14; Plescia, *Oath and Perjury*, 16–17; and W. Burkert, *Homo Necans: The Anthropology of Ancient Greek Sacrificial Ritual and Myth* (Berkeley, Los Angeles, and London: University of California Press, 1983) 65.

22. See, for example, the oaths of the Athenians to observe Solon's laws (Herodotus 1.29.2; Aristotle, *Ath. Pol.* 7.1 (with the comments of G. R. Stanton, *Athenian Politics c. 800-500 BC: A Sourcebook* [London and New York: Routledge, 1990] 50 n. 3, 70 n. 3). See also the oath of amnesty sworn by all Athenians in 403 B.C.E. (Andocides 1.90; Aristotle, *Ath. Pol.* 39.6–40.4).

by law to swear that they would kill anyone who attempted to suppress the democracy or install a tyrant (Andocides, *Or.* 1.97–98). From time to time, citizens were also required to take oaths in connection with various activities of the *polis,* such as the ratification of a new law, the confirmation of a treaty, or the approval of a public contract. Failure to take a mandatory oath entailed serious consequences.[23]

Governmental officials, such as councilmen, heliasts, archons, and magistrates of demes, were required to take a number of additional oaths.[24] These

---

Similar oaths of allegiance to the city's *politeia* as well as oaths of amnesty and reconciliation were not unique to Athens but were taken throughout Greece. See especially Xenophon, *Mem.* 4.4.16: "everywhere in Greece there is a law that citizens shall promise under oath to agree, and everywhere they take this oath. The object of this . . . [is] that they may obey the laws." For examples and discussion, see Plescia, *Oath and Perjury,* 17–23. In monarchial states, oaths of allegiance by both kings and people (or their representatives) functioned similarly. See Theognis 823–24; Xenophon, *Lac.* 15.7; Plutarch, *Pyrrh.* 5.2; and K. Latte, "Zwei Exkurse zum römischen Staatsrecht," in his *Kleine Schriften* (ed. O. Gigon, W. Buchwald, and W. Kunkel; Munich: Beck, 1968) 345–46, 353. For military oaths of loyalty to the king or emperor, see especially Polybius 15.25.11; Seneca, *Ep.* 95.5; Epictetus, *Diss.* 1.14.15; and A. D. Nock, "Hellenistic Mysteries and Christian Sacraments," in his *Essays on Religion and the Ancient World* (ed. Z. Stewart; 2 vols.; Oxford: Clarendon, 1972) 2:816–17, who notes that *sacramentum* "meant the soldier's oath of loyalty in particular."

23. Failure to take an oath of loyalty and obedience to a superior power could be especially grievous. For instance, the Athenian treaty with Chalkis in 446–445 B.C.E. (Meiggs and Lewis, *Greek Historical Inscriptions,* No. 52) required all Chalkidians to take an oath of loyalty to Athens. The penalty for failure to take the oath was as follows: "any man who does not take the oath shall be disfranchised, his property shall be confiscated, and a tithe of his property shall be consecrated (in Chalkis) to Olympian Zeus" (trans. N. Lewis, *The Fifth Century B.C.* [Greek Historical Documents; Toronto: Hakkert, 1971] 15–16). Conversely, the names of all who took this oath were recorded on a list. For the text of this inscription and discussions of its provisions, see Tod, *Greek Historical Inscriptions,* 1:82–86; and Meiggs and Lewis, *Greek Historical Inscriptions,* 138–44.

24. Although specific evidence is lacking, it is extremely likely that all Athenian officials were obliged to swear some kind of oath before taking office. See Gilbert, *Constitutional Antiquities,* 221; and Bonner and Smith, *Administration of Justice,* 2:151. For officials outside Athens, see P. Gardner and F. B. Jevons, *A Manual of Greek Antiquities* (New York: Scribner, 1895) 232.

For the oath of induction by members of the Athenian Council (βουλή) of Five Hundred, see Andocides, *Or.* 1.91; Aristotle, *Ath. Pol.* 22.2; and the discussion by Bonner and Smith, *Administration of Justice,* 1:190, 192–93, 200, 204, 342–44; 2:151–52; Plescia, *Oath and Perjury,* 25–26; and Stanton, *Athenian Politics,* 169 n. 4. For the installation of an Athenian-like democratic council at Erythrai and the loyalty oath to be sworn by members of this council, see Meiggs and Lewis, *Greek Historical Inscriptions,* No. 40 (pp. 89–94). (The document is No. 29 in the collection of Tod, *Greek Historical Inscriptions,* 1:46–49.) A translation of the document is available in Lewis, *Fifth Century B.C.,* 7–8.

The Heliaia was a judicial assembly of six thousand citizens over the age of thirty. They were drafted for judicial service into sections or panels known as dicasteries. See Bonner, *Lawyers and Litigants in Ancient Athens* (1927; repr. New York and London: Blom, 1969) 35–37, 75–76; also Bonner and Smith, *Administration of Justice,* 1:154–57, 162.

For oaths by archons, see Aristotle, *Ath. Pol.* 3.3; 7.1; 55.5 (which indicates that they swore their oath of investiture on two separate occasions and in two different places); Plutarch, *Solon* 25.3, and the discussion by Bonner and Smith, *Administration of Justice,* 1:62; 2:150–51; Ostwald,

included their oath of investiture as well as whatever oaths were essential to the fulfillment of their official duties.[25] In a similar way, citizens who refused public appointments, military service, or various civic obligations were required to take a disclaimer oath (ἐξωμοσία) in support of their refusal.[26]

Oaths also were indispensable to the ancient Greek judicial system, both in Athens and elsewhere.[27] They were required of various jurors and public arbitrators (οἱ διαιτηταί), and they were also taken by private arbitrators under certain circumstances, such as when the dispute involved significant sums of money or when conciliation failed and a decision was necessary.[28]

Nomos, 3–4; Plescia, *Oath and Perjury*, 29–30; and Stanton, *Athenian Politics*, 8 n. 5, 70–71 nn. 3–4, 84 n. 3.

On magistrates of demes, see Plescia, *Oath and Perjury*, 30. Serious actions by the deme, such as exclusion from its list of citizens, were taken under oath (Aeschines, *Or.* 1.78). See also Demosthenes, *Or.* 57.63.

25. Athenian dicasts took the amnesty oaths annually; see Cronin, *The Athenian Juror and His Oath*, 47–54. Other oaths were occasioned by particular historical events; see, for example, the oath by the five hundred members of the Athenian Council and the six thousand dicasts in regard to treatment of the Chalkidians (Meiggs and Lewis, *Greek Historical Inscriptions*, No. 52 [pp. 138–44] = Tod, *Greek Historical Inscriptions*, No. 42 [1:82–86]). A translation of the inscription is available in Lewis, *Fifth Century B.C.*, 15–16. (For the Chalkidians' oath of loyalty to Athens, see n. 23 above.)

26. See Aeschines, *Or.* 2.94; Aristotle, *Ath. Pol.* 49.2; *Pol.* 4.10.6 (1297a20–21); Aristophanes, *Eccl.* 1026; Demosthenes, *Or.* 19.122–27; and the discussions by Lipsius, *Attische Recht*, 2:407; Bonner and Smith, *Administration of Justice*, 2:163; and Plescia, *Oath and Perjury*, 31–32, 100. For another use of the disclaimer oath, see n. 46 below.

27. For oaths in the judicial system of Chios as early as 575–550 B.C.E., see Meiggs and Lewis, *Greek Historical Inscriptions*, No. 8 (pp. 14–17), and the analysis by L. H. Jeffrey, "The Courts of Justice in Archaic Chios," *Annual of the British School at Athens* 51 (1956) 157–67. For a brief summary of Jeffrey's conclusions, see Gagarin, *Early Greek Law*, 89–91. Oaths also played a crucial role in the judicial procedure of Eretria; see E. Vanderpool and W. P. Wallace, "The Sixth Century Laws from Eretria," *Hesperia* 33 (1964) 381–91; and Gagarin, *Early Greek Law*, 91–93. For oaths in legal disputes involving property at Halicarnassus, see the inscription printed in both Tod, *Greek Historical Inscriptions*, No. 25 (1:36–40); and Meiggs and Lewis, *Greek Historical Inscriptions*, No. 32 (pp. 69–72); see also the discussion by C. D. Buck, *The Greek Dialects* (Chicago: University of Chicago Press, 1955) 184–86; and Ostwald, *Nomos*, 167–70. On the use of oaths in the legal systems of Crete (at Dreros and Gortyn), see n. 17 above, and also J. W. Headlam, "The Procedure of the Gortynian Inscription," *Journal of Hellenic Studies* 13 (1892–93) 48–69; Gardner and Jevons, *Manual of Greek Antiquities*, 560–74; J. Koehler and E. Ziebarth, *Das Stadtrecht von Gortyn und seine Beziehungen zum gemeingriechischen Rechte* (Göttingen: Vandenhoeck & Ruprecht, 1912) 82–84; G. M. Calhoun, *The Growth of Criminal Law in Ancient Greece* (Berkeley: University of California Press, 1927) 109; W. Wyse and F. E. Adcock, "Law," in *A Companion to Greek Studies* (ed. L. Whibley; 4th rev. ed.; Cambridge: Cambridge University Press, 1931; repr. New York and London: Hafner, 1963) 464–70, esp. 467. A translation of the laws of Gortyn is available in Lewis, *Fifth Century B.C.*, 93–103.

28. For the so-called "Heliastic Oath" of the dicasts, see n. 11 above. For oaths by other Athenian juries—the ephetai and members of the Areopagus—see Plescia, *Oath and Perjury*, 38–39. For a similar oath to be sworn by judges in Erythrae, see Ostwald, *Nomos*, 45. For oaths

These oaths functioned not only to remind jurors and arbiters of their responsibility to decide justly but also to assure the litigants of their impartiality in rendering a verdict. In some cases, the jurors even swore oaths affirming the just fulfillment of their duties both prior to and following the proceedings.

Litigants also took oaths, of which some were voluntary and others were required.[29] Three basic types of party oaths may be distinguished—the decisory, the evidentiary (or probative), and the declaratory.[30] The decisory oath was the most ancient form, sometimes called the oath of Rhadamanthus (Plato, *Leg.* 948B).[31] This was originally a voluntary oath taken by one party to the suit in response to the challenge of the other party; later, in at least part of the Greek world, it became a compulsory oath prescribed by law for dealing with certain types of cases.[32] This oath was decisive and settled the suit without any decision by the judge.[33] In archaic Greece, it was

---

by judges at Gortyn, see Gardner and Jevons, *Manual of Greek Antiquities*, 568, 571, 573 (where this practice is also claimed for Ephesus); and Buck, *Greek Dialects*, 323.

On public arbitrators, see especially Aristotle, *Ath. Pol.* 55.5, and the comments of Lipsius, *Attische Recht*, 228; K. Latte, *Heiliges Recht* (Tübingen: Mohr, 1920) 42; H. C. Harrell, *Public Arbitration in Athenian Law* (University of Missouri Studies 11.1; Columbia, Mo.: University of Missouri, 1936) 22–23; Bonner and Smith, *Administration of Justice*, 2:156–57; and Plescia, *Oath and Perjury*, 36–37. On the topic of public arbitration, see especially Harrell, *Public Arbitration*, 1–42, and Bonner and Smith, *Administration of Justice*, 1:346–54; 2:97–116.

On private arbitrators, see especially Isaeus, *Or.* 2.30–31; 5.31–32; and Demosthenes, *Or.* 29.58; 52.30–31. Opinion is divided in regard to the oaths taken by private arbitrators; see the discussions by Wyse, *Isaeus*, 261, 450–51; Lipsius, *Attische Recht*, 1:222–26; Harrell, *Public Arbitration*, 22 n. 12; Bonner and Smith, *Administration of Justice*, 2:157; and Plescia, *Oath and Perjury*, 37–38.

29. For oaths by those who appeared before arbitrators, see Isaeus, *Or.* 2.32–33; 5.31, 33. For the failure to swear an oath in appealing an arbitrator's decision, see Demosthenes, *Or.* 21.86.

30. Terminology in regard to the types of oaths varies from author to author. Some scholars, such as Bonner and Smith, for example, use the term "evidentiary oath" to describe both decisory oaths and evidentiary/probative oaths, whereas others correctly seek to distinguish them. My categories are similar to those of Plescia, *Oath and Perjury*, 13–14.

31. It is usually assumed that Plato presupposes that Rhadamanthus, the legendary king of Crete, tendered an oath to both parties, on the assumption that only the innocent party would take it.

32. Bonner and Smith suggest that the decisory oath "began as an exculpatory oath allowed to the defendant alone; soon it was allowed to the plaintiff as well" (*Administration of Justice*, 2:83). At Gortyn, for example, a slave girl who had been raped by her master was apparently allowed to swear a decisory oath against him. This extension of the decisory oath to the plaintiff was accompanied by a transformation of the voluntary procedure into a mandatory one. See Gardner and Jevons, *Manual of Greek Antiquities*, 570; G. Smith, *The Administration of Justice from Hesiod to Solon* (Chicago: University of Chicago Libraries, 1924) 32–43, 56–57; Wyse and Adcock, "Law," 467; and Plescia, *Oath and Perjury*, 42–43.

33. Bonner and Smith, *Administration of Justice*, 2:146, 158. The tendering of an oath to Antilochus by Menelaus (Homer, *Il.* 23.566–611) is an early example of this type of oath; on this passage, see the comments by Latte, *Heiliges Recht*, 8; Bonner and Smith, *Administration of Justice*, 1:26–28; L. Gernet, *The Anthropology of Ancient Greece* (Baltimore and London: Johns

often a purgatory oath by which a defendant cleared himself of the charges that had been brought against him.[34]

In later Greek history, a litigant's oath usually[35] was not decisive in and of itself, but was simply evidentiary or probative.[36] Solon, for example, "permitted the oath only when there was no other evidence available and allowed both parties to take it."[37] In such a case, the judges were called upon to decide which of the two litigants had sworn rightly.[38] In other cases, one litigant might tender an oath to the other, but it was far more common for a litigant to volunteer to give his own statement under oath.[39] "Either of the parties," moreover, "might swear to the truth of his statements in court without a challenge."[40]

A declaratory oath was required of both parties at Athens from an early date. It was taken at the preliminary hearing (ἀνάκρισις) and functioned to attest the sincerity and veracity of the plaintiff's and defendant's claims.[41]

Hopkins University Press, 1981) 189–90; Gagarin, *Early Greek Law*, 36–38; and N. Richardson, *Books 21-24*, Vol. VI of *The Iliad: A Commentary* (ed. G. S. Kirk; Cambridge: Cambridge University Press, 1993) 230–36. On the decisory oath in general, see Plescia, *Oath and Perjury*, 13–14, 41, 52–55, 95–97, 101–2; for an account that includes both decisory and evidentiary oaths, see Smith, *Administration of Justice from Hesiod to Solon*, 55–77. The decisory oath was not at all unique to ancient Greece. It was also used, for example, in the ancient Near East (as reflected in both the Code of Eshnunna and the Code of Hammurabi), ancient Israel (see esp. Exod 22:10–11), and imperial Rome (Quintilian 5.6.1–6; 9.2.95); see H. J. Boecker, *Law and the Administration of Justice in the Old Testament and Ancient Near East* (Minneapolis: Augsburg, 1980) 35, 167–69. A dissenting view in regard to archaic Greece is offered by Gagarin, who denies that there are any clear cases of decisory oaths in early Greek literature (*Early Greek Law*, 37 n. 55, 42 n. 64, 43 n. 66).

34. See, for example, Aeschylus, *Eum.* 429, where Orestes' refusal to take an exculpatory oath is condemned by the chorus but defended by Athena. On this passage, see Bonner and Smith, *Administration of Justice*, 2:148; Gernet, *Anthropology of Greece*, 191–92; H. Lloyd-Jones, *Aeschylus: Oresteia: Eumenides* (London: Duckworth, 1979) 37–38; and Gagarin, *Early Greek Law*, 41–42.

35. For an exception in a case of arbitration, see Demosthenes, *Or.* 40.10–11, where the oath by Menecles is decisive.

36. As Bonner and Smith note, "in practically all cases [the oath] becomes subject to rebuttal" (*Administration of Justice*, 158). An oath that is subject to rebuttal is no longer decisory but belongs to the art of persuasion. The intent of such an oath is probative; it is offered either as evidence or in support of evidence. Aristotle thus treats the oath, along with laws, witnesses, contracts, and torture, as one of the five proofs of forensic oratory (*Rhet.* 1.15).

37. Plescia, *Oath and Perjury*, 43. For a full discussion of Solon's innovation in regard to judicial oaths, see Bonner and Smith, *Administration of Justice*, 1:173–75; see also Bonner, *Evidence in Athenian Courts* (Chicago: University of Chicago Press, 1905) 75.

38. According to the *Lexica Segueriana* (s.v. "Doxastai"), "Judges are those who determine which one of the litigants swears rightly. For Solon ordains that the defendant, when there are neither contracts nor witnesses, should swear, and the plaintiff in like manner" (trans. Plescia, *Oath and Perjury*, 43 n. 34).

39. Plescia, *Administration of Justice*, 43–47.

40. Bonner, *Evidence in Athenian Courts*, 79.

41. In cases involving homicide, the preliminary oath (διωμοσία)—especially on the part of the plaintiff—was both more solemn and more detailed than in other cases. See Bonner and Smith, *Administration of Justice*, 2:83 n. 1, 165–172; and Plescia, *Oath and Perjury*, 14, 47–49, 53.

In addition to these three basic types of oaths, other oaths might be taken by litigants, such as a dilatory oath to obtain a delay in the proceedings (ὑπωμοσία). In the time of Aeschines (2.87–88), the victor in a homicide suit "had to cut in pieces a sacrificial victim and take a solemn oath on it, affirming that those of the dicasts who had voted on his side had voted what was true and right, and that he had spoken no falsehood."

Witnesses in trials were sometimes sworn. In the archaic period, as the famous code of Gortyn shows, some witnesses were so-called "oath-helpers," who supported one of the litigants by testifying in his behalf. Their oaths did not originally concern the facts at dispute, but simply attested their belief in the truthfulness of the oath sworn by the litigant whom they supported.[42] Whether witnesses were sworn in later Greek history often depended on the nature of the trial. In Athens, witnesses in homicide cases were always sworn,[43] but those in civil cases usually were not.[44] Furthermore, "the oath was not administered by the magistrate, but by one of the parties. Since the administration of an oath to the opponent's witnesses was of the nature of a privilege, it could be omitted at will by either party."[45]

Individuals who were summoned as witnesses had only two legal choices: to testify or to deny under oath that they knew anything about the facts of a case (ἐξωμοσία).[46] To refuse to answer a summons, to testify, or to swear an oath of ignorance was not a real option, for it aroused suspicions of bribery and feigned forgetfulness (Lycurgus, *Or.* 1.20) and could result in a stiff fine (Aeschines, *Or.* 1.46).[47]

42. Gardner and Jevons, *Manual of Greek Antiquities*, 571–72; Wyse and Adcock, "Law," 467; Bonner and Smith, *Administration of Justice*, 2:175–91; and K. Latte, "Der Rechtsgedanke im archäischen Griechentum," in *Kleine Schriften*, 237–38. Even in Gortyn, however, not all witnesses were sworn; see Gardner and Jevons, *Manual of Greek Antiquities*, 570; and Wyse and Adcock, "Law," 467.

43. Bonner, *Evidence in Athenian Courts*, 76; and Smith, *Administration of Justice from Hesiod to Solon*, 77.

44. When witnesses were put on oath, they may have been taken away from the site of the proceeding and led to the oath-stone (Aristotle, *Ath. Pol.* 55.5) or, at least to an altar, in order to take their oath. Naturally, this would cause a delay in the proceedings. See especially Demosthenes, *Or.* 54.26 and, for the textual problem involved in the Demosthenes' passage, the comments of Harrell, *Public Arbitration*, 22 n. 14.

45. Bonner, *Evidence in Athenian Courts*, 77. For three situations in which a witness might take an oath, see pp. 78–79.

46. For the oath of ignorance, see especially Aeschines, *Or.* 1.46; Demosthenes, *Or.* 45.58–61; 57.59; Isaeus, *Or.* 9.18; Plato, *Leg.* 936E; and the discussions by Wyse, *Speeches of Isaeus*, 637–38; Lipsius, *Attische Recht*, 3:878–79; Bonner and Smith, *Administration of Justice*, 2:136–37, 163–64; and Plescia, *Oath and Perjury*, 56. On other uses of disclaimer oaths, see n. 26 above.

47. For the procedure against recalcitrant witnesses, see Bonner and Smith, *Administration of Justice*, 2:137–38. In the case of witnesses who were willing to testify but unable (because of illness, travel, etc.) to appear at the trial, arrangements were made for the testimony to be given in writing and later presented in court (see especially Demosthenes, *Or.* 46.7; Isaeus, *Or.* 3.18-27). It is unlikely that such extrajudicial depositions (ἐκμαρτυρίαι) were normally accom-

In addition to judicial life, oaths also played an important role in international affairs.[48] They were an essential element in concluding truces between warring states and in forming treaties of alliance.[49] In a similar way, oaths were central to the various Greek leagues, such as the Amphictyonic League.[50] Oaths of allegiance to cities, kings, and emperors were also prominent, as were the oaths used in disputes that required international arbitration.[51] In addition, oaths played a key role in relations between a city and its colonists.[52]

The oath was also integral to the Greeks' public and private social life. Inclusion in the phratry, for example, not only depended on the oath, but its members and officers swore various oaths. In a similar way, the various associations, clubs, and guilds usually had membership oaths, oaths of office, and judicial oaths.[53] For example, if members of the Society of Iobac-

---

panied by an oath; see Lipsius, *Attische Recht*, 3:886–87; Bonner and Smith, *Administration of Justice*, 133–35, 174.

48. Plescia, *Oath and Perjury*, 58–74.

49. See, for example, the importance of oaths in the truce between Sparta and Athens (Thucydides 5.18–19) as well as in the alliance treaty between Athens and Argos, Mantinea, and Elis (printed in Tod, *Greek Historical Inscriptions*, No. 72 [1:175–78]; see also Thucydides 5.47). For a general discussion of the former, see A. W. Gomme, *A Historical Commentary on Thucydides* (corrected ed.; Oxford: Clarendon, 1962) 3:666–82; for the latter, see Gomme, A. Andrewes, and K. J. Dover, *A Historical Commentary on Thucydides* (Oxford: Clarendon, 1970) 4:54–63. For oaths in the treaties involving Crete, see Willetts, *Ancient Crete*, 158, 205–6, 208. The official who administered the oath in such treaties was sometimes referred to as ὁ ὁρκωτής ("the commissioner of oaths"); see, for example, Xenophon, *Hell.* 6.5.3; cf. Meiggs and Lewis, *Greek Historical Inscriptions*, No. 52, lines 17–18, 38.

50. See Aeschines, *Or.* 2.115; 3.109–12, 118–21; and Bonner and Smith, "Administration of Justice in the Delphic Amphictyony," *Classical Philology* 38 (1943) 1–12.

51. For oaths of loyalty to Athens, see Meiggs and Lewis, *Greek Historical Inscriptions*, Nos. 40 (Erythrai), 47 (Kolophon), and 52 (Chalkis). The first and third of these oaths are discussed in nn. 23 and 24 above. On the oath by the people of Kolophon, see Meiggs and Lewis, *Greek Historical Inscriptions*, 121–25, and Ostwald, *Nomos*, 41–42.

On kings, see the oath of loyalty required of the Greeks by Philip of Macedon (Tod, *Greek Historical Inscriptions*, No. 177 [2:224–31]).

For an early example of an oath of allegiance to the Roman emperor—the Paphlagonian oath of loyalty to Augustus that was taken by both natives and Roman citizens—see L. R. Taylor, *The Divinity of the Roman Emperor* (Middletown, Conn.: American Philological Association, 1931) 206–7.

52. See, for example, the law of the East Lokrians with regard to their colonists at Naupaktos, printed in Tod, *Greek Historical Inscriptions*, No. 24 (1:31–36); and Meiggs and Lewis, *Greek Historical Inscriptions*, No. 20 (pp. 35–40). See also Buck, *Greek Dialects*, No. 57 (pp. 248–53), and Ostwald, *Nomos*, 45, 170–73.

53. On the various associations, see Plescia, *Oath and Perjury*, 77. For a brief overview of the various voluntary associations in the Greek world, see M. N. Tod, "Clubs, Greek," in *The Oxford Classical Dictionary* (ed. N. G. L. Hammond and H. H. Scullard; 2nd ed.; Oxford: Clarendon Press, 1970) 254–55; for a more detailed analysis, see F. Poland, *Geschichte des griechischen Vereinswesens* (Preisschriften . . . der fürstlich Jablonowskischen Gesellschaft 38; Leipzig: Teubner, 1909). On the relevance of such Greek and Roman associations for the understanding of early Christianity, see W. A. Meeks, *The First Urban Christians: The Social World of the*

chi in Attica saw one member insult or abuse another, they were asked to give testimony to that effect under oath.[54] The most famous oath by members of a professional guild was that taken by physicians, the so-called Hippocratic oath.[55]

Participation in athletics also entailed the taking of oaths. They were taken not only by the athletes themselves, but by all those connected with the games—their fathers, brothers, trainers, and judges (Pausanius 5.24.9–10). In some cases, the setting for these athletic oaths could be quite solemn, similar to that which prevailed at an initiation into a mystery religion.[56] Similarly, even the trainers of choruses and the judges of literary and musical contests swore oaths (Demosthenes *Or.* 21.17, 65; Ps.-Andocides, *Or.* 4.21).

In the world of business, oaths were not only common but absolutely essential. Virtually all contracts depended on oaths for their legality. As one might expect, all public contracts—whether for the drainage of a swamp, the cultivation of public land, or any other public project—required the swearing of oaths for their ratification. But oaths were common even in the making of private contracts. As Plescia notes, "Leases, loans, in fact all business transactions were sealed by more or less solemn oaths."[57] According to Theophrastus, for example, "A contract of buying and selling is sealed in regard to the acquirer [only] when the price is paid and the legal formalities such as the oath are fulfilled."[58] Thus, merchants swore that their wares had

---

Apostle Paul (New Haven and London: Yale University Press, 1983) 31–32, 68, 77–80, 134, 159, 162.

On oaths and pledges in the Athenian political clubs (ἑταιρεῖαι), see especially G. M. Calhoun, *Athenian Clubs in Politics and Litigation* (Austin, 1913; repr. Rome: "L'Erma" di Bretschneider, 1964) 34–35. The term συνωμοσία ("sworn association") was occasionally used of these clubs, whose members supported one another in lawsuits and in elections (Thucydides 8.54.4; see Bonner and Smith, *Administration of Justice*, 2:19–20). More commonly, it was used of those who bound themselves by oaths and other pledges to participate in a conspiracy of some kind (Calhoun, *Athenian Clubs*, 4–7, 34–35; Plescia, *Oath and Perjury*, 77–79).

On the guilds and their relevance for understanding the associations of early Christians, see A. J. Malherbe, *Social Aspects of Early Christianity* (Baton Rouge: Louisiana State University Press, 1977) 87–91.

54. See the excerpt from this organization's statutes in E. Ferguson, *Backgrounds of Early Christianity* (Grand Rapids: Eerdmans, 1987) 108–10; the pertinent section appears on p. 109.

55. The translation of the oath in the Loeb Classical Library is by W. H. S. Jones (*Hippocrates* [London: Heinemann; New York: Putnam, 1923] 291–301), who offers a fuller discussion in his *The Doctor's Oath* (Cambridge: Cambridge University Press, 1924). See also L. Edelstein, *The Hippocratic Oath* (Baltimore: Johns Hopkins University Press, 1943) and A. J. Festugière, *Hippocrate, L'ancienne médecine* (Paris: Klincksieck, 1948).

56. See especially Plutarch, *Thes.* 25, on the Isthmian games at Corinth. According to one ancient tradition, these were held in honor of Palaimon, and it is extremely likely that the oaths taken by contestants prior to the competition were sworn in his shrine, the Palaimonion. Consequently, "an encounter with Palaimon at night in the underground vault preceded the days of competition." So Burkert, *Homo Necans*, 197–98.

57. Plescia, *Oath and Perjury*, 81.

58. *Apud* Stobaeus, *Flor.* : :.?2; cited and translated by Plescia, *Oath and Perjury*, 80.

not been adulterated (Plato, *Laws* 917B), and bankers gave oaths of assurance that they would return whatever had been deposited with them. The sacral manumission of slaves was typically accompanied by an oath and took the form of a sales contract whereby a god purchased the slave.[59] Again, oaths were also involved in the ancient equivalent of the modern search warrant. Before an Athenian could conduct a search for stolen property believed to be in another person's house, he had to remove his garment and swear that he fully expected to find the missing article in the suspect's house (Plato, *Leg.* 954A).[60] In short, anything that involved money or property was almost certain to be accompanied by an oath, and the greater the amount, the more solemn the oath. Consequently, even private agreements over the settlement of an estate and the division of an inheritance were sealed with an oath.[61]

Finally, oaths were intimately connected with Greek religion. After all, swearing involved the invocation of one or more gods to witness and guard the oath. Again, many oaths were taken in temples or other holy places (e.g., Isaeus, *Or.* 2.31), and the taking of any significant oath almost always involved sacrifice (e.g., Andocides, *Myst.* 97–98).[62] Indeed, one of the earliest attested meanings of ὅρκος —and perhaps its root meaning—is "oath-offering." That is, in Homer the word ὅρκος often signifies not the words spoken when swearing, but the victim that was sacrificed at the oath ceremony.[63] Thus, Homer speaks not of "taking an oath" but of "cutting an oath."[64] For

---

59. Plescia, *Oath and Perjury*, 81. For discussion and examples of such sales contracts, see A. Deissmann, *Light from the Ancient East* (4th ed.; London: Hodder & Stoughton, 1927) 320–23; H. Rädle, "Untersuchungen zum griechischen Freilassungswesen" (Ph.D. diss., Ludwig-Maximilians-Universität zu München, 1969) 56–88; and S. S. Bartchy, *MAΛΛON XPHΣAI: First-Century Slavery and The Interpretation of 1 Corinthians 7:21* (SBLDS 11; Missoula, Mont.: Society of Biblical Literature, 1973) 121–25.

60. The garment was removed to prevent the accuser from smuggling the missing article into the suspect's house so as to frame him with the implicating evidence. See Aristophanes, *Nub.* 499–500 and the note by Dover, *Aristophanes: Clouds*, 163. On the oath taken in connection with the search, see Latte, *Heiliges Recht*, 22, and "Beiträge zum griechischen Strafrecht," *Hermes* 66 (1931) 131.

61. For the view that witnesses in Athenian inheritance cases were sworn, see Bonner and Smith, *Administration of Justice*, 2:83 n. 1.

62. On this orator, see now A. Missiou, *The Subversive Oratory of Andokides* (Cambridge: Cambridge University Press, 1992).

63. See especially *Il.* 3.245–46, 268–69. For discussion, see W. Leaf, *The Iliad* (2 vols.; 2nd ed.; London: Macmillan, 1900, 1902) 1:137; J. R. S. Sterrett, *Homer's Iliad: First Three Books and Selections* (New York, Cincinnati, and Chicago: American Book Co., 1907) 149; J. T. Hooker, *Homer: Iliad III* (Bristol: Bristol Classical Press, 1979) 55; M. M. Willcock, *The Iliad of Homer* (2 vols.; London: St. Martin's, 1978, 1984) 2:275; and G. S. Kirk, *Books 1-4*, Vol. I of *The Iliad: A Commentary* (ed. G. S. Kirk; Cambridge: Cambridge University Press, 1985) 274, 310.

64. See *Il.* 2.124; 3.73, 94, 105, 252, 256; 4.155; 19.191. Similar language was employed by both ancient Israelites and Romans in the making of covenants and treaties. See E. Bickerman, "Couper une alliance," *Archives d'Histoire du Droit Orientale* 5 (1951) 133–56; and Burkert, *Homo Necans*, 35.

the Greeks, therefore, to swear an oath—even in connection with the most mundane matter—was ultimately a religious act.

Consequently, the use of oaths in Greek religion was natural. For instance, at the festival of flowers known as the Anthesteria, which was closely associated with the worship of Dionysus, the fourteen "venerable women" swore oaths over the sacrificial baskets; the oath itself was administered by the wife of the king-archon, who played a key role in the ceremony and was later united with Dionysus in a sacred marriage.[65] Furthermore, initiation into a mystery religion typically involved a pledge of fidelity to the cult gods[66] and a promise not to divulge the contents of the mystery.[67] A similar oath was taken by the Pythagoreans.[68] Other oaths involved the promise to live a moral life. A private religious association at Philadelphia in the first century B.C.E., for example, placed a marble stele at the entrance of the house where it met. The stele, which contains a number of commandments that are said to have been given by Zeus, reads in part as follows:

> Those who enter this house [i.e., temple], both men and women, both bond and free, are to take oath before all the gods that, conscious of no guile toward man or woman, they will not [administer] an evil drug to men, nor will they learn or practice wicked charms, nor [give] any philter, or any abortive or contraceptive drug, nor [commit] robbery or murder, either carrying it out themselves or advising another or acting as witness [for his defense], nor overlook complacently those who rob [or withhold—i.e., offerings] in this house; and if anyone shall do any of these things or advise them, they will not consent or

---

65. See, for example, Demosthenes, *Or.* 59.73, and the discussion by Burkert, *Homo Necans,* 230–38.

66. R. Reitzenstein, *Hellenistic Mystery-Religions* (Pittsburgh Theological Monograph Series 15; Pittsburgh: Pickwick, 1978) 20, 127, 132, 237–38, 240–41. One such mystery oath, printed and briefly discussed by M. P. Nilsson (*Geschichte der griechischen Religion* [Handbuch der Altertumswissenschaft 5.2.1–2; 2 vols.; 3rd ed.; Munich: Beck, 1967] 2:695–96) exists in two exemplars that come from the first and the third centuries C.E. This fact suggests that it enjoyed long and sustained use. On this important oath, see now R. Merkelbach, "Der Eid der Isismysten," *Zeitschrift für Papyrologie und Epigraphik* 1 (1968) 55–73; M. Totti, *Ausgewählte Texte der Isis- und Serapis-Religion* (Subsidia Epigraphica 12; Hildesheim: Olms, 1985) No. 8 (pp. 19–20); and W. Burkert, *Ancient Mystery Cults* (Cambridge, Mass., and London: Harvard University Press, 1987) 50.

67. See, for example, Reitzenstein, *Hellenistic Mystery-Religions,* 240–41; S. Angus, *The Mystery-Religions* (2nd ed; London: Murray, 1928; repr. New York: Dover, 1975) 78–79; and L. H. Martin, *Hellenistic Religions* (New York and Oxford: Oxford University Press, 1987) 60–61. Mithraism, moreover, not only required an oath of secrecy but also depicted Mithras as the guardian of oaths; see Ferguson, *Backgrounds of Early Christianity,* 231, 236. For an example of a Mithraic oath "to observe the secrecy of the mysteries," see M. J. Vermaseren, *Mithras, the Secret God* (New York: Barnes & Noble, 1963) 130–31.

68. G. S. Kirk and J. E. Raven, *The Presocratic Philosophers* (Cambridge: Cambridge University Press, 1957) 220–21.

pass over it in silence, but will bring it out into the open and see that [the crime] is punished.[69]

A similar moral promissory oath, of course, was attributed to the early Christians by Pliny the Younger: "They maintained . . . that they bound themselves with an oath, not for any crime, but not to commit theft or robbery or adultery, not to break their word, and not to deny a deposit when demanded" (*Ep.* 10.96).[70] A metaphorical oath of allegiance to virtue was also popular among the Stoics (Seneca, *Ep.* 35; see also Epictetus, *Diss.* 1.14.15–16).

Additional examples of oaths taken by Greeks could easily be given, but the preceding should suffice to indicate the extent to which the practice of oath taking permeated the public, judicial, international, social, and religious life of the Greeks. It is against this pervasive practice of swearing and sacrifice that references to perjury in both Hellenistic and early Christian literature are to be understood.

THE MORALISTS' CRITICISMS OF OATHS

From a history-of-religions perspective, the Matthean Jesus' criticism of oath-takers in Matt 23:16–22 and his prohibition of oaths in Matt 5:33–37 belong to the widespread Greco-Roman polemic against the use of oaths. In general, serious moralists were disturbed by the widespread practice of resorting to oaths for the most trivial of reasons.[71] Consequently, they sought to minimize the occasions when individuals swore oaths on the presupposition that oaths were superfluous for the person of integrity. That idea was by no means a new one. In Sophocles' *Oedipus at Colonus* (648–51), for instance, Theseus promises Oedipus that he will not cheat him. In response, Oedipus says, "I will not make you swear to it. I trust you." The-

---

69. The translation is that of F. C. Grant, ed., *Hellenistic Religions* (Indianapolis and New York: Bobbs-Merrill, 1953) 28–29. See U. von Wilamowitz-Moellendorff, *Der Glaube der Hellenen* (2 vols.; 5th ed.; Darmstadt: Wissenschaftliche Buchgesellschaft, 1976) 2:364; A. D. Nock, *Conversion* (Oxford: Oxford University Press, 1961) 216–17; idem, *Early Gentile Christianity and Its Hellenistic Background* (New York: Harper & Row, 1964) 20–22; and Meeks, *Moral World*, 114. For a suggestion that this "cult" group was a household organization and thus that the oath reinforced the patriarchal household structures (along the lines of the *Haustafel*), see L. M. White, *Building God's House in the Roman World* (Baltimore: Johns Hopkins University Press, 1990) 45.

70. The translation is that of J. Stevenson, ed., *A New Eusebius* (London: SPCK, 1957) 14. For a comparison of the Christian oath in Pliny with the oath sworn in the shrine of the goddess Agdistis at Philadelphia, see A. D. Nock, "The Christian Sacramentum in Pliny and a Pagan Counterpart," *CR* 38 (1924) 58–59; idem, *Early Gentile Christianity*, 22.

71. See, for example, Plutarch, *Mor.* 46A: "Exceedingly displeasing also are those who use an oath in testifying to their approval of the speakers as though in a law court" (trans. LCL). See also the view of Favorinus *apud* Plutarch, *Mor.* 271C.

seus replies, "My word is my bond. No oath could make it stronger."[72] Cicero twice recounts a story about Xenocrates (head of the Platonic Academy from 339 to 314 B.C.E.), whose reputation for veracity was so strong that the Athenian jury refused even to allow him to take an oath (*Balb.* 12; *Att.* 1.16.4). Herakles was said by some to have been "so circumspect regarding an oath that he swore but once and for Phyleos, the son of Augeas, alone" (Plutarch, *Mor.* 271C; trans. F. C. Babbitt, LCL). The truly good man, therefore, needs neither oath nor witness to confirm his statements.[73] In light of this, Epictetus advises his students, "Refuse, if you can, to take an oath at all, but if that is impossible, refuse as far as circumstances allow" (*Ench.* 33.5).[74] Similar advice is given by Philo:

> To swear not at all is the best course and the most profitable to life, well suited to a rational nature which has been taught to speak the truth so well on each occasion that its words are regarded as oaths; to swear truly is only, as people say, a "second best voyage," for the mere fact of his swearing casts suspicion on the trustworthiness of the man. Let him, then, lag and linger in the hope that by repeated postponement he may avoid the oath altogether. But, if necessity be too strong for him, he must consider in no careless fashion all that an oath involves, for that is no small thing, though custom makes light of it. (*Dec.* 84; trans. F. H. Colson, LCL)

Finally, in some cases the critique of frivolous and unnecessary oaths may have developed into a virtual rejection of oaths. The traditions about Pythagoras vary; in some instances, he is said to have counseled his followers to use oaths sparingly (Diodorus Siculus 10.9.1–2), whereas in others he rejects all oaths (Diogenes Laertius 8.22; Iamblichus, *VP* 9.47; 28.144, 150). Similarly, the Essenes are said by Philo to show their love of God by abstaining from oaths (*Prob.* 84). Indeed, according to Josephus, "Any word of theirs has more force than an oath; swearing they avoid, regarding it as worse than perjury, for they say that one who is not believed without an appeal to God stands condemned already" (*Jewish War* 2.135; trans. H. St. J. Thackeray, LCL). Yet in neither case does the aversion to oaths appear to have been absolute. It is fairly certain that the Pythagoreans did take an oath of secrecy and even swore "by him who into our souls has transmitted the Sacred Quaternary."[75] Similarly, the Essenes, despite their general rejec-

72. The translation is that of P. D. Arnott, *Sophocles: Oedipus at Colonus and Electra* (Northbrook, Ill.: AHM Publishing Corp., 1975) 25.

73. See Marcus Aurelius, *Med.* 3.5, with the commentary of A. S. L. Farquharson, *The Meditations of the Emperor Marcus Antoninus* (2 vols.; Oxford: Clarendon, 1944) 2:566.

74. The translation is that of W. A. Oldfather in the LCL. Epictetus certainly does not wish entirely to prohibit oaths. See *Diss.* 3.19.3; 4.1.50; and esp. 1.14.15–16, where he gives a Stoic's oath of allegiance to god.

75. On the Pythagorean oath of silence, see n. 68 above. The quotation is from the anonymous Neopythagorean poem known as the *Golden Verses*, which was often attributed to Pythagoras himself; the translation of the verse is taken from K. S. Guthrie, *The Pythagorean*

tion of oaths, required "tremendous oaths" of loyalty to God and of secrecy in regard to the community's mysteries (Josephus, *Jewish War* 2.138–42).

GRECO-ROMAN PERSPECTIVES ON PERJURY

The Hellenistic moralists' critique of oath-taking was but one part of their polemic against perjury. In combating perjury, they were attacking not only a moral and social problem but also a religious offense. This is unusual, for, in general, the concern with morality in the Greco-Roman world was grounded in philosophy and rhetoric rather than in religion, and the latter "had little directly to do with ethics."[76] Perjury was a major exception,[77] for it involved the profanation of the divine's name, and while "the gods [may] have nothing against straightforward lying, . . . they do object to their names being taken in vain."[78] Oaths, therefore, linked religion to morality. Furthermore, as K. J. Dover observes,

> Since the swearing of oaths played so large a part in commercial transactions, it was hard to be fraudulent or dishonest without at the same time being impious; when Hermogenes in Xen. *Smp.* 4.49 defines religious duty as fidelity to oaths and abstention from blasphemy, he is going much further towards the equation of religion with morality than we might think, and in Ar. *Wealth* 61–105 "faithful to his oaths" and "of good character" seem to be treated as synonyms.[79]

Perjury was thus a conspicuous form of ἀσέβεια ("impiety").[80] For that reason, perjury and impiety are often mentioned together. For example, Antiphon declares: "I will prove that my accusers are the most reckless perjurers (ἐπιορκοτάτους) and the most impious scoundrels (ἀσεβεστάτους) alive" (6.33). The impious (ἀσεβής) person is by definition ἀνόσιος, "unholy" and "profane."[81] Consequently, Antiphon can also call his opponents "the worst perjurers (ἐπιορκοτάτους) and the most profane (ἀνοσιωτάτους)

Sourcebook and Library (ed. D. R. Fiedler; Grand Rapids: Phanes Press, 1987) 164. The "Sacred Quaternary" is the famous Pythagorean "tetractys." See W. Burkert, *Lore and Science in Ancient Pythagoreanism* (Cambridge, Mass.: Harvard University Press, 1972) 72–73.

76. Meeks, *Moral World*, 114. See also A. J. Malherbe, "Life in the Graeco-Roman World," in *The World of the New Testament* (ed. A. J. Malherbe; Austin: Sweet, 1967) 34; and Ferguson, *Backgrounds of Early Christianity*, 135.

77. For the recognition that the use of the gods' names in oaths constitutes an exception, see Nock, *Early Gentile Christianity*, 17.

78. E. R. Dodds, *The Greeks and the Irrational* (repr. Berkeley and Los Angeles: University of California Press, 1966) 32.

79. Dover, *Greek Popular Morality*, 249.

80. See, for example, Plutarch, *Mor.* 275D ("an impious and perjured man") and Aristophanes, *Thesm.* 356–67, where the breaking of oaths is one of the deeds of impiety.

81. For sacrilegious behavior involving oaths, see Demosthenes, *Or.* 18.217.

scoundrels alive" (6.48). A perjurer is thus both ἀσεβής and ἀνόσιος;[82] conversely, a person who swears truly and keeps his or her oaths is both εὐσεβής ("pious") and ὅσιος ("holy" and "devout").[83] For that reason, Socrates tells the dicasts that "we ought not to get you into the habit of breaking your oaths, nor ought you to fall into that habit; for neither of us would be acting piously" (Plato, *Ap.* 35C; trans. H. N. Fowler, LCL). Moreover, whereas the pious person speaks the truth, a perjurer states what is false or what proves to be false and thus is ψευδής, a "liar." Xenophon presents Hermogenes as the friend of the gods, because, as he says, "I never intentionally lie (ψεύδομαι) in matters wherein I have invoked them to be my witnesses" (*Symp.* 4.49).[84] Given these conceptual and terminological links, it is not at all surprising that the author of 1 Tim 1:9 uses ἀσεβής, ἀνόσιος, and ψευδής together with ἐπίορκος in his list of sinners. His original readers would have immediately recognized the connection between these terms.

Because the Greeks considered perjury to be a religious offense, they traditionally believed that the gods would punish perjurers. Indeed, this idea appears already in Homer and continues throughout antiquity, though it is also mocked in some circles (as, for example, in Lucian, *Tim.* 2). The divine penalty for perjury was not set; it could be woes of various kinds (Homer, *Il.* 19.264–65), shipwreck (Euripides, *El.* 1355), death (Homer, *Il.* 3.298–301), or even involve postmortem punishment (Homer, *Il.* 3.278–79; Aeschylus, *Eum.* 269–75; Aristophanes, *Ran.* 146–51). Indeed, inasmuch as the oath was a self-curse, the sanction for the infraction was sometimes specified by the oath-taker at the time of the oath. In this case, the gods' responsibility was not to determine what the penalty should be, but to punish the perjurer according to the terms that he or she had indicated in the oath. The punishment could be corporate, so that the perjurer's family suffered along with the offender (Homer, *Il.* 3.298–301). Or, in keeping with the ancient Greek idea of inherited family guilt, the punishment could be postponed so that the perjurers' children suffered instead of the offenders themselves.[85] Belief in the divine punishment of perjury did not, of course, necessarily result in people keeping their oaths. Maximus of Tyre laments that humans all too

82. For the combination of these two terms, see Philo, *Spec. Leg.* 1.327; cf. Xenophon, *Cyr.* 8.8.27.

83. For the connection between piety and oaths, see Euripides, *Hipp.* 656–58; Plato, *Apol.* 35C; Demosthenes, *Or.* 9.16; 18.7. For the link between piety and holiness, see Plato, *Euthphr.* 12E; 14B.

84. I have slightly modified the rendering in the LCL. For perjury as a form of falsehood, see especially W. Luther, *"Wahrheit" und "Lüge" im ältesten Griechentum* (Borna: Noske, 1935) 90–97, 143–44, and *Weltansicht und Geistesleben* (Göttingen: Vandenhoeck & Ruprecht, 1954) 85–90. See also Maximus of Tyre, *Or.* 29.2e, where Philip of Macedon is said to have committed perjury and lied, and the vice list in Lucian, *Calumn.* 20.2, where lying and perjury are listed consecutively.

85. On this point, see especially R. Parker, *Miasma: Pollution and Purification in Early Greek Religion* (Oxford: Clarendon, 1983) 198–206.

often "feared [the gods] as avenging powers, yet committed perjury, as if the gods had no existence" (*Or.* 36.2n).

It is important to emphasize that, for the ancient Greeks, perjury was a religious offense punishable by the divine, *not* a legal offense punished by the court. In Athens, for example, the legal offense was the giving of false testimony. Most witnesses, as we have seen, were not sworn, and a false witness was subject to prosecution whether the testimony was given under oath or not.[86] To give false testimony was, moreover, a civil offense, not a criminal one. Or, to be more precise, it was a quasi-criminal offense, for, though prosecuted by a private citizen, the penalty was assessed by the state.[87] Prosecution took the form of a lawsuit for false testimony (ψευδο-μαρτυρίων δίκη) and, if successful, typically resulted in a fine or, after three convictions, the loss of civil rights.[88]

Within a legal setting, perjury was an *additional* offense. Witnesses who swore falsely were guilty of giving false testimony; if they did so under oath, they were also guilty of perjury. If convicted of the former, they were punished by the state for the legal offense involved; if guilty of perjury, they were subject to punishment by the divine for the religious offense of taking the god's name in vain.[89]

The situation was similar in ancient Israel, for no text in the Hebrew Bible indicates that witnesses were placed under oath.[90] Stated in terms of the Decalogue, therefore, perjury was a violation of the third commandment ("You shall not take the name of the LORD your God in vain"), whereas false witness was a violation of the ninth commandment ("you shall not bear false witness against your neighbor"). Because perjury and false witness were similar but not the same,[91] the author of the *Didache* was not being

86. Latte, "Meineid," 349. Sworn testimony may have been more prevalent in other cities, but the fundamental point is not thereby affected. For Ptolemaic Alexandria, see Seidl, *Der Eid im ptolemäischen Recht*, 104–5.

87. Calhoun, *Growth of Criminal Law*, 131. For a unique exception, see p. 117 n. 33. Completely excluded from consideration here is perjury involving the name of the Roman emperor, which was a potentially serious, even treasonable, offense against the imperial majesty (*crimen laesae maiestatis*). See Tertullian, *Apol.* 28; Minucius Felix, *Oct.* 29; and Wenger, "Der Eid in den griechischen Papyrusurkunden," 268–69. For Tiberius's lenient attitude toward offenses of this kind, see Tacitus, *Ann.* 1.73, and Dio Cassius 57.8.3.

88. See especially G. M. Calhoun, "Perjury Before Athenian Arbitrators," *Classical Philology* 10 (1915) 1–7; idem, "ΕΠΙΣΚΕΨΙΣ and the ΔΙΚΗ ΨΕΥΔΟΜΑΡΤΥΡΙΩΝ," *Classical Philology* 11 (1916) 365–94; idem, *Growth of Criminal Law*, 131; and A. R. W. Harrison, *The Law of Athens* (2 vols.; Oxford: Clarendon, 1968, 1971) 1:156–62; 2:127–31, 192–99.

89. For the Roman attitude, see especially Cicero, *Leg.* 2.9.22: "For the perjurer the punishment from the gods is destruction; the human punishment shall be disgrace" (trans. C. W. Keyes, LCL). In short, it is the gods' responsibility to punish injuries against themselves; see especially the famous maxim of Tiberius in Tacitus, *Ann.* 1.73: *deorum iniurias dis curae.*

90. Boecker, *Law and the Administration of Justice in the Old Testament*, 35: "We do not know of any case of an oath taken by a witness."

91. See D. Patrick, *Old Testament Law* (Atlanta: John Knox Press, 1985) 57: "One might think

redundant when he incorporated prohibitions against both perjury (οὐ ἐπι-ορκήσεις) and false witness (οὐ ψευδομαρτυρήσεις) into the Two Ways tradition (2:3).[92] Matthew, on the other hand, was concerned with the problems of oaths and perjury, which were broader than the legal setting assumed by the ninth commandment. For that reason, he did not preface Jesus' prohibition of oaths with a quotation of the ninth commandment, but provided an interpretive summary of the third commandment. In so doing, he was like Philo, who also understood the third commandment to be essentially a prohibition of perjury (*Dec.* 82–91).

THE MEANING OF "PERJURY"

From a chronological standpoint, Greek oaths can be divided into two basic types—the assertory and the promissory. Oaths about the past and present are assertory, and those that contain pledges concerning the future are promissory. The Greeks used the term ὅρκος in regard to both types as well as to mixed oaths that contain both assertions and promises. In a similar way, they applied the term ἐπιορκία to all the kinds of oaths discussed above, both promissory and assertory. The Romans did the same with *perjurium*. As a consequence, the ancient Greco-Roman terms for perjury generally indicate "false" as well as "broken" oaths. The semantic range of ἐπιορκία and *perjurium* creates enormous difficulties for the contemporary English-speaking translator, for the English word "perjury" no longer suggests to most modern speakers of English both broken and false oaths.[93] Therefore, when rendering ἐπιορκία and ἐπιορκεῖν, modern translators typically use "false oath" and "to swear falsely" when an assertory oath is in view, and "broken oath" and "to break an oath" when a promissory oath is being discussed. The translator's difficulty becomes acute when faced with a text that treats both types of oaths or when the type of oath is not clearly indicated.

This is certainly the case in regard to Matt 5:33. Almost all English versions render the verb ἐπιορκεῖν in this verse with "to swear falsely," which suggests falsification in regard to an assertory oath. This is highly problematic, because the context clearly suggests that promissory oaths are particularly (and perhaps even exclusively) in view. One of the reasons the

---

that the third commandment would cover false testimony, but this is not the case, because testimony was not given under oath."

92. In a similar way, the author of 1 Tim 1:10 can associate "liars" with "perjurers" without identifying the two.

93. "Perjury" once indicated both "false oath" and "broken oath." See the meanings given for "perjury" in J. A. Simpson and E. S. C. Weiner, *The Oxford English Dictionary* (2nd ed.; Oxford: Clarendon, 1989) 11:571.

Matthean Jesus gives for prohibiting oaths concerns human inability in regard to future actions: "Neither swear by your head, for you are not able to make one hair white or black" (Matt 5:36). Again, Matthew's recasting of Deut 23:22 LXX indicates that he understands ὅρκοι ("oaths") to be equivalent to εὐχαί ("vows"), for he substitutes the former for the latter. The very notion of keeping an oath or vow, of course, entails action in the future (ἀποδώσεις). Such an understanding of oaths is quintessentially Greek, for, as Rudolf Hirzel noted long ago in his classic study of Greek oaths, the Greeks thought of oaths as essentially promissory.[94] In light of such considerations, it is much more preferable to translate the key phrase in Matt 5:33 as "You shall not break your oaths, but you shall keep the oaths you have sworn to the Lord."

The literary contexts of 1 Tim 1:10 and *Did.* 2.3 provide little help in determining a more specific meaning for the term "perjury." It is extremely likely, however, that assertory as well as promissory oaths are presupposed in both instances. In that case, ἐπίορκος in 1 Tim 1:10 has reference to those who break their oaths as well as those who swear false ones. In a similar way, the prohibition in *Did.* 2.3 means (translated expansively) "you shall neither swear false oaths nor break those that you take."

94. Hirzel, *Der Eid*, 4. On Stoic attempts to restrict the meaning of ἐπιορκεῖν to promissory oaths, see Plescia, *Oath and Perjury*, 84–85.

CHAPTER 12

The Social World of James:
Literary Analysis and
Historical Reconstruction

Luke Timothy Johnson

IN THE HISTORY of New Testament scholarship, the name Wayne A. Meeks inevitably and appropriately will be associated with the social analysis of early Christianity. Both by his writing and by his teaching, Meeks has demonstrated that a "sociological" approach to the New Testament is not a scholarly fad but a fundamental contribution to historical knowledge. His seminal contributions to the discussion of Christianity's social world have revealed the rich possibilities of the approach and have helped secure at the very least a conviction that earliest Christianity can no longer be understood simply in terms of a "history of ideas." But Meeks's own highly successful forays into the analysis of early Christian social realities have also suggested certain intractable limitations on what this approach can yield by way of real knowledge.

In *The First Urban Christians*, for example, Meeks built on his own and others' previous studies to provide a rich profile of the Corinthian congregation during the years of Paul's work there.[1] By combining the close analysis of the Corinthian correspondence with archaeological evidence, and reading these texts for signs of social structures and relationships, Meeks was able to illuminate not only the social realities underlying the specific problems dealt with by Paul but also something of the umbrella of meaning

---

1. Wayne A. Meeks, *The First Urban Christians: The Social World of the Apostle Paul* (New Haven: Yale University Press, 1983). See also, for example, W. A. Meeks, "Social Functions of Apocalyptic Language in Pauline Christianity," in *Apocalypticism in the Mediterranean World and the Near East* (ed. D. Hellholm; Tübingen: Mohr-Siebeck, 1982); idem, "The Image of the Androgyne: Some Uses of a Symbol in Earliest Christianity," *HR* 13 (1974) 165–208; E. A. Judge, "The Social Identity of the First Christians: A Question of Method in Religious History," *Journal of Religious History* 11 (1980) 201–17; A. J. Malherbe, *Social Aspects of Early Christianity* (Baton Rouge: Louisiana State University Press, 1977); G. Theissen, *The Social Setting of Pauline Christianity: Essays on Corinth* (trans. J. Schutz; Philadelphia: Fortress, 1982).

that provided an ideological framework for the nascent Christian movement. So brilliant was his achievement that it may have raised unrealistic expectations of accomplishment elsewhere.

Meeks would be the first to acknowledge that the success of his Corinthian analysis depended on an unusual combination of factors: a successfully excavated and archaeologically rich urban setting that was also described in ancient literature; a correspondence that not only dealt with specific problems in the community but did so with an unparalleled degree of particularity and specificity, down to the naming of names; and, finally, the existence of other Christian literature (Acts, Romans) which helped locate this correspondence chronologically and confirm some of the social realities suggested by 1 Corinthians. To a remarkable degree, in fact, Meeks's analysis focused almost exclusively on the Corinthian congregation, with evidence from other Pauline letters and communities offered mainly by way of corroboration.

Where a like combination of converging evidence is lacking, sociological analysis of early Christianity can easily mean a return to a slightly more complex version of the history of ideas, with the use of sociological/developmental models filling in for the lack of genuine data.[2]

Think what our knowledge of the Corinthian church itself would really amount to, if 1 Corinthians—so rooted in the real and urban world—were no longer extant. 2 Corinthians could lend itself to any number of "mirror readings" concerning Paul's rivals, as in fact it has.[3] R. Hock has offered a slight foothold in reality by sketching the background to debates concerning payment for services among Hellenistic philosophers, which helps make sense of Paul's language in 2 Corinthians 10–12.[4] But otherwise, 2 Corinthians and the other Pauline letters tend to be read as evidence for theological debates between "Paul and his Opponents," with the letters themselves being chopped into ever finer pieces and arranged in sequence to supply the appropriate reconstruction of the "stages" of such debates.[5]

---

2. An early advocate of an explicit commitment to such models was J. G. Gager, *Kingdom and Community: The Social World of Early Christianity* (Englewood Cliffs, N.J.: Prentice-Hall, 1975); for the options, see H. E. Remus, "Sociology of Knowledge and the Study of Early Christianity," *SR* 11 (1982) 45–56.

3. The most elaborate and influential example has been D. Georgi, *The Opponents of Paul in Corinth* (1964; Eng. trans. Philadelphia: Fortress, 1985); see also C. K. Barrett, "Paul's Opponents in II Corinthians," *NTS* 17 (1971) 233–54. Criticism of this approach is found in C. J. A. Hickling, "Is the Second Epistle to the Corinthians a Source for Early Church History?" *ZNW* 66 (1975) 284–87, and in C. R. Holladay, *Theios Anēr in Hellenistic Judaism: A Critique of the Use of this Category in New Testament Christology* (SBLDS 40; Missoula, Mont.: Scholars Press, 1977).

4. R. F. Hock, *The Social Context of Paul's Ministry* (Philadelphia: Fortress, 1980) 50–65.

5. On 2 Corinthians, see the recent attempt along these lines by A. de Oliveira, *Die Diakonie der Gerechtigkeit und der Versöhnung in der Apologie des 2 Korintherbriefes: Analyse und Auslegung von 2 Kor 2,14-4,6; 5,11-6,10* (NTAbh n.F. 21; Munster: Aschendorff, 1990); for other Pauline letters, see J. Tyson, "Paul's Opponents in Galatia," *NovT* 10 (1968) 241–54;. R. Jewett, "Conflicting

The recent attempt by J. Neyrey to read Galatians in terms of anthropological concepts such as "witchcraft" shows the intrinsic limitations of social-scientific approaches for Pauline letters where rich supporting evidence is lacking: his readings are fascinating and suggestive, but cannot reach much beyond that.[6] When it comes to the disputed Pauline letters, the evidence is even thinner. M. MacDonald's study of institutionalization in Pauline churches, for example, is forced to make the production of pseudonymous letters itself the major evidence for that particular stage of institutional development![7]

It seems clear that the more we move from occasional literature such as letters to compositions intended for a wider readership, the more the factors of rhetoric and literary artistry necessarily interpose themselves between the contemporary reader and the social world that may have been presumed by the composition. Likewise, when the text itself reveals little specific information about its social world, the investigator becomes more dependent on theoretical models concerning social groups and their development. The sheer multiplicity of possibilities suggested for the various "communities" presupposed or addressed by the Gospels raises severe doubts concerning the usefulness of the search.[8]

Not that stunning invention is impossible. By his use of sociological categories concerning sectarianism, Meeks himself masterfully exploited the possibilities of such a theoretical model for unlocking the intricate rhetoric of a narrative text.[9] No one acquainted with Meeks's analysis of the Fourth Gospel's textual ironies as reinforcing the sectarian views of Johannine Christianity can, I suspect, ever totally shake the force of that reading. Yet even so great an accomplishment did not significantly add to our knowledge of John's social world, although it immeasurably sharpened our appreciation of its ideology and literary rendering.

Movements in the Early Church as Reflected in Philippians," *NovT* 12 (1970) 361–90; W. A. Meeks and F. O. Francis, *Conflict at Colossae* (SBLSBS 4; rev. ed.; Missoula, Mont.: Scholars Press, 1975).

6. J. Neyrey, *Paul in Other Words: A Cultural Reading of His Letters* (Louisville: Westminster/John Knox, 1990) 181–206.

7. M. Y. MacDonald, *The Pauline Churches: A Socio-Historical Study of Institutionalization in the Pauline and Deutero-Pauline Writings* (SNTSMS 60; Cambridge: Cambridge University Press, 1988) 86–97; somewhat similar is the argumentation of M. Wolter, *Die Pastoralbriefe als Paulustradition* (FRLANT 146; Göttingen: Vandenhoeck & Ruprecht, 1988) 115–30. As I noted in my review of MacDonald's study in *JAAR* 58 (1990) 716–19, her work has the significant virtue of methodological clarity and consistency; in my view, however, that very quality makes even more doubtful the validity of the development as she exposes it.

8. I have tried to suggest some of the difficulties for finding a "community" behind the Gospel narratives in "On Finding the Lukan Community: A Cautious Cautionary Essay," in *Society of Biblical Literature 1979 Seminar Papers* (ed. P. J. Achtemeier; Missoula, Mont.: Scholars Press, 1979) 87–100.

9. W. A. Meeks, "The Man from Heaven in Johannine Sectarianism," *JBL* 91 (1972) 44–72.

More pedestrian attempts to derive from the layered texture of John's narrative or from the sequential arrangement of the Gospel and Johannine letters a "history" of Johannine Christianity must be viewed as interesting but nonconclusive paper chases rather than history.[10] Beyond the signals obvious to any careful reader—that this literature reflected experiences of being embattled from without and divided from within; that such division sharpened its symbols into polar opposites; that the causes of embattlement from without and division from within involved the central figure of Jesus—efforts at reading a "history" out of such fragmentary sources become less plausible the more highly they are developed. Once more, access to the social world of John or his readers is blocked by the lack of controls offered by a convergence of diverse sources from a specific time and place, as well as by the literary character of the texts.[11]

These observations on the possibilities and problems of reconstructing the social world behind New Testament writings bring me in a chastened mood to the real topic of this essay. What, if anything, can be determined from the Letter of James about the social world of its author or readers? Can the Letter of James be rooted in history at all? If so, by what means or with what benefit to the understanding of the letter? On the one hand, we are offered hope because James is so obviously enmeshed in the realities of life and practical wisdom. On the other hand, our hope is qualified by the realization that James's no-nonsense practicality is never clothed with the sort of specific information we desire. In the remainder of this essay I propose to survey some of the ways the social world of James might be approached and assess the chances of success offered by each.

A Social World Suggested by Traditional Authorship

The most encouraging possibilities would seem to be offered by the identity of the author, if we could assume that James "the Brother of the Lord"—universally considered the "James" of the letter's greeting[12]—was the

---

10. For example, J. L. Martyn, *History and Theology in the Fourth Gospel* (rev. ed.; Nashville: Abingdon, 1979); idem, *The Gospel of John in Christian History* (New York: Paulist, 1978); R. E. Brown, *The Community of the Beloved Disciple* (New York: Paulist, 1979); J. Painter, "The Farewell Discourses and the History of Johannine Christianity," *NTS* 27 (1980–81) 525–43.

11. Chances are obviously improved if the book of Revelation is taken seriously as a source for the history of Johannine Christianity: see, e.g., E. Schüssler Fiorenza, "The Quest for the Johannine School: The Book of Revelation and the Fourth Gospel," in *The Book of Revelation: Justice and Judgment* (Philadelphia: Fortress, 1985) 85–113.

12. See the very full discussions in J. B. Mayor, *The Epistle of St. James* (3rd ed.; London: Macmillan, 1910) i–lxv; J. H. Ropes, *A Critical and Exegetical Commentary on the Epistle of St. James* (Edinburgh: Clark, 1916) 53–74; M. Dibelius, *James: A Commentary on the Epistle of James* (rev. H. Greeven; trans. M. A. Williams; Hermeneia; Philadelphia: Fortress, 1976) 11–21; R. P. Martin, *James* (WBC 48; Waco, Tex.: Word, 1988) xxxi–lxix.

real and not simply the eponymous author. What we would gain by this supposition is a writer whose position and importance as a pillar of the church in Jerusalem are attested by other New Testament writers,[13] and who is sufficiently prominent in the public affairs of Jerusalem to have his martyrdom in 62 noted as well by Josephus.[14] By this means we would gain as well the sort of geographical and chronological controls otherwise so difficult to come by in the analysis of New Testament literature. Geographically, the greeting to "the twelve tribes in the dispersion" (1:1) would be unproblematic if written by one residing in Jerusalem,[15] as would the assumption that his readers were, indeed, fellow Jews "holding the faith of our Lord Jesus

13. Paul lists James as a witness to the resurrection in 1 Cor 15:7, and may include James in his passing reference to those who traveled with a woman/sister: "the rest of the apostles and the brothers of the Lord and Cephas" (1 Cor 9:5). In Galatians, Paul recounts having seen James in Jerusalem on his trip to that city ἱστορῆσαι Κηφᾶν ("to visit Cephas"), although his language does not make clear whether he regards him as one of the apostles (1:19; compare the language in 1 Cor 15:7). James is included first in his list of those "reputed to be pillars" (δοκοῦντες στῦλοι εἶναι) in that city who made agreement with Paul concerning the allocation of mission work (2:9). Finally, there are the mysterious "people from James" (τινας ἀπὸ Ἰακώβου) who catalyze the problem between Paul and Cephas in Antioch (2:12). In contrast to Mark 6:3 and Matthew 13:55, who mention James among Jesus' brothers in a somewhat negative context (see J. D. Crossan, "Mark and the Relatives of Jesus," *NovT* 15 [1973] 81–113), Luke makes no certain mention of this James (see the ambiguity of Luke 6:16; Acts 1:13) until Peter's escape from prison in Acts 12:1–17: before "departing to another place," he told the assembly to "inform James and the Brothers of these things" (12:17). The language, together with that in 1 Cor 9:5, suggests the picture of James at the center of a special group called "brothers of the Lord" (see also Acts 1:14). James appears twice more in Acts as spokesperson for the Jerusalem church, first at the Apostolic Council, where his response to the debate concerning circumcision of Gentile converts is definitive (Acts 15:13–21), and second at Paul's final trip to Jerusalem, where James and the elders with him recommend that Paul deflect charges concerning his rejection of the law and circumcision for Jews by performing a symbolic act of solidarity (21:18–25). Finally, the author of the Letter of Jude identifies himself as "servant of Jesus Christ and brother of James" (Jude 1:1; compare Mark 6:3; Matt 13:55).

14. Josephus, *Antiquities* 20.200. In contrast to an older criticism that tended to reject the authenticity of the notice (see F. C Baur, *Paul the Apostle of Jesus Christ* [2nd ed., edited by E. Zeller; trans. A. Menzies; London: Williams & Norgate, 1875] 1:160), more recent scholars have tended to credit it; see the discussion, with literature, in J. P. Meier, *A Marginal Jew: Rethinking the Historical Jesus*, Vol. 1: *The Roots of the Problem and the Person* (New York: Doubleday, 1991) 58–59, 72–73. James's death is also recounted (with variations) by the account from Hegesippus found in Eusebius, *Church History* 2.23, and in the Nag Hammadi writing the *Second Apocalypse of James* 61–62.

15. An alternative to the straightforwardly geographical understanding of "diaspora" (διασπορά) is to understand it as symbolizing the Christian condition of being "exiles, aliens, and sojourners" with respect to their heavenly homeland (compare especially 1 Pet 1:1; 2:11; 2 Cor 5:1–10; Gal 4:26; Phil 1:21–24; 3:20–21). And the opposition between faith and a certain understanding of "the world" is certainly central to James (see 2:5; 4:4). See L. T. Johnson, "Friendship with the World/Friendship with God: A Study of Discipleship in James," in *Discipleship in the New Testament* (ed. F. Segovia; Philadelphia: Fortress, 1985) 166–83. But the two levels of meaning are compatible.

Christ" (2:1). References to "Gehenna" (3:6), "fig-tree, olives, grape-vine" (3:12) or the "early and late rain" (5:7) might even be taken as spontaneous evidence for the influence of local conditions.[16]

Chronologically, connecting the letter to James the brother of Jesus makes more plausible the simple social structures and activities suggested by the text. The letter contains no sign of the institutional complexities that are supposed to be the marks of a community developing over time. The gathering of the community can be called the συναγωγή ("assembly or synagogue"; 2:2) as well as ἐκκλησία ("assembly or church"; 5:14).[17] As for authority figures, the author designates himself simply as a δοῦλος ("servant") of God and the Lord Jesus Christ (1:1) before modestly receding behind his message. He demands no further recognition from his readers and asserts no further role among them, with the exception of carrying, with fellow teachers, the burden of "a greater judgment" (3:1).[18] Otherwise, the letter speaks of the "elders of the church" (πρεσβύτεροι τῆς ἐκκλησίας) who are to be called to pray over the sick.[19] Apart from this collegial leadership—if, in fact, πρεσβύτεροι ("elders") here suggests a position of official leadership rather than age—there is no indication of a formal structure, with only a

16. For commentaries that consider James of Jerusalem to be the author of this letter it is characteristic to entertain the possibility of "real life" perceptions behind passages such as 3:12 (see Mayor, *Epistles*, 124; Martin, *James*, 121; J. B. Adamson, *The Epistle of James* [NICNT; Grand Rapids: Eerdmans, 1976] 129), whereas commentaries holding for pseudonymous authorship lean entirely on literary sources (Dibelius-Greeven, *James*, 204–5). Mayor (*Epistle*, cxliii) is convinced that the supposition of early authorship is "confirmed by incidental allusions to the early and latter rains (v. 7), to the effect on vegetation of the burning wind (i.11), to the existence of salt and bitter springs (iii.11), to the cultivation of figs and olives (iii.12), and to the neighborhood of the sea (i.6, iii.4)." The case of γέεννη ("Gehenna") in 3:6 is particularly interesting. Since it does not occur in the LXX and is absent as well from Philo and Josephus or any other New Testament writings except the Gospels, it seems in particular to suggest a knowledge of local Palestinian usage (see J. Jeremias, γέεννη, *TDNT* 1:657–58).

17. Compare the use of ἐπισυναγωγή in Heb 10:25. Although the terms ἐκκλησία and συναγωγή would come in some contexts to signify opposition between Christianity and Judaism (see Justin, *Dialogue with Trypho* 134.3), there also continues a more flexible usage in which the terms are virtually interchangeable: see Ignatius, *Polycarp* 4.2 (or the combination of συνέδριον/ἐκκλησία in *Tral.* 3.1); *Shepherd of Hermas*, *Mand.* 11.9, 13–14; Justin, *Dialogue with Trypho* 63.5.

18. The title of δοῦλος ("servant") for leaders is attested in several places in the first-generation Christian literature (Rom 1:1; 2 Cor 4:5; Gal 1:10; Phil 1:1; Col 4:12; 2 Tim 2:24; Titus 1:1; 2 Pet 1:1; Jude 1; Rev 1:1).

19. According to Acts, the leadership of elders was found not only in Jerusalem (15:2, 4, 6, 22–23; 21:18) but also in "diaspora" churches of the first generation (14:23; 20:17). Although it is popular to dismiss this portrayal as anachronistic for Pauline churches (see, e.g., F. Prast, *Presbyter und Evangelium in nachapostolischer Zeit: Die Abschiedsrede des Paulus in Milet (Apg 20, 17-38) im Rahmen der lukanischen Konzeption der Evangeliumsverkündigung* [Stuttgart: Katholisches Bibelwerk, 1979]), the evidence of 1 Tim 4:14; 5:1, 17, 19; Titus 1:5 should not altogether be disregarded, nor that of 1 Pet 5:1, 5.

passing warning against many seeking to become "teachers" because of the inherent dangers of that role (3:1–2).[20] Such minimal structure fits well within what little we know of the diaspora synagogue in Judaism.[21] The same can be said about the straightforward activities of the community mentioned by the text: judging cases (2:1–4), assisting the needy (1:27; 2:14–17), teaching (3:1–2), praying and singing (5:13), anointing the sick (5:14), and practicing mutual correction (5:16, 19).[22]

If James the brother of the Lord wrote the letter sometime around the middle of the first century, other aspects of this composition also make sense. It has frequently been noted that, despite mentioning Jesus by name only twice (1:1; 2:1), this letter appears to know and make use of the Jesus sayings traditions (see, e.g., 1:5, 9, 12; 2:5, 8; 5:9, 12).[23] At the same time, the letter combines a profound appreciation for wisdom (1:5; 3:13–18),[24] together with a vivid sense of the nearness of the παρουσία ("coming") of the Lord for judgment (2:12–13; 3:1; 4:11–12; 5:7–9).[25] Although I have misgivings about some of the ways in which the hypothetical document Q has been hypostatized, it is striking that just this combination of features (a concentration on the sayings of Jesus and his return as judge) is taken in Q as characteristic of a distinctively Palestinian form of earliest Christianity.[26]

20. For the διδάσκαλος (also ὁ διδάσκων, ὁ κατηχῶν) as a first-generation position within the assembly, see Acts 13:1; Rom 12:7; 1 Cor 12:28–29; Gal 6:6; Eph 4:11. For teaching as a possible double-duty for the elder, see 1 Tim 5:17.

21. See Josephus, *Antiquities* 14.260; the inscriptional evidence has been gathered by L. H. Kant, "Jewish Inscriptions in Greek and Latin," *ANRW* 2.20 (1987) 692–98.

22. For the range of activities in the synagogue, see Josephus, *Antiquities* 4.211; *Against Apion* 2.10; *Life* 294–302; Philo, *Life of Moses* 2.216; *Special Laws* 2.62; *b. Ber.* 6a; *Ber.* 64a; *Ket.* 5a; *B. Meṣ.* 28b; *Pes.* 101a; *Yeb.* 65b.

23. See, e.g., M. Shepherd, "The Epistle of James and the Gospel of Matthew," *JBL* 75 (1956) 40–51; P. Minear, "'Yes and No': The Demand for Honesty in the Early Church," *NovT* 13 (1971) 1–13; P. J. Hartin, "James and the Sermon on the Mount/Plain," in *Society of Biblical Literature 1989 Seminar Papers* (ed. D. J. Lull; Atlanta: Scholars Press, 1989) 440–57.

24. See B. R. Halston, "The Epistle of James: 'Christian Wisdom'?" in *Studia Evangelica* 4 (1968) 308–14; J. A. Kirk, "The Meaning of Wisdom in James: Examination of a Hypothesis," *NTS* 16 (1969) 24–38.

25. There are three lines of evidence supporting the position that the coming of the Lord in 5:7–9 refers to the return of Jesus rather than the visitation of God. (1) The term παρουσία occurs only four times in the LXX and always in the secular sense (Neh 2:6; Judg 10:14; 2 Macc 8:12; 15:21; 3 Macc 3:17). The use in *Testament of Judah* 22:2 for "the appearing of the God of righteousness" may be an interpolation. In the New Testament, the term can be used in the secular sense (1 Cor 16:17; 2 Cor 7:6–7; 10:10; Phil 1:26; 2:12), but its dominant usage is as virtually a *terminus technicus* for the return of the Son of Man (Matt 24:3, 27, 37, 39; 1 Cor 15:23; 1 Thess 2:19; 3:13; 4:15; 5:23; 2 Thess 2:1, 8; 1 John 2:28; 2 Pet 1:16). (2) The use of the verb ἐγγίζω ("draw near") in the perfect tense to express "the Lord is near" is similar to the usage in Mark 1:15; Matt 3:2; 4:17; 10:7; Luke 10:9, 11; Rom 13:11; 1 Pet 4:7; Phil 4:5; Rev 1:3; 22:10. (3) The statement of 5:9b, "the judge is standing at the doors" (πρὸ τῶν θυρῶν), seems to fit within the development of the cluster of statements found in Mark 13:28–29 and Matt 24:32–33; Rev 3:20.

26. Already James Ropes had observed, "James was in religious ideas nearer to the men who collected the sayings of Jesus than to the authors of the Gospels" (*James*, 39). It is striking to

Even with such a simple and straightforward hypothesis, of course, great caution would need to be exercised in drawing conclusions from the text about James's social world.[27] In the first place, the self-presentation of the document itself suggests a broad readership, and one not located in the same place as the author (1:1)! Throughout the diaspora, furthermore, readers could live in a variety of social situations. Such specific and lively examples as that provided in 2:1-7 must, therefore, be handled gingerly. They can reflect general or typical situations just as easily as they could local ones known to the author.[28] Similarly, language that seems to derive from knowledge of local meteorology and horticulture might equally come from the reading of Torah,[29] or acquaintance with popular moral traditions.[30] The language of "rich and poor" in James is likewise complex and not easily reducible to conclusions about the economic status of the readers.[31] James's frequent and fluent use of *topoi* from Hellenistic philosophy equally resists

---

observe the complete lack of any references to James in the analyses of Q which describe precisely those preoccupations that have long been associated with James: the theme of judgment in a context of wisdom and prophecy; see, e.g., R. A. Edwards, *A Theology of Q: Eschatology, Prophecy, and Wisdom* (Philadelphia: Fortress, 1976). It is especially startling when the argument about Q is precisely its similarity to other wisdom traditions and therefore its comfortable fit within early Palestinian Jewish Christianity; see J. S. Kloppenborg, *The Formation of Q: Trajectories in Ancient Wisdom Collections* (Studies in Antiquity & Christianity; Philadelphia: Fortress, 1987). The link with James called out to be made, and has been recently by P. J. Hartin (*James and the Q Sayings of Jesus* [JSNTSup 47; Sheffield: JSOT Press, 1991]), reaching conclusions concerning the provenance of James similar to those in the present essay (see esp. pp. 220–44).

27. The most obvious error in method is to deduce from the circumstances of the author the situation of the readers.

28. This, of course, is the point made emphatically by Dibelius-Greeven, *James*, 2, 46. Yet it is perhaps noteworthy that the analysis that has provided the fullest understanding of even a hypothetical social context for Jas 2:1-7 finds its basis in specifically Jewish traditions: see R. B. Ward, "Partiality in the Assembly," *HTR* 62 (1969) 87–97.

29. For the "early and late rain," in 5:7, see LXX Deut 11:14; Hos 6:4; Jer 5:24; Joel 2:23; Zech 10:1.

30. Despite the broad resemblance of 3:12 to Matt 7:16//Luke 6:44, Dibelius-Greeven (*James*, 204-5) lists an impressive number of Stoic parallels; see also Mayor, *Epistle*, 125.

31. An adequate analysis of this language complex requires: (a) making approriate distinctions between terms for the "poor" (πτωχοί, 2:2, 3, 5, 6) and the "rich" (πλούσιοι, 1:10, 11; 2:5, 6; 5:1), which naturally bear an economic sense, and terms for "lowliness" (ταπεινός, etc., 1:9, 10; 4:10) and "exaltation" (ὕψος, 1:9; 4:10), which may have an economic sense but need not; (b) determining the ways such language may serve to demarcate community boundaries (e.g., 2:5-7; 5:1, 6); (c) correlating such language with the various characters and activities described in the letter: Is the "rich man" who enters the assembly (2:2) a member of the community or an outsider (2:6)? Is the rich man who "[boasts] in his humiliation" (1:10) a member of the community or an outsider (1:11)? Are those who thoughtlessly engage in commerce (4:13-15) and oppress day-laborers (5:1-5) the wicked outsiders, or insiders who have been seduced by the measurement of "the world" (4:4)? Likewise, what do we make of the ability of members of the community to feed and clothe the needy (2:14-16)? It is easier to affirm that the author and his readers shared the *ideology* of the poor than it is to deduce from that a realistic appreciation of the actual economic conditions within which they lived.

simplistic conclusions concerning the social situation being addressed;[32] it is surely a mistake, for example, to take James 4:1-2 out of its literary context, that is, of a *topos* on envy, to conclude that the author was responding to Zealot activity in first-century Palestine.[33]

Despite such warnings, it is obvious that the hypothesis of authorship by the historical James of Jerusalem at least provides the *possibility* for genuine investigation into the social world of the composition.[34] It may be appropriate, therefore, to ask why that hypothesis is now so seldom entertained. There is certainly nothing in the letter that prevents its having been written from Palestine in the middle of the first century. All the usual criteria for positing a late dating for New Testament writings are absent: there is no institutional development, no sense of tradition as a deposit, no polemic against false teachers, no highly developed Christology, no delay of the parousia. On the face of it, everything in the letter suggests an early dating rather than a late one.

The rejection of traditional authorship is based on a perceived conflict between what we think we know of the "historical James" from other sources and the evidence suggested by this letter. Sometimes the distinctive Greek style of the letter has been cited as a factor against its being composed by James of Jerusalem,[35] but that argument has no real weight; it is now universally acknowledged that Palestine was thoroughly Hellenized and that writers from there could write sophisticated Greek.[36] The real problem has to do with what is believed to be the attitudes and actions of the "historical James" concerning the question of circumcision and the keeping of the Law of Moses. Although it is rarely stated in such bald terms, James is taken to be not only a representative of Jewish Christianity but

32. See my own attempts to identify some of these *topoi* of Hellenistic moral teaching in "James 3:13–4:10 and the *Topos PERI PHTHONOU*," *NovT* 25 (1983) 327–47; "The Mirror of Remembrance (James 1:22–25)," *CBQ* 50 (1988) 632–45; "Taciturnity and True Religion (James 2:26–27)," in *Greeks, Romans, and Christians: Essays in Honor of Abraham J. Malherbe* (ed. D. Balch et al.; Minneapolis: Fortress, 1990) 329–39.

33. See M. T. Townsend, "James 4:1–14: A Warning Against Zealotry?" *ExpT* 87 (1975) 211–13.

34. Notice, for example, that by working with traditional authorship, Mayor is able to locate the poor in the Christian communities of the diaspora, and the rich oppressors in their Jewish compatriots (*Epistle*, cxxxviii–cxli); whatever one thinks of his argument, his premise at least enables the inquiry.

35. "Nor does the language of our text point to an author who spent his life as a Jew in Palestine" (Dibelius-Greeven, *James*, 17).

36. Thus, Dibelius himself adds a footnote (*James*, 17 n. 42) that cancels the opinion just cited; see also J. N. Sevenster, *Do You Know Greek?* (NovTSup 19; Leiden: Brill, 1968) 3–21; M. Hengel, *Judaism and Hellenism: Studies in their Encounter in Palestine during the Early Hellenistic Period* (trans. J. Bowden; Philadelphia: Fortress, 1974) 56–106. But the habit is hard to break. Even after answering the objections to James's ability to write such Greek, Martin (lxxiii) is compelled to add: ". . . on the several grounds of the letter's style, its Jewishness in tone and content, its post-Pauline ambience . . . it seems hardly to have been written *as it stands* by James of Jerusalem." So Martin invokes a two-stage theory of composition (*James*, lxxvii).

specifically the source of the so-called judaizing movement that was fundamentally hostile to Paul's Gentile mission.

CHALLENGE TO TRADITIONAL AUTHORSHIP

The essential body of evidence comes from the only firsthand source contemporary with James, Paul's Letter to the Galatians. In the *narratio* that forms the first part of his argument in Galatians,[37] Paul mentions James three times. When Paul went up the first time to Jerusalem after his conversion, he visted Cephas, "but I saw none of the other apostles except James the Lord's brother" (Gal 1:19). When he went up by way of revelation after fourteen years with Titus, "James and Cephas and John, who were reputed to be pillars, gave to me and Barnabas the right hand of fellowship, that we should go to the Gentiles and they to the circumcised" (Gal 2:9). So far, nothing but Paul's acknowledgment of James's position and James's reciprocal acknowledgment of Paul's. Then, when recounting his altercation with Cephas in Antioch, Paul attributes Peter's change of behavior and "insincerity" to the arrival of "certain men from James": before they came, Cephas had eaten with Gentiles, but after they came, he withdrew from such fellowship (Gal 2:12).

Now the difficulty of this text for learning much at all about the "historical James" is obvious. Paul's dispute is with Cephas, not with James, nor even the men from James. Nor does Paul suggest that the "men from James" were on an official mission from that leader. The way these comments get turned into a portrayal of James as Paul's opponent is, first, by identifying the "false brethren" who threatened Paul's liberty in Gal 2:4 with these "men from James," as representatives of a circumcising party, and, second, by connecting "those unsettling" the Galatians by advocating circumcision (Gal 5:12) with emissaries sent out by James.[38] By an even further extrapolation, Paul's "opponents" in Philippi and Corinth as well are then connected to a coherent program of repression ultimately deriving from the Jewish Christianity of the Jerusalem church over which James ruled.[39]

37. For the rhetorical function of the *narratio*, see H. D. Betz, *Galatians* (Hermeneia; Philadelphia: Fortress, 1979) 58–62, 83.

38. See Baur, *Paul, the Apostle of Jesus Christ*, 1:122–23 n. 1; 1:136; the men from James are "his declared foes and opponents" (1:203); Baur is circumspect, however, in attributing the troubles in Galatia directly to James, although Paul's opponents there represent James's party (1:250–57). More recently, see M. Hengel, *Acts and the History of Earliest Christianity* (trans. J. Bowden; Philadelphia: Fortress, 1980) 112–26. See also his argument for the early dating of James and its character as a contemporary and sustained if indirect polemic against Paul, in "Der Jakobusbrief als anti-paulinische Polemik," in *Tradition and Interpretation in the New Testament: Essays in Honor of E. Earle Ellis* (ed. G. F. Hawthorne with O. Betz; Grand Rapids: Eerdmans, 1987) 248–78.

39. See Baur's discussion whether the "Christ Party" in Corinth might be explicitly associ-

It should be obvious that these connections are not required by the text of Galatians. If Paul himself saw his problems either in Jerusalem or in Galatia as stemming from James, he was remarkably reticent and roundabout in his complaint. In fact, James may well not have had anything to do with Paul's troubles in either place. The tone of Paul's comments in Gal 1:19 and 2:10 is entirely positive (as, for that matter, is his reference to James in 1 Cor 15:7). But once Galatians is read this way, then the evidence of Acts 12:17; 15:1–21; and 21:17–26 is taken not as a historically accurate portrayal of cooperation between James and Paul but as a partially successful cover-up for a relationship characterized by mutual hostility.[40] Then, the admittedly legendary account in Hegesippus concerning the death of James[41] is taken at least as confirmation of James's place in the "Jerusalem Caliphate"[42] and, together with an unreasonably high valuation of the Pseudo-Clementine literature, is thought to reflect the character of Jewish Christianity in some sort of continuity with an earlier historical reality.[43]

---

ated with James; he seems almost convinced, but of course the demands of his system require that there be only two real "parties," so James is associated with the Jewish Christianity of Peter (*Paul, the Apostle of Jesus Christ*, 1:265); see also the discussion of the "superapostles" in 2 Corinthians, and James's association with them (1:277). For a more recent rendering of this view, see P. Achtemeier, *The Quest for Unity in the New Testament Church* (Philadelphia: Fortress, 1987) 59–61.

40. An essential part of Baur's reconstruction of the conflict between the Pauline and Jewish-Christian parties, of course, was the destruction of the credibility of Acts in the key passages dealing with Paul's relationships with Jerusalem (*Paul, The Apostle of Jesus Christ*, 1:110–21, 125–26 n. 1; 129). See Achtemeier, *The Quest for Unity*, 29–55.

41. That the account in Eusebius, *Church History* 2.23 is filled with patently fictitious elements is obvious to anyone who carefully examines it (see the comments of Dibelius-Greeven, *James*, 15–17; and Martin, *James*, xlviii–liv). What is more surprising is the hold it has on scholars' imaginations: "This legend from Hegesippus cannot be considered a serious rival to the short, clear, and prosaic statement of Josephus. However, it is valuable as evidence of Jewish Christian piety, and moreover it sketches the image of the 'just' James which was current in certain circles of Jewish Christianity" (Dibelius-Greeven, *James*, 17).

42. Other primary texts support the picture of James's special role. See the account in Eusebius (derived from Clement's *Hypotyposes*) concerning the installation of James on the "throne of the bishopric of the church in Jerusalem" by the apostles themselves; Clement had also made James a direct recipient of "the tradition of knowledge" (γνῶσις) by Jesus after the resurrection, a portrayal that accords exactly with that in the Nag Hammadi writings associated with James (see Eusebius, *Church History* 2.1.2–5. There is also the fragmentary passage from *The Gospel of the Hebrews* (cited by Jerome in *De Viris Illustribus* 2) that appears to make James the first witness of the resurrection. For the language of "caliphate," see, e.g., K. Aland, "Der Herrenbrüder Jakobus und der Jakobusbrief: Zur Frage eines urchristlichen Kalifäts," *TLZ* 69 (1944) 97–104.

43. "The Ebionites are generally regarded as mere heretics, but their connection with the original Jewish Christianity is unmistakeable. Thus their view of the Apostle Paul is no isolated phenomenon" (Baur, *Church History of the First Three Centuries*, 1:90). More recently, see H. J. Schoeps, *Theologie und Geschichte des Judenchristentums* (Tübingen: Mohr-Siebeck, 1949) 69. The parts of the extraordinarily complex collection called the Pseudo-Clementine literature that are regarded by advocates of such views as deriving from the Ebionites and reflecting early perceptions are the *Epistula Petri Ad Jacobum* and the *Contestatio* (Schoeps, *Theologie*, 50).

A number of observations need to be made about this reconstruction of the "historical James" as an opponent of Paul. The first is that it is even on its own terms a fragile restoration, dependent more than it might like to think on presuppositions concerning the rival "parties" in early Christianity derived from the Tübingen school,[44] and requiring the connection of a good many pieces that need not be connected at all.[45] Second, the discovery of the Nag Hammadi writings shows us that the figure of James could be developed in quite a different direction by later parties seeking legitimation in the founding figures of the Christian movement. In the Nag Hammadi writings, James is not connected to circumcision or the observance of the Law or hostility toward Paul. The place of honor held by James in this Gnostic collection suggests that, like other eponymous figures in earliest Christianity, he was capable of various exploitations.[46] We are thereby given the salutary reminder that the "James" of Hegesippus and the "James" of the Pseudo-Clementines is not necessarily any closer to the historical James than is the "James" of the Nag Hammadi Library.

Third, and most critically, the Letter of James—at the very least one of the earliest witnesses concerning James—simply does not support this picture.

The major sections that contain the most explicit polemic against (supposedly) Paul under the guise of Simon Magus are *Recognitions* 1.43–72 (including a role played by "the enemy" in the death of James, 70–71); and *Homilies* II, 16; XI, 35; XVII, 13–19. The identification of those called Ebionites (Irenaeus, *Adversus Haereses* 1.26.2; Origen, *Contra Celsum* 2.1) is essential for Baur's position. But see L. Keck, "The Poor among the Saints in the New Testament," *ZNW* 56 (1965) 109–29; idem, "The Poor among the Saints in Jewish Christianity and Qumran," *ZNW* 57 (1966) 54–78. The historicity of the Ebionites' "flight from Jerusalem" to Pella—essential to making the connection between this group and the Jerusalem community—has been challenged. G. Lüdemann has described it as a legend serving to legitimate this version of Jewish-Christianity; see "The Successors of Pre-70 Jerusalem Christianity: A Critical Evaluation of the Pella Tradition," in *Jewish and Christian Self-Definition* (ed. E. P. Sanders; Philadelphia: Fortress, 1980) 1:161–73.

44. For a critique of the entire premise that undergirds so much of the Tübingen project and remains as a staple of historical reconstructions, namely, the theological distinction between the "Hellenists" and the "Hebrews" in the Jerusalem church, with the figure of Stephen providing the necessary bridge between the "Hellenists" and Paul (as still in Hengel, *Acts and the History of Earliest Christianity*, 71–80), see now C. C. Hill, *Hellenists and Hebrews: Reappraising Division within the Earliest Church* (Minneapolis: Fortress, 1992); among other things, Hill argues for the fictional character of the Hegesippus story that has proven so influential in shaping the image of James (pp. 184–91); argues that the Jerusalem church on the basis both of Acts *and* of Galatians is shown by our best sources to be in fundamental agreement with Paul (pp. 143–47); and claims that James is explicitly *not* an opponent of Paul (pp. 183–92).

45. For more neutral discussions of "Jewish-Christianity" that recognize the complexities of categorization and historical identification, see J. Daniélou, *Théologie du Judéo-Christianisme* (Bibliothèque de Théologie; Tournai: Desclée, 1958) 17–98; S. K. Riegel, "Jewish Christianity: Definitions and Terminology," *NTS* 24 (1977–78) 410–15.

46. James the Righteous is called one "for whose sake heaven and earth came into being" and recommended as a leader after Jesus' departure in *Gospel of Thomas* 12. He appears with Peter as the source of a "secret book" revealed by the Lord in the *Apocryphon of James*, and as a Gnostic teacher in the *First Apocalypse of James* and the *Second Apocalypse of James*.

Despite the lingering influence of Luther's dictum that James "drove you back to the law,"[47] contemporary readers are increasingly coming to agree with Calvin that such an opinion was a form of "absurdity."[48] James's references to the "perfect law, the law of liberty" (1:25), we now see, have nothing to do with a demand for circumcision or the keeping of ritual commandments. Nothing in James could possibly be construed as part of a judaizing program, much less one directed against Paul. Rather, James's understanding of "the royal law" (2:8) involves the keeping of the Decalogue and the moral commandments of Lev 19:11–18.[49] James takes the same moralizing approach to the Law as we find in such Jewish parenetic texts as the *Testaments of the Twelve Patriarchs* and the *Sentences of Pseudo-Phocylides*.[50] Far from being a point-by-point rebuttal of Paul's teaching in Gal 2:15–16, James's discussion of "faith and works" in 2:14–26 uses those terms in quite a different fashion,[51] elaborating the moralist's concern that profession be enacted by specific deeds (compare Jas 3:13), and agrees substantially with the position stated by Paul in Gal 5:6.[52]

47. See the preface to the Letters of James and Jude in his "Preface to the New Testament" of 1522, in *Luther's Works 35: Word and Sacrament I* (ed. E. T. Bachmann; Philadelphia: Muhlenburg Press, 1959) 395–97.

48. J. Calvin, *Commentaries on the Catholic Epistles* (trans. and ed. J. Owen; Grand Rapids: Eerdmans, 1948) 314–15.

49. See L. T. Johnson, "The Use of Leviticus 19 in the Letter of James," *JBL* 101 (1982) 391–401.

50. The resemblances to the *Testaments* were noted especially by J. H. Ropes, *James*, 20–21; see also Johnson, "James 3:13–4:10 and the *Topos PERI PHTHONOU*," *NovT* 25 (1983) 341–46. See also the article by M. de Jonge in this volume. On Pseudo-Phocylides, see P. W. van der Horst, *The Sentences of Pseudo-Phocylides* (SVTP 4; Leiden: Brill, 1978) 126, 295; idem, "Pseudo-Phocylides and the New Testament," *ZNW* 69 (1978) 202.

51. The main problem with the putative James–Paul opposition on this point is that it simply refuses to take into account the full range of meaning in *either* author. Paul is reduced to parts of Galatians/Romans, and James is reduced to 2:14–26. Yet it is obvious that Paul in those places is arguing a contrast between ἔργα τοῦ νόμου ("works of the law") and πίστις Χριστοῦ ("faith of Christ"), whereas James is arguing that πίστις θεοῦ ("faith of God") requires expression in ἔργα πίστεως ("works of faith"). Thus, James says in 2:22, "*faith* coworked his works and out of the works *faith* was perfected." The connections in each author, furthermore, are more complex than the discussion usually takes into account. The use of ἔργον in Jas 1:4 and 3:13 must be considered. Equally, Paul's use of ἔργον is much wider than often supposed (see Rom 13:3, 12; 14:20; 15:18; 1 Cor 3:13–15; 9:1; 15:58; 16:10; 2 Cor 9:8; 11:15; 1 Thess 1:3; 5:13; 2 Thess 2:17). If the entire Pauline corpus is considered, over fifty occurrences of ἔργον fit perfectly with the meaning in James, whereas only seventeen fit Paul's narrower polemic purpose. Note that Paul can speak without embarrassment about "your work of faith" (ἔργον τῆς πίστεως) in 1 Thess 1:3 and of the "work of faith in power" (ἔργον πίστεως ἐν δυνάμει) in 2 Thess 1:11; and if we can make bold to use the Pastorals, Titus 1:16, "They claim to know God but deny him by their works," accords perfectly with Jas 2:19.

52. This is the conclusion reached by an exquisitely argued letter written by Severus, the Monophysite patriarch of Antioch (ca. 465–538) to a Julian, who was probably the Monophysite bishop of Halicarnassus (d. after 518); see Zachary the Rhetorician, *Capita Selecta ex Historiae Ecclesiasticae*, sect XIX (PG 85:1176–78). The entire patristic and medieval tradition

Remarkably, however, despite three substantial objections to the standard historical reconstruction of James of Jerusalem, the portrayal still has sufficient influence to make scholars uncomfortable with the notion that the jerry-rigged portrait is wrong, and that this letter may actually represent the straightforward views of the historical James. Instead, it is simply assumed that something in the traditional picture must be right and that the Letter of James must come from a later, pseudonymous author. Despite a grudging admission that James and Paul were talking about two different sorts of things, scholars have not been able to rid themselves of the besetting sin of virtually all historical reconstructions of earliest Christianity, namely, *that Paul has to figure in the equation somewhere.* Although it is a historical fallacy of the plainest sort to infer from Paul's canonical importance data relevant to his historical importance, scholars continue to read whatever is different from Paul with reference to Paul, rather than allow it to stand as simply different.[53]

PSEUDONYMOUS AUTHORSHIP
AND THE HISTORY OF IDEAS

Deciding for pseudonymous authorship does not by itself mean abandoning hope for finding the social world of James, but it makes the quest more difficult, if only because the number of variables automatically increases. In reality, the decision to regard James as pseudonymous has tended to place James not in a specific social context but within a temporal development of ideas. If the letter is not by the historical James but by a pseudepigrapher, then it must be not only later than James but also later than Paul. Why? Not because there are any indications within the text of the letter itself that suggest a situation inconsonant with that of the first generation, but because Paul is the only stable point of reference available. And if the letter cannot be taken as a response of the historical James to the historical Paul, then it must represent a response of a certain kind of Christianity to a certain brand of Paulinism.

The conflict model used by the Tübingen school is demonstrated by F. Kern's 1835 study of James. Although he designates James as a "sitt-

---

concerning the apparent contradiction was that there was none, a view nowhere more trenchantly conveyed than by Erasmus, "Verum Paulus illic opera vocat observationem Legis Mosaice, hic sentit de officiis pietatis et charitatis"; see *In Epistolan Jacobi* in *Opera Omnia* (1516; repr. London: Gregg, 1962) 6:1031.

53. See, e.g., E. Lohse, "Glaube und Werke: Zur Theologie des Jakobusbriefes," *ZNW* 48 (1957) 1–22. In the light of my remarks below about Dibelius's inconsistency, it should be noted that he clearly saw the fallaciousness of trying to pull Paul into every equation: "Yet, only too easily we fall into the error—which, to be sure, is fostered by the character of the materials preserved from the early Christian period—of thinking that Paul influenced every branch of early Christianity. This is, in fact, an error . . ." (*James*, 118).

liche-paraenetische" letter,[54] he nevertheless works to place it within the movements of early Christianity. To do this, he aligns two major themes of the letter: that dealing with the rich and poor, and that dealing with faith and works. By this means he locates the intended recipients of the letter as second-generation Jewish Christians who are being marginalized by Gentile Christians.[55] James's teaching of faith and works is, therefore, something of a *rapprochement* between these competing parties.[56] Likewise F. C. Baur (who expressly approved Kern's reading) considered the Letter of James—though incompatible with Paul's teaching on righteousness[57]—to be part of that synthesizing movement that helped shape catholic Christianity.[58] In the same tradition, Han Joachim Schoeps refuses to consider James in his elaborate reconstruction of "Jewish Christian Theology," but in an excursus devoted to the letter, he defines it as a postapostolic writing of "Jewish Christian but not Ebionite" character and of basically an "antignostic" tendency.[59] More recently, J. Jeremias argued in similar fashion that James's teaching on faith and works was intended to correct a misunderstood and misused Paulinism.[60]

Whatever the merit of these respective positions, their inadequacy for enriching our understanding of James's social world is obvious. Because they need Paul as a control, they isolate within James only that aspect which can be brought into conversation with Paul, namely, the section on faith and works (2:14–26). Not only does this perpetuate the fallacy of treating Paul as the essential pivot point for all early Christian history; it distorts James's discussion in 2:14–26 by treating it as a "response" to a theoretical position putatively held by Paul, rather than as an integral part of James's own argument. Finally, by making 2:14–26 the only section of James of compelling interest, it fails to take into account those other features of James's text that might prove instructive precisely concerning the "world" inhabited (or at least imagined) by this text.

54. See F. H. Kern, *Der Character und Ursprung des Briefes Jacobi* (Tübingen: Fues, 1835) 5.
55. See Kern, *Character*, 24, 36; Kern argues that James had to know Paul's letters even though it is not a direct attack on the person of Paul (p. 25), and that on the issue of righteousness Luther was correct: James and Paul are incompatible (pp. 11–17, 44). The similarity of James to the Letter of Clement and the Pseudo-Clementines suggests a time after the apostolic age but before the writing of the Pseudo-Clementines (p. 86). Note here the assumption of continuity between the Jerusalem church of the first generation ("the poor among the saints," Rom 15:26; Gal 2:10) with the later group identified as "the Ebionites." It is not shocking that Kern made the identification; but despite work such as that noted in n. 43, above, the equation is still sometimes made as if it were obvious; see Hengel, *Acts and the History of Earliest Christianity*, 118.
56. Kern, *Character*, 38.
57. Baur, *Paul the Apostle of Jesus Christ*, 2:297–313.
58. Baur, *The Church History of the First Three Centuries*, 1:128–30.
59. Schoeps, *Theologie und Geschichte des Judenchristentums*, 343–49.
60. J. Jeremias, "Paul and James," *ExpT* 66 (1955) 368–71.

SOCIAL SETTING THROUGH GENRE?

The magisterial commentary by M. Dibelius placed its entire interpretive weight on a decision concerning the genre of James. Dibelius regarded the epistolary format as nothing more than a formal adornment. James was really a form of *parenesis*.[61] This meant, for Dibelius, that James was a relatively structureless compendium of wisdom traditions with no specific reference to time or place. Topics are taken up as much because they are the expected topics for the genre as because they addressed specific social situations.[62] It was possible to describe certain broad aspects of James's outlook, such as that concerning wealth and poverty,[63] but the characterizations were ideational rather than social. In effect, Dibelius's decision on genre seemed to cut James off from any connection to the real world, allowing it to float in the sea of generalized wisdom traditions with little distinctive character of its own. Given his overall commitment to the exegetical consequences of this generic decision—so much so that he treated each unit atomistically, disallowing in principle the possibility of contextual analysis[64]—it is surprising to find Dibelius still insisting on James's connection to *Paul* in 2:14–26, proving how powerful that particular assumption has been![65]

Recently, however, L. Perdue has taken the generic analysis of James in the opposite direction. He has suggested that the genre of James might actually provide a sort of back-door entry to the social world of the writing. Perdue agrees with the designation of James as *parenesis*.[66] But he is convinced that this literary genre, as a subset of wisdom literature such as we find it reaching back into antiquity,[67] demands a certain kind of social set-

61. See Dibelius-Greeven, *James*, 1.

62. Ibid., 3–5.

63. In Dibelius's lengthy discussion ("Poor and Rich," 39–45), he sketches the piety of the "poor of the Lord," within which James stands. But despite his earlier warning (p. 11), "the admonitions in James do not apply to a single audience and a single set of circumstances: *it is not possible to contruct a single frame into which they all fit*" (his emphasis), the legacy of Kern and Baur remains strong. Dibelius suggests that the "most likely place" where this pauperistic piety would have survived was in the churches of diaspora Judaism "where the consistency of Paul is alien" (p. 43).

64. Dibelius-Greeven, *James*, 2–3. He could scarcely be more emphatic. With original italics, he declares (p. 6): "*It seems to me that the literary evaluation of Jas depends completely upon the resolution of this question,*" and in his exegesis, he sticks to that principle (see, e.g., pp. 207–8).

65. Just how deeply conflicted Dibelius was can be indicated by his painful discussion on pp. 17–18 (where he insists that Jas 2:14–26 "cannot be comprehended without the previous activity of Paul . . . yet the letter presupposes not only Paul's formulation of the question about the Law but also the resolution of Paul's struggles regarding the Law") and pp. 29–30, where he must argue that the passages in James which seem to have an obvious affinity with Paul (e.g., Jas 1:2–4 and Rom 5:3–5) are to be explained on a basis other than a knowledge of Paul's letters.

66. L. G. Perdue, "Paraenesis and the Letter of James," *ZNW* 72 (1981) 241–46.

67. L. G. Perdue, "The Death of the Sage and Moral Exhortation: From Ancient Near Eastern Instructions to Greco-Roman Paraenesis," *Semeia* 50 (1990) 81–109.

ting. Specifically, the formality of "father to son" transmission of wisdom so typical of wisdom/parenetic texts fits the state of liminality (and therefore danger) that occurs in moments of transgenerational change. Parenetic literature provides a medium for safe passage across such moments of crisis.[68] With this sort of rough-and-ready equivalency model, the identification of James as parenetic would seem to demand its production at such a moment in the history of Christianity, and its function as an instrument of resocialization and relegitimation of the social world of the readers. Perdue suggests a situation when the author is either separated from the readers (and must write a letter) or about to leave them because of age and approaching death (a farewell address).[69]

When I read Perdue's first effort along these lines, I was not convinced,[70] primarily because I considered parenetic literature more diverse in character and capable of being fitted to a variety of social situations. I doubted that direct conclusions could be drawn from genre to social world.[71] Recently, however, more careful attention has been paid to these connections. J. G. Gammie has pursued the variety in *literary* (material and formal) characteristics within wisdom/parenetic writings.[72] And L. G. Perdue has greatly refined his analysis of the *social worlds* of parenesis, recognizing that parenesis can function variously within them for purposes of conversion or socialization or legitimation. In such situations, parenesis serves to establish or confirm order.[73]

But it is Perdue's perception of some parenetic texts as serving a "conflict" function that is particularly interesting. In these cases, parenesis serves to "subvert" the broader cultural values (that of the *Gesellschaft*) in order to reaffirm the values of an inner group that has withdrawn from that larger society (as a *Gemeinschaft*). Here "a different social reality is con-

---

68. L. G. Perdue, "Liminality as a Social Setting for Wisdom Instruction," *ZAW* 93 (1981) 114–26.

69. Perdue, "Paraenesis and the Epistle of James," 250–51.

70. I commented on it negatively in "Friendship with the World/Friendship with God: A Study of Discipleship in James," in *Discipleship in the New Testament*, 179 n. 13, and "The Mirror of Remembrance (James 1:22–25)," *CBQ* 50 (1988) 632 n. 1.

71. See, e.g., A. J. Malherbe, *Moral Exhortation: A Greco-Roman Sourcebook* (Library of Early Christianity; Philadelphia: Westminster, 1986) 23–29. For Malherbe's views on the relationship between literary production and social settings, see *Social Aspects of Early Christianity* (2nd ed.; Philadelphia: Fortress, 1983) 29–59. Malherbe had in view A. Deissmann's famous thesis. An attempt to derive something of an "implicit sociology of letter writing" (p. 87) has recently been essayed by S. K. Stowers on the basis of the ancient classifications of letter types; see "Social Typification and the Classification of Ancient Letters," in *The Social World of Formative Christianity and Judaism* (ed. J. Neusner, P. Borgen, et al.; Philadelphia: Fortress, 1988) 78–89.

72. J. G. Gammie, "Paraenetic Literature: Toward the Morphology of a Secondary Genre," *Semeia* 50 (1990) 41–77.

73. L. G. Perdue, "The Social Character of Paraenesis and Paraenetic Literature," *Semeia* 50 (1990) 19–26.

structed, and efforts are undertaken to protect it from the threat of outside worlds," clearly a "sectarian position." Perdue locates the Letter of James as an example of such subversive parenesis.[74] Although he does not himself explicitly make a connection between James and Q, it is striking that Perdue lists as another example of such "conflict" parenesis "the sayings source Q, produced by an early Christian community before the fall of Jerusalem."[75] Thus, the genre analysis tends to confirm the connection between James and the early Palestinian traditions about Jesus suggested earlier.

To some extent, Perdue is pursuing the principle already enunciated though not systematically applied by Dibelius, namely, that an author's "voice" can be heard even in parenetic literature through analysis of the "selection and arrangement of traditional thought and of the new emphasis which he gives to it,"[76] as well as his own conviction that the way toward the analysis of social function is through comparative analysis.[77] But that project might be pushed much further. What might we learn if we *systematically* compare James to other recognizably parenetic/wisdom writings across the cultural spectrum of the Mediterranean world, as a way of checking what James might be expected to include but does not, and what it does include that might not be anticipated?

Among the distinctive (though not necessarily unique) characteristics of James that emerge from this comparison is the letter's focus on a community *ethos* rather than simply individual behavior,[78] on moral behavior rather than on manners,[79] on an ethics of solidarity rather than of competition.[80]

---

74. Ibid., 26–27; in this article, the earlier type distinctions make the final determination concerning James more convincing than they were in "Paraenesis and the Epistle of James." 255–56.

75. Perdue, "Social Character of Paraenesis," 14.

76. Dibelius-Greeven, *James*, 21.

77. ". . . any suggestions about conceivable social settings for the parenesis of James must necessarily be inferential and analogical, based on a variety of other paraenetic texts" in "Paraenesis and the Letter of James," 247.

78. The group is always being addressed in James even when individual cases are being considered; the exhortation in the majority of ancient parenetic texts is to the individual: see, e.g., *Instruction of the Vizier Ptah-Hotep* (*ANET*, 412–14); *Instruction for King Meri-Ka-Re* (*ANET*, 414–18); *Instruction of King Amen-Em-Het* (*ANET*, 418–19); *Instruction of Prince Hor-Dedef* (*ANET*, 419); *Instruction of Ani* (*ANET*, 420–21); *Instruction of Amen-Em-Opet* (*ANET*, 421–24); *Counsels of Wisdom* (*ANET*, 426–27); *Words of Ahiqar* (*ANET*, 427–30); the book of Proverbs; Qoheleth; Sirach; the *Sentences of Pseudo-Phocylides*; Pseudo-Isocrates, *To Demonicus*; the *Sentences of Sextus*; the *Sentences of Syriac Menander*; a partial exception is the *Testaments of the Twelve Patriarchs*.

79. See Prov 23:1–9; Sir 4:27–31; 7:14; 9:18; 31:12–30; 32:1–9; *Words of Ahiqar* x.142ff.; *Counsels of Wisdom* 20; *Sentences of Syriac Menander* 11–14; 57–62; 99–101; 148–53; 181–84; *To Demonicus* 15, 20, 27, 41; *Sentences of Sextus* 149, 157, 164, 252, 265; *Sentences of Pseudo-Phocylides* 81–82, 98, 123, 147–48, 156–58, 211–12; *Instructions of Vizier Ptah-Hotep* 139; *Instruction of Amen-Em-Het* 1.4–5; *Instruction of Ani* 6.1, 7.7; *Instruction of Amen-Em-Opet* 9, 23.

80. That one of the motivations for being "wise" is to be a greater success in the world than others is frequently implied, but nowhere more obvious than in Pseudo-Isocrates, *To Demoni-*

But equally worth considering are the elements typical of parenesis that are entirely lacking in James. It is not remarkable that James should use kinship language, for it is universal in wisdom writings.[81] What is remarkable is that James lacks completely any generational kinship language, such as is found even in Paul.[82] Instead, James's use of kinship language is entirely egalitarian.[83] Far from reflecting the tensions of generational change, James lacks even the conventional use of generational language. It is also remarkable that James should find no need to speak of sexual ethics[84] or of marriage,[85] since these are, once more, common fare in parenesis, including the parenetic sections of other early New Testament letters.[86] Nor does James take up the subject of the care and disciplining of children so frequently found in such literature.[87] In a word, the sort of topics that work for the establishing of order and socializing people within it tend to be absent from James.

Taken together with the characteristics sketched earlier in this essay, these deviations from the generic norm help support the suggestion that James is not simply a compendium of wisdom themes or a free-floating piece of parenesis, but a vivid exhortation that emerges from and addresses real human beings in specific social settings. Everything in the letter and

---

cus 2, 3, 13, 15, 17, 21, 24, 26, 32, 33, 35, 38; nothing could be at greater odds to such "pursuit of nobility" than the "lowly-mindedness" encouraged by James (4:7–10).

81. The transmission of wisdom from father to son is, of course, the standard *mise-en-scène* of parenesis, from the most ancient (*Instruction of the Vizier Ptah-Hotep*) to works close in time to James (*Testaments of the Twelve Patriarchs*), and enables the play on the convention in Pseudo-Isocrates, *To Demonicus* 1–3, 9–10.

82. Thus, it is Paul's claim to be the "father" of the community that legitimates his moral instruction (1 Cor 4:15; 1 Thess 2:11); see also his language about individuals like Onesimus (Phlm 10) and Timothy (Phil 2:22). It is not surprising that the most obviously "parenetic" of the letters attributed to Paul explicitly employs this kinship *topos* (2 Tim 1:2; 2:1).

83. James never designates himself or anyone else as "father," but identifies his readers consistently as "brothers" (1:2, 9; 2:1; 2:14; 2:15; 3:1, 10, 12; 4:11; 5:7, 9, 10, 12, 19) or as "beloved brothers" (1:16, 19; 2:14), the only exception being the reference to the "sister" in 2:15.

84. For commandments concerning sexual ethics, see *Sentences of Pseudo-Phocylides* 3, 198; Sir 7:24–25; 9:1–9; 25:21–26; 26:11–12; Prov 2:16–22; 6:24–32; 7:10–27; 9:13–18; Pseudo-Isocrates, *To Demonicus* 15, 21; *Sentences of Sextus* 60, 67, 70, 71, 73, 75, 102, 139, 240, 346, 449; *Testament of Reuben* 4:1–6:5; *Sentences of Syriac Menander* 170–72; 240–49; *Instruction of Ani* 3.13.

85. For discussions of marriage, see *Sentences of Syriac Menander* 45–51, 118–22; *Instruction of Prince Hor-Dedef*; Sir 7:25–26; 26:1–9, 13–18; 40:19; Prov 5:15–20; 31:10–31; *Instruction of Vizier Ptah-Hotep* 320–40; *Counsels of Wisdom* (Obverse 23); *Sentences of Pseudo-Phocylides* 3, 175–97; 201–6; *Sentences of Sextus* 235–39; *Instruction of Ani* 3.1; 8.4; 9.1.

86. See Rom 13:13; 1 Cor 5:1–5; 6:12–20; 7:1–24; Eph 5:21–6:4; Col 3:18–25; 1 Thess 4:4–5; 1 Tim 2:9–15; Titus 2:3–5; Heb 13:4; 1 Pet 3:1–7.

87. See, e.g., *Words of Ahiqar* 6.79, 7.106, 9.138; *To Demonicus* 14, 16; *Sentences of Pseudo-Phocylides* 207–17; Prov (LXX) 10:1–8; 13:1–2; 30:11–14; Sir 3:1–16; 7:28; 16:1–5; 30:1–6; *Sentences of Sextus* 254, 256–57; *Sentences of Syriac Menander* 5–6, 9–10, 20–24, 94–98, 194–212; *Instruction of Vizier Ptah-Hotep* 565–95; *Instruction of Meri-ka-re* 55–60; *Instruction of Ani* 7.17.

everything lacking from the letter help confirm the impression that this social world was that shared by a leader of the Jerusalem church and Jewish messianists of the diaspora during the first decades of the Christian movement.[88]

88. Readers familiar with the history of scholarship on James will recognize that the basic points in my argument, although responding to more recent contributions to the discussion, do not differ dramatically from the ones laid out so simply by G. Kittel, "Der geschichtliche Ort des Jakobusbriefes," *ZNW* 41 (1942) 71–105.

CHAPTER 13

The Footwashing in John 13:6-11: Transformation Ritual or Ceremony?

Jerome H. Neyrey, S.J.

INTRODUCTION AND HYPOTHESIS

THE NARRATIVE in John 13:4-20 is notoriously complicated.[1] The evangelist narrates Jesus' washing of the disciples' feet (13:4-5), a conversation with Peter (13:6-11), and then a general discourse about footwashing (13:12-20). But the remarks in vv. 12-20 hardly serve as an adequate or proper commentary on the events in vv. 6-11.[2]

Similarities abound between 13:6-11 and 12-20, but the differences deserve attention.[3] (1) Peter becomes Jesus' conversation partner in vv. 6-9, whereas all the disciples are addressed in vv. 10-20. (2) Peter is told "You do *not* know" (v. 7) but will understand later, whereas all of them are clearly "in the know" during the general explanation of the rite: "You know what I have done" (v. 12). . . . If you know these things, honored are you if you do them"

---

1. On the distinction between 13:6-11 and 12-20, see Fernando Segovia, "John 13:1-20: The Footwashing in the Johannine Tradition," *ZNW* 73 (1982) 31; Arland Hultgren, "The Johannine Footwashing (13:1-11) as Symbol of Eschatological Hospitality," *NTS* 28 (1982) 539-40; Karl Kleinknecht, "Johannes 13, die Synoptiker und die 'Methode' der johanneischen Evangelienüberlieferung," *ZTK* 82 (1985) 366-68.

2. Rudolf Bultmann (*The Gospel of John* [Philadelphia: Westminster, 1971] 466-67) insisted that there are two interpretations of the footwashing, vv. 6-11 and 12-20. Similar observations can be found in Edwyn Hoskyns, *The Fourth Gospel* (London: Faber & Faber, 1947) 436-39; M.-E. Boismard, "Le lavement des pieds (Jn, XIII, 1-17)," *RB* 71 (1964) 5-24; and Herold Weiss, "Footwashing in the Johannine Community," *NovT* 21 (1971) 301-2.

3. Commentators distinguish the two interpretations (vv. 6-11 and 12-20) in three basic ways: Boismard ("Le lavement," 6-8, 18-20) contrasted sacramental with moral interpretations (see also Rudolf Schnackenburg, *The Gospel According to St. John* [New York: Crossroad, 1982] 3:21); Georg Richter distinguished a christological interpretation from a sacramental one (*Die Fusswaschung im Johannesevangelium* [Regensburg: Pustet, 1967] 252-78); Bultmann juxtaposed a cleansing by hearing of the revealer's word with a gesture of humility (*Gospel of John,* 467).

(v. 17). (3) Jesus tells Peter, "Unless (εἰ μή) I wash . . ." (v. 8), whereas they "ought" (ὀφείλετε) to wash others' feet (v. 14)—different notions of obligation. (4) Jesus' action will make Simon and others "pure" (καθαροί, vv. 10–11), whereas their washing of others' feet will make them "honored" (μακάριοι, v. 17). (5) The remark in v. 10 identifies someone who is not pure, "You are clean, but not every one of you." The evangelist says that this refers to Jesus' betrayer: "He knew who was to betray him; that was why he said, 'You are not all clean'" (v. 11). In contrast, when Jesus mandates washing of feet, he alludes to a traitor, "I am not speaking of you all; I know whom I have chosen" (v. 18); he quotes Ps 41:9 about a treacherous table companion. "Clean" and "chosen" are different things, as are Jesus' own words and a snatch of psalm. (6) The "now/later" distinction functions differently: Peter does not understand now, but will later (v. 7), whereas all of them know "now," so that "later" when the prophecy comes true, they will remain faithful (v. 19).

The action in 13:6–11 signifies something quite different from what is discussed in vv. 12–20. Some event on Jesus' part warrants notice as an "example," which Jesus commands to be repeated (vv. 15, 17).[4] But what was described in vv. 6–11 is a distinctively Johannine conversation[5] about an unrepeatable action. Jesus' action in vv. 6–11 and his remarks about "purification" simply do not parallel what is discussed in vv. 12–20, an action repeated whenever the group gathers.

Notions of "ritual" and "ceremony" from cultural anthropology can serve as important lenses for sharpening our perception of 13:6–11 and explaining the differences between the two accounts of Jesus' symbolic action. "Ritual" refers to rites of status transformation, such as baptism, marriage, consecration, in which individuals change status and role. "Ceremony" refers to rites that confirm roles and statuses, such as anniversaries, priestly rites, triumphal parades, and the like. In 13:6–11 Peter is urged to undergo a status transformation *ritual* to become "wholly clean" and so have a special inheritance or place with Jesus. In 13:12–20, however, the disciples are told to practice a *ceremony* in which their role and status are confirmed by acts of hospitality to group members. Peter's footwashing *ritual* has to do with his transformation into the role of an elite, public witness to Jesus with accom-

---

4. Some identify 13:4–5 as the "action," which is then interpreted; see Robert T. Fortna, *The Gospel of Signs: A Reconstruction of the Narrative Source Underlying the Fourth Gospel* (SNTSMS 11; Cambridge: Cambridge University Press, 1970) 155–56.

5. The Johannine redactional elements include: (1) Simon Peter as a "representative character" (see R. F. Collins, "Representative Figures in the Fourth Gospel," *DRev* 94 [1976] 26–46, 118–32); (2) statement/misunderstanding/clarification (see J. H. Neyrey, *An Ideology of Revolt* [Philadelphia: Fortress, 1988] 42, 234 ##10, 11); (3) dialogue with a disciple (see Schnackenburg, *John*, 3:18); (4) knowing versus not knowing; (5) purification (2:6; 15:3); (6) "unless . . ." demands (see Neyrey, *Ideology of Revolt*, 41, 138); (7) laying down/taking up (see R. E. Brown, *The Gospel According to John XIII–XXI* (AB 29A; Garden City, N.Y.: Doubleday, 1970) 551.

panying risk of death—a one-time event. Conversely, the *ceremony* the disciples will perform for members of their circle confirms their role and status as leaders of the group—an action to be repeated regularly. Two different rites are described in 13:6–11 and 12–20, and the use of materials from anthropology offers a fruitful way of clarifying the social dynamics of the narrative.

CULTURAL ANTHROPOLOGY: RITUALS AND CEREMONIES

Victor Turner described the difference between ritual and ceremony:

> I consider the term "ritual" to be more fittingly applied to forms of religious behavior associated with social *transitions*, while the term "ceremony" has a closer bearing on religious behavior associated with religious *states* . . . . Ritual is transformative, ceremony confirmatory.[6]

The following diagram compares and contrasts the elements of status-change *rituals* and *ceremonies* that confirm status.[7]

Elements of a Ritual	*Elements of a Ceremony*
1. frequency: irregular pauses	1. frequency: regular pauses
2. schedule/calendar: unpredictable, when needed	2. schedule/calendar: predictable, planned
3. temporal focus: present-to-future	3. temporal focus: past-to-present
4. presided over by: professionals	4. presided over by: officials
5. purpose: status reversal; status transformation	5. purpose: confirmation of roles and statuses in institutions

(1) *Frequency:* Both rituals and ceremonies represent pauses in life's rhythms. Certain pauses occur irregularly (sickness, uncleanness), which

---

6. Victor Turner, *The Forest of Symbols: Aspects of Ndembu Ritual* (Ithaca, N.Y.: Cornell University Press, 1967) 95 (emphasis added); see also Raymond Firth and John Skorupski, *Symbol and Theory: A Philosophical Study of Theories of Religion in Social Anthropology* (Cambridge: Cambridge University Press, 1976) 164.

7. See Bruce J. Malina, *Christian Origins and Cultural Anthropology: Practical Models for Biblical Interpretation* (Atlanta: John Knox Press, 1986) 139–43. See also Jerome Neyrey, *Paul in Other Words: A Cultural Reading of His Letters* (Louisville: Westminster/John Knox, 1990) 76–80; and Mark McVann, "Rituals of Status Transformation in Luke-Acts: The Case of Jesus the Prophet," in *The Social World of Luke-Acts: Models for Interpretation* (ed. J. H. Neyrey; Peabody, Mass.: Hendrickson, 1991) 334–36.

we call *rituals*, that is, pauses which allow us to assume new and different roles and statuses. Other pauses that occur routinely in our lives we call *ceremonies* (meals, festivals). These do not effect change of role or status but confirm them. (2) *Calendar:* Ritual pauses occur unpredictably; we undergo them when necessary. No one plans to be ill or unclean; but when sickness or pollution occurs, rituals for changing from those states are handy. Some rituals are unrepeatable status changes, such as birth, coronation, death, and the like. On the other hand, ceremonial pauses occur on fixed calendar dates, such as sabbath and Passover. We anticipate and plan for them. (3) *Time focus:* Ritual pauses take us from present needs to the future, as we change our current status and assume a new role in the future. Ceremonies, however, look to the past and celebrate its influence on the present. Past roles and statuses continue to exist in the present and influence present social dynamics. (4) *Presiding:* Different kinds of people preside over rituals and ceremonies. *Professionals* (physicians, prophets) preside over or direct status transformation rituals. These are the "limit breakers" whom society allows to deal with marginal people as they cross fixed social lines.[8] *Officials* (father at Passover meals, temple priests) preside over or direct the appropriate *ceremonies* in their institutions.

(5) *Purpose:* Ceremonies leave in place the lines of the maps of society, because they function to confirm the values and structures of society and to celebrate the orderly classification of persons, places, and things in the cosmos.[9] For example, birthdays, anniversaries, pilgrimage feasts and the like confirm the roles and statuses of individuals in the group as well as the group's collective sense of holy space and holy time which pertain to its festivals. Ceremonies look to the stability of the lines of society's maps. Conversely, rituals attend precisely to those lines but focus on their crossing. Rituals are stable ways of dealing with necessary instability in the system: a boy and a girl cross lines to become husband and wife in a marriage ritual; sick people cross lines and become healthy (Leviticus 14; Mark 1:44); sinners become purified (Luke 18:13–14). The converse is also true: a seemingly innocent person may become guilty through a ritual trial. The status of those who cross lines is thereby changed, and so these rites are called "status-transformation" rituals. If ceremonies look to the center of the map and the stable lines that make up the map, rituals look to the map's boundaries. These should be stable, but may be legitimately or fraudulently crossed.

---

8. "Limit breaker" is the term Bruce Malina uses to identify the professional presider at rituals of status transformation, whom society authorizes to lead people across lines and boundaries usually judged dangerous (*Christian Origins and Cultural Anthropology*, 144–54).

9. On "purity systems" and "symbolic universes," see J. H. Neyrey, "The Symbolic Universe of Luke-Acts: 'They Turn the World Upside Down,'" in *The Social World of Luke-Acts: Models for Interpretation*, 271–304; and Neyrey, *Paul in Other Words*, 21–55.

Footwashing (13:6–11) as Ritual of Status Transformation

Using our model of a ritual, let us examine Jesus' washing of Peter's feet. (1) *Frequency:* This ritual occurs just once in the Fourth Gospel.[10] Since the meal had begun when Jesus rose to wash his disciples' feet, this ritual occurs as an irregular pause in a ceremonial meal. (2) *Calendar:* The narrator locates the general meal in the context of Passover, a fixed calendar date (13:1). Because the footwashing in 13:4–5 is not a fixed element of Passover or any other known Jewish meal, it is an irregular, unpredictable pause; it arises then because it was needed ("Unless . . ."). (3) *Time focus:* The present footwashing looks to the future: "Unless I wash you, you have no part in me" (13:8). The narrator evokes no past action of Jesus here, as in 13:14–15; rather a new status with Jesus depends on what is presently happening. (4) *Presiding:* Jesus presides over the ritual. Were this an act of etiquette that welcomed guests to a ceremonial meal, Jesus would be an official of the kinship institution which celebrated its commitment through commensality. But his washing of Peter's feet has nothing to do with welcoming etiquette or meal participation. This action will make Peter "wholly clean," a status he cannot now enjoy, unless Jesus performs this ritual. Jesus, then, acts here as a professional, not an official. He allows Peter to cross from one status ("already bathed") to a better status ("wholly clean").

(5) *Purpose:* Whatever role and status Peter enjoyed prior to 13:6, Jesus requires that he undergo this ritual for two reasons. First, unless he accepts this, "You will have no part in me." Second, when completed, Peter will be "wholly clean." As regards the former purpose, this footwashing resembles other status transformation rituals in the Fourth Gospel, many of which are presented using a formula introduced by "unless" (ἐὰν μή):

3:3	*Unless* one is born anew, he cannot see the kingdom of God.
3:5	*Unless* one is born of water and the spirit, he cannot enter the kingdom of God.
6:53	*Unless* you eat the flesh of the Son of Man and drink his blood, you have no life in you.
8:24	*Unless* you believe that "I AM," you will die in your sins.
12:24	*Unless* a grain of wheat falls into the earth and dies, it remains alone.
13:8	*Unless* I wash you, you have no part in me.

10. We should contrast it with two others in which Jesus is the recipient of the action. In Luke 7:37–38 a woman interrupts a meal to wet his feet with her tears; Luke interprets this as a *ceremonial* act of welcoming etiquette which the host failed to extend to Jesus (vv. 44–46); such actions should confirm his status as "honored guest." In John 12:1–8, Mary interrupted Jesus' meal with the family to anoint Jesus' feet (vv. 2–3). Although this is an anointing and not a "footwashing," we label it a *status-transformation ritual*, for it constitutes part of Jesus' burial ritual (v. 7). Ceremonial etiquette can be extended repeatedly, not so ritual anointing for burial.

15:4   As the branch cannot bear fruit by itself, *unless* it abides in the vine, neither can you, *unless* you abide in me.

John 3:3 and 5 refer to the status-transformation ritual of baptism.[11] Outsiders become insiders by virtue of this entrance ritual.[12] Jesus demands of prospective disciples in 8:24 that they acclaim him by a confession of his divinity, thus changing status from outsiders or lukewarm disciples to that of first-class insiders. Later even this confession is deemed insufficient; something more is required. Like grains of wheat, disciples must be willing to die (12:24; see 16:1–2; Mark 8:34–37). Jesus tells Peter, who is already a member of the circle, that still more is needed, that his current status is inadequate and that, although he is "bathed," he is not yet "wholly clean." Finally, unless branches abide through thick and thin, they bear no fruit.

Most of these "unless" statements, then, describe moments of status-transformation passage in the Johannine group's identity. Some represent the radical change of status from that of outsider to insider (3:3, 5). Others indicate a change of insider status, from less complete to more complete disciple and from imperfect to perfect follower. Indeed, there seems to be a sense of escalation in these statements: first, mere membership (3:3, 5); then, elite confession (8:24); then, elite behavior (12:24).

According to the story's logic, Peter is a disciple who has passed one loyalty test (6:67–69) and so enjoys basic membership and is part of the general circle of disciples (see 9:28). The "part" Jesus offers in 13:8 would seem to be a new elite status.[13] The footwashing, then, stands as the last, and perhaps the climax, of these transformation rituals.

As regards the second stated purpose of this ritual, what does it mean to be "wholly clean?"[14] Purity and cleanness are issues of considerable impor-

---

11. See Ignace de la Potterie, "'To be Born Again of Water and the Spirit'—The Baptismal Text of John 3,5," in *The Christian Lives by the Spirit* (Staten Island, N.Y.: Alba House, 1971) 1–36; David Rensberger, *Johannine Faith and Liberating Community* (Philadelphia: Westminster, 1988) 57–59, 66–70.

12. Rensberger indicates that Nicodemus is a symbolic character, namely, a representative of Jewish leaders who were unwilling to come publicly to Jesus (*Johannine Faith and Liberating Community*, 40). See Raymond E. Brown, *The Community of the Beloved Disciple* (New York: Paulist, 1979) 68–73, 77–82, 89. Nicodemus's "baptism" would elevate his status to that of a confessing member of Jesus' circle (see 9:22; 12:42), truly the elite "inner circle."

13. Μέρος has been particularly difficult to interpret. Often it means (1) *a region or place* (Matt 2:22; 15:21; Mark 8:10; Acts 2:10; Eph 4:9; Rev 16:19), (2) *a party or faction* (Acts 23:9; Josephus, *Jewish War* 1.143), (3) *an inheritance* (Rev 21:8; 22:19), or (4) *a member of the body* (Eph 4:16). All of these meanings find a ready equivalent in the Johannine symbolic world: (1) Jesus speaks about "where" he is going and the mansions awaiting his disciples (14:2); (2) we recognize many factions within the Johannine church, among them the elite (12:24) and the cowards (9:22; 12:42); (3) rewards and inheritance ("peace," 14:27; the Holy Spirit, 15:26; "bring forth much fruit," 15:2–6); and (4) member of Jesus' group (i.e., vine and branch, 15:1–7).

14. "Clean" is one aspect of the semantic word field that has to do with purity and pollution; see J. H. Neyrey, "Unclean, Common, Polluted and Taboo," *Forum* 4,4 (1988) 72–82, and *Paul in*

tance in this Gospel. The references are clustered in John 2–3 and 13–15. Jesus' initial sign has to do with "purification," for the six jars at Cana which he filled stood there "for the Jewish rites of *purification* (καθαρισμόν)" (2:6).[15] The Gospel's logic argues that Jesus replaces former rites, feasts, places of worship, etc. with new and better ones.[16] The sign at Cana heralds the beginning of new and better "purification" rituals, even status-transformation rituals. The narrator then presents a discussion of baptism between Jesus and Nicodemus (3:3–5), a status-transformation ritual for "entering the kingdom of God" (3:5). A brief notice is then made of "a discussion between John's disciples and a Jew over *purification* (περὶ καθαρισμοῦ)" (3:25). The Gospel argues that Jesus' "purification" is superior to all others, as well as essential for special status.

Talk about purification occurs again in 3:6–11 and 15:1–3. In the latter place, Jesus states that the vinedresser "takes away" unfruitful branches, but "prunes" (καθαίρει) fruitful ones (15:2). "Pruning" masks the implied verb, namely, "to purify" (καθαρίζειν). Hence, more cleansing awaits disciples, despite the fact that they were already cleansed in baptism. In 13:10 Jesus affirmed that some have already "bathed and do not need to wash"; nevertheless, they still need to have their feet washed so as to become "wholly clean." Likewise in 15:3 Jesus affirms, "You are already made clean (καθαροί) by the word I have spoken to you"; nevertheless, they will be made "clean" when pruned/cleansed by the vinedresser. In 15:1–3, then, a status-transformation ritual is envisioned, whereby an already "clean" disciple will take on a new status of "cleanness" (a branch that bears more fruit), when cleansed by the vinedresser. This ritual transforms mere insider status to that of elite or perfect insider status. This status transformation occurs through suffering (see 12:24 and 16:1–2).

These references to purification influence how we interpret "wholly clean" in 13:10. At a minimum, Jesus' washing of Peter's foot is a washing whose aim is purification. Like other washings, it too is a status-transformation ritual, not a mere entrance ritual, but a ritual whereby an insider gains a better status, a more perfect role. Peter will be *wholly* clean, something impossible without this ritual. The comparison of 13:6–10 with 15:1–3 suggests that this footwashing is more than a mere washing ritual; perfect

---

Other Words, 54–55. Generally "clean" either has to do with the removal of pollution, consecration for entrance or participation in a holy rite.

15. These presumably include the washing of hands and perhaps vessels (see Mark 7:2–4); the volume of the six jars correlates with a house filled with wedding guests needing to wash their hands before the wedding feast.

16. See Neyrey, *Ideology of Revolt*, 130–41. See James VanderKam, "John 10 and the Feast of the Dedication," in *Of Scribes and Scrolls* (ed. Harold Attridge, John Collins, and Thomas Tobin; New York: University Press of America, 1990) 203–14. See Francis Moloney, "From Cana to Cana (Jn 2:1–4:45) and the fourth Evangelist's concept of correct (and incorrect) faith," *Salesianum* 40 (1978) 817–43.

καθαρισμός comes about by public confession and even risk of death (16:1–2).[17]

Footwashing (13:12–20) as a Ceremony

If 13:6–11 describes a ritual of status transformation, a different type of ritual action is portrayed in 13:12–20. Because this does not involve change of role or status but rather confirmation of them, let us read vv. 12–20 according to the model of ceremony.[18]

(1) *Frequency:* Jesus mandates in 13:12–15 that the feet of church members be regularly washed as a standard part of their gatherings. Whereas Peter would be washed once and then be "wholly clean," the feet of the members of the group would be washed again and again. How often? If this footwashing is, as I suspect, an act of etiquette which welcomes people to a ceremonial meal (see Luke 7:44–46; 1 Tim 5:10), then it would be repeated whenever the group gathered. We simply do not know how frequently they gathered, whether only at Passover (13:1) or at sabbath or the first day of the week (Acts 20:7). But as often as they gathered, this act of etiquette would be appropriate. (2) *Calendar:* This footwashing is expected with every gathering and should occur regularly at the beginning of the ceremony. It is not the emergency ritual which interrupted the meal in progress when Peter's feet were washed. (3) *Time focus:* It harks back to the past example of Jesus which should be presently imitated by the group's leaders. Jesus calls attention to his past action as the warrant for its continuation in the present: "Do you know what I have done to you? . . . If I have washed your feet,

---

17. J. A. T. Robinson noted the parallel with Mark 10:32–45 and its offer of "baptism" to James and John; Jesus' "way of the cross/way of glory" must be imitated by his disciples ("The Significance of the Foot-Washing," in *Neotestamentica et Patristica* [NovTSup 6; Leiden: Brill, 1962] 144–47). Robinson also links Peter's remarks in John 13:36 about willingness to follow Jesus, even unto death.

18. Although we focus on only one ceremony (13:12–20), this Gospel notes two other types which correspond to two key social locations: (1) the temple and pilgrimage feasts to the nation's shrine and (2) the household and meals. As regards the temple, Jesus participates in certain feasts such as Passover (2:13ff.; 13:1ff.), Tabernacles (7:2–8:20), Dedication (10:21), and an unnamed feast (5:1ff.). Ideally these should confirm his membership, role, and status in the political institution, but in the Fourth Gospel he challenges and replaces them, thereby disrupting their function as confirming ceremonies. As regards the household, Jesus confirms his association with circles of intimate friends (12:1–8; 13:1–17:26; 21:9–13) and general disciples (6:1–15). Meals confirm his special role as host and provider when he feeds others or his status as honored guest when they fete him. This sketch suggests that in this Gospel ceremonies are not functioning properly on the public level of participation in the nation's ongoing socialization, which indeed is challenged by Jesus. But on the level of private associations in households they do function to confirm membership, as well as specific roles and statuses. On the importance of the temple/household distinction, see John H. Elliott, "Temple versus Household in Luke-Acts: A Contrast in Social Institutions," in *The Social World of Luke-Acts*, 212–17, 230–38.

you also ought to wash one another's feet" (13:12, 14). Present roles and relationships among the Johannine group depend on the past action and example of Jesus. (4) *Presiding:* Jesus presides at this footwashing as an official. If footwashing belongs in the orbit of etiquette and etiquette denotes commensality, then Jesus presides over that ceremony.

(5) *Purpose:* The *purpose* of this footwashing in 13:12–16 is manifold. Jesus confirms his own role and status by this act: "You call me 'Teacher' and 'Lord'; and you are right, for so I am" (13:13). Then he alludes to himself as "Master" (13:16). Yet the appropriate act of this Teacher-Lord-Master is to wash the feet of disciples and servants, thus offering them welcome. By presiding at this ceremonial washing, Jesus confirms his unique role as Teacher-Lord-Master and his exalted status, even if the action done is "humble" in our eyes. Only the person of this exalted role and status within the group is expected to perform this action.

So when those whose feet Jesus has washed in turn wash the feet of others, they do so precisely as leaders of the group. In Jesus' absence, they enjoy roles and status comparable to that of Jesus, who enjoyed a superior role and exalted status. Hence, Jesus' word legitimates their position. In their ceremonial actions they are like the master; they are not "greater than their master" so as to avoid this action. Rather, as "servants" they imitate their "master": "A servant is not greater than his master; nor is he who is sent greater than he who sent him" (13:16). They too will be officials presiding at this ceremony. Their performance of this action will serve to confirm their role as leaders and teachers of Jesus' group. Moreover, they wash the feet of members of the church, and so the status of those washed is confirmed as authentic members of this Jesus synagogue.

WHO PARTICIPATES IN THESE RITUALS AND CEREMONIES?

Who gets elevated to *what* role or status in the ritual in 13:6–11? Was the transformation *successful?* Was the new status *acknowledged?* I ask these questions in light of recent studies which argue that readers must attend to the whole of the story in John 13.[19] Although focusing on Peter, we compare and contrast him with other candidates for ritual transformation in John 13. The narrator highlights four characters: Jesus, who presides at all the rituals and ceremonies, and three candidates for the rituals: Peter (vv. 6–10, 36–38), Judas (vv. 11, 18, 24–29), and the Beloved Disciple (vv. 23–26). Since Collins's work readers are sensitive to the representative nature of the

---

19. In particular, Francis J. Moloney, "A Sacramental Reading of John 13:1–38," *CBQ* 53 (1991) 242–48; and F. Manns, "Le lavement des pieds: essai sur la structure et la signification de Jean 13," *RevScRel* 55 (1981) 159.

dramatis personae of the Fourth Gospel.[20] This pertains to our analysis of status-transformation rituals, for we should inquire about the characterization of the candidates for ritual transformation.

Peter. He is typically presented in this Gospel in terms of comparison and contrast.[21] On the narrative level, he is contrasted in 13:6–11 with Judas, just as he was in 6:67–71. If Jesus washes him he will be "wholly clean," which juxtaposes him with Judas, who is "not clean." Yet he is also contrasted with the Beloved Disciple. In seeking to know the traitor's identity, Peter asks the Beloved Disciple to ask Jesus.[22] Peter's alleged primacy among the Twelve stands in contrast to the actions of the Beloved Disciple. He is "in the know"; Peter is not. He enjoys the place of honor next to Jesus, whereas Peter reclines farther away. As we shall see, the Beloved Disciple and Peter will be contrasted first as shepherd and sheep (18:15–16) and then as loyal disciple (19:26–27) and disloyal coward (18:17, 25–27).

Jesus converses with Peter again in 13:36–38. His remark to him there resembles that in 13:7 and clearly anticipates Peter's denial in 18:25–27. Peter cannot follow Jesus now, just as he does not know now what Jesus is doing. But "you will follow afterward," just as "afterward you will understand." This suggests that Peter remains in a liminal or candidate state of transformation, incomplete both in knowledge and following. Jesus refuses to acknowledge that Peter has achieved the new status signaled in 13:6–11. He will not prove a loyal disciple, willing to die for the Master.

Thus, the narrator compares and contrasts Peter with both Judas and the Beloved Disciple. The Beloved Disciple knows and follows most closely—not so Peter. Judas disguises himself and plots malice—not so Peter, who openly professes loyalty but will fail the test of courage in 18:25–27. Yet the narrative says that Peter will know afterward and follow afterward, an allusion to chapter 21. Hence he remains in a liminal stage; his status and role

20. Collins, "Representative Figures in the Fourth Gospel," 26–46, 118–32; idem, *These Things Have Been Written* (Grand Rapids: Eerdmans, 1991) esp. 38–46; see Alan Culpepper, *The Anatomy of the Fourth Gospel* (Philadelphia: Fortress, 1983) 105, 118–23.

21. Increasingly New Testament scholars are studying the rhetorical device called *synkrisis*, or comparison, especially as this is found in the *progymnasmata*; see James Butts, "The Progymnasmata of Theon: A New Text with Translation and Commentary" (diss., Claremont Graduate School, 1986) 494–512. See Christopher Forbes, "Comparison, Self-Praise and Irony: Paul's Boasting and the Conventions of Hellenistic Rhetoric," *NTS* 32 (1986) 1–8; Peter Marshall, *Enmity at Corinth: Social Conventions in Paul's Relations with the Corinthians* (WUNT 2.23; Tübingen: Mohr, 1987) 53–56, 325–29, 348–65; D. A. Russell, "On Reading Plutarch's Lives," *Greece and Rome* 13 (1966) 150–51; P. A. Stadter, "Plutarch's Comparison of Pericles and Fabius Maximus," *GRBS* 16 (1975) 77–85.

22. Compare this with a parallel process in 12:20–23. Certain "Greeks" ask to see Jesus. They ask Philip, who asks Andrew, who takes them to Jesus. Hence certain people in this Gospel function as mediators or brokers of access and information, thus indicating their special role and status.

have not yet been fully transformed. He is not yet an elite figure, but neither is he a hostile outsider.

Judas. Readers were told that the devil had already put it into Judas's heart to betray Jesus (13:2), a remark that echoes 6:70–71, where loyal and disloyal disciples were contrasted. Jesus then labels him "not clean" (13:10b–11). Despite Jesus' washing of his feet, Judas certainly will not be transformed to elite status, especially if it means public loyalty to Jesus. Judas, then, appears disloyal and demonic (3:27).

According to 13:12–15 Jesus' ceremonial washing of the disciples' feet confirms both membership status and specific roles. But this does not apply to Judas. After giving the mandatum, Jesus excepts Judas from the ceremony: "I am not speaking to you all; I know whom I have chosen" (13:18). Indeed, he identifies Judas as the one who violates the basic laws of commensality: "He who ate my bread has lifted up his heel against me" (13:18b). He certainly did not participate in the status-transformation ritual (he was *not* made "clean"), nor was he confirmed as a group member in the ceremony. He fails as regards both ritual (vv. 6–11) and ceremony (vv. 12–20).

Beloved Disciple. We learn abruptly that he is "the one whom Jesus loved." His intimacy is symbolized by "lying close to the breast of Jesus" (13:23); from Jesus he receives special information hidden to all else: "Lord, who is it?" (13:25–26). Thus, he acts as Peter's broker or mediator; what Peter lacks, the Beloved Disciple has or can get. He is, then, the consummate insider, a true elite, who has access to knowledge of deviants in the group. Finally, he follows Jesus most closely, both to Caiaphas's house and to the cross, displaying public loyalty at the risk of his life. He would appear to have achieved the new status suggested by the footwashing ritual in 13:4–5, as well as confirmed group membership according to 13:12–20.

When we survey the characters in John 13 and ask about their participation in the rituals and ceremonies described there, we find the following characterization:

Person	*Ritual (13:6–11)/Ceremony (13:12–20)*	*Characterization*
Peter	1. Ritual: still a candidate for status transformation 2. Ceremony: confirmed group member	failed loyalty
Judas	1. Ritual: no status transformation ("One is *not* clean") 2. Ceremony: group membership denied ("I am *not* speaking of you all")	hostile disloyalty
Beloved Disciple	1. Ritual: elite status transformation 2. Ceremony: confirmed group member	courageous loyalty

PETER: CLAIMANT FOR THE ROLE OF GOOD SHEPHERD

We turn now to "the Noble Shepherd" materials, for these involve Peter and influence how we should read the narrative in John 13. Jesus enjoys the role of the Noble Shepherd. When calling the sheep by name, leading them out or laying down his life for them, he acts as the Noble Shepherd and confirms his role. Yet Peter too lays claim to this role.

In 13:37 Peter protests to Jesus that "I will lay down my life for you" (13:37), which is what the shepherd does. We compare this with Jesus' remark to Peter in 13:6–11 and note striking formal similarities between the two conversations.

13:6–8	*13:36–38*
1. *Question by Peter* "Lord, do you wash my feet?" (13:6)	1. *Question by Peter* "Lord, where are you going?" (13:36)
2. *Answer from Jesus* Jesus answered and said to him: "What I am doing you do not know now, but afterward you will understand" (13:7)	2. *Answer from Jesus* Jesus answered him: "Where I am going you cannot follow now, but afterward you will follow" (13:36b)
3. *Peter's Boast* Peter said to him: "You shall never wash my feet" (13:8)	3. *Peter's Boast* Peter said to him: "Lord, why cannot I follow you now? I will lay down my life for you" (13:37)
4. *Response from Jesus* Jesus answered him: "Unless I wash you, you have no part in me" (13:8)	4. *Response from Jesus* Jesus answered: "Will you lay down your life for me? Amen, amen I say to you, the cock will not crow, until you have denied me three times" (13:38)

Both conversations are formally similar in terms of topics discussed and rituals of status transformation described. In both, Jesus tells Peter that he does not know and cannot follow Jesus *now*; but *afterward* he will understand and follow. When Peter speaks in 13:36, he remains a candidate for the elite status which the "footwashing" symbolized. Yet his present boast of loyalty unto death implies that he presents himself as no mere candidate for elite status, but a tested and acknowledged holder of that status. Peter's boast of loyalty, moreover, denotes another claim, namely, the role of a "noble shepherd," who lays down his life for another.

The Noble Shepherd (10:11)	*Peter, the Shepherd? (13:37)*
The good shepherd lays down his life for the sheep	I will lay down my life for you

After Jesus commands that his disciples "love one another" (13:34–35), he defines that "love" in terms of what the noble shepherd does: "Greater love has no one than this, that a man lay down his life for his friends" (15:13). *Noble Shepherds*, then, *love by laying down their lives for their sheep/friends.* Peter claims in v. 37 both the status of an elite disciple and the particular role of "noble shepherd." But has he been formally initiated to that role? Does anyone acknowledge it?

Jesus challenges his claim to this new status, indicating that Peter remains but a candidate for the new role and status. Instead he predicts that Peter, far from being the noble shepherd, will instead act like a hireling, who sees the wolf coming and flees (10:12). If this is true, then the narrator issues a serious challenge to Peter's role vis-à-vis the group. According to Johannine logic, the hireling has no relationship with the sheep: "He who is a hireling, whose own the sheep are not . . . He flees because he is a hireling and cares nothing for the sheep" (10:12–13). Whatever the Johannine group knew of the traditional role and status of Peter, that would be severely challenged by Peter's association here with the hireling and not the shepherd.

Who, then, is the Noble Shepherd? The Beloved Disciple fulfills that ceremonial role. Returning to Jesus' parables of shepherds, doors, and sheep in 10:1–4 and 11–13, we learn that the true shepherd enters the door; the doorkeeper recognizes and admits him; and he calls the sheep by name. This fully describes what the Beloved Disciple does in 18:15–18.

Metaphorical Description of the Noble Shepherd	*Johannine Description of the Beloved Disciple*
1. *Shepherd Enters by the Door* "He who enters by the door is the shepherd of the sheep" (10:2).	1. *Beloved Disciple Enters By the Door* "As this disciple was known to the high priest, he entered . . . while Peter stood outside the door" (18:15)
2. *Gatekeeper Recognizes Him* "He who enters by the door is the shepherd of the sheep.	2. *Gatekeeper Recognizes Him* "So the other disciple, who was known to the high priest,

To him the gatekeeper opens."
(10:2–3).

went out and spoke to the
maid who kept the door"
(18:16).

3. *He Leads the Sheep In/Out*
"He calls his own sheep by name
and leads them out. When he has
brought out all his own, he
goes before them, and the
sheep follow him" (10:3–4).[23]

3. *He Leads the Sheep In*
"Peter stood outside the door.
... The other disciple
spoke to the maid who kept
the door and brought Peter
in" (18:16).

In fact, using the perspective of this study, we should label the actions described in 18:15–18 as a ceremony. The respective roles of Beloved Disciple and Peter are confirmed as shepherd and sheep. Far from being either shepherd or noble, Peter acts out the inferior role of the sheep.

Yet the conflict over who is the group's shepherd ends only in John 21. There the evangelist presents Peter again in terms of rituals of status transformation. The scene opens with Peter assuming the role as chief fisherman: "I am going fishing" (21:3). When six others join him, Peter's role as leader of Jesus' followers is ceremonially confirmed (see Luke 5:1–11). Yet Peter's ideal role is not Fisherman, but Shepherd. Yet this scene alerts us to examine the role and status of Peter once more.

Jesus serves a ceremonial meal confirming his role as host and provider, that is, shepherd who feeds his flock. Then he addresses Peter in a way that signals a radical transformation of his status. Readers know that Peter failed thrice in loyalty (13:38; 18:17, 25–27). Despite his claims to the contrary (13:36–38), he has been presented neither as "noble" nor as "shepherd" but as a hireling or sheep. Now Jesus questions Peter, and in doing so transforms his status to that of loving/loyal disciple and publicly acknowledges his role as shepherd.

Question:	*Answer:*	*Status Transformation:*
"Simon, son of John,	"Yes, Lord; you	"Feed my lambs"
do you love me more	know that I love	"Tend my sheep"
than these?"	you."	"Feed my sheep"
(21:15a, 16a, 17a)	(21:15b, 16b, 17b)	(21:15c, 16c, 17c)

This Gospel labors to affirm that Peter finally becomes the group's shepherd. Through ritual loyalty oaths, the status transformation of Peter is accomplished. Jesus himself acknowledges it as he invests Peter with the role and status of Shepherd of all the sheep ("Feed my lambs ... Feed my

23. According to the parable, the sheep know the voice of the shepherd (10:4–5); this seems to be ironically illustrated in 18:15–18 when the maid recognizes the voice of Peter and identifies him as a follower of Jesus, an association he denies.

sheep").[24] It is now legitimate for Peter to act as "shepherd." But is he also a "noble" shepherd?

The scene concludes with the prediction of Peter's death (21:18–19). Earlier Peter had boasted that he would lay down his life for Jesus, only to have this challenged (13:38). Now Jesus' prediction acknowledges Peter's earlier claim. But is this too a status transformation ritual? Does it add anything to the role and status of Peter?

At this point, we should ask about the relationship of 13:6–11 to 21:18–19. In the former passage, Jesus would make Peter "wholly clean." But at that point, can Peter be "clean," much less "wholly" clean, for he will fail in loyalty (13:36–38)? Jesus told Peter "What I am doing you do not know now, but afterward you will understand" (13:7). When did Peter finally know? These questions call attention to the problem of understanding fully what is being communicated in 13:6–11. It narrated an incomplete ritual, whose completion lies later and whose meaning will only be understood "afterward." But when?

The answers come in 21:18–19. Peter becomes "wholly clean" though a death whereby "God will be glorified" (21:19). The failure in loyalty is replaced by a declaration of "love" (21:15–17).[25] The ungrasped meaning of Jesus' actions is met with full understanding of Jesus' words in 21:19.

According to ritual analysis, Peter the initiand should experience status elevation by becoming "wholly clean" (13:10); but Jesus refused to acknowledge any change of status (13:36, 38). Peter remains a candidate for status transformation, as Jesus twice tells him that completion of the ritual lies in the future ("afterwards you will know," v. 7; "you will follow afterward," v. 36). In 21:15–17 and 18–19 the Fourth Gospel finishes Peter's status transformation. He is finally acknowledged to be the official and unchallenged Shepherd ("Feed my lambs . . . Feed my sheep," 21:15–17). Likewise his status as "noble" shepherd is acknowledged; he can truly "follow Jesus" and "lay down his life for him" (13:37). His death as faithful witness will seal his status as an elite disciple, courageous, loyal, and perfect according to the canons of this Gospel. In his death, he will become "wholly clean."

In conclusion, by itself cultural anthropology cannot fully interpret the symbolic meaning of the footwashing in 13:6–11. Nothing replaces the

---

24. Just as Jesus acted as the host of the ceremonial meal just finished (21:13), so Peter will assume that role too, as Jesus tells him, "*Feed* my lambs. . . . *Feed* my sheep" (21:15, 17). Whether we understand Jesus' command literally (Peter as host at genuine community meals) or symbolically (Peter as shepherd who pastures the flock), Jesus designates him as a ceremonial official.

25. Recall "greater love no one has than 'to lay down one's life'" (15:13); but "laying down one's life for the sheep" is the mark of a noble shepherd (10:11). Hence "love" is linked with the heroic loyalty of the shepherd. It is hardly incidental, then, that Jesus asks Peter "do you *love* me?"

study of background materials[26] and redactional inquiry.[27] But its use aids in clarifying what Jesus intends for Peter in vv. 6–10 (a status change) and what his example means for the disciples in vv. 12–20 (confirmation of their ceremonial roles).

A model of rites of status change and status confirmation greatly assists our reading of the Fourth Gospel. This Gospel records precious few successful ceremonies. Since attention is focused on boundary crossings and status changes (i.e., "unless . . ."), we are urged to focus on the social conflict within and without the Johannine community; this is helped by noting the shifting demands made of disciples, which are expressed in terms of new rites of status transformation. This model, moreover, greatly clarifies the rivalry between the symbolic figures Peter and the Beloved Disciple, when we see the latter successfully if temporarily acting as the ceremonial Noble Shepherd. The figure of Peter, moreover, remains in a state of change and uncertainty until the final ritual in 21:15–19.

26. For example, the Torah speaks of two kinds of footwashings: (1) a ceremonial act of hospitality to travelers before they eat (Gen 18:4; 24:32; Judg 19:21) and (2) a ritual purification of priests before entering and ministering to the Lord (Exod 30:19–21; 40:31). Philo gave a moral meaning to priestly footwashing, namely, blamelessness or walking in the way of the Lord (*Mos.* 2.138; *Q. Exod.* 1.2); when a sacrificial animal's feet are washed, it no longer walks on earth, but in God's realm (*Spec. Leg.* 1.206); see Herold Weiss, "Foot Washing in the Johannine Community," (see n. 2 above) 315–17.

27. On the relationship of the footwashing in 13:6–11 to Jesus' death, see Hoskyns, *Fourth Gospel*, 435; Brown, *Gospel According to John*, 2:551; J. D. G. Dunn, "The Washing of the Disciples' Feet in John 13,1–20," *ZNW* 61 (1970) 249.

CHAPTER 14

Rich and Poor, Proud and Humble in Luke-Acts

David L. Balch

Hendrik Bolkestein has misled many New Testament scholars into thinking that Greco-Roman social ethics were not concerned with the relationship between rich and poor, a misconception corrected by Alexander Fuks of the Hebrew University in Jerusalem.[1] Bolkestein argued that Greek society did not recognize an obligation toward the poor, widows, or orphans, that although Greeks valued being "lovers of humanity," the objects of their love were foreign guests, not the poor in their own society.[2] Fuks sees, on the contrary, that significant Greek philosophers, rhetoricians, comedians, historians, poets, and rulers were forced by social conflicts in their cities to relate to the poor who did not have daily necessities. He concludes, for example, that "the problem of πενία καὶ πλοῦτος, of poverty versus riches, and of the deep gulf between the 'haves' and the 'have nots' is, on examination, one of the major themes in Isocrates" even though it "has never been studied."[3]

1. Hendrik Bolkestein, *Wohltätigkeit und Armenpflege im Vorchristlichen Altertum: Ein Beitrag zum Problem "Moral und Gesellschaft"* (Utrecht: A. Oosthoek, 1939). Alexander Fuks, *Social Conflict in Ancient Greece* (Jerusalem: Magnes; Leiden: Brill, 1984), twenty-four essays originally written between 1951 and 1980, edited after the author's death by Menahem Stern and Moshe Amit. See the essays in *Social Struggles in Archaic Rome: New Perspectives on the Conflict of the Orders* (ed. Kurt A. Raaflaub; Berkeley: University of California Press, 1986), and from a Marxist perspective, see G. E. M. de Ste. Croix, *The Class Struggle in the Ancient Greek World from the Archaic Age to the Arab Conquests* (Ithaca, N.Y.: Cornell University Press, 1981).

2. Bolkestein, *Wohltätigkeit*, 93, 110–11, 138, 149, 420, 432, etc.

3. Alexander Fuks, "Isokrates and the Social-Economic Situation in Greece," *Ancient Society* 3 (1972) 21, 17, now in *Social Conflict* 56, 52. Compare A. H. Sommerstein, "Aristophanes and the Demon Poverty," *Classical Quarterly* 34 (1984) 133: "Having for nearly a quarter of a century spoken unmistakably in the language of the well-heeled, he began to write [in "Assembly-women" and "Wealth"] like a spokesman of the barefoot, because the class he most admired [Attic peasantry] had lost their shoes." I am grateful to Prof. David Konstan for the reference to Sommerstein.

This erroneous perception among New Testament scholars has led to false conclusions about the relationship between early Christian and Greco-Roman attitudes toward the poor. For example, in an otherwise excellent book on the social setting of Luke-Acts, Philip Esler argues that this Gentile author writing for Gentile Christians in a Mediterranean urban setting corrects his congregations' attitudes by a Palestinian, apocalyptic work, *1 Enoch*.

> The area in which Luke-Acts most resembles 1 Enoch 92–105 is in its reiter-ated prediction of a forthcoming reversal of the conditions of the rich and the poor. To the Hellenistic elite, a message such as that conveyed in these chap-ters of 1 Enoch would no doubt have appeared novel and surprising.
> The rich members of the community were the source of funds and meals for the poor. In Luke's eyes wealth was likely to have been unjustly acquired (Lk 16.9), and if its possessors did not distribute at least some of it to the poor in this world they faced the prospect of eternal punishment in the next. This teaching was a radical challenge to the deeply held beliefs in his Hellenistic milieu, where the ruling elite not only treated the lower orders unjustly and with contempt, but congratulated themselves on doing so. Luke not only attacks the propriety of their attitudes, but also instructs them to modify the very behaviour which expresses their superiority in status, wealth and power (Lk 14.12–14). Let there be no doubt that those people from the upper strata of this society who tried to live a Christian life as Luke defines it were required to abandon some of their most cherished beliefs and practices. . . . The Lukan Gospel imposes on the rich an indispensable requirement, quite at odds with the social values of their own society.[4]

Fuks has shown such a view to be incorrect with respect to both Greek theory and practice.[5]

A further misreading of Luke-Acts has been stimulated by recent discus-sions of genre. Charles Talbert has argued that the Gospel is a biography, and Richard Pervo that Acts is an ancient novel.[6] Either of these conclusions would mean that Luke-Acts is to be read in an individualistic manner, that the Gospel is the biography of an individual, Jesus, and that Acts consists of

---

4. Philip Francis Esler, *Community and Gospel in Luke-Acts: The Social and Political Motivations of Lucan Theology* (SNTSMS 57; Cambridge: Cambridge University Press, 1987) 199. A similarly mistaken assumption is made by authors in a recent collection, *The Social World of Luke-Acts: Models for Interpretation* (ed. Jerome H. Neyrey; Peabody, Mass.: Hendrickson, 1991), e.g., by Richard L. Rohrbaugh, "The Pre-Industrial City in Luke-Acts: Urban Social Relations," 125–49 (see esp. 142, 145–46). Cf. George W. E. Nickelsburg, "The Apocalyptic Message of 1 Enoch 92–105," *CBQ* 39 (1977) 309–28.

5. Alexander Fuks, "Τοῖς ἀπορουμένοις κοινωνεῖν: The Sharing of Property by the Rich with the Poor in Greek Theory and Practice," *Scripta Classica Israelica* 5 (1979–80) 46–63, now in *Social Conflict*, 172–89.

6. Charles H. Talbert, "Ancient Biography," *Anchor Bible Dictionary* (ed. D. N. Freedman; New York: Doubleday, 1992) 1:745–49. Richard I. Pervo, *Profit with Delight: The Literary Genre of the Acts of the Apostles* (Philadelphia: Fortress, 1987).

the adventures of other individuals, Peter and Paul.[7] David Aune is correct, however, that Luke-Acts is more indebted to the genre of political historiography than to biography or novel.[8] The social-political theme of rich and poor in Luke-Acts should be compared to similar stories in the historians Polybius and Dionysius of Halicarnassus. I will focus on comparing the stories in Luke with those in Dionysius. I write this essay about tensions within Greco-Roman cities in gratitude for Prof. Wayne Meeks, a teacher at Yale and a mentor, who more than anyone else has taught us about the social setting of the first urban Christians.

The Lukan language I have in mind includes the following. In Luke's birth narrative, Mary praises the Lord for looking upon her, a humble slave girl (ταπείνωσιν τῆς δούλης, 1:48). Mary continues her praise of the One who "has brought down the powerful from their thrones, and lifted up the lowly; [God] has filled the hungry with good things, and sent the rich away empty" (1:52–53). In Luke's Galilean section, Jesus proclaims the gospel to the poor in 4:18, and he pronounces blessings on the poor and woes on the rich in 6:20–26.

In the long, central section of the Gospel, the third petition of the Lord's Prayer is for daily bread (τὸ καθ᾽ ἡμέραν), and the fourth asks for forgiveness of sins on the grounds that "we have forgiven everyone owing a debt to us" (ἀφίομεν παντὶ ὀφείλοντι ἡμῖν, 11:3–4), which includes an economic concern. Chapter 12 has the parable of the rich person who possesses many good things (12:18–19) but is a fool, a story introduced with a strong caution against greed (πλεονεξία). The next paragraph concerns anxiety and includes the imperative to sell one's goods and give alms (12:33). Chapter 14 recalls the Magnificat: guests are to sit in the lowest place "for all who exalt themselves will be humbled, and those who humble themselves will be exalted" (14:11). This time Luke employs the verb ταπεινόω. Jesus draws the consequences that a host is to invite not the rich but the poor, who cannot repay (14:13–14); the word "poor" here (πτωχός) recalls Jesus' inaugural sermon in 4:18.[9] Then follows the awesome parable of the great banquet, opening with a phrase from the Lord's Prayer about eating bread in the kingdom of God (14:15; cf. 11:3). The invitation is rejected by those who have just bought land, so the owner of the house sends out a slave to invite the poor, again the same word from Jesus' sermon in chapter 4.

The parable of the dishonest manager in chapter 16 is directed explicitly

7. Albrecht Dihle confirms that biography focuses on individuals ("Die Entstehung der historischen Biographie," in *Sitzungsberichte der Heidelberger Akademie der Wissenschaften* [Philosophisch-historische Klasse (1986/3); Heidelberg: Universitätsverlag, 1987] 9, 17, 18, 20, 27).

8. David E. Aune, *The New Testament and its Literary Environment* (Library of Early Christianity 8, ed. Wayne A. Meeks; Philadelphia: Westminster, 1987) 78. See now H. Cancik, "The History of Culture, Religion, and Institutions in Ancient Historiography: Philological Observations Concerning Luke's History," *JBL* (forthcoming).

9. See Sommerstein, "Aristophanes," 318, 329.

to disciples; the manager is charged with squandering his rich master's property. "So, summoning his master's debtors (χρεοφειλετῶν) one by one, he asked the first, 'How much do you owe (ὀφείλεις) my master?'" (16:5). The language once again recalls the Lord's Prayer: the manager reduces each debt. The conclusion is that "his master commended the dishonest manager because he had acted shrewdly. . . . And I tell you make friends for yourselves by means of dishonest (ἀδικία) mammon, so that when it is gone they may welcome you into eternal homes. . . . You cannot serve God and mammon" (16:8-9,13). In the following verse the Pharisees are called lovers of wealth (16:14), and the affirmation is made that "it is easier for heaven and earth to pass away, than for one stroke of a letter in the law to be dropped" (16:17), which may, in this context, refer to the sabbatical year and the forgiveness of the debts owed by the needy (see Acts 4:34, which cites Deut 15:4).

The final story in chapter 16 relates the rich man and Lazarus, the former feasting sumptuously "every day" (καθ' ἡμέραν, 16:19) while the poor man, Lazarus, is hungry. By contrast, the daily feasting recalls the third petition in the Lord's Prayer. Both men die, and the rich man is humbled to Hades while the poor man is exalted to Abraham's bosom (the verbs in my interpretation come from the Magnificat). Chapter 18 has a story of the Pharisee who exalts himself and the tax collector who humbles himself (18:14). Next there is the rich ruler whom Jesus commands to "sell all that you own and distribute the money to the poor, and you will have treasure in heaven; then come follow me" (18:22). Jesus observes that it is hard for those with wealth to enter the kingdom of God (18:24). Jesus heals a blind beggar near Jericho, a man who had called repeatedly to the son of David for mercy (18:37, 39). Chapter 19 has still another story about a rich tax collector; this one gives to the poor, so is pronounced both "saved" and a "son of Abraham" (19:2, 8, 9). The final story before the triumphal entry into Jerusalem concerns a severe (αὐστηρός, vv. 21, 22) nobleman who hands out ten pounds to slaves, who know that he gives to every one who has and takes away from those who do not have (19:26). This is a selective survey of stories and sayings on the rich and poor, exalted and humble in the Magnificat, and in Luke's Galilean and central sections.[10]

Dionysius's *Roman Antiquities* belongs to the genre of ancient history, to which Luke-Acts is indebted, and this has consequences for understanding

---

10. For complete interpretations, see Hans-Joachim Degenhardt, *Lukas, Evangelist der Armen: Besitz und Besitzverzicht in den Lukanischen Schriften: Eine traditions- und redaktionsgeschichtliche Untersuchung* (Stuttgart: Katholisches Bibelwerk, 1965) and Jacques Dupont, *Les Béatitudes*, Tome III, *Les Évangélistes* (Ebib; Paris: Gabalda, 1973) 99–206. L. T. Johnson, *The Literary Function of Possessions in Luke-Acts* (SBLDS 39; Missoula, Mont.: Scholars Press, 1977). Cf. John R. Donahue, "Two Decades of Research on the Rich and Poor in Luke-Acts," in *Justice and the Holy: Essays in Honor of Walter Harrelson* (ed. Douglas A. Knight and Peter J. Paris; Atlanta: Scholars Press, 1989) 129–44.

the stories about rich and poor, proud and humble, even though modern studies of the terms rich and poor, proud and humble virtually ignore the material.[11] I will survey some of the Greco-Roman texts and stories, and, following the survey, I will comment on their relationship to the Lukan Magnificat, the Lord's Prayer, and some of the material sketched above. I am assuming that some Christians in Luke's congregations would have been familiar with the rhetorical, historical, and philosophical material which follows and that these stories would have influenced how they heard the Gospel and Acts.[12]

The historian Dionysius of Halicarnassus was decisively influenced both by the rhetorician Isocrates and perhaps less directly by some Stoic ideas about relationships between rich and poor.[13] First I will cite some texts from Isocrates concerning rich and poor, and these are not simply random texts; all are from Isocrates' treatises that the historian Dionysius knew and studied. In both Isocrates and Dionysius, poverty has forced some from their homes who have had to become wanderers, and then the question arises whether some foreign culture will "receive" these immigrants. Through forty years of writing orations, Isocrates' basic conception is the same: he urges a war of conquest against Persia, which would enable Greeks to settle the poor, those unable to find a livelihood in Greece. A Persian war would enable those persons ejected from their cities and displaced to find livelihood in the conquered territory. Isocrates wrote:

> It were well to make the expedition in the present generation, in order that those who have shared in our misfortunes may also benefit by our advantages and not continue all their days in wretchedness. For sufficient is the time that is past, filled as it has been with every form of horror; for many as are the ills which are incidental to the nature of man, we have ourselves invented more than those which necessity lays upon us, by engendering wars and factions among ourselves; and in consequence, some are being put to death contrary to law in their own countries, others are wandering with their women and children in strange lands, and many compelled through lack of the necessities of life (δι᾽ ἔνδειαν τῶν καθ᾽ ἡμέραν) to enlist in foreign armies, are being slain, fighting for their foes against their friends.

11. See Eduard Schweizer, *Erniedrigung und Erhöhung bei Jesus und seinen Nachfolgern* (Zurich: Zwingli, 1955); and Albrecht Dihle, "Demut," *RAC* 3 (1957) 735–78, esp. 746–50. On the terms rich and poor, see Bolkestein, *Wohltätigkeit*, 177, 420, 435, 456, 484, and esp. Sommerstein, "Aristophanes," 318, 329.

12. Cf. the reference to Dionysius, *Ant. Rom.* 2.15.3 by François Bovon, "Israel, die Kirche und die Völker im lukanischen Doppelwerk," in *Lukas in neuer Sicht: Gesammelte Aufsätze* (Biblisch-Theologische Studien 8; Neukirchen-Vluyn: Neukirchener, 1985) 121–22.

13. See Clemence Elizabeth Schultze, "Dionysius of Halicarnassus as a Historian: An Investigation of His Aims and Methods in the Antiquitates Romanae" (dissertation, Oxford, 1980) 270, who notes the "pervasive" influence of Isocrates on Dionysius, especially in his treatment of rich and poor. And since Dionysius wrote a work on Isocrates, we know what speeches he knew and admired.

Against these ills no one has ever protested; and people are not ashamed to weep over the calamities which have been fabricated by the poets, while they view complacently the real sufferings, the many terrible sufferings, which result from our state of war; and they are so far from feeling pity (ἐλεεῖν) that they even rejoice more in each other's sorrows than in their own blessings. (*Panegyricus* 167–68, written ca. 380 B.C.E., trans. Norlin, LCL)[14]

In the same work, Isocrates refers to a time following the Peloponnesian War when Sparta set up rulers in other Greek cities, including Athens, and

under the rule of these men, because of the multitude of our own calamities, we ceased feeling pity for each other (ἀλλήλους ἐλεοῦντες), since there was no man to whom they allowed enough of respite so that he could share another's burdens. (*Paneg.* 112)[15]

In the *Archidamus*, written about 366 B.C.E. to urge Sparta to war against Thebes, Isocrates mentions those whose

fields have been laid waste, their cities sacked, their people driven from their homes, their constitutions overturned, and the laws abolished. . . . They feel such distrust and such hatred of one another that they fear their fellow-citizens more than the enemy; instead of preserving the spirit of accord and mutual helpfulness which they enjoyed under our [Spartan] rule, they have become so unsocial that those who own property had rather throw their possession into the sea than lend aid to the needy, while those who are in poorer circumstances would less gladly find a treasure than seize the possession of the rich (τὰ τῶν ἐχόντων)[16] . . . and more people are in exile now from a single city than before from the whole of the Peloponnesus. But although the miseries (κακῶν) which I have recounted are so many, those which remain unmentioned far outnumber them; for all the distress and all the horror have come together in this one region. (*Archid.* 66–68, trans. Norlin, LCL)[17]

Toward the beginning of this work, Isocrates marvels

at the men who have ability in action or in speech that it has never occurred to them seriously to take to heart the conditions which affect all Greeks alike, or even to feel pity (ἐλεῆσαι) for the evil plight of Hellas, so shameful and dreadful, no part of which now remains that is not teeming full of war, uprisings, slaughter, and evils innumerable. [He refers to] renegades who, if we had any sense, we should not be permitting to come together into bands or, led by any chance leaders, to form armed contingents, composed of roving forces more numerous and powerful than are the troops of our own citizen forces. These armies do damage to only a small part of the domain of the king of Persia, but every Hellenic city they enter they utterly destroy, killing some, driving others

---

14. Cited by Alexander Fuks, "Isokrates and the Social-Economic Situation in Greece," 26 n. 33, now in *Social Conflict*, 61, with other key passages.

15. Cited by Fuks, "Isokrates," 37 n. 67.

16. This expression occurs quite often in Luke-Acts referring to the rich.

17. Cited by Fuks, "Isokrates," 33 n. 58.

into exile, and robbing still others of their possessions, furthermore, they treat
with indignity children and women, and not only dishonour the most beautiful
women, but from the others they strip off the clothing which they wear on
their persons, so that those who even when fully clothed were not to be seen
by strangers, were beheld naked by many men; and some women, clad in rags,
are seen wandering in destitution from lack of the bare necessities of life.
(*Archid.* 9–10)[18]

In a later work *On the Peace*, written about 355 B.C.E. just at the end of the
social war, he also speaks of the "Hellenes who are in need and, because of
their poverty, are now wandering from place to place" (24, trans. Norlin,
LCL).[19] And in the preface to the *Areopagiticus*, also written in the postwar
period about 355, he says he is anxious,

for I observe that those cities which think they are in the best circumstances
are wont to adopt the worst polities, and that those which feel the most secure
are most often involved in danger. The cause of this is that nothing of either
good or of evil visits mankind unmixed, but that riches (πλούτοις) and power
are attended and followed by folly, and folly in turn by license; and whereas
poverty and lowliness (ταπεινότησι) are attended by sobriety and great moder-
ation.... For we shall find that from a lot which seems to be inferior, men's fortunes generally advance to a better condition; whereas from one which
appears to be superior they are wont to change to a worse. (*Areopag.* 2–5)[20]

Based on these passages, which he says have never been studied, Alexander
Fuks draws several conclusions. First, "the problem of πενία καὶ πλοῦτος, of
poverty versus riches, and of the deep gulf between the 'haves' and the
'have nots' is, on examination, one of the major themes in Isokrates."[21] Second, the mass of the poor in Greece consisted of two groups—those who
have stayed at home and those who have left their homes.[22] Those who
stayed home were the urban poor, but the others were refugees, those who
have been ejected from the life of the *polis*, many of whom took up employment as mercenaries to make a living. The basic reason for their refugee status was poverty, the lack of daily necessities, and the expression Isocrates
used repeatedly to refer to daily necessities is the same as that found in the
Lord's Prayer (Luke 11:3, τὸ καθ' ἡμέραν).[23] The danger to the well-being of
Greek cities and the outrages committed are painted in lurid colors. The
dimensions of the problem are indeed problematic: if Philip decides on war
against Persia, "such is now the state of affairs in Hellas that it is easier to
get together a greater and stronger army from those who are wandering
from place to place than from those living as citizens in their own states"

18. Cited by Fuks, "Isokrates," 26 n. 33.
19. Cited by Fuks, "Isokrates," 28 n. 42.
20. Cited by Fuks, "Isokrates," 32 n. 52.
21. Fuks, "Isokrates," 21, also quoted above n. 3.
22. Ibid., 25.
23. Cf. *On the Peace* 46; *Panegyricus* 34, 168; *To Philip* 120.

(*Phil.* 96).[24] Third, Fuks concludes, Isocrates often described the situation of the poor, less often that of the rich.

This sketches the picture of the poor versus the rich in Isocrates. As noted above, in her Oxford dissertation on the rhetorician/historian Dionysius, Clemence Schultze argues that Isocrates was perhaps *the* major influence on Dionysius.[25] The vocabulary and some of the concerns in Isocrates and especially in the historian Dionysius reappear in a modified form in Luke-Acts. As had Isocrates, so Dionysius writes of political turmoil, of στάσις, in which he sees both political and socioeconomic factors. Like Isocrates, Dionysius writes of desperate poverty, of plebeians driven into exile, of the intransigence of the rich, and the potential for violence. And he stresses how close society is to a breakdown of the social order, yet one of Dionysius's major theses is that, unlike the Greeks, the Romans avoid chaos.[26] Instead of the evils, the κακά of Greece, actions in Rome are not ἀνήκεστον, not "beyond remedy"; in Rome there is a different and surprising outcome, that is, harmony or concord, ὁμόνοια.[27] Schultze concludes that as a central aspect of his historiographical purpose, Dionysius narrates history combining Greek stories of civic turmoil with an emphasis on Roman concord.[28] Dionysius's argument is that the Romans are Greeks, but Greeks in an even better, fuller sense. Dionysius presents Roman history as one of conflict, including the conflict of rich and poor, proud and humble, but the conflict reaches a *resolution* (*Ant. Rom.* 7.66.1).[29] I will briefly retell Dionysius's story of the first στάσις, that is, the first open conflict between rich and poor, proud and humble, in Rome. The first eleven volumes of Dionysius's history are still extant. Books 6 and 7 concern conflict between rich and poor, and they include many statements about and by the poor that Bolkestein denies were expressed in Greco-Roman culture and society.

This story about conflict between the rich and the poor, whom Dionysius also calls the proud and the humble, is found in *Ant. Rom.* 6.22–90 [unless otherwise specified, all following references will be to book 6]. The Romans have just put an end to foreign wars, but, Dionysius notes, civic strife

24. Fuks, "Isokrates," 30.

25. Schultze, "Dionysius"; and Emilio Gabba, "Political and Cultural Aspects of the Classicistic Revival in the Augustan Age," *Classical Antiquity* 1/1 (1982) 43–65. I will cite the edition and translation of Dionysius's *Roman Antiquities* by Earnest Cary (7 vols.; LCL; Cambridge, Mass.: Harvard University Press, 1937–50).

26. Schultze, "Dionysius," 48, 168, 175, 181, 221, and esp. chapter 10 (pp. 263–72) on Dionysius's narrative and Rome.

27. That is, the rich and poor in Rome listen and respond to each other's speeches. Note the context of Dionysius 7.66.1–3. The Greek ὁμόνοια was usually used to render the Latin *concordia*, a chief virtue in Roman political and domestic/social life. Personified *Concordia* was often depicted in marriage contexts. She had a temple on the west end of the Forum but was also associated with the vestal virgins. Cf. Suetonius, *Tiberius* 20; *Vitellius* 15.4.

28. Schultze, "Dionysius," 271.

29. Ibid., 272.

(στάσις) sprang up (22.1). The controversies resulted, he reports, in outrageous and shameless behavior—the plebeians, on the one hand, pretending that they were unable to pay their debts, and the moneylenders (δανεισταί), on the other hand, alleging that the misfortunes of war had been common to all (22.1; cf. 5.53, 63). At this point in Roman history, new consuls were elected, one of whom had the reputation of being a harsh, arrogant Republican, Appius Claudius (23.1; 24.1).[30] The consuls decide to divert the uproar in the city in the direction of a foreign war. They order the men of military age to report, but the plebeians refuse to do so. The second consul, Publius Servilius Priscus, thinks they ought to cure the cause of the sedition and abolish or diminish the debts of the plebeians. The Greek word used for the "abolition" of debts is ἄφεσις (23.3), the same verbal root that refers to forgiving debts in the Lord's Prayer (Luke 11:4). At the least, Servilius says, the debtors whose obligations are overdue ought not to be hauled off to prison, for men who are in want of the daily necessities of life (τῶν καθ' ἡμέραν, 23.3; cf. 56.3; 83.4, the same prepositional phrase as in the Lord's Prayer, Luke 11:3) might get together and adopt some desperate course.

At this point, several enemies attack Rome. The plot thickens: an elderly man appears in the Roman Forum dressed in rags, crying to the citizens for assistance, and many flock to hear him. As is typical in ancient historiography, he gives a speech:

> Having been born free, and having served in all the campaigns while I was of military age, and fought in 28 battles and often been awarded prizes for valour in the wars; then, when the oppressive times came that were reducing the commonwealth to the last straits, and having been forced to contract a debt to pay the contributions levied upon me; and finally, when my farm was raided by the enemy and my property in the city exhausted owing to the scarcity of provisions, having no means with which to discharge my debt, I was carried away as a slave by the money-lender, together with my two sons; and when my master ordered me to perform some difficult task and I protested against it, I was given a great many lashes with the whip. (26.1)

He then threw off his rags and showed his bleeding back, which produced a general lamentation. Poor persons ran about the city, and many who had been so enslaved ran out of the houses, their hair grown long, most of them being in chains and fetters. So the Forum was full of debtors who had broken their chains. Appius flees from the Forum, but Servilius begs the debtors to be quiet and demands that no moneylender should be permitted to hale any citizen to prison for a private debt. The next day the two consuls debate, Appius calling his fellow consul a flatterer of the people and a leader of the poor, Servilius in turn calling Appius harsh and arrogant, the

---

30. Cf. T. P. Wiseman, "The Legends of the Patrician Claudii," in *Clio's Cosmetics: Three Studies in Greco-Roman Literature* (Leicester: University, 1979) 57–139.

cause of evils in the state (27.1). The result is that with enemies invading, the plebeians refuse to enlist in the army and fight, and the city is full of disorder (31, 34). There is a trilogy of speeches with a full range of opinions evaluating the actions of the poor (35–36, 37, 39–43). The poor secede from the patricians and Rome (45), withdrawing to a nearby sacred mountain. They charge the patricians with having driven them from their country and with transforming them from free men into slaves; they challenge the patricians who come out to reconcile them to return to Rome "undisturbed by the poor and humble" (ὑπὸ τῶν πενήτων καὶ ταπεινῶν, 45.3). There is another trilogy of speeches to the senate: Menenius adopts a middle course (49–56), Valerius speaks for the poor (58), and Appius Claudius opposes them (59–64). The Roman senator Menenius is the moderate arguing for an accommodation between rich and poor:

> We are not the only people, nor the first, among whom poverty has raised sedition against wealth, and lowliness against eminence (ταπεινότης πρὸς ἐπι-φάνειαν), but *in nearly all states*, both great and small, the lower class is generally hostile to the upper (and in all these states the men in power, when they have shown moderation, have saved their countries, but when they have acted arrogantly, have lost not only their goods, but their lives as well).... (54.1)

The Lukan audience, presumably urban Christians located in some significant city in the eastern Mediterranean, would have heard the Magnificat in light of the tensions between rich and poor in its city as sketched in this speech; Menenius says this hostility is present "in nearly all states." To return to the story: one key problem is that the plebeians, the poor, have the right to declare or terminate war (66). Therefore the consuls choose ten senators to reconcile them by any means (69), and Valerius addresses them with a speech (71).

Lucius Junius [Brutus], one of the poor plebeians, responds with a speech (6.72–80) that Schultze claims is one of the most carefully constructed speeches in all of Dionysius's history, with numerous reminiscences of Demosthenes. Brutus gives a masterly account of the justice of the plebeian cause, the cause of the poor.[31] I recount some of this speech here because the Greek ideas in it help us understand key Lukan terminology beginning with the Magnificat, themes basic to Luke's two-volume history. The speech is delivered by one of the "poor" in Dionysius, with poor laborers, clients, and artisans gathered around him (51.1; 52.1). Note that, in general, the poor are those who must work for a living in contrast to those who have leisure. Yet the cultivated argument and concepts of the speech present a nobler character, again in keeping with the historiographical concerns of Dionysius.

He addresses those who are "humbled" before the patricians (72.3), arrogant men (οἱ ὑπερήφανοι) at whose hands they have suffered (72.3; cf. Luke

---

31. Schultze, "Dionysius," 212.

1:48, 51–52). The cause of the humble is just (72.5). He makes three points against the senators, the primary one having to do with justice. Brutus objects that the senators come to them as if they were the ones who had offended (ἡμαρτηκόσιν, 53.1) and offering the plebeians a favor. Rather, "having yourselves wronged us, you [arrogant patricians] stand in need of pardon and an amnesty. But as it is, you profess to be giving the pardon for which you ought to be asking, and prate boastfully of acquitting us (ἀφεῖσθαι) from the wrath of which you yourselves seek to be acquitted" (73.2). Brutus then surveys Roman history from the time of the early kings, surveying how the plebeians have been treated. The conclusion is that the plebeians have wasted their bodies in supporting the patricians' greed for power (75.2). The patricians have abused them like slaves (76.1). Even then, the humble folk (οἱ ταπεινοί) who had been treated so outrageously, allowed themselves to go on fighting for the patricians (76.2), having good hopes for the future. Repeatedly in wartime, they, the proud and stern, had been obliged to appeal to the humble and the despised (77.1). And now they offer no honors, no magistracies, and no relief from poverty (78.1). Brutus then repeatedly asks what might induce the plebeians to "trust" the patricians (the verb is πιστεύω).

> No [says Brutus], let them have the whole city to themselves and enjoy it with-out us, and let them reap alone every other advantage after they have driven the *humble and obscure* plebeians from the fatherland. As for us, let us depart whithersoever Heaven shall conduct us, feeling that we are leaving an alien place and not our own city. . . . We have not even the liberty of our own per-sons which we have purchased with many hardships. For some of these advan-tages have been destroyed by the many wars, some have been consumed by the scarcity of the necessaries of daily life (τὰ τῶν καθ' ἡμέραν[32] ἀναγκαίων), and of others we have been robbed by these haughty money-lenders (ὑπερ-ηφάνων δανειστῶν), for whom we poor wretches are at last obliged to till our own allotments, digging, planting, ploughing, tending flocks, and becoming fellow-slaves with our own slaves taken by us in war, some of us being bound with chains, some with fetters, and others, like the most savage of wild beasts, dragging wooden clogs and iron balls. . . . Accordingly, now that we are freed by Heaven from so many and so great evils (κακῶν), let us gladly fly from them, . . . taking as guides of our journey Fortune and the god who ever pre-serves us, and looking upon our liberty as our country and our valour as our wealth. For any land will receive us as partners (ὑποδέξεται . . . κοινωνούς). . . . (79.1–3)

And just as Luke picks Abraham, Moses, and David as ancestors of the *Gen-tile* Christian church, so Dionysius in this speech by Brutus, picks early *Greek* forefathers for the Romans. The humble poor are abandoning Rome:

> Of this let many Greeks and many barbarians serve us as examples, particu-larly the ancestors of both these men and ourselves; some of whom, leaving

32. On daily necessities, cf. 56.3; 7.37.2; and Luke 11:3.

Asia with Aeneas, came into Europe and built a city in the country of the Latins, and others, coming as colonists from Alba under the leadership of Romulus, built in these parts the city we are now leaving. . . . Those who removed from Troy were driven out by enemies, but we are driven hence by friends. . . . But fare you well and lead the life you choose, you who are so unwilling to associate as fellow-citizens and to share your blessing with those of a humbler estate (ἀκοινώνητα πρὸς τοὺς ταπεινοτέρους φρονοῦντες. (80.1–4)

The last phrase in this speech is an accusation that the proud are unwilling to have *koinōnia* with the humble.[33]

In a few sentences I conclude retelling this story. The senator Menenius responds, reminding the poor of a metaphor "quoted in all ancient histories: as the human body has many parts, so society has many classes" (86.1). In the end this symbol is so powerful that it persuades the poor to return to Rome. Menenius makes the following promise:

> We think it just that all those who have contracted debts and are unable to pay them should be relieved of their obligations (πάντας ἀφεῖσθαι τῶν ὀφλημάτων); and if the persons of any who are in default in their payments are already held under restraint . . . , it is our wish that these also shall be free, and we set aside their sentences. (83.4)

The phrase the senator here employs for relieving obligations includes the same verb and participle that occur in the Lord's Prayer: "forgive us our sins, for we ourselves *forgive* every one who is *indebted* to us" (Luke 11:4a).

Menenius asks Brutus to name a safeguard, and he asks for magistrates with power to relieve the threatened plebeians (87, 89; also 7.45, 55). For the first time in Roman history, the senate appoints five tribunes, including Brutus; these tribunes are declared inviolate by an oath of all the Romans over sacrificial victims and by prayer (89). Finally, an army is raised from among the plebeians to defend Rome against the invaders.

Without retelling another long story, I simply assert that the following narration in Dionysius's history tells of Coriolanus,[34] the "most illustrious man of his age" (6.94.2), who hated the poor plebeians (7.21.1), assumed a haughty air, and came to a disastrous end (7.21.4; 46.2, 6; 63.1; 65.2–3). Coriolanus says of himself, "though I was once looked upon as the most powerful of all men in the greatest city, I am now cast aside, forsaken, exiled, and humble" (ταπεινός; 8.1.5; 25.3; 32.3). He takes up arms against Rome, and when Romans ask him to reverse himself, he speaks about the gods as follows:

> since I enjoy the favouring breeze of Fortune in the wars I wage and everything that I attempt goes steadily forward for me, it is evident that I am a pious

33. This reference is to be added to those collected by Fuks, "Isokrates."

34. See Eralda Noè, "Ricerche su Dionigi d'Alicarnasso: la prima stasis a Roma e l'episodio de Coriolano," in *Ricerche de storiografia Graeca di età Romana* (ed. Emilio Gabba; Ricerche di storiografia antica I; Pisa: Giardini Editori e Stampatori, 1979) 21–116.

man and that my choice of conduct has been honourable. What, then, will be my fate if I change my course and endeavour to increase your power and humble theirs? Will it not be just the reverse, and shall I not incur the dire wrath of Heaven which avenges the injured, and just as by the help of the gods I from a low estate have become great (ἐκ ταπεινοῦ μέγας διὰ τοὺς θεοὺς ἐγενόμην), shall I not in turn from a great be brought again to a humble estate, and my sufferings become lessons to the rest of the world? These are the thoughts that occur to me concerning the gods.... (8.33.3)[35]

Finally, Coriolanus is stoned to death (8.59.1), although in death, honored by Rome (8.62). Nearly two volumes in Dionysius tell how the deity humbled this proud man.

I draw the following conclusions after reading these stories of the empowerment of the Roman poor and of the humbling of their proud opponent, Coriolanus. First, both in Dionysius's story of the first sedition in Rome and in Luke's Magnificat (Luke 1:48), the deity watches over the humble. Second, in Dionysius's narrative of the haughty Coriolanus and in the Magnificat, the deity humbles the proud, the rich (Luke 1:51). Third, both in Isocrates, in Dionysius's stories, and in the Lord's Prayer (Luke 11:3), a key need of the poor is for the necessities of daily life; Dionysius and Luke use the same Greek phrase to refer to these needs. Fourth, one primary need expressed by the poor is for their debts to be forgiven; in Dionysius a Roman senator promises the poor the forgiveness of their debts/ obligations, and in the Lukan Lord's prayer, employing the same verbs, the one praying tells the Lord that he or she has forgiven debts as he or she asks for forgiveness of sins.

I have already argued that this language in the historian Dionysius has one source in the rhetoric of Isocrates. I point now to two further sources, especially for the language about forgiving debts. As Robert Sloan has discussed the demand in Lev 25:10 that debts be forgiven, which proclaims a "release" (ἄφεσις) for the land after forty-nine years.[36] And if a fellow Israelite is humbled by slavery, he too is to be released (Lev 25:39–40; cf. Isa 61:1). The language about the sabbatical year in the Book of the Covenant is even closer to Luke: in the seventh year, Israel is to let the land rest, so that their poor shall eat (οἱ πτωχοὶ τοῦ ἔθνους σου, Exod 23:11 LXX; the same word for poor as in Jesus' inaugural sermon in Luke 4:18, which quotes Isa 61:1). This language is revised by the Deuteronomist, and the language exhorting Israel to care for the poor is expanded: a poor person (ἐνδεής) is to be lent as much as he wants (Deut 15:8) and needs (15:10). The law is to be

---

35. Hildebrecht Hommel, "Der bald erhöhn, bald stürzen kann," in *Sebasmata: Studien zur antiken Religionsgeschichte und zum frühen Christentum* (WUNT 32; Tübingen: Mohr-Siebeck, 1984) 2:3–9, a reference I owe to Prof. Hans Dieter Betz.

36. Robert Bryan Sloan, Jr., *The Favorable Year of the Lord: A Study of Jubilary Theology in the Gospel of Luke* (Austin: Scolia, 1977).

read at the feast of Tabernacles every seven years in the time of the year of release (31:10; cf. Neh 10:31). There is some evidence in Josephus and 1 Maccabees that this year of release for the land was kept in the time of Alexander the Great (Josephus, *Ant.* 14.343), during the Maccabean revolt (1 Macc 6:49, 53), and later under Herod the Great (*Ant.* 14.475).

But how are we to understand the relationship between these texts, the first from the Book of the Covenant, the earliest body of Hebrew law, the second, a revision and expansion of the earlier law by the Deuteronomist, and the third a phrase in the Lord's Prayer that also refers to forgiving debts. Luke's congregations are often understood as Gentiles who are engaged in intense Bible study, who then take the terms, values, and institutions they read in their Bibles and employ them in Greco-Roman society where they were totally foreign.

This opinion, expressed by both Bolkestein and Esler, is incorrect. On the contrary, Luke is reinforcing and reinterpreting values based on some of the most important stories in Roman tradition, values supported, for example, in one of the most carefully constructed speeches in Dionysius's twenty-volume history about the origins of the office of Roman tribunes, stories as important to them as are stories about George Washington, Abraham Lincoln, and Martin Luther King, Jr., leaders during times of revolutionary change, are to North Americans. Both we and the Romans remember, value, and learn from such stories.

These values that relate rich and poor, proud and humble, and hold open a possibility of the reversal of roles are not only Roman but also Greek; in fact they are Stoic. Andrew Erskine, in a recent book on the Hellenistic Stoa's political thought, has argued this case.[37] His primary evidence comes from four of Plutarch's biographies, his lives of *Agis* and *Cleomenes*, both kings of Sparta, and of *Tiberius Gracchus* and *Gaius Gracchus*, Roman consuls.[38] In one of these biographies, we are told that king Cleomenes' teacher was Sphaerus the Stoic (Plutarch, *Cleomenes* 2.2; 11.2) and that Tiberius Gracchus's teacher was Blossius (*Tiberius Gracchus* 8.4; 17.4; 20.3), also a Stoic. I accept Erskine's argument, but there is a continuing debate among classicists about the amount of Stoic influence. Here I am primarily concerned not to argue that these ideas are Stoic but to illustrate the appeal to these ideas beyond Isocrates and Dionysius.

Cleomenes became king of Sparta about 241 B.C.E. He sent eighty rich senators into exile, charging them with subverting the ancient form of government (Plutarch, *Cleomenes* 10.1, 3). He wanted to rid Sparta of imported

37. Andrew Erskine, *The Hellenistic Stoa: Political Thought and Action* (Ithaca, N.Y.: Cornell University Press, 1990) esp. chapters 5–7.

38. On these stories, see Bolkestein, *Wohltätigkeit*, 357–59, 372–73; Fuks, *Social Conflict*, 230–59; and now especially Caluse Mossé, "Women in the Spartan Revolutions of the Third Century B.C.," in *Women's History and Ancient History* (ed. Sarah B. Pomeroy; Chapel Hill: University of North Carolina Press, 1991) 138–53.

curses—namely, luxury and extravagance, debts and usury—and evils older than those—namely, poverty and wealth; thus he wanted to cure the disease of his country like a wise physician (10.4). For the salvation of Sparta, Cleomenes changes the constitution back to that of their founder, Lycurgus: "the whole land should be common property, debtors should be set free from their debts (χρεῶν τοὺς ὀφείλοντας ἀπαλλάττειν), and foreigners should be examined and rated, in order that the strongest of them might be made Spartan citizens and help to preserve the state by their arms" (10.6). Sphaerus the Stoic helped him arrange all this. But Cleomenes was opposed by the Achaeans, especially by their general, Aratus (15.1), and this attitude delivered the cause of Greece to the Macedonians (16.1). Instead of accepting Cleomenes, a descendant of Heracles and king of Sparta who was attempting to restore the ancient constitution, Aratus denounced him, saying that he had abolished wealth and restored poverty, and so Aratus cast all Greece down before the Macedonians, according to Plutarch (16.5). In his discussion, Erskine concludes: "It was the [Spartan] revolution itself which was responsible for elevating the equality of property into its central position and in this respect the revolution reflected contemporary Stoic ideas about equality."[39] But the later members of the Stoa were embarrassed by this association of Stoics with the Spartan revolution in third century B.C.E., and distanced themselves from it.[40]

Plutarch also narrates the life of *Tiberius Gracchus*. In war Romans won some land from their neighbors and sold some of it, but the rest they made common land, which for a small rent they assigned to the poor and indigent among the citizens. The rich offered larger rents and drove out the poor (8.1). The poor, ejected from their land, no longer showed eagerness for military service. In Dionysius this is already a familiar pattern.[41] Italy was filled with gangs of foreign slaves, by whose aid the rich cultivated their estates, from which they had driven away the free citizens. Tiberius Gracchus was elected tribune and, incited by Blossius the Stoic (who had been a friend of Antipater of Tarsus [8.5]), decided to recover for the poor the public land, proposing an agrarian law to do so (8.7). But the men of wealth were led by their greed to hate the law and the lawgiver and accused him of stirring up a general revolution (9.3). Tiberius took the rostrum and "pleaded for the poor" (λέγοι περὶ τῶν πενήτων, 9.4):

> The wild beasts that roam over Italy ... have every one of them a cave or lair to lurk in; but the men who fight and die for Italy enjoy the common air and light, indeed, but nothing else; houseless and homeless they wander about with their wives and children [cf. Isocrates]. ... [T]hey fight and die to support

---

39. Erskine, *Hellenistic Stoa,* 142.
40. Ibid., 149.
41. E. Badian, "Tiberius Gracchus and the Roman Revolution," *ANRW* 1.1 (1972) 668–731; p. 701 n. 100 points out that Dionysius, *Ant. Rom.* 6.68–80 seem to be modeled on Gaius Gracchus.

others in wealth and luxury, and though they are styled masters of the world, they have not a single clod of earth that is their own. (9.5, trans. Perrin, LCL)

There was high conflict over the agrarian law. Tiberius Gracchus illegally ejects his fellow tribune, Octavius, from office, after which the law passed. When the king of Pergamum in Asia Minor died in 133 B.C.E., naming the Roman people as his heir, Tiberius proposed giving the money to the citizens who received a parcel of the public land (14.1). During the vote, the party of the rich determine to kill Tiberius (18.2), and they beat him to death with sticks and stones (19.6), the first sedition at Rome to end in the death of citizens.

Before concluding, I need to make some observations about the date of these stories and then to discuss the relationship between the theory in the stories and actual practice. The stories' date and their relation to the historiographical tradition has been examined most effectively by Jürgen von Ungern-Sternberg.[42] The conflict between patricians and plebeians began with the first secession, dated in 494–493 B.C.E.,[43] centuries before Dionysius wrote under Caesar Angustus.[44] Von Ungern-Sternberg argues that "the problems of the present were included in the presentation of the past either in order to make the narrative more lively, or to comment indirectly on matters of contemporary concern."[45] He characterizes "matters of contemporary concern" as follows:

From the time of the Gracchi (i.e., the last third of the second century B.C.) political life in Rome was dominated by two political methods fundamentally opposed to each other. On the one side were those politicians who consistently tried to realize their goals in association with the majority of the Senate; they were called *optimates*. On the other side were those who at least occasionally aimed at succeeding primarily through the popular assembly; these were the *populares*. . . . It is easy to recognize a resemblance between this antithesis (*optimates/populares*) and the opposition between patricians and plebeians. For contemporaries such a resemblance was even more obvious. . . .[46]

In other words, "the Roman historians used as a model the propaganda of the *optimates* against the great *populares* of the late Republic, especially the

42. Jürgen von Ungern-Sternberg, "The Formation of the 'Annalistic Tradition': The Example of the Decemvirate," in *Social Struggles in Archaic Rome*, 77–104; idem, "Überlegungen zur frühen römischen Überlieferung im Lichte der Oral-Tradition-Forschung," in *Vergangenheit in mündlicher Überlieferung* (Stuttgart: Teubner, 1988) 237–65; and "Die Wahrnehmung des 'Ständekampfes' in der römischen Geschichtsschreibung," in *Staat und Staatlichkeit in der frühen Römischen Republik: Akten eines Symposiums, 12-15 Juli, Freie Universität Berlin* (Stuttgart: Steiner, 1990) 92–102. I am grateful to Prof. Kurt Raaflaub for these references.

43. Von Ungern-Sternberg, "Formation," 92.

44. Emilio Gabba observes that the date of 7 B.C.E. in Dionysius, *Ant. Rom.* 1.7.2 is of little help for a precise date since the preface was published separately (*Dionysius and the History of Archaic Rome* [Berkeley: University of California Press, 1991] 1 with n. 2).

45. Von Ungern-Sternberg, "Formation," 87.

46. Ibid., 90–91.

events of the year 133 and the tribunate of Ti. Sompronius Gracchus."[47] Nevertheless, because it is interested in providing practical examples for the statesman and citizen, Roman historical tradition is separate from the historical novel.[48] The stories retold above were first written down by the rulers of Rome, the nobility, around 200, and their memory reached as far back as their fathers or grandfathers, that is, as far as 287 B.C.E., the last secession of the plebeians.[49] Von Ungern-Sternberg concludes that the story of the first secession was told according to the model of the last one.[50] That Roman historical traditions were first written down about 200 and then "transformed by each generation of Roman historians"[51] makes these stories all the more relevant to understanding cultural values at the time of the rise of early Christianity and to understanding its first historian, Luke.

A final question before summing up: Are these stories about the rich forgiving the debts of the poor in Dionysius (e.g., *Ant. Rom.* 2.56.3; 3.8.4; 9.2) and in Luke (11:3–4; 16:5) simple theory without any practical results? Were they merely an ideology that salved the consciences of the rich? Fuks has already discussed a number of cases in which the theory became practice.[52] I will not repeat his observations here, but will add a later example of the practice of forgiving debts and one touching the disputed relationship between debts and imprisonment.[53]

Ephesus issued two decrees concerning the war with Mithridates ca. 86–85 B.C.E. The first includes a declaration of loyalty to Rome and sketches the historical circumstances of the war "without great regard for the truth."[54] The second establishes a commission and records Ephesus's preparations for war.

> To the end that the city and the sanctuary of Artemis might be successfully defended, all those who by reason of indebtedness to the Goddess or to the city had been deprived of citizenship or imprisoned were now restored to their former status; likewise those against whom judgements had been ren-

47. Ibid., 92.

48. Ibid., 100. This reinforces the view that Luke-Acts is more indebted to the genre of political history than to the novel.

49. Von Ungern-Sternberg, "Ständekampfes," 98–101.

50. Ibid., 101.

51. Von Ungern-Sternberg, "Formation," 89. For suggestions about Plutarch's motives in retelling these stories, see Heinz Gerd Ingenkamp, "Plutarchs 'Leben der Gracchen': Eine Analyse," *ANRW* (1992) 2.33.6.4298–4346, at p. 4326: "The positive evaluation of M. Octavius [Tiberius' co-consul] shows that Plutarch is not taking a political position but recommending a quality of political relationships" (my translation).

52. Fuks, "Τοῖς ἀπορουμένοις κοινωνεῖν: The Sharing of Property by the Rich with the Poor in Greek Theory and Practice," 56–63 on practice.

53. I am grateful to Prof. Richard Oster for assistance in locating these inscriptions. For one example of his own work, see "The Ephesian Artemis as an Opponent of Early Christianity," *JAC* 19 (1976) 24–44.

54. David Magie, *Roman Rule in Asia Minor to the End of the Third Century after Christ* (Princeton: Princeton University Press, 1950) 1:224.

dered because of their debts were released from their obligations. The decree also promised full citizenship to all resident aliens, freedmen and strangers who took up arms, and freedom and the status of resident aliens to all the city's slaves who did likewise....

Encouraged by the example of Ephesus, other communities also began to rid themselves of the liberator now turned tyrant.... Mithridates ... then resorted to a desperate expedient. All the Greek cities which had not revolted he restored to their previous status of freedom and autonomy; he added, however, the provision that all debts should be cancelled and all slaves set free. This dubious step did, indeed, win him, as he had purposed, the support of a considerable element of the population, but it also won him the hatred of the richer citizens and the owners of slaves.[55]

Relevant lines of the inscription read as follows:

From whatever has been borrowed from temple resources, all debtors (πάντας ὀφείλοντας) and administrators (of loans) are free from the debts (ἀπολελύσθαι ἀπὸ τῶν ὀφειλημάτων), with the exception of those who by the committee or the ones appointed by the money-lenders gave loans in exchange for encumbrances (ὑποθῆκαι) they are passed by during the coming year, until the situation of the people improves (lines 35–40).[56]

Dionysius narrated Rome's legendary origins in a social context in which these events were recent history, and Luke's Christian readers were aware of both.

A second example of practice, relating to the question of imprisonment for debts, is an edict of Tiberius Julius Alexander, a Jewish prefect of Egypt, granting relief to oppressed Egyptians; it was published on 6 July 68 C.E.[57] The prefect contrasts those from the upper classes with those from the farms (line 6: ... εὐσχημονεστάτων καὶ τῶν γεωργούντων), "and all of them were finding fault with abuses" (line 5) about which they made petitions (line 8).

Whereas some (officials) have had loans of others (ἀλλότρια δάνεια, line 15) assigned to themselves and then on pretense of interest due to the State (δημοσίων) have had some persons thrown into debtor's prison (εἰς ἄλλας φυλακάς) or other confinement facilities, which I know for a fact to have been abolished (ἀναιρεθείσας, line 16) so that recovery of money may be had out of properties and not out of the persons (who owe the money), I, in keeping with the decision of Divine Augustus, order that no one shall assign to himself, under

---

55. Ibid., 225.

56. *Inschriften Griechischer Städte aus Kleinasien*, Band 11.1: *Die Inschriften von Ephesos*, Teil 1a, Nr. 1–47 (Texte) (ed. Hermann Wankel; Bonn: Rudolf Habelt, 1979) #8, p. 51.

57. M. McCrum and A. G. Woodhead, *Select Documents of the Principates of the Flavian Emperors including the Year of Revolution A.D. 68–96* (Cambridge: Cambridge University Press, 1961) #328, pp. 88–92. Also *CIG* III #4957, pp. 445–54, 1236–38. Trans. Frederick W. Danker, *Benefactor: Epigraphic Study of a Graeco-Roman and New Testament Semantic Field* (St. Louis: Clayton, 1982) #51, pp. 305–9.

pretense of seeking the interests of the State, loans from others for which he did not himself originally contract (ἃ μὴ αὐτὸς ἐξ ἀρχῆς ἐδάνεισεν, line 17), and in general no free persons, except a criminal, are to be subject to any kind of confinement, and except for those who are in debt to (Caesar's) privy purse they are not to be remanded to debtor's prison. . . . (μηδ᾽ ὅλως κατακλεῖσθαί τινας ἐλευθέρους εἰς φυλακὴν ἡντινοῦν, εἰ μὴ κακοῦργον, μηδ᾽ εἰς τὸ πρακτόρειον ἔξω τῶν ὀφειλόντων εἰς τὸν κυριακὸν λόγον, lines 17–18).[58]

Whether debtors, and if so which ones, could be sent to prison was an issue at the time of the legendary founding of Rome as narrated by Dionysius, and it remained a primary social question in the century in which Luke wrote.

I make some concluding observations about these stories and their relationship to Luke-Acts. There is a cluster of key Greek terms and values: in nearly every Greek city there is tension between the rich and the poor. Dionysius calls these same two groups the proud (οἱ ὑπερήφανοι) and the humble (οἱ ταπεινοί). One of the major themes of Greco-Roman historiography, as exemplified in Dionysius, is that this tension does not lead to chaos; rather the Roman rich listen to speeches of the poor and work out an accommodation, so that there is *koinōnia* and concord. The stories recounting the opposition of Appius Claudius and of Coriolanus to the humble poor that I recounted are set about 500 B.C.E., but they reflect the concern of later centuries with similar conflicts. In these stories, the humble, poor, unknown Brutus is elevated to be tribune of the Roman people, and the haughty, proud Coriolanus, the most illustrious man of his age, is humbled and finally stoned to death because of his opposition to the poor. And in Isocrates, "mercy" for the poor is a positive value. Further, the constant concern of the poor is for daily necessities, for daily bread. Their major problem is their poverty, and their need and demand is that the moneylenders forgive their debts, not sending them to labor in chains.

Bolkestein's and Esler's typical opinion that Luke is introducing novel values to Gentile Christian congregations fundamentally misunderstands the social ethics of the Gospel. Rather, Luke is reinforcing these Gentiles' pre-Christian values. Greeks and Romans who retold the stories of Brutus and Coriolanus, of Cleomenes and the Gracchae, knew that providence watches over the poor, who live with the rich in Greco-Roman cities, and that the rich who mistreat them will be humbled. The Gospel of Luke reinforces these values. The Hellenistic Christian confession in Philippians 2, surely known by the author of our Gospel, confesses that Christ "*humbled* himself, being obedient unto death, and that God *highly exalted* him" (2:8–9). Analogously, Peter's sermon on Pentecost proclaims that Christ was not abandoned in *Hades*, but rather *exalted* to the right hand of God (Acts 2:27, 31, 33, citing Ps 15:8–11 LXX). However, the rich man who feasted daily

---

58. *CIG* III, insert between pp. 446 and 447; also p. 449. Trans. Danker, *Benefactor*, 307.

while ignoring the poor man at his gate was indeed abandoned in *Hades*, while Lazarus was exalted to Abraham's bosom (Luke 16:19–31). Key terms (died, buried, resurrection from the dead, the prophets, repent, and especially "Hades") connect the reversal in Luke 16 with the christological reversal in Peter's Pentecost sermon in Acts 2. Greeks and Romans knew analogous stories, those concerning the elevation of Brutus to the tribuneship and the humiliation of Coriolanus, the most illustrious man of his age, who hated the poor. The deity worshiped by Gentiles before and after their conversion watches over the poor. Rich Christians know that if they mistreat the poor, they, like the one of their number portrayed in Luke 16, will be humbled by the God who exalted the slave girl Mary and who raised the humiliated Christ from Hades, exalting him to God's right hand. Every time they pray the Lord's Prayer in their liturgy, asking God to forgive their sins, they must testify to God that they have forgiven debts of the poor.

Finally, I suggest that this interpretation of Luke-Acts as Hellenistic historiography is closer to the Mosaic story of salvation than are the individualistic interpretations of Luke as a biography of the individual hero Jesus or of Acts as a novel recounting the adventures of the individuals Peter and Paul. Luke-Acts is a political history of the economic responsibility of the rich among the people of God for the poor, affirmed already in the Book of the Covenant. Responsibility of the rich for the poor occurs in the constitution of this people, that is, in the institution of Jubilee and sabbatical years in Exodus 23, Deuteronomy 15, and Leviticus 25. But just as Deuteronomy updates and reinterprets Exodus, so Luke updates and reinterprets both in light of stories, values, and terminology well known, although intensely disputed, in Greco-Roman culture. The disputes whose terms Luke is employing were so intense that they resulted in the death of Spartan kings, Roman consuls, and their supporters. Luke-Acts is the translation and interpretation of the word of God given first in the Book of the Covenant into the language of Isocrates, Dionysius, and Plutarch. Ancient Israel knew that God cares for the poor. Greeks and Romans knew stories about the powerful *daimōn* humiliating powerful leaders who hated the poor. Lukan Christians who worship God pray that all might have the necessities of daily life and confess that they have contributed toward that end by forgiving debts of the poor. Luke's Gospel proclaims that God raised the humiliated Jesus from Hades to the right hand of God and exalted Lazarus, starving at the rich man's gate, to the bosom of Abraham.

CHAPTER 15

Visualizing the "Real" World of Acts 16: Toward Construction of a Social Index

L. Michael White

In previous generations of scholarship on earliest Christianity it was possible to conceive of ideas and abstractions, especially the eternal truths of theology, as distinct and detachable from social and historical reality.[1] The realization that such detachment is not possible, that theological postulates are part and parcel of larger constructs of human knowledge, and hence are socially conditioned and maintained, has produced a revolutionary change of perspective for current scholarship, and no less for contemporary culture. In this current endeavor Wayne Meeks holds a singular position. Meeks's own use of the archaeological and historical materials as background to understanding and describing the social context of Pauline cities is, therefore, exemplary, not only for its innovation but also for its prudence. For the full appreciation of the *realia* remains one of the most complex tasks still open to those who wish to explore the social world of the early Christians.[2] Far too often it is assumed that one need only

1. See my article "Adolf Harnack and the 'Expansion' of Early Christianity: A Reappraisal of Social History," *TSC* 5 (1985–86) 97–127, esp. 99–104.
2. In 1973 when a new working group on the Social World of Early Christianity was constituted in the Society of Biblical Literature, Wayne Meeks co-chaired the proceedings. In one of their first sessions a paper presented by Jonathan Z. Smith (subsequently published as "The Social Description of Early Christianity," *RSR* 1 [1975] 19–25) set the stage for much of the research that has carried on to the present, just as the study of social history has become a regular component of the SBL program through the continuation of the Social History group. In his paper, Smith identified four main areas of research: social description of early Christians, analysis of social organization and institutions, the application of sociological theory, and "the achievement of a genuine *social history*" that would "incorporate a comprehensive knowledge of the *realia* [meaning archaeological and documentary data] with social and political history and theology within an informed theoretical framework" (p. 19). Much of the field since that time has followed one of the first three lines, or some middle ground between them. The integration of the *realia* remains the most complex.

describe the archaeological remains in order to "visualize," as it were, the very footprints of Paul on the Areopagus in Athens or along the Via Egnatia in Philippi. To be sure, the guidebooks and curio shops are glad to assist. But the process is more complicated than that, and for the guidance of Wayne Meeks in helping us to see this more clearly, this small case-study is offered as a token of gratitude.

"Visualizing" in Focus

What is the task or goal of applying archaeological data and methods to the field of New Testament study? To some it might seem that "visualizing" the New Testament world implies nothing more than bringing the story to life. One thinks, then, of Adolf Deissmann or, even more so perhaps, of Sir William Ramsay, tracing the footsteps of Paul.[3] Theirs was a quest to reconstruct the world of Paul through the burgeoning fields of archaeology, epigraphy, and papyrology.

Yet it must be remembered that in Ramsay's day the goal of that quest was governed by different attitudes toward both archaeology and the New Testament. For Ramsay, working before the turn of the century, it was a mere two decades since Heinrich Schliemann had rediscovered Troy (and then Mycenae), at about the same time that a French team was just beginning an archaeological survey of ancient Macedonia, including Thessalonika and Philippi. Also visiting with the French team during this period, and eagerly expecting fresh materials for New Testament research, was Ernest Renan.[4] But it is that image of Schliemann, with a shovel in one hand and a copy of Homer in the other, that should also cause us to be cautious. Rashly using Homer as his guidebook, Schliemann probably destroyed the very part of Troy which he so fervently sought. Now the field of archaeology uses different measures, and the most important is "context." So, too, we must be cautious in applying social description approaches using archaeological data to literary texts. All too often reckless enthusiasm for "bringing the biblical story to life" has resulted in scurrying hither and yon for "facts" by which to bolster meager elements in the text, but with no real evidence for a historical connection. While such use of the archaeological record may provide background, it does not guarantee concrete data by which to generate an index of historical contexts. Such an approach runs

3. See, e.g., A. Deissmann, *Paul: A Study in Social and Religious History* (2nd ed.; New York: Harper, 1927) 29–51; William Ramsay, *St. Paul the Traveler and Roman Citizen* (London: Hodder & Stoughton, 1897) 213–37 (which, of course, presupposes much of his earlier work and travels).

4. L. Heuzey and H. Daumet, *Mission archéologique de Macédoine* (Paris: Bocard, 1869–76). Renan's *Paulus* appeared in 1869.

the risk of becoming nothing more than an "illustrated Bible" and may well distort rather than clarify.[5]

As a test case for future discussions, I should like to suggest some lines of contextual analysis, by integrating archaeological, social, and exegetical data, for the story in Acts 16:11–40—Paul's arrival at Philippi during the so-called second missionary journey. The raw itinerary may well be loosely based in fact, since we also have Paul's own firsthand references to his initial visit and its difficulties, although the details are otherwise obscure (1 Thess 2:2; Phil 1:3–6; cf. 2 Cor 8:2; 9:2). That the travelogue reflected in Acts 16:11–12 is typical is substantiated by Paul's own accounts (2 Cor 2:12), albeit from a later trip not fully accounted for in Acts. Still, the story in Acts 16 offers two cases of historical interest, since they support the establishment of Christian communities in households, a pattern reflected in Pauline epistolary address and central to the situation of several of the letters.[6] Thus, there seem to be points of correlation to the historical events and social environment of the Pauline mission even though the details of Acts 16 are otherwise unsubstantiated from other historical sources, including Paul himself. But how can one go farther in drawing precise historical correlations without also giving too much credence to the Acts narrative or to later legendary materials based on it, such as the so-called "prison of St. Paul" (part of a fifth-century basilical complex)?

Here it may be the case that the house-church and the early development of the synagogue would offer a likely candidate for application of archaeological data to the discussion.[7] It has been observed previously that some of the descriptive language in Luke-Acts corresponds directly to patterns of building and donation, noting the two cases in Luke 7:4 and Acts 18:7.[8] At this point, however, the task of focusing the picture becomes more difficult in two areas. First, the attempt to correlate the details of the accounts in Acts either with direct evidence from Philippi or with the information available from Paul's own correspondence proves to be more

5. See Eric M. Meyers and L. M. White, "Jews and Christians in a Roman World," *Archaeology* 42 (1989) 26–33; I have also made some of these observations on the need for "social indexing" (in contrast to the creation of an "illustrated Bible") in an article entitled "Scaling the Strongman's Court (Luke 11:21)," *Foundations and Facets Forum* 3 (1987) 11.

6. Acts 16:5, 33–34; cf. 1 Cor 16:19; Rom 16:5, 23; Phlm 2. Cf. W. Meeks, *The First Urban Christians: The Social World of the Apostle Paul* (New Haven and London: Yale University Press, 1983) 74–84; A. J. Malherbe, *Social Aspects of Early Christianity* (2nd ed.; Philadelphia: Fortress, 1983) 60–91.

7. So J. Murphy-O'Connor, *St. Paul's Corinth: Texts and Archaeology* (Wilmington: Michael Glazier, 1983) 153–67. Even so, the treatment of archaeological materials in this work should be used with due caution.

8. L. M. White, *Building God's House in the Roman World: Architectural Adaptation among Pagans, Jews, and Christians* (Baltimore: Johns Hopkins University Press, 1990); repr. as *The Social Origins of Christian Architecture*, vol. 1: *Architectural Adaptation among Pagans, Jews, and Christians* (HTS; Minneapolis: Fortress, 1995) 86.

problematic than Ramsay and others have assumed. Second, the simple terms οἶκος and οἰκία present us with a broad range of architectural, social, economic, and symbolic indicators, depending on historical and semantic contexts. Thus, one can neither rationalize simply the data from literary and archaeological sources nor pit them against one another as irreconcilable.

CONSTRUCTING A SOCIAL INDEX

For this reason, I prefer to speak of constructing a social index by which to correlate archaeological, historical, and literary evidence in descriptive categories.[9] Let us take the example of housing for a moment. In order to create such a correlation scale for literary and archaeological data, one might wish to arrive at economic, topographic, demographic, or sociographic indices for a given locality or context. Such information might be that of a census record—better still, supplemented with a realtor's guide—and given such data one may develop a profile by which to place any house and its occupants within the measurable scales of the society at large. The basic housing descriptors, then, are easily imagined: a peristyle house in the theater quarter of Delos; an insula just off the Decumanus at Ostia; a Roman villa-estate on the road from Pompeii to Herculaneum; or a private bathing establishment off the Decumanus at Philippi. To the social historian these phrases may deliver a wealth of information about the social context just as would comparable descriptors relative to scales of our own day: a two bedroom Cape in an older neighborhood of Cambridge; a brownstone on the Lower East Side; a six-bedroom "Mediterranean" (with pool) on an ocean-view bluff in Malibu; or a townhouse on Prince's Gardens (just behind the V & A) in Knightsbridge. Intuitively we perceive the social and economic scales behind even minimal descriptive detail. Our mental decoders decipher and assess them in a flash because we have the appropriate contextual knowledge, acquired through experience and convention, by which to understand what is not clearly detailed in these coded descriptions of social reality. The scales are time and location specific. We may next put these data together with demographic and prosopographic information in order to develop a more complete picture. Developing the same resonance for the ancient contexts takes more time, and caution. The key is social context. After all, much of this context is left unstated precisely

9. I first made some of these suggestions in my article "Scaling the Strongman's Court," which deals with four "householder" parables in Luke in order to suggest what kind of housing or social reality might be in the author's view. The analogy that follows on housing patterns is drawn from the same, although it has been elaborated for the present discussion. I will also return, by way of the conclusion, to some of the analysis of Lukan Gospel materials treated there by suggesting lines of continuity with the sections of Acts to be discussed in the body of this article.

because it is commonly assumed information, at least in the conventional-ized knowledge of a defined social context. It is part of the *realia* just as much as the fact that one hardly needs to explain, at least for those from a certain socially defined realm of knowledge, that the "Lower East Side" clearly refers to Manhattan, or "the V & A" to a London landmark, the Victo-ria and Albert Museum.

There are, in addition, the more symbolic uses of the semantic field of house and household, which are equally determined by the historical con-texts of the environment. To hear an Archie Bunker say, "A *man's* home is *his* castle," reflects interwoven semantic and conceptual categories, which form part of the implicit template of symbolic social structures reaching beyond physical dwelling places to familial ideals and gender relations. Indeed, despite its roots in English common law of a past century, one notes an implied familial social structure (with quasi-legal ramifications) that is con-text specific both in time and place. One will also detect a subtle economic inversion in this application of the term "castle." Thus, the literary fiction (a satire not unlike elements in Lucian for the Roman world, perhaps) func-tions within a contextualized social matrix and is made more "real" by its appropriation of a semantic convention. In this case, it must be noticed that the historical and cultural contexts behind such implied social structures, and even the rhetorical stance of the participants (whether actual individu-als or fictionalized characters), are equally in evidence, while the precise nature of the "housing" reference (at least in architectural or spatial terms) may become secondary.

To sharpen the focus, consider overhearing our Londoner (mentioned above) talk about going back to the Knightsbridge "flat" after spending the weekend at the country home. The "flat," as cued by the neighborhood, turns out to be a complete townhouse with living quarters on three levels above a ground floor and basement let out for a chic art-and-antiques shop and with apartments for the domestic staff on the top floor. One person's "flat" is another's "castle" in the relative world of socioeconomic status scales. At times, also, the two types of scales overlap and converge, as in the common description of another character type, Willy Loman: "He was look-ing for the American dream— a house in the suburbs with a two-car garage." This seemingly simple phrase yields an array of sociographic indices (including topographic, architectural, and economic scales) *as well as* a sym-bolic reference scale ("American dream"), all of which are only locatable within a specific historical and cultural context. It captures a certain reality, even though both the character and the story are entirely fictional.

That we may expect similar kinds of symbolized rhetorical and semantic conventionalization in the ancient sources will be seen readily enough when one observes Pliny the Younger saying that he possessed only "moderate resources," which were strained by his senatorial position.[10] Compared to whom? Elsewhere he describes his villa retreat at Laurentinum, one of six estates he owned outside of Rome itself. Even with his rather elaborate detail of the plan and amenities, the task of reconstructing the architecture without direct archaeological evidence remains precarious. Clearly, Pliny has not given a complete picture, and he himself says that it was "spacious enough but not sumptuous."[11] Again, one wonders about the relative scales for comparison. Moreover, Pliny was self-conscious of the fact that the goal of such literary description was not precise physical detail but rather an emotive visualization, or what we might call a not-quite-factual rendering for the sake of aesthetic and rhetorical effect.[12] While there were certainly richer individuals in the early principate, Pliny was still extremely wealthy. Despite his own rhetorical claims to "living frugally," he lived well and was lavishly honored for his extensive public benefactions. In other words, for Pliny liberality (*liberalitas*) and frugality (*frugalitas*) in matters relating to the management of his wealth and his villa estates were cultivated and corre-lated out of his sense of social status (*dignitas*).[13] In this case, even without the direct archaeological evidence one is able to gain a rather clear sense of the scale and social setting of Pliny's villas by using comparative domestic architecture as an approximate guide for the physical plan and by factoring the rhetorical, literary, and semantic nuances into the total picture.

10. Pliny, *Ep.* 2.4.3: *Sunt quidem omnibus nobis modicae facultates, dignitas sumptuosa, reditus propter condicionem agellorum nescio minor an incertior; sed quod cessat ex reditu, frugalitate supple-tur, ex qua velut fonte liberalitas nostra decurrit* ("Indeed, my resources as a whole are modest, while my 'dignity' is expensive to maintain; since it depends upon the circumstances of my (farming) estates, I know not whether my revenue will be smaller or more uncertain. But what fails to come from revenues is made up for by frugality, and from it, as from a spring, flows our liberality"—my translation).

11. The description is in *Ep.* 2.17; noting especially 2.17.3: *Villa usibus capax [est], non sumptu-osa tutela.* On past attempts to use this description for architectural reconstruction (one of which is used as the illustration for the LCL edition [2:554–55]) and their difficulties, see A. N. Sherwin-White, *The Letters of Pliny: A Historical and Social Commentary* (Oxford: Clarendon, 1966) 186–88.

12. In *Ep.* 5.6.41–42 Pliny himself characterizes his foregoing description of another of his villas (in Tuscany) as following the type of description used by Homer of Achilles' armor, what is now usually called *ekphrasis* and is typically florid and elastic in detail. Yet he clearly does it for the thematic effect of making the reader visualize the place. On *ekphrasis* as a tool of narrative and fiction see the article by G. Downey in *RAC* 4 (1959) 921–44.

13. The terms are all Pliny's own (taken from *Ep.* 2.4.3 quoted in n. 10 above) and are loaded with symbolic value for his age. The key seems to be a distaste for ostentatious display of wealth through luxurious living. So note the *topos* or convention of criticizing luxury, espe-cially in matters relating to housing, among the following Roman writers: Cicero, *De legibus* 2.1; Sallust, *Catilina* 12; Horace, *Odes* 1.38; 3.1.33; 3.24; Pliny, *Natural History* 34.34; 35.26. For the relative scale of Pliny's wealth and his benefactions, see Richard Duncan-Jones, *The Econ-omy of the Roman Empire: Quantitative Studies* (2nd ed.; Cambridge: Cambridge University Press, 1984) 17–24.

In dealing with ancient sources, therefore, we must be doubly cautious, as the record is seldom as complete as a modern census and we are less familiar with the semantic and symbolic terrain. Certainly archaeological and documentary data must provide the fundamental sociographic scale by which to correlate information from literary sources to provide the semantic and symbolic reflections. Still, the case of firsthand letters is one thing, while novelistic literature represents an even more complex set of problems. So, the task of visualizing the ancient world using archaeological data seems much more viable for the letters of Pliny or Paul, though one finds precious little in the way of kitchen-to-streetcorner detail in the latter. Yet the task is even more daunting for satirical and propagandistic fiction (such as Lucian or Apuleius) or for historiographical narratives (such as Josephus or Dionysius of Halicarnassus). The same will hold true, as we shall see, for Luke-Acts. Surely there are points of historical reality in all these types of literature, but the means of correlation and analysis is less direct. There may be a high degree of intentional realism, or verisimilitude, in such fictional narratives, even when they are not based on real historical events or extant localities. After all, how typical was Petronius's Trimalchio?[14] On analogy one may call to mind the case of the very well known London flat at 221b Baker Street and the social world it evokes. To this day, as many people go looking for this landmark as for those associated with the stories of Paul, and alas with the same results. That it never existed hardly seems to matter to most, until one tries to use Conan Doyle to write a social history of Marylebone parish.

Hence, we must attempt to locate our story—the occasion of Paul's arrival and missionizing at Philippi—within the appropriate historical contexts. These I would arrange according to three categories: (1) *sociographic contexts* (which include archaeological and historical information), (2) *functional semantic contexts* (which include social conventions reflected in language from both documentary and literary sources), and (3) *cultural symbolic con-*

---

14. Cf. Duncan-Jones, *Economy*, 239–56. On "realism" as a trait of ancient fiction, see Richard Pervo, *Profit with Delight: The Literary Genre of the Acts of the Apostles* (Philadelphia: Fortress, 1987) 109. The use of realism or verisimilitude for drawing subtle distinctions between historical and novelistic narratives in antiquity (where both use nonreal or nonhistorical events and characters) is based largely on the definitions of E. Auerbach, *Mimesis: The Representation of Reality in Western Literature* (Princeton: Princeton University Press, 1953) as followed in more recent discussions, such as that of T. Hägg, *The Novel in Antiquity* (Berkeley: University of California Press, 1983) 3–4. More recently, see C. Gill and T. Wiseman, eds., *Lies and Fiction in the Ancient World* (Austin: University of Texas Press, 1993). I have also found the suggestions of David Konstan ("The Invention of Fiction" [unpublished paper, 1993]) to be very helpful, and I offer thanks for being allowed to see his paper in draft form. It is not my intention to deal directly with the question of the genre of Luke-Acts (i.e., whether Hellenistic novel or history), but rather to examine the social stance and purview of its narrative construction. In this way, however, we may come to some new insights regarding the genre question as well as the purpose of the writing.

texts (which reflect the underlying template of understanding). In this way we may hope to draw together the respective concerns of archaeological and exegetical analysis to understand a particular New Testament text in its context.

PHILIPPI: SOCIOGRAPHIC CONTEXTS

Since the time of Lightfoot and Ramsay, working just after the first French archaeological survey of Macedonia, it has been typical in commentaries on Paul's Philippian correspondence to begin by discussing Paul's arrival as described in Acts 16. Hence, an implicit set of historical correlations have been assumed. It is significant, therefore, that such attention has been given to the social and historical circumstances of the city in order to make sense of the texts. One problem, however, arises from the fact that New Testament scholars ever since have tended to accept information and observations from Lightfoot and Ramsay or from the early French excavators, where elements from Acts were read into the archaeological record, as if it were archaeological data. In fact, there have been two subsequent phases of excavation. The second ran from 1914 to 1938 under the direction of the École Français d'Archéologie at Athens; the third, commenced in 1958 and continues to the present, by the Philippi Archaeological Society.[15] Thus, a number of new historical or sociographic insights need to be brought into the discussion.

The basic history of the city, known largely from the Roman writers, need not be recited here, except to note that the small Macedonian settlement came under Roman control after the battle of Pydna (168 B.C.E.). It was elevated to the status of colony (*Colonia Victrix Philippensium*) by Antony in 42 B.C.E. in celebration of the decisive victory over the Republican forces of Brutus and Cassius.[16] Later, in 30 B.C.E., after the civil war, Octavian renamed it *Colonia Julia Augusta Philippensis* when he repatriated the population of several Italian towns as a means of consolidating his power (Pliny, *Natural History* 4.18). The location was important, since Philippi was the first major city on the Egnatian Way approximately ten miles inland from its termina-

15. For excavation reports from 1920 to 1938, see "Chronique des Fouilles: Philippe," *BCH* 44 (1920) to 62 (1938); for reports since 1958, see "Chronique des Fouilles: Philippe," *BCH* 82 (1958) and continuing to the present; see also S. Pelekanidis, "Excavations in Philippi," *Balkan Studies* 8 (1967) 123–26; R. Stillwell, "Philippi," in *Princeton Encyclopedia of Classical Sites* (Princeton: Princeton University Press, 1976) 704–5; M .I. Finley, *Atlas of Classical Archaeology* (New York: McGraw-Hill, 1977) 176–77. I am grateful for the kind hospitality of Charalambos Bakirtzes, the Ephor of Byzantine Antiquities for Eastern Macedonia and Thrace (Kavalla), who made it possible for me to work at Philippi and gain further insights into the historical and archaeological problems.

16. Strabo, *Geogr.* 7, frg. 41; Diodorus Siculus, *Hist.* 16.3, 8; Appian, *Bell.Civ.* 4.10.

tion at the Aegean port of Neapolis (modern Kavalla). The Via Egnatia runs through the city by two main gates on the east and west; it doubled as the *Decumanus maximus* of the town running past the north face of the agora. The earlier agora was rebuilt in the Antonine period as a Roman forum, as it now stands. From there the Via Egnatia ran west to Amphipolis and Thessalonika, and thence across Macedonia to the Adriatic coast.[17]

Here we note several points of archaeological and historical information that may be useful corrections to some of the traditional assumptions of the story in Acts 16. First, it should be noted that Philippi was *not* (as has sometimes been assumed)[18] primarily a *military* colony in the Julio-Claudian period. While veterans were settled by Antony and a number of veterans do appear in later inscriptions, especially from the Antonine period,[19] the settlers of the Augustan colony were largely Italian partisans of Antony who were expatriated to make room for the settlement of Octavian's soldiers in new military colonies in Etruria and Umbria (Dio Cassius, *Hist.* 51.4.6). In fact, similar Augustan colonies (populated by Italian expatriates) were established in Macedonia at Byllis, Cassandreum, Dium, Pella, and the Adriatic port of Dyrrachium.[20] The main free cities were Amphipolis, Beroea, and Thessalonika. They, like the colonies, had the right to mint coins and set levies.[21] Also, there was intermittent competition among these cities for imperial favors, reflected in terms of social orders and imperial cult.[22] The

17. F. Papazoglou, "La territoire de la colonie Philippes," *BCH* 106 (1982) 517–42; M. Seve, "Rapports: Philippes," *BCH* 106 (1982) 651–53.

18. J. B. Lightfoot, *Saint Paul's Epistle to the Philippians* (12th ed.; London: Macmillan, 1913) 50; R. P. Martin, *Philippians* (NCBC; Grand Rapids: Eerdmans, 1976) 3; cf. A. N. Sherwin-White, *Roman Law and Roman Society in the New Testament* (Oxford: Oxford University Press, 1963; repr. Grand Rapids: Baker, 1978) 92.

19. *CIL* III.645, 647; P. Lemerle, "Nouvelles inscriptions latines de Philippes," *BCH* 61 (1937) 418; A. Salac, "Inscriptions du Pangee, de la region Drama-Cavalla et de Philippes," *BCH* 47 (1923) 87. By way of contrast, note the prominence of magistrates at Philippi who were not veterans, e.g., *CIL* III.650: P. Cornelius Asper, *flamen, decurion,* and *duovir* under Nero (see below n. 23).

20. J. A. O. Larsen, "Roman Greece," in T. Frank, *An Economic Survey of Ancient Rome* (Baltimore: Johns Hopkins University Press, 1938) 4:448; M. I. Rostovtzeff, *The Social and Economic History of the Roman Empire* (2nd ed.; Oxford: Clarendon, 1957) 1:253; 2:554 n. 32. While most bear names signifying their Augustan enfranchisement, only the more important or more privileged were granted the *ius italicum* (which is here indicated by * after the name): Byllis (*Colonia Byllidensium*), *CIL* III.600; Pella (*Colonia Julia Augusta Pella*), *CIL* III.598; Dium* (*Colonia Julia Augusta Diensium*), *CIL* III.7281; Dyrrhachium*/Epidamnus (*Colonia Dyrrhachium*), *CIL* III.611; Cassandrea* (*Colonia Julia Augusta Cassandrea*), Pliny, *Natural History* 4.36; Philippi* (*Colonia Julia Augusta Philippensis*).

21. Pliny, *Natural History* 4.36–38. One reason was that the region around Philippi, including the nearby island of Thasos, was known for mining operations (cf. Larsen, in Frank, *Economic Survey,* 4:461–62, 486); however, many of these mines were in decline by the early principate. Cf. Strabo, *Geogr.* 9.399; Plutarch, *Mor.* 434A.

22. Larsen, in Frank, *Economic Survey,* 4:449–55; Rostovtzeff, *Social and Economic History,* 1:253; 2:650 n. 97. For epigraphic evidence of this competition between local municipalities of

result was that while the countryside remained largely native Macedonian or Thracian, there were (a) large provincial landholders (of senatorial, equestrian, or decurional ranks), (b) a high degree of romanization of the local urban population, and (c) an active trade with other Roman cities of Greece (Macedonia as well as Achaia), the islands, and the Aegean coast of Asia Minor. These factors will have implications for the social makeup and administrative organization of Philippi and for its relations to other cities.

Here, as a way of staking out some sociographic markers, we should perhaps begin to check the nature of the story in Acts (and its uses in later commentaries) with the information from archaeological and epigraphic sources. As Sherwin-White observed, there are a number of difficulties with the wording of Acts 16:12a "which is the leading city of the district of Macedonia" (ἥτις ἐστὶν πρώτη μερίδος τῆς Μακεδονίας πόλις) and with the Greek designation στρατηγοί (16:20, 22, 35, 36, 38) for the city's magistrates (presumably the Latin *duumviri*).[23] The term *duovir* is well attested in the Philippi inscriptions, but στρατηγός as the Greek equivalent is not known, even as a local variant. The term στρατηγός generally means a military officer; however, it is regularly found in the papyri as the equivalent for the Latin *praetor*, or compounded as στρατηγός ὕπατος for the Latin *consul*. In the New Testament the term στρατηγός is found only in Luke-Acts, and then only in reference to the Temple administration in Jerusalem and these magistrates in Philippi; so, the choice of wording is hardly incidental. These difficulties are not minor, given the assumptions that have often been advanced regarding Luke's eyewitness account of the Philippi narrative.[24] Ramsay, it must be remembered, went farther to suggest that this "vividness" resulted from the fact that Philippi was actually Luke's hometown and that he was the one who brought Paul there from Troas.[25]

---

the region during the Antonine period, see M. N. Tod, "Greek Inscriptions from Macedonia," *JHS* 42 (1922) 167–80.

23. Sherwin-White, *Roman Law and Roman Society*, 92–93 (cf. 74–77); cf. Martin, *Philippians*, 2. Also, as Ramsay (*Paul the Traveler*, 217–18) pointed out, there are difficulties knowing whether the term ἄρχοντες (16:19) is supposed to refer to the same. On the Latin equivalents, see Moulton-Milligan, 592–93. From Philippi *CIL* III.650, which dates from the reign of Nero (thus contemporaneous with Paul's actual visits), is rather typical and suggestive for the social location of the local magistracy: *P. Cornelius Asper Atiarius Montanus/equo publico honoratus, item ornamentis decu/rionatus et IIviralicis, pontifex, flamen, Divi Claudi, Philippis, ann XXIII, H·S·E*. The abbreviation *IIvir.* is standard for *duovir*. The only way I can see to salvage the Lukan wording relative to the actual political organization at Philippi is to suggest that the ἄρχοντες (16:19) are meant to represent the *duovirs*, the στρατηγοί (16:20, etc.) represent *praetors*, and the ῥαβδοῦχοι (16:35, 38) represent *lictors* (as usually suggested).

24. Lightfoot, *Philippians*, 53; cf. Ramsay, *Paul the Traveler*, 206–7. The assumption is based on the beginning of the first-person narrative in 16:11 (while third person resumes at 17:1) and again in 20:5–6 (also at Philippi).

25. Ramsay, *Paul the Traveler*, 200–202. Ramsay conjectured (pp. 204–6) that Luke himself was also the "man of Macedonia" who appeared to Paul in the vision at Troas (Acts 16:6–10). He explains the circumstances by the fact that Luke had been in Troas plying his trade as

Now we continue to see a good bit of "grasping at straws" of illustrative detail, handed down from generation to generation in the commentary tradition, often without checking for more recent archaeological discussion. One example is a fragmentary Latin inscription that preserves the term [*pu*]*rpurari* (*CIL* III,644), often suggested as a correlate to the designation of Lydia as a "purple dealer" (πορφυρόπωλις, Acts 16:14) and to prove trade with Thyatira. While Thyatira was known for this export, the Macedonian-Thessalian coast was also a known production center for the dye. But the inscription gives no clear evidence what aspect of purple dye work was being commemorated. Hence, the inscription really "proves" nothing in relation to details of the story in Acts; there is no direct link to the sociographic context.[26] The appearance of the name Porphyrios, a fourth-century bishop at Philippi, in an edifice epigraphically designated the βασιλικὰ Παύλου suggests that the later Christians took the story of Acts 16 (and even Paul's founding of *their* church) most seriously.[27] On the other hand, we cannot accept as contextual evidence Lightfoot's attempt to use the name Gaios Klodios Epaphrodeitos from a Thessalonian inscription to equate Paul's coworker (Phil 2:25) with the Gaius of Acts 19:29, especially in light of the fairly common use of these names in inscriptions from Philippi and its

physician, when Paul came to encounter him in need of medical attention (apparently assuming as previous the ailment in Gal 4:13). In the case of the Philippian magistrates (Acts 16:20, cf. n. 23 above), therefore, he was forced to explain Luke's lack of precision in terminology on the use of titles of courtesy (p. 218).

26. *CIL* III.664. Larsen, in Frank, *Economic Survey*, 4:485; cf. Ramsay, *Paul the Traveler*, 214. Actually, Thyatira was more known for producing red dye, while the chief center for purple dye production was Hierapolis.

27. Πο[ρφύ]ριος ἐπίσκο/πος τὴ[ν κ]έντησιν τῆς Βασιλικῆ/ς Παύλο[υ ἐπ]οίησεν ἐν Χρ(ιστ)ῷ ("Bishop Porphyrios made the mosaic [floor] of the basilica of Paul in Christ"), *BCH* 100 (1976) 685 and fig. 236. Cf. Πρακτικά Ἀρχαιολογικῆς Ἑταιρείας [hereafter *PAE*] 1975:101; D. Feissel, *Recueil des inscriptions chrétiennes de Macédoine du IIIè au VIè siecle* (BCH Suppl. 8; Athens: École Français, 1983) 192 (no. 226)—an inscription in the floor mosaic of the recently excavated fourth-century church found beneath the later Byzantine Octagon. The rectangular "hall church," which incorporated an earlier Hellenistic *herōon*, probably antedates by at least a few years the installation of the mosaic floor, to which the inscription refers. A bishop Porphyrios from Philippi is named among the participants in the Council of Serdica of 344 C.E. (CSEL 65:133), and this evidence corresponds to others for the fourth-century date of the early edifice. It should be noted that the edifice is not a true *basilica* in architectural terms; therefore, the appearance of the terminology in the inscription is evidence of a fourth-century nontechnical usage among Greek Christians. On the inscription, see also S. Pelekanidis, "Kultprobleme in Apostel-Paulus-Oktagon von Philippi im Zusammenhang mit einem ältern Heroenkult," in *Atti del IX Congresso Internazionale di Archeologia Cristiana* (Rome and Vatican City: Pontifical Institute of Archaeology, 1978) 2:393–99; "Οἱ Φίλιπποι καί τά χριστιανικά μνεμεῖα τους," in Ἀφιέρωμα τεσσαρακονταετηρίδας Ἑταιρείας Μακεδονικῶν Σπουδῶν (Thessalonika: Institute for Balkan Studies, 1980) 108–9; and V. Abrahamsen, "Bishop Porphyrios and the City of Philippi in the Early Fourth Century," *VC* 43 (1989) 80–85. On the edifice, see S. Pelekanidis, "Ἀνασκαφή Ὀκταγώνου Φιλίππου," *PAE* 1978:64–72; and L. M. White, *The Social Origins of Christian Architecture*, vol. 2: *Texts and Monuments of the Christian Domus Ecclesiae and Its Environment* (Minneapolis: Fortress, 1995) no. 50.

environs.[28] What stands out all the more is the fact that Acts so stresses the geographical mobility and social standing of tradespeople like Lydia and Paul himself.

Current scholarly opinion is rather sharply divided on what to make of the historical reality behind this story. While most scholars continue to follow the views of E. Haenchen and H. J. Cadbury, at least some have recently returned to the view that Luke was the traveling companion of Paul and that certain sections, notably including 16:10–40, were eyewitness accounts.[29] Others have taken an opposite view that the story is essentially novelistic fiction, with no basic historical value. In this view the story of the imprisonment follows the paradigm of a travails of the road, found commonly in the Hellenistic novels.[30] Others, still, would opt for a mediating course, preferring to think that the core events, such as those in Acts 16, are based loosely on actual events even if highly stylized or fictionalized in their portrayal in Lukan redaction to suit some thematic intent.[31] To claim that the individual episodes in Acts are based on historical events and persons in real locations is dependent to some extent on assuming a direct connection between the narrative and the sociographic reality of that locality.

One problem for this type of assumption in Acts 16 is the lack of detail regarding events, persons, and locations, including the style and spatial circumstances of the houses of Lydia and the jailer. Virtually nothing can be said about Lydia's house from the story, other than that it was large enough to accept guests and serve them a meal. If she were a purple dealer, it would not be atypical for her house to include facilities and shops for the trade. An extended retinue of household and business personnel would also be consistent with such a situation. Yet Acts gives no such details.

The case of the jailer is a bit more interesting, even though Acts in no way indicates whether he is to be taken as local resident or a posted provincial officer from elsewhere. The situation of his house is also noteworthy, since the narrative has a curious sequence of movements for Paul and Silas between the prison and the house (16:23–40). Not the least of the diffi-

---

28. Lightfoot, *Philippians*, 62; cf. Salac, "Inscriptions du Pangee," *BCH* 43:92 (= no. 23). For the name Aurelios Epaphrodeitos in a dedication to Isis and Serapis, dating to the third century (perhaps fourth), see L. Vidman, *Sylloge inscriptionum religionis Isiacae et Sarapiacae* (Berlin: de Gruyter, 1969) no. 27.

29. This is the view of Martin Hengel, *Acts and the History of Earliest Christianity* (Philadelphia: Fortress, 1979) 59–68, esp. 66. It is followed in publications recently by some of his students.

30. So Pervo, *Profit with Delight*, 21–24, esp. 23. Compare the view of Robert Tannehill, *The Narrative Unity of Luke-Acts: A Literary Interpretation* (2 vols; Philadelphia: Fortress, 1986) 1:7–8; 2:196–205.

31. G. Lüdemann, *Early Christianity according to the Traditions in Acts: A Commentary* (Minneapolis: Fortress, 1987) 177–84, esp. 183. Compare P. Esler, *Community and Gospel in Luke-Acts: The Social and Political Motivations of Lucan Theology* (SNTSMS 57; Cambridge: Cambridge University Press, 1987) 14.

culties from the archaeological perspective is the fact that no jail facility has been identified to date, and there is no indication of general earthquake damage in the city from this period. So it should be noticed that after being thrown into the innermost part of the jail (16:23–25), when the earthquake struck and the jailer returned, Paul and Silas immediately preached to his entire household (16:32). Only then, after dressing their wounds and being baptized, does the jailer take them "up into his house" (ἀναγαγών τε αὐτοὺς εἰς τὸν οἶκον, 16:34) in order to prepare a meal for them. But then, after some negotiation with the embarrassed magistrates, when it is time for Paul and Silas to leave the city, the story concludes: "So they left the prison" (ἐξ-ελθόντες δε ἀπὸ τῆς φυλακῆς, 16:40a). This is quite peculiar, since it seems to presuppose that they never left the prison even while enjoying the hospitality of the jailer. Are we to assume that he lived upstairs from the dungeon (with his entire "household") and that Lydia (and her "household") lived virtually next door? Thus, note the parallelism of the verb construction in 16:40b: εἰσῆλθον πρὸς τὴν Λυδίαν (literally, "they went in to Lydia"). Is this the "real" situation in Philippi? Or is this a disparate series of story vignettes loosely stitched together by the Lukan author? Unfortunately, there is nothing to substantiate these peculiar details so as to demonstrate a direct sociographic correlation with historical contexts in Philippi. On the other hand, perhaps one can come to see some of the typical scenes of urban life assumed as texture for these episodes by the author.

Perhaps the greatest difficulties in correlating the story in Acts with the archaeological data arise in connection with the occasion of Paul's encounter with "God-fearer" Lydia on the sabbath at the riverside προσευχή (Acts 16:13–14; cf. v. 16). It is clearly the intent of Acts, in keeping with its own thematic interests, to suggest the presence of a Jewish community at Philippi as the typical starting point for Paul's missionary activities. But the setting by the river has produced notable efforts to effect the correlation. The discovery of a Roman arch spanning the Via Egnatia about two kilometers west of the city gate, near the River Gangites, has been argued for this boundary location since the time of Heuzey and Renan.[32] Alas, it continues to be cited as "proof" of the essential veracity of the story despite good archaeological evidence to the contrary.[33] Three assumptions are gen-

32. The argument is based especially on P. Collart, *Philippes, ville de Macédoine depuis ses origines jusqu'à la fin de l'époque romaine* (Paris: Bocard, 1937) 319–22, 458–60. It is followed by W. A. McDonald, "Archaeology and St. Paul's Journeys in Greek Lands," *BA* 3 (1940) 20; and J. Finegan, *Light from the Ancient Past* (Princeton: Princeton University Press, 1946) 270–71 (which were the first New Testament studies to make use of the excavations of the École Français). So also Martin, *Philippians*, 6; and W. Elliger, *Paulus in Greichenland: Philippi, Thessaloniki, Athen, Korinth* (Stuttgart: Katholisches Bibelwerk, 1978) 87–89. While the latter expresses some reservations, the former does not even cite the more recent discussions.

33. P. Lemerle discovered tombs just outside the west city gate, which means that the *pomerium* (at least as traditionally assumed for a Roman city) could not have extended to the triumphal arch, two kilometers farther west (*Philippes et la Macédoine orientale à l'époque chré-*

erally made: (1) that a Jewish community existed but that its "prayerhall" was *by law* restricted to the area outside the gates (16:13) of the city (on the presumed model of the *pomerium* at Rome); (2) that "God-fearers" (such as Lydia) represent either proselytes or some sort of "partial" converts to synagogue Judaism and became the core of Paul's church; and (3) that there was an inherent anti-Semitic bias among the Roman population against Jewish religion.[34] The last feature, of course, is an essential thematic element for the story of the arrest and imprisonment in Acts 16:20-38.

Some unusual features of the account raise serious doubts about the historical reliability of all these assumptions, especially when examined in the light of the archaeological evidence. The term προσευχή (as a Jewish place of meeting/prayer, in distinction from the more typically Lukan term συναγωγή) is found only here in Luke-Acts, despite its common use in inscriptions elsewhere.[35] Recent archaeological work on the diaspora synagogue would support the diverse and informal nature of architectural setting, especially using houses, in the early periods.[36] One might as easily expect a congregation to meet in someone's house or in a renovated edifice inside the city proper. Still, the situation is less than clear for Philippi. Indeed, apart from Acts itself, there is very little evidence (either literary or archaeological) for Jewish activity at Philippi, and what is extant is generally of a later date.[37] The most direct evidence that has come to light is a Jewish funerary inscription discovered in 1987.[38] Given the paucity of evidence,

tienne et byzantine: Récherches d'histoire et d'archéologie [Paris: Bocard, 1945] 24–25). Lemerle argued instead that the προσευχή must have been on the little stream nearer the western gate, where there is a chapel dedicated to Lydia. This is the view adopted by L. Portefaix, *Sisters Rejoice: Paul's Letter to the Philippians and Luke-Acts as Seen by First-century Philippian Women* (ConBNT 21; Stockholm: Almqvist & Wiksel, 1988) 73. Still, it must be noted that this conclusion is making extraordinary effort to preserve the veracity of Acts in conjunction with the archaeological remains. Yet the whole argument is suspect, as we shall suggest below.

34. Cf. Martin, *Philippians*, 6–8.

35. Cf. F. W. Beare, *The Epistle to the Philippians* (New York: Harper, 1956) 10–11; M. Hengel, "*Proseuche* und *Synagoge:* Jüdische Gemeinde, Gotteshaus und Gottesdienst in der Diaspora und in Palästina," repr. in *The Synagogue: Studies in Origins, Archaeology, and Architecture* (ed. J. Gutmann; New York: Ktav, 1975) passim.

36. A. T. Kraabel, "Unity and Diversity among Diaspora Synagogues," in *The Synagogue in Late Antiquity* (ed. L. I. Levine; Winona Lake, Ind.: Eisenbrauns, 1987) 49–60; E. M. Meyers and A. T. Kraabel, "Archaeology, Iconography, and Nonliterary Written Remains," in *Early Judaism and Its Modern Interpreters* (ed. R. A. Kraft and G. W. E. Nickelsburg; Atlanta: Scholars Press, 1986) 183–89; see also my "The Delos Synagogue Revisited: Recent Fieldwork in the Graeco-Roman Diaspora," *HTR* 80 (1987) 133–37; idem, *Building God's House*, 62–67.

37. I am disinclined to make anything particularly Jewish out of the name *Mofius* (a Latin orthographic variant for Greek Μωϋσης, "Moses"), which comes from a second-/third-century Isiac dedication at Philippi by one Q. Mofius Euhemerus, in Vidman, *Sylloge inscriptionum religionis Isiacae et Sarapiacae* (hereafter just *Sylloge*) no. 121. The name could be, therefore, a hellenized Egyptian derivative, while not necessarily Jewish.

38. The text is as yet not formally published; however, I was allowed to see it while it was undergoing initial study at the Kavalla Museum.

this recent find is all the more striking because it was located *within* the city, and thus might shatter previous assumptions about the existence of a *pomerium* governing the jurisdiction of the city (i.e., in terms both of burials and of location of "foreign" cults). In this vein, too, recent archaeological work has revealed the existence of Hellenistic hero-cult tombs (*herōon*, ἡρῷον) in connection with at least two prominent monuments near the Roman forum, that is, within the supposed *pomerium*.

One might argue that it is merely a fluke of archaeological survival that no more evidence of Jewish presence has been discovered, and that this view may still need to be modified. As with all archaeological evidence, so it may. We do know, of course, of Jewish communities in Macedonia, as at Stobi and (the most recently discovered) at Philippopolis. But these also tend to be of a later date, as does the Samaritan enclaves at Thessalonika and perhaps Neapolis, known from fourth-century inscriptions.[39] So it must be noted that the recovery rate for inscriptions from all periods at Philippi (Republican through Byzantine) is fairly high, even though much of the city still needs to be excavated. Moreover, and despite the similar account in Acts 17:1–5 of an initial core of Jewish converts at Thessalonika, Paul's own firsthand correspondence with these Macedonian churches (both 1 Thessalonians and Philippians) suggests that they were predominantly, if not overwhelmingly, Gentile in makeup.[40]

Now, supposing that new evidence to the contrary is not revealed in the future, it is possible to make one tentative suggestion regarding the social and historical implications of this point. Much of the diffusion of Jewish communities through the Aegean reflected in the known archaeological and literary remains commences in the Hellenistic cities, so that by the late Republic we regularly see Roman decrees asserting ancestral rights of resident Jews. But then the great growth of these Jewish communities in observable archaeological terms comes largely from the second or third centuries C.E. and afterward. For example, in the case at Sardis, Josephus

---

39. B. Lifshitz and J. Schiby, "Une Synagogue samaritaine à Thessalonique," *RB* 75 (1968) 368–78. It should be noted that one name found in connection with these Thessalonika Samaritan texts (Siricius) also has connections to Neapolis (cf. *CIJ* I², pp. 71–75). Yet another Samaritan appears in a second-century B.C.E. inscription from Thasos: Ῥοδικλῆς Μενίππου Σαμαρίτας (*IG* I,2, 8.439; cf. Lifshitz and Schiby, "Une Synagogue samaritaine," 377). Even so, the lateness of these texts makes direct connections to first-century Philippi/Neapolis impossible to demonstrate for sociographic purposes. What one might want to do instead is to create a longitudinal tracking for the development of these groups over time.

40. On Thessalonika, see 1 Thess 1:9; cf. A. J. Malherbe, *Paul and the Thesslonians* (Philadelphia: Fortress, 1987) 6, 8, 12–16. On Philippi, I have suggested in another study that the character of the letter reflects little if any Jewish background, even in the hymn of 2:6–11 (that is, in its present form and despite any claims to a Jewish *Vorlage*); see White, "Morality Between Two Worlds: A Paradigm of Friendship in Philippians," in *Greeks, Romans, and Christians: Studies in Honor of Abraham J. Malherbe* (ed. D. L. Balch, W. A. Meeks, and E. Ferguson; Minneapolis: Fortress, 1990) 201–15.

provides evidence of an early community (during the time of Julius Caesar), but it should be noted that there is a marked gap in the evidence between the Republican and later Roman period, commencing with the acquisition of the municipal building, probably not before the early third century.[41] Here the civic history of Philippi is perhaps something of an anomaly since it was, in effect, refounded (not once but twice!) in precisely the same period when the position of Jewish communities in other Hellenistic cities was being ratified. Even so, on the basis of the "evidence curve" of other Jewish communities we might well have expected a new phase of Jewish activity sometime in the late second century C.E. and after. But for Philippi, the evidence of this same period begins to point instead to the emergence of a well-established Christian community.[42] A Jewish community was certainly present by the late third to fourth century, if not before, but so far there does not seem to have been a large presence. From the first century on, the city of Philippi itself does not seem to have experienced exceptional growth under imperial patronage, except for a period under the Antonines and Severii, when the forum and a number of other public buildings were rebuilt.[43] Only in the fourth-fifth centuries does a new wave of building commence, and that under a clear Christian influence.

41. Josephus, *Antiquities* 14.231–50; cf. Meyers and Kraabel, "Archaeology, Iconography, and Nonliterary Written Remains," 178–90. I am indebted to Prof. Helmut Koester for a comment which, I think, helps to focus this issue. The gap is one whose full implications are yet to be realized.

42. Thus, at Philippi it is the period from Ignatius and Polycarp (ca. 112–120) down to the fourth century (ca. 344), which is evidenced in the prosopography of the "basilica" of Paul edifice below the Octagonal Church. Also a Christian funerary inscription from Philippi may be noted: Ἀυρ(ήλιος) Καπίτων πρεσβύ(τερος)/ νέος τῆς καθολει/κῆς ἐκ(κ)λησίας ἀνέ/στησα τὴν στή/λην ταύτην τοῖς/ ἰδίοις γωνεῦσιν/ καὶ τῇ εἰδίᾳ συνβίω/ Βεβίᾳ Παύλα καὶ/ τῷ γλυκυτάτῳ μου υἱῷ Ἐλπιδίῳ./ υ΄ κὲ δέκα ("[I,] Aurelius Capito, new [or junior?] presbyter of the catholic church, set up this stele to [my] own parents, and to [my] own wife Vibia Paula, and to my dearest son Elpidius. [In the year] 410"). See J. Coupry and M. Freyel, "Inscriptions de Philippes," *BCH* 60 (1936) 53. The dating is based on the reading of the number 410 in the last line. Lemerle (*Philippes et la Macédoine*, 94–95, following Collart, *Philippes ville de Macédoine*, 306–11) dates it to 262/263 C.E. based on the provincial foundation in 148 B.C.E.; however, a colonial dating based on the year of the founding (or refounding) of Philippi would yield either 368/369 or 380/381. Either of the latter two dates is preferable in my view given two factors in the text: the ecclesiastical titles used and comparison with other similar inscriptions using the name Aurelios, all datable from the fourth century. Feissel, *Recueil des Inscriptions*, 197–98 (no. 233) accepted the dating 379 C.E.; compare nos. 231 (epitaph for Aurelios Kyriakos and his wife Aurelia Markellina) and 232 (epitaph for Aurelios Severos and his wife Aurelia Klaudia).

If this proposal turns out on further investigation to be correct for the evidence at Philippi, it would point to a local phenomenon which runs in the opposite direction of the local fortunes of Christians and Jews at Sardis in the later second century, as suggested by A. T. Kraabel, "Melito the Bishop and the Synagogue at Sardis: Text and Context," in *Studies Presented to G. M. A. Hanfmann* (ed. D. G. Mitten; Cambridge, Mass.: Harvard University Press, 1971) 77–85.

43. Michel Seve, "Rapports: Philippes," *BCH* 103 (1979) 619–31; idem, "Rapports: Philippes," *BCH* 105 (1981) 918–23; idem, "Rapports: Philippes," *BCH* 106 (1982) 651–53.

In the final analysis, then, the case of the riverside προσευχή begins to look like a thematic element woven into the narrative by the author in order to provide continuity at two different levels of the story. First, it connects the Timothy episode (16:1-5), which also serves as a summarizing statement, to other encounters with Jewish antagonists that follow (17:1-9, 13; 18:7-17; 19:8-10). Second, it provides the narrative thread linking the Lydia vignette (16:13) to that of the mantic girl (16:16), and thereby the imprisonment. Thus, the final verse of the section (16:40) serves to wrap up all the vignettes narratively as well as thematically.

On the basis of both the archaeological evidence and the literary analysis we must question the assumption, first suggested by Renan,[44] that by analogy to Rome (in granting the *ius italicum* to a colony), foreign cults (including the Jews) would necessarily be restricted outside the *pomerium*. As noted, this assumption is also tied directly to the reading of the legal charge upon which Paul is arrested in Acts 16:20-22. The sociographic context of Philippi, while giving only minimal evidence of the place of Jews, does reveal a very prominent position in the early first century for numerous foreign cults, not all of which would have been admitted inside the *pomerium* at Rome by this period.[45] In particular, we may note the local popularity of the Egyptian cults, which were already well established at Philippi before 42 B.C.E.[46] There was a sanctuary of the Egyptian gods within the city, on the hillside approach to the acropolis above the Hellenistic period theater. It dates in all probability from before the principate, and it contained multiple chapels dedicated to the various Egyptian gods by individuals and cultic sodalities.[47] For example, a group called θρησκευταὶ τοῦ Σεράπιδος ("worshipers of Sarapis," a parallel to the phrase σεβομένου τὸν θεόν ["worshiper of God"] in Acts 18:7) honored the benefaction (εὐεργέτην) of their most praiseworthy patron, Quintus Flavius Hermadion. It is suggestive of the acceptance of the Egyptian cults that Q. Fl. Hermadion (the son of the former), who is titled priest and gymnasiarch, is honored with the office of ἀγωνοθέτης (judge or honorary president of the annual games) in another parallel inscription by a cultic sodality of θρησκευταί, but the only god

44. Heuzey and Daumet, *Mission archéologique de Macédoine*, 117; cf. Collart, *Philippes, ville de Macédoine*, 278–79; Lemerle, *Philippes et la Macédoine*, 26.

45. Charles Picard, "Les Dieux de la colonie de Philippes vers le Iᵉʳ siècle de notre ère, d'après les ex-voto rupestres," *RHR* 80 (1922) 117–201.

46. Appian, *Bell. Civ.* 4.41. Picard, "Les Dieux de la colonie de Philippes," 172; R. E. Witt, "The Egyptian Cults in Macedonia," in *Ancient Macedonia* (ed. B. Lourdas and C. I. Makaronas; Thessalonika: Institute for Balkan Studies, 1970) 324–32; idem, *Isis in the Graeco-Roman World* (Ithaca, N.Y.: Cornell University Press, 1971) 97. The episode involves one M. Volusius, who escaped the camp of Brutus disguised as an Isiac priest. Also for the name, cf. *CIL* III.640 and Valerius Maximus 7.3.8.

47. Vidman, *Sylloge*, no. 110; Witt, *Isis in the Graeco-Roman World*, 204.

named is Asklepios.[48] At Thessalonika the same term is used of cultic sodalities dedicated to both Hermanubis and Sarapis; the latter group is designated συνθρησκευταὶ κλείνου θεοῦ μεγάλου Σαράπιδος ("fellow worshipers of the illustrious deity great Sarapis").[49] Moreover, the use of the titles and epithets reflects the common practice among various clubs and foreign cultic associations of adopting the nomenclature of office from the immediate social environment, a further sign of social placement and acculturation.

The sociographic evidence from Philippi indicates an active interplay between the Egyptian cults and other local deities with romanized identity. Isis Regina was identified with Bendis-Artemis and associated as Isis Pelagia with the healing cult of Telesphorus.[50] Sarapis was identified with Silvanus, one of the most prominent cultic associations of the city as it was attached both to the local decurionate and to the imperial cult.[51] Thus, foreign cults were indeed prominent within the religious life of Philippi. On this basis, R. E. Witt has noted a number of features of the story in Acts 16 which he thinks intentionally reflect elements of Isis-cult practice or symbolism.[52] These include the python mantic, the location of a sanctuary near water, and the name Lydia (or "the Lydian") as an epithet for Isis.[53]

48. P. Lemerle, "Inscriptions Latines et Grecques de Philippes," *BCH* 59 (1935) 140–43 (nos. 40–41). The texts are as follows:

No. 40
Ἀγαθῇ Τύχῃ/ Κ(οίντον) Φλάβιον Ἑρ/μαδίωνα τὸν/
ἀξιολογώτα/[το]ν οἱ θρησκευ/[τὲ] τοῦ Σέραπι/
[τὸ]ν εὐεργέτην/ [μνή]μης χάριν.

No. 41
Κο(ίντον) Φλάβιον Ἑρ/μαδίωνα υἱὸν/ Κο(ίντου)
Φλαβίου Ἑρμαδίωνος· /τοῦ κρα(τίστου)· γυμνα/σιάρχου
κα(ὶ) ἀρχιερέως οἱ θρησκευ/τὲ τὸν ἴδιον ἀγωνοθέτην/
τῶν μεγάλων Ἀσκληπείων.

49. Ibid., 142; cf. *BCH* 37 (1913) 94–95.

50. Cf. Vidman, *Sylloge* nos. 123–24 (*BCH* 53 [1929] 87; *BCH* 94 [1970] 809–11; Picard, "Les Dieux de la colonie de Philippes," 159–72, 173–83; Witt, *Isis in the Graeco-Roman World*, 81, 145, 192. Also for Egyptian cults on Thasos, see Claude Rolley, "Le cultes égyptiens à Thasos: À propos de quelques documents nouveaux," *BCH* 92 (1968) 187–219 (esp. 187–96) and for Isis Pelagia, see Philippe Bruneau, "Isis Pelagia à Délos," *BCH* 85 (1961) 435–46; idem, "Isis Pelagia à Délos," *BCH* 87 (1963) 301–8.

51. For the *Cultores Collegi Silvani*, cf. *CIL* III.633 (items I–IV). It is interesting that the title *Augustales* (usually found in connection with local imperial cult) and *dendrophoroi* (usually found in connection with the official cult of Cybele, especially at Rome) are here found together in conjunction with the *Cultores Silvani* (cf. P. Lemerle, "Inscriptions Latines et Grecques de Philippes," *BCH* 58 (1934) 466. The list of names includes numerous local elites and officials (all men). By the same token, prominent individuals are also attested among the dedicants to Isis/Sarapis, e.g. L. Valerius Priscus, a *duovir* and decurion (cf. Collart, "Inscriptions de Philippes," *BCH* 62 [1938] 428–29 [no. 10] = *CIL* III.14206[27]). For connections with the imperial cult note also the formula *ob honorem divinae domus* (in honor of the divine house) on the second-century dedication to Isis of Q. Mofius Euhemerus (Vidman, *Sylloge*, no. 121).

52. Witt, *Isis in the Graeco-Roman World*, 192, 260, 322.

53. Cf. Vidman, *Sylloge*, no. 371.

SOCIAL SEMANTIC CONTEXTS

It seems to me that despite the clear intention of Acts 16 to create a Jewish social context for Paul's mission, Witt has in fact hit on the problem, at least indirectly. The upshot is *not* to claim, as does Witt, historical and archaeological (or what I term sociographic) "reality" for such Isis allusions in the case of Luke-Acts. Instead, it points to an array of conventionalized terms and practices which were operative in the environment, that is to say, based on the typical aspects of these sociographic contexts though not themselves historically verifiable. Thus we have now shifted to the functional semantics of social context. This is not to say, of course, that such semantic complexes are not rooted in the realities of the day. Quite the contrary, they are a major force in shaping that reality. Still, one can see that the conventionalization and idealization of such social practices through key terms or phrases functioned in literature apart from direct historical events and persons.[54]

Take the example of our epigraphic data from Philippi for the father and son Q. Flavius Hermadion (cited above). As anyone knows who has ever attempted to decipher ancient Greek or Latin inscriptions, there is an old adage that goes "inscriptions are easy to read as long as you know what they are supposed to say." The adage rings true precisely because so much in epigraphy depends on accepted patterns, use of abbreviations, and set formulas or conventions, all of which were fairly rigid. Thus, for any given formulaic inscription, its *sociographic context* would refer to the specific person(s), location, date, and actions designated. Its *functional semantic contexts* would represent the ability, need, or expectation of a different person, in another town or another time, to describe an analogous action using the same basic formula. Hence, in order for a modern historian to understand a given piece of archaeological data, one must be aware of both its sociographic context and its semantic contexts. So, we may take the case of a

54. This point has also been made recently by Dennis E. Smith in regard to dining practices. He cites the case of Plutarch's Banquet of the Seven Sages (*Convivium septem sapientium*), an account of a dinner in the days of Socrates told in first person. Apart from the historical difficulties here, Smith notes that the account is really a conventionalized portrayal of dining practices based on the idealization of the symposium. At the same time, he argues, these idealized accounts seem to have informed and influenced the actual practices of people, at least in polite society, when they convened formal dinners. Thus, actual social practices are conventionalized into literary fictions which in turn influence actual social practices. See D. Smith, "What Really Happened at Ancient Banquets: Evaluating the Evidence for Ancient Meal Practice," paper presented at the 1993 SBL Annual Meeting; also his forthcoming monograph *From Symposium to Eucharist*. In the case of Acts, one may note the idealized legal process depicted in Paul's treatment by Festus, especially noting Acts 25:16. Provincial governors are known to have exercised extraordinary judicial power (under their *imperium*) in cases of Roman citizens, even to the point of capital punishment. Hence, Festus's statement is more ideal than real. For narrative linkages between Acts 16 and chapters 25–27 see below ad loc. nn. 57, 60.

member of the prominent Muscii family from Philippi in the Antonine period. In the sociographic context Julius Maximus Mucianus held the offices of *aedile* and *praetor* and was accorded decurion rank both in the colony of Philippi and in the province of Thrace. The last line of one of his honorific texts reads simply: *L·D·D·D*, which is the abbreviated formula *l(oco) d(ato) d(ecreto) d(ecurionum)* ("set [this honorific] in place by decree of the decurions").[55] Here the semantic context includes both the formula of honorific conferral and the social conventions it reflects. We might call this the "grammar of etiquette," a parallel to what Ramsay MacMullen has called the "lexicon of snobbery." Both phrases, I think, accurately grasp the sense of *convention* in the Roman social order and in the semantic fields associated with it.

Often it is just this social semantic convention that finds its way into the romance and satire of novelistic literature in the Roman age, and it is this fact that allows us to identify the form and function, that is, the sociographic background, of various literary, rhetorical, philosophical, or social *topoi*—"commonplaces." Thus, a *topos* is certainly a real reflection of the age, though it may not always depend on the historical reality of the situation described. Such features in the story of Acts 16 are suggested not only by the observations of Witt (noted above) but also by Sherwin-White's discussion of the legal issue of Paul's citizenship, which becomes an issue for the first time in Acts at Philippi. Although Sherwin-White holds to the "essential veracity" of the account, he does observe that the story is closer to the rhetoric of abuse of citizens found in the Republican sentiments of Ciceronian oration than to actual legal claims of citizenship rights by provincials in the first century C.E.[56] This observation is pertinent to our question, especially given the ongoing debate over the historicity of Paul's Roman citizenship as depicted in Acts.[57]

We may begin to take account of the semantic conventionalization of Acts 16 by noticing the basic structure of the Philippi episode: (a) arrival (vv. 11–12); (b) conversion of Lydia and table fellowship/exhortation (vv. 13–15); (c) encounter with the mantic, complaint before civil authorities, and

55. Collart, "Inscriptions de Philippes," 422 (no. 8) = *CIL* III.7339:

[.] *Iul(io) C. f(ilio) Vol(tinia)/ [M]aximo Muci/ano,*

viro cl(arissimo), la/toclavo hono/[r]ato a divo Pio,

[q(uaestori)] pr(o) pr(aetore) Ponto-Bithy(niae),/

[a]ed(ili) cerial(i), praet(ori)/ desig(nato), idem

dec(urioni) Phil(ippis)/ et in provinc(ia) Thra(cia),

C. Iul(ius) Teres, thra/carc(ha), pater sena/torum, fratri,/ l(oco) d(ato) d(ecreto) d(ecurionum).

56. Sherwin-White, *Roman Law and Roman Society*, 76–92 and esp. 172–73.

57. Thus, despite Sherwin-White's conclusion affirming Paul's Roman citizenship, I am very doubtful. See the discussions by E. R. Goodenough, "The Perspective of Acts," in *Studies in Luke-Acts* (ed. L. E. Keck and J. L. Martyn; 2nd ed.; Philadelphia: Fortress, 1966) 55; and J. Jervell, *The Unknown Paul: Essays on Luke-Acts and Early Christian History* (Minneapolis: Augsburg, 1984) 68–76.

imprisonment (vv. 16–24); (d) earthquake, conversion of the jailer, and table
fellowship (vv. 25–34); (e) resolution of the civil encounter (vv. 35–39); and
(f) final exhortations and departure (v. 40). The parallelism of the chapter
occurs in the repetition of conversion/encounter/conversion/encounter
sequence, which is typical of several episodes in this section of Acts.[58]

Thematic links are created in this section by the use of several catch-
words or *topoi*, in addition to narrative elements suggested earlier. Most
notable is the conversion of the entire household, or *Oikosformel*, followed
immediately by table fellowship (in vv. 15, 32–34). Also, the house of Lydia
as the locus of exhortation (using the term παρεκάλεσαν) serves to bracket
the conversion/encounter parallelism (vv. 15, 40, cf. 20.1–2). The term
ὑπάρχοντες (simply translated "being") serves as a flag for the legal status of
"being Jews" or "being Romans" in the two encounters with the civil magistrates (vv. 20, 37) that bracket the imprisonment. On this sense of ὑπάρχων,
used to designate nationality or citizenship, it should be noted that the only
other occurrence in Acts is at 16:3, that is, at the beginning of the so-called
second journey in connection with Timothy's family situation (again Jew
and non-Jew) at the Roman colony of Lystra. Finally, the verb καταγγέλλειν
(used of proclamation to non-Jews) is a thread in the "second journey" narrative. It runs from 15:36 (the commission of Paul by the Apostolic Council)
to 16:17, 21 (the first encounter with the Philippian authorities) to 17:3, 13,
23 (the parallel preaching/encounters at Thessalonika, Beroea, and
Athens).[59] While the term was used earlier in 13:5 and 38, it does not occur
again until Paul's speech before Agrippa (26:23). A number of these uses, it
should be noticed, are direct discourse (13:38; 15:36; 16:17, 21; 17:3, 23; 26:23),
all but the two in chapter 16 spoken by Paul himself, usually in sermons.[60]
The remaining instances, however, are in sections of connecting narrative.
Moreover, several are in the so-called "we" sections of the narrative (again,
this applies to 16:17, 21, while 26:23 is somewhat ambiguous), but they
weave in and out of the first- and third-person narrative units and appear in
clearly Lukan redactional elements (so 17:13). In other words, this term suggests a catchword in the interweaving of the disparate units of the Lukan
narrative, especially in the travelogue of the "second journey" section.

What is striking in this thematic structure is the use of the semantic conventions of hospitality and table fellowship in connection with the conver-

---

58. On the parallel organization and type of scene, see also Tannehill, *Narrative Unity*, 2:202.

59. J. T. Sanders, "The Prophetic Use of the Scriptures in Luke-Acts," in *Early Jewish and
Christian Exegesis: Studies in Memory of William Hugh Brownlee* (ed. C. Evans and W. F. Stine-
spring; Atlanta: Scholars Press, 1987) 197–98. Also, the opening comment of his essay (p. 191)
is entirely consistent with our findings regarding the semantic structures in Acts 16.

60. On the speeches, see *inter alia* E. Schweizer, "Concerning the Speeches in Acts," in *Studies in Luke-Acts*, 208–16; J. Jervell, "Paul: The Teacher of Israel, The Apologetic Speeches of Paul
in Acts," in *Luke and the People of God* (Minneapolis: Augsburg, 1979) 153–77; Tannehill, *Narrative Unity*, 309–29.

sion episodes, first by a Greek woman from Asia and then by a Roman man, both of whom are heads of households. The technical vocabulary of hospitality/fellowship (16:15: εἰσελθόντες εἰς τὸν οἶκόν μου μένετε ["come into my house and stay"]; and 16:33–34: παραλαβὼν αὐτοὺς . . . ἀναγαγών τε αὐτοὺς εἰς τὸν οἶκον παρέθηκεν τραπέζαν ["welcomed them . . . and taking them up into the house he prepared a table"]) is used here to reflect the social conventions.[61] These same conventions are to be seen earlier in Acts in the case of the pious benefactress Dorcas (9:36–43) and the precedent-setting case of the centurion Cornelius (10:1–48), another "God-fearer" converted with his entire household. Still earlier, in the ministry of Jesus, the Lukan author elaborates the account of another pious centurion by exploiting the technical language and social obligations of benefaction (Luke 7:2–10, noting especially vv. 4–5: παρεκάλουν αὐτὸν σπουδαίως λέγοντες ὅτι ἄξιός ἐστιν ᾧ παρέξῃ τοῦτο· ἀγαπᾷ γὰρ τὸ ἔθνος ἡμῶν καὶ τὴν συναγωγὴν αὐτὸς ᾠκοδόμεσεν ἡμῖν ["they besought him earnestly, saying, 'He is worthy to have you do this for him, for he loves our nation, and he built us our synagogue'"]).[62] It is no mere accident, then, that Acts 16, the pivot point to the "second journey" narrative, draws together these important social factors using the semantic conventions. The conversions involve only prominent individuals, the Greek woman and the Roman jailer, who function as patrons and/or "God-fearers." The point of convergence is yet another theme or motif with great significance in Acts, the *Oikosformel*, as both are heads of households. This theme carries through the "second journey" narrative in chapter 17 and 18 (the cases of Jason and Titius Justus). The sociographic issues here have been addressed recently in discussions of the "God-fearers." It has been argued on epigraphic grounds that the "God-fearers" constitute a thematic literary convention in Acts but are difficult to place in the historical contexts of diaspora synagogues.[63]

61. Cf. Malherbe, *Social Aspects*, 94–102; idem, *Paul and the Thessalonians*, 15.

62. On the technical benefaction language in this case, see especially F. W. Danker, *Benefactor: Epigraphic Study of a Graeco-Roman and New Testament Semantic Field* (St. Louis: Clayton, 1982) 317–92, 406.

63. Acts 17:4; cf. Malherbe, *Paul and the Thessalonians*, 12–17. On the issue of the "God-fearers," see A. T. Kraabel, "The Disappearance of the Godfearers," *Numen* 28 (1981) 113–26; J. Gager, "Jews, Gentiles, and Synagogues in the Book of Acts," in *Paul Among Jews and Christians: Studies in Honor of Krister Stendahl*, ed. G. W. E. Nickelsburg and G. MacRae, HTR 79 (1986) 91–99. The question is yet to be resolved. In my view the publication of the inscription from Aphrodisias has not settled the matter definitively, as was suggested by many. For the inscription and discussion, see J. Reynolds and R. Tannenbaum, *Jews and Godfearers at Aphrodisias* (Cambridge: Cambridge Philological Society, 1987). *Pace* Tannenbaum (who reads rabbinic norms and terminology into the text), I do not see in the inscription evidence for the actual synagogue community per se, but rather a social organization (a *collegium* with philanthropic interests, most likely) attached loosely to the synagogue, but made up of Jews as well as non-Jews. In this context, the term θεοσεβής/-εῖς does not clearly mark a penumbra of near-converts in the synagogue community itself. On the contrary, it may show an instance of Jewish accommodation to avenues of social interaction with non-Jews that allowed for both

THE "WORLD" OF ACTS 16:
THE CULTURAL CONTEXT OF NARRATIVE

There are, then, a number of details in the narrative of Acts that ring true to the historical and social environment. The host (and patron) Jason's posting a peace bond before the πολιτάρχαι at Thessalonika (17:5–9) and the house of Titius Justus situated "hard up against" (συνομοροῦσα) the synagogue under the leadership of an ἀρχισυνάγωγος (18:7–8) both "fit" the environment.[64] Still, in neither case is there sociographic evidence by which to make a direct historical correlation. Instead, the narrative itself has been shaped and conventionalized to make a thematic point in Acts, and the semantic social contexts set up this point by stressing typicalities. In other words, rather than reflecting the social and historical particularities of individual localities, the narrative revolves around the conventional.

In this semantic and thematic context, then, it is most significant that the mantic girl (of Acts 16:16–17) does not necessarily become a convert.[65] In fact, Paul only confronts her Pythonic spirit when she persists in announcing their role as proclaimers of θεὸς ὕψιστος, the only time the term appears in Acts. Also, Paul's formula for revoking the "demonic" spirit is the same as that of Jesus in the lone occasion in Luke where θεὸς ὕψιστος, appears.[66] Of course, the term does not appear in Paul, even though it is found commonly among diaspora Jews; however, it is also found in clearly pagan contexts, including a precisely contemporary inscription to Cybele by an imperial client (a Thracian king) at Philippi/Neapolis.[67] Thus,

---

civic activities as well as social dining, yet set apart in some measure from the worship activities of the congregation. See my preliminary discussion of the text in *Building God's House*, 88–90; a fuller treatment of the issue, following the suggestions made there and above, is in preparation.

64. Sherwin-White, *Roman Law and Roman Society*, 96; A. T. Kraabel, "The Social Systems of Six Diaspora Synaogues," in *Ancient Synagogues: The State of Research* (ed. J. Gutmann; Atlanta: Scholars Press, 1981) 79–91; White, "The Delos Synagogue Revisited," 133–38.

65. *Contra* Lightfoot, *Philippians*, 57 (which is the occasion for his theological excursus; cf. below n. 68).

66. Cf. Luke 8:28, where it is also a demonic voice, in the context of Greek city of the Decapolis, which is then summarily silenced by Jesus using the invocation παρήγγειλεν γὰρ τῷ πνεύματι τῷ ἀκαθάρτῳ ἐξελθεῖν ("for he had charged the unclean spirit to come out"). Compare the similar formulation in Acts 16:18: παραγγέλλω σοι ἐν ὀνόματι Ἰησοῦ Χριστοῦ ἐξελθεῖν ("I charge you in the name of Jesus Christ to come out").

67. Θρακικά 1935:302:

Διὶ Ὑψίστωι εὐχαρισ[τή]ριον ὑπὲρ κυρίου βασιλέος Θρακῶν Ῥοιμη/τάλκα Κότυος καὶ τῶν τέκνων αὐτοῦ Εὔτυχος ὁ ἐπὶ τῶν λατόμων καὶ οἱ ὑπ᾽ αὐτὸν πάντες.

Cf. *OGIS* 378:

Θεῷ ἁγίῳ ὑψίστῳ ὑπὲρ τῆς Ῥοιμητάλκου καὶ Πυθοδωρίδος ἐκ τοῦ/ κατὰ τὸν Κοῖλα {λ}ητικὸν πόλεμον κινδύνου σωτηρίας εὐξάμενος καὶ/ ἐπιτυχὼν Γαίος Ἰούλιος Πρόκ{λ}ος χαριστήριον.

On the term θεὸς ὕψιστος, see A. T. Kraabel, "Hypsistos and the Synagogue at Sardis," *GRBS* 10 (1969) 81–93; White, "The Delos Synagogue Revisited," 139, 145–46. I would suggest,

the "charge" brought against Paul by the mantic girl would have had no real weight in the particular sociographic context of Philippi, since it is a known and accepted divine epithet in common pagan usage. Its purpose, instead, comes in the thematic and theological structures of Luke-Acts but has nothing really to say about events peculiar to Philippi.[68] Here it should be remembered that Lightfoot saw *three* conversions in Acts 16 (Lydia, the mantic, and the jailer) as instrumental to the social progress of the gospel.[69] The mantic girl, he said, was the first recorded conversion of a slave. In the case of Lydia, he made much of the uniquely high social position of women in Macedonia (citing also the "leading women" in 17:4) as establishing a precedent for the church.

For Lightfoot, the newly found inscriptions of his day revealed women in more prominent positions. Of course, he went on to hint his own suspicions that either Euodia or Syntyche (of Phil 4:2) might be the personal name by which Paul addressed the "Lydian" woman. While there is important evidence for the role of women, both in the environment and in the narrative theme of Acts, the sociographic evidence for Philippi does not quite bear out Lightfoot's point regarding the situation for Macedonian women, despite recent discussions of this point. Indeed, the *realia* that reflect the prolific women's cultic activities peculiar to Philippi are not the aspects reflected in the story of Acts 16.[70] Instead, the story of Lydia

therefore, that the term was intentionally "neutral" in common usage, and thus did not serve to distinguish Jews in the common religious environment. For recent evidence from Asia Minor of this term in conjunction with local cults of angel worship, but in pagan contexts, see also A. R. R. Sheppard, "Pagan Cults of Angels in Roman Asia Minor," *Talanta* 12/13 (1980–81) 77–101.

68. On the structure and function of these exorcism episodes as thematic in Luke-Acts, see S. Garrett, *The Demise of the Devil: Magic and the Demonic in Luke's Writings* (Minneapolis: Fortress, 1989) 93 et passim. Cf. Tannehill, *Narrative Unity*, 197–201.

69. Lightfoot, *Philippians*, 55–58.

70. Lightfoot's claim, partially following Ramsay, seems to be repeated in almost every commentary on Philippians without critical discussion. The most elaborate treatment of the issue in following out this line is that of Lilian Portefaix (*Sisters Rejoice*, 177–88, et passim), which attempts to do a reader-response interpretation of Acts 16 (particularly the conversion of Lydia) as it would have been received by women at Philippi. While she is certainly aware of the critical issues in the composition of Acts, she nonetheless blurs the literary setting with the real sociographic situation of Philippi in a way that the text itself does not permit. Also on the religious activities of women at Philippi see Valerie Abrahamsen, "Christianity and the Rock Reliefs at Philippi," *BA* 51 (1988) 46–56; eadem, "Women at Philippi: The Pagan and Christian Evidence," *Journal of Feminist Studies in Religion* 3 (1987) 17–30; eadem, "Pagan Funerary Practices in Northern Greece during the Early Christian Era," *Macedonian Studies* 6 (1989) 58–72. I am in no way disputing the evidence collected by Abrahamsen, especially for the uniqueness and the popularity of the cult of Diana among women at Philippi. Her argument, in fact, runs counter to that of Lightfoot, since she suggests that the prominence of women in the pagan cults would have militated against any need for them to convert to Christianity (so her "Women at Philippi," 22). However, demonstrating the popularity of such a cult for women, or even egalitarian tendencies in funerary cult, is not the same as claiming an overall social prominence of women in other arenas of social life.

revolves around the more typical type of urban social phenomenon of geographical mobility and relative economic independence. More generally, my own rapid "scatter count" of Philippi inscriptions (both Greek and Latin) suggests a mix of prominent women in other areas of public social life that is fairly typical of major urban centers in the Greek east.[71]

So, Paul converts a prominent Greek woman and her household but not the mantic girl. Paul does not convert slaves, Acts seems to say. But why? The social semantic categories, usually arising in conjunction with the *Oikosformel* motif, point to an emphasis on the conversion of a *pater-* or *mater-familias*, many of whom are already actively demonstrating sympathies (both intellectual and social) toward synagogue Judaism. Upon conversion they in turn demonstrate the implications by exercising the accepted social conventions of hospitality and patronage toward Paul. Acts 16, then, marks an important turning point, both geographically and socially, in the Lukan portrayal of the Pauline mission. Geographically, the "second journey" marks the first foray in the major urban centers of the Greek East, thus setting up the important encounters in Athens, Corinth, and Ephesus. Socially, it marks a turn more toward "God-fearers" and Gentiles-at-large, while the synagogue becomes increasingly a source of animosity and civil strife.[72] The social litmus test for the larger urban environment is that they deal with heads of households. The social and theological test for Paul's apostolic commission, then, comes in his willingness to accept the hospitality of these converts.

It seems to me, then, that the convergence of two conversion/encounter episodes in which Paul's Jewishness stands in tension with his "Roman

71. On a survey of 202 inscriptions from Philippi, mixed Greek and Latin, I come up with the following "raw" breakdown based on the gender of the dedicant (Male, Female, N/A [= information Not Available]). For *CIL* III (all Latin inscriptions) a total of 112 inscriptions: M=54; F=16; N/A=42. For a mixed lot (Greek and Latin) taken randomly by yearly publications in *BCH* a total of 90 inscriptions: M=50; F=9; N/A=31. The aggregate of the two would be: M=104; F=25; N/A=73. Thus, the ratio of male to female for discernible cases within this sample is roughly 4:1; or, put more precisely, women make up 19.4 percent of the dedicants, where identifiable. But of the total count, identifiable women constitute only 12.4 percent. While this "scatter count" in no way claims to be exhaustive, it is likely to be within the range of indicative ratios for the surviving corpus of inscriptions. On this assumption, then, general areas of participation by women at Philippi do not seem to stand out as appreciably higher than the proportion of inscriptions by prominent women from other regions of the empire; however, I have seen no comparable "scatter counts" for other localities on which to base more precise calculations or comparisons. For suggestions regarding the empire at large, drawing on a similar type of sampling from Asia Minor, see R. MacMullen, "Women in Public in the Roman Empire" and "Women's Power in the Principate," both reprinted in *Changes in the Roman Empire: Essays on the Ordinary* (Princeton: Princeton University Press, 1990) 162–68, 169–76, respectively. (See especially his conclusions on pp. 175–76, which concur with my suggestions for Philippi.)

72. J. T. Sanders, *The Jews in Luke-Acts* (Philadelphia: Fortress, 1987) passim; J. B. Tyson, *Images of Judaism in Luke-Acts* (Columbia, S.C.: University of South Carolina Press, 1992) 35–39, 143–44.

citizenship" is central to the narrative impact of Acts 16. We have here yet
another case of apologetic interests, along the lines suggested by Cadbury,
Haenchen, and others.[73] But I think the convergence of sociographic and
social semantic categories may carry us beyond previous suggestions as to
the precise nature of this apologetic intent, at least in one regard. Luke-Acts
seems to be making a claim about the nature of the Christian mission using
an established social model from the environment. That model asserts the
position of the extended household (including the *pater-* or *mater-familias*,
children, slaves, friends, freedmen, and other clients) is the locus of the
movement. I have suggested previously that these same motifs are at work
in the four householder parables of Luke (chapters 11–13). There the model
of the householder and extended household provides a structural analogy
for the cosmic order, with God (or the Messiah) as the *paterfamilias*. At the
same time these four parables are positioned around and directed at concerns over a Jesus logion (Luke 12:49–53, cf. 11:17) on division within households.[74] Thus, the image of the householder and the social function of
patronage are important thematic elements drawn explicitly from the
Roman environment and disseminated through semantic conventions.[75]

73. H. J. Cadbury, *The Making of Luke-Acts* (2nd ed.; London: SPCK, 1958) 251–53, 360–68; cf.
The Book of Acts in History (London: Adam & Charles Black, 1955) 50–82; E. Haenchen, "Judentum und Christentum in der Apostelgeschichte," *ZNW* 54 (1963) 169–72 (especially in regard
to the "placarding" or caricature of Jews); idem, *Die Apostelgeschichte* (16th ed.; Göttingen;
Vandenhoeck & Ruprecht, 1977) 431–43, esp. 442–43 on the literary artistry of Acts. More
recently on the apologetic interests, see the discussion by Esler, *Community and Gospel in
Luke-Acts*, 205–18 (and further bibliography cited there). See also below n. 75.

74. White, "Scaling the Strongman's Court," 15–19.

75. While I find much in Esler's work (*Community and Gospel in Luke-Acts*) to be helpful and
informative for sociohistorical analysis of Luke-Acts, there are some basic areas of disagreement reflected here. First and foremost, I do not quite accept his distinction between what he
calls an "apologetic" over against a "legitimating" function for the document. Implicit within
his use of the term "apologetic" is the assumption that it must be directed toward outsiders (so
pp. 207–8). Such a definition misunderstands the way much of the so-called apologetic literature of antiquity really functioned socially, in that it need not have actually been intended to
be read by outsiders. Instead, most apologetic literature was really addressed to insiders who
were looking toward that margin with the larger society as the arena of acculturation and
self-definition. Thus, I see little difference in the two ways of talking about the function of the
document. Second, and given the "legitimating" community function just discussed, I am still
uncomfortable with adopting sectarian definition models and language for these communities.
Indeed, Esler's own conclusions do not correspond well with a more precise definition of the
sectarian dynamics. So see my "Shifting Sectarian Boundaries in Early Christianity," *BJRL* 70
(1988) 7–24, esp. p. 17. Third, it seems that the attitude toward wealth and the patronal class
that controlled it in the Roman world is not met with the type of antithetical attitude suggested by Esler (esp. pp. 185–87). Instead, Luke-Acts seems to be holding up heads of families
and householders (both male and female) as ideal types who are attracted to the gospel and
who in turn follow its social ethic in caring for their economic dependents. In my view, this
too is part of the apologetic/legitimating function of the narrative at a social semantic level.
This view is consistent with that suggested by David Balch's article in this volume. His discus-

In this connection, we may note the competition of provincial cities for imperial patronage, which, more often than not, took the form of an imperial grant or *senatus consultum*. A good example, though from Miletus rather than Philippi, is the *senatus consultum* granting status as *amici* of Rome to three Asclepiades.[76] Among the privileges granted with this status were exemptions from taxes and liturgies and the right to *hospitium* ("hospitality," that is a housing and allowances while in Rome). *Amicitia* here, though a term derived from the *patrocinium* and social dependencies of the household, comes to be used of the organs and ideology of Roman statecraft in the Greek east as part of the consolidation of the empire already in Republican times.[77] By the early principate, however, the terminology came to be used also of direct grants to individuals and cities by the emperor, and it was used as a weapon in the competition of cities for largesse.[78] A good example here is Augustus's grant of freedom (ἐλευθερία), which is termed φιλάνθρωπον to the Aphrodisians.[79] In the case of Macedonia, we see similar grants issued by Nerva to the Macedonian κοινόν in Beroea, at the embassy of Q. Popillius Python.[80] While these texts deal with free cities, they come closer to home in that they were still in competition with the provincial colonies for imperial benefations, as seen in the case of Thessalonika.[81] In particular, we may note the grants to the clients under Augustus and Tiberius, who were of a Thracian royal family and residing in Philippi and Neapolis.[82] These recipients of imperial εὐεργεσία, in turn, paid honors to the imperial household, particularly Livia, and they regularly use dedications to θεὸς ὕψιστος.[83] Thus, dedications to individual patron deities also

---

sion aptly suggests the range of sources (as well as a genre of literature) for the semantic conventions that I have been trying to identify here.

76. *IGRR* I.118 (= *CIL* I².588); cf. R. K. Sherk, *Roman Documents from the Greek East: Senatus Consulta and Epistulae to the Age of Augustus* (Baltimore: Johns Hopkins University Press, 1969) 124–32 (no. 22), dated ca. 78 B.C.E.

77. E. Gruen, *The Hellenistic World and the Coming of Rome* (2 vols.; Berkeley: University of California Press, 1984) 1:48–51. So also notice the use of *amicitia* in terms of statecraft in the *Res gestae divi Augusti* 29–32, where in the parallel Greek text (from the Ancyra inscription) the rendering is φιλία. On the earlier use of this term among Hellenistic rulers, see also G. Herman, "The Friends of the Early Hellenistic Rulers," *Talanta* 12/13 (1980) 103–49, in which acts of benefaction are requisite to the status of φιλία as a political relationship.

78. F. Millar, *The Emperor in the Roman World* (Ithaca, N.Y.: Cornell University Press, 1977) 420–34; Larsen, in Frank, *Economic Survey*, 4:449–56.

79. F. Millar, *Emperor*, 431.

80. Rostovtzeff, *Social and Economic History*, 2:650 n. 97; Millar, *Emperor*, 432.

81. B. Levick, *Roman Colonies in Southern Asia Minor* (Oxford: Clarendon, 1967) 68–80, 86–88; 103–29. See also H. Hendrix, "Benefactor/Patronage Networks in the Urban Environment: Evidence from Thessalonica," *Semeia* 56 (1991) 39–58.

82. Salac, "Inscription du Pangee," 87; cf. *BCH* 56 (1932) 203; *CIL* III.656, 703, 707 for rich Thracian landowners in the environs of Philippi.

83. *ILS* 8784, cf. *OGIS* 378 (from the same dedication quoted above in n. 67).

served in obligatory displays of gratitude for imperial patronage, a pattern not unlike the request made to Jesus in Luke 7:5–6.[84]

Patronage and the household model point to larger concerns of the environment which emerge out of the sociographic and semantic contexts. At this point, the "world" of Acts 16 seems to have opened up into a whole cosmos of cultural symbolic concerns as well. This is, I suspect, a large part of what is at stake to the author of Luke-Acts in this presentation of the mission of Paul. But at this point the "real" world of Acts 16 is far removed from Philippi in the historical circumstances of Paul's day.

84. Danker, *Benefactor*, 489; White, "Scaling the Strongman's Court," 18–19. In this connection we may take note of an often overlooked textual variant in 16:38–39, when the στρατηγοί come to the house of the jailer to exhort (παρακαλεῖν) Paul to leave peaceably. Codex Bezae adds the fact that the authorities sent their "friends" (φίλοι), a use of the term as clients or retainers, which accurately reflects the social semantic conventions of patron–client relationships in the environment. It is also worth noting that Luke-Acts has by far the highest use of this technical vocabulary of friendship and patronage, in contrast to Paul, who *never* uses φίλος/φιλία (though he does incorporate many of the other semantic conventions). In Luke-Acts it can be seen particularly in the four "householder" parables of Luke 11–13; cf. "Scaling the Strongman's Court," 15–17.

Part Three

The Religious and
Social Environment
of Early Christianity

CHAPTER 16

The Red Hall
in Pergamon

Helmut Koester

PERGAMON, in the northeastern part of the Roman province of Asia, was once the proud capital of the wealthy Hellenistic kingdom of the Attalids. During the Roman imperial period it was in competition with Ephesos, which had become the capital of the province, for the title of "the first city" of Asia. Indeed, Pergamon had received the first imperial neocorate, the title of "warden of the temple for the worship of the emperor," in the province of Asia,[1] well over a hundred years before Ephesos. The latter did not achieve this honor until the reign of Domitian at the end of the first century C.E., and it had to wait for Hadrian to achieve a second. Pergamon was granted its second imperial neocorate under Trajan (98–117 C.E.). The temple of Trajan on the Akropolis of Pergamon was a large peripteral podium temple surrounded by stoas on three sides and was completed during Hadrian's reign (117–138 C.E.).[2] However, this was by no means the only major building that was erected in Pergamon at that time. The Asklepieion, situated 2 km west of the city, was rebuilt according to a completely new general design. The plan incorporated stoas surrounding a large square measuring 120 m by 90 m, with a propylon, theater, library, and a large round temple for Zeus-Asklepios, modeled on Hadrian's Pantheon in Rome.[3] It also seems that the theater in the lower city, the amphitheater, and the stadium were built, or completed, during Hadrian's reign.[4]

1. The temple serving this first provincial cult in Asia, built during the time of Augustus, has not yet been found or identified. See Wolfgang Radt, *Pergamon: Geschichte und Bauten, Funde und Erforschung einer antiken Metropole* (DuMont Dokumente; Cologne: DuMont, 1988) 46–47.

2. Ibid., 239–50; for bibliography see pp. 376–77.

3. Ibid., 250–71; O. Ziegenaus and G. de Luca, *Das Asklepieion* (Altertümer von Pergamon 9,1–4; Berlin: de Gruyter, 1968–84).

4. Radt, *Pergamon*, 292–95.

While all these major constructions were under way, another monumental building project was undertaken in the lower city of Pergamon—a sanctuary for the worship of the Egyptian gods. It is one of the most impressive structures in the Greek world from the Roman period. The central building, which is still standing to a height of 19 m, is known as the "Red Hall" (often erroneously called the "Red Basilica"). This enormous structure, however, is only the central part of a much larger sanctuary complex, which in its dimensions dwarfs even the Jupiter temple of Baalbek. Unfortunately, this sanctuary is still not fully excavated and published, and its interpretation remains a conundrum.[5] Some badly needed repairs have been made in the main building, and the German Archaeological Institute conducted a thorough architectural survey shortly before World War II. Yet the results of this survey were never published. This is unfortunate, because this sanctuary at Pergamon is testimony to the great popularity of the Egyptian cult in a region where also the new Christian religion was rapidly expanding and becoming established during the same period. The following discussion will try to introduce the results of the preliminary investigations into the discussion of the religions of the early Christian period.[6]

THE TEMENOS
(Figure 1)

The Red Hall is the central temple structure of a much larger sanctuary. It was flanked by two round temples on its northern and southern sides. These three temples stood at the eastern end of the monumental *temenos* (sacred precinct/enclosure), and the Red Hall sits on its main axis, against its eastern wall. Most of the central and western parts of the *temenos* are now occupied by houses of the modern city of Bergama. However, of the *temenos* wall the northwestern corner and parts of the western and southern side are still standing to a height of 13 m. The entire *temenos* measures ca. 270 m from east to west and ca. 100 m from north to south. The *temenos* wall was built of small rectangular blocks to a height of at least 13 m. The

5. Ibid., 228–39, bibliography, 275–76. A brief discussion, including a rather unsatisfactory map, can be found in Regina Salditt-Trapmann, *Tempel der ägyptischen Götter in Griechenland und an der Westküste Kleinasiens* (EPRO 15; Leiden: Brill, 1970).

6. This discussion is to some extent based on the description provided by Wolfgang Radt (*Pergamon*, 228–39) and for the most part on on-site inspections under the guidance of Professor Dr. Klaus Nohlen of Wiesbaden, the architect of the German Archaeological Institute in Pergamon, who has also read a draft of this paper and to whom I wish to express my gratitude for all that I have learned during my visits.

The enclosed plans have been drawn on the basis of the often only approximate measurements given in previous publications. They may be somewhat inaccurate—as exact measurements are not always available—but should be helpful for a better understanding of the description and arguments of this essay.

Figure 1

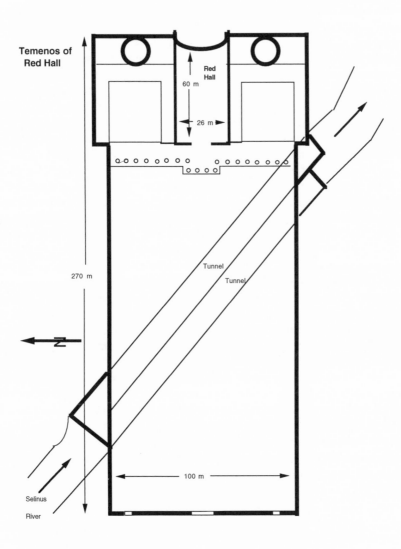

western *temenos* wall contained the entrances to the sanctuary, consisting of one large central door and two narrower doors close to its northern and southern end. This triportal western façade, of which portions are preserved, must have provided a magnificent sight. It was entirely faced with marble revetments; the three entrance gates were built of marble blocks. In front of this western wall stood a row of columns that were joined with the wall's protruding joists and, according to some recent finds, must have been constructed of gray granite. The central door opened onto a central *dromos*, which proceeded some 200 m to the *propylon* of the Red Hall with its 14 m high columns.

In order to create the necessary space for this immense sanctuary, the Selinus River had to be channeled into two vaulted tunnels, over which the *temenos* was built. After passing under a Roman bridge, which is fully preserved today (and is used even by automobile traffic), the Selinus River passes diagonally underneath the *temenos* from northwest to southeast for a distance of ca. 150 m. The reason for the construction of these water tunnels is most likely that the sponsor of the building wanted to situate the sanctuary in the center of the city rather than in an outlying district. Using the area over the river would also reduce the number of houses that had to be torn down in order to create the space needed for this gigantic project. The building of the tunnels is an example of the ingenuity of Roman engineering; the tunnels still function perfectly today as they drain without any difficulties the large amounts of water which swell the Selinus River during winter and spring rains.

There were probably three protruding *exedras* in the north and south walls of the *temenos*; the eastern and western *exedras* seem to have been rectangular, the central *exedras* semicircular. But there is no definitive evidence for the existence of these *exedras* (they are not featured on the plan). It is likely that porches surrounded the open western interior area of the *temenos*, and that a *dromos* ran from the central gate of the western *temenos* wall to the *propylon* of the Red Hall.

At the eastern end of the *temenos* stood the three temples, a rectangular temple in the center, namely, the Red Hall, flanked by two round structures. The spaces in front of the two round structures were occupied by square colonnaded courts. It seems that a colonnaded portico, running from north to south, with a central *propylon* in front of the entrance to the Red Hall, separated these structures from the central and western parts of the *temenos*.

THE RED HALL
(Figure 2)

The central rectangular structure, the Red Hall, measures 60 m from east to west and 26 m from north to south. Its southern, western, and northern

Figure 2

Eastern Part of Red Hall Temenos

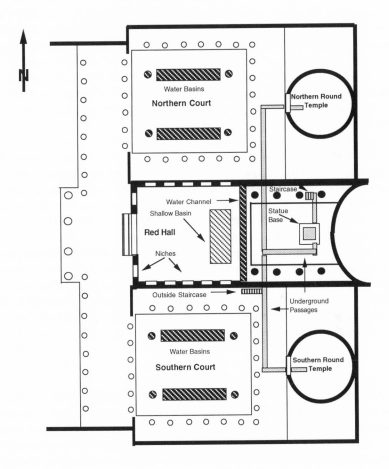

walls are preserved up to a height of 19 m. The eastern wall was destroyed when the building was remodeled into a Christian basilica with an eastern apse. Nonetheless, the foundations of the eastern wall that are preserved demonstrate that this wall was originally curved so as to form an apse on the outside. It is not possible to say definitively whether there were windows in this eastern wall; however, this may have been the case in order to provide special effects from the light of the rising sun.

The building is not a basilica, but a huge hall that was covered by a wooden roof without any interior support or colonnade.[7] The walls were constructed entirely of brick—a feature that has no parallel anywhere in Anatolia but is typical of buildings of this period in Rome and Italy. All its walls, inside and out, were covered with marble revetments in various colors. Important structural parts, like the frames of the door and the gable of the building, were constructed of solid marble blocks.

Stoas were attached on the outer long walls of the Red Hall (see below). Above the roofs of these stoas narrow balconies ran along the entire length of the building, probably serving for the maintenance of the roofs and windows, which were situated in the uppermost parts of the long wall above these balconies. There were five windows on each side in the western half of the building. In the eastern part the row of windows is continued on the outside by three arched niches on each side, which are in fact false windows. Thus, the eastern portion of the Red Hall did not receive any natural light, unless there were windows in the eastern wall, which is not preserved.

The door in the center of the west side of the Red Hall was more than 7 m wide and approximately 14 m high. The preserved doorsill was constructed of one large marble monolith, weighing approximately 30 tons. There are cuttings for the bronze pins for the hinges of the huge wings of the door. In front of these a second set of cuttings indicates the presence of an iron grating. The doors themselves must have been kept open all the time because no traces of rollers for the door have been found. Access to the interior was probably controlled by a gate in the iron grating in front of the doors.

The interior of the Red Hall is divided into two sections of approximately equal length which are separated by a water channel (1.40 m wide and 1.37 m deep) extending from the north wall to the south wall. The floor and walls of the channel are revetted with Egyptian alabaster. A water pipe ends in the center of the eastern wall of the channel. The western part of the hall was lit by the windows in the upper story of the north and south walls and

---

7. For its later Christian use, the building was changed into a basilica by the construction of two inner colonnades, of which the foundations are still preserved.

was accessible to the public; the eastern part was reserved for the monumental cult statue and for the attending priests.

In the western part of the Red Hall five arched niches are preserved in the inside of the north and south walls, situated below the upper-story windows. In addition there are two niches on the inside of the western wall, flanking the door, for a total of twelve niches. The niches begin 2.70 m above the floor; each one is 3.12 m wide and ca. 6 m high. They probably served for the placement of statues of deities. The pillars between the niches, measuring 2.55 m in width and 2.25 m in depth, together with the massive pillars at the four corners are the most important structural elements of the building. The floor consisted of plates of red Rhodian and green Indian marble and black Egyptian granite. At the point of the fourth window the floor was interrupted by a shallow basin, 22 cm deep, apparently occupying the entire space from wall to wall and extending 5.20 m west to east. Three rectangular tubs were standing in this basin, placed parallel to each other.

The eastern part of the Red Hall behind the water channel is dominated by a podium. It begins abruptly behind the water channel, rises 1.50 m above the floor and is 8.82 m wide. The base for the temple statue rises another meter above the podium and measures 4.60 m square. One can estimate that the statue was at least 10 m high. A central well in the base for the statue, measuring 1.5 m square, indicates that the statue was hollow and could be accessed from the inside. A staircase 2.8 m north of the podium gave access to a passageway that leads to the opening underneath the inside of the statue[8] and connects to the tunnel system of the sanctuary complex. This tunnel system could also be reached from a staircase outside the southern wall of the Red Hall, in the southern court.[9]

Two massive towers form the eastern end of the north and south walls. These towers contain staircases, which lead to narrow balconies that protruded from the walls right and left of the temple statue. The original east wall of the Red Hall is not preserved because it was replaced by an apsidal wall when the building became a Christian basilica. But the foundations show that it originally formed an inverted apse convex on the inside and open to the outside—a strange feature for a wall that also served as part of the eastern terminating wall of the entire *temenos*.

8. Thus, priests were able to climb, probably by means of a wooden ladder, into the inside of the statue and issue statements as if coming from the mouth of the deity.

9. My plan does not try to present the entire tunnel systems; they need to be investigated once more. The tunnels shown on the map of Salditt-Trapmann (*Tempel der ägyptischen Götter*) are confusing because they fail to distinguish between the higher and wider access tunnels, connecting the interior of the three temples and linking up with the staircase outside the south wall of the Red Hall, and the narrower drainage tunnels that were designed to channel the water from the roofs of the buildings into the Selinus River.

THE TWO COURTS AND THEIR TEMPLES

The spaces north and south of the Red Hall were occupied by two courts measuring about 35 m square. The courts were surrounded on all sides by stoas, 5 m deep, with eight columns on each side. It appears that marble benches and intervening pedestals were placed in the northern, eastern, and southern stoas as some remains have been found along the outside of the southern wall of the Red Hall. The stoas on the western sides of the two courts opened onto the portico that connected to the *propylon* in front of the Red Hall. Together with this *propylon*, the portico served at the same time as the eastern boundary of the large western courtyard of the *temenos*.

Many of the low bases for the columns have been found *in situ;* the corner bases measure 2.25 m; the others are 1.60 m square. Caryatids and Atlantes, of which many parts and fragments have survived, served instead of columns in the stoas of the two courts. Each consisted of two figures, sometimes a male and a female, sometimes two females, which stood back to back on a 2 m high square pedestal that was set on a low square base. On their high Egyptian headdress they carried a capital that was shaped like a chalice but was flat in front and in back. The dressed parts of the figures along with the pedestal and capital were of white marble, but the faces, arms, hands, and feet were made of a dark gray marble. The dark-colored marble of the naked parts of these figures undoubtedly indicates that they represented Egyptians. The lowest course of the architrave was curved downward between each of these double figures, giving the appearance of hanging garlands. The points at which the beams of the roof of the stoas were joined to the walls of the Red Hall demonstrate that their total height (column bases, caryatids, capitals, entablature, and roof) was 14.5 m.

There were water basins in the two courts, of which several are preserved. They were not situated in the center of the courts, but at a distance of 5.6 m from the colonnades of the northern and southern stoas. They are 11.5 m long, 2.5 m wide, and .85 m deep. At each end of these basins are smaller round basins of 1.75 m diameter.

Two round temples, flanking the Red Hall on the north and on the south, were set in the center behind the eastern stoas of the courts against the eastern back wall of the *temenos.* Both temples are well preserved; the one in the northern court now serves as a mosque. The inner diameter of these round temples is 12 m, and their height rivals that of the Red Hall; the domed roof begins at a height of 16 m; the doors are 11.5 m high.

CONCLUSION

This impressive building complex, one of the largest from the entire Roman period, was certainly a sanctuary of the Egyptian gods. An inscription referring to this sanctuary tells that Euphemos and Tullia Spendousa, the ἱεροφόροι ("bearers of holy objects"), gave to the gods what the goddess had commanded: "Sarapis, Isis, Harpokrates, Osiris, Apis, Helios on a horse... Ares, and the Dioskouroi...."[10] Another inscription from Pergamon mentions Sarapis,[11] and a small terra-cotta head of Isis with sun disk and horns was found in the area of the *temenos*.

It is difficult, however, to assign the three temples to any of the particular Egyptian deities. The main temple—that is, the Red Hall—must have been dedicated to either Sarapis or Isis. Sarapis appears on two coins from Pergamon from the periods of Antoninus Pius and Commodus. *Oxyrhynchus Papyrus* 1380 calls Isis ἐν Περγάμῳ δεσπότις (mistress or she who rules in Pergamon). The two round temples may have been dedicated to Horus and Anubis.

The complexity of the buildings, the underground passageways, and the water installations invite hypotheses about cult, ritual, and procedures of initiation. It is difficult to use Apuleius's description (*Metamorphoses* 11) as a guide for the interpretation, but some of the architectural features can be interpreted. Most important is the fact that this Egyptian temple does not follow the classical pattern of a Greek temple, according to which the temple itself is strictly the house of the deity. Rather, the place for the deity is restricted to the eastern part of the building, whereas the western part provides space for the worshiping community. This has analogies in the Sarapeion of Ephesos,[12] the Sarapeion of Miletos,[13] and the Isis temple of Thessalonike. The *temenos* of the Egyptian sanctuary of Pergamon was surrounded by very high walls, which did not allow outsiders to witness activities or rituals inside the *temenos*. Such enclosures of a *temenos* are otherwise found only in Greek mystery sanctuaries, such as Eleusis.

The western two-thirds of the *temenos*, about 200 m long, would certainly have featured a central *dromos*, to be used by the procession leading from the central entrance in the west *temenos* wall to the *propylon* of the Red Hall. The twelve niches in the western part of the Red Hall may have contained images of the Twelve Gods of the Zodiac, representing the universe.[14] Access to the underground passages by a staircase outside of the Red Hall gave the opportunity to lead an initiand to the interior of the Red Hall and

10. *Die Inschriften von Pergamon*, ed. R. Merkelbach et al. (Bonn, 1979–83) no. 336.

11. Ibid., no. 337.

12. The large structure west of the commercial agora of Ephesos, erected in the first half of the second century, is commonly identified as the temple of the Egyptian gods. However, this identification is not certain.

13. This is a three-aisled basilica that also dates from the second century; a *propylon* with an architrave inscription that mentions Sarapis was added in the third century.

14. The two passageways inside the north and south wall of the Sarapeion of Ephesus also featured a total of twelve niches. See also the report in Apuleius (*Metamorphoses* 11.23.8): Deos inferos et deos superos accessi coram et adoravi de proxumo ("I saw the gods infernal and the gods celestial, before whom I presented myself and worshiped").

of the two round temples. The initiand could then, at the end of the initiation, emerge inside the eastern part of the main temple and be presented to the worshipers, standing on the podium in front of the statue of the god or goddess,[15] but separated from the crowd by the deep water channel that divided the Hall into a public and a sacred area. At the same time, the public western space of the Red Hall was large enough to provide room for hundreds of worshipers who came to witness the presentation of the person who had just been initiated. Water basins inside the Hall gave the opportunity for generally accessible purification rituals, while the water basins in the courtyards may have been purely decorative. However, the pedestals between the benches in the stoas of the two courtyards allowed for the placement of votive offerings.

There can be no question about the incredible wealth and economic power of the city of Pergamon at that time. The building techniques of the Red Hall and the style of the sculptures indicate a date in the first half of the second century C.E. However, the use of brick for the erection of such an immense structure is a unique feature of the architecture of Anatolia in the imperial period. It must be assumed, therefore, that the emperor himself, most likely Hadrian, dispatched a Roman architect and workshops of brick masons to Pergamon to accomplish this task.[16] The sanctuary of the Red Hall is thus important evidence for the Hadrianic sponsorship and patronage of the Egyptian cult. The same emperor who issued the rescript regarding the treatment of Christians to Minucius Fundanus,[17] the proconsul of Asia, also lavishly provided money and sent Italian masons, skilled in large brick structures, for the building of this Egyptian sanctuary in the venerable royal city of Pergamon, whose mistress—as the Egyptian papyrus says—was Isis, the queen of the universe.

15. Ibid., 11.24.2: Namque in ipso aedis sacrae meditullo ante deae simulacrum constitutum tribunal ligneum . . . ("There in the middle of this sacred temple before the image of the goddess I was made to stand on a wooden pulpit . . .").

16. Cf. Trajan's answer to Pliny's request that an architect from Rome be sent to him in Bithynia: "I do not even have a sufficient number of architects for the buildings that are erected in Rome and its vicinity" (Pliny, *Epistulae* 10.18).

17. Justin, *Apology* 1.68.3–10; Eusebius, *Church History* 4.8.7–4.9.3.

CHAPTER 17

On the Nature of Magic:
A Report on a Dialogue
between a Historian and a Sociologist

Alan F. Segal

IT IS A GREAT PLEASURE to submit this paper to the Festschrift in honor of Wayne Meeks. When asked to contribute, I thought it particularly apt to write up these thoughts because Wayne had taken time to attend and comment on the work contained herein at a faculty seminar I attended at Yale in 1992. Furthermore, my interest in the problem of magic and religion began at Yale. Several years ago, I wrote an article on the subject in Hellenistic Judaism. It grew out of work done with Professors Meeks and Malherbe and appeared in the Gilles Quispel Festschrift. In the interim many new and very interesting studies have been done; so it is time to return to the subject again.

In addition to the many interesting studies on the data, the problem of the definition of magic has further occupied my time. It was especially important to the first chapter of a book jointly authored by TP (fictitious initials), a retired sociologist at Barnard, and me. Although the manuscript exceeded four hundred pages and received a contract from Harvard University Press, theoretical differences necessitated abandoning it. But some important differences emerged between my approach as a historian of Hellenistic religion and that of TP, as a sociologist, even as early as the first chapter, which concerned the definitions of magic and religion. I will trace some of the issues that are articulated in the now unpublished manuscript.

FIRST DRAFT

The best way to introduce the theoretical issues that TP and I discussed is by comparing various versions of chapter 1, which concerns, among other things, the definition of magic and religion. I reproduce (with my

comments along the way) parts of the various versions that went back and
forth between TP and me. This forms a kind of dialogue about magic and
religion.

This version is the result of several drafts now lost and several series of
comments back and forth; but, in this version, it comes from TP. It should
serve as the basic manuscript text:

> We must not confuse an analytical from a concrete view of religious belief and
> practice. Our definition is intended to be rigorously analytic, useful for pick-
> ing out the religious aspect or component in a complex of concrete activities
> and beliefs. For example, much that goes on in churches, synagogues, and
> mosques is not religious by our analytical definition. The religious element is
> there, but so also may be some science, some political beliefs, even, as we shall
> see in a moment when we give an analytical definition of that phenomenon,
> some magic. . . .
>
> The importance of distinguishing the analytical from the concrete is
> nowhere clearer than in seeing how religion, as we have defined it, differs
> from science and magic. We may define these three analytically, in order bet-
> ter to understand their concrete intermixtures, by returning to our original
> definition of religion. All human action, we said, is oriented to goals or ends
> and uses a variety of means to achieve those ends. Both the means and the
> ends may vary: some are empirical, this-worldly, profane; some are not, but are
> rather sacred, transcendental. Thus, we may characterize science and scientific
> common sense as consisting of the use of empirical knowledge to achieve
> empirical goals, for example, vaccination to prevent smallpox. Magic consists
> in the use of non-empirical means to achieve empirical goals—for example,
> prayer to make rain or improve the harvest. And religion, of course, consists of
> the use of non-empirical means to achieve non-empirical, transcendental
> goals, for example, prayer to achieve salvation. All three—science, magic, and
> religion—have their uses in coping with the physical, biological, and social
> worlds. None of them can be reduced to either of the other two. They are
> related concretely but each also has its measure of independence.

The point of this strategy of definition from TP's point of view was to
find what he wanted to call an analytic definition, which he considered *the
most general possible definition*. It was intended to cover not only data that
comes to us from anthropological fieldwork but also the many definitions
that have characterized human interactions throughout history and even
contemporary life. It is a very exact definition until one realizes the difficulties in defining transcendental. But, going along with the definition would
mean, practically, that many activities in churches and synagogues, that
would normally be considered religion in our culture would actually fit our
definition of science on the one hand or magic on the other:

> Since magic is so often intermixed concretely with religion—who has not seen
> little metal reproductions of parts of the body pinned up before statues of
> saints in Mexican churches in the hope that the saints will induce cures of ill-

ness in those parts? or, who has not seen the plaques put up on the walls of a Paris church giving thanks for success in school examinations?—it will be helpful to say some more about it. What we have defined as magic is widespread not only in "primitive" societies but in our own "scientific" Western societies today. As the great anthropologist Malinowski made clear some fifty years ago, magic occurs when there is some important empirical goal in view that is surrounded by difficulty and uncertainty and where the relevant common sense or empirical scientific knowledge does not guarantee success. In the case of the Trobriand Islanders, whom Malinowski studied so intensively, a great deal of magic occurred in connection with food-gathering. Thus, there was much magic, in addition to all the relevant empirical knowledge, to insure the success of agriculture. And there was also much magic in connection with fishing, another large source of food for the Trobrianders.

This analysis owes a great deal to Talcott Parsons, who commented on Malinowski's work:

> There were in fact two distinct systems. On the one hand, the native was clearly possessed of an impressive amount of sound empirical knowledge of the proper uses of the soil and the processes of plant growth. He acted quite rationally in terms of his knowledge and above all was quite clear about the connection between intelligent and energetic work and a favorable outcome. There is no tendency to excuse failure on supernatural grounds when it could be clearly attributed to failure to attain adequate current standards of technical procedure. Side by side with this system of rational knowledge and technique, however, and specifically not confused with it, was a system of magical beliefs and practices. These beliefs concerned the possible intervention in the situation of forces and entities which are "supernatural" in the sense that they are not from our point of view objects of empirical observation and experience . . . entities with a specifically sacred character. Correspondingly, the practices were not rational techniques but rituals involving specific orientation to this world of supernatural forces and entities.

It ought to be clear now that one of the things especially important about an "analytic" definition of magic, in TP's view, is that it expresses a universal definition of magic. It can be applied by use to any situation and yield a definition of magic which is both comprehensive and comprehensible but often at odds with what the society defines as magic or religion:

> In our society similarly, magic—the use of non-empirical means for empirical ends—more frequently occurs where the end or goal is important, where empirical knowledge is not enough, where success is problematical, and where the magic may help and probably won't hurt. Thus, in areas like agriculture, commercial fishing, love, school examinations, health, and war combat we find actors frequently using magic. Some apprehensive actors seem to use magic for everything, witness the widespread use of astrology to guide everyday behavior.

It is this "generalizability," so to speak, which TP feels is a characteristic of laws of science, which gives TP confidence to go on to the next step, an observation about the characteristic of "objectivity" in social scientific discourse:

> We need to address a question that is bound to be asked of a book like this: Is it possible to be objective, social scientific about religion? Indeed, when social scientists and others talk about the "value-freedom" problem, they often assert that objectivity about any social problem is impossible. Even further, there are now some radical relativists, some extreme believers in the social construction of reality principle, who assert that the observer's values taint all physical and biological knowledge of the relevant aspects of the world. We disagree with such views. It is our conviction that one can be objective enough about religion and other matters. Those who believe that the fact that all action is produced, in part, by values makes objectivity impossible do not understand the matter. This is a fact we not only accept, but insist upon. But we go on to point out that there are values and values and some values and their associated structures and processes may impede the effects of other values. Thus, all forms of science, natural and social, result from a certain set of values and from the structures and processes closely connected therewith that produce a kind of objectivity about the physical, biological, and social worlds that insulates it in important measure from other values. There may be no absolute value-freedom for science and any other kind of human action but objectivity is still possible. That is our principled conviction for this book and we hope to realize that conviction as much as is possible.

SEGAL'S RESPONSES

It is, of course, too difficult and time-consuming to print the entire draft that Segal sent back to TP in response to this one. Some of Segal's editing was merely technical and was meant only to clarify the joint case. Other changes were illustrative examples designed to further and expand on the arguments already expressed in concise form—in other words, purely supportive arguments. Still other changes were meant to moderate the arguments TP propounded strongly, and this is where the problems in this chapter arose. Segal was extremely nervous about the notion that anything is "objective," the term seeming to have no practical definition at all. Furthermore, he was critical of TP's conception of "universalizability," being identical with analytical, understanding past generalizations as provisional when dealing with every new case. The "we" in some of the paragraphs above was in fact TP alone. While Segal shared TP's skepticism of some extreme relativists, he did not insist on TP's contention that there be but one analytic approach to complex social phenomena, especially when no real criteria were adduced for discovering when universality was achieved, apart from the opinion of the Western scientist. Instead Segal wanted to stress the issues of perspective and the problems associated with the fact that religion and magic are defined quite differently in different cultures.

As a historian, Segal found that the definition expressed in the first draft amounted to a kind of Humpty-Dumptyism, a professorial language with no cognizance of specific culture. Furthermore, it was difficult to understand how one might convince a person with another definition that this one was better. The one thing that one could say is that the definition was specifically designed for the making of comparisons and was not an attempt to describe magic or religion as these are used within a specific society.

Some of Segal's additions to the text show this intention:

> *We* may characterize science and technology as consisting of the use of empirical knowledge to achieve empirical goals—for example, vaccination to prevent smallpox. Magic consists in the use of empirical means to achieve transcendental, non-empirical goals—for example, buying a ritual performance by a trained class of practitioners to ensure well-being.

The point here was to emphasize that this is a very intellectualist definition which fits a Western scientist's notion of what the differences between magic and religion are. It may have no relationship to the way in which the terms are defined within the specific cultures under study.

And again:

> Of course, the terms *transcendental* and *empirical* are relative and have different meanings in different cultures. We feel smallpox is a medical issue but salvation is a transcendent issue. On the other hand, an individual Westerner may at the same time think that his recovery from a disease is his salvation and offer prayers of thanksgiving to God but he can be just as capable of simultaneously ascribing it to the automatic result of the medication. Others in our society and many in other cultures think that deliverance from a disease is always and primarily a transcendent issue of salvation. Furthermore, what happens when a culture thinks of smallpox not as a disease with a natural etiology but as possession by a demon? Then, it may seem completely appropriate to hold an exorcism for a smallpox sufferer rather than treat the disease with Western medicines. Thus, to apply the definition of magic and religion, we must always remain consciously aware of the consequences of our own cultural definitions; we must always make a decision as to whether we are going to adopt our own theories of causation or the culture's under consideration. If we take account of the indigenous theories of causation, no matter how incorrect we may think them, we discover that the substance of what the culture defines as magic and religion will be quite different. Indeed, it may not make any distinction between the two phenomena. Or, it may distinguish between magic and religion in ways that seem illogical or inconsistent or merely different from ours. Thus, we must always be aware of the differences between our analytic systems and those in use within the culture.

In consonance with the program to bring historical context into the analysis—in effect, to propound that the issue of perspective is fundamental to the distinction between magic and religion—Segal added more examples of the ambiguities:

> But, let us return to the differences between magic and religion in an analytic framework. One kind of magic entails the use of non-empirical techniques like prayer to achieve empirical ends. The converse, the use of empirical means to achieve non-empirical goals—for example, prayer to make rain or improve the harvest—will also appear to our analytic categories to be magic but it may not necessarily be so to the participants. Prayers for this purpose are regularly offered in many mosques, churches, and synagogues, where they are viewed as proper religious actions, not magical at all. In our analytic discourse, which corresponds to no particular actual culture, all magic is, by definition, a kind of category mistake and is necessarily false. According to this scheme, religion would consist of the use of non-empirical means to achieve non-empirical, transcendental goals—for example, prayer to achieve salvation. (Indeed, in some varieties of predestinarian Protestantism, even this would be considered a mistaken and magical attempt to coerce God into doing something upon which He has logically already determined from the origin.) . . .
>
> In actual practice, however, in various cultures and religions, there are no totally independent variables. Even in our own Western churches, mosques, and synagogues, there is often no way to distinguish among them. Magic is so often intermixed concretely with religion. We think of magic and religion as being well mixed in foreign or primitive cultures. But a seasoned traveler of the religious sites in the Americas or Europe will have seen many examples of the mixing. Mexican churches contain little metal reproductions of body parts in the hope that the saints will cure the illness, just as the ancient Greeks and Romans left votive offerings and thanksgivings to Asklepius for having cured them. In Parisian churches plaques commemorate success in school examinations. The people who put up these plaques would be scandalized to think that they are indulging in magic. They understand that their own behavior, which is sanctioned by the church, must be religion rather than magic, because magic is defined in Christianity as being anti-Christian and forbidden. In Ancient Rome too, offerings to savior gods and goddesses for physical cures were considered legitimate religion. And they used the terms magic and religion to refer to their own understandings.

For Segal, then, the important issues for the scholar are not what we think of as magic and religion but how our "analytic" categories interact with and may distort our understanding of others' definitions. The question is not which definitions are adopted but knowing why and when specific definitions are adopted and defining the effect of the perspective:

> As historians and sociologists we must be willing to distinguish between the understanding of the actors and the comparative theory we are propounding. What we have defined as magic is widespread not only in "primitive" societies but in our own "scientific" Western societies today. . . .

Another interest Segal showed in his editing of TP's text was to add more detail on some of the social functions of witchcraft:

> Witchcraft beliefs are functional to a society because they help preserve and make understandable a morally structured universe. In many African societies, for instance, witchcraft is an incentive to economic sharing and redistribution of wealth, which is socially sanctioned and is probably a necessary value. Conspicuous prosperity or excess wealth is almost everywhere regarded as the grounds for hostility from evil spirits, sorcerers, and witches. As Ronald Green says: "The sheer wickedness of witchcraft and sorcery therefore presents no bar to our understanding its place in the morally structured African religious universe: Witches help (negatively) to define moral conduct, their existence explains misfortune in a morally understandable way and their wrath or the threat of being accused of witchcraft helps deter selfish and immoral conduct."[1]
>
> But charges of witchcraft or magic are a more subtle phenomenon. For a charge to be made, there has to be a presumption of harm committed by one person against another. Charges of witchcraft involve very complicated social interactions where there is usually no empirical distinction between the religious actions of the various actors. Yet, what one person does is called religion whereas what another person does is labelled witchcraft. In European society, sometimes a woman who gathered herbs in the forest was considered as a lay healer. Other times, especially if she were successful and respected at her trade, she might risk the charge of witchcraft from offended medical personnel and priests.

Segal finished his additions along with additions about specific witchcraft accusations—for example, the Salem witchcraft trials:

> To Americans the most famous outbreak of witchcraft accusations is surely the Salem witchcraft trials. They have certainly entered Americans' imagination as the opposite of the cultural pluralism and respect for differences which we want to promulgate in our own society. It was, however, in its own time, understandable as the last gasp of a mania of witch hunting which infected Protestant and Catholic Europe and which only spread briefly to the United States.[2] The larger process, in which witchcraft trials proliferated in the early modern period, may be ironically partly due to the construction of a new, more scientific worldview in which the many intermediaries of the Medieval world were gradually eliminated, especially in Protestantism. Those accused of witchcraft were typically poor, socially marginal, and often widowed old women who were pariahs in their communities. In place of the more medieval

---

1. See Ronald M. Green, *Religion and Moral Reason: A New Method For Comparative Study* (New York: Oxford, 1988) 38.

2. See Peter W. Williams, *Popular Religion in America: Symbolic Change and the Modernization Process in Historical Perspective* (Englewood Cliffs, N.J.: Prentice Hall, 1980) 151ff.; and the classic work, Keith Thomas, *Religion and the Decline of Magic*, as well as Alan D. MacFarlane, *Witchcraft in Tudor and Stuart England* (London: Routledge & Kegan Paul, 1970).

code of charity, these women were victimized by the notion of individualistic self-help.

In the American context, Chadwick Hansen has written a very interesting account of the actual psychological mechanisms of hysteria in *Witchcraft at Salem*.[3] He persuasively argues that the fear of witchcraft was based upon actual practices and that the hysterical symptoms of the victims were authentic and not faked. Another possibility is also present. The children who first felt the effects of witchcraft had been eating barley cakes. These may, in fact, have been infected with ergot poisoning, which is a naturally occurring psychotropic drug quite akin to LSD. Their symptoms were interpreted within the available explanations of the day. In the following century, Jonathan Edwards may have begun his career within the Great Awakening with another case of ergot poisoning, but in this context, the symptoms were interpreted as the effects of a benevolent deity seeking the salvation of enthusiastic converts. The question then remains, why interpret these effects in terms of witchcraft in one context or the effects of God in the next?

Thus, to call someone a witch, or practitioner of black magic, may tell us nothing about the particular behavior of the person accused. A striking example of this occurs in Azande society where a witch, as opposed to a sorcerer, was believed to operate unconsciously within the spirit of the offending witch and without special techniques. For the Azande, the sorcerer was a person who practiced a number of malevolent arts, all of which entailed learned techniques. And sorcery was actually practiced, although it was considered a lesser offense than witchcraft. Thus, anyone could be charged with witchcraft if she or he had reason to inflict damage on someone else, whether or not sorcery was attempted. In other words, witchcraft was entirely outside of the realm of observable phenomena, except in its effects, which were palpable, terrible, and threatening. The Azande definitions of magic and witchcraft, however important they may be for understanding the moral universe of the Zande people, should not be blindly applied to every other culture, as was done by so many enthusiastic readers of Evans-Pritchard. Instead, what Evans-Pritchard really wanted to point out was the way in which in each culture the variously defined different supernatural forces operate together as a single theoretical structure to make the moral world comprehensible.

Of course, the mere existence of a complete system does not guarantee its benign operation. In many situations, including Salem, unfortunate people died as a result of witchcraft accusations, because the crime, when proven, was punishable by death.[4] Each society defines what it means by magic and witchcraft, regulating its own definitions. The purpose of the definition is to try to keep a human being from thinking that she or he has the ultimate power

3. (New York: Braziller, 1969).

4. See *Witchcraft Confessions and Accusations* (ed. Mary Douglas; London: 1970). Also see Alan F. Segal, "Hellenistic Magic: Some Questions of Definition," in *Studies in Gnosticism and Hellenistic Religion: Essays for Gilles Quispel* (Leiden: Brill, 1981) 349-75 and now reprinted in *The Other Judaisms of Late Antiquity* (Brown Judaic Studies 127; Atlanta: Scholars Press, 1987) 79-108. This account shows the difficulty that not only the Hellenistic but also contemporary scholarly observers have in distinguishing between religion and magic because of their perva-

over whether salvation is achieved, even by doing morally correct actions. David Brion Davis provides a convenient term to designate these witch hunting crazes—countersubversion.[5] Movements against Masons, Mormons, Catholics, Jews, Southern slave-holders are similar in structure to the witchcraft trials and witch hunting of the Seventeenth Century. And of course, the McCarthy anti-communist hunts of the 1950's have very similar functions and structures.[6]

We may discover a society in which these questions of moral meaning are not asked, though none have yet turned up, and we may one day decide to live in a society where the questions are no longer asked. All of these are possible. But they do not seem plausible. Or it may be that the answers to these questions will be mediated by other institutions than ones traditionally called religious in our society. But it does seem that the questions are perennially human and that various classes of educated people will always devote their lives to answering them. Human beings appear to want to ask these questions.

TP'S RESPONSE TO SEGAL

This was the version which was sent out to editors and accepted for publication at Harvard University Press. However, the readers' reports suggested that the material could be better integrated, that less space should be devoted to resuming others' opinions, and that the writing could be tightened. Segal and TP set out to meet the criticisms, which seemed prudent and agreeable. TP began to edit the text which he and Segal had produced.

Upon reflection, TP was not happy with the additions Segal had made. He did not appreciate the insertion of the issue of perspective, against which he had published some critical remarks in an occasional writing. He also sought to shorten and tighten up the argument. He felt Segal had entered some illogicalities into the text. This is the version which TP sent back to Segal:

> . . . Only through analytic definition can we see how they differ from one another and when and how they may also be intermixed. For example, much that goes on in churches, synagogues, and mosques turns out, on analytic definition, not to be just religion but rather partly science and partly magic. While

---

sive intermixture in a variety of concrete contexts. Of course, definitions of what religion and magic were in the Hellenistic world were constructed also as weapons in social and religious conflict. What one group defined as its "good" religion, a hostile group could define as "bad" magic. This article also has a useful general bibliography on magic. On religion and social conflict, see also the classic Clyde Kluckhohn, *Navaho Religion* (New York: Penguin, 1976).

5. David Brion Davis, "Some Themes of Countersubversion: An Analysis of Anti-Masonic, Anti-Catholic, and Anti-Mormon Literature," *Mississippi Valley Historical Review* 47 (September 1960) 205-24; in abridged form in Davis, ed. *The Fear of Conspiracy: Images of Un-American Subversion from the Revolution to the Present* (Ithaca, N.Y.: Cornell University Press, 1971) 9-22.

6. Arthur Miller, *The Crucible* (New York: Viking Press, 1953; New York: Penguin, 1976).

the liturgy is religious, the sermon may express common sense or scientific views on marital relations, social problems, and politics, and, finally, some prayers (e.g., for rain) may be more magic than religion.

Our analysis proceeds as follows. All human action is oriented to ends and goals and proceeds by a variety of means to attain those ends. Both the ends and the means may vary: some are empirical, this-worldly, profane; others are non-empirical, sacred, transcendental. Thus, we may define science and technology as consisting of the use of empirical means to achieve some empirical end. For example, it is scientific to use the appropriate vaccines to prevent smallpox, or measles or mumps in children. Magic occurs when non-empirical means, such as rituals or prayers are used to achieve some empirical goal. For example, crossing one's fingers and saying a prayer to ensure safety while taking off on a jet airplane is magic. And finally, religion exists when non-empirical means are used to achieve non-empirical goals. For example, taking communion in a Christian church, participating in the Eucharist, saying the Kaddish in a synagogue, in order to achieve salvation for oneself or others, in order to enter into Heaven, is genuine religion.

The fact of concrete intermixture comes about for a number of reasons. First, social organizations and groups are often not mono-functional. Churches, mosques, synagogues, as we have suggested above, may have different ends in view, both the non-empirical and the empirical. And they may see these ends as concretely interconnected. The church official may see his discussion of social problems as contributing to helping the church members know better how to realize the behavior and values of the church and thereby achieve salvation. Or, judging by the profusion of metal reproductions of body parts in Catholic churches in places like Mexico or France or Italy, where they are put up near the shrines of saints to insure or regain good health in those body parts, the Church sees this bit of magic (which it may not acknowledge as magic but consider legitimate religion, since magic is formally defined as anti-Christian) as useful for aiding the good religious life. In some Parisian parish churches, walls are covered with ceramic plaques giving thanks for success in school examinations. Just so did ancient Greeks and Romans leave votive offerings and thanks at shrines of the patron god of health, Asklepios, for having cured their illness.

Notice that TP has incorporated Segal's examples into the text but has, at the same time, rephrased the text in such a way that any definition of magic and religion that differs from those offered "analytically" becomes simply error. To Segal's notion that a society's assumptions about how to categorize events imposes an evaluation on the data, TP answers with the notion that people seem determined to misuse scientific notions of causation:

Second, there may be socially structured goal-situations which people feel to be both important and uncertain. In pursuit of such goals, people feel they need all the help they can get; as a result, they use both science and magic. Among the many situations of this kind that have been noticed by observers or studied directly are health, combat in war, agriculture, commercial fishing, love, and school, college, and university examinations. For example, the student striving for a good grade on an examination will probably both study hard and then add on some little bit of magic (a special piece of clothing, a favored seat, or anything else) "just for extra safety." The soldier in combat will see to all of his gear but also use some idiosyncratic magic. Of course, he may also say a truly religious prayer, though not necessarily, at least in the modern world; nobody has ever proved the common saying, "there are no atheists in foxholes." . . .

The basic notion here is that definition of social processes, like science, is an inherently rational category, derivable through methodological analysis. But the method for finding out what the definition is appears to be *Verstehen*, theoretical description, without data or experiment. Along the way, we are reminded that there is nothing inevitable about religious faith—foxholes do not inevitably produce faith. This is a good corrective to the notion that humanity is destined to religious expression, *homo religiosus*, just as humanity is *homo faber* or *homo ludens*.

TP also reinserts his paragraph on water-witching, presumably a practice that he considers valid technology but not yet adequately understood:

We should note, of course, that the term "witch" is often used in loose and various ways. For example, in rural areas of the United States, where underground sources of water where wells may be dug are often hard to locate, and where faulty drilling may result in undesired expense, some men offer themselves as "water-witches" who can locate underground sources by the use of a forked willow switch. In this case, again, magic is considered a reasonable addition to common sense knowledge and science.

THE RESULTING VERSION

Here then is the next version, again as edited by Segal. Because of the length of the section and repetition with previous quotations, I will quote only one small section of it:

Magic, Science, and Religion

Because the empirical world of science and the nonempirical world of transcendent values may sometimes be concretely intermixed, sometimes hard to distinguish from one another because of the rituals that help define the boundaries, and because both the empirical and religious worlds are sometimes confused with "magic," it is necessary to discuss these three concepts analytically. Through analytic discussion and deductive reasoning we can see how we understand the concepts to interact and when and how they may also be intermixed. Then we shall be in a better position to evaluate the differences between what we want to call "magic" and "religion" and what specific societies mean by them. . . .

Of course, our definitions of magic and religion apply to our comparative perspective and not to the actors themselves. While the liturgy of a particular Western religion is normally religious, the sermon may express commonsense views about science or marital relations or social problems or values or even politics. Finally, some prayers—for example, those for rain— may be more magic than religion. But for the participant, all may loosely be classified as religious. The difficulty is that "religion" is an English word with a context in our society. In societies that are very different from ours, there may be entirely different words to describe the phenomena we know as magic, science, and religion.

Our analysis of the differences between magic and religion proceeds from our theory of action and our understanding of the problem of moral meaning and the transcendent. Human action is normally oriented toward ends and goals, proceeding by a variety of means to attain them. Both the ends and the means may vary. Some are empirical, this-worldly, profane; others are nonempirical, sacred, transcendental. Thus, we may define for ourselves science and technology as consisting of the use of empirical means to achieve some empirical end. For example, it is scientific to use the appropriate vaccines to prevent smallpox, measles, or mumps in children. We can therefore have a relatively clear distinction between science and religion.

But the definition is moot when the intentions of the actors are not entirely clear. One kind of magic occurs when nonempirical means, such as rituals or prayers, are used to achieve some empirical goal and sometimes *vice versa*, when empirical means are used to achieve what turns out to be a religious goal. For example, crossing one's fingers as protection when taking off on a jet airplane is magic. Religion consists in nonempirical means used to achieve nonempirical goals; for example, taking communion in a Christian church is a religious ritual that defines the community of the saved. Thus, magic appears to be a kind of category mistake, where means are wrongly understood to have a specific goal which they do not have.

Even in this analytic definition there are many gray areas that depend on motivations and interpretation of actions. Saying prayers at airplane takeoffs is neither inherently religious nor magical. It depends on the goal of the actor. If the religious system defines petitionary prayer as merely trying to get the attention of the deity or perhaps orienting the will of the believer for the crisis, then it may be religious. If the prayer is believed to protect the individual automatically, it is magic. If it is believed automatically or invariably to help the individual into a proper attitude or consciousness in life's difficult moments, it may be magical in spite of its proven technique. The cases are difficult and need to be sorted out by analysts. Indeed, within a given society the definitions of religion and magic are often disputed and the source of conflict. We shall soon analyze cases of witchcraft accusations, where the actors try by political actions to sort out the distinction between magic and religion. But it is clear that the analytical definition depends entirely on the goals and motivations of the actor. Thus, the definitions function as conceptual tools which we may choose to use for the purpose of comparison, while the native categories should be explained for the purposes of description.

As analysts we must be willing both to describe what we see and to compare it with other related phenomena. But we must also take account of the ways in which a culture describes the same phenomenon. We need to have some idea about what we want to study as we enter a culture but the conceptualizations employed in the society must be noted because the actors and the society itself may have a very different view of the nature of the actions from the analyst. This is true even when we are studying our own society. In other words, our conceptual tools are designed to clarify what comparative observers, a small group of religionists and social scientists, may mean by magic, science, and religion, but they have to take account of, interact with, and sometimes compete with what a culture defines as its religion. In short, we may see prayers for success in war or for healings as magic, but we must be well aware that, in the churches in which these activities take place, it is religion.

Sometimes these analyses have the result of underlining the differences between modern scientific society and traditional ones. Shaking a rattle at a smallpox victim may seem like magic because it will do nothing to cure the illness. But if the goal is to allude to the transcendent realm, where questions of the meaning of an individual's sickness or health are appropriate, then it is a religious action, nevertheless. On the other hand, if the goal is to cure the disease, the action is magical, according to our definition.

One corollary of these comparative definitions is that a society itself may change its understanding of a ritual, even while preserving it. We can see in the theoretical example of the smallpox rattle that as a culture modernizes, its understanding of the nature and goals of its own religious actions can change. In one generation, a person may simply shake the rattle in the presence of smallpox. The next generation, when medical knowledge is available, may continue to shake the rattle for different reasons. We may see this in the continued importance of traditional healers in societies where pharmacological medicines have recently become available. But we should also note that this evolution in the aims of religious rituals has also occurred in our own culture. Western culture has sometimes had the luxury of adapting more slowly to new conceptions of natural and social scientific causation. . . .

This discussion of the social justification for continuing to allow the mixture of magic and religion, even in a society like our own, which eschews magic, contains an implicit second, more individual reason for the admix-

ture: there are situations where people feel the need to practice magic both
because the goals are important and because the outcomes are uncertain. In
our society magic is considered wrong in various ways, but the consola-
tions of magic are considerable if it is conveniently recategorized as religion. As in the examples of healing and success in examinations, there are
situations in which even "religious" people want all the help they can get so
they use both science and magic as well as religion to help them get it.
Among the many situations of this kind that have been studied by scholars
interested in distinguishing magic and religion are health, combat in war,
agriculture, commercial fishing, love, and university examinations. Anxiety
over success leads to the knowing employment of magical means, even
where they are forbidden or known to be false.

To take a familiar example, a student striving for a good grade on an
examination might both study hard and then utilize some bit of magic, such
as wearing a lucky piece of clothing or sitting in a favored seat, just for the
extra help, or even the psychological confidence it might bring. Most of the
time, Western religion does not condone these magical procedures, but
occasionally one finds them caught up into religious beliefs and structures.

We must add also that a soldier may ignore both magic and religion.
Nobody has ever proved the common saying that there are no atheists in
foxholes. In all these cases we are dealing with more subtle nuances of
magic which come out of the interplay between our analytic, comparative
perspective and a specific culture's historical definitions—in particular our
society's Judeo-Christian dislike, distrust, and scientific disproof of magic.
We could say that our society tends to use science to distinguish between
magic and religion. Magic becomes any wrong causal relationship in a situa-
ton of stress. Wearing a rabbit's foot for protection is false because it has no
bearing on one's safety, only on one's confidence. But this definition is a
corollary of our analytic definition in a specific historical situation.

But there are cultures where magic is considered true and important. . . .

Witchcraft

Thus, to call someone a witch or practitioner of black magic may tell us
nothing about the particular behavior of the person accused. A striking
example of this occurs in Azande society, where a *witch*, as opposed to a *sorcerer*, was believed to operate unconsciously within the spirit of the offending witch and without special techniques. For the Azande, the *sorcerer* was a
person who practiced a number of malevolent arts, all of which entailed
learned techniques. And sorcery was actually practiced, although it was
considered a lesser offense than witchcraft. Witchcraft was also a crime, but
it did not necessarily have anything to do with techniques or conscious
desires. Thus, anyone could be charged with witchcraft if she or he had reason to inflict damage on someone else, whether or not sorcery was

attempted. In other words, witchcraft was entirely outside of the realm of observable phenomena, except in its effects, which were palpable, terrible, and threatening.

The Azande case illustrates a difficulty in understanding any particular society's definition of magic, religion, and science. Evans-Pritchard's analysis of Azande witchcraft was so powerful in the scholarly community that researchers frequently used the Azande definitions of sorcery and witchcraft in trying to analyze other cultures. This is as mistaken as trying to adopt Western notions, instead of trying to distil an analytic notion of the notions for comparative purposes. The Azande definitions of magic and witchcraft, however important they may be for understanding the moral universe of the Zande people, should not be blindly applied to every other culture, as was done by so many enthusaistic readers of Evans-Pritchard. Instead, what Evans-Pritchard really wanted to point out was the structure of the relationship between magical and religious beliefs, the way in which various different supernatural forces operate together as a single theoretical structure to make the moral world comprehensible.

Of course, the mere existence of a complete system does not guarantee its benign operation. In many situations, including Salem, unfortunate people died as a result of witchcraft accusations, because the crime, when proven, was punishable by death.[7] Each society defines what it means by magic and witchcraft, regulating its own definitions. One function of the definition is to try to keep a human being from thinking that she or he has the ultimate power over whether salvation is achieved, even by doing morally correct actions. David Brion Davis provides a convenient term to designate these witch hunting crazes—countersubversion.[8] Movements against Masons, Mormons, Catholics, Jews, are similar in structure to the witchcraft trials and witch hunting of the seventeenth century. And, of course, the McCarthy anti-communist hunts of the 1950s have very similar functions and structures.[9]

---

7. See *Witchcraft Confessions and Accusations*; see also Segal, "Hellenistic Magic." This account shows the difficulty that not only the Hellenistic but also contemporary scholarly observers have in distinguishing between religion and magic because of their pervasive intermixture in a variety of concrete contexts. Of course, definitions of what religion and magic were in the Hellenistic world were constructed also as weapons in social and religious conflict. What one group defined as its "good" religion, a hostile group could define as "bad" magic. This article also has a useful general bibliography on magic. On religion and social conflict, see also the classic Clyde Kluckhohn, *Navaho Religion*.

8. David Brion Davis, "Some Themes of Countersubversion: An Analysis of Anti-Masonic, Anti-Catholic, and Anti-Mormon Literature," *Mississippi Valley Historical Review* 47 (September 1960) 205-24; in abridged form in Davis, ed. *The Fear of Conspiracy: Images of Un-American Subversion from the Revolution to the Present* (Ithaca, N.Y.: Cornell University Press, 1971) 9-22.

9. See n. 6.

SOME CONCLUSIONS AND DISCUSSION
OF THE HELLENISTIC WORLD

The resulting section appears to me to have many advantages. It balances TP's concerns for an "analytic" definition with Segal's concerns to acknowledge the volatility and variability of definitions of religious phenomena. TP's fear of illogicality is avoided, although he might not entirely agree, while Segal's concern to treat the data with respect is expressed, though it is done without any use of the term "perspective," which would have made the whole analysis easier.

Yet within this chapter one can see some of the reasons why the partnership failed. TP insisted on making analytic definitions of magic and religion, which entailed for him the agreement on but one formulation of definitional issues. In retrospect, Segal should have insisted on invoking the issue of perspective more systematically because the seeming agreement partly unravels the moment a real historical example was proferred.

As an example I take the Hellenistic world, in which there were several different and competing definitions of magic and religion, which interacted in different and complex ways. This is quite clearly parallel to our own society as well. In our society the analytic definition of the difference between magic and religion contains within it the luxury of merely condemning competing definitions of magic. Anyone who understands astrology as true can be faulted from the point of the analytic definition as a mistaken analysis of cause and effect. Anyone who thinks that a St. Christopher medal will protect a car from accident is mistaking a magical thought process for a religious one because it contains a seeming religious justification (although, to be sure, in the case of St. Christopher's medal, the church has itself denied the efficacy). We justifiably say that our analytic definition of magic should distinguish between various competing definitions in our own culture, implying that the definitions of the social scientist should rank higher than the definitions of the native exegete.

But the situation appears quite different when one attempts to understand what happens in a particular historical situation.[10] In that case, the purpose of the analysis is not to establish one particular definition of magic or religion over another but merely to analyze what the differing perspectives were in a particular situation. For instance, the term "magician" (μάγος, *magos* in the Hellenistic Greek world) was sometimes sought out and respected yet at other times and by other people avoided in the Hellenistic world. We find the competing definitions within the New Testament, one of the important documents of the Hellenistic world. The "three kings" or *magoi* (Matthew 2) who are pictured as visiting the birthplace of Jesus were called *magoi* because they are pictured as powerful religious practitioners,

10. See n. 7.

without a negative value judgment. They follow a star, which gives astrological credence to the birth of the savior, but in this case it must be viewed as a religious sign and wonder. Thus, in this story, the *magi* (in Latin) or the *magoi* (in Greek) are priests and co-religionists. They may even be considered scientists because they rest their conclusions upon observations of the natural world.

So too the adepts of the magical papyri seem to have no problem calling themselves *magoi*. But there is a potential conflict in native definitions of *magos* here because not everyone respected those who used the magical papyri. Apuleius, in his defense against the charge of magic (*Apologia*), plays with the ambiguity by maintaining that if he is being charged with being a Persian priest there is nothing wrong with the title. Yet, on the contrary, if his accusers are implying that he has the power to do as he wills and especially to do others ill, then he is surprised that his accusers are so blithely risking disaster. Of course, he appears to be ridiculing the nature of the charge. In so doing, he seems tacitly to be ridiculing the notion that magic in the hostile sense is real, though he may only be doing so to ridicule his accusers.

However far Apuleius's skepticism goes, several Hellenistic ambiguities in the use of the term *mageia* (magic) underline the notion that most people thought magic real and potentially dangerous. What was illegal for the Hellenistic world was unjustly attempting to do others harm by any supernatural means, regardless of whether such practices would be regarded by us as possible. That means, essentially, that much of what we would consider magic would be considered religion by the authorities, if it did no one any harm.

Yet in the case of the accusations of magic made against Jesus, we have a further complication: we are dealing with a particular Hellenistic subculture—the Jewish world—which did not deny the existence of magic; rather, it denied that any use of magic could be licit religion. To take a complicated issue and simplify it for a moment, magic—even helpful—had the additional difficulty of risking idolatry, recognizing gods other than the One God. Of course, from modern definitions of magic, much of what was called religious in Hebrew culture might be called magic by us—the drinking of bitter waters by the suspected adulterer or the use of the ashes of a red heifer to purify—but in the Hebrew context it was not magic because it did not recognize gods other than Israel's. Thus, as opposed to the prior case, any substantiation of the term magician as applied to Jesus would be tantamount to condemnation, even if there are ample records that Jews indulged in the same kinds of magical practices that we see in the magical papyri. In this context, it is important to note that no Christian accepts the title *magos* for Jesus, nor is there such a self-affirmation in the Gospels' characterization of the words of Jesus. Indeed, the accusation comes from Jesus' detractors and is renewed by modern scholars such as Morton Smith who wish to under-line the similarity between Jesus' own religious actions and those of other people called magicians. But this ignores the obvious problem with the texts, which are trying, to the contrary, to fight against the notion that Jesus could be called a magician, as he evidently was by his ancient enemies.

The relationship between magic and science in the ancient Hellenistic world is equally difficult to square with contemporary definitions. Both magic and medicine in the Hellenistic world were almost equally false from the point of view of modern science, as were the procedures for correcting mistakes. A similar problem actually occurs in our modern "analytic" uses of the term but we are less likely to be sensitive to them. In the modern world, a practitioner of astrology is more likely to say that astrology is science than to admit that he or she is functioning as a magician, simply because the term *magician* in our society in this context is almost univer-sally understood to mean a charlatan and certainly implies faulty logic.

But that does not excuse us from the equally important occupation of describing the nature of the astrologer's thinking process. From this per-spective, the "analytic" definition of magic appears to be nothing more than the definition of a small group of scientists and social scientists who hap-pen to inhabit the academy, as Wayne Meeks himself said to me at the fac-ulty seminar on magic in which I took part in the fall of 1992. It may be "universally" valid or merely more valid than the ancient definition, but it is irrelevant to the job of describing the ancient case, except that it must be known and stated as part of the assumptions of the reader in order for the ancient case to be described accurately. That is to say, we cannot entirely do without it, if we want to know what we are looking for when we begin our search in other societies. We must, in fact, define what we think magic is before we can begin to deal with the terminology in use in any specific soci-ety. Thus both the analytic and the historical enterprise must be pursued in parallel fashion, and they must mutually recognize the other's validity—indeed, report on the conclusions of the other's analysis—if one is going successfully to describe the phenomenon.

This train of thought leads naturally to the question of whether the whole enterprise of attempting a sociology of religion written jointly by a sociologist deeply influenced by Talcott Parsons and a historian can suc-ceed. The partnership can succeed as long as the issue of perspective is addressed fully. But it must fail if the issue of perspective is not allowed to be addressed, because the minute one notes conflicting definitions and the way that they may power a social situation, one must somehow address the problem of dramatic and perspectival presentment.

CHAPTER 18

Greeks Who Sacrifice and Those Who Do Not: Toward an Anthropology of Greek Religion

Stanley K. Stowers

IMAGINE A COMMUNITY in the contemporary United States that renounced not only television viewing but also any products, persons, and ideas promoted by television. The group would not vote in elections, drive automobiles, shop in supermarkets, watch athletic contests, or form conventional families.[1] These people would remain citizens of the United States but to a large extent would have abandoned American and Western culture. Understanding what it meant for a Greek, Roman, or Syrian to renounce animal sacrifice requires some such act of comparative imagination. The investigation of ancient sacrifice, however, requires comparisons not only with modernity but also within the ancient societies.

My discussion begins with the assumption that we cannot understand nonsacrificers, including early Christians, until we have understood the sacrificers, who dominated the society. Here I will limit myself to discussing Greek sacrifice but will keep in view the fact that minority communities of those who rejected animal sacrifice existed throughout the historical period. I will also assume that exchange between the various ethnic peoples of the ancient Mediterranean was a constant factor in the production of culture for all groups. The historian must be fully open to the possibility of both differences and commonalities in ritual meaning and practice that cross boundaries we represent as "paganism," "Judaism," and "Christianity."[2] We have not understood the renunciation of sacrifice in

---

1. I would like to thank the members of the Brown Seminar on the Religions of the Ancient Mediterranean for their discussion of an early version of this article and the following individuals for their criticisms and comments: Nancy Evans, Howard Eilberg-Schwartz, Peter Laipson, and Saul Olyan.

2. Jonathan Z. Smith, *Drudgery Divine: On the Comparison of Early Christianities and the Religions of Late Antiquity* (Chicago: University of Chicago Press, 1990).

early Christianity as well as we have assumed. In a conventional theological account, the problem appears quite simple: Gentiles gave up many gods, idols, and attendant immorality for the one transcendent God and right-eousness. Perhaps more profoundly than anyone else, Wayne Meeks has shown the poverty of such answers and the rich rewards of another approach.[3] As Meeks has shown, if we want genuinely to understand these ancient peoples as fellow human beings and not merely to mark their exis-tence with a caricature for our own uses, we must attempt to reweave the complex webs of their cultures without forgetting that we are the weavers.

In this discussion I aim to establish constant features of Greek sacrifice from the classical period into the early Roman Empire. I have tried not to underestimate historical change and the great diversity of practices among Greeks, but I want to emphasize aspects of commonality and persistence. At the very least, I believe that the following account will place the burden of proof on those who would hold that Greek sacrifice fundamentally changed or even lost its cultural significance and social "functions" between the classical age and the early empire. I will first discuss seemingly persis-tent fundamental aspects of sacrifice concerning procreation, gender, descent, and place that make sacrifice a powerful means of organizing all kinds of social relations. Next will follow a discussion of these principles in organizing agnatic groups and the other social relations in the *polis*. Finally, I will suggest directions for the study of early Christians as renouncers of sacrifice and say something about theory of sacrifice.

FEATURES OF GREEK SACRIFICE
IN COMPARATIVE PERSPECTIVE

Except under extraordinary circumstances, Greeks ate only meat that had been sacrificed.[4] An early imperial inscription from Pisidia tells how the servants of Meidon ate unsacrificed meat. An offended god, Zeus Trosos, struck Meidon dumb for three months until the god gave instruc-tions in a dream to record the incident for posterity.[5] With some effort we

3. Among his discussions of approaches to early Christian social history, see *The First Urban Christians: The Social World of the Apostle Paul* (New Haven: Yale University Press, 1983) 1–8; *The Moral World of the First Christians* (Library of Early Christianity; Philadelphia: Westminster, 1986) 11–17; "A Hermeneutics of Social Embodiment," in *Christians among Jews and Gentiles: Essays in Honor of Krister Stendahl on His Sixty-fifth Birthday* (ed. G. W. E. Nicklesburg and G. W. MacRae; Philadelphia: Fortress,1986) 176–86.

4. Paul Stengel, *Die Griechischen Kultusaltertümer* (3rd ed.; Munich, 1920) 105–6.

5. Published and commented on in Peter Herrmann and Kemal Ziya Polatkan, *Das Testament des Epikrates und Andere Neue Inschriften aus dem Museum von Manisa* (Österreichische Akademie der Wissenschaften; Philosophisch-Historische Klasse, Sitzungsberichte 265; Vienna: Hermann Böhlaus, 1969) 58–62.

can begin to imagine the ubiquity of sacrifice in the Greco-Roman world.[6] At a birthday party, a city festival, a social club—wherever people ate meals with meat—a sacrifice took place. When the gods were thanked, placated, or beseeched for blessings—beginning a meeting of the city council, setting out for war, after the birth of a child, entering manhood—Greeks sacrificed. All significant political bodies in the Greek city (e.g., *ekklēsia, boulē,* prytany, boards of officials, boards of generals, archons)[7] were male sacrificing bodies that conducted no significant political activity without sacrifice.

Sacrifice stood at the center of a complex set of cultural, social, and political institutions. With the "official" cults of the particular city and the imperial cult at center, worship of the gods under the empire occupied many groupings of people in many different contexts from the mystery cults, much overemphasized by modern scholarship, to societies of freedmen, household sacrifices, kinship groups, and artisans' clubs. These cults were not different religions like Judaism and Christianity but modulated articulations of one somewhat riotous religious system.[8] Animal sacrifice together with plant offerings, a cult locus, belief that the endless variety of local gods somehow belonged to one family, and the religious dominance of a "lay" aristocratic elite were the bonds of Greco-Roman "paganism."

Due to the greater number of sources and the intense focus of scholarship, classical Greece proves the best starting point for investigation. Greek sacrifice can be greatly illuminated by the comparative and theoretical work of a long and distinguished line of investigators.[9] Since the sacrifice of ani-

6. The most important contexts of sacrifice in the early imperial period were houshold, larger agnatic groups such as the deme, polis-sponsored cults and the imperial cult, voluntary associations, and private votive sacrifice. For an introduction to these respectively, see H. J. Rose, "The Religion of the Greek Household," *Euphrosyne* 1 (1957) 95–116; S. C. Humphreys, *The Family, Women and Death: Comparative Studies* (London: Routledge & Kegan Paul, 1983); Martin Nilsson, "Roman and Greek Domestic Cult," *Opuscula Romana* 18 (1954) 77–85; Robert Parker, "Festivals of the Attic Demes," in *Gifts to the Gods: Proceedings of the Uppsala Symposium 1985* (ed. T. Linders and G. Nordquist; Acta Universitatis Upsaliensis; Uppsala: Almqvist & Wiksell, 1987) 137–48; Walter Burkert, *Greek Religion* (Cambridge, Mass.: Harvard University Press, 1985) 216–75. The following contain useful essays on both Athenian classical religion and the imperial cult: *Pagan Priests: Religion and Power in the Ancient World* (ed. Mary Beard and John North; Ithaca, N.Y.: Cornell University Press, 1990); Francesco de Robertis, *Storia delle corporazione e del regime associativo nel mondo romano* (2 vols.; Bari: Adriatica Editrice, 1973); F. T. van Straten, "Gifts for the Gods," in *Faith, Hope and Worship* (ed. H. S. Versnel; Leiden: Brill, 1981) 65–104.

7. Antiphon 6.45; Demosthenes 19.190; 21.114–15; 54.39; Isaeus 3.79; 8.18; Pollux 8.107; Theophrastus, *Char.* 21.11; Aeschenes 1.22–23 and scholiast.

8. I use "system" with some hesitation. I do not mean to imply a functionalist sense that underplays the degree of incoherency and contradiction. Immense local variety is also patent even if a family of commonalities marks Greek religion through time and place.

9. The best discussion of theory and theories is Nancy Jay, *Throughout Your Generations Forever: Sacrifice, Religion and Paternity* (Chicago: University of Chicago Press, 1992) esp. 1–29, 128–46. Valerio Valeri's *Kingship and Sacrifice: Ritual and Society in Ancient Hawaii* (Chicago: University of Chicago Press, 1985) is also full of important theoretical insights. For Greek sac-

mals has been so ubiquitous across the globe and clearly tied to societies that transmit property, power, and status through descent, the subject has been central to the development of the social sciences. Classic studies include those by W. Robertson Smith, E. Durkheim, S. Freud, H. Hubert, and M. Mauss.[10] More recent work by E. E. Evans-Pritchard, V. Turner, C. Lévi-Strauss, J.-P. Vernant, and M. Detienne, V. Valeri, and N. Jay have made sacrifice central for understanding human societies.[11]

With Jay, Valeri, and the French classicists, our cross-cultural and theoretical understanding of sacrifice has reached a level of maturity unusual for the human sciences. Such scholarship has seemed to make possible a number of cross-cultural generalizations. "In No Other Major Religious Institution is gender dichotomy more consistently important, across unrelated traditions, than it is in sacrifice."[12] Furthermore, sacrifice never exists in hunter-gatherer societies and is barely able to exist in achievement-oriented, monetary-market-based societies. Sacrifice belongs to societies that center on the inheritance of real property.[13] In spite of the enormous variety in sacrificial practice, so that each society's practices must be understood in its own historical and cultural contexts, sacrifice always seems to involve two movements. Historians, ethnographers, and theorists have given various

---

rifice, the work of Marcel Detienne, Jean-Pierre Vernant, and collaborators (*The Cuisine of Sacrifice among the Greeks* [Chicago: University of Chicago Press, 1989]; *Mortals and Immortals: Collected Essays of Jean-Pierre Vernant* (ed. Froma I. Zeitlin; Princeton: Princeton University Press, 1991] 291–302) constitutes a major advance over other theorists of Greek sacrifice even though they underinterpret sacrifice's role in the construction of gender and social hierarchy, greatly underemphasize the importance of nonalimentary expiatory sacrifice, and tend to romanticize classical Greek democratic equality. I consider the work of René Girard a sacrificial ideology based on Christian and Freudian thought rather than a theory of sacrifice.

10. W. Robertson Smith, *The Religion of the Semites: The Fundamental Institutions* (1889; repr. New York: Shocken Books, 1972); Emil Durkheim, *The Elementary Forms of Religious Life* (New York: Free Press, 1965); Sigmund Freud, *Totem and Taboo: Some Points of Agreement between the Mental Lives of Savages and Neurotics* (London: Routledge & Kegan Paul, 1950); Henri Hubert and Marcel Mauss, *Sacrifice: Its Nature and Function* (London: Cohen & West, 1964).

11. E. E. Evans-Pritchard, *Nuer Religion* (Oxford: Oxford University Press, 1956); idem, introduction to *Sacrifice* by Hubert and Mauss (1964); idem, "Sacrifice as Quintessential Process: Prophylaxis of Abandonment," *HR* 16 (1977) 189–215; Claude Lévi-Strauss, *Totemism* (Boston: Beacon, 1963). For Vernant and Detienne, Valeri, and Jay, see n. 9 above.

12. Jay, *Throughout Your Generations*, xxiii.

13. This is a conclusion that follows from the coincidence of sacrificial practice and certain ways of organizing descent and kinship; see Meyer Fortes, "The Structure of Unilineal Descent Groups," *American Anthropologist* 55 (1953) 24; Karen E. Paige and Jeffery M. Paige, *The Politics of Reproductive Ritual* (Los Angeles: University of California Press, 1981) 56–57; M. G. Nimkoff and Russell Middleton, "Types of Family and Types of Economy," *AJS* 66 (1960) 215–25. See also the comments on pastoralism, agriculture, and domestication by Jonathan Z. Smith in *Violent Origins: Walter Burkert, René Girard, and Jonathan Z. Smith on Ritual Killing and Cultural Formation* (ed. R. G. Hamerton-Kelly with an introduction by Burton Mack and a commentary by Renato Rosaldo; Stanford, Calif.: Stanford University Press, 1987) 197, 199–201, 224.

names to these movements: communion and expiation; integration and differentiation; joining and separating; conjunction and disjunction; the collective and the piacular.[14] Communion sacrifices unite participants and are always eaten. Expiatory sacrifices eliminate innumerable undesirable conditions and are rarely eaten. I suggest that sacrificing cultures build countless other logical structures around this central dichotomy, which correlates in some way with gender distinctions.

Greek alimentary communion sacrifice was known as θυσία, expiatory nonalimentary sacrifice as ἐναγισμός.[15] The clear-cut terminology can be misleading, however, since a sacrifice can be both expiatory and communal at the same time. Communion sacrifice formed a much more common part of everyday life than expiatory sacrifice, but nonalimentary expiatory sacrifices were crucial gifts and manipulations for keeping society and the larger world working properly. Two great dangers above all others threatened the order of the household and city requiring scrupulous expiation—death and childbirth.

Our modern understanding of sacrifice makes a grasp of the ancient practices most difficult. The meaning of "sacrifice" is so loaded with Christian connotations that researchers have constantly been misled.[16] Thus we think of sacrifice as being about killing, substitutionary death, or self-giving suffering for others, so that scholars talk about sacrifice as "ritual killing."[17] Generally, however, members of sacrificing cultures view the slaughter of the animal as only an unremarkable necessary prelude to what is important about sacrifice.[18] Greeks seem to have thought that the meaning of communion sacrifice was primarily in the distribution, cooking (including the god's portion), and eating of the meat. Greeks minimized the violence of the killing, acting almost as if slaughter played no part in the

14. Hubert and Mauss, *Sacrifice*, 7–8, 17; Evans-Pritchard, *Nuer Religion*; Luc de Heusch, *Sacrifice in Africa* (Bloomington: Indiana University Press, 1985); Jay, *Throughout Your Generations*, 17–19.

15. To my knowledge, no good discussion exists of ἐναγισμός and its role over against θυσία. For a discussion of terminology, see Jean Casabona, *Recherches sur le vocabulaire des sacrifices en grec* (Aix-en-Provence: Ophrys, 1966) 18–26, 70–85, 204–8; Jean Rudhardt, *Notions fondamentales de la pensée religieuse et actes constitutifs du culte dans la Grèce classique* (Geneva: Droz, 1958) 238–46, 285–94.

16. See Jean-Louis Durand's comments in Detienne, *Cuisine*, 88–89.

17. This terminology has been repopularized in scholarly discussion by Girard and his followers. Thus, for instance, *Violent Origins* (see n. 13 above). The superb introduction by Mack and the chapter by Smith provide subtle critiques of this equation of sacrifice and "ritual killing," which has been discredited by a century of ethnological studies and the work of the French classicists.

18. See also Renato Rosaldo's comments about guilt (*Violent Origins*, 241–42). The "gift" to the god is not the death but what remains after death. The metaphorical, mapping, and indexing qualities of sacrificial practices usually focus on the division (or lack thereof in holocaust sacrifices), distribution, and consumption or other use of the sacrificial products.

practice.[19] They attached no particular significance to the animal's death. (Neither would we, were it not that our Western conceptions of sacrifice have been filtered through the lens of Christian theology concerning Christ's death.)

Typically a sacrifice involving a larger animal would begin with a festive procession.[20] Often the wearing of garlands, singing, and flute playing characterized this parade to the altar with the "willing animal." The inner circle of participants purified themselves from the dangers of childbirth and death with a washing and clean clothes. If splashing water onto the animal's head and tossing a handful of grain caused the animal to shake, the participants took the response as a sign of consent.[21] Suddenly the animal was struck down unconscious or dead and then bled with two knives hidden in a basket of grain and salt. The blood was very carefully collected and poured over the altar. Sacrificing men handled the blood, symbol of creative and procreative power, in an act of exchange between themselves and the gods. All of this served as prelude to the distribution and consumption of the lifeless animal, which had thus been ritually rendered suitable for eating. In a major civic sacrifice, the μάγειρος (butcher-sacrificer-cook) who actually wielded the knife was a professional civic-religious functionary and not the aristocratic male, magistrate, or head of some social subgrouping who offered the sacrifice (*sacrifiant*).[22] The μάγειρος quickly skinned and carved the animal in a sequence and manner of division loaded with social-religious significance. The bones wrapped in fat were the god's portion burned on the altar. The central moment and focus of the sacrifice were the eating of the roasted σπλάγχνα, the noble viscera (liver, lungs, heart, kidneys), while the god's portion ascended as smoke from the altar.[23] In this high point of the sacrifice, only an elite inner circle of men near the altar ate the holy meat of the viscera cooked on skewers.[24] In the second phase, quarters of meat were placed in a caldron to boil and were distributed in various ways for a nearby wider feast or to be eaten elsewhere.

With a very few exceptions, modern interpreters have wanted to see the

19. Detienne, *Cuisine*, 9, 90–91, and passim.

20. For accounts of the ritual and evidence, see Durand (in Detienne, *Cuisine*, 97–118 and passim), who corrects earlier accounts. Burkert's basically excellent account (*Greek Religion*, 55–57) is limited by an interpretation that employs the misleading concepts of "sacred" and "profane" (see Durand [in Detienne, *Cuisine*, 87–89] and Jay [*Throughout Your Generations*, 134–37] on the sacred/profane concept) and by an anachronistic and psychosocial explanation from origins. See also Rudhardt, *Notions fondamentales*, 257–66; and Paul Stengel, *Opferbraüche der Griechen* (Leipzig: Teubner, 1910).

21. My account is not complete, lacking many details: for example, just before the animal was killed, some of its hair was cut from its forehead and thrown into the fire. This was called the "beginning." The scope of this article precludes discussion of vegetable and grain offerings.

22. Guy Berthiaume, *Les rôles du mágeros* (Mnemosyne Suppl. 70; Leiden: Brill, 1982).

23. Detienne, *Cuisine*, 92.

24. Ibid., 177, 131–33, 104–5.

"cultic meal" as separate from the sacrifice and have thus misunderstood the significance of sacrifice. Again, the problem seems to stem from interpreters making Christian assumptions. The constant refrain that "Greeks and Romans seemed more interested in feasting than religion" simply misses the significance of their religion.[25] This refrain also reveals to what a great extent scholars have associated "religion" with the guilt, expiatory solemnity, and ascetic ethos so dominant in the varieties of traditional Christianity. Dio Chrysostom's remarks (3.97) reveal what Greeks thought important for worship:

> What festivity could delight without the presence of the most important thing of all [friendship]? What symposium could please without the good cheer of the guests? What sacrifice is acceptable to the gods without those celebrating the feast?

STRUCTURAL FEATURES OF GREEK SACRIFICIAL PRACTICE

I have sketched major moments of the ritual, but the so-called meaning is more difficult for us who live at a vast remove from the lives and societies of ancient Greeks and who are accustomed to separate "political," "social," and "religious" in a way utterly foreign to antiquity. Sacrifice must be understood in light of particular cults to particular gods at definite times and places. When one adds an analysis of associated myths in local variations, the extreme complexity and polyvalence of Greek sacrifice become apparent. Interpreters have almost always provided misleading accounts by choosing one dimension of sacrifice's multivalency as *the* meaning of sacrifice.[26] A better approach involves illuminating what one might call persistent structural features of the ritual that allow it to bear multiplication of "meaning" and to show the actual work which the practice performed in the particular society at a specific time. Nancy Jay's brilliant researches have shown that across many cultures the oppositions created by sacrifice concern gender and paternity. This centrality of issues regarding paternity immediately explains why sacrificial practices have been produced only in societies based on inheritance. I will argue that sacrifice served in the construction of maternity at the same time that it lent itself to the construction of paternity. I will also argue that a focus only on paternity (and maternity) is much too narrow and misunderstands the way ritual works.

25. For examples of such comments, see Martin Nilsson, *Greek Folk Religion* (New York: Harper & Row, 1940) 87; W. S. Ferguson, "The Attic Orgeones," *HTR* 37 (1944) 123, 129: Paul Veyne, *Le Pain et le Cirque* (Paris: Seuil, 1976) 286, 363 n. 299, 364 n. 306; F. Puttkammer, *Quodo modo Graeci victimarum carnes distribuerint* (Königsberg, 1912) 51–56; R. L. Gordon in *Pagan Priests*, ed. Beard and North, 218.

26. Even Jay focuses too narrowly on descent and gender (*Throughout Your Generations*).

Wherever sacrifice occurs, one seems to find that whatever else sacrifice does, it also binds some group of men together in opposition to childbearing women, often creating rights of inheritance between fathers and sons.[27] Here one must understand how the separating and averting qualities of expiatory sacrifice stand over against the uniting effects of communion sacrifice. Sacrificing cultures associate that which must be expiated and averted with femaleness and childbearing.[28] In many cultures, for example, menstrual blood and anything associated with childbirth are polluting and cause danger, including alienation from the divine, which can only be averted with some kind of sacrificial ritual.[29] For ancient Greeks, childbirth severely polluted anyone who came in contact with the mother or the house where the birth took place.[30] During either the principate of Augustus or about the time Paul wrote his letter to the Romans, anxiety that the temples and sacrifices of Attika had been polluted by "childbirth and death" led to a massive project of restoration and purification through expiatory sacrifices.[31] Greeks believed that the pollution caused by women giving birth to children could threaten the very existence of the city.

Blood, Sacrifice, and Procreation

Sacrifice seems often to serve as a male counterpart to childbirth. This "social fact" about sacrifice may or may not be openly expressed in a partic-

---

27. Ibid., 30–60.

28. Ibid., xxiii, xxiv, 29, 35–37, 39–40, 45, 147; Evans-Pritchard, *Nuer Religion*, 233–34; Valeri, *Kingship and Sacrifice*, passim. For the Greeks, see below. For Roman religion, see Plutarch, *Roman Questions* 60, 102; Festus, *Glos. Lat.* 107L; Suetonius, *Nero* 6.2; Arnobius 3.4; Tertullian, *De Idol.* 16; Daniel Hanson, "The Family Festivals of Rome," *ANRW* 2.16.2 (1978) 1596–98. The *dies lustricus* for purification from childbirth centered on a series of sacrifices.

29. On menstrual pollution, see Howard Eilberg-Schwartz, *The Savage in Judaism: An Anthropology of Israelite Religion and Judaism* (Bloomington: Indiana University Press, 1990) 24, 32, 33, 36, 174, 179–87, 205, 214; Shaye J. D. Cohen, "Menstruants and the Sacred in Judaism and Christianity," in *Women's History and Ancient History* (ed. Sarah B. Pomeroy; Chapel Hill: University of North Carolina Press, 1991); *Blood Magic: The Anthropology of Menstruation* (ed. T. Buckley and A. Gottlieb; Berkeley: University of California Press, 1988). In practices of "native" Greek cults menstruation was not polluting to nearly the same degree as lochial bleeding, but the evidence suggests that popular lore made menstrual blood dangerous and that Greeks easily accepted stronger degrees of pollution in the case of hellenized foreign cults and perhaps in a few of their own. See Susan Guettel Cole, "ΓΥΝΑΙΚΙ ΟΥ ΘΕΜΙΣ: Gender Difference in the Greek LEGES SACRAE," *Helios* 19 (1992) 111; *LSG Suppl.* 54.7–8; 91.16; 119.13; *BCH* 102 (1978) 325.9; *LSG* 55.5; Porphyry, *Abst.* 2.50.

30. Good on evidence but weak on interpretation is Robert Parker, *Miasma: Pollution and Purification in Early Greek Religion* (Oxford: Clarendon, 1983) 33–73, 352–56.

31. *IG* II² 1035; *SEG* xiv 78; *SEG Suppl.* 26 (1976–77) 34–38. For the expiatory sacrifices, see lines 11–13, and Gerald R. Culley, "The Restoration of Sacred Monuments in Augustan Athens (IG 2/3² 1035)" (Ph.D. diss., University of North Carolina, 1973) 68–71. On the debate over dating, see Culley, "The Restoration of Sanctuaries in Attica: *IG* II², 1035," *Hesperia* 44 (1975) 207–23; Elias Kapetanopoulos, "Gauis Julius Nikanor, Neos Homeros Kai Neos Themistokles," *Rivista di Filologia* 104 (1976) 375–77.

ular culture. In ancient Greek culture, the analogy sometimes came to expression in literature and especially in medical writings that explained "female nature." The latter explicitly draw comparisons between women's procreative blood and the blood of sacrifice and sacrificial procedure and the process of birth. Although the medical writers very frequently discuss bleeding of all types, of both men and women, they only draw analogies between sacrificial blood and the procreative blood of menstruation and childbirth.[32] Attention to these medical texts, and to certain patterns of Greek thought that they reflect, suggests qualifications to Jay's theory of sacrifice as a means of effecting paternity. Jay writes as if paternity were an artificial construct stolen from the mother through sacrificial practices, and that while paternity is socially constructed, maternity is a natural fact.[33] Thus, Jay fails to notice the widely varied conceptions and meanings given to procreation for both genders in different societies and the inherent polyvalence of sacrifice. Maternity no more has an intrinsic meaning than paternity. The evidence from the medical texts and elsewhere strongly suggests that Greek sacrificial practices where concerned with constituting and interpreting both paternity and maternity, with defining the male and female roles in procreation and, more broadly, with gender itself, since the Greeks took the procreative roles as central to the meaning of male and female.

In *De morbis mulierum* (1.6), the Hippocratic writer says that during normal menstruation blood "flows as from a sacrificed animal."[34] According to Aristotle (*HA* 581b1–2), menstrual blood is "like that of a freshly slaughtered animal." Aretaeus, in the first century C.E., uses nearly the same expression for blood loss in women (2.11; *CMG* 2.34). Two Hippocratic texts (*Nat. Puer.* 18 [L 7:502]; *Morb. Mul.* 1.72 [8:152]) apply the same sacrificial analogy to post-birth, lochial bleeding that the first Hippocratic text and Aristotle use for menstruation. Wording like Aristotle's is also applied to blood following the decay of a fetus (*Morb. Mul.* 2.113 [L 8:242]). All of these texts reflect the ancient medical belief that the blood following childbirth is menstrual blood unused by the child in its growth.[35] These writings take the blood as a vivid sign of the mother's contribution to the creation of the child and thus of her potential claims upon its future.

32. Helen King, "Sacrificial Blood: The Role of *Amnion* in Ancient Gynecology," *Helios* 13 (1987) 119. King concludes that the analogy points to the different nature of women with "absorbent flesh" and their social roles in Greek culture.

33. See, e.g., Jay's statements in *Throughout Your Generations*, 35, 36, 39, 147. The assumption of maternity's obviousness and naturalness is important generally for Jay's argument, but see especially her comments about the "natural certainty," "sole criterion," and availability to the senses of childbirth (p. 36). Even more important, however, is simply her silence about maternity as a cultural construct.

34. É. Littré, *Oeuvres Complètes D'Hippocrate* (Paris, 1853; repr. Amsterdam: Hakkert, 1982) 8.30 (hereafter cited as L with volume and page).

35. King, "Role of *Amnion*," 117–18.

Other texts occur showing Greek writers intuitively assuming an analogy between women's procreation and Greek sacrificial practices. In one, a certain flux is "like the juice from roasted meat," an allusion echoing the most central part of the sacrifice, when the elite men roasted the sacred σπλάγχνα (*Mul.* 2.115 [L 8:248]). In another text, abnormal lochial blood is "like water from meat when bloody meat has been washed" (*Mul.* 1.30 [L 8:74]), perhaps suggesting the boiled portion of the sacrifice, and abnormal menstrual blood can be described in virtually the same way (*Mul.* 1.6 [L 8:124]).

Helen King has perceptively discussed a passage from Empedocles (*Frg.* 70) used by the medical writer Rufus of Ephesus and the lexicographer Pollux.[36] Rufus says that the covering enclosing the fetus is called the ἀμνίον by Empedocles and that this is why Eileithyia, goddess of childbirth, is called 'Αμνίας.[37] The word ἀμνίον is the Homeric term for the vessel that collected the blood of the sacrificed animal and from which the blood was poured out over the altar to the god (*Od.* 3.44). Eustathius's commentary on the Homeric passage says that Cretans employ the same word for their sacrificial blood vessels (1476.35). King shows that medical writers likened female flesh and the fetal sack to an absorbent sheepskin, ἀμνεῖον.[38] The fetal covering, like the bowl for collecting the blood of the sacrificed animal, collects and pours out the blood in the procreative process. Women's procreative blood was not the kind of subject that the male writers of Greek antiquity normally deemed fit for the page. But when the medical writers do broach the subject while staking out a new domain of professional expertise, they betray a reflex of thought that makes animal sacrifice analogous to women giving birth.

Greek discussions of procreation and the blood of men and women illuminate the logic of the analogy or homology between men's sacrifice and women's procreation. According to Aristotle, the heart turns food into blood, charging it with vital pneuma so as to provide nourishment for the whole body (*Part. An.* 647b5; 666a8).[39] The production of the blood is a kind of cooking or ripening.[40] The ultimate goal of this heating process is semen (*Part. An.* 726b3–11). In the female, however, due to her colder nature, the heating process fails its goal and produces menses instead (*Part. An.* 726b30). While certain other writers attributed seed, albeit inferior seed, to women, Aristotle denies women this contribution to procreation and makes

36. Ibid., 120–26.

37. *Oeuvres de Rufus d'Ephése* (ed. Charles Daremberg; Paris, 1879) 229 p. 166.11; cf. Pollux, *Onom.* 2.223.

38. King, "Role of *Amnion*," 121–23.

39. On the pneumatization, see A. L. Peck's discussion in *Aristotle, Generation of Animals* (Cambridge, Mass.: Harvard University Press, 1943) 592–93.

40. Πέψις and πέπτω were used both of cooking food and the ripening of fruits.

menses correspond to male seed as a byproduct of heated blood.[41] Milk also comes from the heating of blood (739b25). Male seed or semen is strongly charged with the vital essence of pneuma, giving the form and vital principle to the child whereas the mother provides only the material of the embryo. The male semen provides the potential for sentient soul and the female menses the potential for nutritive soul. The male semen contains an element that is ungenerated, indestructible, divine and analogous to elements of which the stars consist (736b35–39; cf. *Cael.* 269–270). Aristotle describes the mother's nutritive contribution as "earthy."[42] The male seed connects him with the divine; woman's blood ties her to the earth.

I want to make three points about Aristotle's account. First, blood is the basic vital substance common to humans and animals, and the vehicle for the spark of procreation. This biological conception thus coheres with common language that speaks of related people as being of the same seed/semen or blood. As in the medical texts, so also in sacrifice, men alone own and control the creative and generative use of blood. Only men could collect the blood and pour it over the altar to the gods (see below). Hesiod's account of creation makes men of a different "race" from women, that is, of a distinct bloodline (*Theog.* 590; cf. Semon. 7; Plato, *Tim.* 90e).[43] More importantly, the "lineage of men" trace themselves back to the gods. Zeus is the "father of gods and men (*andres*)." In the medical writers, and probably in Hesiod, however, men and women are not biological opposites but social and cultural competitors who differ because of their differing abilities to "cook" the same basic substance, blood.[44] Greek sacrifice implied a hierarchical contrast between its own ritualized practice of men cooking meat and the ordinary practice of women cooking bread.

Second, the medical ideas about blood and procreation naturalize the roles given to men and women in Greek society and culture. Men and their

41. There were ancient theories that gave women a greater role, but the seed/soil view certainly dominated; and the theories allowing women some contribution did not usually lessen in any marked way the inferiority attributed to women. See G. E. R. Lloyd, *Science, Folklore and Ideology* (Cambridge: Cambridge University Press, 1983) 108–11; E. Lesky, *Die Zeugungs- und Vererbungslehrn der Antike und ihr Nachwirken* (Mainz: Akademie der Wissenschaften und der Literatur, 1951) 125–59; Ann Elis Hanson, "Conception, Gestation, and the Origin of the Female Nature in the *Corpus Hippocratorum,*" *Helios* 19 (1992) 31–71; Page duBois, *Sowing the Body* (Chicago: University of Chicago Press, 1988); J. Morsink, "Was Aristotle's Biology Sexist," *Journal of the History of Biology* 12 (1979) 83–111. For an important discussion of the seed/soil metaphor in modern rural Turkey and reflections on the construction of paternity and maternity, see Carol Delaney, *The Seed and the Soil: Gender and Cosmology in Turkish Village Society* (Berkeley: University of California Press, 1991). I would like to thank Howard Eilberg-Schwartz for the reference to Delaney.

42. Peck, *Aristotle*, lxvi–lxvii.

43. Nicole Loraux, "Sur la race des femmes et quelques-unes de ses tribus," *Arethusa* 11 (1978) 43–88.

44. Thomas Laqueur, *Making Sex: Body and Gender from the Greeks to Freud* (Cambridge, Mass.: Harvard University Press, 1990) 25–62.

blood/semen are active, creative, dominant, and the source of human identity; while women and their blood/menses are passive, supportive, nurturing, imperfect, and need men's active power for biological fulfillment. Third,
the medical logic and metaphors concerning procreation depend on an
analogous everyday language about gender and procreation. Throughout
antiquity, Greeks employed the metaphor of the seed and the soil for procreation.[45] Men provided the seed. Women provide a space and nutrients for
a creation of which they bear no essential part. The common cliché likened
sexual intercourse to ploughing the soil; the man ploughed and the woman
was the soil. In another image, Greek writers likened procreation and sexual
intercourse to baking bread in an oven.[46] The woman passively provided the
space; the man the active creative role and material. For Aristotle, procreation involves a cooking of the fetus, although the male semen must itself
provide the necessary heat. The Hippocratic treatise "The Nature of the
Child" (12.325) explicitly compares the development of the embryo to the
baking of bread.

An otherwise puzzling story from Herodotus (1.59) betrays the connection between sacrifice (cooking food) and procreation. Hippocrates, father
of Pisistratus, was sacrificing at Olympia when the kettles full of meat
began to boil without fire until they overflowed. Chilon, accounted one of
the seven sages, happened to see the wonder and warned Hippocrates "not
to take a childbearing wife into his house, if he were going to have one; and
if he already had one, to send her away; and if he had a child, to disown
him." The sacrificial meat in the kettle signifies for Chilon the pregnant
womb and the kettle's self-heating an ill omen regarding the offspring.

From the second century C.E., Artemidorus's book (2.10) on the interpretation of dreams connects the household altar with bearing children. "If a
man dreams that he sees fire that burns brightly in the hearth or an oven, it
is propitious and signifies the birth of children. For both a hearth and an
oven are similar to a woman in that they receive things that are productive
of life. Seeing fire in them means that a man's wife will become pregnant."
These passages suggest the stories of children who were born of hearths
(Apollodorus 1.8.2; Aeschylus, *Choer.* 607f.; *H. Hymn Dem.* 239). In Cly-
temnestra's dream Agamemnon regains the rule of his house and bloodline
by planting Aegisthus's staff in the household altar. He takes control of his
seed at the place of sacrifice and it sprouts into a mighty lineage (Sophocles, *Ele.* 416–23). As I shall try to show in my discussion of Greek agnatic
groups, it is not that sacrificial practices merely acted out symbols. Rather,
Greek texts intuit an analogy between sacrifice and men's control of child-

---

45. For numerous examples, see duBois, *Sowing the Body,* 39–85. For the metaphor's importance in later times, see Plutarch, *Coniug. Praec.* 144a–b; Soranus, *Gyn.* 1.39–40.

46. DuBois. *Sowing the Body,* 110–29.

birth because sacrifice actually effected paternal control of children. Else-where (1.74) Artemidorus writes that the tripod caldron and the hearth sig-nify life or the dreamer's wife. He also makes the blood–childbirth connection. A man who sees a great amount of blood will have a child and if the blood flows into a vessel, the child will grow to adulthood (1.31).

Insight into the way that the sacrificial system participated in the con-struction of gender roles centered on conceptions of procreation can be gleaned from the ultimate women's festival sanctioned by the polis, the Thesmophoria.[47] Greek cities celebrated the festival in connection with the fall planting, honoring Demeter, goddess of agriculture. I would argue that it plays on the seed/soil opposition but reverses the focus of normal sacrifi-cial practice by centering on the soil rather than the seed. This focus tends to represent women as having predominantly a nurturing role in pro-creation and the necessity of the active-creative seed but also gave women room for ritual play that was threatening to Greek men. My account will be very restricted and one-sided, pointing only to some aspects of the festival involved in a series of oppositions homologous to the seed/soil contrast.

In Attika at least, participation in the festival was required of all of the cit-izen's wives (Menander, *Epit.*, Isaeus 3.80). Virgins who ordinarily were able to come closest to sacrificial practice, since lacking the ability to bear chil-dren, were forbidden to participate.[48] Viewed as a "fertility cult," scholars have thought it strange or paradoxical that sexual intercourse was strictly forbidden to the wellborn wives who particpated, but the isolation of women from men and their creative blood/seed belonged to the meaning of the event. On the first day or night, the women made an offering without draining blood, in symbolic opposition to the normal sacrifice of men: piglets were thrown into a chasm in the earth and left to decay.[49] Decayed remains from past years were then taken from the chasm and mixed with seed for the new planting and placed upon altars, thus enacting the earth's and the woman's role of being a medium for the seed. Here the women pro-duce new fertile soil and show their affinity to the nurturing earth. In oppo-sition to men, who offer the vital blood and send up smoke to the gods above, women bring soil from the depths of the earth to be united with seed which only lies on the altar, as if waiting to be given life. Sacred objects rep-resenting the male role in reproduction were also thrown back into the chasm.

47. In addition to the standard works on the Thesmophoria and Greek religion, the follow-ing are important: Detienne, "The Violence of Wellborn Ladies," in Detienne, *Cuisine*, 129–47; Froma I. Zeitlin, "Cultic Models of the Female: Rites of Dionysus and Demeter," *Arethusa* 15 (1982) 129–57. I have followed the evidence as collected by K. Dahl, *Thesmophoria: en graesk kvinefest* (Copenhagen: Museum Tusculanum, 1976).

48. On the exclusion of virgins, see Detienne, *Cuisine*, 137.

49. Ibid., 134–35.

On the second day, the women reenacted Demeter's grief over the loss of her daughter by sitting on the ground in mourning. The separation of mother and daughter, I suggest, reflects women's dilemma in the agnatic order of descent and virilocal marriage effected by sacrificial practice. The wife leaves the house of her birth and lives in a house where she has no part in the blood lineage. She must in turn see her own daughter suffer the same loss of the identity and power available ony through the recognition of bloodline. In the classical ideology, then, women's only identity and power came from attachment to lines and households produced by the seed of men. The mourning in the Thesmophoria ended when a man was quickly hustled in and out to wield the knife in the sacrifice of animals for a great feast.[50] The ritual defining male supremacy in the reproduction of the society ended the mourning and ushered in the third day, dedicated to the goddess Kalligeneia, "She of Beautiful Birth." During the festival, the women were to sit upon the *agnus castor* plant reputed to quench active sexual desire but to also promote menstruation and lactation.[51] The whole festival celebrates and even glorifies a passive supportive role for women in the city's procreation while pointing to the male role as the necessary active and creative complement.

Sacrifice, Gender, and the Order of Power

The preceding discussion will, I hope, show that the sacrificial order was involved in the construction of gender by evoking symbols of men's and women's roles in procreation. To say that sacrifice asserted men's claims of paternity over those rights naturally belonging to women illuminates the male side but mystifies and naturalizes the woman's side. Sacrificial practices also played a key role in constructing Greek conceptions of maternity at the same time as they constructed paternity and placed the two in a complementary but hierarchical order.

The evidence of the male writers cited above shows that Greek sacrificial practices were able to evoke tropes relating blood/seed, food production, and the cooking and eating of food to human procreation, and setting the procreation of men over against the procreation of women. In sacrifice, men collected the blood, gave it back to the gods, reorganized the body of an animal bred by men, roasted and ate certain portions of the animal among themselves, and then boiled and distributed parts of the animal to others in a way that reproduced the social body. This ritual activity had to be strictly guarded from the impurity of women who had given birth. In the home, not the wife but the virgin daughter was the symbolic guardian of the virgin hearth/Hestia which was the place of both cooking and domestic sacrifice

50. Ibid., 142–44.
51. Ibid., 147; Zeitlin, "Cultic Models," 146.

(see below). Here the father purified by sacrifice the newborn child from the birth pollution of its mother (see below).

What does one make of these patterns of homology relating cooking, blood, and procreation to sacrifice? Vernant, Detienne, and Durand have, I think, rightly insisted that Greek sacrifice used food and feasting to produce a system of classifications central to the culture. The limitation of their analysis reflects their heritage from Lévi-Strauss and consists in their rendering of sacrifice's meaning in a small set of broad cognitive categories and oppositions (e.g., animals/humans/gods) without showing concretely how sacrifice effected and reflected the Greek social order. The analysis of the French classicists also fails to develop the key connection between the discourse of food production-consumption and the code of procreation. This link allows one to see how sacrificial practices actually helped to effect men's and women's roles and the negotiation of power in the city. Accounting for the analogies with sacrifice requires a more adequate understanding of ritual activity. I will first discuss a general approach to sacrifice and ritual activity and then move to some specifics of Greek sacrifice.

Theories which present sacrifice and ritual in general as a functional mechanism or an expressive medium producing social control and social (and psychological) integration have proved unable to account adequately for ritual.[52] Ritual does not produce coercive power with its constant threat of force or contractual power with its constant need to change and reaffirm the contract but a distinct set of power-producing strategies.[53] Ritual practices form a particular political technology of the body, so that the body comes to have certain objectified schemes that it can produce and modify.[54] Ritual practices are not the instrument of some more basic power or of social entities outside of ritual but a particular environment within which participants come to embody and negotiate power relations.[55] James Fernandez and others have shown that while ritual activities require a minimal assent to participation in the activities, they do not require, nor do participants usually have, consensus of thought or unified beliefs and common understandings of symbols.[56] Ritual in fact works on the basis of ambiguity, partial misrecognition, and constraint of power at the same time that it

52. See the brilliant critique and discussion of ritual by Catherine Bell, *Ritual Theory, Ritual Practice* (New York: Oxford University Press, 1992). My discussion of ritual owes the most to Bell and the following: Pierre Bourdieu, *Outline of a Theory of Practice* (Cambridge: Cambridge University Press, 1978); idem, *The Logic of Practice* (Cambridge: Polity Press, 1990); idem, *Language and Symbolic Power* (Cambridge, Mass.: Harvard University Press, 1991) esp. 105–26; and the works by Michel Foucault in nn. 54 and 60 below.

53. Bell, *Ritual*, 212–13.

54. Michel Foucault, *Discipline and Punishment* (New York: Vintage Books, 1979) 25–28; Bell, *Ritual Theory*, 202, 207.

55. Bell, *Ritual*, 196.

56. James Fernandez, "Symbolic Consensus in a Fang Reformative Cult," *American Anthropologist* 67 (1965) 902–29.

reproduces an order of power.[57] One who consents to participate obtains dispositions in the body that both reproduce the social order and also empower the participant to perform the practices and wield some sort of power in the society.[58] Ritual practices both constrain and permit negotiation and resistance.

This understanding of ritual suggests insights into the importance of sacrificial practices for the Greeks. The play of ritual and the way it constrains conscious and overt exercise of power allow it to produce social solidarity based on fragmentation.[59] Ritual practices work through a strategy of indirection.[60] Although ritualization does socialize the body, its indirection can create community without threatening the autonomy of individuals and subgroups.[61] An extreme fragmentation into independent sacrificing groups characterized classical Greece. The sense of community and indirect negotiation of power produced by animal sacrifice created a strong sense of solidarity among citizens precisely because it kept power fragmented and produced social cohesion without the inevitable conflict produced by overt rationalization of power and ideology. I suggest that sacrificial practices produced an arena of stable power that allowed classical Athens to survive the conflict in the overt political arena. Thus, it is no accident that Athens' period of most intensely elaborated sacrificial activities (e.g., households, clans, phratries, demes, tribes, clubs, polis) was also its time of democracy.

This understanding of sacrificial practice also sheds light on non-sacrificers. Since participation did not require or produce consensus of belief or common symbolization, sacrificial polytheism made participation easy and refusal to participate radical. Catherine Bell writes concerning ritual in general: "The only real alternative to negotiated compliance is either total resistance or asocial self-exclusion."[62] Sources of various types agree in representing Orphics, certain philosophers, some Jews, and Christians as both strongly resisting participation in Greek sacrificial practices and as asocial (see below). The system made differentiated participation of diverse actors easy, but refusal to play the game at all difficult.

Ritual can only be understood in the context of other local practices from

57. See Bourdieu on these characteristics of practices (*Outline*, 5–6, 14–15, 21–22, 171).

58. Emphasized by Bell, *Ritual*, 197–203. On dispositions or *habitus*, see Bourdieu, *Outline*, 78–83, 95–97.

59. Bell, *Ritual*, 189, 222; John B. Thompson, *Studies in the Theory of Ideology* (Berkeley: University of California Press, 1984) 62–63.

60. Michel Foucault, "The Subject and Power," in *Michel Foucault: Beyond Structuralism and Hermeneutics* (ed. Hubert Dreyfus and Paul Rabinow; 2nd ed.: Chicago: University of Chicago Press, 1983) 224–26; *Power/Knowledge: Selected Interviews and Other Writings 1972-77* (ed. C. Gordon; New York: Pantheon, 1980) 202–6.

61. Bell, *Ritual*, 221–22. Bell, I believe, underestimates the degree to which ritualization may limit freedom, although her emphasis certainly forms a needed corrective.

62. Ibid., 215.

which it distinguishes itself and over against which it creates oppositions.[63] Ritual employs various strategies of differentiation to give itself a privileged position over against other activities, for example, festival time versus ordinary time, sacred versus ordinary space, formalized activity versus normal activity, informal activity versus normal activity. In Greek animal sacrifice, the ritual actors were individuals who had developed a *habitus* (deep dispositions) that enabled them to elaborate gestures and manipulate objects so as to produce an environment of homologous oppositions that were for the most part beyond conscious articulation by themselves and the other participants in the sacrifice.[64] Greek sacrifices featured positions, postures, and the manipulation of objects over against speech and moved from the more formalized procession and dismantling of the animal to the informal festivity of the wider feast. The environment created by the orchestration of sight (e.g., smoke rising to the gods, the spatial arrangement of participants), smell, taste, and the allusion to mundane practices (e.g., eating meals, childbirth) created an ambiguous and indeterminate but patterned play of oppositions.

It would be impossible to know a wide range of these homologies since our evidence is unyielding, since even the participants lacked conscious awareness of them, and since the oppositions were vastly variable precisely in relation to changing contemporary mundane activities. Nevertheless, some features were so persistent and important that we can deduce some of the oppositions. Moreover, answering the question raised above, concerning what to make of the unexpected analogies to sacrifice in Greek writers, can extend the evidence. I suggest that these analogies reflect the instincts of Greek men socialized by the environments of sacrificial practice. Intuiting "obvious" similarities between the birth of a child and the sacrifice of an animal was a reflex of a sacrificially constructed *habitus*.

By its very constitution, Greek θυσία (alimentary sacrifice) set itself in contrast to ordinary eating. Let me thus suggest the following homologies created by the ritualized, religious eating of sacrifice: sacrificial feast/mundane meal, meat/bread, men's cooking/women's cooking, viscera eaters/eaters of other meat, eaters of roasted meat/eaters of boiled meat, humans who eat/gods who do not eat. This list represents a very limited sample of the oppositions that Greeks would have embodied as a competency in sacrificial practices. The list, even represented in writing, allows the reader's "thinking" to slide from categories of physical objects and activities to categories of gender and social order. One contrast echoes and evokes another. Such schemes of oppositions privilege one term over the other creating patterns of hierarchy.[65] Another set already inferred in my previous discus-

---

63. Ibid., 90–91.
64. Ibid., 98–104.
65. Ibid., 102–3.

sion includes men's sacrificial blood/women's blood of childbirth and evokes another set concerning degrees and categories of liability to pollution so that the pure blood poured out by men in sacrifice, which honors the gods, stands over against the polluting blood of women's childbirth, which repels the gods. The sacrificial organization of space suggests another set of homologies, including a particular sacred space/ordinary space, land around the cult site/other land, participants centered at cult site/dispersed inhabitants, central actors (e.g., viscera eaters)/peripheral participants, mediators to the gods/those for whom mediation is made. Another set of homologies might be formed from types of rites: domestic/wider communal, local/central, men's normal sacrifice/women's festivals, Apatouria/Thesmophoria. One could produce similar sets with sacrificial time/ordinary time and many other features of sacrificial practice.

This exercise makes clear how very often the oppositions are gendered and yet how natural the assumptions evoked by the sacrificial arrangements, gestures, and manipulations might seem. I want to continue by focusing on gender and the sacrificial reproduction of the social order but must first say more about the significance of impurity.

Sexual contact and semen were polluting for Greeks but much less so than childbirth.[66] At first sight, Greek sexual pollution might seem unrelated to descent and the separation of children from the mother and attachment to the father. But sexual activity very literally meant the loss of the man's control over his "seed."[67] The pollution of sexual activity marked the beginning of a man's loss of control over his descendants, which was only regained by the lines of male descent created in sacrifice. Between the time of the man's loss and regaining of control, the seed is possessed by a woman. Women are both necessary for and the great threat to man's lineage. Thus Hesiod as exegeted by Jean-Pierre Vernant emphasizes the dilemma women cause for men:

> They may decide to shun the feminine "evil" and refuse to marry. Then for the rest of their lives they spend their days without care or misery.... But because of the lack of sons to continue their lineage and carry on their place in the house, the wealth they have been able to accumulate during their lives because of their celibacy is dispersed among distant kin at their death.[68]

Thus, Greeks forbade approaching temples, altars, or participation in sacrifices when unpurified from sexual activity. These taboos included Hesiod's canonical strictures against having sexual intercourse before the hearth where the man's lost semen might pollute the place of household sacrifice

66. Parker, *Miasma*, 74–94.

67. On loss of control and pollution in Israelite and other cultures, see Eilberg-Schwartz, *Savage in Judaism*, 186–92.

68. In Detienne, *Cuisine*, 65.

(*Op.* 733-36; cf. Hipponax fr. 104.20). Since sexual activity involves contact, both partners were polluted but sacred laws and inscriptions tend to speak as if it is a problem for men caused by women.[69]

The Greeks strongly associated birth with death and the pollution of death echoed the pollution of childbirth.[70] In Hesiod, all humans were originally male, immortal, and did not have to labor for sustenance or guard against deceit and injustice.[71] When Zeus caught this race of men colluding with Prometheus to defraud the Olympian at the first sacrifice, he punished them by sending "the beautiful evil," woman. Henceforth men would die and only continue as a son was born carrying the image of his father. "Unfortunately," men are only born of women and so must separate themselves by ritual in order to continue the pure generations of men.[72] So strong was the Greek association of birth with death that abstinence from procreation and thus death would become a major motif of Christian asceticism.[73]

Hesiod's myth mirrors the Greek organization of society. The significant components of society were organized by agnation, that is, descent reckoned through males only.[74] The most important of these agnatic groups are the household, the γένος, the tribe, the phratry (and Dorian counterparts), and, in Athens and elsewhere after the reforms of Kleisthenes, the deme.[75] I shall argue that one must also include the πόλις itself, since citizenship rested on membership in the major sacrificing agnatic groups. The importance and shape of these groups varied greatly from archaic times through the high Roman Empire and from city to city but the significant forms of Greek life were always organized by agnation and the criterion for membership was not birth but sacrifice.[76]

69. Thus, one often finds expressions like "enter pure from a woman" and "a man coming from a woman" (e.g., *LSG Suppl.* 115 A 11; 124.9, 151 A 42).

70. Parker writes, "They clearly saw the two pollutions as similar, since they constantly spoke of them together" (*Miasma*, 54-55).

71. My discussion of Hesiod draws on the following: Jean-Pierre Vernant, *Myth and Society in Ancient Greece* (New York: Zone Books, Harvester Press, 1980) 143-201; Vernant in Detienne, *Cuisine*, 21-86.

72. Jay, *Throughout Your Generations*, 30-40.

73. Peter Brown, *The Body and Society: Men, Women and Sexual Renunciation in Early Christianity* (New York: Columbia University Press, 1988) e.g., 119-20, 296-98; Robin Lane Fox, *Pagans and Christians* (New York: Alfred A. Knopf, 1987) 366.

74. Jay, *Throughout Your Generations*, 42; John K. Davies, "Athenian Citizenship: Descent Group and the Alternatives," *Classical Journal* 73 (1977) 105-21.

75. Nicholas F. Jones, *Public Organization in Ancient Greece: A Documentary Study* (Memoirs of the American Philosophical Society 176; Philadelphia: American Philosophical Society, 1987); David Whitehead, *The Demes of Attica: 508/7-ca. 250 B. C.* (Princeton: Princeton University Press, 1986); J. Wiesner, "*Phyle*," *RE* 20.1, cols. 994-1013; Karl Latte, "*Phratrie*," *RE* 20.1, cols. 746-56; idem, "*Phyle*," *Kleine Schriften* (Munich, 1968) 435-54; Davies, "Citizenship"; D. Roussel, *Tribu et cité* (Annales litt. Univ. de Besacon 193; Paris, 1976). See further below.

76. On developments in Athens, see James H. Oliver, *The Civic Tradition and Roman Athens*

Studies of Greek religion have tended to emphasize the larger, more public, and more spectacular cults and festivals. Precisely this emphasis, I
believe, distracts our vision from the most important and basic features of
Greek religion. Most sacrificing was so mundane that it might be compared
to setting and clearing the dinner table, absolutely essential but not worthy
of note except that it was relatively extraordinary in relation to other practices with which it evoked comparison. We can get closer to this "basic"
dimension of sacrificial practice by focusing on the agnatic groups. I will
depend heavily on the case of classical Athens since it provides the fullest
evidence by far. But I will also draw on evidence to show similar patterns in
other cities and to show the persistence of certain features into the early
empire. I shall argue that Greek society was organized around agnatic kinship groups and that sacrificial practice was central to the maintenance of
these groups. Cults were never just expressions of personal piety but ways
of organizing social relations.

SACRIFICE AND THE RITUAL CONTROL OF KINSHIP

Before clarifying the relationship between these groups and Greek religion, I must deal with a fundamental confusion regarding the character of
such groups. Until recently scholars explained γένη (clans), φρατρίαι (broth-
erhoods), and the older φυλαί (tribes) in terms of an evolution from kinship
groups to territorial and political (here usually meaning modern-like) organizations.[77] These entities were originally supposed to have been "pure kinship groups" of the nomadic and tribal early Greeks.[78] Membership was
solely through birth. When these tribes settled, they began to lose their
basis in kinship and to acquire a territorial and political basis. Tribes became
public divisions of the city, and phratries and γένη became private clubs,
vestigial groups with "honorary" religious functions. Kleisthenes' reforms
provided the final break from the old tribal organization. Writing separately,
books appearing in the same year by Denis Roussel and F. Bourriot demol-
ished the old evolutionary scheme.[79] According to the new view that was

---

(Baltimore: Johns Hopkins University Press, 1983) esp.1–33; for evidence from numerous
cities, see Jones, *Public Organization;* for demes in Antioch (founded by the Seleucids!), see
Gerald Downey, *A History of Antioch* (Princeton: Princeton University Press, 1961) 115; and for
tribes, Libanius, Or. 19.62; 11.245; for Alexandria, Diana Delia, *Alexandrian Citizenship During
the Roman Principate* (American Classical Studies 23; Atlanta: Scholars Press, 1991) 7–70.

77. For a good synthesis of traditional interpretation, see Robert J. Littman, "Kinship in
Athens," *AncSoc* 10 (1979) 5–31; and the discussion by Roussel, *Tribu*, 3–25, 109–15.

78. I see not only the influence of nineteenth-century evolutionary sociology here but also
Herodotus's nomadism.

79. F. Bourriot, *Récherches sur la nature du génos* (Lille, 1976).

built on insights of Max Weber and first hailed by P. Gauthier and Moses Finley, the three groups were "artificial" creations of the polis, "pseudo-kinship groups."[80] Only the family was a true or pure kinship group.[81] The territorial demes and organizational tribes of Kleisthenes thus were a logical final step on the way to the rationalized organization of the classical polis.

In my view, the new interpretation suffers from as many defects as the old. It supposes an overschematized understanding of both the groups and the polis that supposes something like the utilitarian premises and liberal individualism of the modern Western nation-state. Above all, both the old and the new interpretations assume that kinship beginning with the nuclear family is essentially natural and arbitrary while political-territorial arrangements are willed and rational. The dichotomy is false. Rather, Greek society always rested heavily on kinship, but kinship is never merely natural, physiologically determined. Physiology and biology do not create descent groups and patterns of kinship. People do. Thus, the organization of kinship is always political.[82] "Genetic" biological relationships branch into immense trees in a very short time and yet societies draw straight lines of descent through these excluding numerous other possible lines. Even for the selected lines, the chosen "genetic" plan is insufficient for continuity. Studies have shown that even in fully reproducing societies that a significant proportion of the male lines will fail in each generation.[83] The continuity of societies requires adoption and fictive kinship. In addition to this reality, one must also add considerations of ideology and power that often supersede the criterion of biological parenthood. Sacrificial systems are ways of regulating kinship, descent, and the inheritance of property in the face of such facts.

Greek society was sacrificially regulated by a pattern found in numerous societies across the globe including societies existing in recent time such as the eighteenth-century Hawaiian and the twentieth-century Tallensi in West Africa. Sacrificial practices at a fixed cult locus regulate patterns of land tenure, inheritance, and kinship.[84] Greek households, γένη, phratries,

---

80. M. Finley, *Ancient History, Evidence and Models* (New York: Viking, 1986) 88–93 on Weber and Roussel; Gauthier, *Revue historique* 259 (1978) 509–15. "Pseudo-kinship groups" is used by Finley and others. Most recently Philip Brook Manville (*The Origins of Citizenship in Ancient Athens* [Princeton: Princeton University Press, 1990]) has followed Roussel, Bourriot and the new view with some enthusiasm and sensitivity. Although my criticisms of the new view apply also to his book, he has succeeded in presenting a reconstruction that avoids the usual overschematization.

81. Finley, *Ancient History*, 91.

82. M. Gluckman, *Politics, Law and Ritual in Tribal Society* (Chicago: University of Chicago Press, 1965).

83. Kenneth Wachter and Peter Laslett, "Measuring Patriline Extinction for Modelling Social Mobility in the Past," in *Statistical Studies of Historical Social Structures* (ed. K. W. Wachter et al.; New York: Academic Press, 1978) 113–37.

84. Meyer Fortes, *The Dynamics of Clanship among the Tallensi* (London: Oxford University

demes, and πόλεις (cities) all possessed cult sites. In Attika, altars outside of the city center are usually centered in the areas of agriculturally most productive land.[85] From other societies, one could predict that access to participation in these cults and the hierarchies of participants within them would correspond to patterns of ownership and land use.[86] A γένος might have its most important altar in an area surrounded by high-quality land divided between corporate ownership and possession by individual households of the γένος, interspersed with plots owned by lesser, unrelated or distantly related houses, rented plots and less productive areas that were treated as unclaimed public land. The way the γένος operated the cult would legitimize its land use. Passing on the sacrificial rights to an heir meant also passing on the land use rights and traditional patterns of interdependence with neighbors. The same principles could be applied to urban nonagricultural property. The cult centered and hierarchically organized a particular area of land. Patterns of sacrificially distributing meat and grain, products of the land, would mirror property rights.

Such cultic regulation permitted both continuity of control and great flexibility. No matter how hallowed a shrine might be, it was always possible to move it or transfer it to others. By the same token, the claims maintained by the cult locus permitted those who controlled it to live elsewhere. Thus members of phratries did not necessarily live near their shrines and demesmen often did not reside in their demes. In Roman Egypt, papyrus records show Alexandrian demesmen and citizens living throughout Egypt.[87] They, like their Athenian counterparts, only had to return to their deme altars from time to time for important festivals and registration sacrifices.[88] Pilgrimage is thus an essential part of such locative religions. Even the polis was movable (one of the many features that distinguish it from the modern state). The people could transport themselves and their altars to another site and reestablish the same patterns. This portability permitted the Greek style of colonization. Perhaps the most famous case involving this principle is the Athenian threat in 480 to move the polis to Siris in Italy (Hdt. 8.63). According to Herodotus, the Spartan commander and the allies took the threat very seriously. The Phokaians moved their polis to Elea in Italy and Teos moved to Abdera in Thrace (Hdt. 1.163–68).

The Greek sacrificial "system" could not have existed without the οἶκος (household) or something very much like it. The household's cult locus was the hearth. By sacrifices at the hearth, children, brides, and slaves became

Press, 1945); idem, *The Web of Kinship among the Tallensi* (London: Oxford University Press, 1949).

85. Manville, *Origins of Citizenship*, 108.

86. On cult and land use, see D. Biebuyck, "Tenure foncière et valeurs religieuses," *African Agrarian Systems* (London, 1963) 35–41.

87. Delia, *Alexandrian Citizenship*, 51, 136–41.

88. Ibid., 58–59.

members of the οἶκος. Pollution requiring sacrificial expiation marks and effects social divisions crucial to the society. For Greeks, pollution marked the void in the social fabric left by death, and it effected the separation of mothers from claim to the property, power, and status that were passed through inheritance between generations. Thus, childbirth represented a time of potential danger to the control of generations by men. Human childbirth is a cultural production and not merely a natural process, and the Greeks gave it a highly ritualized structure.[89] We know only bits and pieces about it, from many different places and periods, primarily because it was an event hidden in the γυναικών, women's quarters.[90] We know that midwives, like priestesses, had to be above childbearing age and were responsible for helping to control the pollution of childbirth.[91] They, for example, gave the first bath of purification to the mother and child after birth.[92] Medical writers also assume that the midwife in the birthing room acted in the stead of the father to decide if the newborn was healthy enough and "normal" enough to be allowed to survive at that point.[93]

A child did not become a member of the household at or by virtue of birth.[94] That would have allowed claims by the mother or the mother's kin. Rather, membership was effected cultically by sacrifice as the child was separated from the pollution of its mother and bonded to the father. It is not clear whether the child became fully a member of the household at the Amphidromia on the fifth day after birth or whether membership was a two-step process including the tenth-day rite.[95] In the first ritual, the father ran or walked the newborn around the purified hearth and offered a sacrifice that was both expiatory and communal. Ephippos mentions lamb, but various animals were probably sacrificed and eaten depending on the means of the οἶκος.[96] In the tenth-day ceremony, the father declared the child either legitimate or illegitimate and gave it a name. Testing of legitimacy in connection with sacrifice for the purpose of agnatic filiation occurs in all of the Greek kinship groups. The mother seems to have remained polluted until rites that occurred on the fortieth day.[97] Although the periods of pollution and the rituals may have varied, the child only

89. Robert Garland, *The Greek Way of Life From Conception to Old Age* (Ithaca, N.Y.: Cornell University Press, 1990) 59–93.

90. Most of the evidence, however, concerns Athens.

91. Garland, *Greek Way*, 62, 64.

92. *Hom. Hymn Aphr.* 120; Kall., *Hymn Zeus* 15–17; Soranus, *Gyn.* 2.12–13.

93. Soranus, *Gyn.* 2.79.

94. Jay, *Throughout Your Generations*, 43.

95. Some sources also speak of a seventh-day rite. There is clearly some confusion in the later sources probably due to variations in practice over time and region. On the rites and sources, see Garland, *Greek Way*, 93–98. Plato (*Theait.* 160e–61a) clearly shows that the rite was both a purification and an adoption by the father in which the mother was powerless.

96. *Comicorum Atticorum fragmenta* (ed. T. Kock; Leipzig: Teubner, 1884) 2, p. 251, 3.

97. Parker, *Miasma*, 51–52; Garland, *Greek Way*, 97.

became a member of the household at least several days after birth in connection with sacrifice at the purified hearth.[98] These practices bypassed family relations that in other societies could be claimed through birth from the mother and set the polluting blood of the mother in opposition to the purifying blood of sacrificing males.[99]

Clearly membership and status in the οἶκος were cultic, not natural. The ritual declaration of legitimacy meant that the child now separated from its mother was of the father's seed and line of descent. The ritual probably varied depending on whether the child was male or female. The father would have already decided to raise the child. Some scholars argue that girls were often exposed, yet another "rational choice" to this supposedly natural unit of kinship.[100] Sentiments like Aeschylus's line (*Eum.* 658) that the mother is not the child's parent but only the nurse of the man's seed reflect both ancient biology and the social reality effected by sacrificial practice. Hippolytus imagines a more direct cultic arrangement when he criticizes Zeus for requiring women for procreation and proposes that men could make offerings in temples in exchange for the seed of offspring. Then men could live entirely without women in the οἶκος (Euripides, *Hipp.* 616–24).

The γένος (often translated as "clan") formed another patrilineal agnatic group organized by sacrificial practice.[101] In the greatly overschematized traditional scholarship, γένη were often seen as subdivisions of phratries. But γένη had no standard constitution beyond that of being an extended agnatic kinship group with a common cult center or centers. In the classical period they did often have a relationship with a specific phratry.[102] They have also been understood as solely aristocratic groups, but this is clearly not the case.[103] Rather, a γένος is a locative sacrificing kinship group larger than the οἶκος but smaller and less diverse in its kin relations than a phratry. Such a grouping of households was of maximal size for effectively wielding power and still maintaining tight kinship and descent relations. This is why the important aristocratic families appear in this form. The

98. L. Deubner, *Rh. Mus* 95 (1952) 374–77; Parker, *Miasma*, 48–52; *Ath. Pol.* 42.1–2; Demosthenes 29.22; Isaios 3.30.

99. This sentence virtually summarizes Nancy Jay's major thesis, with the added caveat that I am not implying that claims by the mother are simply natural.

100. For instructions from husbands away from home to expose a newborn if it is a female, see *P. Oxy.* 4.744; Apul., *Met.* 10.23.3. For the major issues, see C. Patterson, "Not Worth Rearing: The Causes of Infant Exposure in Ancient Greece," *TAPA* 115 (1985) 103–23; Sarah B. Pomeroy, "Infanticide in Hellenistic Greece," in *Images of Women in Antiquity* (ed. A. Cameron and A. Kuhrt; Detroit: Wayne State University Press, 1983) 207–22.

101. In some cities it was known as πάτρα or πατρία. Generally on the γένος, see Bourriot (*Nature du genos*), who is overly skeptical about the γένος as a familial kinship group but in understandable reaction to earlier scholarship.

102. A. Andrews, "Philochoros on Phratries," *JHS* 81 (1961) 1–15.

103. So, e.g., Andrews ("Philochoros" 1–10) and many others; but compare Bourriot (*Nature du genos*).

most powerful and propertied γένη in Attika such as the Bouzygai, Kerykes, Eulmolpidai, and Praexiergidai controlled cults that served as the most important religious centers in the city ("polis cults"). We hear much of such elite γένη in the Roman period, since Rome extended its rule over the Greek world by forging alliances between its aristocracy and the Greek elites.[104] Γένη are well attested until the end of the third century of the Roman era.

Γένη organized themselves around the sacrificial cult of an eponymous ancestor and claimed descent from this common ancestor.[105] In reality, members were accepted by participation in sacrificial communion. These groups of men also had laws of their own and corporately owned property.

Γένη and phratries have been understood as "mere kinship groups," holdovers from the pre-Kleisthenic era that in contrast to demes had no territorial principle.[106] The location of the fifteen known phratry shrines from classical Attika shows that most phrateres lived near their phratry altars.[107] Even though the phratries were not officially organized by residence, this coincidence of membership and residence should not be surprising in light of their locative cult-centered character, discussed previously. One might also expect that the majority of γεννῆται would live near their altars. We do not possess evidence to reach similar conclusions about the Hellenistic and Roman periods. Writers often assume that phratries died out during the Hellenistic period but they are known to have existed in several cities during the early empire and to still be performing many of the same functions.[108] What clearly changed for these kinship groups was their relationship to the exercise of political power in the city and the existence of an increasingly comprehensive body of polis law. Some phratries may

104. Daniel Geagan, *The Athenian Constitution after Sulla* (Hesperia suppl. 12; Princeton: American School of Classical Studies at Athens, 1967) 35–36, 170–71, 184; Paul MacKendrick, *The Athenian Aristocracy 399-31 B. C.* (Cambridge, Mass.: Harvard University Press, 1969); Oliver (*Civic Tradition*, 9–26) contains a discussion of important documentation for later γένη, but his attempt to argue for a type of military γένος is totally unconvincing. Roman senators and knights do not seem to have accepted offers of citizenship until Domitian, probably because of an ancient prohibition of dual citizenship. They did, however, accept membership into kinship groups as when M. Porcius Cato accepted an offer of membership in the Eumolpidae. See E. W. Bodnar, "Marcus Porcius Cato," *Hesperia* 31 (1962) 321–39.

105. Johannes Toepffer (*Attische Geneologie* [Berlin: Weidmannsch Buchhandlung, 1889]) provides a list of the ancestors.

106. On shrines of γένη, see W. S. Ferguson, "The Salaminioi of Heptaphylai and Sounion," *Hesperia* 7 (1938) 1–74; Bourriot, *Nature du genos*, 1043–49.

107. Charles W. Hedrick, Jr., "Phratry Shrines of Attica and Athens," *Hesperia* 60 (1991) 241–67.

108. M. Guarducci, "L'InstitUzione della fratria nella Grecia antica e nelle colonie greche," *Atti della reale Accademia dei Lincei* 6.6 (1937) 5–108. In *IG* XIV 759, for example, a man in the early empire performs an εἰσαγωγή for a woman in a process suggesting something like the gamelia or Alexandrian testings for legitimate marriage. *IG* XIV 759 records a sacrifice to the gods of a phratry in Roman Sorrento. For evidence of phratries in Hellenistic Egypt, see *P. Hib.* 1.28.

have continued in places like southern Italy because they became vehicles for asserting Greek ethnicity as a minority culture. The fact that records and decrees were kept on papyrus rather than carved in stone has also made later phratries invisible.

In Athens and Ionian cities the most important sacrificial transactions of the phratries took place at the festival of Apatouria.[109] Dorian and West Greek cities celebrated similar festivals of comparable kinship groups at the festival called Apellai.[110] The active kinship making of the Apatouria stands over against the nurturing passivity evoked in the Thesmophoria.[111] Three sacrifices occurred on the third day of the Apatouria, called Koureotis. In the first, the *meion*, fathers who had sons born in the previous year offered a sheep, presenting the male infants as their own. The *koureion* was a sacrifice that made the adolescent male a member of the phratry and the *gamelion* was a sacrifice where young grooms introduced the names of their brides so as to show that her father was a legitimate Athenian. In each case, sacrifice established agnation or the potential for agnation connected with the life stages of birth, adolescence, and marriage. The sacrificial procedure of such scrutinies appears in a decree of the Dekeleians (deme?):[112]

> Whoever have not yet been scrutinized according to the Nomos of the Demotionidi, the Phrateres shall make scrutiny of them forthwith, after swearing by Zeus Phratrios, carrying their votes from the altar. Whoever seems not being a Phrater, to have been introduced, his name shall be expunged by the priest (cf. Isaios 6.22). . . .

A member of the phratry who doubted the legitimacy of the initiate would lead the animal away from the altar. If the sacrifice were allowed, the kinship was considered effected. In Roman Alexandria, it took priests known as ἱεροθύται to certify the legitimacy of marriages with the status of offspring in view and membership in a tribe and deme which was the basis for citizenship.[113] In classical disputes over inheritance, citizenship, or agnatic

---

109. Among the literature on the Apatouria, see especially Susan G. Cole, "The Social Function of Rituals of Maturation: The Koureion and the Arkteia," *ZPE* 55 (1984) 233–44; H. W. Parke, *Festivals of the Athenians* (London and Ithaca, N.Y.: Cornell University Press, 1977) 86–92.

110. Walter Burkert, "Apellai und Apollon," *RhM* 118 (1975) 1–21.

111. Zeitlin, "Cultic Models," 140. I do not mean to imply that women did not resist and negotiate in the Thesmophoria. Aristophanes and other sources show that they surely did resist, but the festival also reproduced the dominant social order of the city.

112. *IG* II² 1237; trans. from Davies, "Athenian Citizenship," 118. Charles Hedrick, Jr., (*The Decrees of the Demotionidai* [American Classical Studies 22; Atlanta: Scholars Press, 1990]) argues that the "Dekeleians" represent the deme of that name and that they have intervened in the affairs of the phratry of the Demotionidai regarding an extraordinary scrutiny for membership. Hedrick notes that the procedure for both kinds of scrutiny would have been similar (p. 78).

113. Hans Julius Wolff, *Written and Unwritten Marriages in Hellenistic and Postclassical Roman Law* (APA monograph 9; Haverford, Penn.: American Philological Association, 1939) 37–47; Delia, *Alexandrian Citizenship*, 108–9. As in most cities with Ionic origins, demes also met at least once a year for the testing and admission of males who had reached majority. Unfortunately we know little about how this was done at Alexandria.

membership, proof in the courts over rights hinged not on one's birth from a particular mother, much less father, since physical paternity was virtually impossible to prove, but whether one had entered into the particular relationship by sacrifice.[114]

If we understand that social groups and not biological parentage create kinship, then the distinctions between "physiological" and "fictive" kinship will become much less important to our analyses of ancient societies. Laws and forensic orations show that Greeks often disputed kinship. In such cases, the strongest claims were made by those who could show relationships with male heads of households verified by sacrificial communion. Testimony by a claimant to the estate of Kiron illustrates the point.[115]

> Now we have other proofs to demonstrate that we are the children of Kiron's daughter. For, as was fitting, since we were the sons of his own daughter, Kiron never offered a sacrifice (θυσία) without our presence. Both at small and great sacrifices we were always present and actually shared in the sacrifices. And not only were we invited to such sacrifices but he also always took us into the country for the Dionysia, and we also always went with him and sat beside him at the [public?] festivals, and were with him for all the [household?] feasts. And when he sacrificed to Zeus Ktesios [protector of the household's possessions] (a sacrifice for which he had special enthusiasm, to which he invited neither slave nor free men who were not of his family and at which he himself performed all the rites) we shared in these rites and laid hands together with his upon the victims and gave our offerings with his.

The litigant goes on to say that both brothers were initiated at birth into their father's deme without controversy and that their mother was chosen by the wives of the demesmen to preside at the Thesmophoria. Both cases carry the implication that persons without legitimate rights of kinship would not be permitted the sacrifices involved in deme initiation and as a leader of the women's festival.

Demes were not so much residential areas as agnatic groups with eponymous hero (or royal) ancestors. A deme did have a territory, but residence there was not a requirement of membership whereas ritually and legally certified kinship was necessary.[116] The sacrificial calendars of demes clearly show the corporate life of the demes centering on sacrificial practice.[117] Scholars have persistently obscured accounts of these agnatic groups by adopting the ideology of kinship, ancient and modern. Writers contrast the "private" household, γένος, and phratry with the "public" tribe or deme and

114. Demosthenes 43.82 (The one who is challenging a boy's inheritance should have led the animal away from the altar if he doubted his legitimacy).

115. Isaios 8.15–16. My translation.

116. W. E. Thompson, "The Deme in Kleisthenes' Reforms," *Symbolae Osloenses* 46 (1971) 72–79.

117. G. Dunst, *ZPE* 27 (1977) 243–64; J. Labarbe, *Thorikos Test.*, no. 50, 56–64 and articles by Mikalson and Parker n. 146 below.

"natural" "biological" kinship groups with "artificially created" demes, thousands, and tribes.[118] Even when cities created new demes or tribes, future membership, status, and rights in such units were determined by legitimating some offspring (born to the parents or adopted) or claimed offspring (other biological offspring becoming illegitimate children) and sacrificially creating hierarchies among the legitimate, beginning with gender. Agnatic groups continually changed, overlapped, competed and reorganized, providing the peculiar struggle and balance of powers among essentially self-governing entities that we recognize as the Greek polis. A full account of sacrificially constituted groups would include ὀργεῶνες (known as late as the third century C.E.), θίασοι, σύσσιτοι, ὁμόταφοι, and a number of groups unique to Dorian cities.

SACRIFICE AND THE ORDER OF THE GREEK CITY

One should not too sharply set the polis over against the other traditional kinship groups. The polis was created largely as a move to produce ἰσονομία between the kinship groups. This centralizing reorganization was not a move away from descent groups toward a primitive version of the modern state but the creation of a new kind of descent group where some residents (citizens) of the territory were marked off from others (noncitizens). Precisely at this point we see the creation of a new center of cultic activity in a polis religion that transcended but by no means replaced the smaller agnatic groupings.

The extent to which the polis's central institution, the prytaneion, was a great common οἶκος helps us to understand the city in Greek terms.[119] The scholiast to Thucydides, in fact, calls the prytaneion a great house(hold), οἶκος μέγας (2.15.2). Γένη phratries and demes sometimes had meeting places that they called an οἶκος.[120] Perhaps here we should resist the temptation to translate οἶκος merely as "building" and thus introduce modern utilitarian conceptions. The agnatic groups in many ways acted the part of a larger οἶκος. Modern scholarship on the prytaneion speaks of its two major functions, political and religious, or describes it as a political and social welfare institution with occasional ceremonial aspects that became increas-

118. E.g., Jones, *Public Organization*, passim. My comments are not meant to detract from the importance of this impressive and essential book.

119. Sayings about the prytaneion betray its centrality to Greeks, e.g., "What the prytaneion is to the city, this city (Athens) is to all Greeks in common" (Ael. Arist. 179.11; cf. Athenaeus 6.254b; Plato, *Protagoras* 337d). The prytaneion is "the symbol of the city," and its presence distinguishes a polis from a village (*Scholion* D, Ael. Arist. 103.14).

120. *IG* II² 1672, 24; Zenobios 2.27; Hedrick, *Demotionidai*, 48–51. Hedrick's arguments for understanding *oikos* as "building" in such instances do not make sense to me and seem to suppose a host of unquestioned assumptions.

ingly important in Hellenistic and Roman times.[121] Such descriptions constitute a modernizing hermeneutic that abstracts the political from the religious and other aspects of the institution. Precisely the integration of what for us are separate domains characterizes the prytaneion. The ancient sources most frequently mention two features about the prytaneion, the city's common hearth within it and the right of certain individuals to take meals there.[122] The hearth, the place of Hestia, was the site of sacrifice in the οἶκος. The constant, perhaps daily, sacrifices at the city's common hearth have a certain claim as the center of polis sacrificial practice. While other institutions and civic buildings disappeared, the prytaneion persisted as a standard feature of Greek cities well into late antiquity.[123] Dionysius of Halicarnassus and Dio of Prusa specifically call the prytaneion a sacred or religious building (*Ant. Rom.* 2.65; Dio, *Or.* 50.1).[124] Plutarch explains that if the flame of the common hearth were to go out it cannot be rekindled from an ordinary fire but only from a "pure and unpolluted flame" (*Numa* 9.6). After the battle of Plataea, the Greek cities decided that their hearths had been polluted by the barbarians and rekindled them with pure fire from Delphi (Plutarch, *Arist.* 20.4).

The Greek conception of Hestia helps one to understand the hearth's sensitivity to pollution. Hestia is a virgin goddess. The *Homeric Hymn to Aphrodite* relates that she disliked the works of Aphrodite and refused to marry either Poseidon or Apollo (21–25). Zeus granted her to be a maiden forever, instead of marriage granting her a place in the middle of the οἶκος where she receives the fat of sacrifice (27–30). Thus, every temple of the gods honors her (32). Every altar and every hearth honor Hestia. In third-century C.E. Ephesus, Hestia was designated the perpetual virgin (ἀει-πάρθενος), a title later given to the Virgin Mary.[125] Ancient codes forbade procreative acts before the hearth (Hes. *Erg.* 733) and tending the hearth was the duty of maidens. In Naukratis, women were forbidden to enter the prytaneion except for flutegirls (Athen. *Dein.* 4.150a). The perpetual fires in common hearths were tended by women past the age of childbearing (Plutarch, *Numa* 9.5).[126] In sum, the prytaneion served as the collective οἶκος for the men who were citizens in the city. Like the ordinary οἶκος, the social

121. The principal treatment is now Stephen G. Miller, *The Prytaneion: Its Function and Architectural Form* (Berkeley: University of California Press, 1978). Miller's otherwise important and excellent study operates with an anachronistic religious/political distinction.

122. Ibid., 134–218.

123. Ibid., 21–24. Miller's evolutionary shift from politics to religion is misleading. Rather, the character of its political-religious uses changed. Some cities did not have a prytaneion but housed the hearth in a different building with analogous functions (Miller, *Prytaneion*, 15 n. 23).

124. Miller (*Prytaneion*, 14) regards Dionysius's statement as exaggeration and does not mention Dio's statement.

125. J. Keil, "Kulte im Prytaneion von Ephesos," *Anatolian Studies Presented to W. H. Buchler* (Manchester, 1939) 119.

126. Hestia was often conceived as an old woman (Artem. *Onir.* 44; Hymn *Aphr.* 32).

organization promoted by the polis center was effected by the sacrificial practices of men set in a basic opposition to childbearing women and bonded to one another by the metaphorical-symbolic, indexing, and *habitus*-producing effects of the practices.

Ephebes, the future citizens and elites of the city, made their rite of passage by offering sacrifices in the prytaneion. From throughout the second century B.C.E. in Athens, inscriptions announce graduating classes of ephebes with formulas like "having sacrificed the initiation sacrifices for registration in the prytaneion on the common hearth" (*SEG* XV, 104, 5–7).[127] The procedure echoes initiation by sacrifice into all of the men's groups beginning with the οἶκος. Commensality and hospitality are other basic characteristics of the οἶκος reenacted in the prytaneion in connection with sacrifice. Visiting ambassadors and honored foreigners were invited to ξενία, the ancient "religious" duty of hospitality toward strangers.[128] Ξενία meant sharing in a sacrificial banquet at the common hearth (e.g., *Ditt.*³, 560, 42–44; *SEG* XII, 373, 49–51). Citizens honored in various ways were "invited to" or "given rights to" δεῖπνον or σίτησις, meals that sometimes included sacrifices.[129] The ancient practice of sanctuary at household hearths was also thought to extend to the common hearth.[130] Oath taking important to the city took place there. Various cults were found within the prytaneion, and it was a regular place for the processions of all sorts of cults to begin.[131]

The social organization of the classical Greek city was at least partly an adaptation to the fragile, often near-subsistence economy. The sacrificial system lay at the heart of this adaptation in two ways. First, it formed what Roy Rappaport has phrased "a ritually regulated ecosystem."[132] Second, sacrificial practice and sacrificing groups largely maintained the moral economy creating interdependence among poor, moderately well-off, and wealthy citizens. In general, classical period sacrificial calendars correspond to the seasonal availability of animals from yearly increase and the culling of older ones.[133] The importance of sacrifice encouraged animal husbandry, which was less immediately efficient and profitable than farming

127. *IG* II² 1006, 6–8; 1008, 4–7; *SEG* XXI, 476, 3–4; *IG*² 1011; 1028; *SEG* XXIV, 189, 3–4; *Hesperia* 16 (1947) 170, 7–10.

128. Miller, *Prytaneion*, 4–11.

129. Ibid.

130. Ibid., 16.

131. *IG* II² 1283, 1011, 1028; C. Michel, *Recueil d'Inscriptions Grecques* (Brussels, 1900) 515, 15–16. Pausanius 5.15,8–9, 12, 15.

132. Roy Rappaport, *Ecology, Meaning and Religion* (Richmond, Calif.: North Atlantic Books, 1979) 41.

133. Michael H. Jameson, "Sacrifice and Animal Husbandry in Classical Greece," in *Pastoral Economies in Classical Antiquity* (ed. C. R. Whittaker; Cambridge: Cambridge Philological Society, 1988).

but an important way of ensuring food for emergencies and crop failures.[134] Xenophon writes of the reasons for raising animals: "The art of animal husbandry is linked to farming so that we may be able to please the gods by sacrificing and so that we can use them ourselves" (*Oec.* 5.3). Finally, sacrifices distributed and redistributed a significant amount of food among the population.[135]

Through the agnatic groups, sacrificial practice created "hierarchically arranged networks of exchange relations."[136] Members of γένη, phratries, and demes were supposed to share a kinship and friendship enacted by sacrificial rites. By the ethos of kinship and friendship, they were to regard and aid one another.[137] The agnatic groups fostered an ideology of equality among citizens sharing cult and table fellowship. In reality, a mass of citizen farmers shared membership and festivals with wealthy, often aristocratic elites. The fiction of equality and kinship allowed common citizens to forge networks of interpersonal bonds with well-to-do patrons. The forge of these bonds was the rhythm of sacred meals where the powerful and the common feasted one another on certain occasions and shared equally in the expenses of other occasions. In the frequent times of crisis, poorer citizens could depend on the aid of the well-to-do and still maintain the ethos of generalized reciprocity that was supposed to characterize kinship and friendship.[138] Sacrifice thus mediated power in an indirect and nonthreatening way that allowed for negotiation and resistance even while reproducing the social order.

One of the major changes from the classical polis in the Hellenistic kingdoms and the Roman Empire was a lessening of moral obligation for elites within the ethos of broadened sacrificial reciprocity that had characterized earlier times.[139] Sacrificial groups came to depend less on equal contributions and more on the resources of a few wealthy patrons.[140] Sacrificing agnatic groups did not disappear, but they no longer bound the elite to the common citizens. New forms of sacrifice arose binding elites to the structures of kingship and empire. Power came from above.[141] The new legitima-

---

134. Ibid.; Thomas W. Gallant, *Risk and Survival in Ancient Greece* (Stanford, Calif.: Stanford University Press, 1991) 122–27, 174–77.

135. The contribution to the overall diet was not very high but was nevertheless significant for many people (Gallant, *Risk*, 174–77; Jameson, "Animal Husbandry," 105–6).

136. Gallant, *Risk*, 168. The phrase belongs to Gallant, although he does not make the strong connection between sacrifice, kinship, and agnatic groups that I am making.

137. Ibid., 143–69.

138. Ibid., 159–66.

139. For the general trends, see J. K. Davies, "Cultural, Social and Economic Features of the Hellenistic World," *Cambridge Ancient History* (2nd ed.; Cambridge: Cambridge University Press, 1984) 257–320.

140. Whitehead, *Demes of Attica*, 175.

141. Gabriel Herman, "The 'Friends' of the Early Hellenistic Rulers: Servants or Officials?" *Talanta* (1981) 103–49.

tion from outside the old face-to-face communities weakened the elites' sense of interpersonal moral obligation and the community's leverage on the elites. Patronage continued, but the elites now followed the models of kings and emperors, who acted as benefactors from above for the city or group as a whole. The new age saw the rise of massive centralized altars where elites contributed sacrifices binding them to rulers above and the community far below. Agnatic groups certainly still maintained a vital role but with a diminished capacity to tie the mass of common citizens to the city's networks of power apart from overtly hierarchical transactions. The disappearance of the phratry in many places and the seemingly lessened activity (to judge by epigraphical evidence) of agnatic groups reflect a loss of the sacrificially centered spell under which elites and commoners had shared power and produced "democracy." These changes coincided with the rise of large and cosmopolitan urban centers. In such centers, sacrifice became less closely attached to the rural farming economy and its ecosystem.

Agnatic descent groups, however, persisted as the basis for Greek ethnicity even in a city such as Corinth, which had been refounded as a Roman *colonia*.[142] Basic principles of kinship, citizenship, and ethnicity continued. One of the great social divides in the empire lay between those who were Greek citizens or the wives and children of citizens and the large noncitizen populations of the cities. The latter often participated in sacrifices but always in a way to mark their social location at the periphery.[143] In Greek cities, the tribes, γένη, and organizations like the Attic demes continued even when citizenship became easier to obtain and these groups no longer had such direct links to city councils increasingly dominated by a small class of wealthy elites.[144] The importance of the imperial cult also

142. Archaeological work of the last fifty years has shown that Strabo's claim that Corinth lay uninhabited until its refoundation is false. In fact, a rather flourishing Greek population continued. In addition to Roman Corinth's large ethnically Greek population that would have kept the household and γένος intact, the city was refounded with *tribus* and *tribuli* rather than the *curiae* and *curiales* that became characteristic of Roman foundations. On changes in Corinth's ethnicity, see Donald Engels, *Roman Corinth: An Alternative Model for the Classical City* (Chicago: University of Chicago Press, 1990) 71–74. On organization by *tribus*, see A. B. Wise, *Corinth VIII 2* (Princeton: Princeton University Press, 1931) nos. 110, 86, 90, 97, 68, 56, 16; J. H. Kent, *Corinth VIII 3* (Princeton: Princeton University Press, 1966) nos. 249, 349, 258, 222; J. R. Wiseman, "Corinth and Rome I: 228 B. C.–A. D. 267," *ANRW* 7.1 (1979) 497–98 n. 221.

143. David Whitehead, *The Ideology of the Athenian Metic* (Cambridge: Cambridge University Press, 1977) esp. 86–89. There seems to have been a widening of participation for women and noncitizens in late Hellenistic and Roman times but with the same general hierarchical implications: see the cautions of Davies ("Features of the Hellenistic World," 309–13).

144. Scholars of Greek political history have puzzled at the "conservatism" of Greek agnatic groups at a time when they no longer played such a direct role in political rule because they have not understood how essential such sacrificing groups were to maintaining the social order (e.g., Jones, *Public Organization*, 23). Historians who wonder why such groups per-

changed the religious landscape.[145] Nevertheless, agnatic groups beginning with the household were sacrificing units that fundamentally defined Greekness. Inscriptions document the religion of agnatic groups in Athens and elsewhere well into the empire, while papyri supply another kind of evidence for the same kinds of institutions at Alexandria and the other cities of Egypt.[146] Γένη, tribes, and demes show remarkable vitality in the early empire and especially as sacrificing groups.[147] Augustus and other emperors encouraged sacrificing male descent groups.[148]

The centrality of animal sacrifice for establishing relations of fictive kinship helps us to understand the Greek enthusiasm for the imperial cult and why it so quickly became a dynastic cult including the whole imperial family. The elites in the Greek East who surged forward to establish these cults were making claims to a relationship with the new power.[149] Again, sacrifice differentiated those with close ties from those with weak or distant claims. Except in Roman *coloniae*, imperial cults in the Greek East took the form of Greek sacrifices.[150] Sacrifice as the key to kinship also helps us to understand the difficulty of the Jewish situation in the empire. The Ionian Greeks petitioned Marcus Agrippa that they alone and not the Jews should enjoy citizenship, arguing that "if the Jews were their relatives (συγγενεῖς) they should worship the Ionian gods" (Josephus, *Antiquities* 12.125–26; 16.12–60). When Dionysius of Halicarnassus wants to argue that the Greeks and Romans are close relatives with common ancestry, the "conclusive" proof comes from his point-by-point comparison showing that Greek and Roman sacrifices are nearly identical (*Ant. Rom.* 7.72.14–18). A Jewish writer would have to be even more imaginative than Dionysius to make the same case. A Greek follower of Christ could make no case at all for kinship.

MAPPING THE ORDER OF GODS, HUMANS, AND ANIMALS

Viewing sacrifice as a map or ideogram of Greek social relations clarifies the social and cultural power of the practice. Again, patterns varied from

---

sisted or who view them as vestiges with "ornamental" religious functions operate with anachronistic and ethnocentric distinctions between religion, society, and politics.

145. Robert L. Gordon, "From Republic to Principate" and "The Veil of Power," in *Pagan Priests*, 177–232; S. R. F. Price, *Rituals and Power: The Roman Imperial Cult in Asia Minor* (Cambridge: Cambridge University Press, 1984) esp. 234–48.

146. There appears to be no direct evidence that Naukratis had demes. Since it was founded before Kleisthenes, it may never have had them. On demes and tribes in Egypt, with bibliography, see Delia, *Alexandrian Citizenship*. On deme religion, see Robert Parker, "Festivals of the Attic Demes"; John D. Mikalson, "Religion in the Attic Demes," *AJPh* 98 (1977) 424–35. On the vitality of the γένη and tribes and sacrifice in Roman Athens, see Oliver, *Civic Tradition*, 19.

147. See Oliver, *Civic Tradition*, 19 and nn. 104, 108 above.

148. Dio Cassius 54.7; Oliver, *Civic Tradition*, 15–19, on *IG* II² 2338.

149. Gordon, "From Republic to Principate"; idem, "Veil of Power"; Price, *Rituals and Power*.

150. Price, *Rituals and Power*, 207–33.

period to period and from city to city, but sacrifice continued to represent or, more precisely, was involved in effecting the roles and structures of honor in the city. The procession ended when a circle was ceremonially drawn around the participants, the altar, and the animal. At the center of this circle stood those who exercised authority in whatever social unit, whether polis, tribe or cult association, upon which the sacrifice effected its powers. From the center of the circle outward and by size and quality of the portion distributed, the practice established a hierarchy.[151] Only in one respect were all equal: the mortal condition. According to Hesiod, Prometheus tried to trick Zeus at the first sacrifice by wrapping the bones in glistening fat as his portion.[152] The trickster god hid the choice portions inside the disgusting stomach to be eaten by men. All-seeing Zeus accepted the distribution but put men in their place by revealing the true significance of the division. The unrotting bones, appropriate to the immortal god, were changed by fire into a fragrant smoke ascending into the heavens and showing the unbridgeable distance between the gods and men.[153] The gods would accept the pious communication from the now mortal men, but sacrifice would always remind men of their finitude. The men indeed got the dead flesh of the lifeless animal and, unlike the needless gods, would have to continually eat dead and decaying flesh in order to stay alive.[154] But men who cooked their meat and communicated with the gods were above the animals, who could neither cook nor sacrifice. Humans organized into cities so as to sacrifice would find exquisite enjoyment in festively eating the cooked meat with one another but at the same time know their finitude. Sacrifice was intensively locative, placing humans between gods and beasts and setting the human hierarchy of the city in its place.[155] The gods benevolently watch from an impenetrable distance. Sacrificial practice keeps the gods in the background and the human conviviality of the god-ordained cities in the foreground because that arrangement constitutes the heart of piety and respect for the gods. Again, sacrifice both joins and separates, thus locating Greeks in society and the cosmos.

By locating humans within the cosmic hierarchy, the myth of sacrifice legitimated and naturalized the social hierarchies of the polis that were also mapped and indexed by sacrifice.[156] The greatest share of the sacrifice went

---

151. Detienne et al. provide a somewhat confusing analysis in pointing to the circles of honor and the inferior participation and portions of women but then also strongly emphasizing the egalitarian nature of the distribution (*Cuisine*, 4, 104–5, 131–33, 136, 177).

152. See n. 71 above.

153. Detienne, *Cuisine*, 7, 35, 39.

154. Ibid., 25.

155. On the concept of locative religions, see Jonathan Z. Smith, *Drudgery Divine*, 121–25; *Map is not Territory: Studies in the History of Religions* (Leiden: Brill, 1978) xi–xv, 67–207.

156. For an important discussion of sacrifice's indexing function, see Jay, *Throughout Your Generations*, 6–7.

to the one making the offering and/or the priest, although priests were by no means always required for sacrifice but were important in the more public kinds of sacrificing.[157] Being the (male) head of household, association, agnatic group, general, or magistrate was more important than being a priest in the larger scheme of sacrifice. The priest ate from the most sacred *splanchna* and received a special portion (γέρας) of the meat, usually a leg, the food laid on the table of the god beside the altar and often the skin. He was usually a man, always a citizen and an elite except in restricted contexts where "lower" social groups might have their own cultic practices.[158] Priesthoods were frequently hereditary and connected with "ancient" aristocratic families who in some cases held priesthoods from archaic and classical times until the end of antiquity.[159] Some could be purchased with large sums of money.[160] Women could be priests in certain cults, but with one requirement essential to the religion: the woman must not be a childbearer. Thus maidens, women past childbearing age, or sexually abstinent women served in temples.[161] Women never performed the actual killing, carving, and distribution.[162] The free and lawfully married wives of citizens and their daughters could receive a portion of the distribution from the meat but usually through the hands of the husband and father.[163] Only by virtue of attachment to husbands did wives possess any rights. Each sacrifice reinforced this "pattern of nature."

Foreigners, noncitizen residents, and illegitimate children were generally excluded or relegated to the periphery of sacrifice and normally could not make offerings themselves except in restricted foreign, metic, or "private" settings that reinforced their marginality in the city.[164] To the extent that

157. Burkert, *Greek Religion*, 96–97; David Gill, "Trapezomata: A Neglected Aspect of Greek Sacrifice," *HTR* 67 (1974) 117–37; Detienne, *Cuisine*, 104.

158. Detienne, *Cuisine*, 131–33; Garland and Gordon in *Pagan Priests*, 73–91, 179–232 respectively.

159. The most famous are the Eumolpidai and Kerkyes at Eleusis, the Branchidai at Didyma, and the Eteoboutadai in Athens.

160. This is especially the case for Asia Minor from the end of the classical period. *IE* 201 is an amazing piece of evidence listing some fifty priesthoods.

161. Burkert, *Greek Religion*, 78.

162. Detienne, *Cuisine*, 133–44. Even an exclusively women's festival such as the Thesmophoria employed a male μάγειρος or slaughterer (see Phillip Bruneau, *Recherches sur les cultes de Délos à l'époque hellénistique et à l'époque impériale* [Paris, 1970]; *LSA* 61, 5–10 and compare *LSA* 6 from the first century C.E.).

163. Detienne, *Cuisine*, 131–32.

164. Ibid., 131. In Ceos, for example, noncitizen residents (those of foreign origin and half-castes) feast with slaves after a sacrifice (*LSG* 98, 10). The most common "private" setting would be votive offerings. In Lucian's *Assembly of the Gods*, which parodies concerns about pure birth in second-century Greek cities, the gods decide to do something about metics, foreigners, both Greek and barbarian, and half-castes who have infiltrated the heavenly polis by fraudulant registration, "feasting [with the other gods] on equal terms" and "sharing equally in the sacrifices" (3). The chief example is Dionysus, half-human and half-god, not even Greek

they could participate in the city's sacrificing, participation was through the mediation of some citizen who represented the outsider.[165] When Greeks in power wanted to form new relationships with outsiders, they did so with sacrifice, as in the imperial cult and the numerous citizenship grants to foreign notables in the late Hellenistic age and beginning of the empire. Those honored by citizenship were registered in tribes and demes.

Sacrifice must always represent the proportion in the social relations of the participants. Thucydides tells (1.25.4) of the bitter hatred engendered toward the Corinthian colony of Korcyra, when during sacrifice the Korcyrans neglected to give the honored portions of meat to Corinthians who were present. The father city ranks higher than the colony. It might help in understanding Thucydides' story and the Greek investment in sacrifice to recount the domains and distinctions that sacrifice helped to shape: perception of the human place in the cosmos, gender, descent, kinship, citizenship, civic particularity (e.g., Athenians vs. Spartans), membership and rank in voluntary associations, ethnicity, social status, basic patterns of conviviality, the distribution of food, civic time, life passages, age grading, and civic space. No wonder that one of the bitterest conflicts in antiquity could be attributed to improper sacrifice.

In such locative religions, the participants do not view sacrificial protocol as "mere ceremonial honor" but as acts that keep their world together and finely tuned.[166] Without constant sacrifice, the world would fall apart. Indeed, their perspective is truer and more realistic than the modern understanding of such activities as empty ritual, merely symbolic, or emotive. Sacrifice actually caused what it signified.[167] Sacrifices at the hearth, of the phratry and deme actually caused membership in an all-male line of descent through which the initiate received property, power, and status, including citizenship. Pollution and expiatory sacrifices actually caused a separation of women from men. Communion sacrifice actually effected membership and bonds of community in hierarchically ranked groups, both identifying and constituting the group. Moreover, sacrifice inscribed these patterns of society and culture in the body. Such meanings and effects occurred through and with the habitual pleasures of eating, drinking, and fellowship, creating deep patterns of emotion, rationality, and other dispositions. Pierre Bourdieu has illuminated these dispositions under the rubric of *habitus*.[168] Religiously produced *habitus* helps us to understand how religions have

"with a female and womanly nature" who has introduced his whole phratry into heaven (4). Zeus calls for a testing that will require certain poof of each one's descent. James H. Oliver ("The Actuality of Lucian's *Assembly of the Gods*," *AJP* 10 [1980] 304–13) relates the story to *SEG* XXI 508 and a previously unpublished fragment of the same inscription.

165. Casabona, *Vocabulaire des sacrifices*, 108–9.
166. Smith, *Drudgery Divine*, 121–25 and n. 13; *Map Is Not Territory*, xi–xv, 67–207.
167. Jay, *Throughout Your Generations*, 6–7.
168. See nn. 52 and 58.

been a basic means for constructing virtually all known cultures and societies and why what moderns tend to think of as ethnic attributes are so deep and so nearly ineradicable. In addition to an indexing (i.e., pointing to various people in various ways—e.g., the roasted meat goes to aristocratic males), sacrificing actors created environments that also generated very basic schemes of oppositions and hierarchies embodied by those with sacrificial *habitus* and empowering them to reproduce similar environments. Taking apart the animal in a certain way and distributing the meat, for example, elicited patterns that reinforced the relationships of honor and power in the city.[169]

But why did animals and the bodies of animals serve as the most important ritually productive symbols for ancient Greeks? Greeks did not sacrifice all animals but only domestic animals produced by their own husbandry.[170] Sacrificial animals were only the "most perfect" products of Greek breeding practices.[171] Since they controlled the descent of these animals with the goal of attaining the purest and most excellent offspring, the animals easily served as metaphors for relationships among Greeks. Above all, the animals, like humans, had the vital fluid, blood; and the Greeks used blood to think about procreation and the manipulation of procreation. From citizenship in the polis to gender and the family, Greeks thought of descent and birth (nature) as the most important criteria for membership in a class and for providing the attributes fitting to particular roles in society. Sharing the goods from the body of a nobly bred animal with the gods and among themselves provided a way of thinking about and effecting their own social relationships. The selection of an adequate animal was an extremely important part of sacrificial practice.[172] Greeks inspected animals in the same way that patriarchs of the οἶκος (exposure, legitimacy), phratries, tribes, demes, and the guardians of the ephebate inspected potential members. In the case of each agnatic group, the inspection and sacrifice of an animal accompanied the δοκιμασία (testing) of members. They controlled the breeding of their animals and the bodies of their animals in the same way that they desired to control the descent and status of each member of the city. Sacrificial ritual seems to belie the myth that each person's status is given by nature at the same time that it enacts that very myth.

---

169. On this sense of metaphor, see Eilberg-Schwartz, *Savage in Judaism*, 118–26. For "disassembling" the animal and its "topology," see Durand in Detienne, *Cuisine*, 87–118.

170. The minor exceptions consist mostly of wild animals sometimes sacrificed to Artemis.

171. E.g., *LSCG* 96.6 (καλλίστευον); Jameson, "Sacrifice and Animal Husbandry."

172. On the qualities of sacrificial animals for festivals of the deme Thorikos, see Dunst *ZPE* 27 (1977) 250–60; *DGE* 251 A 10–13, C 1–5 (Cos third century B.C.E.). In the latter, panels of priests inspect animals according to a very complex procedure of the φυλαί. See also Stengel, *Opferbräuche*, 197–202.

CONCLUSIONS AND PROSPECTS

In concluding, I would like to make some methodological observations and suggest some areas for continuing this line of inquiry. The central problem in the next step of this investigation can be formulated as a question in the history of religions: What happens when a segment of society in a sacrificing, locative culture separates itself from sacrificial practice? To answer this question we must first understand the significance of sacrificial practice in the particular society. The context for reading the alternative society is always the dominant society. In attempting to understand the meaning of sexual abstinence in early Christianity, for example, the fact that virtually all religiously motivated sexual abstinence in the culture was connected to the sacrificial system, and its sacred places should be a baseline for interpretation. A next step would involve the comparative investigation of other groups that had withdrawn from sacrificial practice, for example, Orphics, some philosophers, and perhaps some Jewish groups.

Religion in sacrificing cultures is intimately tied to systems of descent, strategies of inheritance, and the establishment of kinship. The most fundamental problem in these patriarchal societies is how to eliminate, subordinate, or bypass the claims that women might represent with the dramatic and bloody rite of childbirth. Thus, men have employed an equally dramatic and bloody rite of their own, animal sacrifice. Groups who reject sacrifice, like the early Christians, must still deal with women, kinship, and descent. The examples from the Greco-Roman world show such groups either entirely rejecting or reformulating the purity system derived from the dominant sacrificing culture, the primary or only idiom available to them.

One of Nancy Jay's many brilliant contributions comes from showing how easily theory of sacrifice becomes ideology of sacrifice.[173] Any essentialist universal theory will lead in the direction of sacrificial ideology because it will obscure the historical and cultural contingency of sacrifice as one particular family of human practices. On the other hand, although sacrifice is not found in many societies, its importance in such a vast number of often genetically unconnected societies stands as a remarkable fact needing explanation.[174] Looking at sacrificers together with the study of those in the society who refuse to sacrifice can provide a useful perspective on the problem. The nonsacrificers show that sacrifice is a socially and historically contingent practice and not some universal natural or necessary human attribute. The nonsacrificers show just how, in the particular society,

173. Jay, *Throughout Your Generations*, 128–46.
174. The extent of such a particular rite as animal sacrifice indicates to me that Bell may overstate the case for the local expediency of ritualization, as she herself suggests (*Ritual*, 222–23).

it was possible to create an alternative cultural space. If Durkheim, Hubert and Mauss, Girard and many other theorists seriously had considered such nonconformists, it would have been less easy for them to abstract sacrificial practice from particular social contexts and to abstract sacrifice into some supposedly universal psychological, social, or epistemological trait. Even a superficial look at nonsacrificers in Greco-Roman society shows that withdrawing from sacrificial practice meant also forming alternative societies. If sacrificing and any particular form of nonsacrificing are not eternal and natural but the creation of particular groups of human beings, then we must look to particular social and historical conditions for understanding. Particular nonsacrificers will likely share conditions that distinguish them from sacrificers.

Sacrifice, however, is not an unproblematic object of study separable from the constructive activities of investigators. In each society, scholars must establish a syndrome of comparable similarities among the differences of time and place in the killing and ritualized uses of dead animals. We need a complex comparison of thick descriptions.

This study of Greek sacrifice suggests two major contexts for and types of sacrificial practice. In the earlier period, sacrificial practices in the polis were still tied rather closely to the agricultural ecology and helped to regulate land tenure, the distribution of food supply, and interdependence between those who owned and worked the land. Sacrifice may have continued to do much of this sort of work in Hellenistic and Roman times, but the focus of sacrificial practice shifted to serve a cosmopolitan urban culture less directly linked to the agricultural ecology and the inheritance of land among farmer-citizens. The later society, including the various Hellenistic and Roman empires, still had its basis in lineage and family; what Max Weber called patrimonial states. Thus, the work of sacrifice creating lineages through men and bypassing rights established through women remained basic. But sacrifice seems to have increasingly worked to establish and maintain many types of social relations beyond gender throughout the three periods. This scenario suggests a context for the formation of the most significant nonsacrificers of antiquity, the early Christians. As Wayne Meeks has so eloquently shown, the first Christians were a distinctly urban phenomenon. Although primarily Greeks, they lived at a far remove from the society of farmer-warrior-citizen in classical Attika. I would also argue that they tended to occupy a new social space being created by the empire. One of the intriguing questions is why Christians created a new form of nonanimal sacrifice in the eucharistic cult of the fourth and fifth centuries.

What does the Greek example tell us about the way that the rite worked? Greek animal sacrifice worked because it elaborated schemes of hierarchical homologies through an inarticulate medium that inscribed such patterns in the body. It also effectively indexed participants and nonparticipants and involved a concentrated focus on the domains of human experience most central to human continuity and flourishing. To take the last point first, sacrifice brought together eating and procreation. Acts and symbols regarding food production, food distribution, the pleasures of eating, and eating together joyously were made vehicles for transforming "natural reproduction" into the social reproduction of the community. In this process, sacrifice also reinforced the gender roles and other social roles that each participant felt was natural, although in a nonthreatening and negotiable way.

The rite made the body of the animal, including its blood, into a plastic "metaphor" for the social body and its parts, beginning with the problem of defining men and women. The first fact of the rite seems stark and simple. Certain men owned and had control of that body even to the point of taking its life and reorganizing its body for food. Thus, the first rule of Greek sacrifice: No matter whatever other role women might play in the ritual they can never wield the knife, bleed, and cut up the animal. In Greek communion sacrifice, men disorganized a body that was the product of "natural" birth by a female and reorganized it by a pattern of distribution to the polis which incorporated it into its body.[175] Propitiatory sacrifice by holocaust destroyed a body as it rid the social body of a danger or reconstituted a diseased version of the social body. Since the rite controlled a specific source of pollution, the ritual also indexed a specific group as dangerous to the city, usually childbearing women. Nancy Jay has shown why the pollution of childbearing women was linked to the pollution of death.[176] Sacrificing men assured their immortality by creating an eternal line of fathers and sons going back to the gods, the image of the man passed on forever. The constant systemic threat to that immortality was childbearing women. If the society were allowed to recognize descent through them, then the man's line would be destroyed. Death and childbirth repel even the immortal gods.

I hope that ending with a note on the importance of sacrificial practices in the modern world will provoke interest in the subject. Sacrifice does not belong only to the ancients but still shapes the lives of a substantial portion of the world's human population. One need go no further than newspapers and magazines for evidence. A few years ago the *Economist* reported on the international surfeit of fresh meat caused by the worldwide sacrifice by Muslims on the last day of the Hajj.[177] In 1983, 1.2 million animals were flown into Mecca alone from several countries to be sacrificed on that day. On Sunday, November 1, 1992, the *Providence Journal* reported that Protes-

175. Durand in Detienne, *Cuisine*, 155; Jay, *Throughout Your Generations*, 149.
176. Jay, *Throughout Your Generations*, 31, 55, 60.
177. September 3, 1983; cited in Jameson, *Animal Husbandry*, 87.

tant, Catholic, Jewish, and civil liberties groups had banded together to ask the Supreme Court to defend the right of "an obscure African-Cuban sect" to continue practicing animal sacrifice. Such rites are prohibited by local animal ordinances in Hialea, Florida. The newspaper reported that Jewish groups were particularly fearful that "the availability of kosher meat could or would be restricted or inhibited." Some two weeks later the *Providence Journal-Bulletin* reported on the "unusually contentious debate" at the semi-annual meeting of the National Conference of Catholic Bishops over women and the ordination of women.[178] One bishop was reported as explaining why women could never become priests (and thus perform the sacrifice of the mass): "It's as impossible for a woman to be a priest as it is for me to have a baby."

178. November 18, 1992.

CHAPTER 19

Prolegomena to the Study of Ancient Gnosticism

Bentley Layton

INVESTIGATIVE PROCEDURE

1. The aim of these prolegomena is to propose a means of identifying the data that can be used to write a history of the Gnostics, and thus to define the term Gnosticism (§23). The subject of Gnosticism will be treated here as part of the social history of ancient Mediterranean antiquity, because the data make it clear that the word "Gnostic" primarily denoted a member of a distinct social group or professional school of thought (§9), not a kind of doctrine. It was people who were called Gnostics. The artifacts of these people, especially their literary and intellectual artifacts, can be called Gnostic only in a secondary way, by reference to the name of the ancient group whose members produced them. The grounds for such a conclusion are presented below.

2. Any account of the Gnostics can only be tentative. As will be seen below, the data regarding the ancient Gnostics are sparse and survive out of context; are unrepresentative and come from tendentious sources; or else are pseudepigraphic mythography and completely disguise their real author, audience, and place, date, and reason of composition. No historical interpre-

Earlier versions of this text were read as public lectures at the École biblique et archéologique française de Jérusalem, the Israel Academy of Sciences and Humanities (in honor of Gershom Scholem), the Annual Meeting of the Society of Biblical Literature, the University of Illinois classics department (in honor of Miroslav Marcovich), the University of Pennsylvania, the Oriental Club of New Haven, and the graduate philosophy faculty of the New School for Social Research (in honor of Hans Jonas). I am grateful to various colleagues for critical discussion of the paper, and most recently to Zlatko Pleše, Thomas Jenkins, and Stephen Emmel for comments on the final draft.

tation of inadequate data is likely to produce clear and certain results, even if the best procedure of investigation is followed. Yet this accident of the data does not diminish the historical importance of the subject, nor lessen the urgency with which the results are needed for historical understanding.

3. The word "Gnosticism" is a modern word, created by the Cambridge Platonist Henry More in the seventeenth century through application of a productive modern desinence *-ism* to the scholarly loanword *Gnostick* (which itself had been taken directly from ancient Greek texts); see Appendix below. There is no equivalent of the word "Gnosticism" in ancient Greek, Latin, or Coptic. The history of the word "Gnosticism" from the seventeenth century to 1995 is fundamentally irrelevant to the historical study of antiquity (though it might be an appropriate topic in modern intellectual history).

4. However, the word *gnōstikos* (γνωστικός) occurs in Classical and Post-classical Greek (from there, borrowed into Latin), and so this is the term, as describing members of an ancient group called the Gnostics (see §9), that historians will have to interpret before they can draw any inductive conclusion about a characteristic category or ism of the ancient Gnostics, the ancient Gnostic ism, or Gnosticism (§23).

5. The historical investigator of a social group will pay considerable attention to how its members characteristically constituted, constructed, defined, and designated themselves as a specific group. If they had a distinctive proper name (*nomen proprium*, personal name) for themselves, obviously this is the appropriate label for the modern historian to use when referring to them. Furthermore, the modern historian must avoid using that word in any other sense, because ambivalent usage would introduce disorderliness into the historical discourse.

6. In general, proper names and epithets of ancient groups vary among themselves linguistically in formation, syntax, translatability, jargon character, range of reference, and so on. Some have one set of characteristics, while others have another. For example, some proper names of social groups are translatable—that is, allow a possible translation into another language as a common-noun substantive (e.g., οἱ Μεθοδικοί, a first-century medical *hairesis* [αἵρεσις]; cf. μέθοδος, μεθοδ-ικός, "systematic"), while others are not (e.g., οἱ Πλατωνικοί denoting adherents of the school of Plato); some epithets were relatively distinctive group jargon ("the seed of Seth"), while others were less distinctive ("the saved"); and so on. Bearing in mind the existence of a scale of naming words that ranges in gradation from extreme properness to extreme commonness with many points along the

way, the historical analyst should look carefully for the privileged, most distinctive (most "proper") name by which the members of any distinct group designated themselves as a group.

7. The common-noun meaning of any translatable proper name of a social group requires special consideration: (a) whether the common noun already existed before the word's appearance as a proper name; and, if so, the meaning, usage, and connotation of the common noun at the very moment it was adopted as the proper name of a group, that is, the intention of the leader who coined the proper-name usage; (b) whether the common-noun meaning was, or continued to be, vivid to members of the group beyond the moment of its coinage or the moment of their adhesion or rather, faded from consciousness; that is, whether the common-noun meaning tells us anything about typical attitudes or practices of group members. As will be seen below, two more issues arise in the study of "Gnostic" as a proper name in antiquity: (c) possible restoration of the vividness of the common-noun meaning by hostile opponents for the purpose of vilification; (d) possible adoption of the name (including but not necessarily limited to ad hoc borrowing), with possible restoration of the vividness of the common-noun meaning, by a person who did not count as a member of the group. Various ancient social group names presumably differed from one another as to these four points.

Illustration of the four points: (a) The adoption of the common-noun substantive γνωστικός as a proper name is discussed below, §§9–10. (b) Do members of the modern Christian Protestant denomination named Methodists think or talk about themselves as being methodical and do they act methodically? (c) Irenaeus mockingly suggests that the Gnostics do not really supply *gnōsis* when he speaks of "that which is falsely called gnosis" in the full title of his work *Adversus Haereses*. (d) Clement of Alexandria's description of "the *gnōstikos*" (typically in the singular) is of a spiritual type, not a member of a haeresis (see §12).

8. The original meaning of Greek *gnōstikos* was a common-noun meaning. Its history began in the fourth century B.C.E., not as a word of everyday speech but rather as a technical term that belonged to philosophy, as philosophical diction, the language of intellectuals. This flavor clung to the word throughout its entire ancient history. The word made its first appearance in a dialogue of Plato (the *Statesman*) and was invented by him through the process of combining the very productive adjectival desinence *-(t)ikos* (-[τ]ικος) with the stem *gnō-* (γνω-) plus (-*s*- [-σ-]), which is found in γνῶναι ("know"), γιγνώσκειν ("know"), γνῶσις ("knowledge"), and so on (*gnōstikos* would have been perceived as deriving from the stem *gnō-* [γνω-] and not from any specific word.) Plato invented several hundred new Greek terms with the ending *-ic* (in Greek -[τ]ικος), and in this case, as often, he

explained what the new word was supposed to mean. The literary context is a dialogue about the qualities of an ideal ruler. First, the discussants distinguish two possible kinds of science (ἐπιστήμη): one kind is termed *praktikos*, "practical" (πρακτική scil. ἐπιστήμη), for example, the skill of a carpenter. For the opposite kind of science, Plato invents the new word *gnōstikos* (γνωστική scil. ἐπιστήμη). This made-up word, he explains, describes the pure sciences such as mathematics, which merely lead to knowledge, not to practical activity, τὸ δὲ γνῶναι παρέσχοντο μόνον, "they merely furnish the act of knowing" (*Statesman* 258e), παρεχόμενός γέ που γνῶσιν ἀλλ᾽ οὐ χειρουργίαν, "providing knowledge, not manual skill" (259e). Since the science that characterizes a ruler has to do with the "intelligence and strength of his soul," it is more akin to the *gnōstikos* type of science than to the *praktikos:* it supplies knowledge instead of showing how to practice a craft; it is more like mathematics than like carpentry. The science of an ideal ruler must be γνωστική; it must supply the ruler with knowledge. This passage from the *Statesman* with its explicit definition of *gnōstikos* sets the usage of the word for the next five centuries. Like many of the new words formed with *-(t)ikos*, *gnōstikos* was never very widely used and never entered ordinary Greek; it remained the more or less exclusive property of Plato's subsequent admirers, such as Aristotle, Philo Judaeus, Plutarch, Albinus, Iamblichus, and Ioannes Philoponus. Most important of all, in its normative philosophical usage *gnōstikos* was never applied to the human person as a whole, but only to mental endeavors, faculties, or components of personality.

The productive adjectival desinence *-(t)ikos* (-[τ]ικος) basically conveys no more than "(somehow) related to . . ." (rather like the Greek genitive) and is thus ambiguous. Its ambiguity made it widely useful for the creation of new technical vocabulary in Greek; according to Adolf Ammann's count, from the classical period down to the end of late classical antiquity about five thousand new technical terms with the desinence *-(t)ikos* were coined. Because of this inherent ambiguity, when Plato coins a new word in *-(t)ikos* he usually stops to explain exactly what he wants it to mean: word and technical definition are created at the same moment. Such is the case with *gnōstikos:* both the new technical word and its technical definition (τὸ γνῶναι παρεχόμενος, "furnishing the act of knowing," "knowledge-supplying") are launched in the same passage of text. For the rest of its rarefied lexical history, the word was only used as a Platonist technical term. Its adoption in Platonizing (§29) Christian circles as a proper name belongs precisely to this philosophical history.

9. The application of *gnōstikos* to persons as social entities was therefore a significant deviation from established usage of this technical term. The personal application of *gnōstikos* first occurs in the second century C.E., in reference to Christians whom Irenaeus, bishop of Lyons, attacks (180 C.E.) in his work *Adversus Haereses* (he may be using a now lost composition by Justin Martyr, written about 150 C.E., that had been directed against various

schools of thought or *haireseis* [αἵρεσεις]). These persons are collectively called by the plural of *gnōstikos* (οἱ Γνωστικοί scil. ἄνθρωποι, *Adv. Haer.* 1.29.1; etc.) and are said to constitute "the so-called 'Knowledge-Supplying' school of thought" (ἡ λεγομένη Γνωστικὴ αἵρεσις, *Adv. Haer.* 1.11.1). A century later a pagan Neoplatonist observer, Porphyry, also speaks of Gnōstikoi as members of a *hairesis* (αἱρετικοί, *Vita Plotini* 16). In one passage Irenaeus (1.25.6) refers explicitly to those who "call themselves" Gnōstikoi; a contemporaneous non-Christian Middle Platonist Celsus also knows of people "who profess to be" Gnōstikoi (apud Origen, *Contra Celsum* 5.61). About the same time Clement of Alexandria speaks of the leader (προϊστά-μενος) of a certain *hairesis* who "calls himself" a Gnōstikos (*Strom.* 2.117.5); elsewhere, of followers of Prodicus who "call themselves" Gnōstikoi. Passages such as these indicate that Gnōstikos was a self-designating proper name referring to a haeresis. This is the only proper-name usage of the word *gnōstikos* in classical or late classical antiquity, and we may conclude that it was the Gnostics' own professional school name for themselves, rather than a descriptive epithet formulated by their enemies. This conclusion is suggested not only by outright statements of the kind cited above. It is suggested also by the history, meaning, and connotations of the common-noun usage of *gnōstikos* at the time that the proper name was coined, since the quality expressed by the common noun *gnōstikos* was clearly a desirable one: Plato had first illustrated its meaning with the example of an ideal ruler, and subsequent users of the common noun never strayed too far from Plato's passage. Thus, in the second century C.E. the effect of its neologistic application to persons must have been admirative, not pejorative, and so it was presumably a self-applauding designation. Applied to persons, "Gnostic" meant "belonging to the 'Knowledge-Supplying' school of thought," the Γνωστικὴ αἵρεσις.

10. The specific reason why the creator of this *hairesis* chose the name Gnōstikē ("Knowledge-Supplying") is not clear. Actually, the claim to possess and teach *gnōsis* ("knowledge") was certainly common enough in Christian (and Hellenistic Jewish) circles, including nonphilosophical ones, as was the insistence that one's religious opponents did not have it. Thus any implied claim to supply or to have *gnōsis* ("knowledge") was not at all a distinctive claim. The only innovative element in the proper name Gnōstikoi was a matter of word usage: its application for the first time in the history of the word to a school of thought, and (by extension) to members of that school. This application to persons as social entities was a neologism; it must have sounded strange and thus (because of the word's philosophical connotations) very much like professional jargon. The professional or technical sound of the term was also conveyed by the desinence *-(t)ikos* (§8, end). These factors made Gnōstikē eminently suitable as a distinctive pro-

fessional self-designation, despite the absolute banality of the idea of supplying or having *gnōsis* ("knowledge").

11. The only people called by the *proper name* "Gnostics" in late antiquity are members of this *hairesis*. Provisionally, all these references will be considered to attest in some sense to a single Gnostic *hairesis* developing over time in many places and also using or getting additional names.

Critical evaluation of the *Adversus Haereses* literature is made difficult by the polemical strategy of Irenaeus (following Justin Martyr or Hegesippus?), which strings together and homogenizes a largely fictitious *successio haereticorum* from the first-century mythical figure of Simon Magus down to the second generation of Valentinians, sometimes under the extended rubric of Gnōstikoi. But references by Irenaeus and Celsus (both using Justin Martyr's lost *Syntagma?*) to a contemporaneous group that *called themselves* "the Gnostic *hairesis*" or "Gnostics" can be taken as the starting point for social historical investigation.

12. Clement of Alexandria's description (ca. 200 C.E.) of an ideal type called "the *gnōstikos*" (usually in the singular, sometimes qualified as ἡμῖν ὁ γνωστικός, "our [kind of] gnostic") does not refer to membership in a social group and is not a proper name (see §7[d]); Clement does not, for example, call his own contemporary church hoi Gnōstikoi. His use of "gnostic" is comparable to general descriptions of the behavior of *ho sophos* (ὁ σοφός), the ideal "wise person," in Stoic ethical writings.

In Clement's works, five categories will clearly account for most uses of γνωστικ-, of which the first three express Clement's own neologistic meaning. Much of his largest work, the *Stromateis*, is devoted to explaining this neologism. (a) Substantive ὁ γνωστικός in Clement's special sense; defined as ὁ τῆς παντοδαπῆς σοφίας ἔμπειρος οὗτος κυρίως ἂν εἴη γνωστικός (*Strom.* 1.58.2); opposed to ὁ ἄπειρος καὶ ἀμαθής (*Strom.* 5.57.1–2). He once contrasts οἱ γνωστικοί (Christians who might conform to his ideal type) with αἱ αἱρέσεις (*Strom.* 7.94.3). More than 150 instances, mostly singular. (b) Modifying adjective, γνωστικός -ή -όν, with reference to (a). Modifies a wide variety of substantives. More than fifty instances. (c) Adverb γνωστικῶς, with reference to (a). About two dozen instances. (d) Neuter substantive τὸ γνωστικόν, opposed to τὸ ποιητικόν, somewhat like Plato's usage (§8) (*Strom.* 6.91.2). (e) Substantive Γνωστικός -οί. Members of a school that calls itself the Gnōstikoi (*Strom.* 2.117.5; 3.30.2; 4.114.2; 4.116.1; 7.41.3; cf. *Paedagogus* 1.52.2). Among these are the followers of Prodicus οἱ ἀπὸ Προδίκου (*Strom.* 3.30.1).

In Greek literature down to the seventh century, there seems to be no other record of *gnōstikos* applied to specific people. Two apparent exceptions to this statement turn out to be irrelevant or nonexistent upon closer inspection. First, in the manuscripts of Diogenes Laertius, *Vitae Philosophorum* 1.114 (second century C.E.), Epimenides the Presocratic shaman and seer is called γνωστικώτατον. However, editors following J. J. Reiske (*apud* H. Diels, *Hermes* 24 [1889] 307), have been unanimous in emending the transmitted text to ‹προ›γνωστικώτατον. This conjecture is supported by the fact that in Roman Greek literature at least two other figures of remote antiquity, namely, Anaxagoras and Democritus, are called προγνωστικός.

The second passage is in the Greek Alexander Romance, which comes down to us in several distinct ancient recensions, whose interrelationships have been investigated by textual scholars. Recension γ, book III (ed. F. Parthe, p. 452,20) contains an episode in which Bucephalus avenges Alexander's death in the manner of "those people who are λογικώτατοι and γνωστικώτατοι." Whatever the correct text of this passage may be, recension γ has been shown by its modern editors to be an expansion of the somewhat earlier recension ε (ed. J. Trumpf, p. 177,6), which has this same passage verbatim but without the phrase containing γνωστικώτατοι. Since the author of recension γ has been dated to the seventh century C.E. (because of details that are mentioned in describing a chariot race), the phrase containing the word γνωστικώτατοι must be regarded as a seventh-century Byzantine revision. In any case the word as used in recension γ designates an ideal type and not a social group. A third passage has been adduced by Morton Smith, from Ps.-Ecphantus, ed. H. Delatte, but in fact this passage does not contain the word in question, nor does Delatte defend it as a conjecture (*pace* Smith).

13. Where does the social historian find data describing the Gnostics (see §4)? The most certain place to start is the ancient references that mention them explicitly by their own professional name (§9), *hoi Gnōstikoi.* These can be called the *direct testimonia.* Despite the tendentious sources in which they are preserved, the direct testimonia are the fundamental and most certain core of information about the Gnostics, but they are very meager and give an extremely inadequate (and partly contradictory) historical picture. It is therefore desirable to use a compensatory procedure of investigation that will increase the amount of available data that can be associated with the social group called Gnostics and so thicken the ultimate description of the Gnostics (even at the cost of introducing greater uncertainty into the results).

14. All the direct testimonia occur in works by the enemies of the Gnostics, especially Irenaeus, Celsus, Clement of Alexandria, Hippolytus, Plotinus, Porphyry, and Epiphanius, and they report, in a very reduced and ironic way: doctrines (mostly isolated) of the Gnostics, liturgical and sexual practices of the Gnostics, and cosmological myth read by the Gnostics. Of these three, the reports of Gnostic cosmological myth have the greatest chance of being distinctive, because myth is an orderly system with characters, plot, an elaborated structure, a functional narrative dynamics, and a philosophical point of view; because reports of a cosmological myth are, at least in the second century, liable to be based on written works of a philosophical character; and because a myth of origins often functions as part of the apparatus of group maintenance, in a way that abstract philosophical doctrines do not—whereas isolated doctrines are hard to interpret without their full context, and stories about sexual customs and liturgical practices are not likely to be based on very accurate or firsthand information. A priori, then, the summarized reports about Gnostic myth have a special likelihood of being

a touchstone by which other, undenominated textual material can be recognized as being Gnostic and thus added to the Gnostic data base.

15. Also present in the direct testimonia are some lists of titles of Gnostic literary works (§18), and also lists of other names by which the Gnostics were called (either by themselves or by their enemies).

16. The compensatory procedure consists of five steps, in which various textual features are assumed to be a distinctive sign that a work emanates from, or that a testimonium refers to, the Gnostic *hairesis* even though the proper name "Gnostic" does not appear. Using these features, the entire body of surviving ancient Christian literature is surveyed, and those items which show a distinctive feature are added to the corpus of Gnostic data. The uncertainty of this procedure relates to the difficulty of proving that the indicative textual features are *distinctive* indicators of Gnostic authorship.

The procedure is like the method of field archaeologists, who use purely formal archaeological means when they establish which artifacts belong to one and the same stratigraphic level, and only afterwards interpret and describe the culture that these artifacts represent. In the present case the aim is to establish, by formal philological means, which data can be linked with the direct testimonia explicitly naming the Gnostics, and only after these have all been collected, to draw conclusions about the Gnostic *hairesis*.

17. *Step 1.* The first step is collection and critical use of the direct testimonia, to which reference has already been made (§§13–15). These convey five kinds of information: doctrines; liturgical and sexual practices; a summary of Gnostic philosophical myth; lists of some Gnostic books by title; and other names by which the Gnostics also were known.

18. *Step 2.* Here two comparisons are made. First, summaries of Gnostic myth that were registered in step 1 are compared to all the vast corpus of surviving Christian literature (including the manuscript hoard from the Nag Hammadi region), to see if any correspondences can be found, and one such correspondence is easily identified. In his direct testimonium about the Gnostic *hairesis*, Irenaeus (*Adv. Haer.* 1.29) summarizes part of a work (unnamed) which, he says, belongs to the Gnostics; comparison shows that the unabridged version of this work survives elsewhere in no fewer than four manuscript witnesses: in the manuscripts it is entitled *Secret Book According to John*, and it contains an elaborate philosophical creation myth. Irenaeus notes (1.30–31) that several versions of Gnostic myth were circulating about 180 C.E.

Second, the direct testimonia refer to several Gnostic works by title only. A number of these occur in a testimonium by Porphyry in his life of the

Neoplatonist philosopher Plotinus. The circumstances that he describes are those of Plotinus's seminar in Rome, between 262 and 270: "In [Plotinus's] time there were among the Christians many others, members of a school of thought (αἱρετικοί), who were followers of Adelphius and Aquilinus and had started out from classical philosophy. They possessed many works by Alexander of Libya, Philocomus, Demostratus, and Lydus; and they brought out revelations of Zoroaster, of Zostrianus, of Nicotheus, of the Foreigner, of Messus, and of other such figures. They deceived many people, and themselves as well, in supposing that Plato had not drawn near to the depth of intelligible essence" (*Vita Plotini* 16). Three of the works whose titles are mentioned in this testimonium are preserved or excerpted in the Nag Hammadi hoard. They are the *Oracles of Truth of Zostrianos; The Foreigner;* and the *Book of Zoroaster.* Formally this identification is made only by title; however, the contents of all three have significant points of contact with the *Secret Book According to John,* tending to confirm their identification as Gnostic. Thus, in step 2, four surviving Gnostic works have been added to the meager direct testimonia: *The Secret Book According to John, Zostrianos, The Foreigner,* and the *Book of Zoroaster* (the latter known only in excerpted form).

19. *Step 3.* In step 3, attention shifts to the content of these four Gnostic works, and here a common, distinctive system of mythographic features is registered. Hans-Martin Schenke was the first to describe this distinct common system (which he variously called the Sethian Gnostic system or the Gnostic Sethian system). It expresses with more or less variation a distinct type of cosmography and philosophical creation myth, and it has its own general structure, imagery, and cast of characters. It can be considered Gnostic because of Irenaeus's statement that a myth which he summarizes, from the *Secret Book According to John,* belongs to the Gnostics (§18). The distinctive Gnostic mythographic system is now compared with all works of ancient Christian literature in search of correspondences of content, especially similarities of mythical structure (for the reasons stated in §14). This comparison yields an expanded corpus of works; the exact membership of this corpus is to some degree debatable, but the type of myth that it displays seems to stand distinct within ancient Christian literature. Provisionally, ten additional works are added to the corpus in this step: nine are known from the Nag Hammadi hoard and a tenth can be recognized in an Oxford manuscript, and they can be properly described as literary artifacts of the Gnostics. Adding these ten works to the four registered in step 2 of the procedure, a corpus of some fourteen works of Gnostic scripture is accumulated. The method elaborated by Schenke needs further evaluation and refinement, and at present its results (including the exact composition of the corpus) are merely provisional.

Provisionally the fourteen works are the following: *The Secret Book According to John (Apocryphon of John), The Book of Zoroaster* (excerpted in the longer version of the *Secret Book According to John*), *The Revelation of Adam* (*Apocalypse of Adam*), *The Reality of the Rulers* (*Hypostasis of the Archons*), *First Thought in Three Forms* (*Trimorphic Protennoia*), *Thunder: Perfect Mind* (*Thunder, Perfect Intellect*), *The Egyptian Gospel* (*Gospel of the Egyptians*), *Zostrianus*, *The Foreigner* (*Allogenes*), *The Three Tablets of Seth* (*Three Steles of Seth*), *Marsanes*, *Melchizedek*, *The Thought of Norea*, and the untitled text in the Bruce Codex.

The structure of the Gnostic type of myth also has striking parallels in Valentinian mythography, just as Irenaeus (*Adv. Haer.* 1.11.1) states that the Valentinian *hairesis* derived historically from the Gnostic *hairesis*. But many aspects of Valentinian mythography are also significantly different from Schenke's Gnostic type of myth, so that Valentinus and his followers can best be kept apart as a distinct mutation, or reformed offshoot, of the original Gnostics.

20. *Step 4.* Now this enlarged corpus of fourteen works is compared with all ancient testimonia or summaries of esoteric Christian mythmakers, no matter what sectarian name they bear in the sources. This time the goal is to look for two things: first, distinctive parallels to the Gnostic type of myth and cosmography; second, any references to the titles of the corpus of fourteen surviving Gnostic works that were not already registered in step 1. At this point, several more testimonia are added, including Irenaeus's summary of Satorninus of Antioch, Epiphanius's so-called Sethians, his Archontics, and the group called Audians by Theodore bar Konai. These can be called the *oblique testimonia*, since they are not transmitted under the name of the Gnostics, but nevertheless seem to refer to the Gnostics under other names.

21. *Step 5.* In the last step of the procedure, the "other names" registered in step 4 (§20) are assembled with the "other names" registered in step 1 (§17), and compared with all surviving information about early Christian sects called by these names, in order to collect additional testimonia, even if this information does not agree with the distinctive Gnostic type of myth, as represented in steps 3 and 4. The inclusion of information under names other than Gnōstikoi may mean that the result of the survey is a species containing several varieties. It may, of course, also mean that the survey contains some irrelevant data.

22. In the center of the Gnostic corpus is the *Secret Book According to John*, which Irenaeus's summary explicitly assigns to the Gnostics. Around the periphery are works, titles, testimonia, and names whose pertinence will remain a matter of greater uncertainty. Each step of the procedure leads to more comprehensiveness and less certainty.

23. If the proposed procedure is correct, then *only data identified by these five steps should be assumed to describe the Gnostics.* "Gnosticism" thus means an *inductive category based on these data alone* (cf. §§3–4). (Other data, and induc-

tive categories based on different data bases, would have to be called by some other name.)

24. The question is sometimes raised of why the self-designation "Gnostic" does not occur in the corpus of Gnostic writings (as opposed to the testimonia). The answer lies in the fact that the name Gnostic was the name par excellence of the members of the *hairesis*, their most proper name (§6). As such, its function was not to convey information about what they were like, but rather to express their distinctiveness as a group; not to say what they were, but who they were. The claim to supply (or have) *gnōsis* was absolutely banal, but the use of Gnōstikos *as a proper name* was distinctive (§10, end). Now, the works in the Gnostic mythographic corpus are pseudepigraphic and mythic in literary character, disguising their real author, audience, and place, date, and reason of composition. They do not speak of second- and third-century school controversies (as do the testimonia of Irenaeus, Porphyry, or Epiphanius), but rather of primordial, eschatological, and metaphysical events and relationships. In such compositions, there is no context in which a second-century school name such as Gnōstikos might naturally occur. Thus, the absence of the proper name "Gnōstikos" in the mythographic corpus is not a significant absence.

In Gnostic mythography the enlightened religious person *as a type* is described by other terms, which occur there as epithets (i.e., as "less proper" nouns than the term Gnostic, §6): "the offspring of Seth," "the immoveable race," etc.

On the basis of the Gnostic mythographic corpus, it is therefore impossible to comment on whether or not the common-noun meaning of Gnōstikos was vivid to members of the Gnostic *hairesis* (cf. §7[b]). Within some non-Gnostic circles, the polemics of Irenaeus and the other heresiologists (§7[c]), as well as Clement of Alexandria's ad hoc adoption of the term *gnōstikos* for his ideal spiritual type (§7[d]), must have heightened awareness that a claim to bestow knowledge (*gnōsis*) could be implied in the common-noun meaning of the name. Yet this says nothing about the Gnostics' own conscious evaluation of their name.

SOCIAL HISTORY

25. Because of its pseudepigraphic character (§24), the Gnostics' mythographic corpus cannot provide data for a social history of the Gnostics, that is, a thick description of the *hairesis* over time. The historian has to depend entirely on the meager direct (§13) and oblique (§20) testimonia, supplemented by any information known about the textual transmission of the mythographic corpus (region and language of transmission, scribal names, etc.). The testimonia include a great deal of information about Gnostics said to be known (at least by hostile observers) under other names. To some degree these names appear to be pejorative labels used by the enemies of the Gnostics (e.g., Borborites, "filthies"); others may be self-appellations

used by offshoots or subgroups within the Gnostic movement; still others may be the names of groups mistakenly included within the survey. In sum, the term "Gnostic" may turn out to name a species containing several varieties. Ancient names for the Gnostics may have included Archontics, Barbelites, Borborians, Borborites, Coddians, Levites, Naasenes, Ophians, Ophites, Phibionites, Satornilians, Secundians, Sethians, Socratites, Stratiotics, and Zacchaei (Valentinians are purposely omitted from this list, cf. §19, end). At least some of these names, especially Borborites, were polemical tags devised by enemies of the Gnostics.

26. A social history of the Gnostics has not yet been written. Provisionally, the information of the testimonia may be summarized as follows. This summary is not such a history, but it may serve to demonstrate the kind of data that are collected by application of the procedure. Three points should be noted. First, this data base is only provisional, subject to possible refinement and reapplication of the procedure that is described above. Second, the rich data on the Valentinian *hairesis*, which developed out of the Gnostics ca. 150 C.E., are not included here (testimonia on the later history of the Valentinians have been collected by Koschorke). Third, Gnostics under all their "other names" known from the direct and oblique testimonia (§25) are simply called "Gnostic" in the following summary. This simplification probably conceals important distinctions felt and observed at some level by the ancient persons themselves.

(a) The Pre-Constantinian Period, before 325 C.E.

Before 325, Gnostics are noted in Antioch, Alexandria (?), Rome, and probably Coptic-speaking Egypt. The first to be mentioned are Satorninus (Satornilus) of Antioch (sometime before 155), and the Gnostics who influenced Valentinus, either in Alexandria or Rome. The Valentinian reformation of the Gnostic *hairesis* occurs about 150, in Rome. The ascetic ethics of Gnostic piety is noticed by Irenaeus: vegetarianism, celibacy, and (presumably) sexual continence: "[Satorninus] says that marriage and the engendering of offspring are from Satan. And most of his followers abstain from (the flesh of) living things" (*Adv. Haer.* 1.24.2). The mythography, Christology, and soteriology of Gnostics (including the so-called "Satornilians") are attacked in a flood of anti-sectarian publications. The translation of Gnostic literature from Greek into the Egyptian language, Coptic, almost certainly occurs before Constantine's final victory.

(b) The Post-Constantinian Period, after 325 C.E.

The post-Constantinian evidence portrays a situation that has changed. Now Gnostics are noted not only in the Greek-speaking East but also in

Aramaic and Armenian linguistic areas. They are an element *lodged within* non-Gnostic Christianity, both parochial and monastic. As such, they suffer more and more violent forms of ecclesiastical persecution, which is now backed up by the power of imperial Christian Orthodoxy and the Zoroastrian court of Persia. Gnostics are noted in Egypt (335 C.E.), Palestine (350), Arabia (among the Ebionites, 340), various parts of Syria (later fourth century to 578), Cilicia (340), Galatia (350), Constantinople (422), Lesser or Byzantine Armenia (350), Osrhoëne (370 to 436), and Greater or Persian Armenia (360 to 578). In Egypt, Epiphanius finds them "hidden within the church." Peter the Archontic Gnostic is an ordained priest in the Orthodox church, and later he lives undetected as an ascetic in Judean desert monasticism. Fourth-century Gnostics use the canonical Old and New Testaments allegorically to justify or disguise their views. Theodore of Mopsuestia (400 C.E.) considers them difficult to distinguish from non-Gnostics; while Nestorius (422) is said to have found Gnostics freely attending Orthodox services in Constantinople and even to have detected crypto-Gnostics among the clergy of that city. The ascetic or monastic associations of Gnostics, already noted in the case of second-century "Satornilian" Gnostics, are attested from Epiphanius's sojourn in Egypt about 335 down to the flight of Persian Gnostic monks into Syria, about 570. The later phase of the ascetic Audian movement uses the Gnostic *Secret Book According to John* and *The Foreigner*, and teaches a creation myth based on these. Attacks on Gnostic myth and scripture continue strong in the antisectarian literature. A public debate is reported between a Gnostic and a non-Gnostic opponent in Cilicia, about 340. In fourth- to sixth-century Orthodox sources, innuendo is added to substance, and the Gnostics are mainly called Borborites or Borborians, from Greek *borboros*, "filth," "muck"—clearly a satire on the name of Barbēlō or Barbērō, the primary hypostatic aeon in Gnostic myth (the term also evokes *barbaros*, "barbarian"). Together with this innuendo goes a slanderous tradition alleging the existence of sexually promiscuous worship services, which has its origins in the pre-Constantinian period. However, the tenor of such stories is at odds with the asceticism of Gnostic piety and with the participation of Gnostics in Orthodox Christian worship. The only detailed report of Gnostic sexual rituals is given by Epiphanius; its veracity is indeed a matter of dispute. And, of course, sexual innuendo about Christian worship services of all denominations is centuries older than Epiphanius.

With the gradual establishment of an imperial Christian Orthodoxy the established religious party could more and more effectively take legal measures against the Gnostics. Gnostics are "detected" within Orthodox parishes and monasteries and are excommunicated, starting about 335 C.E.; a priest is defrocked as being a Gnostic in 340; scripture manuscripts are now in danger of destruction, as the burial of the Nag Hammadi hoard may suggest; Gnostics are forbidden by imperial law to build churches or conduct services; their baptism is nullified (Syria, late fifth century); and their legal testimony is declared universally invalid. The most violent persecutions occur in Byzantine Armenia, where with imperial backing Bishop Mesrop imprisons, tortures, physically mutilates, and exiles Gnostics (about 400). In Osrhoëne, about the same time, Bishop Rabbula also exiles them, while in northwestern Sassanid Persia at royal instigation they are persecuted and forced to flee abroad (565–578).

Thus, the activity of the Gnostics, in parts of the Roman, Byzantine, and Persian empires, is attested from the early second to the late sixth centuries C.E. Although their mythography is best known from apocrypha transmitted in the Coptic language (among those discovered near Nag Hammadi), the original language of the *hairesis* was clearly Greek, and its scope, international.

27. Accidentally, only a few Gnostic teachers are known by name: Saturninus of Antioch (before 155 C.E.); Adelphius, Alexander of Libya, Aquilinus, Demostratus, Lydus, Philocomus (all before 251); Eutactus of Satala, Peter the Archontic (both about 350); and possibly one Gnostic scribe, an Egyptian named Concessus Eugnostus (the copyist of Codex III from the Nag Hammadi hoard).

28. All ancient opponents of the Gnostics in both these periods, whether Christian or pagan, treat them as a species of Christian—a *hairesis* (αἵρεσις), "sect," "school of thought." However, the exact social relationship of Gnostics to non-Gnostic Christians is unclear. The surviving Gnostic mythography—all of which predates Constantine's victory—shows certain features that look in some sense to be exclusionary: a complex and distinctive myth of origins; a strong expression of group identity; a special jargon or in-group language; and talk about a Gnostic initiatory sacrament of baptism. Pre-Constantinian testimonia do not necessarily tell us whether the Gnostics had separate parishes, or, rather, like the Valentinians of that period, tried to exist undetected as a component of mixed congregations. Certainly the post-Constantinian sources depict them as an unwanted element within the established Orthodox church at large, though fourth-century Gnostic missionary efforts are also recorded. Thus, although the Gnostics may conveniently be called a "*hairesis*," no precise sociological limitation of that term is immediately obvious from the testimonia. Designations and self-designations of medical and philosophical schools would provide very pertinent comparative data for the further study of this question.

INTELLECTUAL HISTORY

29. An intellectual history approach to Gnosticism would have as its main data the evidence of the Gnostics' mythography rather than the testi-

monia, because the mythic data provide extensive firsthand, completely narrated structures, as opposed to very brief, secondhand, tendentious testimonia recorded without context (§14). The Gnostics' mythography consists of multiple versions of a cosmogonic myth of origins, which is reminiscent of Plato's *Timaeus*. Therefore this approach would situate the various versions of the myth within the history of Hellenistic and late antique Greek philosophy, including its orientalizing representatives such as Philo Judaeus, Plutarch, and Numenius. The most obvious comparanda are the interpretations and retellings of the *Timaeus* in the period from Xenocrates to Plotinus. The obviously Platonist context of the Gnostics' mythography on the plane of intellectual history, goes hand in hand with the Platonist context of the common noun *gnōstikos* and the proper name "Gnostic" (§§8–9) on the plane of lexicography. This helps us to understand, at least in terms of school politics, how the Platonic technical term *gnōstikos* might have seemed appropriate as a distinctive proper name when it was coined— strange as it may have sounded—by the founder of the Gnostic school of thought.

A substantial supplement, if used thoughtfully and critically, to the Gnostics' own mythography would be the works of Plotinus (especially *Enneads* 3.8; 5.8; 5.5; and 2.9 [nos. 30–33 in chronological order]) that were written in response to Gnostic myth. The detailed assimilation of this Plotinian evidence has hardly yet begun.

Furthermore, because all ancient observers, whether Christian or pagan, treat the Gnostics as a Christian *hairesis* (§28), the intellectual history approach would also situate the Gnostics' mythography within the development of Christian doctrines, Christian interpretations of the Bible (especially Genesis), and, more generally, the Christian uses of myth. On the functions of myth in ancient Christianity, see recently Wayne A. Meeks, *Inventing Christian Morality*, passim.

APPENDIX: HENRY MORE'S COINAGE
OF THE WORD "GNOSTICISM" (§3)

Henry More (1614–1687), the author of *An Exposition of the Seven Epistles* (1669), stood in a learned tradition that exegeted the New Testament book of Revelation, especially the seven letters to the churches of Asia (Rev 2:1–3:22), partly by reference to Epiphanius's lurid description of the Nicolaitans and Gnōstikoi, two groups that Epiphanius (*Panarion* 25–26) had equated. Among More's sources was Henry Hammond (1605–1660) (*A Paraphrase and Annotation upon All the Books of the New Testament* [2nd ed. 1659]), whose work shows acquaintance with ancient Christian heresiological literature and takes a broad view of "Gnosticks" as a generic name for "all the Heresies then abroad" in ancient Christianity, emphasizing the moral depravity of the "Gnostick-heresie" (p. 878). More, writing English Protestant polemic, interprets the seven letters allegorically as signifying seven periods of church history. In interpreting the church at Thyatira (Rev 2:18–29) he coins the term "Gnosticism" with roughly the same generic meaning as Hammond's "Gnostick-heresie":

> This Woman of Thyatira [Rev 2:20], (whether the wife of the Bishop of Thyatira, or some other Person of quality, for Interpreters of the letter vary in that) according to the Literal sense, is described from her acts, as onely guilty of pretending her self to be a Prophetesse, and that thereby she seduced the servants of Christ to commit fornication and to eat things sacrificed to Idols, which is a chief point of that which was called Gnosticisme. (*Exposition*, 99)

He repeats the new ism word (with a slightly different spelling) in a polemical tract against Roman Catholicism entitled *Antidote Against Idolatry*, which is printed with the *Exposition* as an appendix (unpaginated):

> [fo. O1 verso] 8. The truth is, most men are loath to be μάντεις κακῶν, to be messengers of [fo. O2 recto] ill news to the greatest, that is to say, to the corruptest, part of Christendome; but rather affect the glory and security of being accounted so humane, of so sweet and ingratiating a temper, as that they can surmize well of all mens Religions; and so think to conciliate to themselves the fame of either civil and good Natures, or of highly-raised and released Wits, (though it be indeed but a spice of the old abhorred Gnosticism,) that can comply with any Religion, and make a fair tolerable sense of all. 9. But these are such high strains of pretense to Wit or Knowledge and Gentility as I must confess I could never yet arrive to, nor I hope ever shall: though I am not in the mean time so stupid in my way, as to think I can write thus freely without offence. And yet on the contrary, I can deem my self no more uncivil then [*sic*] I do him that wrings his friend by the nose to fetch him out of a Swound. 10. I am not insensible how harsh this charge of Idolatry against the Church of Rome will sound in some ears, especially it being seconded with that other [fo. O2 verso] of Murther, and that the most cruel and barbarous imaginable, and finally so severely rewarded with an impossibility of Salvation to any now, so long as they continue in Communion with that Church.

On More's life and works, see *Encyclopedia Brittanica*, 11th ed. (1911), s.n.

ANNOTATED BIBLIOGRAPHY

Ammann, Adolf. -IKOΣ *bei Platon: Ableitung und Bedeutung mit Materialsammlung*. Freiburg: Paulusdruckerei, 1953. Reliable account of derivation and meaning of Greek adjectives in -*(t)ikos*.

Chantraine, Pierre. *La formation des noms en grec ancien*. Société de linguistique de Paris, Collection linguistique 38. Paris: Honoré Champion, 1933. Pp. 384–96 ("Dérivés thématiques en -κος"). Best history of Greek adjectives in -*(t)ikos*.

———. *Etudes sur le vocabulaire grec*. Paris: Klincksieck, 1956. Pp. 97–171 ("Le suffixe grec -ικος").

Gero, Stephen. "With Walter Bauer on the Tigris: Encratite Orthodoxy and Libertine Heresy in Syro-Mesopotamian Christianity." In *Gnosticism and Early Christianity*, edited by Charles Hedrick and Robert Hodgson, 287–307. Peabody, Mass.: Hendrickson, 1986. Oblique testimonia concerning "Borborite" Gnostics; many of the data summarized above in §26 were collected by Gero.

Koschorke, Klaus. "Patristische Materialien zur Spätgeschichte der valentinianischen Gnosis." In *Gnosis and Gnosticism: Papers Read at the Eighth International Conference on Patristic Studies (Oxford, September 3rd– 8th, 1979)*, edited by Martin Krause, 120–39. Nag Hammadi Studies 17. Leiden: Brill, 1981.

Layton, Bentley. *The Gnostic Scriptures: A New Translation with Annotations and Introductions.* Garden City, N.Y.: Doubleday, 1987. Part I "Classic Gnostic Scripture" (pp. 3–214). Annotated translations of some, but not all, of the Gnostic mythographic works; and some, but not all, of the direct and oblique testimonia to the Gnostics.

Meeks, Wayne A. *The Origins of Christian Morality: The First Two Centuries.* New Haven: Yale University Press, 1993. Ancient Christian uses of myth.

More, Henry. *An Exposition of The Seven Epistles To The Seven Churches; Together with A Brief Discourse of Idolatry; with Application to the Church of Rome.* London: James Flesher, 1669. Copy in the McAlpin Collection of Union Theological Seminary, New York, New York. First appearance of the term "Gnosticism."

Schenke, Hans-Martin. "Das sethianische System nach Nag-Hammadi-Handschriften." In *Studia Coptica*, edited by Peter Nagel, 165–73. Berliner byzantinistische Arbeiten 45. Berlin: Akademie-Verlag, 1974. Pioneering attempt to describe a set of distinctive features defining a corpus of Gnostic mythography, which Schenke calls "the Sethian system"; cf. step 3 of the procedure described above.

———. "The Phenomenon and Significance of Gnostic Sethianism." In *The Rediscovery of Gnosticism: Proceedings of the International Conference on Gnosticism at Yale, New Haven, Connecticut, March 28–31, 1978*, edited by Bentley Layton, Vol. 2, *Sethian Gnosticism*, 588–616 (and discussion, pp. 634–40, 683–85). Studies in the History of Religions 41, vol. 2. Leiden: Brill, 1981. Further elaboration of his "Das sethianische System."

Smith, Morton. "The History of the Term Gnostikos." In *The Rediscovery of Gnosticism: Proceedings of the International Conference on Gnosticism at Yale, New Haven, Connecticut, March 28–31, 1978*, edited by Bentley Layton, Vol. 2, *Sethian Gnosticism*, 796–807. Studies in the History of Religions 41, vol. 2. Leiden: Brill, 1981. Fundamental history of the common noun *gnōstikos*.

Von Staden, Heinrich. "Hairesis and Heresy: The Case of the *haireseis iatrikai*." In *Jewish and Christian Self-Definition*, edited by Ben F. Meyer and E. P. Sanders, Vol. 3, *Self-Definition in the Greco-Roman World*, 76–100. Philadelphia: Fortress, 1982. Extremely pertinent information on various uses of the term *hairesis* in medical school polemics.

Part Four

The Shaping of
Early Christian Culture

CHAPTER 20

Contesting Abraham:
The Ascetic Reader and
the Politics of Intertextuality

Elizabeth A. Clark

The interpretation of a divine command is necessarily a political act.[1]

CHRISTIANS AT THE CLOSING years of the fourth century and the opening years of the fifth witnessed an unprecedented crisis in sexual/textual politics,[2] near the center of which stood the interpretation of the patriarchal narratives in Genesis. Here, debates over marriage and asceticism forced public scrutiny of the patriarchs' sexual mores at a moment of hermeneutical danger prompted by the Manichaean rejection of Hebrew scripture. How could Christians uphold the authority of the Bible when the behavior of Abraham, Isaac, and Jacob so plainly disqualified them from the ranks of the "eunuchs for the kingdom of heaven" (Matt 19:12)? Although Søren Kierkegaard imagined Abraham as a "knight of the faith,"[3] the assessment of many writers a millennium and a half earlier was far less kind.

Various solutions to the dilemma, I posit, were ventured through "preemptive" interpretations of texts,[4] bolstered by ingenious hermeneutical strategies. Most productive of these was an intertextual style of exegesis that read the passage at hand in light of other texts that served to "decode" it. Daniel Boyarin, in *Intertextuality and the Reading of Midrash*, has explained the function of intertextual exegesis in these words:

1. Stanley Rosen, *Hermeneutics as Politics* (New York and Oxford: Oxford University Press, 1987) 88.

2. The phrase is borrowed from Toril Moi, *Sexual-Textual Politics* (New York: Routledge, Chapman & Hall, 1985).

3. Søren Kierkegaard, *Fear and Trembling* (trans. Walter Lowrie; Garden City, N.Y.: Doubleday, 1955) 51–52.

4. The phrase is borrowed from Lee Patterson's discussion of Augustine in *Negotiating the Past: The Historical Understanding of Medieval Literature* (Madison: University of Wisconsin Press, 1987) 151; see also Harold Bloom, *A Map of Misreading* (New York: Oxford University Press, 1975) 68, on the "pre-emptive force" of imagination.

Intertextuality is, in a sense, the way that history, understood as cultural and ideological change and conflict, records itself within textuality. As the text is the transformation of a signifying system and of a signifying practice, it embodies the more or less untransformed detritus of the previous system. These fragments of the previous system and the fissures they create on the surface of the text reveal conflictual dynamics which led to the present textual system.[5]

Through such intertextual exegesis, scripture could be affirmed as "self-interpreting," as if the preferences of the interpreter had played no role in the production of meaning, as if no "fissures" existed between the texts, and as if no political consequences attended the choice of intertexts. *Which dominant texts controlled the interpretation of others was, in fact, fiercely contested:* the ascetic or nonascetic leanings of late ancient Christian commentators are here revealingly displayed. The religious needs of the present—as understood by Jovinian, Jerome, the anonymous author of *De castitate*, or Augustine—could thus take precedence over a "historical" reading of Genesis, "saving" ancient scriptures while commanding their interpretation. Exegesis, it emerged, could palliate the embarrassing ethical quandaries posed by the Manichaeans or by Christians who held too ascetic or nonascetic a stance.

The Manichaean position will here be represented in arguments advanced by Augustine's North African opponent, Faustus.[6] Although in the *Confessions* Augustine registers his disappointed discovery of Faustus's sparse liberal education (5.3.3; 5.6.10–11; 5.7.13 [CCL 27:58, 61–62, 63–64]),[7] and in the *Contra Faustum* scathingly comments on his inept treatment of scripture (32.16; 33.7 [CSEL 25:775, 793]), he alternatively alludes to Faustus's eloquence and cleverness: Faustus is, he admits, not stupid.[8] It is Augustine's latter judgment, I submit, that should be sustained. Indeed, Faustus's deep knowledge of scripture and adept argumentation provided Augustine with the sharpest opponent he would encounter prior to his debilitating last struggle with Julian of Eclanum. Although Augustine faults

5. Daniel Boyarin, *Intertextuality and the Reading of Midrash* (Bloomington and Indianapolis: Indiana University Press, 1990) 94.

6. According to Augustine in the *Contra Faustum*, Faustus was from Milevum (1.1) and from a poor family (5.5) (CSEL 25:251, 278). For discussions of Manichaeanism in North Africa, see François Decret, *Aspects du Manichéisme dans l'Afrique Romaine: Les controverses de Fortunatus, Faustus et Felix avec saint Augustine* (Paris: Etudes Augustiniennes, 1970); and idem, *L'Afrique Manichéenne (IVe–Ve siècles): Etude historique et doctrinale*, Tome I: *Texte* (Paris: Etudes Augustiniennes, 1978). For an overview of Augustine's relation with Manichaeanism, see Samuel N. C. Lieu, *Manichaeism in the Later Roman Empire and Medieval China* (Manchester: Manchester University Press, 1985) esp. chapter 5.

7. On the unavailability of many literary texts in late antiquity, now see William V. Harris, *Ancient Literacy* (Cambridge, Mass., and London: Harvard University Press, 1989) esp. 297–98.

8. *Contra Faustum* 1.1; cf. 16.26 (CSEL 25:251, 470–71); *Confessions* 5.6.10–11; 5.7.13 (CCL 27:61–62, 63–64).

his opponent's "maliciousness" throughout the *Contra Faustum*,[9] his argument rests centrally on the claim that Faustus is a poor reader who cannot follow the logic of a narrative (*Contr. Faust.* 22.32 [CSEL 25:625–27]), who cites scripture inaccurately (6.9 [CSEL 25:301] on Deut 22:11), who skips over passages necessary to ascertain the context of a story,[10] who inevitably chooses the most flat-footedly literalistic interpretation of a passage (15.6 [CSEL 25:426–27]), and who, contrary to fair exegetical practice, cites only texts that suit his argument, ignoring those that stand against his interpretation.[11] Faustus's deficiencies as a reader, for Augustine, are thus as much at fault as his motivations. In contrast to Augustine's assessment, I think that Faustus read well *for his purposes:* he had no interest, as did Augustine, in "saving the text."

Thus, Faustus consistently and radically detaches Old Testament precepts and stories from New Testament injunctions (6.1 [CSEL 25:284–85])—and the latter are always read from a stringently ascetic point of view. According to Faustus, the promises to the patriarchs regarding the children they would beget and the riches they would accrue are "useless for the soul's salvation" (10.1 [CSEL 25:310]). Trusting in the Old Testament implies a denial that the New Testament promises are sufficient: hence, Catholics, like an adulterous wife, rush to "serve two husbands" (15.1 [CSEL 25:415–17]). The Old Testament curse on those who fail to "raise up seed for Israel" (Deut 25:5–10) is contradicted by the chastity that Jesus recommended in the Gospels and hence must be rejected (14.1 [CSEL 25:403]). The New Testament rather enjoins us to leave wife, children, home, and riches: Faustus confesses that as a true follower of Christ, he has done just that (5.1 [CSEL 25:271]).

Prominent in the litany of passages from the Old Testament that Christians should find offensive, in Faustus's view, are the patriarchal narratives. Here, Abraham's "defiling himself with a concubine" and being spurred by "an irrational craving for children" are ammunition for his arsenal (22.5 [CSEL 25:594]). Moreover, Abraham cannot even be praised for his trust in God (as Christians often claimed): his taking a concubine proves that he disbelieved God's promise to Sarah (22.30 [CSEL 25:624]), his lack of faith thus exacerbating his sexual sin. In addition, Abraham's selling of Sarah to both Abimelech and Pharaoh indicates that he was motivated by greed and

---

9. E.g., *Contra Faustum* 22.23 (CSEL 25:618). Augustine holds that all biblical interpretation must be motivated by the double goal of love for God and neighbor: *De doctrina Christiana* 3.10.14; 3.15.23 (CSEL 32:86, 91).

10. *Contra Faustum* 23.6 (CSEL 25:711–12): Faustus hasn't investigated the context of Sarah's and Abraham's relationship and thus makes slanderous accusations about Abraham's calling Sarah his "sister."

11. E.g., *Contra Faustum* 11.2; 24.2; 32.16; 32.19 (CSEL 25:315, 724, 776, 780). Augustine notes that Faustus even misses passages that could assist his case: *Contra Faustum* 22.73 (CSEL 25:671) (Faustus neglects to rail at Abraham for his would-be sacrifice of Isaac).

avarice (22.33 [CSEL 25:627]). Nor does Sarah's virtue pass Faustus's scrutiny: she too stands guilty for conniving with Abraham in his sexual defilement with Hagar (22.31 [CSEL 25:625]). Thus, Faustus declines the invitation of Matt 8:11 to sit at table with the patriarchs in the kingdom of heaven. On the basis of their behavior, they should rather have been sent to the "dungeons below" (33.1 [CSEL 25:784]: *poenali inferorum custodia*). Moreover, Faustus's argument not only broaches moral issues but also questions the authority of such texts: Did your writers forge these stories, he asks his Christian opponents? (22.5 [CSEL 25:595]). It is not Manichaean critics who have blasphemed the prophets and the patriarchs, for the biblical authors have done well enough at that without assistance! (22.3 [CSEL 25:593]). No ingenious reading of Genesis can "save" Abraham, in Faustus's view.

Yet, when different reading strategies intersect with a less "pre-emptive" ascetic agenda—as was the case with Jovinian—Abraham emerged in a better light. Given Jovinian's anti-Manichaean program[12] and his pro-marital stance, we should not be surprised to discover that his exegetical technique is to read the ascetic passages of the New Testament in light of the Old Testament and the Pastoral Epistles; the latter control the interpretation of the former (e.g., *Adversus Jovinianum* 1.5 [PL 23:227]).

According to Jerome's lengthy rebuttal, Jovinian apparently began his defense of marriage with an appeal to the story of God's creation of man and woman; characteristically, Jovinian reminds his readers that this blessing on marriage was repeated by Jesus in Matt 19:5 (1.5 [PL 23:225]). Dominical authority is here enlisted on the side of marriage, not virginity. Thus empowered, Jovinian searches both the New Testament and the Old for examples of characters who married but were blessed by God, and he implies throughout that their blessedness was linked to their marital status (1.5 [PL 23:225–27]). As for Abraham, Genesis reports that he had three wives (not quite up to Jacob's four, Jovinian notes) and that through his faith, he "received the blessing in begetting his son which he merited by his faith." Likewise Sarah, even in old age, "exchanged the curse of sterility for the blessing of childbearing" (1.5 [PL 23:226]). Parallel New Testament examples should lead readers to understand that the blessing on marriage did not cease with the Christian era. Jovinian thus cleverly defuses two arguments that will be used by Jerome and other champions of asceticism: that childbearing was appropriate only for the beginning of the world when population growth was desired (1.36 [PL 23:271]);[13] and that Paul praised virginity in 1 Corinthians 7 not only because of "the present distress," as Jovinian held, but for its "ontological" status as superior to marriage (1.5 [PL

---

12. On the anti-Manichaean orientation of Jovinian, see David Hunter, "Resistance to the Virginal Ideal in Late Fourth-Century Rome: The Case of Jovinian," *Theological Studies* 48 (1987) 45–64.

13. Cf. *Adversus Helvidium* 21 (PL 23:215).

23:228]). Anyone who forbids or even discourages marriage, in Jovinian's view, sides with the Manichaeans (1.5 [*PL* 23:227]).

Despite Jerome's ardent defense of asceticism and his passionate attempt to refute Jovinian's arguments, he nonetheless shies away from resting his case on the sinful behavior of the patriarchs.[14] Instead, his technique is to press the argument that there is a "difference of times" between the Old Testament and the New: 2 Corinthians 5:17 reminds Christians that "the old has passed away" (1.37 [*PL* 23:273]), and the Song of Songs teaches that the "winter" of the Old Law is past (1.30 [*PL* 23:263]). Our Hebrew ancestors fulfilled God's command under the Law, but Christians are called to fulfill God's (different) command under the Gospel (1.24 [*PL* 23:255]).

Abraham's three wives, however, were too much for Jerome to countenance. If Christians wish to follow Abraham in his marital habits, they had better also follow him in circumcision, he writes in disgust (1.19 [*PL* 23:248]). Like Faustus,[15] Jerome baits his readers: Don't half follow Abraham and half reject him! (1.19 [*PL* 23:248]). Although Abraham served God through marriage, we "upon whom the end of the ages has come" (1 Cor 10:11) should serve him in virginity (2.4 [*PL* 23:301]).[16]

Jerome's gingerly treatment of the Abraham saga reminds us that with good reason he feared Jovinian's charge against him of "Manichaeanism."[17] He had encountered that charge before, and had successfully avoided its possible consequences by (like Abraham) decamping for Palestine.[18] Yet Jerome, not adept at complex theological speculation, apparently did not ponder (at least in writing) what it might mean to urge Christians to abandon the laws of the Old Testament as remnants of "times past." This was a problem that Augustine, with his more acute theological sense, would attempt to circumvent by conciliatory exegetical strategies.

A more strenuous approach to the patriarchal narratives—fed by the debate between Jerome and Jovinian[19]—emerges in the presumably Pelagian

14. Jerome even praises Abraham in *Epp.* 66.11 (CSEL 54:661–62); 125.20 (CSEL 56:142); 108.31 (CSEL 55:349); cf. 39.4 (CSEL 54:301), and uses him and Sarah as exemplars of asceticism in *Adversus Helvidium* 20 (*PL* 23:214).

15. *Contra Faustum* 1.2–3 (CSEL 25:251–52).

16. An earlier stage in the passage from eschatology to asceticism is succinctly noted by Wayne Meeks in *The Moral World of the First Christians* (Philadelphia: Westminster, 1986) 107–8.

17. *Adversus Jovinianum* 1.3; 1.5 (*PL* 23:223, 227); cf. *Ep.* 49.2 (CSEL 54:352).

18. After the death of Paula's daughter Blesilla, apparently from an excess of asceticism (*Epp.* 38–39), and for his encouragement to her daughter Eustochium to adopt a life of perpetual virginity (*Ep.* 22); cf. Jerome's response in *Ep.* 45.

19. Borrowings in the *De castitate* from the Jerome–Jovinian debate include (e.g.) the use of the same biblical texts on "purity" in *Adversus Jovinianum* 1.7; 20, cf. *De castitate* 5.2–3; *Adversus Jovinianum* 1.19, cf. *De castitate* 15.1–4 (on Abraham's wives). The text of *De castitate* was first published by C. P. Caspari, who included it with five other presumably Pelagian texts: *Briefe, Abhandlungen und Predigten aus den zwei letzten Jahrhunderten des kirchlichen Altertbums und dem Anfang des Mittelalters* (Christiana, 1890; repr. Brussels: Culture et Civilisation, 1964).

tract, *De castitate*, whose anonymous author ventures a harder judgment on the patriarchal narratives than did his inspiration, Jerome. The author's approach to the Hebrew scriptures is entirely governed by his own passionate devotion to asceticism as the only worthy form of Christian living: for him, there can be no chastity within marriage until all sexual activity (consistently described as "disease" and "pollution" [2.3.1 (*PLS* 1:1465, 1466)]) is renounced.[20] Given the author's stand, the Genesis stories must be critiqued in light of 1 Corinthians 7, read in its most rigorous sense. Thus, the author claims that it is "wanton" Christians (i.e., Christians troubled by the Jerome-Jovinian debate) who have raised the issue of how the patriarchs "pleased God" when they had not only many wives, but also many concubines? And how, they had pondered, should Christian virgins pray to be taken to the bosom of Abraham if he rests in the company of his concubine?[21]

The author's response precludes Christians from using the patriarchs and other Old Testament figures as moral examples: if we model our lives on the Hebrews of yore, Paul's teaching becomes *otiosa*, *superflua*, and *vana* (11.2 [*PLS* 1:1490]). Thus a sharp breach is registered between the behavior allowable under the Old Law and that acceptable under "grace" (12.2 [*PLS* 1:1490]). Practically no Old Testament injunctions apply to us, the author avers (12.3 [*PLS* 1:1490]): for our rule of life, we should look to the New Testament alone (12.4 [*PLS* 1:1491]).

Focusing on Abraham, the author's opponents—now adopting Jovinian's line—protest that although Abraham had a wife, he was said to be pleasing to God; indeed, he merited the privilege of being the first of the patriarchs (15.1 [*PLS* 1:1496]). The author's reply is crisp: it was hardly because Abraham had a *wife* that he pleased God. Rather, it was his obedience that was pleasing. Since he proved that he scorned the fruit of marriage (i.e., his son) by his readiness to sacrifice him, how much more would he have despised marriage itself! (15.3 [*PLS* 1:1497–98]). How eagerly he would have heeded Paul's words on celibacy, if they had been spoken to him! (15.3 [*PLS* 1:1497–98]).[22]

The author of *De castitate* then switches the focus of his argument from sexual ethics to exegetical practices. There is much in scripture, he claims, that should be read as a "figure." In the Old Testament, marriage (for example) often is a "figure"—and "figures" are meant to pass away when the reality comes. Thus, Gen 2:24 (that a man leaves his parents, cleaves to his wife, and they become one flesh) is merely a "figure" for the relation of Christ to the church, as Paul indicated in Eph 5:31–32. Likewise, and again on Paul's

---

20. *De castitate* 2.9.1; 10.3; 10.4; 10.15; 13.9 (*PLS* 1:1465–66, 1478, 1480, 1489, 1490). Such passages as Lev 7:19–20; Exod 19:10–15; and 1 Sam 21:4 (on "purity") are appealed to in *De castitate* 3.3; 10.4; 5.2; 5.3 (*PLS* 1:1466–67, 1480–81, 1472–73).

21. *De castitate* 11.1 (*PLS* 1:1489). The "bosom of Abraham" also posed a problem for John Chrysostom's audience, according to his *De virginitate* 82 (SC 125:382–86).

22. Cf. Augustine, *De bono coniugali* 23.31 (CSEL 41:226).

authority, Abraham's wife and concubine should be taken as "figures" pointing to the reality, the contrast between "Mount Sinai" and "Jerusalem above" of Gal 4:25-26. But for present-day Christians, marriage does not figuratively foreshadow *any* truth to come—so what could be its function? (15.2 [*PLS* 1:1496-97]). Note that the author does not here claim (as we might) that Ephesians 5 and Galatians 4 provide allegorical interpretations of Old Testament "realities." Rather, the "real" is located, through typology, entirely on the side of the New Testament. Yet Abraham, in the end, is better disposed of than "interpreted": borrowing Jerome's argument, the author of *De castitate* sneeringly concludes that if Christians wish to imitate Abraham by marrying, they should also undergo circumcision and offer animal sacrifice (15.4 [*PLS* 1:1498]). The patriarchs cannot look to this author for their defense.

In a period of about six years,[23] Augustine produced a body of works in which the issues we here address began to coalesce: anti-Manichaean polemics, most notably the *Contra Faustum* in 397-398; treatises on the theory and practice of biblical interpretation whose anti-Manichaean roots lie partially concealed (*De doctrina Christiana* and *De consensu Evangelistarum*); and others on asceticism and marriage (*De opere monachorum; De bono coniugali; De sancta virginitate*). In all these works, Augustine faced hard questions about biblical interpretation. On the one hand, the Bible must be defended against charges of contradiction, inconsistency, and moral unworthiness. On the other, the Christian preference for asceticism must be upheld while an honorable place for chaste nonascetics must be established: the standpoints of *both* Jerome and Jovinian need modification. Whereas Faustus (good postmodernist critic) looked for the disjunctions, gaps, and discrepancies in the text, Augustine's "idealist" project was rather one of harmonization: if readers could but see with the eye of eternity, the seeming discrepancies would evaporate, subsumed in the good news of God's salvific plan.

To accomplish this task, Augustine deployed a variety of reading strategies against his actual and implied opponents that he hoped would win them to his project of scriptural harmonization. Augustine assumes that scriptural texts are self-glossing,[24] and his comments on the Abraham narratives provide an instructive example of these reading practices.

The simplest argument that Augustine mounts against his Manichaean critics is that they should better attend to the "chronology" of the Abraham narratives. Thus, he responds to Faustus's charge that Abraham lacked faith in God's promise to Sarah that she would bear a son (*Contr. Faust.* 22.32 [CSEL 25:625-26]) by arguing that Faustus has not read the text carefully,

23. See the dating of the works that follow in Peter Brown, *Augustine: A Biography* (Berkeley and Los Angeles: University of California Press, 1969) 85, table C.

24. See comments by Gerald Bruns, "Midrash and Allegory: The Beginnings of Scriptural Interpretation," in *The Literary Guide to the Bible* (ed. Robert Alter and Frank Kermode; Cambridge, Mass.: Harvard University Press, 1987) 626, 643-44.

following the narrative line in the proper order. It is at the beginning of the Abraham narrative (Gen 12:2; 13:16), Augustine notes, that God promises Abraham many descendants but does not here reveal how this was to happen; in chapter 15, Abraham still assumes that his servant will be his heir. Only now does God inform Abraham that he will beget his *own* son, but even here, God does not specify by what woman this birth will occur. Thus, in chapter 16 with the appearance of Hagar, Abraham remains ignorant as to the identity of his future child's mother. Neither he nor Sarah should be faulted for imagining that Hagar would be the instrument through which the "many descendants" were to spring. Faustus should further note that only in chapter 18 does God promise Sarah that *she* will bear the child whose descendants will flourish like the stars in the heavens (22:32 [CSEL 25:626]).[25] A closer reading of the text, Augustine implies, would have stayed Faustus from raising such damaging allegations against the holy patriarch.

Moreover, if Faustus had practiced some elementary skills of what we would today call the historical-critical method, he might have avoided other interpretive errors: he should have investigated the historical and cultural practices of the Abrahamic era to discover the context in which the narrative is set. For example, Faustus accuses Abraham of dissimulation for calling Sarah his "sister," when he might better have studied the linguistic and marital conventions of that age. Had he done so, he would have discovered that close kin marriages, including those of first cousins, were not prohibited and that numerous examples stand in scripture of the interchangeability of kinship names: thus, Tobias refers to his bride as his "sister" (Tobit 8:9), and Lot is depicted other than as Abraham's nephew (Gen 13:8; 11:31). Faustus should not have leapt to such hasty and damaging conclusions about Abraham's relationship with Sarah or the title by which he addressed her (22.35 [CSEL 25:628–29]).[26]

A third exegetical strategy used by Augustine for rescuing the text involved the finding of an accepted (by Augustine) moral principle that would justify the patriarch's behavior. Augustine's rejection of sexual desire as a justification for marital intercourse prompted his attempt to exonerate Abraham's behavior by claiming that neither Abraham nor the other patriarchs acted out of lust, but sheerly from the understandable concern that the human race continue (22.30 [CSEL 25:624]).[27] By the same principle, Sarah's virtue remains intact as well: since no wife who loves her husband

25. Cf. 23.6 (CSEL 25:711).

26. Cf. 23.6 (CSEL 25:711–12). Another example of Augustine's appeal to "moral" explanation pertains to Abraham's laudable reluctance to "tempt God" through imagining that he could both save his own life and Sarah's chastity: *Contra Faustum* 22.36 (CSEL 25:629–31).

27. The same point is made in *De doctrina Christiana* 3.12.20 (CCL 32:90) and *De bono coniugali* 15.17–16.18 (CSEL 41:209–12). According to Augustine, the patriarchs would gladly have renounced procreation if only the New Testament call to celibacy had been available to them (*De bono coniugali* 13.15 [CSEL 41:207–8]).

would encourage him in an extramarital affair if he were motivated solely by "animal passion," Sarah too should be seen as acting from the pious motive of wanting the Israelite race to be increased (22.31 [CSEL 25:625]). Female psychology thus conspires with ascetic morality to justify the patriarchal couple's actions.

Our expectation that such a preemptively "moral" reading of scripture would intersect with the argument from the "difference in times" is, however, not borne out in Augustine's writings of this period. The argument that the difference in ethical norms was linked to the division between Hebrew and Christian scripture was not one that Augustine cared to exploit. Although Augustine conceded that polygamy was acceptable then, but not now,[28] he warned Christian celibates not to claim that they were "better" than Abraham and Sarah.[29] Likewise, although following Paul, he admitted that in Abraham's day, the promise was "under a veil" (*Contr. Faust.* 22.23 [CSEL 25:618]), he nonetheless did not press the argument from the "difference" of the Testaments very far. His reluctance to do so is most likely occasioned by his fear of playing into the hands of the Manichaeans. Indeed, in an earlier anti-Manichaean treatise, Augustine had (rather astonishingly) declared that the New Testament does not contain any precepts that are not already contained in the Old (*Contra Adamantium* 3 [CSEL 25:121]), so keen was he to harmonize the books. Augustine prefers not to explain "difference" in the opposition of the Old Law to the New, but to explain it away through reading strategies. Thus, the conflict with Manichaean exegesis is one important source of Augustine's ardently expressed view that scripture must be taken as a whole, both Testaments together, and that all parts must be seen as "true."[30] Yet, as I shall later conclude, Augustine's emphasis on the unity of the Testaments had more than exegetical consequences for the Manichaeans, as well as for the Donatists and Pelagians later.

Since these were the principles that guided Augustine's approach, no part of scripture could be discarded. If there were seeming differences between texts, these must be resolved by interpretation, not by the elimination of disturbing passages. His reading strategy thus required taming and

28. *De doctrina Christiana* 3.12.20 (CCL 32:90); cf. *De bono coniugali* 15.17–16.18 (CSEL 41:209–11). Certainly no Christian should cite Abraham's example to excuse his own sexual relations with servant girls: *Contra Faustum* 22.25 (CSEL 25:620).

29. *De bono coniugali* 22.27 (CSEL 41:222); cf. 23.28 (CSEL 41:223–24).

30. Also important in the development of Augustine's view that every verse of scripture must be true or the authority of the Bible as a whole falls was his argument with Jerome (from 394 or 395 on) concerning whether Paul had staged a mock controversy with Peter in Galatians 2. For an overview of the controversy with Jerome over Galatians 2, see J. N. D. Kelly, *Jerome: His Life, Writings, and Controversies* (New York: Harper & Row, 1975) 148, 218–20, 269–79. Also see Jerome, *Commentarius ad Galatas* I (at 2:11–14) (*PL* 26:363–67); Augustine, *Epp.* 28 and 75; Jerome, *Ep.* 112. It emerged that fear of giving assistance to Manichaeans' denigration of scripture lay at the heart of Augustine's concern.

containment. Two modes of interpretation that he uses to accomplish his hermeneutical task are interrelated: the appeal to figurative modes of interpretation (typology and allegory), and the adoption of intertextual exegetical practices that glossed passages contained in one book with those from another. The difficulty was, of course, to know *which* was the dominant passage that would serve as the interpretive key to decode the others. The resolution of this problem could make a difference in praxis, Augustine unhappily learned, when in 399 or 400 he encountered monks who interpreted the indolent habits of the lilies of the field and the birds of the air (Matt 6:26) literally and Paul's injunction that we must work if we wish to eat (2 Thess 3:10) spiritually to justify their refusal to engage in manual labor (*De opere monachorum* 1.1.2–2.3 [CSEL 41:532–35]).[31] Augustine complained that the Manichaeans, for their part, consistently interpreted figurative passages literally (*Contr. Faust.* 15.6 [CSEL 25:426–27]),[32] with the result that the Old Testament was split from the New, and Gospel from Gospel. The Manichaeans also refused to accept the thesis that the commandments of the "ritual law" could have been meant literally then, but symbolically now.[33] According to Augustine, such details of scripture are edifying, if only they are properly "read."

As for allegorical interpretation, Augustine champions the practice because, he claims, "allegorical narratives" are already in the Bible, although the heretics (i.e., the Manichaeans) err in reading them literally (*Contr. Faust.* 22.95 [CSEL 25:701]).[34] Here Augustine's meaning is ambiguous. He may mean that Paul had already deployed allegorical exegesis, thus entitling Christians of Augustine's time to engage in this method. But Augustine may also imply that allegory lies "in" the text itself rather than existing as the product of his own fertile imagination and rhetorical skill. On the first assumption, we may note that Augustine borrowed from Paul allegories pertaining to the story of Abraham: Abraham's "seed" can mean Christ or, by

31. Paul is no "allegorical" tentmaker, Augustine complains! (19.22 [CSEL 41:567]).

32. A counterexample in which Faustus takes "spiritually" a passage that Augustine believes should be interpreted literally is found in *Contra Faustum* 32.7 (Jesus' crucifixion). Faustus probably spurred Augustine to write the *De consensu Evangelistarum*, judging from *Contra Faustum* 32.2 (CSEL 25:761). Nearly two centuries before Augustine, Origen had well understood the usefulness of allegory in "rescuing" offensive passages of Hebrew scripture. Commenting on a gory passage in the book of Numbers, he writes: "Here even the most contentious defender of 'history' will rush for refuge to the sweetness of allegory" (*Homilia in Numeros* 16.9 [GCS 30:151]). Origen more openly admitted the necessity for such "rescue" operations than did Augustine.

33. *Contra Faustum* 6.2; 6.7; 6.9; 10.2; 22.6 (CSEL 25:285–86, 294–95, 299–301, 311, 596).

34. For the classic study of pagan and Christian allegory, see Jacques Pépin, *Mythe et allégorie: les origines grecques et les contestations judéo-chrétiennes* (2nd ed.; Paris: Etudes Augustiniennes, 1976). For the development of Augustine's "spiritual" exegesis over against the Manichees, see Julien Ries, "La Bible chez saint Augustin et chez les manichéens," *Revue des Etudes Augustiniennes* 7 (1961) 231–43; 9 (1963) 201–15; 10 (1964) 309–29.

extension, ourselves, as descendants of the spiritual Abraham.[35] Likewise, the figures of Sarah and Hagar denote the two covenants (22.51 [CSEL 25:645]).[36]

If, however, Augustine also implies that allegories are already "in" the text rather than an exegetical creation, readers now will remain unpersuaded. Augustine's hand is all too evident in the production of meaning, and his attempt to make his own reading practice seem the "natural" one gives the signal that ideology is at work.[37] Thus, in replying to Faustus, Augustine reads Sarah as an allegory of the church: she is the wife undefiled in a foreign land so that she can be brought "without spot or wrinkle" to Christ her Bridegroom. Here the gloss via Ephesians 5 is evident (22.38 [CSEL 25:631–32]).[38] Likewise, the wives of the patriarchs, according to Augustine, far from being the targets of calumny, stand for the various races who will compose the church, all subject to one man, Christ.[39]

Yet—and this point is to be underscored—even the figurative readings in which Augustine here engages are not produced by allegory proper, in which a person or thing represents an abstract idea that is "hidden." Rather, the figuration is developed by intertextual interpretive practices, in which some texts are acknowledged as the clues that enable the decoding of others,[40] yet no "abstractions" are involved. Passages are piled up to gloss each other, so that the weight of biblical citation will convince the reader of the interpretation's "truth"—and of scripture's commanding authority. Thus the intertexts render the patriarchs' actions not just palatable, but ethically and spiritually uplifting.

Sometimes Augustine's glossing of a text is relatively simple. For example, to Faustus's charge that Sarah "connived" with Abraham in the affair of

35. *Contra Faustum* 22.32; 12.47 (CSEL 25:626, 376) citing Gal 3:6, 8.

36. Also see the interpretation of the olive tree of Rom 11:17–18 as the ancestors of the people of God whom he had discussed in *De sancta virginitate* 1.1 (CSEL 41:235), specifically, the patriarchs and their wives. Even Jesus lends his authority to the exoneration of Abraham in John 8:39, 56 and Luke 16:23, according to Augustine (*Contra Faustum* 33.5 [CSEL 55:790]).

37. See the discussion in Terry Eagleton, *Ideology: An Introduction* (London and New York: Verso, 1991) 59. Also to be pondered is Catherine Belsey's thesis that reading is not "natural," but presupposes a theoretical discourse: see her *Critical Practice* (London and New York: Methuen, 1980) 4.

38. Augustine's use of Eph 5:27 is common in his anti-Donatist writings, starting from *De baptismo* in about 400, to indicate that the church will be "pure," but only at the end of time. See, e.g., *De baptismo* 3.18.23; 4.3.5; 5.16.21; *De correctione Donatistarum* 9.38.

39. *De bono coniugali* 18.21 (CSEL 41:214–15). Augustine goes to considerable lengths to prove here, as well as in *Contra Faustum* 22.37 and *De doctrina Christiana* 3.12.20, that it is "natural" for one man to have many women (but not *vice versa*).

40. Daniel Boyarin has well illustrated how intertextuality differs from allegory in the reading of Midrash (*Intertextuality*, 20). For a fascinating example of Faustus's own intertextual practice, in which the "intertext" is supplied by references to the Apocryphal Acts (thus "escalating" the New Testament's own ascetic charge), see *Contra Faustum* 30.4. Augustine states his preference for "figurative" (i.e., typological) interpretation in *Contra Faustum* 4.2.

Hagar, Augustine responds with 1 Cor 7:4: although the husband usually rules the wife, in the matter of their sexual relation she controls his body as much as he does hers. Thus, Sarah quite appropriately agreed to Abraham's use of his body in this instance (22.31 [CSEL 25:625]). Here apostolic authority provides rationalization for Abraham's otherwise questionable conduct.

Augustine, however, develops intertextual readings not only by an appeal to Paul. Thus, he renders Abraham as the sign of Christ himself, who left the land of his Jewish ancestors to exhibit power among the Gentiles (12.25 [CSEL 25:354]). The Gospel narratives of Jesus' Jewish birth are here brought to bear on the story of Abraham. Moreover, in his rendition of Sarah as the wife who was kept safe "without spot or wrinkle" although besieged by foreign kings, Augustine extends the allegory to his own time with the help of the Song of Songs (1:8) as an intertext; Sarah, "fairest among women," whom the earth's rulers tried unsuccessfully to violate, is a metaphor for the church under the persecuting emperors. Yet later rulers brought gifts to her whom their predecessors had not been able to humble; here the advent of Christian empire is signaled (22.38 [CSEL 25:631-32]). Thus, in Abraham's offering of Sarah to Abimelech and Pharaoh, we have no sordid tale of greed or cowardice, as Manichaean exegesis would have it; we have the story of the church's exalted triumph despite persecution.

That Augustine's retention of the Old Testament whole—the principle he developed in his controversy with the Manichaeans—had political consequences, we are reminded by Peter Brown. For if Hebrew scripture were to remain intact in the new era of grace, the coercive acts of God and Israel recorded therein offer divine sanction to imperial action against alleged heretics.[41] Indeed, Brown argues, it was first in the opposition to Manichaeanism that North African bishops enhanced their power through cooperation with imperial authority in the identification and punishment of these alleged heretics:[42] "The Christian Church," he pithily notes, "appears as a labour-saving institution for the Roman state."[43]

As Boyarin posits, in intertextual exegesis the "detritus" of the old text remains untransformed, surviving as fragments that create "fissures" on the

---

41. Peter Brown, "St. Augustine's Attitude to Religious Coercion," in Brown, *Religion and Society in the Age of Saint Augustine* (New York: Harper & Row, 1972) 272-74. Also see F. Edward Cranz, "The Development of Augustine's Ideas on Society Before the Donatist Controversy," in *Augustine* (ed. Robert Markus; Garden City, N.Y.: Doubleday, 1972) 372-75, on God's incomprehensible actions.

42. Peter Brown, "Manichaeism in the Roman Empire," in Brown, *Religion and Society*, 111-12; and idem, "Religious Coercion in the Later Roman Empire: The Case of North Africa," in Brown, *Religion and Society*, 321-22, 330-31. For the major anti-Manichaean decrees, see *Codex Theodosianus* 16.5, sections 3, 7, 9, 11, 18, 35, 38, 40, 41, 43, 59, 62, 64, 65; Theodosius II, *Novellae* 3.9; Valentinian III, *Novellae* 18. See also Decret, *L'Afrique Manichéenne*, 211-33; Lieu, *Manichaeism*, chapters 4 and 6.

43. Brown, "Manichaeism," 111.

surface of the new text[44]—in this instance, a "text" of moderated asceticism which allowed for the goodness of marriage and supported imperial action against alleged enemies of God.[45] In the hands of Augustine, the "detritus" of ancient Israelite sexual mores could, through "reading," be co-opted in the service of Christian and ascetic norms, while the "detritus" of divine violence lent sanction to an extratextual pressure on his Manichaean opponents. Strategies of containment and compulsion here unite.[46]

44. Boyarin, *Intertextuality*, 94.

45. As Robert Markus reminds his readers throughout *Saeculum: History and Society in the Theology of St. Augustine* (rev. ed.; Cambridge: Cambridge University Press, 1988), this pro-imperialist stance was nuanced in Augustine's later career.

46. I wish to thank Dale Martin and Randall Styers for helpful suggestions.

CHAPTER 21

Augustine's *The Spirit and the Letter* as a Reading of Paul's Romans

Paul W. Meyer

In the recent past, reflection on the importance of the *Wirkungsgeschichte* of religious texts (or the history of their influence) has given fresh impetus to the examination of the history of exegesis. Consideration of a text's post-history, not only the more formal course of its interpretation as deposited in the commentaries but the much more variegated history of its effects, consequences, and repercussions in the continuing life of the community that uses it, can enrich the modern interpreter's encounter with the text in a variety of ways and so help breach that insulation from the contemporary world that seems inevitably to follow upon the necessary historical-critical discipline of locating a text in its original setting. Such consideration of the effect of a text, especially upon its interpreters, is not merely ancillary to understanding but a very part of it.[1]

Although it owes its title directly to the apostle's language (Rom 2:29; 7:6; 2 Cor 3:6), Augustine's treatise *The Spirit and the Letter* (*De spiritu et littera*) would not seem at first sight to provide a "reading" of Paul's letter to the Romans. What we have from Augustine as explicit commentary on Romans is highly fragmentary and, like so much else of his biblical interpretation,

---

1. So concludes Ulrich Luz in the final section of the introduction to *Matthew 1–7: A Commentary* (Minneapolis: Augsburg, 1989) 95–99. His methodological observations have been prompted in part by H. G. Gadamer's emphasis on "effective history" as an essential aspect of the historicality of human understanding (Gadamer, *Truth and Method* [New York: Seabury, 1975] 267–74). In "The Christian Proteus" (in his *The Writings of St. Paul: A Norton Critical Edition* [New York: Norton, 1972] 435–44), Wayne Meeks has summarized in an unforgettable way the results of his own vivid exhibition of the *Nachgeschichte*, or posthistory, of the letters of Paul in an anthology of responses and reactions to the apostle. Paul's texts not only provide access to the apostle, complex and elusive a figure as he may be; they also shed light on and challenge his interpreters in every age.

deeply imbedded in doctrinal, apologetic, and polemic argumentation.[2] This treatise, in one sense, is no exception; it belongs firmly, both by date and in Augustine's own retrospective view of it, to his anti-Pelagian writings.[3] It ought, therefore, to offer evidence primarily for the effects not of Paul on Augustine so much as of Augustine's theological preoccupations upon his reading of Paul. Furthermore, the treatise is strikingly absent from a number of major modern discussions of Augustine's exegesis of Paul, partly because the latter concentrate on specific theological issues or on particular passages in Romans (notably chapters 7 and 9) or on major turning points in the development of Augustine's thought, of which the writing of the *Spirit and Letter* does not seem to have been one.[4] As a matter of fact, it is surprising, when one consults the catalogues and bibliographies, that books or articles devoted to a study of this treatise for its own sake are nearly nonexistent.

This first impression, however, needs correction. Peter Brown calls the *Spirit and Letter* "the book which Augustine himself regarded as his most fundamental demolition of Pelagianism."[5] Yet the three richly documented and informative chapters Brown devotes to the Pelagian controversy contain only two other relatively peripheral references to this treatise. The reason is clear from Brown's own portrayal. Augustine "knew Pelagius only as an author, and he combatted him by books."[6] But the *Spirit and Letter* is a sequel to Augustine's very first anti-Pelagian writing, *On the Consequences and Forgiveness of Sins and Baptism of Little Children*, and this in turn was Augustine's response to Marcellinus's account of the disturbance created in Carthage by Pelagius's zealous disciple, Caelestius, a response composed *before* the flood of materials to which Augustine was later to give detailed attention.[7] The point is that at this inchoative stage (411 C.E.) Augustine was

2. See the introduction in Paula Fredriksen Landes, *Augustine on Romans: Propositions from the Epistle to the Romans; Unfinished Commentary on the Epistle to the Romans* (Chico, Calif.: Scholars Press, 1982) ix–xvi. For a brief survey of Augustine's biblical expositions, see B. Altaner, *Patrologie* (3rd ed.; Freiburg: Herder, 1951) 380–82.

3. *Retract.* 63 (=2.37).

4. See, e.g., Paula Fredriksen, "Beyond the body/soul dichotomy: Augustine on Paul against the Manichees and the Pelagians," *Recherches augustiniennes* 23 (1988) 87–114; W. S. Babcock, "Augustine's Interpretation of Romans (A.D. 394–396)," *Augustinian Studies* 10 (1979) 54–74; idem, "Augustine and Paul: The Case of Romans IX," *Studia Patristica* 16/2 (1985) 473–79; Marie-François Berrouard, "L'exégèse augustinienne de Rom. 7,7–25 entre 396 et 418, avec des remarques sur les deux premières périodes de la crise 'pélagienne,'" *Recherches augustiniennes* 16 (1981) 101–96.

5. Peter Brown, *Augustine of Hippo: A Biography* (Berkeley: University of California Press, 1967) 372. I do not know where Augustine makes this evaluation; the passage in *Retract.* 2.37, to which Brown refers, does not contain it.

6. Brown, *Augustine*, 355.

7. Ibid., 345: "It is extremely difficult to identify the opinions and pamphlets that provided Augustine with the material for his first coherent picture of the ideas he would later ascribe directly to Pelagius." For Brown this makes all the more astonishing Augustine's quick grasp of

confronted with questions for the answering of which he turned afresh to Paul—of course in the context of the prior development of his own thought and understanding of the apostle. That the treatise has not served as a major resource for the reconstruction of Pelagius's teaching or of the main points of Augustine's response is the very reason why it invites fresh examination as a genuine act of "reading" Romans. That it belongs in the *Wirkungsgeschichte* of Romans is confirmed by the way it has served as a major vehicle for Augustine's influence upon the subsequent interpretation of Paul, most notably upon Luther and, through him, the whole of the modern history of the exegesis of Romans, but this lies outside our present concern.[8]

That the *Spirit and Letter* deserves consideration in its own right as a reading of Romans is confirmed above all by closer analysis of the text itself. Of course, like so many writings of the church fathers, this treatise is liberally sprinkled with quotations and allusions from across the breadth of the Bible.[9] But the focus is clearly on Romans; of 171 New Testament citations and allusions, 124 are from the Pauline corpus, and over half of these (72) are from Romans. Such statistics tell only part of the story; it is the long quotations (of Romans, but also of 2 Corinthians 3–5, Jeremiah 31, and Psalm 103), from which verses and phrases not included in the counting are repeated in the ensuing discussion, and the *seriatim* quotation of verses, not always adjoining but nevertheless in their sequence in Paul's letter, that sustain Augustine's argument and capture him in the act of listening to his texts. With good reason, as he nears the end of the book, Augustine lays down the challenge that those who occasioned its writing will have to defend themselves "not against me, but . . . certainly against no less an apostle than Paul, speaking not in a single text but in a long argument of such power, intensity and vigilance . . ." (61).

---

the issues at stake: "Indeed, Pelagianism as we know it, that consistent body of ideas of momentous consequences, had come into existence; but in the mind of Augustine, not of Pelagius" (ibid.). What role may Romans have played in shaping that "grasp"?

8. For the indebtedness of Luther's lectures on Romans to the *Spirit and Letter*, see Wilhelm Pauck, *Luther: Lectures on Romans* (LCC 15; Philadelphia: Westminster, 1961) xxxiv–lxi. It is striking to what extent preoccupation with Augustine's influence on the Protestant Reformation has diverted attention in much scholarship from Augustine's own exegesis in this treatise. See, e.g., W. Anz, "Zur Exegese von Römer 7 bei Bultmann, Luther, Augustin," *Theologia crucis–signum crucis: Festschrift für Erich Dinkler zum 70. Geburtstag* (ed. Carl Andresen and Günter Klein; Tübingen: Mohr, 1979) 1–15; Reinhart Staats, "Augustins 'De spiritu et littera' in Luthers reformatorischer Erkenntnis," *ZKG* 98 (1987) 28–47; Hjalmar Sundén, "Der psychologische Aspekt in der Rechtfertigung durch den Glauben [Augustins *De spiritu et litera* und Luthers 'Turmerlebnis']," *KD* 32 (1986) 120–31.

9. Burnaby's footnotes (see n. 11 below) identify fifty-five quotations from fifteen books of the Old Testament, including two books of the Apocrypha (of these, twenty-eight are from the Psalms) and ninety-nine quotations from sixteen books of the New Testament apart from Romans (of these, fifty-two are from the larger Pauline corpus, not including Hebrews). The count for Romans is seventy-two, but this is a misleadingly low figure; see comment below.

Since I have written a short commentary on Romans myself,[10] it is this aspect of the *Spirit and Letter* that I have found most intriguing and that I propose to examine in what follows, by a cursory review of the structure and movement of Augustine's treatise, especially as he quotes and uses Paul, and by some summary characterizations of Augustine's interpretation in relation to modern understandings in order to identify some significant similarities and differences. The focus, it should be emphasized, is on this treatise alone; I make no claim to sufficient grasp of Augustine's other writings or of his thought in general to reach beyond this modest goal.

THE STRUCTURE AND BASIC ARGUMENT

As one tries to see through and behind the conventional section divisions of this patristic work, certain structural features emerge rather quickly and clearly.[11] After an introduction in 1–7, the main body of the argument ends with a *Q.E.D.* in 42. It is followed by two appendixes dealing with difficulties raised in the course of the argument, one more exegetical in nature (43–51), the other more theological (52–60). A conclusion to the whole work follows in 61–66.

The introduction (1–7) defines the issue. In his first anti-Pelagian writing, *On the Consequences and Forgiveness of Sins*, Augustine had argued that, although God has without doubt the power to make a person entirely free from sin, no one in scripture or experience, apart from Christ, has reached this state. The reason is that

> Men *will* not do what is right, either because the right is hidden from them, or because they find no delight in it. For the strength of our will to anything is proportionate to the assurance of our knowledge of its goodness, and to the warmth of our delight in it. . . . But that what was hidden may become clear, what delighted not may become sweet—this belongs to the grace of God which aids the wills of men.[12]

Marcellinus had asked Augustine to explain the apparent contradiction in claiming both that a sinless human life is possible with God's help and that it has never in fact been realized. Augustine dispenses with this question in 1–3 by showing that the two claims are not mutually exclusive and chal-

10. P. W. Meyer, "Romans," in *Harper's Bible Commentary* (ed. James L. Mays; San Francisco: Harper, 1988) 1130–67. This commentary could never have been completed without the editorial guidance and encouragement of Wayne Meeks.

11. The text used here is the English translation and edition of John Burnaby, *Augustine: Later Works* (LCC 8; Philadelphia: Westminster, 1955) 193–250. The Latin text is available in CSEL 60 (Vienna and Leipzig, 1913) 153–229. References in the body of this essay are to the shorter section divisions of Augustine's text (Arabic numerals in both versions above); references in the notes below to "Burnaby" are to the page numbers of his edition.

12. *On the Consequences* (*de pecc. mer.*) 2.26 (as quoted by Burnaby, *Augustine*, 187).

lenging anyone to provide the example of a sinless life that could falsify the latter.

Augustine then redefines the issue, stating in 4 the main thesis to be opposed and formulating in 5 his own counterthesis. The issue is not *whether* the self needs God's help to achieve righteousness but *why* and by *what* means. That divine help is required, that "God has both created man in possession of a will that chooses freely and teaches him by the gift of his commandments the right way of life" is not in dispute. What is to be vigorously resisted is "that God's help consists in the removal by instruction of man's ignorance," so that a person "by means of the power of free choice belonging to him by nature" may proceed along the path thus opened (4). In Augustine's contrary view (5), that is too narrow a perception of God's assistance, which consists not only in the endowment of freedom to choose, and not only in the instruction how one ought to live, but also in the gift of the Holy Spirit, "whereby there arises in [the] soul the delight in and love of God, the supreme and changeless Good."

> Free choice alone, if the way of truth is hidden, avails for nothing but sin; and when the right action and the true aim has begun to appear clearly, there is still no devotion, no good life, unless it be also delighted in and loved. And that it may be loved, the love of God is shed abroad in our hearts, not by the free choice whose spring is in ourselves, but through the Holy Spirit which is given us. (5)

Free choice, "whose spring is in ourselves (*quod surgit ex nobis*)" fails to provide that transcendent resource that is needed to motivate true devotion and bring about change.

Such formulation of the issue does not fit the popular definitions of Pelagianism on which many theological students have been brought up, as "the heresy that man can take the initial steps toward salvation by his own efforts, apart from Divine Grace."[13] But it fits much better what we know of the ascetic stringency of Pelagius, his sense for the incorruptible majesty of the God of the commandments, and his perfectionism.[14] In 418 the Synod of Carthage, which condemned Pelagius, "expressly emphasized that this grace of God does not consist only in instruction concerning the content of God's commandments, but that, above all, it imparts power for their fulfillment."[15]

It is noteworthy that this opening distinction between knowing the good and doing it parallels precisely Paul's distinction at the start of Romans

---

13. *The Concise Oxford Dictionary of the Christian Church* (ed. E. A. Livingstone; Oxford: Oxford University Press, 1977) 390.

14. Brown, *Augustine*, 340–52 et passim.

15. B. Lohse, *A Short History of Christian Doctrine* (Philadelphia: Fortress, 1966) 121, paraphrasing Canon 4 of the Council of Carthage; the text is in H. Denzinger, *Enchiridion Symbolorum* (24th ed.; Barcelona: Herder, 1946) 104.

(2:13) between hearing the Law and doing it. By charging his Pelagian opponent with narrowing God's grace to divine instruction in right action,
Augustine is positioning him where Paul positions the Jew in Romans 2, a
strategy that becomes explicit later (13–14).

Section 6 takes another arrow from Paul's quiver. So far Augustine has
not indicated why, apart from God's gift of the Holy Spirit, the good is not
delighted in and loved by human beings. Several explanations are given during the subsequent argument, but for now Augustine simply turns rather
suddenly to 2 Cor 3:6 in order to undermine from another side his adversary's "opinion": "The letter killeth, but the Spirit giveth life."[16] That instruction in "the way of truth" with which the Pelagian wants to identify God's
gracious aid is not merely a benign gift. The Spirit has an active role in
"shedding charity abroad in our hearts" (*caritatem diffudens*, echoing the
Latin version of Rom 5:5: *caritas Dei diffusa est in cordibus nostris per Spiritum
Sanctum*), thus inspiring good desire (*concupiscentia bona*). Where the Spirit
is not present, there the law "increases by its prohibition the evil desire
(*concupiscentia mala*)." The "Thou shalt not covet" of Rom 7:7 represents "the
voice of the law forbidding all sin," and Rom 7:11 shows that it is this law
that "killeth" (6). The very law that promises life cannot produce it; quite the
contrary, the law generates the opposite. Once again, it follows that human
righteousness is to be credited only to the operation of God's life-giving
power, which is the Spirit (7).

Rom 2:29 is one of the three verses in which Paul (via the Latin rendering
of *in spiritu non littera* for the Greek ἐν πνεύματι οὐ γράμματι) bequeathed to
Christian theological vocabulary the pair of terms "letter" and "spirit." It is
possible that it served as the springboard for the main argument through its
proximity and parallelism with Rom 2:13, by thus sharply distinguishing the
doing of the good from the knowing of it. While there is no clear evidence
that Augustine had this verse in mind when he opened his argument, it is
striking that he next turns to the second of those eponymous verses (2 Cor
3:6, rendering οὐ γράμματος ἀλλὰ πνεύματος) against the Pelagian. That the
"letter" kills, but the "Spirit" gives life provides the fundamental opposition.
Then he at once appeals to Paul's own elaboration of the third (Rom 7:6 and
the following verses, 7–12, *in novitate Spiritus et non in vetustate litterae*) to
interpret and drive home the second. In the Latin text *littera* ("letter") renders both the sense of "written" and that of "literal." Paul's argument visibly
affects Augustine's in other ways as well. Like Paul, Augustine takes the
commandment "Thou shalt not covet" to be "the voice of the law" and to
stand for the whole of the Decalogue, "for there is no sin whose commission does not begin with coveting" (6).[17] Again, the "letter" now clearly

16. The biblical quotations here follow Burnaby's translations from Augustine's Latin, since
Augustine's biblical text often differs from modern versions; cf. Burnaby, *Augustine*, 14.
17. For Jewish traditions taking the command against coveting as representative of the
Decalogue as a whole, see E. Käsemann, *Commentary on Romans* (Grand Rapids: Eerdmans,

means the command of the Decalogue; Augustine expressly appeals to Paul's language in order to reject the "figurative" and Origenistic uses of "letter" and "spirit" to distinguish the literal and the allegorical senses of scripture.[18] Finally, though Augustine began (4 and 5) with law as neutral instruction (Torah!) in "the right way of life" (both "what is to be avoided" and "what is to be sought"), under the influence of Paul's argument it has become negative and prohibitory in 6 and 7—with immense consequences later in the treatise.[19]

THE BODY OF THE ARGUMENT

The main body of the *Spirit and Letter* consists of sections 8–42 and falls into two major divisions. The first (8–20) continues to draw upon diverse passages in Romans to interpret the topic verse from 2 Cor 3:6. That "the letter killeth" is given another dimension (8 and 9) by turning to Rom 5:20–21: coveting is evil in itself, but when "transgression of law is added to [that] evil," sin is "increased rather than diminished." But the contrast between Adam and Christ in Romans 5 shows that God's real goal is the giving of life: "The apostle's aim is to commend the grace which came through Jesus Christ to all peoples." Something of the universalism of Rom 5:12–21 comes through here. (When Augustine adds, without provocation from the immediate context, "lest the Jews exalt themselves above the rest on account of their possession of the law," his sense for the law as an identity marker reenforcing the Jews' self-consciousness may sound very modern,[20] but the remark may more likely be a passing rebuke to the claims of Pelagian perfectionism.) The reason for the law's "entry" and the consequent "abounding of the offense"[21] is

> so that thus convicted and confounded [man] might see his need for God, not only as teacher but as helper . . . , that he should flee to the help of mercy for

1980) 196; U. Wilckens, *Der Brief an die Römer* (EKKNT; 3 vols.; Neukirchen-Vluyn: Neukirchener Verlag, 1978–82) 2:78–79. For Hellenistic-Jewish identification of coveting as the cause of all sinning, see Wilckens, *Römer*, 2:78.

18. According to *Conf.* 6.4, Ambrose's use of this distinction in interpreting the same text (2 Cor 3:6) played a part in his conversion.

19. Augustine has *not* gotten this from Paul, though it has often been repeated in the interpretation of Romans, his "psychological" explanation of *how* sin "deceives" and "kills," viz., by making "the coveted object [grow] somehow more attractive through being forbidden" (6). For Paul the "deceit" or "trick" lies in the fact that the commandment is unable to deliver what it promises (life) and in truth delivers the opposite, thus defrauding the desire for the good; for Augustine it lies in the way it leads the self to *desire* the evil in place of the good.

20. Cf. "The New Perspective on Paul," in J. D. G. Dunn, *Romans 1–8* (WBC 38a; Dallas: Word, 1988) lxiii–lxxii, esp. lxix.

21. In Augustine's Latin New Testament, what "abounds" is not sin but the *delictum*, the offense or transgression against express prohibition.

his healing, and so . . . grace should yet more abound, not by the desert of the sinner but through the aid of the succourer. (9)[22]

On the heels of this use of Rom 5:20–21, still following Paul's text, Augustine introduces a long quotation of Rom 6:1–11 to explain and describe the "abounding of grace." This benefit, which cannot come "by the letter of the law but only by faith in Jesus Christ," is depicted with two images. One is supplied by the text and its references to Christ's death and resurrection. The other, without basis in Paul, introduced here for the first time in this treatise but loaded with associations that will emerge as Augustine proceeds, is the figure of grace as "healing medicine." Their combination means that death and resurrection are not the apocalyptic turning points by which God reverses the direction of human destiny and behavior, but become metaphors for a moral and spiritual process:

> It is plain enough that by the mystery of the Lord's death and resurrection is signified the setting of our old life and the rising of the new: there is shown forth the destruction of sin and the renewal of righteousness. (10)

By the very same token, however, Augustine is able to appropriate from Paul the indivisible unity of indicative and imperative, justification and sanctification. Illumined by the parallelisms of the Psalmist's language (Ps 36:10), God's mercy and his righteousness are one, and the justification of the ungodly is God's free creation of righteousness where it did not exist before. After quoting a catena of phrases from this psalm (36:7–10 [35:8–11 LXX]), Augustine continues:

> He extends his mercy, not because they know him but in order that they may know him: he extends his righteousness whereby he justifies the ungodly, not because they are upright in heart, but that they may become upright in heart. (11)

Backing off for a moment from the details of his text, Augustine declares the preaching of this grace to be almost the apostle's sole concern in the manifold, persistent, and even wearying (!) arguments of this epistle. (12)

A significant new start is taken with section 13, which opens with a long quotation of Paul's apostrophe to the Jew and its sequel in Rom 2:17–29. Paul's original rhetorical aim seems to have involved three steps: first, to single out the Jew as representative of the best in his religious world, one whose religious identity and distinctiveness revolved around possession of the law; second, to deny that the law provides to those who possess it any exemption from accountability to its demands; third, thus to include the Jew in his argument that all human beings stand on the same footing before

---

22. The assignment of this role to the law, here and elsewhere in the *Spirit and Letter*, clearly anticipates (and prepares for) Luther, who called this the *usus proprius* (the special and characteristic function) of the law—a role it never plays in Paul.

an impartial God and are all under the power of sin. The final words of the section (2:29) remind such a religious person that the ultimate evaluation of human life depends on the "praise" or commendation and vindication that only God can give. Like most Christian interpreters since, however, Augustine takes the passage as Paul's Christian indictment of the discrepancy in the Jew between profession and performance.[23]

The Jews were indeed favored by God's gift of the law; "yet this law of God they supposed themselves to fulfil by their own righteousness, though they were rather its transgressors." Noticing, nonetheless, that Paul's apostrophe does not directly accuse the Jew of breaking the law, he immediately adds, "even those who did as the law commanded." If performance is not wanting, their failure must be found at a deeper level; they

> did it through fear of punishment and not from love of righteousness. Thus in God's sight there was not in their will that obedience which to the sight of men appeared in their work; they were rather held guilty for that which God knew they would have chosen to commit, if it could have been without penalty. (13)

The charge is ruinous. A genuinely Pauline recognition that observance of Torah is not necessarily identical with obedience to God is combined with a wholly non-Pauline preoccupation with the motivation or "will" *behind* human action, to the point where, even when the outward action is right, the guilt that belongs to the action not done is attached to the fear that is presumed and attributed to the doer. The resulting polarizing of "the love of righteousness" (*amor iustitiae*) with the "fear of punishment" (*timor poenae*) becomes an increasingly important ingredient in Augustine's interpretation.

In 14 Augustine gives "their answer," the wording of which shows that he now has his own Pelagian opponent in mind under the cover of Paul's Jew: "We do give praise to God as author of our justification, inasmuch as he gave the law, by the study of which we know how we ought to live." For his rebuttal Augustine draws on the continuity of Paul's text: "from the law shall no flesh be justified before God," and "through the law is the knowledge of sin" (Rom 3:20a, b). With the exegetically correct insistence that by "law" here Paul means the Decalogue, and not any "law of ancient rites" such as circumcision, Augustine goes out of his way to foreclose any move by the Pelagian to deflect Paul's text away from himself and upon the ancient ethnic Jew.

---

23. The pejorative interpretation is aggravated by a forced syntactical substitution of a subjective genitive for an objective, so that "praise" (Greek ἔπαινος; Latin *laus*) is no longer the approbation conferred *by* God on the authentic religious person but the praise rendered *to* God by "the true Jew" in contrast to the self-praise implicitly attributed to the empirical Jew.

As Paul's text reaches a turning point in Rom 3:21 and its following verses, Augustine's reaches a preliminary climax in 15. Insisting on human free will, the Pelagian will not dispute Paul's assertion that "from the law shall no man be justified" (3:20a):

> since the law does but point out what is to be done or not done, in order that the will may carry out its promptings, and so man be justified not by the law's command but by his own free choice. (15)

But for Augustine this is not enough:

> Nay but, O man, consider what follows!—"But now without law the righteousness of God hath been manifested, witnessed to by law and prophets." Can even the deaf fail to hear? . . . "The righteousness *of God*"—not the righteousness of man or the righteousness of our own will—the righteousness of God, not that by which God is righteous, but that wherewith he clothes man, when he justifies the ungodly. (15)

As Paul moves in these verses (Rom 3:21, 31) to more positive remarks about the Mosaic law, Augustine too leaves behind the language about its "killing." Now it is Paul's "without the law" (*sine lege* for χωρὶς νόμου) in 3:21 that serves as his weapon against the Pelagian: "The law . . . contributes nothing to God's saving act." Where for the Pelagian and for Paul's Jew God's gracious gift is the law, for Augustine that gift is "the righteousness of God without law."

> It is indeed a righteousness of God without law, because God confers it upon the believer through the Spirit of grace, without the help of the law. (15)

We have already noted the Pelagian emphasis on free will. In this section (15), just where he is following each verse of Rom 3:21–24, Augustine makes clear how much he shares this preoccupation; "justified freely by his grace" (Rom 3:24a) means:

> not that the justification is without our will, but the weakness of our will is discovered by the law (*uoluntas nostra ostenditur infirma per legem*), so that grace may restore (*sanet*) the will and the restored will (*sana uoluntas*) may fulfil the law, established neither under the law nor in need of law (*non constituta sub lege nec indigens lege*). (15)

The Latin shows that (a) the last words refer to the "restored will": this owes nothing to the law and does not need the law (no *tertius usus legis* [third use of the law] here!); and (b) Augustine is again using the imagery of healing, or making whole what is beset with weakness or infirmity, to describe justification. Most important, this will, "without which we cannot do the good" (20), is fundamental to the human self; this is what is to be healed by God's grace (cf. *Spirit and Letter* 6). How this in turn has affected Augustine's reading of some of the key terms that are of great interest to the modern exegete,[24] is clear from his comment earlier in the section, on Rom 3:22:

> "The righteousness of God through the faith of Jesus Christ": that is, the faith whereby we believe in Christ. The "faith of Christ" here meant is not that by which Christ believes, any more than the righteousness of God is that by which God is righteous. *Both are our own;* called "of God" and "of Christ," because bestowed upon us by his bounty. (15; emphasis added)

AUGUSTINE'S INTERPRETIVE SHIFT

At one point in his introduction to the text, Burnaby comments: "The effect of the Pelagian controversy was to sharpen the dilemma—either God's work *or* ours."[25] That may have been its ultimate effect, but it scarcely fits the *Spirit and Letter.* There seems to be no question, for either Pelagius or Augustine, that the righteous life, when and where it is a reality, is "ours." Augustine's task was to transcend the dilemma and to show that justification is really "ours," that it makes a difference in the way human beings remain human, *and* that it is God's undeserved and gracious gift. But because being human is so closely identified with the freedom of the will (*liberum arbitrium*, freedom of choice),[26] the result is inevitable. Augustine rewrites Paul's text in Rom 3:21 in such a way that "the righteousness of God" is not "manifested" so much as it is "bestowed," being itself now the gift; "without law" (*sine lege*, for χωρὶς νόμου) has become an adjective modifying "righteousness" as much as an adverb qualifying "has been manifested." A shift has taken place, for the form of the "dilemma" in Paul, the true mystery, is not the conjoining of what is God's with what is "ours" but the holding together of freedom and fatefulness, responsibility and destiny, *both* in the behavior of humans, "saints" as well as sinners, and also in the sovereignty and faithfulness of God.[27]

After a somewhat labored excursus in section 16 to deal with "the lawful use of the law" in 1 Tim 1:8–9 (which of course was also attributed to the

24. For the modern discussion, which is voluminous, one may start with Manfred T. Brauch, "Perspectives on 'God's righteousness' in recent German discussion," in E. P. Sanders, *Paul and Palestinian Judaism* (Philadelphia: Fortress, 1977) 523–42; Richard B. Hays, "Pistis and Pauline Christology: What is at Stake?" in *Society of Biblical Literature 1991 Seminar Papers* (ed. D. Lull; Atlanta: Scholars Press, 1991) 714–29; and James D. G. Dunn, "Once More, Pistis Christou," in *Society of Biblical Literature 1991 Seminar Papers,* 730–44.

25. Burnaby, *Augustine,* 192.

26. In his summary of the history of patristic exegesis of Romans, K. H. Schelkle has pointed out that *liberum arbitrium* (freedom of the will, of choice) is closely associated in patristic exegesis with τὸ αὐτεξούσιον (that which is in one's power or discretion), a major term in the vocabulary of Stoicism; it differs greatly from Paul's ἐλευθερία (freedom, the state of having been set free, liberation *from* oppressive and destructive powers, and therefore freedom *for* a new course of life) (*Paulus, Lehrer der Väter* [Düsseldorf: Patmos, 1956] 439–40).

27. Rom 1:21–23; 5:12; 6:17; 8:12–14; 9:33; cf. my "Romans," 1136b, 1145a, 1148a, 1152a, 1157a.

apostle), Augustine returns to Romans 3. What interests him now is v. 27, which exercises interpreters to this day, specifically the contrast here between "the law of works" (which does not exclude "glorying") and "the law of faith" (which does). This contrast sets in motion a new train of thought that dominates the remainder of the body of the *Spirit and Letter*, forming what we may distinguish as its second major part (17–42).

What lies at the heart of this contrast? At first (18–20), Augustine turns to the beginning of Romans, where Paul sets over against the revelation of God's righteousness (1:16–17) the revelation of God's wrath (1:18–2:11). Clearly recognizing the parallelism Paul establishes between a knowledge of God devoid of recognition and gratitude (the human creature of Romans 1) and a possession of the law lacking in true submission to God (the religious moralist and the Jew of Romans 2), Augustine drives home his point once more: as knowledge is not godliness, so ungodliness is not mere ignorance and cannot therefore be cured by instruction apart from the Spirit's help. "Without that aid, the teaching (*doctrina*) is a letter that killeth" (20; cf. 6).

But what are these *two* "laws" of 3:27? In an impressive display of exegetical sophistication, Augustine steadfastly refuses either to relegate "the law of works" to Jewish practices or cultic regulations left behind by Christianity, or to evaporate "the law of faith" into a spiritual principle unrelated to law. The law that produces covetousness (Rom 7:7), "the letter that killeth" (2 Cor 3:6), and the law by which no one is justified (Rom 3:20) are all the very same holy, just, and good commandment of Rom 7:12, 13b (24–25). Both "the law of works" and "the law of faith" say, "Thou shalt not covet"; both refer to the Decalogue that the Christian is "bound to observe" (23).

> Where then lies the difference? To put it in a sentence: what is enjoined with threatenings under the law of works, is granted to belief under the law of faith. ... So by the law of works God says, "Do what I command"; by the law of faith we say to God, "Give what thou commandest." (22)[28]

"The law commands, that we may be advised what faith must do" (22). Here is a nuance different from that of 20; law is now much more closely related to faith. The law does not change; its content is the same in Judaism and Christianity, for both faith and unbelief. Faith knows that performance can come only by the power supplied by God's gift of the Spirit. Unbelief is exhibited by the Pharisee in Luke's parable (Luke 18:9–14), "who gave God thanks for what he had but asked for nothing to be given him—as though he stood in need of nothing for the increase and perfecting of his righteousness" (22). The wording fairly shouts out that "Pharisee" stands for the unnamed Pelagian.

---

28. Burnaby, *Augustine*, 212 n. 61: "The famous prayer of *Conf.*, X, 40, which gave offense to Pelagius (Aug., *De Praedest.*, II, 53)."

The direction of the argument is now established on a new bearing. Subsequent sections draw on a range of passages, from Romans and beyond, to substantiate and to refine its two pillars: (a) "the law of works by which no man is justified" and "the law of faith by which the just lives" are one and the same Mosaic law; the law itself is not simply to be rejected as "letter" and divorced from spirit; and (b) "letter" and "spirit," no longer simply set against each other as polar opposites, the one as the "abounding of sin" and the other as "the abounding of grace," are two dimensions of the same law, two contexts in which the one law functions. A long quotation from Rom 7:6–25 (25) serves to make clear:

> Not that the law itself is an evil thing, but that it holds the good commandment in the letter that demonstrates, not in the spirit that brings aid. And if the commandment be done through fear of penalty and not through love of righteousness, it is done in the temper of servitude not freedom—and therefore it is not done at all. (26; cf. 7)

The law remains one, the Decalogue. But clearly Paul's text provides the materials for constructing a comparison between "the law of works" and "the law of faith." Paul's (synonymous) use of the terms "law" and "commandment" (Rom 7:12) allows Augustine to distinguish (with an assist from 2 Cor 3:2–8 in section 24) one quality of law as "letter" from another in which law is associated with God's Spirit. Indeed, Augustine uses Paul's (for him, Latin) language and plays on it as his own:

> The man in whom is the faith that works through love (*per dilectionem* [Gal 5:6]) begins to delight (*condelectari*) in the law of God after the inward man; and that delight (*delectatio*) is a gift not of the letter but of the spirit. (26)[29]

Again, Augustine mines 2 Corinthians, first with a long quotation of 3:2–8 (24) and then with a series of citations in the order of the text from 3:3 to 5:21 (30–31). The law was always written by the finger of God (Exod 31:18) and that finger is God's Spirit (Luke 11:20). But in the one case it was given to a people "held back by a fearful dread" (Exod 19:21–23); in the other, the Spirit came upon an assembly waiting for his promised coming (Acts 2:1–4).

> There the finger of God worked upon tables of stone: here upon the hearts of men. So there the law was set outside men (*extrinsecus*) to be a terror to the unjust: here it was given within them (*intrinsecus*) to be their justification. (29)

"The law of God is charity (*caritas*)" (29, after quoting Rom 13:9), but in the one case it is "the law of works"; in the other, "the law of faith."

29. It is well known that Augustine changed his mind in the interpretation of Rom 7:7–25, believing at first that Paul's "I" describes "the man who is still under the law and not yet under grace," but coming later to believe that these verses "describe the spiritual man" (*Retract.* 2.1.1). The change is usually dated in 418–419 C.E. (e.g., Wilckens, *Römer*, 2:102). But since "delight" in Augustine's terms presupposes the healing of the will by the Holy Spirit, it seems that the change is already emerging here, in 412 C.E.

> The one is written outside the man (*extra hominem*), to be a terror to him from without (*forinsecus*), while the other is written in the man himself (*in ipso homine*), to justify him from within (*intrinsecus*). (30)

Further, from still another source: a full quotation of Jer 31:31–34, singled out by Augustine as the only passage from the Old Testament in which the new covenant is expressly mentioned (33), supplies another way of distinguishing one law from the other, as the laws of two covenants, the old and the new. We have noted above that an early answer to the question why, apart from God's Spirit, human beings do not delight in God's good, was to appeal to 2 Cor 3:6: "The letter killeth." But now we have another, more nuanced answer, triggered by Rom 8:3–4, showing again Augustine's fondness for healing as an image of salvation:

> The law was given that grace might be sought; grace was given that the law might be fulfilled. For the non-fulfilment of the law was not through its own fault but the fault of the "mind of the flesh"—a fault which the law must exhibit and grace must heal. (34)

Here "fault" (Paul's ἠσθένει [NRSV: "weakened"] in 8:3) was rendered *infirmabatur* ("was weakened, enfeebled") in Augustine's Latin text. But now in his interpretation it has become *uitium*: "a defect, blemish, imperfection," to be made whole by grace. What in Paul is an incapacity in the *law* has become in Augustine a defect in the *self*:

> It is because of the sickness (*noxa* [a close synonym of *uitium*, specifically an injury or damage inflicted upon someone]) of the old man, which the commands and the threatenings of the letter did nothing to heal, that the former covenant is called old, and the latter new with the newness of the Spirit, which heals the new man from his old failing (*uitium*). (35)

The difference between "the law of works" and "the law of faith," between the old covenant and the new, between Judaism and Christianity, does not lie in any change in the content of the law but in a change, a transformation, *within* the human self.

Sections 35–42 elaborate on that important passage from Jer 31:31–34 and the similarities and differences between the two covenants. But the entire argument is summed up and aimed back at the Pelagian in Augustine's *Q.E.D.*:

> Grasp this clear difference between the old covenant and the new: that there the law is written upon tables, here upon hearts, so that the fear imposed by the first from without (*forinsecus*) becomes the delight inspired by the second from within (*intrinsecus*), and he whom the letter that killeth there made a transgressor, is here made a lover (*dilector*) by the Spirit that giveth life. *Then you can no longer say* that God assists us in the working of righteousness and works in us both to will and to do according to his good pleasure, inasmuch as he makes us hear with the outward sense (*forinsecus insonat*) the command-

ment of righteousness. No, it is because he gives increase within us (*intrinsecus incrementum dat*), by the shedding abroad of charity in our hearts through the Holy Spirit which is given us. (42; emphasis added)

This is the real conclusion to the *Spirit and Letter.* What remains are two not insignificant appendixes. One (43–51) directly confronts the difficulty presented to Augustine's understanding of the differences between the two covenants by Rom 2:14–15a.[30] The second appendix (52–60) opens with a paraphrase of Paul's own rhetorical question in Rom 3:31: "Do we then 'make void' freedom of choice through grace? 'God forbid! yea, we establish' freedom of choice." The challenge is to support that claim, so close to Pelagius's own agenda, in a way that will preserve the difference from the Pelagian that the preceding body of the treatise has established. A conclusion (61–66) returns to Marcellinus's question but adds nothing significant to the preceding argument. Its most telling feature is that Augustine ends this "reading" of Paul by adopting as his own the words of praise with which Paul concludes his argument (Rom 11:33–36).

CONCLUSION

How close this argument stays to Paul—and yet how unlike Paul it resonates! One could try to enumerate similarities and differences, but such a list would miss the point, for it is often the case that Augustine displays his distance most clearly just when he is following Paul most closely. One interesting, and perhaps surprising, feature of the *Spirit and Letter* in this respect is that Augustine chooses the question of the law, its nature and function, as the field on which to resist Pelagianism. Why? Of course, this is not Augustine's last word on Pelagianism, perhaps not his most definitive. Has the field of battle been determined here by Paul's letter? Augustine's treatise reflects clearly the variations and the tensions of the apostle's own arguments on this subject—another indication of the closeness of the "reading." But the conclusion of the argument is a measure also of the distance. Since the Christian life is understood in terms of the immanent qualities brought about by change within the believer, Paul's Christology and eschatology suffer heavy erosion. The cross and resurrection are moralized. Paul, on this

---

30. This discussion of Rom 2:14–15a provides a fascinating look into the bishop's exegetical method at its best. He considers first one solution drawn from the context (44) but called into question both by an adjoining verse (45–46) and by a philological difficulty (47). A second solution is tried but proves less than convincing (48). Finally, Augustine advances beyond both by considering the rhetorical aim of the passage, with a surprisingly modern result (49). The upshot: in any case, whatever meaning is assigned the text, it provides no grist for Pelagius's mill (50–51).

reading is left entirely vulnerable to the kind of development that took place in Corinth: the Christian life is a supernatural life. Such a reading fails to grasp the full depth of Paul's understanding of sin as a power that corrupts even the most ardent love and desire of God as the highest Good (Romans 7), and so could not alone check the drift toward Christian triumphalism and legalism. It is ironic that Augustine's assignment of *forensic* distance to God's command and *intrinsic* intimacy to God's grace had to be reversed in the Reformers' insistence on a *iustitia aliena* (alien righteousness) imputed in justification. There are signs that the reversal has raised questions of its own. Perhaps we will not find the balance the apostle had in mind until we put Christology again at the center of his teaching about justification.

CHAPTER 22

Sinned We All
in Adam's Fall?

Rowan A. Greer

Aʟᴍᴏsᴛ ᴛᴡᴇɴᴛʏ ʏᴇᴀʀs ᴀɢᴏ Wayne Meeks wrote of Paul as "the Christian Proteus," whose writings supplied warrants for a wide variety of heresies and orthodoxies. He also cited with approval Harnack's judgment that "Paulinism has proved to be a ferment in the history of dogma, a basis it has never been."[1] More recently he has pointed out how Irenaeus's reading of Paul's Adam typology contributes to a "synthesis" that "points to the way in which the main stream of Christian interpretation would flow for subsequent centuries, until the modern era."[2] The task I wish to accomplish in what follows builds on these observations and focuses on Augustine's reshaping (at least for Latin Christianity) of the "mainstream" by his doctrine of original sin, confirmed in large part by reading Rom 5:12 as though it said "in whom" (i.e., in Adam) all sinned rather than "*because* all sinned."

My argument begins by observing that from Irenaeus to Origen there develops an understanding of the Adam typology central to the way the Great Church proclaims the Christian story.[3] God created Adam that he

---

1. *The Writings of St. Paul* (ed. Wayne A. Meeks; New York: Norton, 1972) 435–44, esp. 435–36.

2. Wayne A. Meeks, *The Moral World of the First Christians* (Library of Early Christianity 6; Philadelphia: Westminster, 1986) 156. See also Meeks's discussion of this same "cluster of images" in *The First Urban Christians: The Social World of the Apostle Paul* (New Haven and London: Yale University Press, 1983) 188.

3. In addition to the texts to which I shall refer in what follows, the reader may consult Clement of Alexandria, *Stromateis* 3.9; 4.3 (enumeration of ANF 2:393, 410); Methodius, *Symposium* 3.6–8; 4.2; Eusebius, *Proof of the Gospel* 7.1; Athanasius, *Letter* 11; Cyril of Jerusalem, *Catechetical Homilies* 2.7; 12.15; 13.1–2, 28, 31; Gregory Nazianzen, *In Defense of His Flight to Pontus* 23; *On the Theophany* 4 (enumeration of NPNF 2.7, pp. 346 and 348). The first four volumes of *Biblia Patristica: Index des citations et allusions bibliques dans la littérature patristique* makes it possible to examine the citations and allusions to Rom 5:12ff. in the ante-Nicene period and in Eusebius of Caesarea and Epiphanius.

might mature and grow to the perfection of the resurrection. His fall, while it was not one from an original perfection, interrupted his growth and brought on him and his posterity the penalty of mortality. Though tragic in the short run, in the long run the fall became part of humanity's growth to perfection. The whole of human history, then, is a process of maturation or, to shift the metaphor, an education for perfection. Humanity learns by its mistakes, and even God's punishments are a part of his educative providence. God teaches, and his culminating lesson is the Incarnation. Humanity learns to train its freedom for maturity in Christ. Within this large framework human sin appears as an ignorance of the good and a weakness in doing it; and both are largely the product of the mortality inherited from Adam. Sin, then, need mean no more than an unfortunate but temporary adolescent rebellion that plays a positive role in humanity's maturation.

There is, however, a Pauline "ferment" that qualifies the optimism of this account of the Christian story and of the Adam typology. However much mortality may explain our sin, the fact remains that we are unable to govern our passions; and death is not only the cause of our sin but also its punishment. The early Augustine adopts this more pessimistic version of the usual Christian Platonist view, but the ferment works upon his thought to transform it into his mature view.[4] We inherit from Adam not only mortality but also spiritual death and the liability to eternal damnation; only God's sovereign and selective grace can rescue people from the mass of perdition. Augustine's radical emphasis on divine sovereignty and human incapacity transforms Christian Platonism into a novel theology and a novel reading of Paul. I shall wish to conclude the argument by reflecting briefly on the question why this shift in understanding takes place.

INTERPRETATIONS OF ROMANS 5:12FF. BEFORE AUGUSTINE

Irenaeus is the first writer of the mainline development of early Christianity to make central use of Paul's Adam typology.[5] Despite one funda-

---

4. Arguing that Augustine transforms an already existing and more or less coherent interpretation of Paul seems more reasonable to me than saying that Paul was ignored before Augustine or that there was an "Eastern" as well as a "Western" interpretation of Paul. For this reason it seems to me that Ernst Dassmann's question may not be the best one to ask ("Zum Paulusverständis in der Östliche Kirche," *JAC* 29 [1986] 27): "Welche Bedeutung Paulus, näherhin sein Römerbrief, für die Rechtfertigungslehre in der abendländischen Kirche gewonnen hat, ist allgemein bekannt. Es genügt, an Namen wie Augustinus und Luther zu erinnern. Gibt es Vergleichbares in der morgenländischen Kirche?"

5. See his citations of verses from Rom 5:12ff. in *Adversus Haereses* 3.16.9; 3.18.7; 3.21.10; 3.22.3; 3.23.8. Cf. Richard A. Norris, Jr., "Irenaeus' Use of Paul in His Polemic Against the Gnostics," in *Paul and the Legacies of Paul* (ed. W. S. Babcock; Dallas: SMU Press, 1990) 79–98, esp. 93: "The source . . . of Irenaeus' notion of recapitulation . . . appears, in the end, to be Romans 5:12ff. . . ." See also my discussion in J. Kugel and R. Greer, *Early Biblical Interpretation* (Philadelphia: Westminster, 1986) 167–71.

mental resemblance (Adam is from virgin soil; Christ, born of a virgin), it is the contrast between the two that Irenaeus underlines. Adam's disobedience produces sin and death; Christ's obedience, righteousness and life.[6] At first it looks as though Irenaeus has a paradise lost/paradise regained pattern. But his insistence that Adam was created childlike means that Christ's reversal of Adam's pattern is not an end in itself. Christ restores what we lost in Adam in order to enable God's plan for Adam to be completed. Redemption, then, is the completion of creation rather than, as the gnostics said, its abolition. Understood this way, there is a progress from the old earthy Adam to the new heavenly Adam; and Christ's "recapitulation" is a heading up or unification that takes place for the first time, even though it was God's intention from the beginning.[7] Finally, the redemption wrought by the second Adam completes humanity's vision of God so that the physical incorruption of the resurrection may be established.[8]

The basic framework that Irenaeus establishes carries with it an emphasis on God's mercy and human freedom. God's response to the fall of Adam and Eve is one of compassion. He removes their penitential fig leaves and clothes them with coats of skin (*Adv. Haer.* 3.23.5). Similarly, Theophilus of Antioch and even Tertullian see God's punishment of Adam as a merciful means of restoring him.[9] This sensibility translates itself into a doctrine of God that insists on mercy more than justice and that refuses to allow any notion that God can coerce. Indeed, since God limits himself to persuasion, his sovereignty attaches to the age to come, when he will have persuaded all to be voluntarily subject to him. Irenaeus's emphasis on human freedom is

6. The typology can be extended to Eve and Mary (3.22.4). Moreover, the seventy-two generations in Luke's genealogy of Christ answer to all the nations that sprang from Adam (3.22.3); and both Adam's death and Christ's, by which he slew death, took place on the sixth day (5.23.2).

7. See *Adversus Haereses* 3.16.6, where it is clear that Irenaeus draws his idea of "recapitulation" from Eph 1:10. The RSV translates the Greek verb "unite." Irenaeus does not think of redemption as the restoration of paradise.

8. Cf. my attempt to describe more fully Irenaeus's theology in *Broken Lights and Mended Lives* (University Park: Penn State University Press, 1986) chapter 1.

9. Theophilus of Antioch, *Ad Autolycum* 2.26–27 (ANF 2:104–5): "God showed great kindness to man in this, that He did not suffer him to remain in sin for ever; but, as it were, by a kind of banishment, cast him out of Paradise, in order that, having by punishment expiated, within an appointed time, the sin, and having been disciplined, he should afterwards be restored." Tertullian interprets God's question of the fallen Adam ("where art thou?") as displaying not ignorance but "the utterance of One who is at once rebuking and sorrowing." God asks the question "with an appearance of uncertainty, in order that even here He might prove man to be the subject of a free will in the alternative of either a denial or a confession, and give him the opportunity of freely acknowledging his transgression, and, so far, of lightening it" (*Adversus Marcionem* 2.25; ANF 3:317). Even though Tertullian's reading of Paul may in some respects differ from the Greek reading (see Dassmann, "Zum Paulusverständnis," 29), his use of the Adam typology allies him with the broad interpretive structure I am describing. See *Adv. Marc.* 3.19; 5.9; 5.13–14; *De res. carnis* 48.

really no more than the other side of the same coin (see *Adv. Haer.* 4.37).[10] Here the implication is that whatever we have inherited from Adam, we remain free within limits to choose between good and evil. Both God's persuasive role as teacher and our free ability to learn find expression in Irenaeus's basic structure of thought.

Let me turn from these general considerations to Origen, who wrote the earliest commentary on Romans to which we have any real access.[11] He retains Irenaeus's basic framework by speaking of a drama that extends from the beginning to the restoration of all things and that plays itself out through the interaction of God's providence and the freedom of rational beings. But he radically transforms that framework by speaking of a pre-cosmic creation of rational beings, who are incorporeal and equal, by explaining the existence of angels, humans, and demons as the consequence of the fall of the rational beings, and by interpreting the resurrection body as spiritual and the sign of perfected contemplation for all. We can say, then, that Origen thinks of the Adam typology as an allegory of deeper truths.[12] Celsus mocks the "resurrection of the flesh from the tree" because "he has misunderstood the symbolical saying that through a tree came death and through a tree came life, death in Adam and life in Christ" (*Contra Celsum* 4.36).[13]

Origen adopts this basic perspective in commenting on Rom 5:12ff. If Rufinus's Latin translation is trustworthy, Origen nowhere explicitly repudiates the narrative level of the Adam story. At the same time, his interest

10. The emphasis on freedom is, of course, at one level polemically aimed at the gnostics.

11. What I mean, of course, is that Origen's specific references to earlier exegetes are to Marcion or the Gnostics. See Peter J. Gorday, "*Paulus Origenianus:* The Economic Interpretation of Paul in Origen and Gregory of Nyssa," in *Paul and the Legacies of Paul* (ed. W. S. Babcock; Dallas: SMU Press, 1990) 143. (He, of course, refers to Elaine Pagels's work.) See also Gorday's book *Principles of Patristic Exegesis: Romans 9–11 in Origen, John Chrysostom, and Augustine* (New York and Toronto: Edwin Mellen Press, 1983). With respect to Origen's Commentary on Romans, the basic problem is that the only full text is Rufinus's Latin translation/paraphrase. For the best discussion of how to examine the Latin in the light of the Greek fragments from the *Philokalia,* the catenae, and the Toura papyri, see Jean Scherer, *Le Commentaire d'Origène sur Rom. III.5-V.7* (Cairo: Imprimérie de l'Institut Français d'Archéologie Orientale, 1957).

12. One way of making the point is to examine Origen's use of Romans in the context of his discussion of John 1:3 ("without him nothing was made"). The question arises whether evil was made through the Word. Origen's answer depends on equating Word and Law and arguing on the basis of Rom 7:3–4, Rom 5:13, and John 15:22 that the Word supplies the standard of being by which evil as non-being is exposed. The argument moves very quickly from the texts to deeper philosophical questions about the definition of evil. See *Commentary on John* 2.15.105ff. (SC 120, pp. 275ff.).

13. Trans. Henry Chadwick (Cambridge: University Press, 1953) 352. Cf. *Contra Celsum* 4.40 (Chadwick, p. 216), where Origen refers to those "concerned to defend the doctrine of providence" and says that "the story of Adam and his sin will be interpreted philosophically by those who know that Adam means *anthrōpos* (man) in the Greek language, and that in what appears to be concerned with Adam Moses is speaking of the nature of man. For, as the Bible says, 'in Adam all die', and they were condemned in 'the likeness of Adam's transgression'. Here the divine Word says this not so much about an individual as of the whole race."

lies in the symbolic meaning of the story. Origen's concern to explain why Paul treats Adam as the source of sin illustrates the first of these two points. The problem is that both Eve and Satan sinned before Adam (1 Tim 2:14; John 8:44). Paul, however, singles out Adam "because all humans who are born in this world were in the loins of Adam while he was still in paradise; and all humans were expelled from paradise with him or in him." This is why Paul can say that all die in Adam, while all are made alive in Christ. Origen, then, conflates Rom 5:12 with 1 Cor 15:22, and he appears to be taking the Adam typology seriously at what we might call the historical level.[14]

As Origen's argument continues, however, it becomes clear that his interest lies in the allegorical meaning of the typology. The contrast between Adam and Christ is really that between the earthy and the heavenly humanities Paul speaks of in 1 Cor 15:47–49. There is a hint that sin entered not only this earthly world but also the heavenly places (Eph 6:12). In any case, "the world" can signify "the earthly and corporeal life where death has its place"; and "death," properly speaking, is the death of the soul (Ezek 18:4). Later in the commentary Origen interprets the contrast between death and life as one between two forms of teaching. The Christian teaching, of course, frees the soul from impiety and gives it eternal life (*PG* 14:1023–24). While Origen does not explicitly appeal to his esoteric understanding of the divine economy that guides the preexistent souls from their incorporeal beginning to the final perfection, it is easy enough to see that he has this picture in his mind.

We can take one further step that helps explain why Origen fails to make his large theological schema explicit. His basic approach to Rom 5:12ff. involves arguing that Paul is a careful teacher. Having explained the mystery that when we were enemies to God, we were reconciled by the Son's death, Paul goes on to explain the causes of the mystery (*PG* 14:1003–4). Origen tells a parable to explain what he means. A king has many treasures in his palace, and he shows different ones to different servants. Paul has seen part of the king's treasure, and he receives a commission to assemble an army for the king. He recruits people by telling them about the treasure, but he can only tell them in part. Moreover, he knows that his message must be tempered to what those hearing it can bear. So for these two reasons the treasure remains largely hidden (*PG* 14:1007–8).

Origen uses this understanding of Paul's aim to explain why Rom 5:12ff. is obscure. The anacolouthon in v. 12 can be completed by appealing to 1 Cor 15:22, but Paul has written it deliberately. It is his custom whenever he speaks of God's goodness to continue by obscuring what he says because he knows many of his hearers are negligent and lazy. In other words, had

---

14. Origen's discussion may be found in *PG* 14:1009–11. The reason we cannot insist on the seriousness with which he takes the historicity of Adam is that elsewhere (e.g., *De principiis* 4.3.1) he denies the narrative level of the story.

Paul given a clear statement of the mystery of God's economy, including its promise of universal redemption, then his hearers would have been tempted to draw antinomian conclusions (*PG* 14:1005-6). The same set of considerations helps explain the baffling shifts from "all" to "many" in vv. 12, 15, 18, and 19 (*PG* 14:1006, 1023, 1030). Origen's basic interpretation of the Adam typology, then, is to see it as an aspect of God's universal redemptive economy.[15] But that economy remains a persuasive one and the context in which human freedom can exercise choice and responsibility.

Origen's basic perspective remains a constant in the interpretation of Rom 5:12ff. in the fourth and fifth centuries. To be sure, most of the fathers reject his idiosyncratic views about the preexistence of souls and the resurrection; and they all take seriously the historicity of Adam.[16] But Origen's twin emphasis on the goodness of God and human freedom remains. Sometimes we can discern this in the way the fathers tell the story of the fall. God's question of the fallen Adam is a sign of his tenderness in seeking to persuade Adam to repent.[17] Even his expulsion of Adam and Eve from paradise was designed to educate and reform them.[18] Free to fall, Adam and Eve remain free to profit by their punishment.

God's goodness and human freedom also characterize the way the fathers read the Adam typology. John Chrysostom is troubled by the possible implication that God would blame us for Adam's sin. We become "sinners" in Adam only because we are mortal and liable to punishment. But the important point is that the superabundance of God's grace in Christ has destroyed condemnation and death.[19] The other side of the coin betrays itself in an insistence that the fall of Adam did not remove human freedom to choose the good. The penalty we inherit is a mortal nature. And, as Theodoret says, "such a nature needs many things . . . and these needs often rouse the passions to disorder. The disorder generates sin" (*PG* 82:100).[20]

15. See Gorday's conclusion in *"Paulus Origenianus,"* 162: "Indeed, as I have argued elsewhere, the best single term for understanding the kind of coherence that Origen and his successors found in Pauline theology is *oikonomia."*

16. The point may be complicated by pointing out that writers such as Athanasius and Gregory of Nyssa, while accepting the historicity of Adam, are concerned to interpret the Adam typology in terms of the broad patterns of an old humanity and a new one in Christ. See Athanasius, *De incarnatione* 10; *Contra Arianos* 1.1; 2.61; Gregory of Nyssa, *Oratio catechetica* 5; *De hominis opificio* 16; and passim.

17. John Chrysostom, *Homilies on the Statues* 7, 8, and 12 (NPNF 1.9, pp. 393, 396, 422).

18. John Chrysostom, *Homily That Demons Do Not Govern the World* 3; *Homily on the Statues* 2 (NPNF 1.9, pp. 180, 353).

19. John Chrysostom, *Homily on Romans* 10 (NPNF 1.11, pp. 402-3). So far as I have been able to discover, no one before Augustine pays particular attention to "because" in Rom 5:12. In the sixth century, however, Oecumenius of Trikka singles the word out to argue that it proves we cannot charge God with punishing people because of Adam's sin. All die *because* all sin (K. Staab, *Pauluskommentaren aus der griechischen Kirche* [Münster: Aschendorff, 1933] 424).

20. It should be noted that in the Greek tradition Origen's and Theodoret's commentaries and John Chrysostom's homilies are the only surviving complete treatments of Romans. Staab

Mortality, then, explains our tendency to sin; but it does not require us to sin. Paul's shift from "all" to "many" in Rom 5:12ff. can be understood as a distinction between nature, which brings death and resurrection on all, and our moral character, which remains free to choose virtue.[21] Chrysostom goes so far as to say that mortality, since it is "not the cause of sin," is no hindrance to virtue.[22] The logic of this reading of Paul's Adam typology is optimistic and designed to baptize the late antique quest for virtue by locating it in the context of God's providential economy.[23]

Although no one before Augustine denies that the mortality we inherit from Adam explains our sinfulness, the point can be expressed in a more pessimistic fashion. And it is this darker view that acts as the Pauline ferment in understanding Romans 5. The logic of the view that predominates is clear. Adam's sin not only prevented him from maturing to incorruptibility but also rendered the whole of human nature mortal. Mortality means not only that we must die but also that the relation between our mind as the governing principle and the body and passions meant to be governed is a disordered one. Consequently, our mortal nature explains why we so easily sin; and yet death remains the penalty for our sin, since it completes the disorder of mind and body. Nevertheless, this logic includes within it a recognition of the disordered state of fallen humanity. Theodore of Mopsuestia argues that death weakened human nature "and generated in it a great inclination towards sin."[24] Strictly speaking, what we inherit from

---

has assembled from the catenae fragments from commentaries by Didymus, Eusebius of Emesa, Acacius of Caesarea, Apollinaris, Diodore of Tarsus, Theodore of Mopsuestia, Severian of Gabala, Gennadius of Constantinople, Oecumenius of Trikka, Photius of Constantinople, and Arethas of Caesarea (*Pauluskommentaren*). Fragments may also be found from the lost commentary of Cyril of Alexandria in *PG* 74.

21. See Theodoret, *PG* 82.104A; also Severian of Gabala (Staab, *Pauluskommentaren*, 218). Gennadius of Constantinople makes the distinction between those who die because of their own sins and those (children) who die only because of their mortal nature (Staab, p. 362). Diodore of Tarsus distinguishes between the "all" who have sinned and the "many" that remain in sin (Staab, pp. 83ff.). Acacius of Caesarea treats the fallen Adam as the first principle of our existence and sinfulness; Photius of Constantinople makes a similar point and explains what he means by saying we take Adam as our point of departure (Staab, pp. 53, 496). I am tempted to compare this interpretation with *Sifra* 112b, where the apparent contradiction between punishing the children for their fathers' sins (Lev 26:39) and individual responsibility for sin (Deut 24:16) is resolved by distinguishing the explanation for sin from the issue of moral responsibility. Does this commonsense solution help explain what Paul means?

22. John Chrysostom, *Homily on 1 Corinthians* 17 (NPNF 1.12, p. 99).

23. Let me note in passing that the popular understanding of God's economy involved the idea that just as Adam had been defeated by Satan, so Christ won the victory over Satan. Baptism enrolled the Christian in the continuing warfare against Satan. See my discussion in *The Fear of Freedom* (University Park: Penn State University Press, 1989) 54–55, 57–61, 69–70, 72–76.

24. Theodore of Mopsuestia, *Catechetical Homily* 12 (trans. A. Mingana; Woodbrooke Studies 6; Cambridge: W. Heffer & Sons, 1933) 21, 27. For the "inclination," see also Commentary on Romans 5:21 and 7:25 (Staab, *Pauluskommentaren*, pp. 120, 133). For an excellent discussion of the problem in Theodore, see Richard A. Norris, Jr., *Manhood and Christ* (Oxford: Clarendon,

Adam is only mortality. Yet this inheritance is what renders humanity badly incapacitated and oriented toward sin.

AUGUSTINE'S TRANSFORMATION
OF THE ACCEPTED PATTERN

We know that as early as the time of his conversion in 386 Augustine was reading Paul's letters. Indeed, when the child's voice chanted "take it up and read," Augustine turned to Romans 13:13, the verse that marked his conversion (*Conf.* 8.12).[25] After his return to Africa and his ordination to the priesthood, he embarked upon a full study of the Pauline letters, partly in order to refute the use made of them by the Manichaeans.[26] Augustine wrote *The Propositions from the Epistle to the Romans* and the *Unfinished Commentary* (which does not go beyond the salutation) shortly before 396. His aim in *The Propositions* is to show that Paul does not condemn the Law, nor does he "take away man's free will." And he fulfills this aim by arguing that Paul has in mind four stages in human life—before the Law, under the Law, under grace, and in peace.[27]

Augustine's understanding of the Adam typology in *The Propositions* is, in general, quite coherent with the predominant view I have just described. The "fleshly desires" that characterize our existence and lead to sin "arise from the mortality of the flesh, which we bear from the first sin of the first man, whence we are all born fleshly." Mortality, in other words, refers to the disordered relation of body and mind that explains our tendency to sin. In two respects, however, Augustine goes beyond Theodore's idea of an inclination to sin. First, the fleshly desires will persist even in the Christian life; they will not pass away until we are in the peace of the resurrection. Second, "prior to grace, [we] do not have free will so as not to sin, but only so much that we do not want to sin."

1963) 173–86. It may be that he is correct in seeing a tension between biblical and philosophical sides of Theodore's thought. I am not entirely convinced that it is so much a question of a contradiction in Theodore's thought as of a "ferment" that works within the logic of his view, one that depends on the idea that the mind is the hegemonikon of the body and its passions. For another attempt to wrestle with the problem, see Ulrich Wickert, *Studien zu den Pauluskommentaren Theodors von Mopsuestia* (Berlin: Töpelmann, 1962) 101–20.

25. Cf. 7.21; 8.6; *Contra Academicos* 2.2.5.

26. See Paula Fredriksen Landes, *Augustine on Romans* (Chico, Calif.: Scholars Press, 1982). Landes has provided text and translation of the *Propositions* and *Unfinished Commentary*. Her introduction is very helpful. See also her essay in *Paul and the Legacies of Paul:* "Beyond the Body/Soul Dichotomy: Augustine's Answer to Mani, Plotinus, and Julian" (pp. 227–51). Cf. Eugene TeSelle, *Augustine the Theologian* (London: Burns & Oates, 1970) 156, where he speaks of a "sudden surge of interest in the epistles of Paul [which] becomes apparent about 394."

27. *Propositions* 13–18; trans. Landes, pp. 5–7.

The second change not only radicalizes the pessimistic reading of the Adam typology found in Theodore but it actually represents a subtle but significant alteration in interpretation. We can appeal to *On Free Will*, completed sometime shortly before 396, to confirm this interpretation. Because of the fall we are born in a penal state, ignorant of the good and unable to do it. Augustine relates this penal state to "the will," a novel concept that refers to the fundamental orientation of the mind that lies behind its acts of free choice. The fall of Adam, then, has left us with a disordered will; and this means that, since our motivation is corrupted, we cannot in any full sense choose the good. Theodore's "inclination to evil" has become a radical incapacity for good. The one choice left to us is a capacity to seek God's help. We can have faith.[28]

Augustine takes the next step toward his mature doctrine of original sin in the treatise *To Simplician*, written in 396. He can continue to speak of the human predicament as "the penalty of his guilt, whereby mortality was brought in as a second nature" and of Paul's "law in my members" (Rom 7:23) as "the burden of mortality under which we groan."[29] But, as we have seen, mortality means that we are "overcome by concupiscence which derives its strength from the fact, not simply that [we] are mortal, but also that [we are] burdened by the weight of custom." In this sense, we all die in Adam as "one mass," and this is "a mass of sin,"[30] Once again, the first change in the view he inherited is to read our inclination to sin as a total incapacity for virtue. The second change is to argue that we cannot even choose grace; rather, grace chooses us. Election cannot be understood as God's foreknowledge of a meritorious use of his grace. Instead, it is God's inscrutable and sovereign choice. Augustine is conscious that he has made a radical

28. The fact that *On Free Will* was written over a long period of time (387 to some time before 396) makes it possible that Augustine's view in the treatise is inconsistent. We can contrast optimistic statements (e.g., 1.13.29 [LCC 6:129]: "whoever wishes to live rightly and honourably . . . attains his object with perfect ease. In order to attain it he has to do nothing but to will it") with pessimistic ones (e.g., 2.20.54 [LCC 6:169]: "But since man cannot rise of his own free will as he fell by his own will spontaneously, let us hold with steadfast faith the right hand of God stretched out to us from above, even our Lord Jesus Christ"). My suggestion is that we need not suppose any contradiction. The optimistic passages refer to what is true in principle but not in fact. (Cf. 1.14.30 [LCC 6:130]: "So when we say that men are unhappy voluntarily, we do not mean that they want to be unhappy, but that their wills are in such a state that unhappiness must follow even against their will.") The choice that remains is to seek God's help. (Cf. 3.20.55 [LCC 6:203]: "But if any of Adam's race should be willing to turn to God, and so overcome the punishment which had been merited by the original turning away from God, it was fitting not only that he should not be hindered but that he should also receive divine aid.")

29. *To Simplician* 11, 13; LCC 6:381, 382.

30. *To Simplician* 16, 17, 19, 20; LCC 6:398, 399, 402, 403. The term *massa* appears in Ambrosiaster's commentary on Rom 5:12. Augustine, however, has not yet discovered Rom 5:12; and it may be better to see here the influence of Tyconius. See Fredriksen, "Beyond the Body/Soul Dichotomy," 238–39.

change in understanding the Adam typology, but can argue with some conviction that his new view is no more than the working out of an emphasis on grace that was his conviction from the beginning.[31]

It is, I think, important to note that as early as 396 Augustine has arrived at his mature theology. There are, of course, details that continue to be sharpened. He will increasingly argue that grace operates by direct infusion rather than by congruous vocation.[32] He will add the grace of perseverance to prevenient grace. He will also discover that "in whom all sinned" in Rom 5:12 puts the seal on his interpretation of the Adam typology in terms of original sin and election by predestination.[33] But I argue that his reading of Rom 5:12 is the product rather than the cause of his interpretation, just as his mature theology is the cause rather than the result of his reaction to Pelagianism. With these points in mind let me turn to a brief consideration of the first of Augustine's anti-Pelagian writings.

On Forgiveness of Sins, and Baptism is a response addressed in 412 to Marcellinus, who was the imperial commissioner appointed to preside over the dispute between Donatists and Catholics in Africa. Augustine is concerned with opinions that are circulating in Carthage and that bear some relation to the opinions of the Pelagian proponent Celestius that had recently been condemned at Carthage (411). The heretical platform involved six points: Adam was created mortal; Adam's sin harmed only himself; children are born in the state in which Adam was created; neither Adam's sin nor Christ's resurrection affects everyone; the law as well as the gospel leads to the kingdom of heaven; even before Christ, some lived without sin. While Augustine does not refute these points in exact order, his treatise must be read with them in mind.

---

31. See *On the Predestination of the Saints* 3.7–4.8 (NPNF 1.5, pp. 500–501) and *On the Gift of Perseverance* 20.52 (NPNF 1.5, p. 547). Cf. *Retractions* 1.9.6 (LCC 6:104). Fredriksen's judgment is that "Augustine's views change more drastically between 394 and 396–98 than between 398 and 430" ("Beyond the Body/Soul Dichotomy," 228). Contrast J. Patout Burns, *The Development of Augustine's Doctrine of Operative Grace* (Paris: Études augustiniennes, 1980) 8: "The foundations of the second and third discussions of divine control, in 418 and 427, are significantly different from the first one in 396." The two views might be reconciled by arguing that the major change regarding original sin takes place by 396, whereas the major changes in understanding operative grace take place later.

32. See Burns, *Development*, 47, 141.

33. The writer known to us as Ambrosiaster (called Hilary by Augustine) wrote in Rome under Damasus (366–384). The Latin text of Rom 5:12 has "*in quo*" for the Greek ἐφ' ᾧ ("because"). While Augustine follows Ambrosiaster in understanding the expression to mean "in whom," that is, in Adam, he does not follow Ambrosiaster's interpretation. Ambrosiaster thinks that all sinned in Adam in the sense that the penalty of bodily death tends to produce sin. The second death of eternal damnation is the punishment of actual rather than original sin. See TeSelle's discussion, *Augustine*, 157–58, 166, 177. It may be noted that Pelagius also in his commentary understands "*in quo*" to mean "in Adam," but argues that we must think of "imitation."

What interests me is that the central chapters of book 1 of *On Forgiveness of Sins* is virtually a commentary on Rom 5:12ff.[34] In chapter 8 we learn that we all inherit death from Adam, as Paul says in Rom 5:12 and 1 Cor 15:21–22. This death is the penalty for Adam's sin and not his created nature.[35] But "death" includes spiritual death, which passes from Adam to all people not by "imitation" but by "natural descent," since "he, in whom all die, . . . depraved also in his own person all who come of his stock by the hidden corruption of his own carnal concupiscence."[36] The scriptural proof of this is Paul's phrase "in whom all sinned," in Rom 5:12. But Augustine also argues that were we sinful only by imitation, Paul would have spoken of the devil rather than of Adam. Moreover, since baptism effects the forgiveness of sins, infant baptism demonstrates that even children who have not committed actual sin require grace.[37]

The basic perspective I have just described governs Augustine's treatment of the rest of Rom 5:12ff.[38] It also informs the whole of the treatise,

---

34. *On Forgiveness of Sins* 1.9.9–16.21 (NPNF 1.5, pp. 18–23). Cf. 3.4.9 (NPNF 1.5, p. 72): "For this phrase ['Adam is the figure of Him that was to come,' Rom 5:14] in reality not only suits the sense which understands that Adam's posterity were to be born of the same form as himself along with sin, but the words are also capable of being drawn out into several distinct meanings. . . . All the rest, however, of the passage in which these doubtful words occur, if its statements are carefully examined and treated, as I have tried myself to do in the first book of this treatise, will not . . . fail to show . . . that believing infants have obtained through the baptism of Christ the remission of original sin."

35. See, e.g., *City of God* 14.11, where Augustine cites Rom 5:12.

36. *On Forgiveness of Sins* 1.9.9–10 (NPNF 1.5, pp. 18–19). Cf. *Enchiridion* 26; *On Man's Perfection in Righteousness* 21.44; *On Marriage and Concupiscence* 1.1.1; 2.2.3; 2.5.15; 2.8.20; 2.22.37; 2.26.42; 2.27.45; 2.28.48; *Against Two Letters of the Pelagians* 4.4.7; *On John* 30.5; 49.12 (NPNF 1.3, p. 246; NPNF 1.5, pp. 176, 263, 284, 288, 290, 298, 300, 301, 303, 419; NPNF 1.7, pp. 187, 274). All these passages include the citation of Rom 5:12, as do the following passages that are less explicit with respect to concupiscence and the propagation of original sin: *De trinitate* 4.12.15; *On Forgiveness of Sins* 3.11.19; *On the Spirit and the Letter* xxvii.47; *On Nature and Grace* 39.46; 41.48; *On the Grace of Christ* 27.55; *On Original Sin* 29.34; *On Psalm* 35.14; *On Psalm* 90.9 (NPNF 1.3, p. 77; NPNF 1.5, pp. 76, 103, 137–38, 236, 249; NPNF 1.8, pp. 82, 443). See also Burns's discussion of "carnal concupiscence," *Development*, 101–7.

37. For the use of Rom 5:12 in the context of the argument from infant baptism, see Letter 98; *City of God* 16.27; *Enchiridion* 45; *On Forgiveness of Sins* 3.1.1; 3.4.7; 3.7.14; *On Nature and Grace* 8.9; *On Marriage and Concupiscence* 2.3.8; 2.11.24; 2.28.47; *Against Two Letters of the Pelagians* 4.8.24; Sermon 65.4; Sermon 94.1; *On Psalm* 51.10 (NPNF 1.1, p. 410; NPNF 1.2, p. 326; NPNF 1.3, p. 252; NPNF 1.5, pp. 69, 71, 74, 124, 285, 292, 302, 427; NPNF 1.6, pp. 455, 538; NPNF 1.8, p. 193). Augustine's argument, of course, depends on equating baptism with the forgiveness of sins. To narrow the meaning of baptism in this fashion is, I think, to allow one theme to exclude others such as incorporation into Christ or into the church. Augustine's understanding, which seems eccentric by comparison with the Greek tradition, draws upon the north African tradition and may also depend on the common custom of deferring baptism to a time after adolescence and youth. This custom assumes that, since baptism cancels sins, it is better to put the sins of youth behind before baptism.

38. For example, v. 14 ("even in those who had not sinned after the similitude of Adam's transgression") means "those who had not yet sinned of their own individual will, as Adam

including the argument of book 3, where Augustine finally turns to Pelagius and to his commentary on Paul. He does not directly attack Pelagius and recognizes that in his commentary Pelagius has not explicitly identified himself with the opinions he is retailing. Nevertheless, according to Pelagius, those who deny the transmission of sin from Adam argue (1) that if Adam's sin harms those not guilty of actual sin (i.e., children), then Christ's righteousness benefits even unbelievers, (2) that if original sin is cleansed by baptism, then the children of baptized parents cannot inherit what the parents no longer possess, (3) that if the body but not the soul is inherited, bodily nature alone is condemned, and it is unjust that a newly created soul should bear a sin foreign to it, and (4) that if God forgives sins, he would not reckon one person's sin to another.[39] The first of these points appears novel to Augustine, but he claims that he has already "sufficiently and clearly replied" to the other points in the first two books.[40]

One need go no further to characterize the view of original sin Augustine has developed. The controversy with Pelagius, which becomes explicit only after 415, will raise a number of detailed points. Augustine will be obliged to discuss the question of the soul's origin.[41] He will argue that his view is the "old theology," supported by Cyprian, Hilary, Ambrose, and others.[42] And his understanding of grace and its operation will undergo a development. His response to the charge that his view undermines the Christian Platonist understanding of God as persuasive and merciful will continue to be an appeal to God's sovereignty. The story continues with the debate in Gaul over Augustine's theology, and it is fair to say that even the Council of

---

did, but had drawn from him original sin. . . ." (On Forgiveness of Sins 1.11.13 [NPNF 1.5, p. 20]). Cf. also vv. 18–19: The reason for "all" is that "as none partakes of carnal generation except through Adam, so no one shares in the spiritual except through Christ. . . ." But these "all" the apostle afterwards describes as "many"; for obviously, under certain circumstances, the "all" may be but a few (On Forgiveness of Sins 1.15.19 [NPNF 1.5, p. 22]).

39. On Forgiveness of Sins 3.2.2 (NPNF 1.5, pp. 69–70). See Robert F. Evans, Pelagius: Inquiries and Reappraisals (London: Adam & Charles Black, 1968) 72–74. The whole of chapter 5 is an excellent summary of the way in which Augustine gradually becomes a foe of Pelagius.

40. On Forgiveness of Sins 3.2.4 (NPNF 1.5, p. 70).

41. For the use of Rom 5:12 in discussions of the soul, see Letter 164; On the Soul and Its Origin 1.17.28; 2.14.20 (NPNF 1.1, p. 520; NPNF 1.5, pp. 327, 341). Augustine never makes up his mind about the origin of the soul. See Burns's discussion, Development, 107–9.

42. See On Forgiveness of Sins 3.5.10; 3.6.12; On Nature and Grace 61.71–65.78; On the Grace of Christ 1.42.46–50.55; On Original Sin 41.47; On Marriage and Concupiscence 1.35.40; 2.29.51; Against Two Letters of the Pelagians 4.8.20–12.32; On the Gift of Perseverance 8.19–20; 19.48–49 (NPNF 1.5, pp. 72, 73, 146–48, 233–36, 254–55, 279, 304, 425–33, 532, 545–46). The passages Augustine cites from Cyprian, Ambrose, Jerome, and others do insist on the necessity of grace and of infant baptism and upon universal sinfulness. What is not clear, however, is that they repudiate the idea that universal sinfulness is the product of the disordered body–mind relation that characterizes mortality. (See, e.g., Ambrose's discussion in his Commentary on Luke 4.66–67 [SC 45:178].) Augustine must also refute Pelagius's use of authorities.

Orange in 529 fails to put an end to controversy.[43] What is clear, however, is that Augustine's conclusion that we all sinned in Adam's fall represents both a transformation of the older view he inherited and a radical novelty. Indeed, his novel reading of Paul has so affected Western thinking that it is nearly impossible for us to understand the Paul of late antique Christian Platonism or, for that matter, of modern Orthodoxy.

CONCLUDING REFLECTIONS

I may not have said enough to describe every aspect of the early church's interpretation of Rom 5:12ff., but I am willing to claim that the texts I have examined demonstrate that Augustine effected a radical transformation in interpretation. This conclusion, however, is more a question than an answer. What explains the shift? To be sure, we can appeal to Augustine's reading not only of Paul but also of Ambrosiaster and Tyconius.[44] But we must also take account of the social setting in which the interpreters found themselves. The interpretation Augustine inherited seems to me rooted in a modified Origenism and a party platform designed to baptize the late antique quest for virtue. Despite appearances, the Christian has the capacity for the free choice of the good and the hope of a time when God will persuade all evil to return to good.

Augustine turns this theology of freedom into a theology of God's sovereignty. Is this because the older theology cannot survive the Constantinian revolution after which Christianity tends to become the religion of society? Augustine the bishop must deal with crowds and with half-Christians. How are we to assess the increasing emphasis in the fourth century on holy places and holy people? Is it that the kingdom of this world has become the kingdom of God and Christ? How are we to assess the impact on Augustine of the controversies in which he was engaged? More elusive than books and harder to interpret than social settings is the human heart. In the long run, however, it seems to me that this explains better than anything the sea change Augustine has worked. Can we not say that his heart teaches him the imperfectibility of humanity and gives him his basic sensibility—human incapacity and divine sovereignty as two sides of the same coin?

43. Rom 5:12, of course, plays an important role in the controversy. The second canon of Orange, for example, uses it to insist on original sin. See the translation of J. P. Burns, *Theological Anthropology* (Philadelphia: Fortress, 1981) 113.

44. See n. 30 above and Fredriksen's discussion.

Modern Authors

INDEX

Ancient Sources

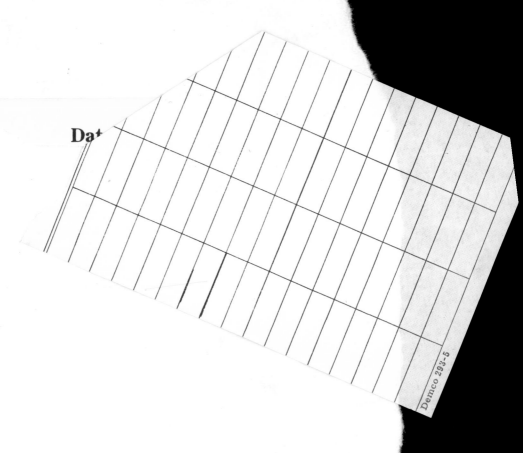

Da†